Indo-Aryan
DEITIES AND WORSHIP
As Contained in the
Rig-Veda

Indo-Aryan
DEITIES AND WORSHIP
As Contained in the
Rig-Veda

ALBERT PIKE

GYAN

Published by

Gyan Publishing House
5, Ansari Road
Daryaganj, New Delhi-110002
Phone: 011-47034999, 9811692060
E-mail: books@gyanbooks.com

Distribution Network
gyanbooks.com
India, USA, Canada, UK, Australia

ISBN: 978-93-6280-040-4 (PB)
First Published, 1930

2nd Impression 2024

Printed at: Gyan Press, Delhi.

INDO-ARYAN DEITIES AND WORSHIPAS CONTAINED IN THE RIG-VEDA
Author: ALBERT PIKE

Indo-Aryan

Deities and Worship

As Contained in the

Rig-Veda

ALBERT PIKE

1872

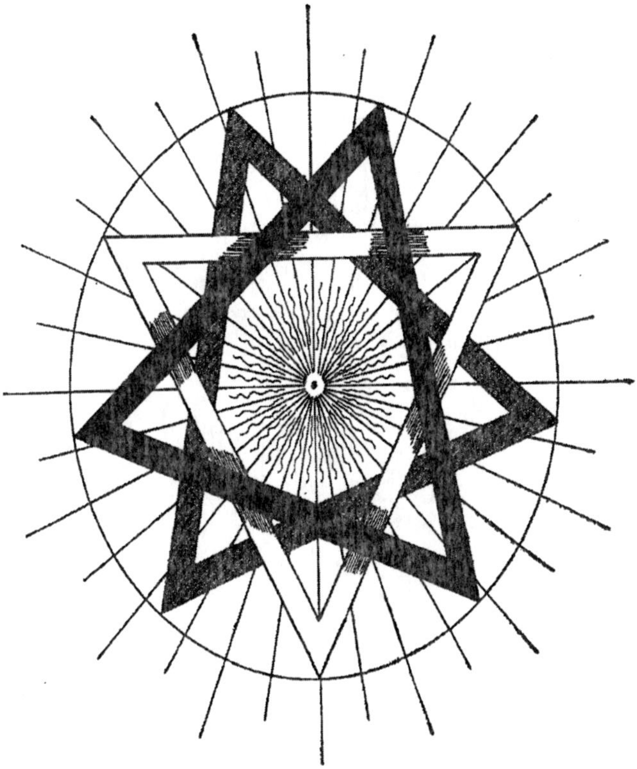

PREFACE.

It is quite uncertain, now that I have this book finished, whether I shall ever care to publish it. It was not commenced for that purpose; and it may always remain a monotype, in manuscript.

For it has been written as a study, and not as a teaching—for myself and not for others. It is not at all the fruit of a meditated purpose, and was not commenced as a diagnosis of the Deities of the Veda, an attempt to discover the distinctive personality and individuality of each, which it afterwards became, and the fruits of itself to myself have been sufficient to reward me abundantly for the labour it has cost. Nothing has ever so much interested me, as this endeavour to penetrate into the adyta of the ancient Aryan thought, to discover what things, principles or phenomena our remote ancestors worshipped as Gods, what Indra, Varuṇa, Mitra, Aryaman, the Açvins, Vayu, Vishṅu, Savitṛi and the others really were, in the conception of the composers of the Vedic hymns.

It has had a singular charm for me, this inquiry into the true meaning of the epithets and phrases, often, in appearance, indiscriminately applied to different Deities, often seemingly inappropriate, and the expressions of a wild and riotous imagination; into the true meaning of names and epithets and phrases that became, literally accepted and misunderstood, the sources, seeds or germs of the legendary myths and many of the Deities of the Grecian mythology and the Brahmanic fables and pantheon.

And I have felt the most intense satisfaction in deciphering, as it seemed to me I did, these hieroglyphs of ancient Aryan thought; in bringing myself into relation (*en rapport*) with these old Poets and Philosophers, understanding them in part, and thinking with them; in deciphering their hieroglyphics, infinitely better worth the labour than all that are engraved on the monuments of Egypt and Assyria, and in solving one by one the enigmas contained in their figurative and seemingly extravagant language, whose meaning was only to be discovered by beginning with their simplest notions and conceptions, and making the curious processes of their thought my own—trying as it were, to *be* them, intellectually, and to think their thoughts.

Thus I satisfied myself that every one of their Deities had for them a perfectly distinct and clear personality and individuality; that their ideas were not in the least vague, incoherent or confused; that their imagination was perfectly well-regulated, and that every epithet and phrase was logically appropriate and correct. So also, upon a partial examination, I found it to be in the ancient Zarathustrian Gâthâs, which are, I do not doubt, even older than the Vedic hymns.

I found in both, the most profound philosophic or metaphysical ideas, which those of every philosophy and religion have merely developed; and that, so far from being Barbarians or Savages, the old Aryan herdsmen and husbandmen, in the Indus country under the Himalayan Mountains, on the rivers of Bactria, and, long before, on the Scythic Steppes where they originated, were men of singularly clear and acute intellects, profound thought and an infinite reverence of the beings whom they worshipped.

The inquiry has opened to me an entirely new chapter of the history of human thought, and given me an infinitely higher conception of the Aryan intellect. I now see how, out of the primitive simplicity of a natural and reasonable religion, and of ideas simple and yet profoundly philosophical, there grew the most monstrous and debasing faiths, the most absurd and delirious fables, and the most abominable superstitions, the worship of animals, legends of the amours and adulteries of the Gods, conceptions of monstrous idols, the most incredible fables, the most irrational mysticism, and the Phallic and Lingam worship with its disgusting obscenities and Priapean abominations, as well as the incoherent notions of the Kabbalah and the vagaries of Gnosticism.

But I also see, growing out of, or rather developing, the same ancient ideas, the doctrines of Plato and Philo which long ruled and in their turn became fruitful of the modern philosophies and psychology, of the doctrines of emanation and of creation by the Word, the self-revealing, and manifestation of the "Inconceivable Deity."

The requital of my labour is already ample; and as to any notoriety that might come of publication, what is that worth to me who can have but little more to do with this world, and the evening of whose life has come?

But to anyone who may read this book, whether it be published or remain unpublished, I wish to offer a few words of explanation.

I am quite aware of my very imperfect qualifications as an interpreter of the antique hymns of the Veda, and how little it becomes me, knowing little of the Sanskrit and less of the Zend, to speak *ex cathedrâ* in regard to the meaning of the texts, either of the Veda or the *Zend-Avesta*, or to think that I can explain what scholars like Wilson, Müller and Muir are obliged to confess they do not understand. Of course I have fallen into many errors, and been unfortunate in my interpretations of many passages. I console myself for the certainty of that, with the reflection that these great scholars have done the same; and that there are hundreds of passages in the Veda, where the "interpretations" of the English and Hindû commentators alike, are only hazardous and wild guesses; and with the certain and positive assurance that if I am not always right, I am not always wrong, but have lifted at least a corner of the veil that hid the real meaning of the Veda.

I was led to study, first, such portions of the Rig-Veda as were accessible to me translated by Professor Max Müller, by a desire to ascertain the origin of the Hindū Ineffable Word OM or A. U. M. of which it is said that the Brahmins themselves knew neither the origin nor real meaning; but which, to them, represents the divine Trimūrti or Triad, of Brahma the Creator, Vishnū the Preserver, and Siva the Destroyer.

I found it in the initials of the names of the Vedic Deities, Agni, Aryaman, the Açvins, Varuṇa, Vayu, Vishnū, Ushas, Mitra, the Maruts, and others; but found myself utterly at a loss to determine what several of these Deities were. I found that the commentators themselves had no clear and definite ideas as to many of them, and did not even attempt to conjecture what they were. Some were sometimes one thing and sometimes another, to the same commentator. The personality that they assigned to some was directly contradicted by the clear letter of texts translated by themselves.

Agni plainly was Fire, domestic, sacrificial and celestial; but also he was Wise, Intelligent, Bestower of Benefits, and invested with a multitude of attributes and characteristics, seemingly incoherent, confused and extravagant, which the commentators made no effort to explain, in any manner, philosophic or otherwise. Ushas was unmistakably the Dawn, and Surya the Sun, and the Maruts the Winds. Soma, the juice of a plant (the *Haoma* of the *Zend-Avesta*), was also a Deity, invested with the most extraordinary powers, and also said to be sometimes the Moon. Indra was said to be the Firmament; but this many texts contradicted. As to Varuṇa, Mitra, Aryaman, the Açvins, Vishṅu, Vayu, Yama, Rudra, Tvashtri, Brahmanaspati, Brihaspati, and Vanospati, there was, as to part of them, not even a conjecture, and as to none, anything more than contradictory guesses or feeble and helpless suggestions.

It seemed as though the most of the Deities were mere names, without intellectual reality; and as though the Vedic Bards had no fixed, distinct, definite and consistent ideas in regard to any but a few of their Gods. The Veda seemed hardly to have been worth the trouble of translating, and the Brahmanic commentaries only made the confusion worse confounded.

At first, I only proposed to ascertain, if I could, by comparison of the texts, to find out what Agni, Varuṇa and Mitra were, to the composers of the hymns; and this, not with the least view to publication, but with reference, entirely, to the ineffable Hindū word, in which, for reasons that do not concern the general reader, I had a special interest.

The process which I adopted, appears in the following pages. Procuring Professor Wilson's translation of the *Rig-Veda Sanhita*, I first copied the principal passages addressed to or speaking of Agni. I then summed up the significant portions of these, referring also to Dr. Muir's *Original Sanskrit Texts*, and to the articles of Professor Müller; and from the whole endeavoured to attain to an understanding of the Vedic conceptions in regard to that Deity. This diverted me from my first purpose, and led me to make a like inquiry, in the same manner, as to Indra, and thence as to the other Deities in succession; until what I wrote grew into a book.

I state these things, to show I set out with no theory as to the nature of any of the Gods. I did not think of looking for other meanings and interpretations of the texts; or of learning more in regard to the Deities, than the learned scholars whose works I had could tell me.

But soon discovering that they did not themselves know what most of the Gods were; that they sometimes considered the same God as one thing, and sometimes as another; that the notions of Sayana and the other Hindū commentators were utterly worthless; and that Indra *could* not be the firmament, nor Savitṛi the sun, nor the Açvins and Varuṇa and Mitra what they were supposed to be, I endeavoured to discover from the texts themselves what first one God, and then the other, was.

In some cases, I was long at a loss, confused by many texts, out of all which it seemed impossible to extract any definite idea, a single one at last gave the key to the rest, and enabled me to comprehend and reconcile them all.

Sometimes I came to a wrong conclusion, before I had collated all the texts relating to a particular God; and afterwards, by the aid of other texts, found what I deemed to be the true solution. That was the case as to the Açvins, whose number, *two*, and the *three* wheels, supports, etc., of their chariot, greatly perplexed me.

I thought, for a time, that Varuṇa and Mitra meant the calorific light of the sun, or Day, and the light, without heat, of the luminaries of the Night. Rudra and Tvashtri were enigmas, as Vishṇu was, which I did not solve to my own satisfaction, without first falling into more than one error.

I knew very little of the Sanskrit, and have had to rely almost wholly upon the translations. But these often themselves enable one to discover the real meaning which they conceal, when, giving the modern sense, secondary and derivative, of the ancient words of the tongue so long dead, they enable one to go back to the more simple, original and radical meaning.

And when one understands the kindred languages, Greek, Latin, and those that have descended from the Latin, and has the original texts given, as Dr. Muir gives it in his fourth volume, and as Professor Wilson commonly does, where the meaning of particular phrases is doubtful, he may not always be bound to take a translation upon trust, and may even sometimes detect an error, where preconceived opinions have caused persistent adherence to particular renderings of words. And this, especially, when the translator uses words which, in their present meaning to us, could not possibly have had equivalents to the Aryan Bards, and perhaps have no definite meaning even to us—such as "heaven," "firmament," and "worlds."

Perhaps what I have written here, even if it be found to be of little value, may help to make our remote ancestors somewhat better known to their descendants, and, followed up by those who are far more competent and better qualified, may result in a truer interpretation of the thoughts of the Aryan Poets. To the reader, whoever he may be, if what I have written is published, I have only to say, in the words of Ovid:

Da veniam scriptis, quorum non gloria nobis
Caussa, deo utilitas officiumque fuit.

March 20, 1872. ALBERT PIKE

NOTE.

There are many more letters in Sanskrit than there are in English—each letter representing a distinct sound; while in our language the same letter often represents two or three different sounds.

The Sanskrit letters, which are not represented by simple English letters, are, in part, not represented by the same marks by the different writers. I prefer to following Eichhoff (*Parallèle des langues de l'Europe et de l'Inde*), and Eastwick's translation of Bopp's Comparative Grammar of the Sanskrit, Zend, etc., where they agree, and one or the other, where they do not.

As to the following, they agree:

â representing *a* long.
î representing *ee* long.
û representing *oo* long.
ṭ representing *t* hard.
ṭh representing *t* hard, aspirated.
ḍ representing *d* hard.
ḍh representing *d* hard, aspirated.
ṇ representing *n* hard.

In the following I prefer Bopp's notation:

ri [Eich. *AR* and *ṛ* liquid; sound *r* with *ee* hardly heard].
rî [Eich. *Â*R and *ṝ* long; sound *ree* Eng. or *ri* French].
ê, equivalent of *ai*, French.
ô, equivalent of *au*, French.
ṅ nasal, French *n*, at end of word, *ngh* or *gn*. Eich. *ñ*.

In the following, Eichhoff:

ṣ, representing *sh* hard.
ṣh, representing *sch*.
Eichhoff also uses ç to represent *sh*, soft, or *s*; as *Açvins*, for *Aṣwins*.

INTRODUCTORY.

The *RIG-VEDA SANHITÂ* is a collection of *Sûktas* (hymns) to the Aryan Deities: the word *Sanhitâ* meaning a "collection."

In the Rig-Vedas are something over a thousand Sûktas.

These are divided into eight *Khandas* (portions), or *Ashtakas* (eighths), each of which is subdivided into eight *Adhyâyas* or lectures.

Another plan classes the Sûktas under ten *Mandalas* (circles), sub-divided into rather more than one hundred *Anuvâkas*, or sub-sections.

The Sûktas are divided into *Vargas* (paragraphs or verses), of about five stanzas each.

The principal part of the Rig-Veda has been translated into English by Professor H. H. Wilson; and it is from this translation that the much larger portion of the texts copied in this book have been taken. A large number of the hymns have been translated by Dr. Muir, in *Volume iv.* of his *Original Sanskrit Texts;* and some by Müller, in his *Lectures on Language,* and *Chips from a German Workshop.* The extracts from the translations of Professor Wilson refer to *Ashtaka, Adhyâya, Anuvâka* and *Sûkta;* those from Dr. Muir and Müller, to *Mandala* and *Sûkta.*

In some cases I have given the later as well as the earlier translation of the same hymn.

Professor Müller's translation of a part of the hymns, lately published in England, I have not seen.

THE VEDA.

The Veda is certainly the second oldest book in the world, and it contains the religious hymns of our ancestors; for we, of whatever mixture of European blood, are wholly of the Aryan race. Germans, Gauls, Franks, Latins, Saxons, Kelts, Sclaves, all are of one blood and family; and the English and all other European languages, and the Sanskrit, Zend and Persian are but varieties of one and the same original language, produced by intermixtures with various others. We are by nature Aryan, Indo-European, not Semitic. There is no mixture of Semitic in the European languages. The indigenous peoples whom the Aryans conquered, and with whom they mixed, were of a race or races totally different from the Semites. Our spiritual kith and kin are to be found in India, Persia, Sclavonia, Greece, Italy and Germany; not in Mesopotamia, Egypt or Palestine.

No literary relic carries us back to so child-like a state in the history of man, as the Veda. The Hebrew books which compose the Pentateuch represent the ancestors of that people as having from the beginning attained to the comprehension of a single creative Deity, above the powers of Nature, and as not regarding these powers as in any sense Deities, but merely forces of Nature. Before the Flood, it assures us, there were performers on the harp and organ, and artificers in brass and iron, and men were gathered together into cities.

The exodus from Egypt, according to the approved chronology, occurred 1,648 years before Christ. The Vedas were compiled 1,400 years before Christ, when the language in which the hymns were written had become a dead language, and kingdoms had been founded and grown grey with age, since they were sung in the country of the Five Rivers.

The book of Genesis records the ancient traditions of the Semitic race, and makes known to us the ancient thought, the ancient feelings, joys, hopes and fears of those who were the ancestors of the Chaldæans, Phœnicians, Kenanim, and Hebrews and of the grand Arabian race. The Vedas bring us face to face with our ancestors, in their tents and pastures, adoring the fire, the light and the luminaries of heaven. Nowhere else is there a sign, a jest or a glimpse of the old Asiatic humanity.

Veda meant "knowing," or "knowledge." It is the same word as the Greek *οἶδα*, "I knew," and appears in the Gothic *vait*, the Anglo-Saxon *wât*, the German *weiss*, and the English "wise, wisdom," and "to wit."

There are four collections of the hymns, the *Rig*-Veda, *Yajur*-Veda, *Sâma*-Veda and *Atharva*-Veda; but for tracing the earliest growth of religious ideas in India, the only real Veda is the *Rig-Veda*.

Rig-Veda means the Veda of "Hymns of Praise, Rich," which before the initial soft letter of Veda is changed to *Rig*, being derived from a root which in Sanskrit means to *celebrate*. The Sanhitâ, a collection of it consists of ten books, containing altogether 1,028 hymns.

Müller ascribes the composition of the Vaidic hymns to a later period than Bunsen does; and in his fear of shocking English prejudices, is exceedingly vague and unsatisfactory upon that point. Even Bunsen is careful not to say that the Veda is older than the Hebrew books. The Biblical chronology, the necessity of considering mere myths and legends as historical, and the supposed inexorable necessity of admitting that all mankind has descended from one man and woman, are sadly in the way of exhaustive inquiry as to the origines of human races and human languages. These sagacious and astute inquirers thoroughly satisfy and convince us that all the European languages are from the same ancient source as the Indian and Persian, but their attempts to show a relationship between these and the Semitic tongues are lamentable failures. As to the Turanian languages, that is, the thousand languages of Asia, Africa and America that have nothing in common with each other, they very faintly suggest a common origin with the Aryan and Semitic tongues; and are not quite bold enough to claim that they also are the descendants of ancestors of our race, and emigrants from Airyana Vaêjâ.

Müller well says that

> the real history of man is the history of religion, the ways by which the different families of the human race advanced towards a truer knowledge and a deeper love of God: that this is the light, the soul and the life of history.

There is nothing of it in the history of the early Semitic races. When the Hebrews were carried away to Babylon, they had made no such advance; for they had no truer knowledge of the Deity than Abraham the Chaldæan had. (*Müller: Chips* i. 21.)

> The oldest, most primitive and simplest form of Aryan faith finds its expression in the Veda. No idols or animals are mentioned in it, as objects of worship.

In fact idols and images are not mentioned at all. They belong only to an anthropological faith. They do not represent the light and the heat. The Veda does not invest its Deities with the human form. It does not represent any of them as coming down in visible shape and having commerce with men.

The Veda, by its language and its thoughts, supplies that distant background in the history of all the religions of the Aryan race, which was missed, indeed, by every careful observer, but could formerly be supplied by guesswork only.

How the Zarathustrian religion had its origin, and while inculcating the worship of the Supreme Being, Ahura Mazda, still permitted fire to be a symbol of him,

how the Buddhists came to protest against temples and sacrifices, how Zeus and the Olympian Gods came to be what they are in the mind of Homer, or how such beings as Jupiter and Mars came to be worshipped by the Italian peasant, we can now understand by a simple reference to the Veda.

The original religion was adoration of the supposed superior beings of which fire and light were manifestations. The Aryan name for God, *Deva*, is the original of the Latin *Deus*, as *Dyaus* is of the Greek *Zeus:* and *Varuṇa* is the *Ouranos* of Hesiod.

The religion of the Veda is not the *source* of all the other religions of the Aryan world,

for it was itself an advance, an improvement upon and the successor of a more ancient faith, as the Sanskrit is not the mother, but the sister, of the Greek and Latin languages. But

we can watch in the Veda, ideas and their names growing, which we meet with in Persia, Greece and Rome only as full-grown or fast decaying. We get nearer to that distant source of religious thought and language which has fed the different national streams of Persia, Greece, Rome and Germany:

and clearly see that the human mind had made a great advance when it had come to worship, not the fire itself but the unseen and intelligent Spirit of the Fire, of which the light was deemed a manifestation.

Many of the Vedic hymns are childish, low, tedious, commonplace. The Gods are constantly invoked for material benefits, for wealth, especially food, horses, cows, large families and a long life. Many prayers are addressed to the Deities for aid against enemies; and Indra is a veritable God of War, the Arēs of the Greeks and Mars of the Romans.

No one supreme God is invoked, like Jehovah or Brahm: and no doubt the religion of the Veda is polytheism.

But whenever one of the Deities is invoked, Agni, Varuṇa, Mitra or Indra, he is not conceived of as inferior, or as limited by the powers of any other. In many respects, the same attributes of power and supremacy are ascribed to all. Each is Supreme and Absolute; each as good as all.

> Among you, Gods, there is none that is small, none that is young. You are all great indeed.

This, Müller says, is indeed the keynote of the ancient Aryan worship. It is the key, we think, by which we may unlock its hidden meanings. All the powers and names of all the other Divinities are distinctly ascribed to Agni; but nothing is said in disparagement of the others. Indra, also, is declared to be greater than all. And Varuña is said to be

> Lord of all, of heaven and earth, king of all, both Gods and men.

Some of the hymns ascribe to the Gods sentiments and passions unworthy of the Deity, as the Hebrew writings do—anger, revenge, cruelty. They delight in sacrifices, as the God of the Hebrews did. Many of the hymns are unmeaning and insipid; and it is only rarely that we find prayers in which we ourselves could join. Nevertheless there are such. And

> in some of the hymns the mercy of the Deities is confidently appealed to, and their readiness to forgive errors due to the inherent frailty of human nature is relied on.
> 'It was not our own doing, Varuṇa,'

the hymn exclaims,

> 'it was temptation, an intoxicating draught, passion, dice, thoughtlessness. The old is there to mislead the young; even sleep brings unrighteousness.'
>
> Words, verses and even whole hymns, of the Rig-Veda, are and perhaps will remain a dead letter to us. But in many we find old thoughts, old hopes, old faith and old errors, the old man altogether—old now, but then young and fresh, and simple and real in his prayers and praises.

There is at least nothing slavish or brutal, sensual or grovelling in these hymns, nothing of the barbarian or savage. A spirit of grave thoughtfulness pervades them; they are highly devotional and reverential; of philosophy there is little; and yet the idea that there was a spirit, of whom no cognition could be had, in fire, a spirit intelligent, wise and powerful, was of the same profound nature as that of the immortal soul, united with the body, or of the divine soul in Nature. It was not the idea of a savage or a child, but of a philosopher and metaphysician; and I think that as these hymns are better understood, and we penetrate more deeply into the thought of the Poets who composed them, we shall find ideas there, of emanation and manifestation, of the principle and essence, itself beyond our cognition, and only attainable by the intellect, limiting itself by form, and positing itself in place, its manifestation of itself, and yet not all or its Very Self, which have re-appeared in all the great philosophies of the world, and been essential in all the great religions.

It is true, as Müller says, truer even than he thought it, that,

> There are hymns in the Vedas so full of thought and speculation, that, at that early period, no Poet in any other nation could have conceived them. (*Chips i.* 77.)

But I doubt whether it is true that

> we find in the Veda that which is really the very essence of all religion, and without which there can be no religion, a belief in personal immortality.

I do not agree that a belief in personal immortality is essential to religion. There is a total absence, in the Hebrew writings, of any teaching or any evidence of a belief that the soul lives on when the body dies: and even in the time of the Apostles, the Sadducees who sat in the same council with the High Priest, openly denied the resurrection. And yet, certainly, the ancient Hebrews had a religion, and were not without one altogether until they learned the doctrine of the immortality of the soul from the Persians. The man who believes in a God or Gods who reward the good and punish the bad in this life, and may be propitiated by adoration or sacrifice, has a religion.

Moreover, the soul may exist after this life, in one or more successive states of existence, and yet not be immortal. It is doubtful if any of the ancients believed in an existence absolutely without end. We have assurance of another life, but not of an eternal life. As God alone is infinite, so, it may be, He alone is by His nature eternal.

Nor do we clearly see that in the Veda there is any evidence of a belief in another life, and still less of a belief in a real immortality. In many places it is sure that the word "immortal" is a mis-translation. Food gives the immortality of the Veda; and the original word, in general, evidently means only continuance, and not even great length, of life.

Professor Müller, from whom our unacknowledged quotations have been made, says:

> We have in the Veda, ancient thought expressed in ancient language. We see reflected in it a phase of the intellectual life of man, to which there is no parallel in any other part of the world. In its hymns we see man left to himself, to solve the enigma of this world and life. (*Chips i.* 69.)

We see him with the simple desires of a simple life in the forests and plains; for almost all the hymns express the wants and wishes of the herdsman, and the dweller in the woods only traversable by paths, or in the plains, where only the luminaries of the day and night could be his guides. Some show the occupation of the worshipper to be that of husbandman. They are villagers, and not denizens of towns and cities. Continually the prayer is for wealth and treasure, but these seem always to mean only horses and cattle, and for food. (Fire is produced by attrition; not, probably, from necessity, for they were not savages, but as perfectly pure when thus procured, and because it had been for ages a part of the ceremonial to produce it so; and evidently the sacrifices were generally offered up in the open air.)

This herdsman or husbandman sees that fire and light are indispensable to human existence, and that they alone reveal to man the existence of the material universe. What they reveal, they seem to create. He is awakened by the dawn or the sun, or, watching before the dawn sees the light-bearer, the beautiful and brilliant Morning Star rise calmly into the sky and smile kindly upon him; and he adored the dawn, the sun, the Morning Star as manifestations of the one great universal light; but I do not find that, as Müller says he does,

> he calls Him whom his eyes cannot behold, and who seems to grant him the daily pittance of his existence. *His life, his breath, his brilliant lord and protector,*

in the sense that he invokes the favour of a God, who is not fire nor light, nor any force or power or essence or principle of Nature, but a being invisible and incomprehensible, *above* Nature and its forces. I think I can most positively assert that there is no such conception in the Veda.

He makes the Fire a *person*, and invests it, as a *universal*, with the characteristics of spirituality. He adores the Fire-Spirit, the universal Light-Principle, the Heat-Principle, as Gods; and they become not merely Powers, but Persons, to him, protectors and benefactors, who hear his prayers and are intelligent and wise. Under various names he adores the same light and fire as variously manifested in shape, place and limitation of forms, as the sun, moon, planets and stars. Even prayer, adoration silent or uttered, and food itself, become Deities, by a strictly logical process of thought, and not by mere vagary of fancy or imagination. He adores the fire and light, also, in the dawn, the Aurora and the lightning. The winds are Gods for him, and even the rivers become Goddesses. The sacrificial Fire fed by the fuel which also he deifies, is the messenger of the Gods and his mediator with them.

> We study in the Veda a theogony [Professor Müller says], of which that of Hesiod is but the last chapter. We can study therein man's natural growth, and the results to which it may lead, under the most favourable conditions.

And we can study the intellect and the intellectual development of the last created and noblest race of men, whose history is that of the civilized world.

That the hymns which compose the Veda, must have existed for ages, before they were compiled, admits of no doubt.

> In different songs the names of different kings occur, and we see several generations of royal families pass away before us, with different generations of Poets. Old songs are mentioned, and new songs are mentioned. Poets whose compositions we possess are spoken of as the seers of older times; their names in other hymns are surrounded by a legendary halo. In some cases, whole books or chapters can be pointed out, as more modern and secondary in thought and language. But on the whole, the Rig-Veda is a genuine document, not later, even in its most modern portions, than the time of Lycurgus. It exhibits one of the earliest and rudest phases in the history of mankind; and brings us as near the beginnings, in language, thought and mythology, as literary documents can ever bring us, in the Aryan World. (*Müller, Chips i.* 74.)

One thing that has an important bearing on the age of the Vedic hymns has not, I think, as yet been noticed. The sea is sometimes mentioned in them. All the commentators agree that all the older hymns, at least, were written or composed while the Aryans dwelt in the Punjab, on the upper Indus, in sight of the Himalayas; and before they crossed the Sutlej and entered the Ganges country. The composers of the hymns, therefore, could have known nothing about the ocean. And it inevitably results that the hymns were not composed in the Punjab, but, at a much later day, in lower India, and when the sea had become a familiar object; or else those who composed them had seen and known and were familiar with, some other sea. This latter hypothesis can only be satisfied by supposing them to have meant the Caspian and the Sea of Aral; and that these hymns in which the sea is spoken of, are of much older date, and were composed in Sogdiana, when the men of the race roamed the steppes as herdsmen. For other reasons, I believe this to be the true solution.

We have some knowledge of times still more ancient—

> of the period during which the as yet undivided Aryan nations formed their myths. Comparative philology has this whole period within the pale of documentary history. It has placed in our hands, a telescope of such power, that where formerly we could see but nebulous clouds, we now discover distinct forms and outlines; nay, it has given us what we may call contemporary evidence, exhibiting to us the state of thought, language, religion and civilization, at a period when Sanskrit was not yet Sanskrit, Greek not yet Greek, but when both, together with Latin, German and other Aryan dialects, existed as yet as one undivided language. (*Müller, Chips ii.* 17.)

What is commonly called Hindū mythology is of little or no avail for comparative purposes. The stories of Siva, Vishṇu, Mahâdeva, Parvati, Kali, Krishṅa, etc., are of late growth, and indigenous to India. But a whole world of primitive, natural and intelligible mythology has been preserved in the Veda. In it there is no *system* of religion or mythology. Names are used in one hymn as appellatives, in another as names of Gods. The same God is sometimes represented as supreme, sometimes as equal, sometimes as inferior to others. The whole nature of these so-called Gods is still transparent; their first conception, in many cases, clearly perceptible. There are as yet no genealogies, no settled marriages between Gods and Goddesses. The father is sometimes the son, the brother is the husband, and she who in one hymn is the mother, is in another the wife. As the conceptions of the Poets varied, so varied the nature of these Gods. The Veda is the real theogony of the Aryan races, while that of Hesiod is a distorted caricature of the original image. If we would know whither the human mind, though endowed with the natural consciousness of a divine power, is necessarily and inevitably driven by the irresistible force of language, as applied to supernatural and abstract ideas, we must read the Veda. (*Müller, Chips ii.* 75–76.)

However imperfect and absurd the notions of Deity of the ancient Aryans may seem to us to be, it must be admitted that no people was ever so anxious to perform the service of the Gods, as these ancestors of our European races. It is the Gods who conquer their enemies, who give them wealth, health, children, friends, and plentiful harvests. They humbly acknowledge their dependence on their Deities, and touchingly express their trust in their beneficence and kindness.

Mr. Cox (*Mythology i.* 40 *et seq.*) says:

The mental condition of the men of those early ages determined the character of their language; and that condition exhibited in them, as in children, how, the waking of a feeling which endowed all outward things with a life not unlike their own. Of the several objects which met their eyes, they had no positive knowledge, whether of their origin, their nature or their properties. But they themselves had life, and therefore all other things must have life also. They were under no necessity of personifying them, for they had for themselves no distinctions between consciousness and personality. They knew nothing of the conditions of their own life, or of any other; and therefore all things on the earth or in the heavens were invested with the same vague idea of existence. The sun, the moon, the stars, the earth, the clouds, winds, fire, storms and lightnings, were all living beings. Could they help thinking that these also were conscious beings like themselves? Their very words would, by an inevitable necessity, express this conviction. Their language would admit no single expression from which the attribute of life was excluded, while it would vary the forms of that life, with unerring instinct. Every object would be a living reality, and every word a speaking picture. For the herdsman of the valleys or the steppes, there would be no bare recurrence of days and seasons, but every morning, the Dawn would drive her bright flocks to the blue pastures of Heaven, before the birth of the Lord of Day from the toiling womb of Night. Round the living progress of the new-born Sun there would be grouped a lavish imagery, expressive of the most intense sympathy with what we term the operation of material forces, and not less expressive of the utter absence of even the faintest knowledge. For every aspect of the material world he would find some life-giving expression; and whose aspect would be scarcely less varied than his words. The same object would, at different times, or under different conditions, awaken the most opposite or inconsistent conceptions.

But it is merely fanciful to say, that

> life would be an alternation of joy and sorrow, of terror and relief;

because of the uncertainty whether, when the Sun set, he would rise again, and Dawn come again to chase away the darkness. It does not need science to assure men of that. The American Indian on the plains feels as certain of it as the man of science does. The feeling of certainty in the permanence of things was never absent from any men, at any time. Hence the terror of the savage at an eclipse.

But the poetic imagination would connect with the Sun

> both mournful and inspiriting ideas, ideas of victory and defeat, of toil and premature death. He would be the Titan strangling the serpents of the night before he drove his chariot up the sky: and he would also be the being who, worn down by unwilling labour undergone for men, sinks wearied at evening into the arms of the mother who bore him in the morning. Other images would not be wanting: the dawn and the clouds would be no less real and living to them than the sun. In his rising from the East, the Sun would leave the fair Dawn, whom he would see no more until his labour drew near its close. And not less would he love and be loved by the Dew and by the Morning herself, while to both his life would be fatal, as his fiery car rose higher in the sky. So he would speak of all other things; of the thunder, earthquake and storm, not less than of summer and winter. (*Cox*, *i*. 41–42.)

We do not find in the Vedas the idea of daily *labour* connected with the luminaries, or that they were regarded as

> free beings kept in temporary servitude, chained for a time, and bound to obey a higher will.

Müller imputes it to the ancient Aryans. But we cannot find that they conceived of any higher will, or of servitude as connected with the sun, moon or stars.

Nor do we agree with Cox that there was no personification in the original notions of the objects which were regarded as living beings. To regard the Sun as a person, or Deity, must have been one of the earliest notions of every people in their infancy. But we agree with him that there was no allegory or metaphor; but it was to them a veritable reality, which they examined and analyzed as little as they reflected on themselves. The Peruvians and Nachis worshipped the Sun as a person and living being; and intellectually these were but children.

Phrases and emblems to which we now attach a purely spiritual signification, have acquired these meanings gradually, as the ruder ideas which belonged to the infancy of the human race faded from the mind: and the translators of the Veda certainly use many words in senses that are spiritual now, and thus misrepresent the ancient ideas, which would be faithfully reproduced, only if the English phrases used had their original material and sensual meaning.

The history of words carries us back to an age far beyond the Veda. When they were composed, it could not be truly said that men had everything to learn, and no experience to fall back upon. They had advanced so far as to conceive of and to adore, in the fire and light and their manifestations, the invisible Spirits of Fire and Light, to which they imputed intelligence, forethought and divine attributes. They had not attained to the conscious acknowledgment of one Deity, or of one life as the source of all the life which they saw around them. We do not think, with Cox, that any of the Vedic hymns "express the hopes and fears of men who had not yet grasped the notion of any natural order whatever." They could not have thought "that the return of daylight might depend on the caprice of the arbitrary being whom they had watched through his brilliant but brief journey across the heaven." The questions asked during the night do *not* "betray a real anguish," nor do the exultations that greeted the dawn show that they really "feared, every night, that the dawn might not come again." The questions and the exultations are merely rhetorical embellishments.

It is truly said by Mr. Cox, that

> the dawns, as they came round, made men old; but the Dawn herself never lost her freshness, and sprang from the sea-foam, as fair as when she first gladdened the eyes of man. Men sickened and died, but the years that brought to them sickness and death, could not dim the light of the sun, or make any change in the familiar constellations.

But these ideas were not expressed by the Poets of the Vedas. For them, the life they lived here seems to have been sufficient, the things of this world all that were to be cared for; and they neither lament the brevity of life, nor concern themselves about or anticipate another.

LANGUAGE AND TRANSLATION.

Professor Müller says,

> It is not in the power of language to express, originally, anything except objects as nouns, and qualities as verbs. The only definition we can give of language, during its early state, is, that it is the conscious expression in sound, of impressions received by all the senses. There were then no abstract nouns.

There are many dialects of the present day that have none. I have found none in several of the American Indian languages of the Southwest.

> An abstract word is an adjective raised into a substantive.

Virtue is not a substantive *thing*, but the habit and succession of virtuous acts, or the natural inclination to act virtuously. It is a quality of the heart, or mind, or character.

> Originally, words like 'day' and 'night,' and 'spring,' 'summer,' 'dawn' and 'twilight,' 'storm' and 'thunder' [Müller says], were abstract, and are so still, in form.

Certainly these are not *things*, but so neither is "life," meaning the time during which we live, nor "light," nor "heat," nor the "rainbow." But time is a reality to the simple and unlearned man. It is only metaphysical subtlety that argues it into nihility, making it a quality raised by language into a substance. Light and darkness are realities to the Indian, and so they were to the ancient Aryans.

To all of these the early men imputed individuality, and to them that individuality was invested with reality, and with each the idea of sex was connected; but that this was "because the name of each had necessarily a termination expressive of gender," seems to us doubtful. Certainly that is not the reason why God is regarded as a male wherever monotheism prevails in the world.

It is true that

> as long as people thought in language, it was simply impossible to speak of morning or evening, spring or winter, dawn or night, the winds or any other natural or ideal object, without giving to these conceptions an individual and active character, nor that it should not at last become personal and sexual. They were not nothings, as they are to our withered thought, but somethings; and being somethings, they could not be conceived of as mere Powers, but as powerful Beings.

We now talk of the powers and forces of Nature, but we cannot conceive of them as existences or entities. There is life and blood now, in all our abstract terms. We call this poetic diction, and regard it as exaggeration in the Poet to address Religion, Humanity, Winter, Ambition, Frost, Snow, Age, the Hours, Storms and Seasons, as persons, as Wordsworth does in a single poem:

> but it is no exaggeration to the Poet, nor was it to the ancient Poets of language. Poetry is older than prose, and abstract speech more difficult than the outpouring of a Poet's sympathy with Nature. It requires reflection to divest Nature of her living expression, to see in the swift-riding clouds nothing but vapourous exhalations, in the frowning mountains mere masses of stone, and in the lightning, electric sparks;

in the light, only undulations of invisible ether, in the rainbow, only an effect and not a thing. It is, indeed, simply impossible for men to talk or write, without personifying visible objects and the various phases of Nature. And when Wordsworth speaks of

> the last hill that parleys with the setting sun,

it is a thought not yet translated into the prose of our traditional and emaciated speech; one such as the men of old would not have been ashamed of in their common everyday conversation. (*Condensed from Müller: Chips from a German Workshop ii.* 54 *to* 58.)

> If we ourselves, in speaking of the sun or the storms, of sleep and death, of earth and dawn, connect either no distinct idea at all with these names, or allow them to cast over our mind the fleeting shadows of the poetry of old; why, if we, when speaking with the warmth which is natural to the human heart, call upon the winds and the sun, the ocean and the sky, as if they would still hear us; why, if plastic thought cannot represent any one of these beings or powers, without giving them, if not a human form, at least human life and human feeling, why should we wonder at the ancients, with their language throbbing with life, and revelling in colour, if, instead of the grey outlines of our modern thought, they threw out those living forms of Nature, endowed with human powers, nay, with powers more than human, inasmuch as the light of the sun was brighter than the light of a human eye, and the roaring of the storms louder than the shouts of a human voice? We may be able to account for the origin of rain and dew, of storm and thunder; yet, to the great majority of mankind, all these things, unless they are mere names, are still what they were to Homer, only perhaps less beautiful, less poetical, less real and living. (*Müller: Chips ii.* 59.)

And I am greatly mistaken, if, when we better understand the thoughts and conceptions of the Poets of the Veda, we do not find still more abundant reason to agree with Müller, that,

> as far as we can trace back the footsteps of man, even on the lowest strata of history, we see that the divine gift of a sound and sober intellect belonged to him from the very first; and the idea of a humanity emerging from the depths of an animal brutality can never be maintained again.

I do not apply these words to races of men like the lowest Africans, Australians and American Indians; but to the great races whose history is the history of civilization. The Aryan race was never a race of barbarians.

> The earliest work of art, wrought by the human mind, more ancient than any literary document, and prior even to the first whisperings of tradition, the human language forms an uninterrupted chain, from the first dawn of history down to our own times. We still speak the language of the first ancestors of our race: and the formation of language attests from the very first the presence of a rational mind. (*Müller: Chips ii.* 8.)
>
> Language [Mr. Swinton says] is a living *original*. It is not made, but grows. The growth of language repeats the growth of the plant. At first it is only root: next it puts forth a stem, then leaves, and finally blossoms.
>
> One must not [says William Von Humboldt] consider a language as a product dead and formed but once: it is an animate being, and ever creative human thought elaborates itself with the progress of intelligence; and of this thought language is a manifestation. An idiom, therefore, cannot remain stationary: it walks, it develops, it grows up, it fortifies itself, it becomes old, and it reaches decrepitude.

The primary and natural signification of words, Frederick Schlegel says, often no longer exists, or at least is rarely traceable: and that there was in the original stem-syllable and radical words of some languages a deep spiritual significance and characteristic meaning.

Professor Franz Bopp says that the Sanskrit is more complete, more distinct, and more organic in its structure, than any other tongue, and exhibits, moreover, a conspicuous originality of grammatical structure. It contains, in its original state, not a single exotic term, and nothing but simple roots in their primitive form; and is, on the other hand, the most successful of inflected languages. In the Sanskrit family of languages, if its oldest state is consulted in those which have continued most pure, the root appears as a circumscribed nucleus, which is almost unalterable, and which surrounds itself with foreign syllables, whose origin we must investigate, and whose destination is to express the secondary ideas of grammar, which the root itself cannot express.

From one of the two classes of roots in the Sanskrit, spring verbs, and nouns (substantives and adjectives), which stand in fraternal connection with the verbs, not in the relation of descent from them; not begotten by them, but sprung from the same shoot with them. All these roots are mono-syllabic, but subject to no further limitation, and may consist of several letters, as *sthâ*, to "stand," and *skand*, to "go." In the earliest period of language, a single vowel is sufficient to express a verbal idea; and nearly all the individuals of the Sanskrit family of languages express the idea to "go," by the root *i*.

Eichhoff, in his *Parallèle des Langues*, gives all the known Sanskrit roots, with words derived from each, in the various languages of the family. To find the root was not difficult, in cases where it appeared in words in several of the languages; but the exact original meaning of the root is generally a matter of deduction.

The tendency of words is always to change their meaning, to put on various meanings, figurative and derivative, among which will at length be found, perhaps, meanings the opposites of each other. Of course it follows that in the more ancient compositions the meanings of the words used will be those that are nearest to the roots, i. e., those most simple and less figurative and abstract. It is only by that rule that the Veda can be truly interpreted.

Professor Wilson has translated the Rig-Veda in accordance with scholastic commentaries, such as we find in India, from Yâska, in the fifth century before Christ, down to Sâyaña in the fourteenth century after Christ. Many hymns, that are mere prayers for food, cattle, wealth or a long life, have been translated, as to whose real intention there can be no doubt; but with the exception of these simple petitions, the whole world of Vedic ideas is so entirely beyond our own intellectual horizon, that instead of translating, we can as yet only guess and combine. Here it is no longer a question of skilful deciphering. We may collect all the passages where an obscure word occurs, we may compare them, and look for a meaning which would be appropriate to all; but the difficulty lies in finding a sense which we can appropriate, and transfer by analogy into our own language and thought. We must be able to translate our feelings and ideas into their language, at the same time that we translate their poems and prayers into our language. We must not despair even where their words seem meaningless, and their ideas barren or wild. What seems at first childish may at a happier moment disclose a sublime simplicity, and even in helpless expressions we may recognize aspirations after some high and noble idea. When the Scholar has done his work, the Poet and Philosopher must take it up and finish it.

We must discover ourselves the real vestiges of these ancient Poets; and if we follow them cautiously, we shall find that with some effort we are still able to walk in their footsteps. We shall feel that we are brought face to face and mind to mind with men yet intelligible to us, after we have freed ourselves from our modern conceits. (*Müller: Chips i.* 75, 6, 7.)

But no translation will reproduce to us the Rig-Veda, if words are habitually used, which in their original sensuous meaning *would* faithfully render the Vedic words, but in their present meaning with us utterly misrepresent it. I think the context often proves that certain words, "truth" for instance, are thus mis-employed by Professor Wilson; and that habitually, the words and phrases that he uses impute to the Vedic Poets ideas much more metaphysical than they possessed.

Even when the Seventy translated the Old Testament, when the Hebrew could hardly be called a dead language, there were many of its words, the original meaning of which the most learned Rabbi would have found it difficult to define with real accuracy. We all know what doubts exist as to the meaning of many words in Shakespeare. Few of the most learned divines in England would find it easy to read and to understand correctly a theological treatise written in England only four hundred years ago. The common English translation of the Oriental books that compose the Old Testament continually misrepresent the ancient Semitic thought: for greater violence is done by successive interpreters to sacred writings, than to any other relics of ancient literature. Ideas grow and change, yet each generation tries to find its own ideas reflected in the pages of their early prophets: and, in the case of the Hebrew books, the ideas of a prosaic Northern race are substituted, by abusive employment of words whose modern meaning in no way reproduces the ancient thought, for the figurative and fervid sensuous ideas of an Oriental and Semitic people.

And in addition to the ordinary influences which blur and obscure the sharp features of old words, artificial influences have been at work distorting the natural expression of words which have been invested with a sacred authority. Passages in the Veda that do not bear on religious or philosophical doctrines, are generally explained simply and naturally, even by the latest commentators. But as soon as any word or sentence can be so turned as to support a doctrine, however modern, or a precept, however unnatural, the simplest phrases are tortured and mangled, until at last they are made to yield their assent to ideas the most foreign to the minds of the authors of the Veda and *Zend-Avesta.*

Not for the same purpose, but to the same effect, by the use of words that cannot be equivalents of the Vedic words, the Veda is distorted and denaturalized by Professor Wilson.

Our word "create" was originally a fit word to represent the Hebrew word *bara*, in the book of Genesis, because the meaning of *creo* was "bring forth, produce, make, create or beget." *Gigno*, whence "Genesis," meant to "beget, bring forth, bear, produce"; and *bara* had these meanings in the Hebrew. We find its correct meaning in the phrase, "the only begotten Son of God." But now the word "create" has come to have the meaning of "cause to exist from nothing," and therefore it is a false rendering of *bara*, as every scholar knows. It would be easy to multiply instances of such translations, all false and some fraudulent. "Lord God" is no manner of a *translation* of *Jehovah-Elohim*, nor "Almighty," of *Al Shaddai*. "Holy Ghost" gives no idea of the real meaning of the original Greek.

To find out, Müller says, how the words of the Old Testament were understood by those to whom they were originally addressed, is a task attempted by very few interpreters of the Bible. The great majority of readers transfer without hesitation the ideas which they connect with words as used in the nineteenth century, to the mind of Moses, or of his contemporaries, forgetting altogether the distance which divides their language and their thoughts from those of the wandering tribes of Israel.

How many words there are in Homer, that have indeed a traditional interpretation, as given by our dictionaries and commentaries, but the exact purport of which is completely lost, is best known to Greek scholars. Ordinary English readers of Virgil do not attach to the word "pius," as applied to Æneas the sense in which Virgil used the word. To translate many French words derived directly from the Latin, by the English derivatives from the same Latin words, would produce a caricature.

As examples of words that have changed their meaning, we need instance only a few, for they meet us everywhere. "Sacrament," originally *Sacramentum*, a deposit or pledge by a party to a suit at Rome, afterwards came to mean a military oath, then any oath whatever; and now means a wholly different thing. "Pagans" (*Pagani*) were originally those who lived in hamlets and villages, and not in cities and towns. Afterwards, when these did not embrace Christianity as soon as the dwellers in the cities, the word came to mean those who were not Christians. "Heathen" were originally the wild Germans who lived on the heaths, when Christianity was introduced there.

"Passion" originally meant suffering; and "passionate" men were suffering men. A "libertine" was originally a free-thinker; now it means a sensual profligate. "Plague" was *plaga*, a blow or stroke; and "pain," *poena*, punishment. It would be a most profitable and interesting study, to take, one after the other, a hundred Latin verbs, and trace the process of thought by which a great number of derivative or figurative meanings became attached to each, until the original meaning of many of them became obsolete.

Take the first word that presents itself, "obsolete." It is from *obsolesco* and *obsoleo*, meaning to lose smell, scent or odor. "Derivative" is from *de-rivo*, to take water from a river; "attached," from *attingo* or *adtingo*, *ad-tango*, to touch or touch against; and "figurative" is from *figuro*, form, fashion or shape. *Firmamentum* is anything used for fortifying or strengthening ("fort," "fortress" and "fortifying" being from *fortis*, strong); thence a stay, support, strength, prop; then reason, proof, main point. Yet it has come to mean the sky.

Now we "endorse" a man's character, from *in dorso*, on the back; and Milton wrote "an elephant endorsed with towers." We speak now of the "virtue" of women, and the virtues of herbs; but the Latin *virtus* meant "virility," ανδρεια: and of a man of good "disposition;" but *dispositio* meant arranging, putting in order; and "provisions" are food; but *provisio* (from *pro-video*) was foresight.

The Vedic hymns unquestionably embody a faith that was already ancient at the time when the earliest of them were composed. When the mythological ideas of those who were their authors are better understood, there will undoubtedly be many additional data for determining the succession, and with some approximation to accuracy, the epochs of the several Aryan emigrations. Already their order of succession has been in part settled by philological evidence, the separation of the Persians from the parent stock being clearly the latest, as the close resemblance between the Zend and Sanskrit languages proves. The streams that flowed into Greece and Italy must have emanated from the source, long before the Persian, but long after the streams that flowed into northern Europe, and intermixing with the native races, formed the Sclaves, the Goths, the Germans, and the various Keltic nations. The greater divergence of language, and the smaller proportion of identical words, proves the greater antiquity of the separation: and the student may with profit devote himself to this study, with the aid of Bopp's *Comparative Grammar*, Eichhoff's *Parallèle des Langues*, and the books of Müller, Bunsen and some others. I have hardly adventured in it beyond the shore.

That those streams which flowed into northern Europe were the earlier outflowings is also evident from the fact that the Aryans, as Dr. Muir clearly shows in his *Original Sanskrit Texts*, came into the Punjab or Indus country from the northwest. A race of men originating in a southern latitude would hardly have emigrated into the cold and inhospitable regions of the north, when they were the superiors in hardihood and bravery and intellect of those resident to the southward of them, in more tempting lands.

It also follows from this that the cradle of the Aryan race must have been north of the Himalayas, and it was undoubtedly this great mountain range of enormous elevation that caused the first streams of emigration to flow to the westward.

That the original seat of Aryan civilization was in that northern region, afterwards known as Sogdiana, and that those remote ancestors of ours ranged as herdsmen, like the Tartar tribes, over the Asian Steppes, is indicated by the first Fargard of the Vendidad, and is proven by many of the hymns. In one of them, the sacrifice of a horse (*Dadikra*) is described, and the eating of the meat by the worshippers, a kind of sacrifice which it is evident had long been obsolete when the later Aryans lived in the Punjab. And everywhere in the hymns we find horses and cattle prayed for, as the chief wealth, while sheep are not once mentioned, except in the designation of Indra as a ram; milk was one of the chief articles of food, and everywhere the herdsman's life seems to have been by far more common than the husbandman's. The sacrifices consisted, for the most part, of clarified (or melted) butter and of the juice of the Soma plant: and the tiller of the ground was probably the inferior of the mounted herdsman of the steppes, careering over those wide plains, ready for any adventure.

There are no pictures of domestic life in the Veda; though the language shows, by its words which still retain the same meanings in our modern languages, that all the domestic relations existed, as they do at the present day.

That their faith and worship were very ancient, when the hymns were written, will be more evident, I think, if my conclusions or conjectures as to the nature of the Deities of the Veda are correct. It is enough for me to say here, that I think the conclusion justifiable, that the earliest Aryans had no other Deities than the sun, moon and other celestial luminaries, and that, after that they had advanced beyond this, to the worship of universals or principles (as fire and light, for example), though they continued to adore the luminaries, they saw in them the limited manifestations, in place and form, of the universals, and worshipped them both as such and as luminous and independent bodies and orbs. For, while these orbs are much more rarely invoked than the Fire Spirit and the Light Spirit, and Sûrya, the Sun, is comparatively unnoticed, there are several Deities of which we have little more than the names, so that it is exceedingly uncertain what they were; and even their names disappear in the later mythologies; and of some that are preserved, their very identity is mistaken.

The Hindūs, it may at once be said, were almost totally ignorant as to the signification of the Vedic Gods; and what they really were must be determined from the Veda itself. Indeed, it seems probable that when the latest hymns were composed, the specific individualities of many of the Deities at first worshipped had become obscured, by larger place filled by others, and by misunderstanding of the epithets applied and attributes ascribed to those more ancient Gods. It is at least certain that as to some, the attributes ascribed at different periods are inconsistent with each in some respects.

Long after the swarms from the original hive had flowed into northern Europe, and those that succeeded them into Greece and Italy and Bactria, we find the ancestors of the Hindūs, a fair-skinned race, living and warring in the Punjab.

This (a Persian word, meaning "Five-Water") is a plain divided into five *doabs*, by the rivers which intersect it, and extending from the Suleiman Mountains, or Himalayas, on the northeast, and the Hindu Kush Range, on the northwest, to the rivers Sutlej and Punjab, forming a delta, its extreme length and breadth being, from north to south, four hundred, and from east to west, three hundred and fifty miles. It lies between the same parallels of latitude as the state of Mississippi, 30° and 35°. The soil is generally sandy, but grain and fruits of all kinds are cultivated; indigo, sugar and tobacco are largely produced; and the date, orange, fig, grape, apple, mulberry, banana and mango are among the fruits. Large trees are scarce, extensive tracts having on them only mimosas, acacias and smaller shrubs. In summer, the climate is hot and dry; but in winter, cold and often frosty. The large alluvial plains are fertile, and are alluded to in the hymns to the River Goddess Sarasvati; and the extensive pasture-grounds still support great herds of buffaloes (which are named in some of the hymns), horses and camels.

In the northeastern part is the Valley of Cashmere, surrounded on all sides by mountains, and noted for its fertility and beauty. Here are produced fruits and flowers, especially roses unrivalled, of both tropical and temperate climates. Rice, tobacco and cotton grow luxuriantly, and vegetables are cultivated in gardens floating on the surface of lakes. This valley, lying within 33° 15′ and 34° 30′, north latitude, may be compared with the northern portions of Mississippi and Alabama. In it are three lakes; and the Sutlej, the Hesudrus of antiquity, issues from a lake.

The upper plain of the Punjab is extremely fertile, and cultivated to the base of the Gangabari or Salt Range of Mountains, which rise 2,000 feet above the plain. The lower plain, also, where irrigation is possible, is abundantly fertile.

Owing to the cold, frosty climate of the winter, the people of the Punjab are vigorous and athletic. Below it is Scinde, and to the northwest, across the Hindu Kush, Tūrkestan, the ancient Sogdiana, now Bokhara, a country of wide steppes or plains, the fit home of a nomadic race, whose wealth consisted in horses and cattle.

Sogdiana, to the north of Bactria, was bounded by the Oxus on the south and west, the Jaxartes on the north, and the Amedarum Montes on the east. It corresponds with part of independent Tartary and Bokhara. It consists of extensive steppes in the west, rising gradually towards the high mountain-chains of Central Asia. Samarcand lay in the fertile valley of the Sogd or Kohik, and north of it stretched for a long distance east and west, a high mountain range, which in the eastern part was a mass of mountains, part of the Indian Caucasus. South of it, between it and the Paropamisus and Indian Caucasus lay Bactria. In the east and south of Bokhara, the mountain valleys are narrow and precipitous; below them a great plain extends, having an elevation of 2,000 feet, and sloping gradually north to the Lake Aral and the Caspian, until it reaches the sea level. The fertile parts of the country are famous for rice, grain and especially fruits; horses and cattle abound, but timber is very scarce. Samarcand is in Latitude 39° 32′ N. and Constantinople in 41° S. The banks of the rivers are extremely fertile. The Indian Caucasus rises to the height of 20,000 feet.

This is a temperate climate, and we find in the hymns nothing to indicate that the country in which their authors lived was a tropical one. There is no reference to the tropical fruits that now grow in the Punjab; and I doubt whether any except the later hymns were composed there. Even the references to the sea are inconsistent with the supposition that the hymns containing them originated in the Punjab, for it was long after that commenced, that the stream of Aryan emigration, crossing the Sutlej, flowed down into Hindūstan, and reached the ocean. May it not be that the sea spoken of was the Caspian? The area of water in the Caspian is 180,000 square miles, and it is of very considerable depth. The Oxus now flows into the Sea or Lake Aral, but it anciently flowed into the Caspian. Nearly 1,200,000 square miles of country are drained by six river systems, three of which run into the Caspian, and two into the Sea of Aral. The Jaxartes, of greater importance than the Danube, flows into the Sea of Aral, its development being not less than 1,200 miles, and the Oxus drains 200,000 square miles of territory, having an extent of development of 1,400 miles.

The Jaxartes is now called the *Syr*, and the Oxus, the *Gihon.* In the time of Peter the Great, gold was reported to have been found about the Oxus, in large quantities. The Sea of Aral is about 370 miles in length, and 124 in breadth. Its area is about 20,000 square miles, and its depth not very great. The Caspian is 700 miles in extreme length, and 420 in breadth, about the same size as the Black Sea. It is about 200 miles from the Sea of Aral. In places, no bottom has been found with 480 fathoms of line. The waters of both these lakes are diminishing, and are probably 300 feet shallower than they were in the early periods of history. Seals, sturgeon and salmon abound in the Caspian, and sturgeon in the Sea of Aral.

In the Khanate of Khiva, which extends west from the Oxus to the Caspian, is a fertile oasis of alluvial land, containing about 20,000 square miles.

In the Khanate of Khokand, on the northeast of Bokhara, which flattens down from the mountainous country in the east and north, towards the west, are extensive tracts of fertile soil, chiefly along the Syr or Gihon, the ancient Jaxartes.

Bokhara lies between 36° and 41° N., and the climate is both pleasant and salubrious. The tree which most abounds is the poplar, which is used for house-building; and rice, wheat, barley, maize and sesamum are the principal grain crops. The cotton plant and hemp are cultivated, and fruit trees are abundant.

North of Bokhara is the great Kirghiz Steppe, and south of it is Afghanistan, a rich mineral country, abounding in gold, silver, copper and iron.

The summers of Bokhara are excessively hot and dry, and the winters very cold, snow falling day and night, making considerable arches over the houses, and remaining on the roofs nearly three months.

Baron Bunsen (*Egypt's Place in Universal History, iii.* 456 *et seq.*), adopts Dr. Haug's conclusion, that the first Fargard of the Vendidad contains the nucleus of a record that dates from the most ancient times,

> and that its contents are nothing less than the reminiscences of the passage of the old Aryans to India—in other words, the succession of the foundation of fourteen kingdoms, the last and most southern of which was the land of the Five Rivers, the Punjab.

Müller considers it to be merely a geographical description of different countries.

Bunsen declares that, according to the Vendidad, the Aryans

> originally inhabited Iran proper, *Airyana Vaêjâ*, the land of pleasantness, and they only left it in consequence of a convulsion of Nature, by which a great alteration in the climate was effected.

This he concludes from the text of the opening of the "record," which is, in the translation of Bleeck, from the German one of Spiegel:

Fargard i.

1. Ahura Mazda spake to the holy Zarathustra.
2. I created, O holy Zarathustra, a place, a creation of delight (but) nowhere was created a possibility (of approach).
3. For had I not, O holy Zarathustra, created a place, a creation of delight, where nowhere was created a possibility,
4. The whole corporeal world have gone after Airyana Vaêjâ.
5. The first and best of regions and places have I created, I who am Ahura Mazda.
6. The Airyana Vaêjâ of the good creation.

7. *Then Añra Mainyûs, who is full of death, created an opposition to the same:*
8. *A great serpent and winter, which the Daevas have created.*
9. *Ten winter-months are there, two summer-months.*
10. *And these are cold as to the water, cold as to the earth, cold as to the trees.*
11. After this to the middle of the earth, then to the heart of the earth,
12. Comes the winter; then comes the most evil.
13. The second and best of regions and places have I created, I who am Ahura Mazda.
14. Gaû, the dwelling-place of Sughda.

It is, it seems to me, a very strained construction of the seventh, eighth and ninth verses, to make them mean a convulsion of Nature.

Bunsen says,

> The country of the sources of the Oxus and Jaxartes, therefore, is the most eastern and most northern point, from which we have to start . . . . wherever the Indians may have fixed the dwelling-places of their northern ancestors, the Uttara-Kuru, we cannot venture to place the primeval seats of Aryans anywhere but on the slopes of the Bolor Tagh, in the Highland of Pawer, between the 40th and 37th degrees of N. Latitude, and 86th and 90th degrees of Longitude . . . . As regards its present climate, it is precisely what our record describes it as having been when the change produced by the above commotion took place. It has only two months of warm weather.

But this is entirely incorrect, and gives a very false idea of the country. The cities of Bokhara and Samarkand are in the same latitude with the northern portion of it, and there the climate is pleasant and salubrious. Of course, it being higher and mountainous, it is colder there than in the vicinity of those cities; but Khokand lies north and west of it, north of 40°, and there the heat is excessive in summer, although it is mountainous and though the winters are cold. Snow falls by the beginning of November, and disappears by March; and cotton is raised and the silk-worm reared there; and fruit is abundant. I think that there is no foundation for the "convulsion" theory.

Lassen remarks that at the present day the old indigenous inhabitants of this region on the slopes of the Bolor Tagh, are Tadshiks who speak Persian, and are all agriculturists. And the Turcomans, Bunsen says, either came after them, or else they are aborigines, whom the Aryans found there.

He says,

> When the climate was altered by some vast disturbance of Nature [how did they live through the "convulsion"?], the Aryans emigrated; they did not, however, follow the course of the Oxus, or they would have come in the first instance to Bactria, and not to Sogd. Their course, therefore, was more northerly.

If they emigrated because of the greatly increased cold, would they have gone further north? Did they go north into Khokand, across the Jaxartes, or northwesterly, down the Jaxartes and between it and the Oxus, towards the Sea of Aral?

> We see, indeed [he says on the next page], evidence of the main direction taken by these travellers having been southerly.
>
> Sughda [he says], was pre-eminently 'the country,' as being the home of the fire-worshippers. The name was afterwards spelled *Sugdia*, and commonly *Sogdiana*. It is in the 38th degree of Latitude, where Maracanda (Samarkand), is situated; a paradisiacal land, fertilized by the river Sogd; so that Sogd and Paradise are used synonymously by later writers.

The subsequent and successive settlements, he thinks, were, Margiana, a fruitful province of Khorassan; Bactria, Northern Parthia; Herat; Sejestan; Cabūl; Candahar; Arachosia; Hilmend; Northern Media; Khorassan; Ghilan; and Hapta Hindu, or the country between the Indus and Sutlej, into which they entered from Afghanistan.

Bunsen concludes that Zarathustra lived in Bactria, about 6,350 years before Christ. He

> opposed the faith in the Gods of Nature, as the highest beings. He found in existence the faith in good spirits, *Ahuras*, 'the Living,' who are also called 'the Dispensers of Wisdom' (*Mazdas*). At their head he placed the one Holy God, Ahura Mazda (*Ormuzd*), 'the Highest Spirit.' He is the Lord of all the Powers of Nature, Creator and Sustainer of all Existence. He rules over the earthly and spiritual life, by which latter Zarathustra understands a better state on this earth. His great axiom, so full of intelligence, was that, 'the Highest Trinity (*drigu*), is Thought, Word, Deed.' These three he considers to be 'pure in the pure, evil in the evil: from the thought emanates the word, from the two together, the deed.'

The "Holy Acts" of the Veda supplied him with this idea. They are the out-shining of the light, in form and limitation, which is an emanation from the fire. Fire is our thought; light, the word; and its emission or manifestation by the orbs, is the act or deed.

The seven rivers of the Indus country are, the Sindhu (Indus), its eastern confluents, Vitastâ (*Hydaspēs*), Asiknî (*Akesinēs*), Purushnî (*Hydraortēs*), Vipâs (*Hyphasis*) Satadru (*Hesudrus*); and the western, Kubhâ (*Kophen*), which comes from Kabūl.

Sughdha, according to Bunsen, is from the root *Suk*, to "burn," whence *Sukhra*, "burning red," as applied to fire, and *dha*, a "where," a "place where something is." Consequently *Sughdha* was *the place* or *land of fire.*

Bunsen thinks that the oldest Vedas "are the Monuments of Aryan life in the country of the Five Rivers." I think they are monuments of an older life, on the steppes.

He thinks that the Aryans immigrated into the Indus country about 4,000 years before Christ, then having the old Bactrian living language, in which the old Zend books were written; and that in that country the Sanskrit grew up. The Agni, or fire-worship, he considers a remnant of the original pre-Zarathustrian doctrine. The emigration from Sogd into Bactria, he places about 5000 B.C. He concludes that the original emigration from the northeast of the primitive land took place from 10000 to 8000 B.C.; that the separation of the Germans, Sclaves and Pelasgians occurred, successively, from 8000 to 5000 B.C.; Zarathustra's reform, about 3500, and the crossing of the Sutlej into the country beyond, where Brahmanism was established, about 3,000 years before Christ. The most modern hymns were composed in the land of the Sarasvati, beyond the Sutlej.

The rainy season commences in the Punjab towards the end of June; but the rivers begin to swell with the first heats of spring and summer, by the melting of the snow on the mountains contiguous to their sources. It appears that Alexander the Great crossed the Indus, and invaded the Punjab, sometime in the beginning of May, and found the rivers swollen and constantly rising. Tamerlane passed the Indus in A.D. 1398, in October, nearly at the same spot where Alexander had crossed it 1,725 years before. Alexander procured on the Hydaspes a fleet of 2,000 vessels, and upon it carried his army down the Indus to the Sea.

Mr. Laing (*Heimskringla iii.* 365) says:

> The most learned Scandinavian antiquaries of our times have ascertained to their own satisfaction, that three distinct populations have inhabited the North; a Mongolian race, of which the type is to be found in the Laplander, the Samoyed, the Esquimaux; a Celtic race; and a Caucasian race, which, almost within the limits of northern history, came from Asia, drove out or extirpated the Celtic and Laplandic races, and are the present inhabitants. (*See, further, as to this, page 27 post.*)

THE VEDAS AND THEIR AGE.

The Vedas are the oldest of all the Indian books. They are, therefore, not only the most authentic source of information in regard to the earliest language of the Indians, but they preserve much more distinct and exact traces of their primeval history than are to be found in later books, composed when the most genuine traditions of the origin of the race had been obscured and corrupted.

Of that which is the most important and interesting portion of the history of every race and nation, the history of the progress of its intellect and of its religious and philosophical ideas, the Vedas contain the *only* authentic record. And of this they contain, as I think, and as I hope to be able to show, very much more than any of the commentators have discovered, though, in one direction they have imagined their ideas to have extended beyond their *real* intellectual horizon.

I do not speak of the Hindū commentators. Making the Vedas the sacred books of their own faith, they utterly denaturalized them, and systematically misunderstood and misinterpreted them. I speak of Professor Wilson, Muir, Roth, Benfey, Müller and others, to whose intelligent labours the student of the Vedas is so infinitely indebted. Mr. Cox, in regard to the meaning of the Vedas, is merely a borrower from the others, and where he ventures to speculate for himself is invariably and persistently wrong.

Dr. Muir says (*Original Sanskrit Texts, ii.* 288),

> From the Vedic hymns, accordingly, it does, in fact, appear, more distinctly than from any other of the Indian writings, that the progenitors of the Hindūs were originally called Aryas.

That is true: but the Vedas should not be called *Indian* writings, for the hymns, or at least the older ones, were the composition of those who were the ancestors of the Hindūs or Indians, of the Persians, and of the Greeks and Latins. This is absolutely certain, because we unmistakably find in them the *Origines* of the Deities of all these branches of the one race, and of their principal religious and philosophical ideas; as we hope very clearly to prove.

Probably none of the hymns can be imputed to a date so early as that of the separation of either the Sclavic, German or Keltic branch, from the great Aryan stock, though the Vedas contain a great number of the roots from which the words in most common use in the languages of those branches were derived or developed.

There is evidence, I think, in the Vedas, that the principal Deities named in them were worshipped, if the oldest of the hymns were not composed, some time before. By means of the precession of the Equinoxes, about 2,455 years before our era, the sun began to enter the Zodiacal sign Taurus at the Vernal Equinox. Three hundred years before our era, he commenced to enter Aries; and at the same rate of precession, he entered Gemini 4,300 years before Christ. Perhaps 2,000, perhaps 3,000 years, or even 4,000, after they were written, and at least 1,000 or 2,000 years after they were compiled, and more than that after the language in which they were written had become a dead language, they were commented on by men whose religious and philosophic ideas were thoroughly contrary to those contained, and in fact concealed, in the hymns themselves.

Dr. Muir continues to say,

> We find this name [*Aryas*] applied to the forefathers of the higher classes among the Indians, in contradistinction to the *Dasyus*, who appear to have been a people of a different race, and to have been settled in India before the Aryas [and who were also of dark complexions, and barbarians or savages].
>
> By means of this word *Arya*, we are able to connect the early Hindūs with the early Persians. For, first, it appears that in ancient times the Medes also, who were eventually included in one empire with the Persians [the ancestors of Kuros or Cyrus being Medes], bore the name of Arians. This is clear from the following passage of Herodotus, in *Book vii.*, Sec. 2 of his *History:* 'They [the Medes] were formerly called "Αριοι by all. But when the Colchian Medea arrived among these *Arioi*, from Athens, they also changed their name. The Medians say these things of themselves.' In Section 66 of the same book, he mentions a nation or tribe bearing the same name: 'The *Arioi* were armed with Median bows, but in other respects like the Bactrians. Sisamnēs commanded the *Arioi*.' Elsewhere he mentions the *Areioi*, with the Chorasmians and Sogdians, as paying 300 talents tribute. Arrian mentions the same people (*iii.* 8. 4), as forming part of the army of *Dareios*.

Dr. Muir further shows that in many ancient authors, proper names are found, compounded with the word *Arios*, e. g. *Ario*mardos, the Kaspian Commander, and the Persian names *Aria*bignes, *Aria*ramnes, *Aria*ces, *Aria*ius, *Ari*mazes and *Aria*rathes (*Aryaratha*): and Æschylus uses the word *Arim* as the synonym of Persian, as applied to a dirge. And he adds:

> It is not only in the Greek authors, that we find the name of *Arians* applied to the Medes or Persians. In the most ancient books of the Zarathustrian religion, also, which are composed in the Zend language, the same word, as a designation of the early Persians, is of frequent occurrence.

And he thus quotes from Professor Spiegel's Introduction to his translation of the *Zend-Avesta:*

It is of special importance that they [the Indians and Persians], call themselves by the same name. *Ârya*, signifying *honourable* in ordinary speech, and derived from *Arya*, which means *Lord* in the Vedas, is the most usual and the most ancient name of the Indian people . . . . According to the Persian laws of euphony, *ārya* had to be changed to *airya*, a name which the Persians long applied to themselves, and out of which the more modern *Irân* has arisen.

Eichhoff (*Parallèle des langues de l'Europe et de l'Inde*, 132) gives from the root *AR* or *ÂR*, to "go, attain, reach, overtake;" *Aris*, "warrior;" *Aryas*, "excellent;" *Âras*, "iron;" *Arus*, "a wound;" and also gives "valiant" as a meaning of *Aryas*. In that sense, the name is eminently appropriate to the race. From the same word come the Greek "αρης, "αρειος, the first meaning, "war, battle, wound, iron or weapon," and the second, "martial, warlike, bellicose;" "Αρης also being *Mars*, the God of War.

The primitive language of this people, was, in the words of Pictet (*Origines Indo-Européennes*, *pp.* 1. 2):

Admirable by its richness, its force, its harmony, the perfection of its forms; in which were spontaneously reflected all the impressions of the race; not merely its mild affections and its simple admirations, but also its nascent aspirations toward a higher world; a language abounding in images and intuitive ideas; bearing within it, in germ, all the future affluence, both of the most sublime poetry and of the most profound reflection. At first one and homogeneous, that language, already perfected to a very high degree, served as a common instrument of expression to this primitive people, as long as it continued within the limits of its native country . . . . The radical affinity of all the Arian languages [Hindū, Persian, Greek, Latin, Sclavonic, Gothic, German and Keltic], necessarily leads us to regard them as having sprung from one single primitive language . . . . And as a language presupposes always a people to speak it, it further follows that all the Aryan nations have issued from one single source, though they may occasionally have become blended at a later period, with some foreign elements. Hence we may with certainty infer the existence, at a pre-historic period, of an Aryan people, free, originally, from all foreign intermixture, sufficiently numerous to have supplied these swarms of men which issued from its bosom, and sufficiently endowed by Nature to have created for itself the most beautiful, perhaps, of all languages [and sufficiently acute of intellect, and thoughtful, to have conceived the profoundest philosophical ideas, and to have furnished the germs of all the profoundest theological truths]. This people, though unknown to tradition, is in a certain degree revealed to us by philological science. [And it is also revealed to us by its thoughts and ideas, its Deities and its notions concerning them, its customs and its manners, and the accounts of its struggles for supremacy, contained and depicted in the pages of the Vedas.]

Each stream of emigration encountered the opposition of an aboriginal race, in every country into which it flowed, and everywhere they were conquerors, or the original language would have died out for each. Each intermingled with one or more aboriginal races, one in greater, another in less proportion; and the language of each mingled with that of the conquered people. Hence the vast differences and also the striking identities between the Welsh tongue and the Sanskrit, the Sclavonic and Persian, the German and the Latin and Greek: and hence also the great differences of physical and intellectual characteristics, and the peculiar and apparently permanent types of the Irish, Grecian, Roman and Hindū face. In fact, the language and the type and cast of features, and the intellectual character of some of the races come chiefly from the conquered aborigines, while others have preserved infinitely more of the Aryan type, probably because the conquerors were, relatively to the conquered, more numerous: and these physical and intellectual differences are also, no doubt, greatly owing to immense original differences of face, form and intellect, among the aboriginal races of Asia and Europe, that the Aryans overcame and mingled with.

The Hindū notions of the dignity and sanctity of the Vedas are curious, but otherwise of no value. When we read the Brahmanic books, as when we read the Kabbalistic books, we are amazed at the vagaries, not of the fancy or of the imagination, but of lunacy and idiotic babble, in which the human mind can indulge.

Manu styles the Veda,

> the Eternal Eye of the Patriarchs, of Gods and of men: beyond human power and comprehension [and it certainly was and is beyond the power of Brahmanic comprehension, saturated, as the Brahmanic mind and intellect were and are, with both the metaphysical subtleties, and the unintelligible nonsense, of its own creed].
>
> The Eternal Veda [Manu says], supports all beings, and is the principal instrument of well-being to man. He who comprehends the essential meaning of the Veda, is prepared for absorption into Brahma, even while abiding in this lower world.

Dr. Muir says of the Vedas (*Orig. Sans. Texts, iii.* 114),

> We find in them ideas, a language, a spirit and a colouring, totally different from those which characterize the religious writings of the Hindūs of a later era. They frequently discover to us the simple germs from which mythological legends current in subsequent ages were derived,—germs which in many cases were developed in so fanciful and extravagant a manner as to prove that the correct tradition had long before disappeared, and that the lost details have been replaced by pure fictions of the imagination. They afford us very distinct indications of the locality in which they were composed [some of them, especially, speaking of the wide alluvial bottom lands of five bold-running rivers subject to overflow]; they show us the Aryan tribes living in a state of warfare with surrounding enemies, many of them, no doubt, alien in race and language; and gradually, as we may infer, forcing their way onward to the east and south. [They picture themselves to us as a people of herdsmen, much more than of husbandmen, with herds of horses and cattle, but no sheep, having villages, perhaps, but no cities—the cities spoken of being all of the Dasyus their enemies, the dark-skinned natives of the land.] They supply us

> with numerous specimens of the particular sort of prayers, viz.: for protection and victory [and for food, and wealth and increase of horses and cattle], which men so circumstanced would naturally address to the Gods whom they worshipped; as well as of those more common supplications which men in general offer up for the various blessings which constitute the sum of human welfare; and they bring before us, as the objects of existing veneration, a class of Deities, principally, if not exclusively, personifications of the elements, and of the powers either of Nature or of reason [of the sun, the planets and stars, and even of the rivers], who gradually lost their importance in the estimation of the later Indians, and made way for Gods of a different description, invested with new attributes, and in many cases bearing new appellations.

For it was a natural advance of the intellect, to reach beyond the personifications of fire and light, flame and heat and other powers, principles and phenomena of Nature, and the planetary and stellar powers, and the Goddesses of the river, and to seek and reach a cause of all, beyond or above them all; especially when the Deities already adored were invested with most of the attributes that must belong to a creator and preserver of the world, a cause of all, Himself uncaused: when it was only necessary to invent a hypothesis or imagine a being, and compose him of those attributes.

But when the idea of that cause was reached, then the Brahmanic intellect tortured itself with a thousand questions in regard to the creation, and at last invented a whole pantheon of Gods, and the most grotesque and absurd theories as to the origination or generation of things; until a hideous idolatry was the consequence.

> We can also [Mr. Muir says], discover from the Vedic hymns that some of them were newer and others older, that they were the works of many successive generations of Poets, and their composition probably extended over several centuries; and that in some places their authors represent them as being the productions of their own minds, while in other passages they appear to ascribe to their own words a certain divine character, or attribute their composition to some supernatural assistance.

Professor Wilson says (*Rig-V. i. Introd. xviii.*):

> To me, the verses of the Veda, except in their rhythm, and in a few rare passages, appear singularly prosaic for so early an era as that of their probable composition; and at any rate, their chief value lies, not in their fancy, but in their facts, social and religious.

Mr. Whitney (*Journ. Am. Or. Soc., iii.* 295) says:

> The Vedas contain the songs in which the first ancestors of the Hindū people, at the very dawn of their existence as a separate nation, while they were still only on the threshold of the great country which they were afterwards to fill with their civilization, praised the Gods, extolled heroic deeds, and sang of other matters

which kindled their poetic fervour . . . . The mass, as it lies before us, is almost exclusively of a religious character; this may have had its ground partly in the end for which the collections were afterwards made, but it is probably in a far higher degree due to the character of the people itself, which thus shows itself to have been at the beginning what it continued to be throughout its whole history, an essentially religious one . . . . Hymns of a very different character are not entirely wanting, and this might be taken as an indication that, had they been more numerous, more would have been preserved to us.

Dr. Muir says (*Orig. Sansk. Texts, ii.* 206):

These hymns are said, by later Indian writers, to have been *seen* by the ancient Ṛishis or bards. The Nirukta says (*ii.* 11) 'a Rishi is so called, from *seeing*. He *saw* the hymns! This is Anpa Manyava's explanation. They became Ṛishis, because Brahma, the self-existent, approached them when they were sunk in devotion. From this, as is generally understood, they acquired their character as Ṛishis.'

There is, however, no doubt [says Dr. Muir], that the Ṛishis were themselves the proper authors of these ancient songs, which they addressed to the Gods, when they were solicitous to obtain any blessing, or composed on other occasions . . . . For many years, the successive generations of these ancient Ṛishis continued to make new contributions to the stock of hymns, while they carefully preserved those handed down to them by their forefathers. The fact of the successive compositions of the hymns is evident from the ancient Index of the Rig-Veda [*anukramani*], as continually quoted in the Commentary of Sayana, which shows that these compositions are ascribed to different generations of the same families, as their seers . . . . We have [in the case of certain hymns of the third Mandala], the seers of hymns extending over five generations or more. The same fact, that a long interval elapsed between the composition of the different hymns, is manifest from various passages in these compositions themselves . . . . And in the Rig-Veda, we find references made in numerous hymns, to earlier Ṛishis (who themselves are yet declared by later writers to have been authors of hymns included in the same Veda), having been delivered by the Gods in ancient times.

In many cases, also, the later composition of a hymn appears by the Brahmanic conceits embodied in it, and its departure from the singular simplicity of the ancient hymns. The same Deities appear in the later hymns, but with the addition of epithets and an accretion of attributes, which, if all were of one age, would greatly embarrass one in the endeavour to determine what the Deity in question really was or represented.

Langlois (*Trans. of Rig-Veda i., Pref. x. xi.*) says:

The Indian Aryas were disposed to piety both by their natural character and by the institutions of Manu. They were sustained in these sentiments by the chiefs of certain families, in which their religious traditions had been more especially preserved. In those primitive ages, the political system was precisely the same as that which Homer depicts; Kings, the veritable shepherds of their people; cultivators or herdsmen united around their chiefs, and prepared whenever necessity arose, to transform themselves into warriors; numerous flocks [herds], and a profusion of rural wealth; towns which were only large villages. Of these villages, some served as retreats to renowned sages, who, while their dependents were tending their fields and herds, were themselves engaged in the cultivation of sacred science, in the company of their sons or their pupils, and fulfilled the functions of a Calchas or a Tiresias, to some Aryan Agamemnon or Œdipus in their neighbourhood. Invited by the chiefs to perform sacrifice, they arrived with their sacred retinue; they ascended the mountain, to where an enclosure of lattice-work had been constructed, for Temples were then unknown. There, beneath the vault of Heaven, they recited their hereditary songs, or a newly-composed hymn; they invoked the grand agents in Nature to grant success to the labours of the field, increase to the flocks, and a succession of brave and virtuous descendants. They implored, they threatened their Gods; and when the sacred rites had been scrupulously performed, they retired loaded with gifts, carrying away cows, horses, and cars filled with provisions, gold and precious stuffs. We see thus by what fortune these hymns have been preserved, forming, as they did, a patrimony to certain families, a species of productive capital, which it was their interest to turn to the very best account. Composed on certain recognized and venerable themes, and sometimes retouched and renovated by the imagination of a new bard, they grew old, as they were transmitted from age to age, bearing on them, sometimes, the date of their composition, which was indicated by the name of the inspired author, or of some generous prince.

Dr. Muir says (*Orig. Sansk. Texts, iii.* 171):

In India, the indistinct and perhaps hesitating belief which some of the ancient Ṛishis seem entertained in their own inspiration, was not suffered to die out in the minds of later generations. On the contrary, this belief grew up by degrees into a fixed persuasion that all the literary productions of those early sages had not only resulted from a supernal impulse, but were infallible, divine, and even eternal. These works have become the Sacred Scriptures of India. And in the popular opinion, if not in the estimation of the learned, most Indian works of any importance, of a religious, scientific or philosophical kind, which were produced at a later period, have come to be regarded as inspired, as soon as the lapse of ages had removed the writers beyond familiar or traditional knowledge, and invested their names with a halo of reverence.

The reader of the Veda will often find power to strengthen the Gods ascribed to prayers and praises and to the Sacrifice, and even peculiar powers ascribed to the metres. And he will even find prayer, silent or uttered, exalted into a Deity, one of the forms of Agni.

As to the value of Hindū interpretation of the Veda, some idea may be formed from this which Müller says in regard to Brahmanas, the oldest of the Hindū books. He says (*Anc. Sansk. Lit.* 432. 434):

There is throughout the Brahmanas such a complete misunderstanding of the original intention of the Vedic hymns, that we can hardly understand how such an estrangement could have taken place, unless there had been, at some time or other, a sudden and violent break in the chain of tradition . . . . Every page of the Brahmanas contains the clearest proof that the spirit of the ancient Vedic poetry, and the purport of the original Vedic sacrifices, were both beyond the comprehension of the authors of the Brahmanas.

Professor Roth says (*Introd. to Nirukta iii.*) that in Greece,

with the exception of Hesiod, who never rose to the same degree of consideration, Homer was the only source of the highest knowledge, and pre-eminently the book of the schools—the book which gave the first occasion to grammatical and almost every other sort of science to develop itself. In India, the Veda occupies the place of Homer. It was to the Veda that the Brahmanical people looked as the sole repository of intellectual culture. As a sacred book, it was the more naturally a subject of research to the learned man, as he was at the same time a priest, and it became the first problem to be solved by grammar . . . . At the same time, the Veda, both as regards its language and its subject matter, stood further removed from the Indian of the two centuries immediately preceding Buddha (700 and 600 B.C.)—in which the sacerdotal system reached its climax—than Homer did from the Greek of the Periclean Era, ... Indian scholarship lay under an incapacity of unfettered movement. It was necessary for orthodoxy to deny the facts of history, and to discover only the circumstances of the present in the monuments of antiquity; for the present was both unable and unwilling to rest on any other foundation than the traditions of an earlier age, surrounded as these were with a halo of glory, and only half understood.

And the Brahmanic notions in regard to the Deities, their origins and their functions, were so totally different from those of the Poets of the Vedas as to render them utterly incapable of understanding the old texts in any other sense than the false ones, which suited their own mythology and metaphysics.

Professor Wilson (*Rig-Veda ii. Introd. xix. xx. xxi.*) has stated the difficulties met with in translating the Veda. They are very great—so great that it will never be possible to translate the whole correctly. All grammar is disregarded in the original, one case or number of a noun substituted for another, one person and tense of a verb for another. Many unusual words are employed in the Veda, the meaning of which, he thinks, can only be arrived at by means of the Hindū interpretations. But these are almost always so utterly unfounded, so evidently the results of preconceived notions, and so continually mere guesses, that I am quite sure they much more tend to obscure the meaning than to elucidate it.

Another great difficulty is that for many words we have no equivalents in our own language, and that the words which are available do not convey the same ideas. *Kavi*, *Vipra*, *vidvat*, *medhâvin*, *Chikitwah*, and many others, mean, it is true, "wise, intelligent, knowing;" but they do not have that meaning, as and where they are employed, and so to translate them is to mistranslate. These and other adjectives are often used without substantives; and there are great numbers of other omissions of words, to be supplied by conjecture, and which the Hindū scholiasts and commentators, having an eye all the time to the later fables as to the Gods, and their changed characters, generally fill erroneously. Often it does not appear what Deity is invoked, or to which one an epithet is applied. Sometimes whole sentences are to be supplied by conjecture: and it is mere guessing when even single words are omitted; as in

> The grandson of the waters has ascended above the crooked——.
> The broad and golden —— spread around.
> Thou removest all —— of men.
> Thou cuttest —— to pieces.

Often the verb is omitted. So, frequently, are the names of the Deities invoked; and it is often evident that the name supplied is wrong. And the same phrase is often explained in two utterly different meanings by different commentators; while they continually disagree with each other, and each often with himself, in regard to what is meant by a particular Deity.

Bunsen says (*Egypt's Place in Universal History iii.* 512):

> In my opinion, none of these Sanskrit sources of information have any historical value, except in so far as they relate to matters within a certain range of sharply distinguished epochs.

And I think that none of our Sanskrit "sources of information" are of the least value, as aids in solving the enigmas which the Vedic pantheon presents to us. As he says on the same page,

> The Vedic Gods, in the Sanskrit period, are completely thrown into the background by others of whom the Vedas either knew nothing at all, Siva, for instance, or else use their names in a totally different sense, as is the case with Brahma and Vishṇu. For these reasons, therefore, the history of the early times may be regarded as systematically adulterated or adjusted by the Brahmans themselves, in those epic poems, and in the notices annexed to the ancient hymns. A large portion is borrowed from historic sources, and dressed up in an ideal shape.

And so the Vedic Gods are transformed and denaturalized, by explanations which are, in Bunsen's phrase applied to their history "Comparatively modern nonsense."

He truly says,

> where detached ballads and the pedigrees of princely families are the only sources of information, genealogical forgery and myth will not be wanting; and where a new Priesthood, founded upon a strict system of caste and a new mythology, holds the literature of a country in its hands, everything of more ancient date will be systematically falsified.

And, we may add with equal truth, the old Gods will either be discrowned or degraded, or they will be invested with new characters and attributes, each becoming something more or less different from what it was in the beginning.

HINDU IDEA OF THE ORIGIN OF THE VEDAS.

Of the elemental origin of the Vedas, according to the Brahmanas, the Upanishads, and the Institutes of Manu, it would be profitless to speak at any length, because the accounts which they give are neither historical nor traditionary, but merely fanciful and fantastical. They will be found collected by Dr. Muir in Volume *ii.* of his *Original Sanskrit Texts.* One account (in the Sâtapatha Brahmana), is that Prajapati was formerly the All. He created and brooded over three worlds, till from them three lights were produced, Fire, Air, and the Sun. He brooded over these three Lights; and from them were produced the three Vedas—the Rig-Veda from the Fire, the Yajur-Veda from the Air, and the Sama-Veda from the Sun. He brooded over these three Vedas, and from them were produced the three seeds or essences—*bhûr*, from the Rig-Veda; *bhûvah*, from the Yajur-Veda, and *svar* from the Sāma-Veda: and the function of the Brahman arose through the essence of the threefold knowledge, i. e., the three Vedas combined.

Manu condenses the account given in the *chhândogya* Upanishad, into this sentence:

> From Fire, Air and the Sun, he milked for the accomplishment of Sacrifice, the eternal triple Veda, distinguished as *Rik*, *Yajush* and *Sâman*.

BRANCHES OF ARYAN LANGUAGE.

It may not be out of place to speak briefly of relationship of the Sanskrit, Zend, Greek, Latin, Gothic, Sclavonic, German and Keltic languages, and those, including our own, formed by the intermixture of some of these; for it is by means of the words common to all or to part of these, that the original identity of all the races that speak these languages, is established.

Recent discoveries have proven beyond dispute the existence all over Europe, long before any emigration of the Aryans, of successive races of men, the most ancient of whom were savages, like the North American Indians, using only implements and weapons of stone. Such of these as remained when the Aryan herdsmen swept over Europe, were subjugated, and amalgamated with the conquerors; and the languages of the victors and the vanquished were intermingled, like themselves. But everywhere, in greater or less degree, the language of the victors was itself victor, and its most important words were everywhere retained.

The case was the same in Asia. The Aryans found an aboriginal people everywhere, different races speaking many different tongues, none of them in the least connected with or resembling their own language: and from these aboriginal inhabitants of Asia and Europe came the differences in type of the existing Aryan races, and in a great measure the differences in language.

How else are we to account for the difference in features between the Irishman and the Hindū, and for the fact that some of these races have not and cannot pronounce particular letters?

That all the languages which we have mentioned are, to the extent stated, outflowings from one original tongue, and that, indeed, much of the difference between them has not been owing to the intermixture of the foreign elements, but to natural changes, modifications and decay, has been too conclusively proven, for doubt to be possible. We need only refer the student to Bopp's *Comparative Grammar*, to Eichhoff's *Parallèle des Langues*, and to Müller's *Lectures on Language* and *Chips from a German Workshop*, for ample proof of this.

We find the names for "Father," "Mother," "Brother," "Sister" and "Daughter" and other grades of relationship, radically the same in most of the Aryan languages, as well as a vast number of other words, indispensable for general use; and by means of these, language has been made to tell much of the history of those ancient times, and of the manners and habits of these men, of whom, not long since, nothing whatever was known. We are thus carried back to the time when the race was not yet broken up into different nationalities, and obtain a character of historical reality for a period, the very existence of which had been doubted. No study is more intensely interesting; and nothing is more curious than many of Müller's demonstrations of historic facts by words.

The names that express the family relations, coming from one source, prove that, at that early day, those relations existed. "Father," too, is derived from a root, *pa*, which means, not to "beget," but to "protect, support, nourish;" and "Mother" is from a root *ma*, meaning to "fashion," whence, among the earliest Aryans, *Mâtar* had the meaning of "maker." As "begetter," the father was called, in Sanskrit, *Ganitár*, as "protector" and "supporter" of his offspring, *Pitár*. Hence in the Veda, the two names are used together, in order to express the full idea of Father. Thus (*i.* 164. 33):

Dyaûs me pitâ' ganitâ'

which in Latin and Greek became

Jovis mei Patēr genitor
Ζεὺς ἐμοῦ πατὴρ γενετὴρ

and the family names in different languages are

	Sanskrit	Zend	Greek	Latin	Sclavonic	Irish
Father:	*pitar*	*patar*	πατὴρ	*pater*		*athair*
Mother:	*matar*	*matar*	μήτηρ	*mater*	*mati* (*gen. matere*)	*mathair*
Brother:	*bhratar*	*bratar*	φρατηρ	*frater*	*brat*	*brathair*
Sister:	*svasar*	*guanhar*		*soror*	*svistar, sestra*	*siur*
Daughter:	*duhitar*	*dughdar*	θυγάτηρ		*dauhtar* *dukte* (Lithuanic)	*dear*

From one of these names we learn something of the habits of this ancient people. *Duhitar*, Sanskrit for daughter, is derived from *duh*, a root which in Sanskrit means to "milk": and the name of milk-maid, given to the daughter of the house, discloses to us how poetical and pastoral the life of the early Aryans was. It shows a kind of delicacy and humour, if we imagine a father calling his daughter his little milk-maid, rather than *sutâ*, his "begotten," or *fīlia*, the "suckling." This meaning had been forgotten long before the Aryans separated; and *duhitar* had ceased to be a nickname, and had become the proper name of daughter. Any one will recall to himself many words now in common use the original meanings of which have long been wholly lost.

Many Aryan words were formed in the same spirit, and were applicable only during a nomadic mode of life, when our forefathers tended their herds on the wide steppes of Toorkistan, with the heavenly luminaries for their guides and to enable them to count the passing of the hours.

"Ox" and "cow" were, in Sanskrit, *go;* and *gâvas* in the plural. The Old High German *chuo, chuowi* were the same words. *Go-pa* meant originally a "herder or keeper of cows," and at last came to mean a "king:" and *goshu-yûdh*, "fighting among or for the cows," is used in the Veda for the name of a warrior in general; while one of the most frequent words for "battle" is *gâv-ishti*, literally "striving for cows;" whence, in the later Sanskrit, *gâve-shaṇa* means simple "research, inquiry," i. e., a striving to attain the truth, physical or philosophical. All these words compounded with *go*, "cattle," prove that the people who formed them led a half nomadic and pastoral life; and they also indicate to us, in the change of the meaning of words that originally referred only to physical things or phenomena, the cause of the false interpretations given by Wilson to the Veda. He gives to certain important words, not the original Aryan meaning, which is the true one, but the meaning which they had, ages afterwards, in the Sanskrit and to the compilers of the Vedas. The result is, the imputation to the old cattle-herders and horse-tamers of the steppes and of the plains of the Five Rivers, of ideas and notions that were not entertained until a much later day.

The name for a wife left husbandless in the later languages comes from the same common source. In the Sanskrit, *dhava* is a "husband" or "man," and this, with the addition of the preposition *vi*, meaning "without," makes *vi-dhava*, "without a husband, a widow." This compound has been preserved in languages that have lost the simple word *dhava*, and we have the Keltic *feadvh*, the Gothic *viduvo*, the Sclavonic *vdova*, Old Prussian *widdewû*, and Latin *vidua*, as well as an English *widow*.

Müller traces the descent of many other words, and says,

> The evidence which we have gone through, must be sufficient to show that the race of men which could coin these words,—words that have been carried down the stream of time, and washed upon the shores of so many nations, could not have been a race of savages, of mere nomads and hunters.

They had homes, and family relations, and names for relatives by marriage, which are yet preserved in our European languages. The Sanskrit *doma*, a "house" or "home," is the Greek δόμος, the Latin *domus*, the Sclavonic *domŭ* and the Keltic *daimh;* as it is the Gothic *timrjan*, to "build," from which the English word *timber;* and the word "door," in ancient times at least, the most essential part of the house, is preserved in Sanskrit *dvar*, *dvâras*, Gothic *daur*, Lithuanian *durys*, Keltic *dor*, Greek θύρα, and Latin *fores*. The "builder" or "architect" has the same name in Sanskrit and Greek, *takshan* being the Greek τέκτων. In the Greek "αστυ, "house," we find the Sanskrit *vâstri*, "house;" in the Sanskrit *puri*, "town," the Greek *πόλις*; and that roads were not unknown, appears from the Sanskrit *path*, *pathi*, *panthan* and *pâthas*, all names for roads, the Greek *πάτος*, the Gothic *fad*.

Most of the names connected with the chase and war differ in the different Aryan dialects, while those connected with more peaceful occupations are generally common to all. This shows that the Aryans had led a long life of peace before they separated, and that it was the new generations which formed new terms connected with the warlike and adventurous life of their onward migrations. Hence it is that not only the Greek and Latin, but all Aryan languages have their peaceful words in common, and that they all differ so strangely in their warlike expressions. Thus, too, the domestic animals are generally known by the same names in England and in India, while the wild beasts have different names even in Greek and Latin. Thus the words for "cattle," "ox," "steer," "heifer," "horse," "fowl," "dog," "sheep," "calf," "she-goat," "sow," "hog," "mouse," "fly" and "goose." "Steer," for example, is, in Sanskrit, *sthûra;* Zend, *staora;* Greek, *ταῦρος*; Latin, *taurus;* Spanish, *toro;* Teutonic, *stiur;* Lithuanian, *taura-s;* Sclavonic, *tour;* and Irish, *tor.*

So the names of some wild animals, common to Asia and Europe, as the bear and wolf; and also the serpent, in Sanskrit *sarpa.*

The oldest term for ploughing is *ar*, which we find in the Latin *arare;* Greek *'αροω*, "to ear"; Old Sclavonic *orati;* Gothic *arjan;* Lithuanian *arti*, and Gothic *ar*. Hence the common name of the "plough" *"αροτρον*, *aratrum;* Old Saxon *erida;* Old Norse *ardhr;* Old Sclavonic *oralo* and *oradlo;* Lithuanian *arkla-s;* Welsh *aradyr* and *arad;* Cornish *aradar.*

So in the Sanskrit, *pada* and *agra* each was a "field;" Greek *πεδον*; Umbrian, *perum;* Latin, *pedum* in *oppidum;* Polish, *pole;* Saxon, *folda;* Old High German, *feld;* English, *field;* and *αγρος*, *ager*, and Gothic *akr-s.*

In Sanskrit, *sveta* means "white," and corresponds to Gothic *hveit*, Old High German *huiz*, and *wiz;* the Anglo-Saxon *hvit* and our *wheat;* Gothic *hvaitei*, and Lithuanian *kwety-s*. "Corn," meant originally what is crushed or ground, Sanskrit *kûrna*, Russian *zerno;* Gothic *kaurn;* Lithuanian *girna*, a millstone, and the plural *girnos* a handmill. The Russian word for millstone is *zernov;* and the Gothic name for mill, *gvairnus*, the later *guirn.*

The name for "clothes" is the same among all the Aryan nations, being *vastra* in Sanskrit, *vasti* in Gothic, *vestis* in Latin, *ἐσθὴς* in Greek, *fassradh* in Irish, *gwisk* in Welsh. To "weave" is *ve* in Sanskrit, and in a causative form, *vap*. With *ve* coincide the Latin *vieo*, and the Greek radical of *Fήτριον*; with *vap*, the Old High German *wab*, the English "weave" and "web," the Greek *ὑφαίνω*. To "sew" is in Sanskrit, *siv*, whence *sûtra*, a "thread." The same root is preserved in the Latin *suo*, in Gothic *siuja*, in the Old High German *siwu*, English "sew," Lithuanian *siuv-u*, Greek κασσύω for κατασύω. Another Sanskrit root, with a similar meaning, is *nah*, which must have existed also as *nabh* and *nadh*. From *nah* we have the Latin *neo* and *necto*, Greek νέω, German *nâhan* and *nâvan*, to "sew"; from *nadh*, the Greek νήθω; from *nabh*, the Sanskrit *nabhi* and *nabha* or *urnanabha*, the spider, literally, "the wool-spinner." *Rak*, in Sanskrit, meant to "make," corresponding with the Greek ῥάπτω, to "stitch together or weave," whence, perhaps ἀράχνη and *aranea*, the "spider," and the classical name of woven wool, λάχνος or λάχνη, and the Latin *lana*.

The value and usefulness of *some* of the metals were known before the separation of the Aryan race, as is proven by a few words; but the names of most of the metals differ in different countries. Iron was known, and its value appreciated; and we find traces of the old names for silver and gold.

It is clear, therefore, that ages before even the composition of the Vedic hymns in the Punjab, the arts of sewing and spinning and weaving were known to our ancestors, and of extracting from the ores and working some of the metals.

But during this early period, they knew nothing about the sea. The names for that are of later growth. They are identical in Greek and Latin, but not in the northern and southern branches of the great family. The words *sara* in Sanskrit, ἅλς in Greek and *sal* in Latin, prove that salt was known; but these words were not applied to the sea until later times. The words "oar" and "rudder" can be traced back to Sanskrit; and the name of "ship," Sanskrit *naus, nâvas;* Latin *navis;* Greek ναῦς; Old High German *nacho;* Anglo-Saxon *naca*, is identically the same in all these tongues.

Remember that all these are proofs of what language was spoken ages before one stream of the great Aryan emigrations took its course towards India, to halt on its way in the land of the Five Rivers: before even the earliest wave of emigration flowed forth, which was to reach Germany and Gaul and the British Isles and Spain, the great Keltic emigration.

At this remote period, the Aryans had a decimal system of numeration, in itself one of the most marvellous achievements of the human mind, based on an abstract conception of quantity, regulated by a spirit of philosophical classification, and yet conserved, matured and finished before the foot of Greek, Roman, Kelt, Sclave or Teuton was set on the soil of Europe.

Such a system could only have been formed by a very small community; and more than any part of language it seems to necessitate the admission of what might almost be called a conventional agreement among those who first framed and adopted the Aryan names for the numbers from one to one hundred.

To form and fix a series of words expressing *one*, *two*, *three*, *four*, etc., it was necessary that the ancestors of the Aryan race should have come to some kind of unconscious agreement to use but one term for each number, and to attach but one meaning to each term. If different names were used for the same numeral, the very object of the names would be defeated, and if one word could be used to mean five as well as ten, all commerce between individuals using the same word in different senses, would have been impossible. Words expressing material objects could, on the contrary, and did, have more than one meaning and more than one word could be used to mean the same object, because things have many qualities, and receive their names from them.

The subjoined table will show the coincidences of the Aryan numerals.

	Sanskrit	Greek	Latin	Lithuanian	Gothic
i.	*ekas*	εἷς (οἴνη)	*unus*	*wienas*	*ains*
ii.	*dvau*	δύο	*duo*	*du*	*twai*
iii.	*trayas*	τρεις	*tres*	*trys*	*threis*
iv.	*katvaros*	τέτταρες (*Æolic*, πισυρες.)	*quatuor* (*Oscan*, *petora*.)	*keturi*	*fidvor*
v.	*panka*	πέντε	*quinque* (*Oscan*, *pomtis*.)	*penki*	*fimf*
vi.	*shash*	ἕξ	*sex*	*szeszi*	*saihs*
vii.	*sapta*	ἑπτὰ	*septem*	*septyni*	*sibun*
viii.	*ashtan*	ὀκτὼ	*octo*	*asztůni*	*ahtau*
ix.	*nava*	ἐννέα	*novem*	*dewyni*	*niun*
x.	*dasa*	δέκα	*decem*	*deszimt*	*taihun*
xi.	*ekadasa*	῞ενδεκα	*undecim*	*wieno-lika*	*ain-lif*
xii.	*dvadasa*	δωδεκα	*duodecim*	*dwi-lika*	*twa-lif*
xx.	*vinsati*	εἴκοσι	*viginti*	*dwi-deszimti*	*twaitigjus*
c.	*satam*	ἑκατὸν	*centum*	*szimtas*	*taihun-taihund*
m.	*sahasram*	χίλιοι	*mille*	*tukstantis*	*thusundi*

Eichhoff says (*Parallèle*, 480):

Everywhere, during the course of this work, we have found, in the principal languages distributed among the peoples of Europe, the traces of their Indian origin, traces certain and ineffaceable, although modified by times and places. The Celts, the first colonists that came from Central Asia, and were forced by successive emigrations to the very ends of the Occident, have preserved of their ancient idiom, then doubtless only in outline [*ebauché*, in outline, rough-hewn, or in the rough], a vague and indecisive remembrance, almost confined to the elementary sounds. Among the Germans, the roots are complete, their connexion logical, their forms fixed, but still impressed with a certain rudeness, that attests the infancy of the language. Among the Slaves, the forms are harmonized, their separation from the mother-country having been later. They are developed and enriched among the Latins,

> and gain in elevation and nobleness, until the genius of Greece, issuing last from ancient Asia to illuminate a new continent, charms us by the graces of a language carried to its highest perfection. Thus the Indian tongue becomes a comparative scale, that determines the places of the different peoples in the great migrations of the human race. It fills the gaps of history, by marking the progress of each epoch, less by its literary traditions in which the imagination riots clad in a thousand colours, than by the aggregate of its vocabulary, the faithful interpreter of our European languages. In our days, too, every nation shares in this as intimately as in the Greek and Latin, and when a grave and solemn thought needs to be worthily expressed, the Muse of the Ganges may, without the least effort, unite with that of the Tiber to proclaim, in the same words, in words everywhere intelligible, a prayer which, dear to French hearts, will find an echo throughout all Europe.

He adds, in a note:

> The words contained in the following text, transcribed in accordance with the rules of Indian euphony, are found sufficiently explained, whether in the chapter on composite nouns, or in the examples of declensions, or in the list of verbal roots, etc., etc.

As the text (an invocation of good fortune for Louis Philippe and his Queen), strikingly shows that the Sanskrit and Latin had a common origin, we reproduce it here:

TEXTE INDIEN.

राजं पालाश्वं राज्ञीं अमलां

युवराजं भ्रातॄन् स्वसॄश्च

तायतां महादेवः

TRANSCRIPTION ET TRADUCTION

RÂJAM PÂLÂÇVAN RÂJNÎM AMALÂN

REGEM PHILIPPUM REGINAM AMALIAM

YUVA-RÂJAM BHRÂTÂN SVASÆÇ-ĆA

JUVENEM REGIUM FRATRES SORORES QUE

TÂYATÂM MAHÂ-DAIVAS

TUEATUR MAGNUS DEUS.

DEITIES OF THE VEDAS.

The far larger number of the hymns in the Rig-Veda are addressed to *Agni* and *Indra*.

Thus, of one hundred and twenty-one hymns in *Ashṭaka i.* thirty-seven are addressed to Agni alone, or associated with others, and forty-five to Indra. Twelve are addressed to the Maruts, and eleven to the Aṣwins.

In *Ashṭaka ii.*, there are thirty hymns to Agni, thirty-nine to Indra, and five to Mitra and Varuṇa.

In *Ashṭaka iii.*, of one hundred and twenty-one *Sûktas*, forty-four are addressed to Agni, and forty-eight to Indra.

And in *Ashṭaka iv.*, of one hundred and forty, thirty-six are addressed to Agni, forty-six to Indra, and eleven to Mitra and Varuṇa.

The Divinities worshipped in the Rig-Veda are not unknown to later systems, but they there perform very subordinate parts, with one or two exceptions; while those Deities that are the Great Gods, *Dii Majores*, of the later period, are either not named at all in the Veda, or are noticed in an inferior and different capacity.

There is no hint in the Veda of the Linga or Phallus, the form in which Siva has been worshipped for thirty centuries, nor any epithet applicable to that Deity; nor is there any hint of the Trimūrti, of Brahma, Vishṇu and Siva, as typified by the Mystic Syllable; nor any mention of Brahm-Maya, the One, Sole, Absolute, First, Self-divided into male and female.

> Come, Nâsatyas, with the thrice eleven Divinities!

it is said in *Sûkta iv.*, of *Adhyâya iii.*, of *Ashṭaka iv.*

And these thirty-three Divinities, it is said (*Vishṇu-Purâṇa, p.* 123, *and note*), are eight *Vasus*, eleven *Rudras*, twelve *Âdityas*, *Prajâpati* and *Vashaṭkâra*.

The chief Deities, as we have said, of the Veda are *Agni* and *Indra*.

We give, hereunder, what Wilson says in regard to the principal Deities, without comment here, preferring to consider how far he is correct at the conclusion of these extracts.

> *Agni* is Fire:
>
> 1. As existing on earth; as domestic and culinary, and as religious or sacrificial; and also as the heat of digestion and life, and the vivifying principle of vegetation.
> 2. As existing in the atmosphere or mid-heaven, as lightning.

3. In the Heavens, as light, the sun, the dawn, and the planetary bodies.

And Agni is identified with Yama, Varuṇa, Mitra, with the Sun, and the Eternal Vedhas.

He is personified as a Divinity, is young, immortal, endowed with infinite power and splendour, giver of victory, wealth, cattle, food, health and life. He travels in a car drawn by red horses. He is the source and diffuser of light, destroyer and reviver of all things.

The Sun is hymned as a Divinity, the soul of all movable and immovable beings; and his manifestations are known as *Âdityas*, including Vishṇu, Mitra, Varuṇa, Aryaman, Pûshan, Bhaga and Twashtṛi, who are the sun diversified, as presiding over each month of the solar year.

Indra is the personification of the phænomena of the firmament, particularly in sending down rain.

The clouds are the Demons that he encounters. They will not part with their watery stores, until he cleaves them with his thunderbolt. Vṛitra, the Demon, becomes a real personage, who wages war against this King of the Gods.

Indra is especially the God of battles, giving victory, destroying the enemies of religious rites, possessor and bestower of riches, granter of temporal blessings, when propitiated by the Soma juice.

Mitra is never addressed alone. He appears among the *Viswadevas* or Gods collectively, or associated with *Varuṇa* and *Aryaman*.

He presides over the day, averts evil and protects cattle, and in conjunction with Varuṇa, is the dispenser of water.

Varuṇa is the Divinity who presides over night. The constellations are his holy acts. The moon moves by his command. He is called King or Monarch, *Râjâ* or *Samrât:* Is Lord of Light, as Mitra is, and supports the light on high; he makes wide the path of the sun. He grants riches, averts evil and protects cattle.

Aryaman is never named alone, but most usually with Mitra and Varuṇa. A text identifies him with the sun, and the scholiast says he presides over the twilight.

Sûrya or *Savitṛi* is the Sun. In the First Book, three Sûktas only are addressed to him. He also is the giver of temporal blessings. He is the source of light, moving swiftly between the heaven and the earth, in a chariot drawn by white-footed horses, or by the Seven. He is golden-handed and golden-eyed.

The *Âdityas*, or lesser Suns, are especially the sons of *Âditi*, who has generally the character of mother of the Gods, identified in the first part of the Veda with the earth, or even with the universe.

There is no separate hymn to *Vishṇu* in the First Book, but he is mentioned as Trivikrâma, or he who took the three steps, the rising, culmination, and setting, of the sun.

Ushas is the dawn.

The two *Aṣwins* are connected, in various places, with the radiance of the sun, and are said to be precursors of the dawn. They are the two sons of the sun, begotten during his metamorphosis as a horse.

Pûshan is said to be the Deity or *Aditya*, or Sun, presiding over the earth.

All the Deities, in the First Ashṭaka, are resolvable into three:—*Agni*, or Fire; *Indra*, or the Firmament; and the *Sun*; or, as the Sun is but a manifestation of Fire, we might resolve all the forms into two, *Agni* and *Indra.*

The Yâska says that there are in the Veda three Gods,— *Agni* on the earth; *Vayu* or *Indra*, in the sky; and *Sûrya*, in heaven,—of each of whom there are many appellations, expressive of his greatness, and of the variety of his functions.

We very much doubt the correctness of these conjectures, as to any of these Divinities, except Agni, Sûrya, Ushas and the Maruts. How far they *are* correct can be ascertained only by carefully grouping and comparing the attributes of each and the epithets applied to each.

Agni is undoubtedly fire, and the spirit or genius of fire.

Ushas is certainly the dawn, or the light of the dawn. Probably it was deemed that this splendidly coloured light was not the light of the sun, which is not yet visible during the glancings of the dawn, and when it rises, puts to flight its beautiful flocks of colours.

Sûrya undoubtedly was the sun; and the Maruts were the winds.

It is also said—

Mitra is the Lord of Day: *Maitram vâ ahar*, the day is dependent on Mitra.

Aryaman is the sun: *Asau vâ âditya aryama*, He, the Sun, is Aryaman.

Vâruṇi râtrî, the night is dependent on Varuṇa.

The Aşwins are heaven and earth; *or* day and night; *or*, the sun and moon..

Âditi literally means, "the independent," "the indivisible."

And, in *Ashṭaka i.*, *Adhyâya vi.*, *Anuvâka xiv.*, *Sûkta v.* (*lxxxix.*):

> 10. Âditi is heaven: Âditi is the firmament: Âditi is mother, father and son: Âditi is all the Gods: Âditi is the five classes of beings: Âditi is generation and birth.

Bunsen (*Egypt's Place in Universal History, iii.* 587) says of the hymns addressed to *Agni*,

> Here we find glimpses of those elements which were developed in later times: by the side of the Agni of the earth, the Agni of heaven (Mitra, sun), and the Agni of the clouds (lightning) or water . . . . Concurrent with this was the worship of the vault of *heaven* as a special Deity, Varuṇa (*Ouranos*). In the most ancient times, human sacrifices were offered to him, subsequently no especial sacrifice. Varuṇa, at a later date, was viewed rather in a moral sense. He is the eternal government of the world, physical, as well as moral. He tries the heart, and judges man. It may, however, be a question, whether we have here two consecutive epochs, or merely two concurring elements.

It will be seen hereafter that, in my opinion, nearly all of these notions find no support at all in the Veda.

Of "the adoration of *æther*, as Indra" (*Zeus*), he says,

> There is no doubt that this belongs to a later time. [But on the contrary, it is not possible to show from the Veda that the adoration of Indra did not commence at the same time with that of Agni. Neither is there any warrant for saying that Indra is the *ether*, nor that he was the same as, or the prototype of, Zeus.] It also has its own peculiar sacred symbol, the sacrifice of Soma, an intoxicating potion, consisting of fermented juice of plants, mixed with milk. [But, although Indra is more frequently spoken of as exhilarated with and strengthened by the Soma juice, than any other of the Deities, yet it was not in any sense his own peculiar sacred symbol. It was not the symbol of any Deity; nor at all peculiar to Indra. As a minor error, it may be noted that the juice of the Soma plant was not fermented, but was pressed out with stones at the very time of the sacrifice.] In this form, however, it reminds us of the Turanian Shamanism, the product of ecstatic excitement.

A .·. U .·. M .·.

Agni	Varuṇa	Mitra
Aryaman	Ushas	Maruts
Âditi	Vayu: Vasu	Maghavan
Ayu	Vishṇu: Vibhwan	Mantras
Aṅgiras	Vedhas	
Aṣwins	Vashtoshpati	
Âdityas	Vanaspati	

> *Âditi* is the mother of the Gods.
> The *Âdityas* are her sons, twelve in number.
> *Vishṇu* is the pervader, or pervading Deity.
> *Vayu* is the God of the wind, identified by the scholiasts with Indra.

These are the conjectures of Wilson.

There are frequent allusions in the Veda, to the birth or production of Agni, by attrition, by the means known to all savages, by rubbing together two pieces of wood.

Fire is manifested in flame, and its effects are light and heat. These give life and productiveness to everything, and flame is the most fearfully destructive of all agents, in city or in forest.

Also, there is a celestial fire, the lightning, which rends and destroys.

And the moon, planets and stars gave, to the primitive men, light unaccompanied by heat or flame. Even the sun, probably, did not give them the idea of fire or flame, but only those of light and heat.

Besides these sources of light, the Aryans north of the Himalayas saw the Northern Auroras in the winter, the flashing meteors, and the strange light of the glow-worm and fire-fly.

At times, also, the clouds were gorgeously radiant with many-coloured light, which must have seemed to the ancients rather to belong to them, than to be the same white light that flowed from the sun.

Those ancients knew nothing about the atmosphere. The winds were as great a wonder to them as light. They did not conceive of wind as a mass of matter in motion; but as a force, the nature of which was as much unknown to them as the nature of heat.

It is reasonable to suppose that all these potencies were deified—the fire, flame, light, heat, lightning, dawn, the winds and the clouds.

Of the firmament they conceived as a smooth and solid concavity, as it seems to children. The sun, moon and other luminous bodies seemed to them to move along its face, at no great distance from the earth. Of the magnitude of these orbs they had no idea, and did not conceive of them as large bodies at all. To them they must have been no larger than they appear. Of the planets, Jupiter and Venus must, morning and evening have attracted their attention, and the seven stars of the Great Bear, as well as the three of the Belt of Orion. Other and single stars must have attracted their attention, such as Aldebarân, Arcturas, Regulus, Leo and Sirius, and the Pole-Star.

VEDIC WORSHIP AND INTERPRETATION.

"The Vedic worship is that of fire and the elements: it is patriarchal and domestic, but is celebrated through the agency of a rather imposing body of priests (Brahmans) although it consists of little more than the presentation, through fire, of clarified butter [the flesh of animals sacrificed] and the juice of the Soma plant to the Gods, who are invoked to be present, whose power and benevolence are glorified, whose protection against enemies and misfortunes is implored, whose displeasure and anger are deprecated, and who are solicited to bestow food, cattle, riches and posterity upon the individuals who conduct the worship, or on whose behalf it is performed. Occasional intimations of the hope of happiness hereafter occur, but they are not frequent nor urgent, and the main objects of every prayer and hymn are the good things of this present life." (*Professor Wilson: Rig-V. ii. Intro. vi.*)

I very much doubt whether there is in the Rig-Veda Sanhita any intimation *at all* of a belief in another life after the present, or of a hope of happiness after this life. The words "immortal" and "immortality" occur in the translation; but they mean only long life, or long-continued existence. The "immortality" of the Veda is to be attained by food.

The Atharva-Veda (*viii.* 48. 3) thus exults:

We have drunk the Soma, we have become immortal, we have entered into light, we have known the Gods: what can an enemy now do to us? What can the malice of any mortal effect, O immortal God!

The ceremony takes place in the dwelling of the worshipper, in a chamber appropriated to the purpose, and probably to the maintenance of a perpetual fire, although the frequent allusions to the occasional kindling of the sacred flame are rather at variance with this practice. There is no mention of any temple, or any reference to a public place of worship, and it is clear that the worship was entirely domestic. (*Wilson: Rig-V. i. Introd. xxiii.*)

I think there are several grave errors in this paragraph. *In general*, at least, as I think clearly appears throughout the Veda, the acts of worship and sacrifice were performed in the open air, the fire being kindled on the grass, and where the flame could ascend toward the stars, to many of which as Deities, hymns were addressed. Wood was gathered there for fuel to feed the fire, and that in considerable quantity, and even of logs, and for some purpose or other posts were set up in rows

like white swans that had alighted on the ground.

I do not find any allusion to a perpetual fire, or one kept continually burning. On the contrary, it seems to have been deemed proper, if not indispensable, to obtain the fire for the sacrifice by attrition of two pieces of dry wood. The fire so obtained was evidently regarded as having peculiar sanctity and is often spoken of.

The sacrifices were often, if not generally, performed early in the morning at sunrise, at or even before the first glancings of the dawn; and at fixed and particular times, when certain constellations were in the East shortly before day, and the Morning Star shone brilliantly.

It is true that no mention is made of temples. In this respect, and in having no idols or images, the ancient Persians, Medes, or Bactrian Zarathustrians simply continued to be Aryans. But the worship was not entirely domestic. If it had been, there would have been no

> goodly array of officiating priests, in some instances seven, in some sixteen,

to recite the *Mantras*, or prayers or hymns.

We need not quote here Professor Wilson's summary of the characteristics of the hymns; because that will amply appear from the extracts that we shall make in subsequent pages. He says,

> There is little demand for moral benefactions, although in some few instances hatred of untruth and abhorrence of sin are expressed, a hope is uttered that the latter may be repented of or expiated, and the Gods are, in one hymn [in the First Ashṭaka] solicited to extricate the worshipper from sin of every kind.

It is quite true that these things appear in the translation, and that the words "Truth" and "Sin" are often used in it. But the reader will readily discover that these words do not reproduce the meaning of the original words. The former, in general, at least, means actuality or reality, and *that* actuality and reality of things, which is produced by making them visible. It is in that sense that light (Indra) is truth; and that the celestial luminaries are "Lords of Truth." And the latter, often, if not generally, merely means losing one's way in the dark, upon the plains or in the woods.

It is constantly the case, it seems to me, that Vedic words which in the lapse of ages had come to have in common acceptation meanings quite other than their original ones, are rendered in the translation into English by words that are the equivalents of the Vedic ones, not in their original meanings, but in those which they had taken upon themselves centuries afterwards.

To understand this, we need only glance at many of our common English words. *Regard* originally meant the act of looking at; *respect*, the act of looking back; *respectable*, one to be looked back at; *umbrage*, a shadow; *extenuate*, to thin out; *refrain*, to rein in; *precocious*, cooked too soon; *premature*, ripe too soon; *candour*, shining whiteness; *nervous*, sinewy; *obsequious* (a holy and obsequious tear), connected with *obsequies*, following one to the tomb; *libel*, a little book; *affront* ("may here affront Ophelia"), meet face to face; *nuisance* (from *nuire*), that which harms; *knave*, an innocent boy or youth, afterwards a servant ("Paul, a knave of Jesus Christ," Duke of Lauderdale's Translation of the Bible); *vulgar*, of the common people; *idiot*, unlearned; *right*, what is ordered; *just*, what is commanded; *animosity*, courage, high spirit; *usury*, interest; *traduce*, to promulgate; *minion*, a favourite; *sophist*, a lover of wisdom; *dogmatic*, doctrinal; *wits*, senses ("thy five wittes"); *pragmatical*, businesslike; *speculation* ("no speculation in those eyes"), contemplation; *officious*, dutiful, attentive (as Dr. Johnson wrote of Levett, "officious, innocent, sincere"); *resentment*, feeling over again; *animadvert*, turn the mind to; *crafty*, skilful in any art; *cunning*, kenning, knowing; *sense*, feeling; *crude*, uncooked; *saucy*, salsus, salted; *moral*, customary; and hundreds of others. If, now, there were an old book in our language, written centuries ago, using these words in their original meaning and one now translating it into French were to take them in their *present* meanings, and translate accordingly, what would the "translation" deserve to be called? Especially if, by taking the words in their modern sense, ideas were imputed to our ancestors which they never had? It is very evident that *many* words are thus habitually abused and misused in the translation of the Vedas.

Even the Fourth Veda (the Atharva-Veda) is of comparatively recent date. The three others were collected together about 1,400 years before our era; but there evidently existed smaller collections before this, especially of the Rig-Veda. When the complete collection was made,

> the compilers had completely lost sight of the original meaning of the old hymns. They treat them as made for the purposes of public worship, whereas it is clear that many of them, and in fact the very ancient ones, were not liturgies at all, but the out-pourings of the free natural inspiration flowing out of the whole material life, and the great events, of the Poet's own time, and the experience of the tribe and of the people.

That is to say, I suppose, translating it into simpler language, they are mere poems, which were composed, not for sacrificial purposes, but as the Welsh and Irish bards composed those which they recited in their ramblings. Whatever it means, it is entirely incorrect. It is perfectly evident that almost all the hymns were composed to be chaunted at the sacrifices. The words of praise and adoration were supposed to mingle with the flame of the sacrifice, and to ascend with them to the Gods and become themselves divine. They are strictly religious. If they speak of wars and battles, of enemies slain and hostile cities demolished, it is in praise of the Deity whom they invoke and to whom they ascribe these victories. Poems containing

> the out-pourings of the free natural aspiration flowing out of the whole material life,

would deal with the ordinary and home life, and the affections of the heart and the charms and beauties of Nature. There is not a word about love or woman or in praise of beauty in the whole Veda: there are no martial strains nor songs of the chase, nothing that tells of home and household, no allusions even to the fruits and flowers and trees, of which every poetic soul loves to sing. It would be better to write accurately and soberly, than to seek to write finely, upon these subjects.

But this is truly said:

> Not only is the scene of these songs, the Indus country, unknown to the compilers, but likewise the religion. Brahma and Brahmanism had dispelled the old religious ideas. The highest Vedic Gods, Agni, Varuṇa, Indra, had degenerated into Gods of the second order, into mere guardians of the world. [The character of Vishṇu had entirely changed, and his original individuality had disappeared.] The form of the language, lastly, is not only different, and far more ancient, but the language of the Vedas is a living language: that of the compilers is more modern, but one already become petrified and obsolete, among the people—a learned language. In the time of Buddha, Sanskrit, in its turn, had become a dead language. He lived in the Sanskrit country; but he preached in Pali. When the Aryans crossed the Sutlej, they took with them the language of the country of the Five Rivers. Then the Brahmanical system sprung up, the old language gradually died away; and the Sanskrit, 'the perfect language,' took the place of 'The language of the seers.'
>
> We find our ancestors [it is said], in this land of the Five Rivers, in possession of all that Nature can bestow. The earth produces for them in profusion its choicest gifts [which are never alluded to in the Veda], the climate is conducive to comfort and to bodily vigour [which is never mentioned], the sky is glowing and transparent; they are surrounded by all the grandeur, and by all the wealth of Nature. And they have a language capable of giving soul to the objects of sense, and body to the abstractions of metaphysics.

And yet, to all this "grandeur and wealth of Nature" there is little or no allusion, except so far as light, the winds and the storms are concerned. Not even the mountains, always in light, with their snow-clad summits are mentioned.

Müller remarks (*Chips i.* 113), that, in the special case of the sacred literature of the Brahmans, we must be guided by their own tradition, which invariably places the poetical hymns of the Rig-Veda before the ceremonial hymns and formulas of the Yajur-Veda and Sâma-Veda. He says,

> The strongest argument that has as yet been brought forward against this view is, that the formulas of the Yajur-Veda and the sacrificial texts of the Sâma-Veda

contain occasionally more archaic forms of language, than the hymns of the Rig-Veda. It was supposed, therefore, that although the hymns of the Rig-Veda might have been composed at an earlier time, the sacrificial hymns and formulas were the first to be collected and to be preserved in the schools, by means of a strict mnemonic discipline. The hymns of the Rig-Veda, some of which have no reference whatever to the Vedic ceremonial, being collected at a later time, might have been stripped, while being handed down by oral tradition, of those grammatical forms, which in the course of time had become obsolete; but which, if once recognized and sanctioned in theological seminaries, would have been preserved there with the most religious care.

METHOD OF INQUIRY.

I propose, now, to copy all those passages of the Veda (principally as translated by Professor Wilson), in which the principal Deities are invoked or named, which will afford us any aid is ascertaining what each Deity was. Many passages, are, of course, for that purpose wholly valueless.

I shall seldom comment upon them, while quoting them; but shall afterwards sum up the information they give us, and see whether they sustain the common interpretations, and whether they enable us, with any degree of certainty, to comprehend the thought of the ancient Aryan Poets.

Commencing with no theory or preconceived notions whatever, except so far as I had unquestioningly accepted as true the dicta of Müller, Bunsen, Wilson and Muir, I hope that I have attained to some comprehension of the meaning of these old hymns, or at least that my suggestions may indicate to others the path on which they may advance towards certainty.

For, so far, in the works of all the scholars, we have but vague guesses at the meaning of most of the Aryan Deities, and the mythology of the Vedas is not only confused and contradictory, but so vague in its outlines as to be absolutely worthless as to lead only to error. It may be truly said that we have no idea what it all means, or whether the Vedic Deities were definite conceptions, or mere shifting and phantasmagorical shadows—words and names, and not realities.

अग्नि AGNI.

TEXTS RELATING TO

Ashtaka i. *Mandala i.*
Adhyâya i. *Anuvâka i.*

Sûkta i. *Varga i.*

1. I glorify Agni, the High Priest of the Sacrifice, Deva,* the ministrant, who presents the oblation and is the possessor of great wealth.

8. The Radiant, the protector of sacrifices, the constant illuminator of truth, increasing thine own dwelling: [*Swe dame, suâ domo*, the chamber in which fire-worship is performed.—*Wilson.*]

Anuvâka iv. *Sûkta i.*

Agni, the messenger of the Gods, their invoker, the possessor of all wealth . . . . Agni, Agni, the lord of men, the bearer of offerings, the beloved of many . . . . Generated by attrition, resplendent, ever young and wise, radiant, remover of disease, the bright resplendent Agni, the purifier, shining with pure radiance, charged with all the invocations of the Gods.

Sûkta iii.

Let the wise invoker bring hither from the shining of the sun all the Divinities awaking with the dawn. With all the Gods, with Indra, Vâyu, and the glories of Mitra, drink, Agni, the sweet Soma juice.

Sûkta iv.

4. Agni, bring the Gods hither! Arrange them in three places, decorate them.
12. Giver of rewards! Being identified with the household fire.

Anuv. v. *Sûkta ii.*

Come, Agni, with the Maruts, who are Divinities abiding in the radiant heaven above the sun; who scatter the clouds and agitate the sea.

Sûkta vi.

Agni, the benefactor of the universe. Agni, abiding in the waters. Agni, confer upon me vigour, progeny and life.

Asht. i. *Adhy. ii.* *Anuv. vi.* *Sûkta i.*

Of whom, or of which Divinity of the immortals shall we invoke the auspicious name? Who will give us to the great Aditi, that I may again behold my father and my mother?

2. Let us invoke the auspicious name of Agni, the first Divinity of the immortals, that he may give us to the great Aditi, and that I may behold again my father and my mother.

**Deva:* bright, shining, radiant; from *div*, to "shine." Also explained, one who dwells in the sky.

3. Ever-protecting Savitṛi, we solicit our portion of thee, who art the lord of affluence.

5. We are assiduous in attaining the summit of affluence, through the protection of thee, who art the possessor of wealth.

6. These birds that are flying, have not obtained, Varuña, thy bodily strength or thy prowess.

Sûkta iii (xxvi).

1. Lord of sustenance, assume thy vestments, and offer this our sacrifice.

3. Thou, Agni, art verily as a living father to a son, as a kinsman to a kinsman, as a friend to a friend.

7. May the lord of men, the sacrificing priest, the gracious, the chosen, be kind to us! May we, possessed of holy fires, be loved by thee!

9, 10. Immortal Agni . . . . Son of strength!

Sûkta iv (xxvii).

6. Thou of variant splendour [*Chitrabhânu*], art the distributor of riches, as the waves of a river are parted by interjacent isles.

11. The vast, illimitable, smoke-bannered, resplendent Agni.

12. May Agni, the lord of men, the invoker and messenger of the Gods, the brilliant-rayed, hear us with our hymns, as a prince.

13. Veneration to the great Gods! Veneration to the lesser! Veneration to the young! Veneration to the old! We worship all the Gods as right-wisely as we are able. May I not omit the praise of the elder Divinities!

Anuv. vii. Sûkta i.

1, 2, 3. Agni, thou wast the first Angiras Ṛishi, a Divinity, thou wast the auspicious friend of the Deities: sapient, manifold, for the benefit of all the world, intelligent, the offspring of two mothers, and reposing in various ways for the use of man. Agni, pre-eminent over the world, become manifest to the worshipper. Heaven and earth tremble. Thou hast borne the burthen in the ceremonial. Thou, Vasu, hast worshipped the Venerable Gods.

4. Thou, Agni, hast announced Heaven to Manu, ... When thou art set free by the attrition of thy parents, they bear thee, first to the East, then to the West. ['Announced heaven to man' is no more a *translation*, i. e., a *transfer* into the English language, of the *meaning* of the original, than the metaphysical ideas of Kant, or the phrases of alchemy would be. The hymn is addressing itself to the *actual* fire, that of the domestic hearth and the altar. It is manifold, the hymn says, i. e., assumes various shapes, can be partitioned, so that all can have the benefit of it. Producing Light, it is the means by which the sky is discerned. That is the 'heaven' which it 'announces'.]

5. Thou, the provider of sustenance, first bestowest light, and then upon all men.

6. Agni, excellently wise, thou directest the man who follows improper paths, to acts fitted to reclaim him. [Which is another attempt to *elevate* the tone of the Veda, by giving its ideas a modern drapery. For the verse simply means that fire giving a light, enables one who loses his way by taking the wrong path (in the woods or elsewhere), to find the right way again.]

7. Thou sustainest the mortal in the best immortality, by daily food. [Which is simply nonsense, because food, which fire supplies by cooking it, does not confer immortality, but sustains life, when, without food, man would perish.]

9. Irreproachable Agni, a vigilant God, in the proximity of thy parents.

13. Thou, four-eyed Agni, blazest as the protection of the worshipper.

14. Thou, who art all-wise, instructest the disciple, and definest the limits of the horizon.

Anuv. viii.

1, 2, 3. The mighty Agni . . . . the augmenter of vigour . . . . who art endowed with all knowledge. The flames of thee, who art mighty and eternal, spread around thy rays, and reach to the Heavens.

4. The Deities Varuṇa, Mitra and Aryaman kindled thee, their messenger from of old.

5. The giver of delight, the invoker and messenger of the Gods, the domestic guardian of mankind; the good and durable actions which the Gods perform, are all aggregated in thee.

7. The Devout adore thee, who art such, bright with thy own radiance.

9. Sit, Agni, on the sacred grass, for thou art mighty. Shine forth, for thou art devoted to the Gods. Adorable and excellent Agni, emit the curling and graceful smoke.

11. The rays of that Agni whom Kaṇwa made more brilliant than the sun, pre-eminently shine.

16. Agni, with the burning rays.

19. Manu detained thee, Agni, Light to the various races of mankind. Born for the sake of sacrifice, and satiated with oblations, thou, whom men reverence, hast blazed for Khañwa.

20. The flames of Agni are luminous, potent, fear-inspiring, and not to be trusted.

Anuv. ix. Sûkta i (xliv).

1. Agni, immortal, and cognizant of all begotten things. Bring from the dawn to the giver, wealth . . . . Bring hither to-day the Gods that awake with the morning.

2. Agni, associated with Ushas and the Aṣwins.

5. Immortal sustainer of the universe . . . . exempt from death, Preserver, Sacrificer.

6. Whose flames give delight; who art universally invoked.

7. All people kindle thee, Agni, the sacrificer, the all-knowing.

10. Resplendent Agni, visible to all, thou hast blazed after many preceding dawns; thou art the protector in villages; thou art the associate of man, placed in the East.

Sûkta ii (xlv).

4. Agni, shining amid the solemnities, with pure resplendence. 6. Radiant-haired.

7. Invoker, ministrant priest, giver of much wealth, quick-hearing, widely-renowned.

9. Strength-generated, giver of rewards, provider of dwellings.

Anuv. xi. Sûkta i (lviii).

1. The strength-generated, immortal Agni . . . . by suitable paths he has made the firmament.

2. Undecaying Agni, combining his aliment and swiftly devouring it, climbs

the dry wood: the blaze of the consuming flies like a race-horse, and roars like a roaring high up in the air.

5. Agni, armed with the flame, and vivified by the wind, with all his might, in a volume of fire, rushed triumphant in the forest.

6. Agni, who sacrificest for men, who art the invoker, the guest at sacrifices, to be valued as an affectionate friend.

8. Son of power, propitiously shining.

9. Variously-shining Agni, be a shelter to him who praises thee. Be prosperity. Protect, Agni, thy worshipper from sin. May Agni, who is rich with right-wise acts, come quickly in the morning.

Sûkta ii (lix).

1. Whatever other fires there may be, they are but branchings, Agni, of thee; but they all rejoice, being immortal, in thee. Thou, Vaiṣwânara, art the navel of men, and supportest them like a column deeply-planted.

2. Agni, the head of heaven, the navel of earth, become ruler over both earth and heaven. All the Gods engendered thee, Vaiśwânara, in the form of night, for the venerable sage.

3, 6, 7. Treasures were deposited in the Agni, Vaiśwânara . . . . The Agni, Vaiṣwânara slew the stealer of the waters, and sent them down on the earth . . . . Vaiṣwânara by his greatness is all men, and is to be worshipped as the diffuser of manifold light.

Adh. iv. Anuv. xii. Sûkta i (lxvi).

4. He (Agni) is the kind kinsman of the waters, like a brother to his sisters. He consumes the forest, as a Râjâ destroys his enemies. When excited by the wind, he traverses the woods, and shears the hairs of the earth.

5. He breathes amidst the waters like a sitting swan. Awakened at the dawn, he restores consciousness to men by his influences. He is a creator, like Soma. Born from the waters, like an animal with coiled-up limbs, he became enlarged and his light flowed afar.

Sûkta ii (lxvi).

4. Agni, as Yama, is all that is born; as Yama, all that will be born.

5. He has tossed about his flames, like running streams of water: the rays commingle, visible in the sky.

Sûkta iii.

Born in the woods, the friend of man—holding in his hand all wealth, and hiding in the hollows, he filled the Gods with alarm . . . . Like the unborn, he upholds the earth and the firmament, and props up the heaven with true prayers.

Sûkta iv.

The conveyer (Agni), mingling them, ascends to the heavens, and invests all things, movable and stationary, and the nights themselves (with light). Radiant among the Gods, and in his single self comprehending the potencies of all of them . . . . Born living, from the dry wood . . . . He who delights in the sacrificial chamber, has studded the sky with constellations.

Sûkta v (lxix).

White-shining Agni, the extinguisher of the dawn, is the illuminator, and fills the united like the lustre of the radiant . . . . Whatever beings I may, along with other men, invoke, thou, Agni, assumest all celestial natures . . . . Agni, who is possessed of manifold light; the giver of habitations and of cognizable forms.

Sûkta vi (lxx).

Agni, who is to be approached by meditation [whose essence is cognizable by the intellect only, the invisible spirit of the fire, not perceptible by the senses], and shines with pure light [is manifested to the sense of Light as simple light] . . . . Agni, who is within the waters, within woods, and within all things, mobile and stationary, immortal, and performing pious acts . . . . The Lord of night, all-knowing—who knowest the origin of Gods and men . . . . whom many variously tinted (flushings of the morning) and nights increase; whom, invested with truth, all things mobile and stationary augment. [Performing pious acts: Sacrificing, or rendering beneficent services. Invested with truth: invested with actuality, manifested and made cognizable by the senses.]

4. When the diffusive vital air excites Agni, he becomes bright and manifest in every mansion.

5. The God bestows light on his daughter (the dawn, Ushas).

9. The sun, who traverses alone the path-way of heaven, with the speed of thought, is at once lord of all treasures. The two kings, Mitra and Varuṇa, with bounteous hands, are the guardians of the precious ambrosia of our cattle.

Sûkta viii (lxxii).

1. Agni, holding in his hands many good things for men, appropriates the prayers addressed to the eternal creator.

Sûkta ix (lxxiii).

Agni . . . . is like the divine sun, who knows the true; preserves by his influences in all encounters; like Nature, he is unchangeable, and like soul, is the source of happiness.

Men keep thee constantly kindled in their dwellings . . . . Thou, in whom is all existence.

Anuv. xiii. Sûkta i (lxxiv).

Let us repeat a prayer to Agni, who hears us from afar.

Sûkta ii.

Most wise Agni, chief of the Angirasas . . . . Worship for us, Mitra and Varuṇa.

Sûkta iii.

What approximation of the mind, Agni, to thee, can be accomplished for our good? [How can our intellect attain any real cognition of thee?]

Sûkta iv.

What may we offer to Agni? What worship is addressed to the luminous, that is agreeable to the Gods? That Agni who is immortal, and observant of truth, the performer of sacrifices . . . . Agni, when he approaches the Gods in behalf of man, knows those, and reverentially worships them.

Sûkta vi (lxxix).

1. The golden-haired Agni is the agitator of the clouds, when the rain is poured forth; and, moving with the swiftness of the wind, shines with a brilliant radiance.
2. Thy falling (rays or shafts), accompanied by the moving (winds), strike against (the clouds). The black shedder of rain has roared; the rain descends, the clouds thunder.

When this (Agni, the lightning) nourishes the world with the milk of the rain . . . . then Mitra, Aryaman, Varuṇa, and the encompassers (Maruts), pierce through the envelope into the womb of the cloud.

Ashṭ. ii. *Adhy. ii.* *Anuv. xxi.* *Sûkta ii (cxli).*

That visible radiance of the divine Agni . . . .

First he reposes as the digestive, the embodied, the acceptor of food, the eternal [i. e. first he is localized and acts, as the digestive heat, within the body, upon the food, and thus perpetuating itself and sustaining life]: Secondly, among the seven auspicious mothers [probably the seven stars of Ursa Major]: Thirdly, the associated generate him, delighting in the ten quarters of space, for the sake of milking this showerer [The 'associated,' rejoicing in the ten regions of the sky, are probably the clusters of stars or constellations, that generate light, in order to send its rays downward to the earth].

By thee, Agni, Mitra, Varuṇa and Aryaman are animated, so that thou hast been born, comprehending them all universally, in all their functions, and encompassing them as the felly does the spokes.

Sûkta iv (cxliii).

His radiance is undecaying. The rays of him who is of pleasant aspect, are everywhere visible and bright; the intensely-shining, all-pervading, unceasing, undecaying (rays) of Agni, never cease to be.

Sûkta vii (cxlvi).

The three-headed, seven-rayed Agni.

He who is, as it were, the generator of men, as well as of heaven and earth, of whom creation has imbibed life, abides with his glories. He it is, who, entering into thy womb, procreates.

Adhy. iii. *Anuv. xxii.* *Sûkta viii (clxiv).*

They have styled him (the sun), Indra, Mitra, Varuṇa, Agni. Agni is all the Divinities (*Agni sarvô devatâh*).

Adhy. v. Anuv. i. Sûkta i.

3. Thou, Agni, art Indra—the adorable Vishṇu. Thou, Brahmaṇaspati, art Brahmá.

4. Thou, Agni, art the royal Varuṇa; thou art the adorable Mitra; thou art Aryaman.

6. Thou, Agni, art Rudra.

7. Thou, Agni, art the divine Savitṛi.

11. Thou, divine Agni, art Aditi, to the offerer of the oblation.

Sûkta x.

The adorable Agni, the first of the Gods, and their nourisher, when kindled by man upon the altar: He who is clothed in radiance, is immortal, discriminating, food-bestowing, powerful.

2. Immortal, of manifold wisdom, and wondrous splendour.

Asht. iii. Adhy. i. Anuv. i. Sûkta x.

5. Offer to the ministering Agni, as if to the creator, the great praise, recited of old.

Sûkta xi.

4. The Gods have made Agni, who is the son of strength.

Anuv. ii. Sûkta i (xiv).

The most wise, the creator, is present at our sacred rites. Agni, the son of force, whose chariot is the lightning, whose hair is flame, manifests his glory on the earth.

Sûkta x.

1. Adorable Agni, thy radiance that is in the heaven, on the earth, in the plants, in the waters; and with which thou overspreadest the firmament; shining and resplendent, beholder of men, great like the ocean.

3. Thou movest, Agni, to the vapour in the heavens; thou congregatest the Divinities who are the vital airs; thou animatest the waters in the bright region above the sun, as well as those that are in the firmament beneath.

Sûkta xiv.

7. I, Agni, am by birth endowed with knowledge of all that exists. I am the living breath of three-fold Nature, the measure of the firmament, perennial heat; I am also the oblation.

8. Thoroughly comprehending the light that is to be understood by the heart, has purified himself, purifying. [It is impossible that any such nonsense was ever put into words by the writer of this hymn, as *these* words are in English. It seems, sometimes, as if Professor Wilson looked only to find equivalent *words*, in English for the Vaidic words, without reading them when he had put them together, to see if they made any *sense*. He certainly did that *here*. Yet the translation shows what the meaning *is;* i. e., Agni, wholly containing in himself the light that is cognizable, while in him, by the intellect only, has sent it forth from himself,

by emanation.] He has made himself most excellent treasure by self-manifestations [he has become of inestimable value and usefulness, by the outward manifestations of his essence (as Agni, Vayu and Aditya), which is not in the text, and is but a *guess*, his manifestations being simply light and heat of the various kinds that men utterly ignorant of physics see in Nature]; and thence has contemplated heaven and earth [which is more nonsense, the evident meaning being, and has thereby been enabled to discern, no longer wrapped in darkness, the heavens and the earth].

Sûkta xvii.

5. Produce by attrition the far-seeing, single-minded, intelligent, immortal, radiant-limbed Agni.

11. When in the word as an embryo, Agni is called Tanûnapât; when generated, the Asura-destroying Naraṣansa; when he has manifested himself in the material firmament, Mâtariṣwan; and the creation of the wind is in his rapid motion.

Asht. iii. Adhy. v. Anuv. i. Sûkta ix.

May that Agni, immortal, pre-eminent among men the descendants of Manu, become the messenger of all the Gods.

Sûkta x.

Agni, who art like a horse, with our wishes, conveying, and like a benefactor, propitious, affectionate, be the conveyer of our sacrifice.

Agni, who like the sun art light, come with all thy hosts to where we are present.

Asht. v. Adhy. v. Anuv. iv. Sûkta xii.

Kindled by us, Agni blazes, the limits of the darkness are visible nigh at hand; the banner (of the sun) is perceived rising in the East with the glory of the Dawn, daughter of Heaven.

Asht. v. Adhy. i. Mand. vi. Anuv. vi. Sûkta xi.

Agni, present in the two sticks, manifested by attrition; Agni, when visible, honoured in every house, well-kindled, youthful, vigourous, pure, eminent, irradiator, purifier.

Asht. Adhy. ii. Mand. vii. Anuv. i. Sûkta ii.

1. Be gratified, Agni, by the sacred fire kindled by us to-day, emitting abundant smoke of adoration. Reach with thy scorching flames the celestial summit. Combine with the rays of the sun.

11. Agni, kindled, come to where we are, in the same chariot with Indra.

Sûkta iii.

1. The most adorable divine Agni; permanently present among men, the observer of truth, crowned with flame.

Sûkta iv.

1. The bright and radiant Agni, who passes with wisdom between all divine and human beings.

2. The sagacious Agni . . . . who, bright-torched, attacks the forest, and quickly devours his abundant food.

3. Whom men have cognizance of as white, in the chief place of manifestation of that Divinity.

Sûkta v.

1. The strong Agni, traversing without hindrance the heavens and the earth.

2. Leader of rivers, showerer of waters, the radiant, abiding in the heavens and on earth.

4. Vaiṣwânara Agni, the firmament, the earth, the heavens, combine in thy worship. Shining with undiminished splendour, thou overspreadest heaven and earth with light.

Sûkta viii.

4. This Agni is largely celebrated by the institutors of the rite, when he shines resplendent, as the sun.

Sûkta ix.

2. The wondrously radiant, he shines before the dawns; the embryo of the waters, he has entered into the nascent plants.

Sûkta x.

1. Agni, like [as, or, in the likeness of] the lover of the dawn, radiant, bright, resplendent . . . . he shines with splendour.

2. Agni, preceding the dawn, is radiant by day, as the sun.

Sûkta xii.

1. The youngest of the Gods, who shines, when kindled, is his own abode [when visible, in the place of his manifestation]; who is blazing wonderfully [thus manifested], between the sky and the earth.

3. Thou art Varuṇa, thou art Mitra, Agni.

Sûkta xv.

4. Agni, to whom as to a swift hawk in the sky, I address this new hymn. [It is curious that the hawk should have been the Bird of the Sun in Egypt, also.]

8. Blaze, Agni, night and day, that by thee we may have the sacrificial fires.

13. Preserve us, Agni, from sin. Divine, who art exempt from decay, consume our enemies with the hottest flames.

Asht. iii. Adhy. v. Anuv. i. Sûkta viii.

He (Agni), knows the ascents of heaven. May he bring the Gods hither. He knows how the Gods are to be worshipped. Knowing the ascent of the sky, he travels between earth and heaven.

Asht. v. Adhy. iv. . . . . Sûkta iv.

Agni, Varuṇa, Mitra, Maruts! Grant happiness, Gods, to him whom you preserve from this; whom you guide here.

The following epithets are, in various places, applied to Agni:

Omniscient and discriminator, intelligent, bestowing faculties, radiant; associated with strength and food, illumines the divine immortal parents of all things heaven and earth; eternal, ancient, irrepressible, powerful, adorable, divine, guide of devout men, observer of truth, liberal giver, brilliant, beautiful, opulent, auspicious, righteous, destroyer, endowed with intelligence, showerer of benefits, the enduring maker, beholder of men, granter of habitations, mighty, vigourous, true, wise, creator; director of sacrifices, of purifying radiance, contributor of food; known of all that is born, eternally renowned; messenger of the Gods, invoker of the Gods, minister of the Gods, ancient banner of sacrifice, purifier, king of men, chief sacrificer.

"Bestower of faculties," i. e., communicating to the orbs of heaven potencies and powers. "Observer of truth," i. e., by his own light beholder of all the reality of things, all that has a real existence. "Guide of devout men," i. e., making visible the paths and ways, and enabling them to find the places of sacrifice. "Righteous," i. e., not deceiving, misleading or ensnaring men, and impartial.

"Truth," Horne Tooke says, "is that which a man *troweth;* and the meaning which it has in the Veda, if it is desired that it should transfer into the translation the sense of the original, is equally as primitive. The Vaidic "truth" is the actuality or reality of visible Nature. And fire and the light are "righteous," because they make visible to men this reality, and are the "observers" of the truth, as a luminary is said to "observe," and "contemplate" that which is made visible by its light.

Messenger, invoker and minister of the Devas (the celestial luminaries), to whom the flame of the fire, ascending, conveys the essence of the meat and Soma juice, consumed by it, and becoming thus a part of itself.

Agni is addressed by various epithets, or under different names. The epithets are, essentially, only adjectives, though used, probably, as proper names and nouns, like many epithets of the Greek Deities. But there are other words, considered by the commentators to be epithets or else synonyms, expressive of particular attributes, by which Deities really different are, I am sure, intended. Vaiṣwânara is the most common of his names; as "the Creator," is an epithet of true Deity in a special and particular mode or function: and "the Almighty," expressive of the attribute of infinite power.

Asht. i. Adhy. i. Anuv. iv. Sûkta ii.

1. Agni, who art Susamiddha . . . .
2. Wise, who art Tanûnapât.
3. I invoke the beloved Narâṣansas, the sweet-tongued, the offerer of oblations . . . .

4. Agni, who art Iḷita, bring hither the Gods in an easy-moving chariot; for thou art the invoker instituted by men.

Susamiddha means 'The thoroughly kindled,' i. e., the 'blazing' and 'flaming:' *Su*, '*well;*' *sam*, 'completely:' *iddha*, 'kindled.'

Tanûnapât, 'the devourer of clarified butter' (*tanûnapa*); or, according to another etymology, 'the devourer of its own substance' (*tanu*) or *fuel*.

Narâṣansa, 'him whom men [*narâ*] praise' (*sansanti*).

Iḷita, the 'worshipped;' from *ila*, to 'adore or praise.'

Sûkta iv (xv).

7. . . . . Praise the divine Draviṇodas, both in the primary and subsidiary sacrifices.

8. May Draviṇodas give us riches . . . .

9. Draviṇodas desires to drink with the Ritus, from the cup of Neshṭri . . . .

10. Since, Draviṇodas, we adore thee, for the fourth time, along with the Ritus . . . .

12. Saṇtya, being identified with the household fire, and partaker with Ritu of the sacrifice, worship the Gods on behalf of their adorer.

Draviṇodas, is either an epithet or an appellative of *Agni*, as the donor (*das*) of wealth or of strength (*draviṇa*).—*Wilson*.

Neshṭri, one of the sixteen officiating priests.

Saṇtya is explained by the scholiast to mean "Giver of rewards," from *shaṅ*, to "give."

The scholiast understands the "*Ritus*" to be the Deities presiding over the months. *Draviṇodas* seems to be *Agni* as the sacrificial fire.

Ashṭ. ii. Adhy. viii. Anuv. iv. Sûkta v.

1. Be gratified, Draviṇodas, by the sacrificial food presented as the offering of the Hotri . . . . Drink, Draviṇodas, along with the Ritus . . . .

2. . . . . He is renowned as a benefactor. . . . . Drink, Draviṇodas, along with the Ritus . . . .

3. May these thy bearers, by whom thou art borne along, be satisfied; Lord of the Forest, be firm, doing no injury, steadfast of resolve. Drink, Draviṇodas, along with the Ritus. . . . .

The sixth verse is addressed to Agni: but it does not certainly identify Draviṇodas with him. The word *Ritus*, it is said, literally means *seasons;* and Draviṇodas would seem to be some personification of light, connected with them or with the months. We find no *express* evidence of his identity with Agni.

Ashṭ. ii. Adhy. ii. Anuv. xxi. Sûkta iii.

1. Agni, who art Samiddha, bring the Gods, today . . . .

2. Tanûnapât, be present at this well-flavoured and butter-fed sacrifice . . . .

4. Agni, who art Iḷita, bring hither Indra, the wonderful, the beloved . . . .

Adhy. viii. Anuv. i. Sûkta iv.

2. Tanûnapât, whom the Deities, Mitra, Varuṇa and Agni worship daily, thrice a day. . . . .

It would seem, from this, that Tanûnapât is *not* identical with Agni. Perhaps Agni here is an error and the name in the original was Aryaman. For we find,

Asht. iii. Adhy. i. Anuv. ii. Sûkta xvii.

11. When as an embryo [unmanifested in the dry wood], Agni is called Tanûnapât; when he is generated, the Asura-destroying Narâṣansa: when he has displayed [manifested himself] in the material firmament, Mâtariṣwan; and the creation of the wind is in his rapid motion.

Asht. ii. Adhy. v. Anuv. i. Sûkta iii.

2. May the bright Narâṣansa, illuming the receptacles, making manifest by his greatness the three radiant, and diffusing the oblation, at the season of sacrifice . . . . satisfy the Gods.

3. Agni, who art the venerable Iḷita, do thou, with mind favourably disposed towards us, offer today sacrifice to the Gods.

10. May Agni, who is Vanâspati, approving, approach. . . . .

1. Agni, the well-kindled, placed upon the earth, stands in the presence of all beings . . . . let the venerable Agni minister to the Gods.

As verse six reads,

Day and Night, perpetually reverenced, are interweaving in concert the extended thread, the web of the sacrifice,

I infer that this hymn was composed to be sung at a sacrifice, just at day-break; and as the fire was burning on the earth, in the presence of all the host of stars [beings, existences, visible manifestations], the sacrifice was in the open air. The "three radiant," though the scholiast reads "regions" to complete the sense, are, I think, three stars, which at a certain season precede the dawn.

Asht. i. Adhy. vii. Anuv. xv. Sûkta vi.

1. We offer oblations of Soma to Jâtavedas . . . . May he transport us over all difficulties. May Agni convey us, as in a boat over a river, across all wickedness [malice or injuries of enemies].

Asht. ii. Adhy. i. Anuv. xix. Sûkta i.

1. I venerate Agni, the invoker, the munificent, the giver of dwellings, the son of strength; *sunum sahaso, Jâtavedasam, vipram na jâtavedasam* [translated by Wilson, 'He who knows all'].

Asht. ii. Adhy. viii. Anuv. i. Sûkta i.

21. The undecaying Jâtavedas, who in every birth is established, is kindled by the Viswámitras . . . .

Sûkta iii.

8. The leaders praise with prostration, for increase, the mighty Lord of people, the guest, the regulator eternally of acts, the desired of the priests, the exposition of sacrifices, Jâtavedas, endowed with energies.

Sûkta v.

1. The sagacious Agni, cognizant of the dawn, is awakened to the paths of the sages: the luminous *Vahni*, kindled by the devout, has thrown open the gates of darkness.

4. Agni, when kindled, is Mitra . . . . Varuṇa is Jâtavedas . . . . Damunas is Vayu . . . .

Sûkta vi.

6. Harness with traces to thy car thy long-maned, ruddy horses. Bring hither, divine Jâtavedas, all the Gods . . . .

Asht. iii. Adhy. i. Anuv. i. Sûkta v.

2. As thou didst offer the burnt-offering, Agni, of earth; as thou, Jâtavedas, didst offer sacrifice, of heaven . . . .

3. Three are thy existences, Jâtavedas; three, Agni, the dawns, thy sisters [*Tisra âjânirushasah*].

Ajani may mean "sisters" or "mothers." "Three are thy existences," probably means, there are three luminaries or phenomena, that are manifestations of thee: and *âjânirushasah* will have *some* meaning, if taken to mean, not "three are thy parent dawns," as Wilson renders it, but "thy three luminaries, sisters of the dawn," or, "thy three luminaries, sisters, of the Dawn." *Ushas* is the Dawn, and is one. Three dawns, existing together and at once, could never have been conceived of. Three *stars*, that were sisters of each other, or of the dawn, could be. *Ushasas*, the plural, is found in the Rig-V. (*i. viii. xvi. viii.*) termed brilliant, in a hymn to Ushas: What these three "stars of the morning" are, we shall consider hereafter.

4. Jâtavedas, we venerate thee, glorifying the brilliant, beautiful, adorable Agni. The Gods have made thee their messenger, the disinterested bearer of oblations.

Anuv. ii. Sûkta xvi.

4. Wise, Jâtavedas, accept the cakes and butter . . . .

6. Agni, who art Jâtavedas, and art thriving upon oblations . . . .

Sûkta xvii.

2. Jâtavedas has been deposited in the two sticks, as the embryo is deposited in pregnant women.

3. Let the intelligent priest place the lower of the sticks with the face upwards, the upper downwards, so that, quickly impregnated it may generate the showerer Agni: then the bright blazing son of Iḷá, whose light dissipates the darkness, is born of the wood of attrition.

4. Agni, who art Jâtavedas, we place thee upon the earth in the centre, in the place of Iḷá, for the purpose of receiving the oblation.

"Son of Iḷá," is simply "son of adoration," i. e., that by which adoration and praise are expressed; expression, utterance of adoration. And the *place* of Iḷá is the place of the sacrifice, offering or adoration.

Ashṭ. iv. Adhy. v. Anuv. i. Sûkta x.

1. Place before you, at the progressive, uninterrupted sacrifice, the divine, adorable, perfect Agni, with prayers; for he, the resplendent Jâtavedas, makes us prosperous in sacred rites.

Anuv. ii. Sûkta i.

29. Jâtavedas, all-beholder, bring us wealth, with good posterity. Doer of good deeds, destroy the Râkshasas.

30. Preserve us, Jâtavedas, from sin; Brahmaṇaskave, protect us from the malevolent.

35. Radiant in the embryo of the maternal; in the imperishable; the cherisher of the paternal; sitting in the seat of sacrifice.

36. Bring to us, Jâtavedas, all-beholder, food, with progeny; such as is brilliant in the expanse.

Ashṭ. v. Adhy. ii. Anuv. i. Sûkta v.

8. Send to us, Agni Vaiṣwânara Jâtavedas, that brilliant sustenance whereby thou conferrest wealth . . . .

Sûkta ix.

4. Thou, Agni, art to be glorified in the ages of men: Thou, Jâtavedas, who art illustrious, when engaged in battle . . . .

Sûkta xii.

2. May that Agni, who by his greatness is the overcomer of all mischiefs, who is praised as Jâtavedas in the chamber, protect us, glorifying him . . . .

Sûkta xvii.

3. Agni Jâtavedas, repair to the Gods, worship them with the oblation . . . .

Asht. v. Adhy. viii. Anuv. ii. Sûkta vi.

3. Do thou, Jâtavedas, drive away from us those who hate us; Agni, the impious hostile hosts.

4. Thou desirest not, Jâtavedas, the sacrifice of the man who is our adversary, although placed before thee.

Tanûnâpat, we may conclude, is the latent fire in the dry wood: and *Narâsansa*, the same kindled and burning. *Jâtavedas* is unmistakably the fire ready for the sacrifices: and *Santya* is the household fire.

INDRA.

Asht. i. Adhy. i. Anuv. ii. Sûkta i.

4. The wise and uninjured Indra, who bestows what is best on thy friends.

10. Sing to that Indra, who is the protector of wealth, the mighty, the accomplisher of good deeds, the friend of the offerer of the libation.

Sûkta ii.

Indra, performer of good works, object of praises, unobstructed. Protector, thou art mighty. Avert violence. [For *unobstructed*, read rather, 'resistless'.]

Sûkta iii.

Those who stand around, associated with Indra, the mighty, the indestructible, the moving, and the lights that shine in the sky.

2. They harness to his car his two desirable coursers, harnessed side by side, bay-coloured, high-spirited, men-bearing.

3. Mortals, you owe your daily birth to Indra, who with the rays of the morning gives sense to the senseless, and to the formless, form.

Sûkta iv.

2. Indra, the blender of all things, the richly decorated, the wielder of the thunderbolt.

3. Indra, to render all things visible, elevated the sun in the sky, and filled the cloud with waters.

6. Shedder of rain, mighty Lord, always compliant, who alone rules over men, over riches, and over the five classes of dwellers on the earth. Lord of wealth, showerer of blessings, dweller in an eternal mansion.

Adhy. ii. Anuv. ii. Sûkta vi (xxix).

1 to 7. [Each ends], Indra of boundless wealth, enrich us with thousands of excellent cows and horses.

Sûkta vi.

Handsome and mighty lord of food.

Sûkta vii.

Indra, mighty, and of a thousand sacrifices; recipient of a hundred pure and a thousand distilled libations; all contained in his belly, as water in the ocean.

9. The man (Indra) who visits many worshippers from his ancient dwelling-place.

11. Drinker of the Soma juice, wielder of the thunderbolt, friend.

Anuv. vii. Sûkta ii.

15. Thou, Indra, the wielder of the thunderbolt, became the sovereign of all that is, mobile or stationary. [After destroying Vṛitra or Ahi, the accumulation of vapour shut up in or obstructed by, a cloud], of hornless and horned cattle: and as he abides the monarch of men, he comprehended all things, as the felly encloses the spokes of a wheel.

Adhy. iii. Anuv. vii. Sûkta iii.

9. Indra, thou enjoyest both heaven and earth, investing the universe with thy greatness.

Adhy. iv. Anuv. ix. Sûkta ii (lii).

The Ram who makes heaven known. When Indra had slain the stream-obstructing Vṛitra, and was pouring down the waters, he stood firm amid the torrents, like a mountain.

He who is victorious over his enemies; who is extended throughout the region of dew.

Indra, whom in heaven the libations sprinkled on the sacred grass replenish, as the kindred rivers hastening to it fill the ocean.

Indra, abiding in thy might beyond the limit of the wide-spread firmament, thou hast framed the earth for our preservation. Thou hast been the type of vigour, thou hast encompassed the firmament and the sky, as far as to the heavens.

13. Thou art the counter-measure of the extended earth [i. e., of like magnitude, co-extensive]: Thou art the lord of the vast God-frequented. Verily, with thy bulk thou fillest all the firmament. Of a truth, there is none other such as thou.

Adhy. iv. Anuv. x. Sûkta ii (lii).

Thou, Indra, of whom heaven and earth have not attained the amplitude, of whom the waters of heaven have not reached the limit; of whom, when warring with excited animation against the withholder of the rains . . . . Thou alone hast made every other thing dependent on thee.

Sûkta iii.

Wise and resplendent Indra . . . . Thou goest from battle to battle . . . . with thy foe-prostrating associate, with thy brightly gleaming spear.

Sûkta iv.

Indra, who purifies both heaven and earth with his irresistible might; who is the sender of showers, and by his bounty gratifies our desires.

Thou hast hurled the sharp and bright-rayed thunderbolt against the assembled Asuras.

Thou hast poured rain on the brow of the breathing (wind), and of the ripening and absorbing (sun).

Sûkta v (lv).

The amplitude of Indra was vaster than the heaven . . . . Earth was not comparable to him in bulk.

2, 3. The firmament-inhabiting Indra . . . . The haughty one takes precedence of all Gods, on account of his exploits.

Sûkta vi.

He is quick in action, and mighty. His faultless and destructive prowess shines in manly conflict, like the peak of a mountain . . . . Suppresser of the malignant . . . . 4. Who with resolute vigour resists the gloom.

Sûkta vii (lvii).

The fatal golden thunderbolt of Indra . . . . Thou, Thunderer, hast shattered with thy bolt the broad and massive cloud into fragments, and has sent down the waters that were confined in it, to flow at will. Thou alone possessest all power.

Anuv. xi. Sûkta iv (lxi).

1, 7. Powerful, rapid, mighty, worship-deserving and resistless Indra . . . . Pervader of the universe. Hurler of the thunderbolt.

8. He encompasses the widely extended heaven and the earth. They two do not surpass thy vastness.

9. His magnitude verily exceeds that of the heaven, earth and sky. Indra, self-irradiating in his dwelling.

12. The quick-moving and strength-endowed Lord.

Adhy. v. Anuv. xi. Sûkta v (lxii).

1, 2. Powerful and praise-deserving Indra . . . . Vast and most powerful Indra.

5. Thou hast scattered the darkness with the dawn, and with the rays of the sun. Thou hast made straight the elevations of the earth: Thou hast strengthened the foundations of the ethereal regions.

7. He parted in two the eternal and united: The graceful Indra cherished the heaven and earth, like the sun in the august and most excellent sky.

Sûkta vi (lxiii).

1. Indra, thou art the Mighty One, who, becoming manifest in alarm, didst by thine energies sustain heaven and earth: then, through fear of thee, all creatures, and the mountains, and all other vast and solid things trembled, like the rays of the sun.

Adhy. vi. Anuv. xiii. Sûkta viii (lxxxi).

He (Indra) has filled the space of earth and the firmament. He has fixed the constellations in the sky. No one has ever been born, or will be born, Indra, like to thee. Thou hast sustained the universe.

Asht. iii. Adhy. ii. Anuv. iii. Sûkta.

8. Indra, who hast upheld earth and heaven and the firmament, and, performer of great deeds, has engendered the sun and the dawn.

10. Born in the highest heaven, thou pervadest the heaven and the earth, and becamest the primary artificer.

Sûkta v.

Indra has overspread the day with his radiance; generating the day; illumining for man the banner of the days (Sûrya or the sun), he obtained light for the great conflict. He animated these dawns and heightened their bright radiance. He gave the sun; bestowed plants and days; gave trees and the firmament, divided the cloud.

Asht. iii. Adhy. iii. Anuv. iv. Sûkta vi.

3. Indra has upheld the yellow-rayed heaven, the green-coloured earth. There is abundant pasture (for his horses) in the two azure spheres of heaven and earth, between which Hari journeys.

4. The azure-coloured showerer illumines as soon as born, the whole luminous region. The Lord of the tawny steeds holds in his hands the yellow weapon, the destroying thunderbolt.

Asht. i. Adhy. i. Anuv. i. Sûkta iii.

Indra, of wonderful splendour. Fleet Indra, apprehended by the understanding and appreciated by the wise. Indra with the tawny coursers. Indra's coursers harnessed in his car.

Asht. v. Adhy. i. Mand. vi. Anuv. vi. Sûkta vii.

In ten stanzas of this Sûkta, Indra and Varuṇa are addressed together.
In *Sûkta viii.*, Indra and Vishṇu:
And in *Sûkta xi.*, Indra and Soma.

Asht. vi. Adhy. ii. Anuv. ii. Mand. vii. Sûkta i.

24. The seven worlds praise Sudâs, as if he were Indra.

The following epithets are applied to Indra: Warrior, lord of wealth, fierce, undecaying, mighty, renowned, resplendent, every way unlimited, wielder of the thunderbolt, adorable, powerful, great, magnificent, lord of all the world, more vast than heaven and earth or the wide-spread firmament; vast and profound, all-pervading, opulent, hero, sage, noble, divine, far-seeing, fracturer of the cloud, sender of waters, demolisher of cities, food-bestowing, lover of horses, lover of the virtuous, lord of men, chief of the Maruts, divine regulator, bestower of strength, vigourous, rushing through things like a war-horse, he has pervaded heaven and earth, sending down rain, upholder of heaven and the firmament, clothed at night [i. e., enveloped, covered, hidden], parent of the sun.

The exuberance of the Aryan imagination in nothing appears more strikingly than in the long list of the *Asuras* slain by Indra. In one hymn, besides Vṛitra and Ahi, we have Dṛibhika, Bala, Uraṇa with ninety-nine arms, Arbuda, Swaśna, the inabsorbable Ṣushṇa, Pipu, Namuchi, Rudhikrâ, and the hundred thousand of Varchin; in others, Vîswarupa, son of Twashṭri; the sleeping son of Danu (Sambara), Ranhiṇa, scaling heaven; Sahavasu, son of Nrimara; Chumuri and Dhuni, the Dasyus, Krivi, Dasa, Asusha, Kuyava, the Godless Piyu, the Danava and Mriga.

Ashṭ. i. Adhy. vii. Anuv. xv. Sûkta viii.

3\. . . . . Indra . . . . whose great power (pervades) heaven and earth; in whose service Varuṇa and Súrya are steadfast [shining permanently by him and his potency, as his manifestations], and whose command the rivers obey [for the rains which he sends down feed and cause to rise and swell and flow, the rivers].

Ashṭ. iv. Adhy. i. Anuv. ii. Sûkta xv.

8\. When thou hadst eaten the flesh of the three hundred buffaloes, when thou, who art Maghavan, hadst drunk the three vessels of Soma, that he should kill Ahi, then all the Gods summoned Indra, full of food, as if he had been a servant, to the battle.

INDRA AND AGNI.

Ashṭ. i. Adhy. ii. Anuv. Sûkta iv.

I invoke hither Indra and Agni, to whom we desire to present our praises.

Praise Indra and Agni, ye men, in sacrifices, decorate them, and sing hymns to them . . . . those two, Indra and Agni, who are mighty.

Adhy. vii. Anuv. xvi. Sûkta iii.

1. Indra and Agni, sitting together in your car, that wonderful car which illuminates all beings, approach, and drink of the effused Soma juice.

3. You have made your associated names renowned, since, slayers of Vṛitra, you have been allied: the showerers of benefits, Indra and Agni, are the two, seated together.

9. Whether, Indra and Agni, you are in the lower, the middle, or the upper region of the world.

11. Whether, Indra and Agni, you are in heaven or on earth, in the mountains, in the herbs, or in the waters.

12. Although, Indra and Agni, in the midst of the sky, on the rising of the sun, you may be exhilarated by your own splendour. . . . .

Sûkta iv.

1. Indra and Agni . . . . I consider you in my mind [my intellect conceives of you] as kinsmen and relations . . . . Wielders of the thunderbolts, overturners of cities.

6. . . . . You are vaster than the earth, than the sky, than the rivers, than the mountains: you exceed all other existent things . . . .

Ashṭ. iii. Adhy. i. Anuv. i. Sûkta xii.

4. I invoke Indra and Agni, the discomfiters of foes, the destroyers of Vṛitra.

7. Indra and Agni, the pious ministers, are present at our holy rite.

9. Indra and Agni, illuminators of heaven, be ever graced in battle, for such thy prowess proclaims.

INDRA AND SOMA.

Ashṭ. iii. Adhy. vi. Anuv. iii. Sûkta vii.

1. Through that friendship, Soma, which has united thee with thy Indra, he has made the waters flow for man . . . .

2. With thee, Soma, for his ally, Indra has quickly taken off by force the wheel of the chariot of the sun, abiding above with the vast and stationary [manifested

and resident in place, by the great orbs of heaven]; the everywhere going wheel of the great oppressor has been taken away.

5. Possessors of wealth, destroyers of enemies, Indra and Soma, you have distributed great numbers of horses. . . . .

Asht. v. Adhy. vii. Anuv. vi. Sûkta xv.

1. Indra and Soma, afflict, destroy the Rakshasas. Showerers, cast down those who delight in darkness.

4. Indra and Soma, display from heaven your fatal . . . . put forth from the clouds the consuming, with which you slay . . . .

6. Indra and Soma, who are mighty . . . . do you, like two kings, accept my homage.

7. Come with rapid steeds . . . .

MITRA.

Asht. i. Adhy. iii. Anuv. viii. Sûkta iii.

13. Praise Brahmaṇaspati, Agni, and the beautiful Mitra.

Asht. iii. Adhy. iv. Anuv. v. Sûkta vi.

Mitra looks on man with unclosing eyes.

Mitra, adorable, and to be served. Sovereign. Endowed with vigour, creator, divine, renowned, victorious; who, among Gods and men, bestows food, as the reward of pious acts.

VARUṆA.

Asht. i. Adhy. ii. Anuv. vi. Sûkta i.

7. The regal [Râjâ, radiant or regal] Varuṇa, of pure vigour, in the baseless [firmament] sustains on high a mass of light, the rays whereof are pointed downward, while their base is above. May they become concentrated in us, as the sources of existence.

8. The Râjâ Varuṇa verily made broad the path of the sun, to travel on his daily course, a path to travel on the pathless. May he be the repeller of every affliction of the heart.

10. The constellations set on high, which are visible by night, and go elsewhere by day, are the undisturbed holy acts of Varuṇa; and by his command the moon moves resplendent at night.

The constellations (Ṛikshâh) may be either, it is said, the seven *Ṛishis*, Ursa Major, or the constellations generally. They and the moon are said to be the "pious acts" of Varuña (*Varuṇaya viâtani*), because they shine by his command. What the meaning of the phrase "pious acts" is, we are not told. It is hardly to be supposed that it means acts of worship and devotion. "Beneficent manifestations" probably expresses the *real* meaning. They are Varuṇa made cognizable by our senses.

13, 14. Varuṇa, wise and irresistible . . . . Averter of misfortunes, wise and prosperous.

Sûkta ii (xxv).

Divine Varuṇa . . . . Varuṇa, eminent in strength, the guide of many.

7. He who knows the path of the birds flying through the air, he, abiding in the ocean, knows also the course of ships.

8. He, who, accepting the rites, knows the twelve months, and their productions, and that which is supplementarily engendered [i. e., the intercalary month of the luni-solar year].

10. He, Varuṇa, the accepter of holy rites, the doer of good deeds, has seated himself among the progeny, to exercise supreme dominion.

11. Through him, the sage beholds all the marvels that have been or will be wrought.

12. May that very wise son of Aditi keep us all our days in the right path, and prolong our lives.

13. Varuṇa clothes his well-nourished (person), wearing golden armour, whence the rays are spread around.

19. Hear, Varuṇa, this my invocation! Make us happy to-day! I have appealed to thee, hoping for protection.

Asht. ii. Adhy. i. Anuv. xviii. Sûkta iii.

Ushas, sister of Varuṇa.

The same to-day, the same to-morrow, the irreproachable precede the distant course of Varuṇa.

Adhy. vii. Anuv. iii. Sûkta vi.

To Varuṇa alone: the sage, the self-radiant Varuṇa; chief guide, the upholder; supreme monarch, endowed with truth.

20. Thou who art possessed of wisdom, shinest over heaven and earth, and all the world. Hear, and reply with prosperity!

Asht. iii. Adhy. iv. Anuv. i. Sûkta i.

2. Bring to the presence of the worshippers, Agni, thy brother Varuṇa, the ruler of the water, the Aditya, the sustainer of men, the sovereign venerated of mankind.

4. Mayest thou, Agni, who art wise, avert from us the wrath of the divine Varuṇa.

Asht. iv. Adhy. iv. Anuv. vi. Sûkta xiii.

Imperial and renowned Varuṇa, who has spread the firmament as a bed for the sun; extended the firmament over the tops of the trees, given strength to horses, milk to cows, determination to the heart. He has placed fire in the waters, the sun in the heaven.

3. Monarch of all the world, watering the soil. 4. Varuṇa waters earth, mid-air and heaven.

5. Renowned Varuṇa, the destroyer of the Asuras, who, abiding in the mid-heaven, has meted the firmament by the sun, as if by a measure.

Mitra, in its ordinary sense, Wilson says, is a name of the sun; *Varuṇa*, of the regent of the waters. They cause rain, by producing evaporation.

But it is doubtful if these ancients knew that the clouds were formed by evaporation, which is, for the most part, invisible. And we will inquire hereafter, how it is that Deities of fire and light are said to be in the waters, which quench fire.

In *Sûktas v.* and *vi.*, of *Anuv. iii. Adhy. vii.* of *Asht. ii.*, Varuṇa is implored to ward off poverty and to give wealth. *Sûkta vi.* is addressed to Varuṇa alone. He is styled "The Sage, the self-radiant Aditya, the sovereign Varuṇa, a Deity propitious to his adorer." It is said,

> May we, Varuṇa, deeply meditating on thee, earnestly praising thee, and in thy worship, be prosperous; glorifying thee daily, as the fires at the coming of the luminous dawns.

He is styled "Chief guide of men, endowed with great prowess; the upholder, by whose power the rivers flow." He is implored to keep off all danger, to cast off sin from the worshipper; and it is said,

> No one rules for the twinkling of an eye, apart from thee. He is everywhere present; and in him, who is difficult of attainment, as in a mountain, all holy acts are gathered, not to be dissevered.

INDRA AND VARUṆA.

Asht. i. Adhy. i. Anuv. iv. Súkta vi.

I seek the protection of the sovereign rulers, Indra and Varuṇa. May they both favour us accordingly.

For you are ever ready, guardians of mankind, to grant protection.

Satisfy us with wealth, Indra and Varuṇa, according to our desires.

I invoke you both, for manifold opulence. Make us victorious.

Indra and Varuṇa, bestow happiness speedily upon us. May the earnest praise that I offer to Indra and Varuṇa, reach you both.

Asht. iii. Adhy. ii. Anuv. iii. Súkta ix.

Sovereign Indra and Varuṇa, guardians of heaven. Royal Indra and Varuṇa, guardians of heaven.

Asht. v. Adhy. vi. Anuv. v. Súkta xii.

1. Indra and Varuṇa . . . . 2. One of you is styled Supreme Monarch, so is the other: you are called *Samraj* and *Swaraj*, Indra and Varuṇa: all the Gods in the highest heaven, showerers, have combined your united strength, united vigour.

Sayana ascribes the epithet *Samraj* to Varuṇa, and *Swaraj* to Indra, and gives the meaning of the former, *royally splendent*, and the latter *self-splendent;* which is appropriate in each case, if Indra is Universal Light, and Varuṇa the regal Morning Star. The "Gods in the highest Heaven," are the stars, each of which is imagined to shine with the light of Indra and Varuṇa, which is one, Varuṇa being a manifestation of Indra.

3. Indra and Varuṇa, you have forced open by your strength the barriers of the waters: you have established Sûrya as the Lord, in heaven . . . .

4. The bearers invoke you, Indra and Varuṇa, in wars, in battles; on bended knees, for the begetting of posterity . . . . Lords of both celestial and terrestrial treasures [of the light in the sky and on the earth].

5. Indra and Varuṇa, inasmuch as you have created by your might all these beings of the world [supplied light and being to all the stars], therefore Mitra returns praise to Varuṇa for prosperity, whilst the other, the fierce Indra, associated with the Maruts, acquires glory.

Súkta xiii.

4. Indra and Varuṇa, you protected Súdas, overwhelming the yet Bheda with your fatal weapons: hear the prayers of these Tṛitsus in time of battle, so that my ministration may have borne them fruit.

5. Indra and Varuṇa, the murderous of my enemy distress me, foes amongst the malignant: you two are sovereigns over both wealths. Protect us, therefore, on the day of battle.

Sûkta xiv.

1. Royal Indra and Varuṇa . . . .
2. Your vast kingdom of heaven gratifies . . . .

Sûkta xv.

1. . . . . Indra and Varuṇa, of which the members are radiant as the celestial Dawn.

MITRA, VARUṆA AND ARYAMAN.

Asht. i. Adhy. i. Anuv. iv. Sûkta iv.

6. Mitra and Varuṇa, propitious to pious acts, be present with Ritu at our sacrifice. [Elsewhere styled, lords of the twilight, Divinities abiding in heaven.]

Asht. i. Adhy. ii. Anuv. viii.

4. The Deities Varuṇa, Mitra and Aryaman kindle thee, their messenger from of old [Agni].

Adhy. ii. Sûkta vi.

We invoke Mitra and Varuṇa, becoming present at the sacrifice . . . . I invoke Mitra and Varuṇa, who, with true speech, are the encouragers of pious acts, and are lords of true light.

May Varuṇa be our special protector! May Mitra defend us with all defences! May they make us most opulent!

Asht. i. Adhy. i. Anuv. i. Sûkta ii.

7. Mitra, of pure vigour, and Varuṇa, devourer of foes, joint accomplishers of the act of bestowing water.

8. Mitra and Varuṇa, augmenters of water, dispensers of water.

9. Sapient Mitra and Varuṇa, prosper our sacrifice.

Adhy. ii. Anuv. vi. Sûkta iii (xxvi).

4. Let Varuṇa, Mitra and Aryaman sit down upon the sacred grass, as they did at the sacrifice of Manu.

Adhy. iii. Anuv. vii. Sûkta v (xxxv).

1. I invoke Agni first, for protection. I invoke for protection Mitra and Varuṇa. I invoke Night who brings rest to the world. I invoke the divine Savitṛi for my preservation.

2. Revolving through the darkened firmament, arousing mortal and immortal, the divine Savitṛi travels, in his golden chariot, beholding the worlds.

3. The divine Savitṛi travels by an upward and by a downward path [rises, ascends, descends and sets?]. Deserving adoration, he journeys with two white horses.

4. The many-rayed, adorable Savitṛi, having power to disperse darkness from the world.

5. His white-footed coursers, harnessed to his car with a golden yoke, have manifested light to mankind. Men and all the regions are ever in the presence of the divine Savitṛi.

6. The spheres are three; two are in the proximity of Savitṛi, one leads men to the dwelling of Yama. The immortals depend upon Savitṛi, as a car upon the pin of the axle.

7. . . . . Where now is Sûrya? Who knows to what sphere his rays have extended?

8. He has lighted up the eight points of the horizon, the three regions of living beings, the seven rivers. May the golden-eyed Savitṛi come hither!

10. The golden-handed, life-bestowing, well-guiding, exhilarating and affluent Savitṛi.

11. Thy paths, Savitṛi, are prepared of old, are free from dust, are well placed in the firmament. By those paths, easy to be traversed, preserve us to-day.

Anuv. viii. Sûkta v (xv).

5. Brahmaṇaspati proclaims the sacred prayer, in which the Divinities, Indra, Varuṇa, Mitra and Aryaman, have made their abode.

Sûkta vi (xli).

1. The man whom the wise Varuṇa, Mitra and Aryaman protect, quickly subdues.

7. How shall we recite praise of the great glory of Mitra, Varuṇa and Aryaman.

Sûkta viii (xliii).

3. By which, Mitra and Varuṇa and Rudra, and all the Gods, being gratified, may show us favour.

Adhy. vi. Anuv. xiv. Sûkta vi (xc).

May Varuṇa and the wise Mitra lead us by straight paths; and Aryaman, rejoicing with the Gods.

May Mitra be propitious to us! May Varuṇa, may Aryaman, be propitious.

Sûkta vii.

Thy acts are of the royal Varuṇa: thy glory, Soma, is great and profound. Thou art the purifier, like the beloved Mitra: thou art the augmenter of all, like

Aryaman. [*Soma* is a plant (*Asclepias*) whose juice was used in sacrifices. Also, it is said, the moon.]

Anuv. xv. *Sûkta i (xciv).*

May this one (O Agni), enjoy the support of Mitra and of Varuṇa.

Do thou, divine Agni, who knowest what is good fortune, on this occasion prolong our existence; and may Mitra, Varuṇa, Aditi (ocean, earth and heaven), preserve it to us.

Adhy. xii. *Anuv. xvi.* *Sûkta i.*

We invoke for our preservation, Indra, Mitra, Varuṇa, Agni, the might of the Maruts, and Aditi.

Sûkta ii.

May Indra, may Varuṇa, may Agni, may Aryaman, may Savitṛi bestow upon us that food!

Adhy. viii. *Anuv. xvii.* *Sûkta x (cxv).*

1. The wonderful host of rays has risen, the eye of Mitra, Varuṇa and Agni; the sun, the soul of all that moves or is stationary, has filled the heaven, the earth and the firmament.

2. The Sun follows the divine and brilliant Ushas.

5: The Sun, in the sight of Mitra and Varuṇa, displays his form in the middle of the Heavens, and his rays (or horses), extend, on one hand his infinite and brilliant power, or on the other bring on the blackness of night.

Asht. ii. *Adhy. i.* *Anuv. xviii.* *Sûkta ii (cxxii).*

6, 7. Mitra and Varuṇa, hear these my invocations! . . . . I praise you, Mitra and Varuṇa, for your gifts of numerous cattle.

9, 1. Mitra and Varuṇa . . . . Royal bestowers of delight . . . . You who traverse the sky.

15. Let your spacious and bright-rayed chariot, Mitra and Varuṇa, blaze like the sun.

Anuv. xx. *Sûkta iii (cxxxvi).*

1. Those two Deities who have existed from of old.

2. The most excellent dawn has been seen . . . . the path of the revolving sun has been lighted up by rays . . . . the brilliant mansion of Mitra, of Aryaman, of Varuṇa.

3. Sons of Aditi, lords of munificence. Of those two, Mitra is the animator of mankind, and so is Varuṇa. Aryaman is the animator of mankind.

5, 6. Adoration to Mitra and Varuṇa . . . . worship addressed to both . . . . Veneration to the mighty sun, to heaven and earth, to Mitra, to the benevolent Varuṇa.

7. May we enjoy the felicity which Agni, Mitra and Varuṇa are bestowing.

Sûkta iv (cxxxvii).

To Mitra and Varuṇa jointly.

Sûkta vi.

2. Mitra and Varuṇa, bestow abundantly that unenduring water which you obtain from the sun, through your own energy, through the energy of the vigourous.

Anuv. xxi. *Sûkta xii.*

The tresses of Agni minister, Mitra and Varuṇa, to your sacrifice.

Sûkta xiii.

1. Robust Mitra and Varuṇa, you wear vestments (of light).

3. Mitra and Varuṇa, it is your doing that the footless Dawn is the precursor of footed beings, and that your progeny (the sun), sustains the burthen of the world, diffuses truth and disperses falsehood.

Inseparable and diffusive radiance, the abode of Mitra and Varuṇa . . . . the radiance in Mitra and Varuṇa.

Asht. ii. *Adhy. viii.* *Anuv. i.* *Sûkta v.*

4. Agni, when kindled, is Mitra, and as Mitra is the invoker. Varuṇa is Jâtavedas: Mitra is the ministering priest. Damunas is the agitator (Vayu): Mitra, associate of rivers and mountains.

Asht. iii. *Adhy. iii.* *Anuv. v.* *Sûkta ii.*

1. When the preceding dawns appear, the great imperishable (light) is engendered in the sphere of the waters.

4. The universal sovereign (Agni) is conveyed to many directions. He sleeps in the places of repose; he is connected with the forests: one mother (heaven) nourishes the child; another (earth) gives him a dwelling.

5. Existing in ancient plants, abiding afterwards in new, he enters into the young, as soon as they are produced; impregnated, they become pregnant and bear fruit.

6. The child of two mothers sleeps in the West; but the single infant proceeds (in the morning through the sky). These are functions of Mitra and Varuṇa.

7. The child of two mothers, the invoker of the Gods at sacrifices, the universal sovereign, proceeds thenceforward: the root of all, he abides.

10. Pervading and protecting all, possessing grateful and immortal radiance, he preserves the supreme path; for Agni knows all these worlds.

Sûkta vii.

The mighty Ushas, the golden light, as it were, of Mitra and Varuṇa.

Adhy. v. *Anuv. ii.* *Sûkta iii.*

The divine Savitṛi diffuses his light on high, dispersing the dew. Then Varuṇa and Mitra and others hasten to their offices, where they elevate the sun in the sky.

Adhy. viii. Anuv. i. Sûkta iii.

Thou, Agni, art born Varuṇa, thou becomest Mitra when kindled: In thee, Son of Strength, are all the Gods. Thou art Indra, Son of Strength, to the mortal who presents oblations. Thou art Aryaman, in relation to maidens.

Asht. iv. Adhy. ii. Anuv. iii. Sûkta viii.

Sûrya speaks, to Indra.—Thou art Mitra, whose wealth is truth. Do thou and the royal Varuṇa both protect me.

Asht. iv. Adhy. iii. Anuv. i. Sûkta vi (lxii).

I have beheld the permanent orb of the sun, your dwelling, where a thousand rays abide together; the one most excellent of the forms of the Gods.

Exceeding is your greatness, Mitra and Varuṇa, whereby the ever-moving sun has, through days, milked forth the stationary waters. You augment all the rays of the self-revolving (sun).

8. At the break of dawn, at the rising of the sun, ascend, Mitra and Varuṇa, your golden-bodied, iron-pillared car, and thence behold the earth and its inhabitants.

9. Munificent Mitra and Varuṇa, protectors of the universe.

Adhy. iv. Anuv. v. Sûkta vii.

Imperial rulers of this world, you shine, Mitra and Varuṇa, at this sacrifice, the beholders of heaven. Your forms traverse earth and heaven.

Imperial and mighty showerers, lords of heaven and earth, beholders of the universe, you approach, Mitra and Varuṇa, with variegated clouds.

Your device is manifested in heaven, when the light that is the sun, your wonderful weapon, moves. Him you invest in the sky, with cloud, with rain.

You illumine the whole world with water, you sustain the sun, the adorable chariot in the sky.

Sûkta xi.

Divine sons of Aditi, Mitra, Varuṇa, Aryaman, possessors of omniscience, all associated at our rites. 4. Observers of truth, distributors of water. Protectors of the holy rites among men. Guides in the right way, liberal givers, benefactors.

Sûkta xii.

Mitra and Varuṇa, sovereign rulers, originators of the rain, eminent Deities among the Gods.

Sûkta xiii.

Mitra and Varuṇa, you uphold the three realms of light, the three heavens, the three regions of earth. The immortal Gods impair not your eternal works. You two divine Adityas, upholders of celestial and terrestrial worlds.

Asht. iv. Adhy. v. Anuv. i. Sûkta iii.

Agni, sympathizing in satisfaction with Mitra and Varuṇa.

Anuv. ii. Sûkta i.

Giver of dwellings (Agni), worship the two regal Divinities, Mitra and Varuṇa.

Adhy. viii. Anuv. v. Sûkta i.

Invoke with adorations, for the sake of felicity, the divine Aditi, and Varuṇa, Mitra and Agni, Aryaman, Savitṛi, and Bhaga, and all protecting Divinities.

Sûkta ii.

The radiance of the sun, grateful to Mitra and Varuṇa, having risen, shines.

Praise the protectors of the solemn sacrifice, the well-born Aditi, Mitra and Varuṇa, and Aryaman and Bhaga.

The very potent Varuṇa, Mitra, Agni, practisers of truth.

Adhy. vii. Anuv. iii. Sûkta v (xxvii).

1. To the royal Adityas! May Mitra, Aryaman, Bhaga, the multi-present Varuṇa, the Power Ansâ, hear us.

2. May those of equal exploits, Mitra, Aryaman, Varuṇa, be pleased to-day, by this my praise; they who are Adityas, luminous, purified by showers.

5. Aryaman, Mitra and Varuṇa, may I, through your guidance escape the sins that are like pitfalls.

6. Aryaman, Mitra and Varuṇa, easy is the path and free from thorns, and pleasant. Therefore, Adityas, lead us by it.

7. May we, blessed with many descendants, and safe from harm, attain the great happiness of Mitra and Varuṇa.

8. They uphold the three worlds, the three heavens.

Sûrya, divine eye of Mitra and Varuṇa.

We worship you, Mitra and Varuṇa, when the sun has risen.

Asht. v. Adhy. i. Mand. vi. Anuv. vi. Sûkta i.

1. I praise the two leaders of heaven, the presiders over this world. I invoke the Aṣwins . . . . who at dawn scatter the investing glooms to the ends of the earth.

2. Coming to the sacrifice with their bright splendour, they light up the lustre of their car, emitting vast and infinite radiance. They drive their horses over deserts, with water.

9. Mitra and Varuṇa recognize him, who of all the world worships the royal (Aṣwins) in one season.

10. Come with your shining and well-guided chariot.

Sûkta vi (lxvii).

1. By my praises to exalt you, Mitra and Varuṇa, the eldest of all existing things; you, two, though not the same.

3. Come, Mitra and Varuṇa, beloved of all.

4. Observers of truth, whom Aditi conceived.

6. You manifest vigour daily; you strengthen the summit of the sky, as if with a pillar; the solid form, and the universal Deity (the sun) replenish earth and heaven with the nourishment of man.

Sûkta vii.

3. Praise Mitra and Varuṇa renowned for all glorious energies and enjoyments.

Asht. v. Adhy. iii. Anuv. ii. Sûkta xvi.

10. When Mitra and Varuṇa beheld thee, Vasishṭha, quitting the lustre of the lightning.

11. Verily, thou art the son of Mitra and Varuṇa, born, Brahman, of the will of Urvaṣi, after the seminal effusion.

13. Consecrated for the sacrifice, propitiated by praises, they, Mitra and Varuṇa, poured a common effusion into the water-jar, from the midst of which Mana arose, and from which also Vasishṭha was born.

Adhy. viii.

The three wheels of the Aṣwins, which were invisible, have become manifest. Do you two, who are cognizant of the past, come by the paths of truth, to the presence of living beings.

Asht. i. Adhy. iii. Anuv. ix. Sûkta i.

1. Agni with sharp ears, hear me; let Mitra and Aryaman, and (other) early-stirring Deities, with all the accompanying oblation-bearing Gods, sit down at the sacrifice, upon the sacred grass.

14. . . . . Let the rite-fulfilling Varuṇa, with the Aṣwins and with Ushas, drink the Soma juice.

Asht. ii. Adhy. iv. Anuv. xxiii. Sûkta iii.

8. Mitra and Varuṇa and Aryaman, defend the sacrifice from the reprehensible, and destroy unworthy [i. e., let there be nothing in this sacrifice that shall be censurable, and free it of all unworthiness]. They cause the unfallen and showering to descend . . . .

Asht. ii. Adhy. vii. Anuv. iii. Sûkta v.

2. May those of equal exploits, Mitra, Aryaman, Varuṇa, be pleased to-day, by this my praise; they who are Âdityas, luminous, purified by showers, who abandon none, who are irreproachable, unassailable.

3. Those Âdityas, mighty, profound, unsubdued, subduing, having many eyes, behold the innermost, whether wicked or virtuous, whether far from or nigh to those royal (ones).

4. The divine Âdityas are the upholders of (things) moveable or stationary, the protectors of the universe, the provident in acts, the collectors of water [or, of the vital powers] . . . .

8. They uphold the three worlds, the three heavens; and in their sacrifices three ceremonies . . . .

9. The Âdityas, decorated with golden ornaments, purified by showers, who never slumber, nor close their eyelids, who are unassailable, and praised by many, uphold the three bright heavenly regions . . . .

10. Varuṇa, destroyer of foes, thou art the sovereign over all, whether they be Gods or mortals.

Ashṭ. iii. Adhy. iii. Anuv. v. Sûkta i.

10. . . . . The soft-bellied, fire-tongued Mitra, royal Varuṇa, the youthful Âdityas all cognizant of the past, and proclaiming, hear it.

Ashṭ. iv. Adhy. iv. Anuv. v. Sûkta viii.

7. Deities who are to be worshipped at the sacrifice to the Gods, at the shining ray, at dawn, ... hasten with rapid steeds, leaders . . . .

Sûktas ix, x.

. . . . The graceful Varuṇa or Mitra . . . . they two, excelling in radiance, royal, who hear from the greatest distance, lords of the virtuous . . . . Mitra grants even to the sinful the repairing to his spacious dwelling: the favour of Mitra, the destroyer of foes. . . . . You come, Mitra and Varuṇa, to this man and guide him . . . . Varuṇa, whose form is water . . . . You two, possessed of irresistible and Asura-destroying strength . . . . we glorify you both, that your chariots may precede ours . . . . Adorable and wonderful Deities . . . . of pure vigour . . . . Mitra and Varuṇa, who are far-seeing, may we proceed to your spacious and much frequented kingdom.

Ashṭ. v. Adhy. v. Anuv. iv. Sûkta v.

1. Sûrya, when rising to-day, declare the truth to Mitra and Varuṇa, that we are void of sin. May we, Âditi, be among the Gods: praising thee, Aryaman, may we be dear to thee.

2. Thus Sûrya, the beholder of man, rises, Mitra and Varuṇa, upon both, moving . . . .

3. He has harnessed his seven bay steeds, Mitra and Varuṇa, from your common dwelling place . . . .

4. The sun has ascended the shining firmament, for whom the Âdityas, and the consentient Mitra, Varuṇa and Aryaman make ready the paths.

5, 6. Mitra, Aryaman, Varuṇa, ... unconquered sons of Aditi . . . . the unsubdued Mitra, Varuṇa and Aryaman animate with energies the unconscious.

7. With unclosing eyes, and cognizant of heaven and earth, they conduct the ignorant man . . . .

10. The association of these is of mysterious lustre: by their secret strength they overcome . . . . Have mercy upon us in the mightiness of your strength.

Sûkta vi.

1. Spreading around the beautiful light, Mitra and Varuṇa, of you two Divinities, Sûrya rises: he who beholds all existing things apprehends the acts of mortals.

3. You are vaster, Mitra and Varuṇa, than the ample earth, vaster, bounteous donors, than the glorious and expansive heaven: you maintain beauty in plants and in people . . . .

4. Praise the splendour of Mitra and Varuṇa, whose strength, by its mightiness, keeps heaven and earth asunder.

Sûktas viii. ix. x. xi.

Sûrya, the eye of all, the divine eye of Mitra and of Varuṇa . . . . we worship you, Mitra and Varuṇa, when the sun has risen . . . . May Mitra, Varuṇa, Aryaman, grant affluence to us . . . . Ruling over the waters that are in heaven and earth . . . . may the auspiciously manifested Mitra, the royal Aryaman, the powerful Varuṇa accept our oblation . . . . Sovereigns, mighty preservers of waters, powerful lords of rivers, come to our presence: send down to us, munificent Mitra and Varuṇa, from the firmament, sustenance and rain . . . . May Mitra, Varuṇa, the divine Aryaman conduct us by the most practicable paths . . . . Mitra and Varuṇa, bedew with water him who fabricates your chariot in his mind . . . . Mitra and Varuṇa . . . . whose imperishable and superior might is triumphant in the crowded conflict, over all enemies . . . . They verily are mighty among the Gods; they are rulers . . . . Mitra and Varuṇa, of reiterated manifestations . . . . You whom the Gods uphold for their invigoration, both mighty, masters of strength, and of diffusive radiance . . . . I glorify you, Mitra and Varuṇa, and Aryaman, the consumer of enemies when the sun has risen . . . . Manifold, radiant as the sun, Agni-tongued augmenters of sacrifice, you who have limited the three universal sacrifices, with comprehensive rites. [Agni-tongued augmenters of sacrifice—i. e., you who emit light and so augment the sacrifice; imagined, perhaps, as thus themselves sacrificing in heaven, each with a limited manifestation of the universal sacrifice of light.]

11. Who have established the year, and then the month and the day [by their risings at certain times indicating the returns of festivals], the sacrifice, the night, and the holy text, they, the royal Deities, Varuṇa, Mitra, Aryaman, enjoy unrivalled might.

AṢWINS.

Asht. i. Adhy. iii. Anuv. vii. Sûkta iv.

1. Wise Aṣwins, be present with us thrice, to-day . . . . Your union is like that of the shining and the dewy.

2. Three are the solid wheels of your abundant-bearing chariot, ... three are the columns placed above it for support, and in it you journey three times by night and three times by day.

8. Come, Aṣwins, thrice, with the seven mother-streams. The three rivers are ready; the triple oblation is prepared. Rising above the three worlds, you defend the sun in the sky, who is established for both night and day.

9. Where, Nasatyas, are the three wheels of your triangular car? Where the three fastenings and props? When will be the harnessing of the powerful ass?

Asht. i. Anuv. ix. Sûkta iii (xlvi).

1. The beloved Ushas, until now unseen, scatters darkness from the sky. Aṣwins, I profoundly venerate you.

2. Who are divine, whose appearing causes rejoicing, children of the sea.

The scholiast says that the Aṣwins are said to be born of the sea; and in the opinion of some, are the sun and moon. The Veda gives no countenance to *that* notion, for they *precede* the dawn, and ride together in one car.

Asht. i. Adhy. iii. Anuv. iv. Sûkta iv.

10. Come, Nasatyas, to the sacrifice . . . . Before the dawn, even, Savitṛi sends (to bring you) to the rite, your wonderful car shining with clarified butter.

"Implying," Professor Wilson says, "that the Aṣwins are to be worshipped with this hymn at the dawn." No doubt: but does it not also imply that they are luminaries of the dawn?

Asht. i. Adhy. i. Anuv. i. Sûkta iii.

3. Aṣwins, destroyers of foes (or diseases) [*dasrâ*], exempt from untruth [i. e., real and actual beings or bodies], *rudra vaittani*, come to the mixed libations sprinkled on the cropped sacred grass.

Rudra-vaittani is translated, "leaders in the van of heroes." *Vaittani* means a "road" or "way": *rudra*, it is said, from the root *rud*, to "weep" or "lament," means those who *cause* to weep, and hence, "heroes," who make their enemies weep: and *vaittani* means the "front" of the way, the *van*. It is quite evident that this is only conjecture. The Deity *Rudra* cherishes the Maruts, and is bountiful and mighty. The scholiast says that the word means, "he who makes to weep;" but Professor Wilson finds nothing in the hymns to sustain that interpretation. The root *rudh* meant, to "care for, defend," and the name may have come from that; or, if it came from *rud*, to "weep," it may have alluded to *rains* or *dews*. Also, *ruh* meant "rise up, increase, grow," and thence *rûdhis*, "growth, vigour."

Asht. i. *Adhy. ii.* *Anuv. vi.* *Sûkta vii.*

17. Aşwins, come hither, with hands borne on many steeds. Dasras, be filled with cattle and with gold.

18. Dasras, your chariot, harnessed for both alike, is imperishable. It travels, Aşwins, through the air.

19. You have one wheel on the top of the solid, while the other revolves in the sky.

Asht. i. *Adhy. iii.* *Anuv. ix.* *Sûkta iii (cont.).*

7. Come as a ship, to bear us over an ocean of praises: harness, Aşwins, your car.

8. Your vessel, vaster than the sky, stops on the shore of the sea: your chariot: the drops are expressed for your worship.

9. Kaņwas, do the rays from the sky? Does the dawn in the region of the waters? Where do you desire to manifest your own persons?

14. May Ushas follow the lustre of your approach, circumambient Aşwins, and may you be pleased with the oblations offered by night.

15. Aşwins, may you both drink, and bestow upon us happiness, through your irreproachable protection.

Adhy. iv. *Anuv. ix.* *Sûkta iv.*

2. Come, Aşwins, with your three-columned triangular car.

6. Good-looking Aşwins . . . . bring to us the riches that many covet, whether from the expanse or the sky beyond.

7. Nasatyas, whether you abide far-off or close at hand [whether near the earth in the east or west, or higher in the sky?], come to us in your well-constructed car, with the rays of the sun.

9. Come, Nasatyas, with your sun-clad chariot . . . .

Adhy. vi. *Anuv. xiv.* *Sûkta viii.*

17. Aşwins, who have sent adorable light from the sky to man . . . .

18. May the steeds awakened at dawn bring hither . . . . the divine Aşwins, who are the givers of happiness, the destroyers of foes, seated in a golden chariot.

Asht. ii. Adhy. ii. Anuv. xxii. Sûkta i.

1. Agni is awakened upon earth: the sun rises: the spreading dawn, exhilarating by her radiance, has dispersed (the glooms): Harness, Aṣwins, your chariot, to come, that the divine Savitṛi may animate all beings . . . .

3. . . . . the three-wheeled car of the Aṣwins, drawn by swift horses, laden with honey, three-canopied, filled with treasure . . . .

5. You Aṣwins, sustain the germ in all moving creatures, you are in the interior of all beings . . . . Supply fire and water and the trees of the forest.

6. You two are physicians, with medicaments . . . .

[So we read elsewhere]: Dasras, you would repair to heaven: your charioteers harness for your heavenward journey, the horses that injure not on your journey to heaven: we have placed you, Dasras, in your golden, three-shafted chariot, going by an easy road to heaven . . . . Dasras, showerers, granters of dwellings, Rudras, cognizant of many, increasing . . . . Aṣwins, Creators, the perpetual threefold hymn addressed to you, has been uttered . . . . whether moving or resting, hear his invocation . . . . May the praise of your resplendent forms in the hall of sacrifice, bring prosperity . . . . Dasras, in truth Indratamâ [superlatively Indra], adorable, swifter than the winds, ... bring hither your car . . . . and with it come, Aṣwins. . . . .

Asht. ii. Adhy. iv. Anuv. xxiv. Sûkta iv.

1. Showerer of benefits, harness the car which has three benches, three wheels, and is as quick as thought: with which, embellished with three metals, you come . . . .

2. . . . . May this hymn . . . . be associated with your forms, and do you unite with the Dawn, the daughter of Heaven.

Adhy. v. Anuv. xxiv. Sûkta v.

1. We invoke you two, to-day, the same two on any other day: when the morning dawns. Nasatyas, grandsons of Heaven, wherever you may be . . . .

3. Divine Aṣwins, in whom is no untruth, like arrows to acquire glory, and to carry off Sûrya . . . .

6. Aṣwins, we cross over the limit of darkness: to you this has been addressed: come hither by the path traversed by the Gods.

Adhy. vii. Anuv. iii. Sûkta ix.

4. . . . . May Ilâ, the resplendent Bhaga, heaven and earth, the sagacious Pushan, and the Aṣwins, the two husbands, urge on the chariot.

Asht. ii. Adhy. viii. Anuv. iv. Sûkta vii.

1. Descend, Aṣwins, like falling stones . . . . like two Brahmans repeating hymns . . . . and come like messengers in the land.

2. Moving at dawn like two heroes in a car; like a pair of goats; like two women lovely in form; or like husband and wife . . . .

3. Come to us, the first, like a pair of horns or like two hoofs, ... like a pair of Chakravâkas, awaiting day . . . .

4. Bear us across like two vessels, or like the poles of a car, the axles, the spokes, the fellies: Be like two dogs, warding off injury to our persons, and, like two coats of mail, defend us from decay.

Asht. iii. Adhy. ii. Anuv. iv. Sûkta i.

3. The parent of twins has brought forth the twins on this occasion, ... they two, the dispersers of darkness, combine, assuming bodies as a pair, at the origin of the day.

Adhy. iv. Anuv. v. Sûkta v.

1. . . . . The praiser awakes the Aşwins preceding the dawn.

Adhy. vii. Anuv. iv. Sûkta xii.

1. We invoke, Aşwins, to-day, your rapid car, the associator of the Solar ray; the banked car which bears Sûryâ [the daughter of the Sun] . . . .

2. Aşwins, grandsons of Heaven, Divinities . . . . powerful horses draw you in your chariot.

Sûkta xiii.

2. Your food-bearing, Soma-laden, well-horsed chariots appear at the opening of the dawn, scattering the surrounding darkness like the sun, and spreading bright radiance over the firmament.

4. . . . . Swift of speed, gentle, unrefractory, golden-winged, bearers, wakers at dawn . . . .

5. . . . . Praise the associated Aşwins at the break of day . . . .

Adhy. viii. Anuv. v. Sûkta vii.

2, 3. . . . . the radiant mother of the rays of light [Ushas, the Dawn], is the friend of the Aşwins: thou art the friend of the Aşwins . . . .

Asht. v. Adhy. v. Anuv. iv. Sûkta xii.

2. Kindled by us, Agni blazes, the extremities of the darkness are seen nigh at hand, the banner is perceived, rising with the glory in the east, of the Dawn, the daughter of Heaven:

3. Verily, Aşwins, the pious priest repeating glorifies you, Nasatyas, with hymns: Come therefore by formerly trodden paths to our presence.

4, 5, 7. Relying on you, Aşwins, as protectors, ... Mâdhwîs, I invoke you . . . . Protect us, Aşwins! . . . . this treasure given by us has been placed, Mâdhwîs, before you . . . . Nourisher of all, the chariot of you two, who are associated in a common purpose, traverses the seven flowing . . . . [Qu. The *weeping* ones, *Rudras*, the Seven Pleiades?]

Sûkta xiii.

9. Thus your devoted worshipper, waking before the dawn, praises you with hymns . . . .

Sûkta xiv.

1, 2, 3, 5. . . . . Your golden chariot, drawn by your vigourous horses, ... radiant with wheels . . . . renowned among the five orders of beings [Qu. The stars of five different magnitudes?] furnished with three benches, ... well horsed and celebrated, come, Aṣwins . . . . drink, Dasras, the sweet pledge: your chariot, conveying you with your spouse, furrows with its two wheels the extremities of the sky . . . . the daughter of Sûrya made choice of your chariot at the approach of night . . . . Riders in the chariot, Aṣwins, come . . . . to this our sacrifice, at the dawn of day.

Asht. v. Adhy. v. Anuv. v. Sûkta i.

1, 2, 3, 4. Night retires before the dawn, ... the dark night leaves the path clear for the radiant . . . . Come, ... bringing desired wealth in your chariot . . . . day and night, Mádhwis, protect us . . . . May your docile and vigourous horses bring hither your chariot at the approaching dawn . . . . that chariot which has three benches . . . . and is the precurser of the day, come, Nasatyas to us; with that chariot which traverses, as your all-pervading form.

Sûkta ii.

3. Praises waken up the Aṣwins (kindled adorations), and the celestial dawns.

4. When the dawns arise, your worshippers, Aṣwins, proffer you praises: the divine Savitṛi casts his splendours on high.

5. Come, Nasatyas, from the west, from the east; Aṣwins, from the south, from the north; from every quarter . . . .

Asht. v. Adhy. viii. Anuv. i. Sûkta v.

1. When the shining dawn, advancing hither from afar, whitens [illuminates], she spreads the light on all sides.

'2. *And you, Aṣwins, of goodly aspect, accompany the dawn like leaders, with your mighty chariot harnessed at a thought.*

7. Come, Aṣwins, to our adoration, hastening quickly, with your rapid, falcon-like horses.

8. With which in three days and three nights you traverse from afar all the brilliant . . . .

9. *Bringers of the day* (bestow) upon us food . . . .

Anuv. ii. Sûkta iii.

23. The three wheels of the Aṣwins which were invisible, have become manifest.

Sûkta iv.

12. Although, Aşwins, you should be riding in the same chariot with Indra, although you should be domiciled with Vayu, although you should be enjoying gratification along with the Âdityas and Ribhus, although you be proceeding in the tracks of Vishṇu . . . .

16, 17, 18. I awake with the pious praise of the Aşwins . . . . Ushas, truth-speaking, mighty Goddess, awake the Aşwins . . . . When, Ushas, thou movest with thy radiance, thou shinest equally with the sun, and this chariot of the Aşwins proceeds to the hall of sacrifice . . . .

Sûkta v.

Whether, Aşwins, you now are where the spacious halls of sacrifice are; whether you are in yonder bright sphere of heaven, or whether you are in a dwelling constructed above the firmament . . . . In the west, in the east . . . . I invoke you: whether you traverse the firmament, or pass along earth and heaven.

Asht. iii. Adhy. iv. Anuv. v. Sûkta v.

The Aşwins, preceding the dawn . . . . Endowed with power, ever young, in whom is no untruth, unwearied, munificent.

Adhy. vii. Anuv. iv. Sûkta xii.

We invoke, Aşwins, your rapid car, the associator of the Solar ray, the banked car which bears Sûryâ.

Sûkta xi.

6. That quick-moving chariot whereby you become the lords of Sûryâ.

Sûkta xii.

2. Guardians of heaven . . . . Divinities.

Sûkta xiii.

The sun rises: Your chariot, Aşwins, traversing, is associated with the divine (orb) on the summit.

Asht. iv. Adhy. iv. Anuv. vi. Sûkta i.

When Sûryâ has ascended your ever easy-moving car, then bright-waving resplendent rays encompass you, Aşwins.

Lords of water: Invincible: Showerers of wealth: Lords of the chariot. The two who come first at dawn. The Aşwins claim the morning sacrifice. The ancient sages praised them at dawn. Worship the Aşwins at early dawn.

Car plated with gold, honey-tinted, water-shedding, laden with ambrosia, quick as thought, rapid as the wind.

Sûkta vi.

Aşwins, come hither! Alight like two swans, like two deer, like two wild cattle in pasture; like two swans alight on the libation.

Asht. v. Adhy. i. Anuv. vi. Sûkta i.

The two leaders of heaven, the presiders over this world, the Aşwins who at dawn scatter the investing glooms to the ends of the earth.

Coming to the sacrifice with their bright splendours; emitting vast and infinite radiance.

Two swift-moving, good-looking, ancient Aşwins: Riders on car: showerers; bountiful givers.

Asht. v. Adhy. v. Anuv. iv. Sûkta xii.

Lords of men. Adorable Deities.

Sûkta xiii.

Your chariot, Aşwins, in which you ride with Sûryâ [the daughter of the Sun].

Sûkta xiv.

The daughter of Sûryâ made choice of your chariot at the approach of night.

Anuv. v. Sûkta i.

Night retires before the dawn, the sister (of the Aşwins). The dark night leaves the path clear for the radiant sun.

Adhy. viii. Anuv. i. Sûkta v.

You, Aşwins, accompany the dawn like leaders, with your mighty chariot. Bringers of the day: Magnificent lords of good fortune.

DEITIES OFFERED BY NATURE TO THE ARYANS.

But for the immense antiquity which it would compel us to ascribe to them, one reading the simpler and probably older hymns of the Rig-Veda, would as unhesitatingly impute them to the bards of a people who led a nomadic and pastoral life on the steppes of Bokhara, as he would impute the poetry of the Bedouins to a people leading a like life in the Arabian deserts.

They smell of the free air of the plains. They tell us of a simple people, whose wealth consisted chiefly in their flocks and herds, and to whom horses and mares were of especial value. The juice of the Soma plant, producing exhilaration and perhaps intoxication, was their sacred beverage, and milk their ordinary and favourite one, while to the Deities they offered oblations of butter, burned in the open air.

Undoubtedly, at any rate, they had in the Punjab the old original worship, more spiritualized than at first, which they had long before when wandering on the steppes and tending their herds. Probably the older hymns were composed and sung there.

To understand these hymns, it is necessary to inquire with what special objects for adoration Nature in those latitudes surrounded a primitive and simple people, who bequeathed fire-worship to their remote descendants, and knew no Gods superior to the Fire and Light.

The word *Deva*, the general name for the Gods in the Veda, means in Sanskrit, "bright;" and it is the Latin *Divus* and *Deus*.

Narrien (*Historical Account of the Origin and Progress of Astronomy*) says that it seems difficult to imagine that the first men could avoid recognizing the fact that the earth is isolated in space, seeing that the celestial bodies must perform part of their revolutions below the earth, in order to enable them to reappear in the East, after having set in the West:

But it is quite certain that they had no such idea. So far from considering it as suspended in air, æther or space, they believed it to be firmly and stably set on solid foundations. It is true that the accounts collected from the most ancient authors of Greece and Rome coincide nearly with each other in representing the earth as a plane figure, bounded on its whole circumference by an ocean of vast extent. Herodotus so describes it, and says that geographers so represented it in his time. Diodorus Siculus says that the Chaldæans considered the earth to rest on the waters like a boat; and Plutarch ascribes a like opinion to Heraclitus.

But these were the notions of a comparatively late day. Everyone is familiar with the Hindū idea that the earth rested upon the back of an immense elephant, standing upon a more vast tortoise: and their ancestors, the Aryans, on the steppes or in the Punjab, knew nothing about the ocean, more than the American Indians do, who inhabit the central plains and the Rocky Mountains. They probably did not attempt to explain to themselves how the sun returned to the East during the night, any more than the children do. Everything in the heavens was wonderful to them, since they understood neither the nature of the luminaries, nor the causes of their motions; and they attempted to explain nothing. Nor had they any idea of the extent of the earth. It was there, and they were on it, and they knew little more.

It was evidently the opinion, Narrien says, of the Eastern sages, in very ancient times, that the surface of the earth was nearly a plane, and that in its central part, which was conceived to be situated northward of the regions then occupied by men (that is, beyond the frontiers of India, Persia and Greece), was a very high mountain, intercepting the view of the sun during part of his daily revolution, and thus producing the darkness of night; this mountain was believed to be of a conical form; and it was supposed that, according as the sun was more or less elevated above the earth (for it appears that he was supposed to describe about the mountain a spiral curve, alternately ascending and descending), he remained concealed during a less or greater portion of time, respectively; and that thus the days and nights were rendered of variable length. This idea bears the marks of an origin that may be dated from a time preceding that of the formation of the opinion that the celestial bodies, in their daily revolutions, pass under the visible surface of the earth; and it seems to be a part of the ancient hypothesis, that the earth constitutes the general basis of the universe.

The mountain is the Alborj of the Būndehesh, up which the sun ascended during 180 days, and then descended during as many; which surrounded the earth, and reached the heavens; and the Meru of the Brahmanical fables, with its three peaks or summits and its seven steps or terraces, encompassing the whole earth, and on which the Gods are seated.

The Poets of the Veda certainly believed the earth to be stable and fixed; for they so speak of it, and as sustained and upheld by pillars. To consider it so, without doubt or question; to accept it as it appears to the senses, without speculation as to what or how great it really is; and to yield belief, slowly and reluctantly, to the different idea demonstrated by science and denied by the senses—all this was not only natural for them, but after it was forgotten that they had ever lived, a wise student of Nature was imprisoned by a church, in the name and by the authority of God, for teaching that the earth was not a stable and stationary mass round which the heavenly luminaries revolved, to serve it; but itself a mere obedient subordinate revolving round the sun. So the old Semitic ancestors of another race might have done; for the doctrine of Galileo was a heresy for the Catholic Church and the Inquisition, because it was contrary to what was said in the old Semitic books, of that hated, detested, despised people, then accursed of all Christendom, whose sacred books Christendom had adopted, and accepted the descendant of a Hebrew and a woman of Moab as its God and Saviour, acknowledging, at the same time, the whole human race to be the fruit of the incestuous connection of brothers and sisters, and a large part of it of that of a father and his daughters.

The modern faith need not smile contemptuously at the ideas of these ancients, in regard either to Nature or the Deity. We know more than they did about the extent, arrangement and movements of the universe; the qualities and attributes of matter; the formulas of the mathematical, chemical and physical laws that apply to matter and regulate movement, and the action and effect of the forces of Nature: we have larger and higher ideas of the attributes that we impute to the Source, Author or Creator, the Ruler and Sustainer of the universe: but we are as ignorant as they were, of what *matter* really is, and what the forces of Nature really are. Of light, heat and electricity in their essence, we know nothing at all; and, after all, in God we only worship either an infinite man, or a force of a Nature utterly unknown to us, to which we ascribe two human attributes or faculties, will and intelligence, and by compounding all His attributes with infinity, make him, to our limited comprehension incomprehensible, an impossible congeries of infinite contradictions and incongruities.

A force of Nature is but a name to us. What attraction, magnetic, of cohesion, of gravitation, or any other *is*, we have no idea. We have the sciences of optics and acoustics, but we no more know *how* we see and hear, than they did. The veil that Isis, the Great Nature, wears, is as thick and impervious for us as it was for them. We investigate the phenomena of Nature, but we know no more about final causes than they did. We are satisfied that the body is not our *very self*, and believe that *we* are immortal; but *what* the soul *is*, and how it acts upon and governs or is governed by the body, we are as profoundly ignorant as they were; nor can we, any more than they could, obtain any distinct consciousness of ourselves, any self-cognition, to the exclusion of, or isolated from, the body. Of what life is, we know as little: nor do we even understand how *we* feel pain, by means of any action upon the nerves of the *body*, nor how *matter* can, by means of vitality, be gifted with the capacity of feeling pain. Generation is as wonderful a mystery to us, as it was to them, and the formation and production of every egg of a bird is a miracle to us.

Those ancient men were alone in the world, with Nature and its manifestations of force, power and life. Stability, permanency and life were the three great facts, patent and palpable to them, about which they could not doubt, and as to the *causes* whereof it did not occur to them to inquire. Whatever was apparent to their senses, visible or audible, was real, and nothing else was so. The conception of invisible powers and forces was of later growth. In everything that was real, they saw life, and knew no difference between their own life, and that of all Nature around them. The first men that lived quickly saw that some of the animals thought and reasoned, as they themselves did, could come to understand the meaning of certain often repeated words, could remember and dream, were capable of love, attachment and gratitude, and that propagation was effected by them in the same manner as by themselves.

The old Aryan herdsman or priest had no conception of his *self* as a *soul* or *spirit*, distinct from his body, dwelling in it or clothed by it as by a garment, or using it as an instrument. He no more imagined that of himself than he did of his horse. Nor did he conceive of any God whatever, as a spirit in our sense of the word, i. e., a somewhat that is *no*-thing, *not* matter, and wholly separate from all that is appreciable by the senses.

There was in them, as there is in our American Indians, a curious mixture of acuteness and shrewdness, wisdom, prudence, energy, resoluteness, reason and good sense, with childishness of intellect in some respects, credulity and simplicity. The Comanche çannot calculate mentally how much is due to three men, for a horse hired by each, at two dollars per day, for six days. They have to find out whether 36 dollars is the correct amount, by means of a number of spears of grass, divided and subdivided, occupying several minutes in the calculation. They will not burn the bones of the bison, with the dry ordure of that animal, which is their only fuel, lest they should anger the animals, and cause them to leave the hunting grounds or to decline to permit themselves to be killed; and when they have slain one, they address to him an oration, apologizing for killing him and assuring him that they have only done so out of necessity, that they and their children may not want for food. One band which I met had with them a ram, with an immense fleece, which was medicine, i. e., sacred. Yet, in all ordinary matters, they are shrewd, sensible, practical men.

Upon the steppes, and on the plains of the Punjab, the sky would seem to our ancestors a solid hemispherical vault, resting all around them on the horizon, of a circumference vastly wider than at any one point it seemed to be. This they would very soon have discovered, each for himself, by finding that, drive their herds as far as they might, towards the sunrise or the sunset, northward or southward, they could come no nearer to the horizon; and no traveller could tell of any one who had ever reached it. The sun, moon and other luminaries would appear to them to be bodies moving between the earth and the solid sky. And of those luminaries they would have very much such ideas as are embodied in the Semitic Cosmological legends with which the Hebrew book *Barasith* commences. According to the first of these, the luminaries in the expanse of heaven were made to divide the day from the night, to be for signs and seasons, days and years, and also to give light upon the earth. Alohayim made one great luminary to rule by day, and the smaller to rule by night, and the stars (*Kocabim*): and he placed them in the expanse of heaven (*rakaya h' samayim*), to give light upon the earth, to rule by day and by night, and to divide the light from the darkness. The luminaries were the host (*tsaba*), the armies of heaven.

For all these purposes, they were the servants and attendants of the earth, bodies emitting light, and the largest of them heat, for the sole benefit of the earth and men. Other purposes than this, they were not imagined to be created to subserve.

Of the real nature of these bodies, they of course knew nothing, nor of their distance from the earth, or their size. No doubt they supposed their relative sizes to be as they appeared to be, and the distance of all from the earth nearly or quite the same. Plutarch says that there were men who supposed the stars to be extinguished when they ceased to be seen, and to be relighted again when they appeared: and the Iberians pretended that they could hear, when the sun descended into the ocean, a hissing sound, like that of heated iron when plunged into water.

The natives of the Society Islands imagined that the sea which surrounded them was a level plain, joined at the horizon by the sky, which enclosed the islands like a vault. Some of them considered the sun as an animated being; and others, that it resembled fire. They imagined that it sunk into the sea every evening, and passed, during the night, by a submarine passage from the West to the East, where it again rose from the sea in the morning.

These ancients never imagined that the stars were placed in empty space. They supposed them set and fixed in a vault, of durable and firm structure. Hence the word *firmament* (from *firmamentum*, that which "strengthens, stays, supports, props up," itself from *firmo*, "fortify, strengthen, support, make durable, permanent, lasting"), by which our version renders the word רקיע *rakaya*, in the book *Barasith*, which De Sola, Lindelthal and Raphall render "expanse."

The word "expanse" is a mistranslation; for לקע means to "beat" or "beat out," to "flatten" or "expand by beating," to "stretch out," as Jehovah is said to have stretched or spread out the earth (*Ps.* 136: 6; *Isa.* 42: 5; 44: 24) and the heavens (Ps. 37:18). In Syriac, *propped up, planted firmly*, etc. The Semitic idea never was that the sky was a void expanse. The Greek word, *στερέωμα*, used in the Septuagint, from *στερεὸς*, "firm, solid, stable," as *στάω* and *στω*, and the Latin *sto*, means "stand, be upright, stay, remain."

The opinions of the ancient philosophers as to the stars may be far from representing those of the more ancient Aryans. Many supposed them to be only bright ornaments, or, as it were, nails, fixed in the crystalline sphere, or firmament. Anaxagoras said that they were stones flung up from the earth, and kindled by the whirling motion of the æther. Heraclides and the Pythagoreans taught that each was a world like the earth. What the Poets of the Veda thought, we shall learn from their hymns.

One of the Vedas, according to the translation of Mr. Colebrooke, says,

> Who knows exactly, and who shall in the world declare whence and why this creation took place? *The Gods are subsequent to the production of this world;* then who can know from whence it proceeded? Or whence this varied world arose? Or whether it upheld itself or not? He who in the Highest Heaven is the Ruler of the Universe indeed does know; but not another can possess that knowledge. (*Asiatic Researches, viii. Sec. 8.*)

Even among the comparatively modern philosophers, it was a general opinion that the earth was the most important body in the universe, and even the source of the principle of existence in all the others. The air was supposed to be nourished by the humid vapours exhaled from its surface, the ether by the air, and the stars by the ether. Cleanthes, according to Cicero, maintained that the stars are proved to be constituted of fire by the evidence of two senses, the touch and the light; and that consequently they are fed by the vapours of the ocean. It is of the sun, however, that Cicero speaks:

> *Nam solis candu illustrius est, quăm ullius ignis, quippe qui immenso mundo lam longe, lateque collocat; et is ejus tactris est non ut tepefaciat solum, sed etiam sæpe ambruat: quorum neutrum faceret, nisi esset igneus. Ergo, inquit, cum Sol igneus sit, oceanique alatur humoribus (quia nullus ignis sine pastu aliquo possit permanere), necesse est, antei similis sit igni, quem adhibemus ad asum atque ad victum, aut ei qui corporibus animantium continetur.*

And so we find in the Veda, that Agni (*Ignis*) is both the domestic fire, which men apply *ad usum et victum*, and that vital heat which *continetur animantium corporibus*.

A general and circular movement of the bodies in the firmament must have been the first phenomenon recognized by the men of our race. The herdsman on the steppes, where the horizon was the only boundary of the plain, would soon perceive that the sun and many stars, and part of the time the moon, rose out of the plain, to the eastward, and each, after describing a curve in the heavens, sunk into the plain to the westward. He would see that in the north were some which performed their revolution without descending so low in any part as to reach the horizon; and finally, that one star seemed to be stationary in the heavens, during all the time that the absence of the sun permitted it to be visible. These phenomena could not fail to suggest the idea of the revolution of some geometrical figure, a cone, a cylinder, or a sphere, about a certain line passing through the eye of the observer, and situated obliquely to the plane of the terrestrial horizon. Probably they soon concluded that the heavens were spherical in form. The argument of Proclus contains what would probably suggest itself to them; that the stars which rise and set evidently describe complete circles daily in the heavens, about one fixed point; that the inequality in the length of the days and nights in different seasons, and the changes gradually made during the day in the position of any shadow cast by an object, prove the circular movement of the sun; and that the sun is, at all seasons, on the surface of one sphere, because his apparent magnitude is invariable, which would not be the case if, from midwinter to midsummer he had moved northward on the surface of a cylinder or cone, since, in one situation, he would then, evidently, have been nearer to the spectator than in the other, and would consequently have appeared greater.

It appears to have been, from the first, generally understood, that the celestial bodies were attached to the concave surface of a spherical shell, which revolved in a certain time round the earth, which was situated in or near the centre of the concavity. Hence the most ancient symbol of the universe that we know, was an egg. It was compared to the yolk, the white and the shell. Beyond it, Aristotle said, nothing can exist.

The sun was that object which, of all in the universe, would first attract the attention of the first men that lived, would more and more engross it, and become infinitely the most important to him. His welfare, comfort, subsistence and very life, would quickly be found to depend upon the great orb of day. As the great radiator of light and only source of heat among the celestial bodies, the cause of all production, melter of the snow and ice that in the springtime freed the chilled earth of her winter covering and set free the streams from their icy bonds, cause of all production, creator of greenness and of flowers and fruits, and ripener of the harvests, regulator of the seasons, and lord of the days and nights, investor of the clouds and sky with the many-coloured glories of the morning and the evening, he must soon have seemed to them the true sovereign and ruler of the universe. His risings

and settings, and his stately and regular march in the great semicircle would enable them to measure intervals of time for regulating the ordinary occupations of life; and his movements northward and southward would soon enable them approximately to measure the years.

> There was no bound or limit to the images suggested by the sun in his ever-varying aspects. For every one of these aspects those early men would have a fitting expression, nor could human memory retain the exact meaning of all these phrases, when the men who used them had been scattered from their original homes. Their words would truthfully express the impressions which the phenomena left on their senses, and their truthfulness would impart to their language an undying beauty. Of whatever object or phenomenon they spoke, this would be the case; but the most fruitful source of mythical phrases, of epithets afterwards to become the names of new beings and give birth to legends, would be found in the daily and yearly course of the sun. In the thought of those early ages, he was the child of night or darkness; the dawn came before he was born, and died as he sprang up out of the plain. He strangled the serpents of the night; he went forth like a bridegroom out of his chamber, like a giant to run his course. He had to do battle with clouds and storms: Sometimes he disappeared behind their gloomy veil, and the children of men shuddered at the anger of the hidden Sun. Sometimes he looked benignly on the face of his bride who came to greet him at his journey's end. His light and heat might give life or destroy it. His chariot, driven swiftly onward, drawn by his red steeds, might scorch with drouth the regions over which it passed, and prepare the forests to be devoured by the terrestrial Agni.

But the images that owed their birth to his brightness, his power, his magnificence, his bounty and beneficence, would far outnumber all the rest.

> A new life flashed up every morning before the eyes of those primitive men, and the fresh breezes of the dawn came to them like greetings wafted across the golden threshold of the sky, from distant realms beyond the clouds, beyond the dawn, which seemed to them to open golden gates, for the sun to pass through.

Next to the orb of day, the queen of night, the moon, would attract attention, and suggest a thousand images. Rising at different hours, hanging as a thin crescent in the west at regular intervals, and growing by degrees to the perfectness of her full-orbed beauty, her variations of form and differences of time of rising would soon enable the first men to measure weeks and months. The new moon would soon come to mark the times of festivals and solemnities, and the full moon to be available for like purposes. She also would be deemed the enemy of darkness, and hated by the clouds and storms. It was long, no doubt, before it was supposed that her light was but the reflected light of the sun, but she would be deemed an independent luminary, source of light, but not of heat. Originally the female sex was not assigned to her, but she, like the sun was characterized as male.

Supposing the moon to shine, like the sun, with her own light, they must have been entirely unable to account for her eclipses, or for the changes which she continually underwent in shape and size. Her soft, mild light must have given them an idea that she was a gentle and beneficent luminary, friend of man in the hours that would without her have been dark. At the full, nothing in Nature is more magnificently beautiful than the moon, and she has therefore, in all ages, received the homage of the Poets.

Those who have slept, as I have, month after month, in year after year, in the open air, in the forests and on the great Western plains, in the Rocky Mountains and the Mexican Valleys, who have risen habitually before day, and measured the hours of guard-duty by the westward marches of Jupiter or the three Kings of Orion, can in some faint degree appreciate the sensations inspired in the minds of the old Aryan herdsmen, leading the same life in nearly the same latitudes, by the bright armies of the skies. No one who has led that life, and become familiar with the principal planets and constellations and single stars, will wonder that they were almost from at first, regarded as protectors, consolers and guides of men; gracious, beneficent and bestowers of benefits.

Among these apparently lesser luminaries, two, apparently the largest, and distinguishable from the rest by their steady radiance, and also by their difference of movement in the heavens, must at once have attracted attention and been deemed of superior importance. These were the stars of the morning and evening, *Jupiter* and *Venus*. There is no reason to suppose that in those early days a difference of sex was imputed to them. Chiefly by the steady and regular movement of Jupiter, I counted the weary hours of my watches on the plains. Sometimes, as the Morning Star, he was the welcome herald of the approaching daylight; while Venus sometimes shone, as she arose in the East before the dawn, with a strange and amazing brilliance, like a large, irregularly-shaped mass, rather than like a star—a phenomenon owing probably to some peculiar condition of the atmosphere, and which caused it to be, for several mornings, mistaken for a comet.

The first men could have known nothing of the real nature or movements of these planets. Of course they knew nothing of their revolving in orbits round the sun, nor that they were bodies of vast magnitude, and resembling the earth, shining only by a reflected light. It is not probable that they formed any hypotheses concerning them. They were, to them, like the sun and moon, satellites of, or lamps ministering to the earth.

They may even have regarded Venus as the morning and as the evening star, as two different luminaries; but they could not long have remained ignorant of the identity of Jupiter, wherever and whenever he appeared in the heavens: though Pliny says that Pythagoras, learning the fact in Egypt, was the first who made known to the Greeks the identity of each as the Morning and as the Evening Star.

Mercury and Saturn were probably for a long time not distinguished from the mass of the stars; but the red Mars must soon have attracted attention, and have been sometimes noticed flaming in the West in the early night, with Jupiter and Venus.

They could have had no proof of the different distances of the planets from the earth, except such as might be furnished by the difference in degree of their brightness, or of their apparent velocities around the earth. It is not likely that either of these suggested a difference in their distances from the earth. The distance of all appears, to the naked eye, to be the same. Ages afterwards, differences of opinion existed as to their relative distances; some of the ancients supposing that the sun and moon revolved with the other planets round the earth, in orbits within that of Mars, and that the moon's orbit was nearest to the earth; while some placed the sun between the spheres of Venus and Mercury; the Egyptians, Achilles Tatius says, placing Mercury between the spheres of Mars and the sun, probably because Venus and Mercury were never seen to pass over the sun's disc; and they supposed Venus to be nearer the earth than Mercury, because it was larger and brighter. In the system of the later Greeks, and, as Alpetragius states, in those of the Babylonians and Hindūs, the orbits of Venus and Mercury are placed between those of the sun and moon, that of Mercury being nearest to the moon or earth, because his conjunctions with the sun occur more frequently than those of Venus.

These discrepancies of opinion among the learned, when astronomy had been studied for ages, teach us how little must even have been guessed, before it became a science: and the statement that the disciples of Epicurus asserted that the sun, moon and stars were no larger than they appeared to be, shows what the opinion of the unlearned was, even in those later days.

Of the fixed stars, those would become most noticeable which were largest and brightest, and thence, or from their groupings, of unmistakable identity, or at least not with difficulty recognized.

In the Odyssey, Ulysses, in his bark, on leaving Calypso, is represented as observing

> the *Pleiades* and *Boötes*, the *Hyades* and the bold *Orion*, the Bear, which is called the wagon, and the unwearied sun and full moon, and all the stars by which, like a crown, the heavens are surrounded.

Perhaps the most constantly watched of all were the seven stars now known as *Ursa Major*, which, in the North, travelling in a perpetual circle, never set. It would soon be noticed that this and other groups of stars retained always the same shape, the stars of which they were composed never changing their relative positions in the group; and to the herdsman, wandering or lost on the plains, no group would be so sure a guide as these that were always in sight, and that enabled him to go with certainty in any desired direction.

Mr. Cox says (*Mythol. i.* 47), that these derived their name from a root that meant to "shine;" but that, in India, afterwards, the meaning of *riksha* was forgotten; and though, possibly or probably,

> to the same roots belongs the name of the Golden Bear (*ἄρκτος* and *Ursa*), and the epithet had, by some tribes, been confined to the Bear, and the Seven Shiners were transformed first into Seven Bears, then into one with Arktouros (Arcturus) for their bear-ward [the Indians], instead of referring the word to bears, confounded it with *rishi*, and the seven stars became the abode of the seven Poets or Sages, who enter the ark with Menu (Minos), and reappear as the Seven Wise Men of Hellas, and the Seven Champions of Christendom.

Mr. Cox says,

> The same lot, it would seem, befell another name for this constellation. They who spoke of the Seven *Triones* had long forgotten that their fathers spoke of the stars as *taras* (*staras*), or strewers of light, and converted the bear-ward into Boôtes the Ploughman; while the Teutonic nations, unconscious that they had retained the old root in their word *stern* or 'star,' likewise embodied a false etymology, in 'wagons' or wains.

Elsewhere (*i.* 413), he says that

> the seven Ṛishis are the media or instruments through which the divine Veda was imparted to mankind; and that their names are variously given, Manu with Bhrigu, Angiras and others, being sometimes reckoned among them; but of the whole number, seven attained a pre-eminent dignity.

And, referring to the mistake by which *riksha* was changed into *rishis*, he says,

> The notion of making bright conveyed also the idea of gladdening and cheering, and hence *arkshah* became a name, not only for the sun, but for a hymn or song of praise, and the makers or singers of these hymns were naturally termed *Ṛishis*, or *gladdeners*. It was not less natural that, as the Ṛishis or sages took a stronger hold on the imagination of the people, the seven *Arkshas* or stars should be converted into Ṛishis, and that the Ṛishis should be said to have their abode in them.

And, he thinks, with Müller, *arktos* became a name for the bear, among the Western Aryans,

> and stood to the Sanskrit *riksha* in the relation of the Greek τέκτων, or 'carpenter,' to *takshan*, and the Latin *pectus*, 'a breast,' to *vakshas;* and then the seven stars were *necessarily* converted into Seven Bears, while the sages whom the Hindū placed in those shining orbs survived as the Seven Wise Men of Hellas, to reappear under different forms, as we have already seen elsewhere.

I confess to having little faith in these etymological conclusions. It is quite certain that the earliest names, everywhere, by which particular groups of stars were designated, were those of animals and other visible objects, fanciful resemblances to which the savage, like the child, readily sees and traces. Nor is one name alone given to each group; but the same group may have been, as in some cases the same group now is, known by more than one name. The Great Bear is now known, also, as Charles's Wain, the Dipper and the Pointers.

The roots *riṣ* and *riç* रिष and रिश mean to "cut," or "cut off" (*couper*, *trancher*), and from the former comes *riṣṭas*, "cut off," *ristis*, "measurement." Hence, perhaps, *rishi*, as one who composed measured lines, i. e., "a poet." ARKS or *raks* means to "crush, wound, break, etc.," whence *rakṣhas* (*ARkṣas*) a "bear," and in Greek ἄρασσω, αρκος; and Latin *ursus*, "a bear." I do not find in Eichhoff the root meaning to "shine." *Raj* is the only one, with that meaning, commencing with *r*, whence *raj*, *rajas*, *rajni*, etc.

The student of the Veda will find that many of the ancient chieftains and Ṛishis were reported to have been transferred to the skies; and all of them, I am satisfied, were deemed to have become stars. Among them were the seven sons of the Rishi Angiras, known as the Angirasas, and they, I am sure, were regarded as being the seven stars of Ursa Major, long before the Vedic hymns were composed. It is most probable that its name of Bear was older still.

Four thousand years ago, the space now distinguished by the constellation Draco was immediately in the vicinity of the northern extremity of the axis about which the celestial sphere seemed to revolve; and one of the stars, now designated as α in that constellation, was then so near the pole, that it must have appeared stationary during the whole revolution, though now it has, by means of that slow movement to which all the stars appear subject, deviated from the pole as much as about 25 degrees.

The polar star of the Phœnicians was the brilliant one of the first magnitude, β of the Little Bear; whereas, in Homer's time, the Greeks made use of a star in the Great Bear,

> from its never being dipped in the floods of ocean,

as their guide in navigation. For 3,000 years before our era β in the Little Bear was nearer the pole than any other large star. It was the largest, in the *square* of that constellation, and the Greeks called it *Phoinikē* or *he Phoinikē;* but it was not near enough to the pole to serve as a guide to navigators, before the middle of the third millennium before Christ (about 2500 B.C.); and from the olden times, long before Homer, the brightest star in the constellation of the Great Bear was the pole-star of the Phœnicians. (*Bunsen: Egypt, iv.* 349.)

The various groups of stars that we see in the heavens have always exhibited the same appearances and configurations, and the stars in each group, as well as the different groups, occupy the same relative positions now that they did in the most ancient times. No changes have taken place in the general arrangement; at least, none but minute changes, which are not sensible to the eye, unaided by instruments.

These "radiant rulers, bringing winter and summer to mortals," were, if not the very first, at least among the earliest objects of human worship. They were the "heavenly host" of the Hebrews, "the Sons of God, who sang the Jubilee of Creation." Oannes, Oe or Aquarius rose from the Red Sea to impart science to the Babylonians; and the Bright Bull legislated for India and Crete; while the Persians invoked the stars Tistṛya and Vanaṇt; and everywhere in the East the stars were imagined to be animated intelligences, presiding over human weal and woe; the potentates and "Holy Ones" of heaven.

Among the array of sparkling points which to the first men the superincumbent vault revealed, occupying the night with their unspeakable beauty, most of them apart and alone, but many grouped into graceful clusters, none presented an appearance so strikingly beautiful and splendid as the stars of Orion and Taurus, recognizable at once by their great brilliance and the peculiarity of their arrangement.

Before calendars were known, the rising and setting of the constellations were the chief guides of the herdsmen and shepherds, and the tiller of the ground, in determining the progress of the seasons; and this made men in general much more familiar with the appearances of the stars than they are now. I found that the Comanches knew and had a name for the Great Bear.

Hesiod says:

> But when Orion and Sirius have come into the middle of the heavens, and the rosy-fingered Aurora has beheld Arcturus, then, O Perses, gather all the grapes home.
>
> But when, at length, the Pleiades and the Hyades, and the Mighty Orion have set, then be mindful of ploughing in time.
>
> But if the desire of dangerous navigation has possessed you, when the Pleiades, flying the fierce strength of Orion, have at length set in the dark sea, then surely storms of wind will blow on every side.
>
> At the rising of the Pleiades, the daughters of Atlas, begin to reap; but when they set, to plough. These stars become invisible for forty days and nights; but they appear again, as the year rolls round, when first the scythe is sharpened.

Orion ['Ωρίων] with its great stars Betelguese, Bellatrix, Rigel and the three Kings in his girdle, and Aldebaran, Sirius, Procyon, Castor and Pollux, occupy the same quarter of the heavens, and excel in splendour every other assemblage of stars, while above the Pleiades are, forming a triangle, the great stars Algol, Algenib and Almaack in Perseus and Andromeda. And it is reasonable to suppose that to these stars and to Arcturus, Regulus, Antares, Vega and Spica, the souls of the ancient Ṛishis had been transferred, when they exchanged earth for the skies.

The great stars also differ in colour, and the difference is perceptible to the eye. Sirius, Vega, Altair and Spica are white: Aldebaran, Arcturus and Betelguese are red: Capella and Procyon are yellow. And these differences are far more striking, in countries where the atmosphere is clear and dry, not humid and hazy. In Syria, for instance, one star shines like an emerald, another like a ruby; and the whole heavens sparkle as with various gems.

The systematic arrangement of the stars in constellations, is of course comparatively modern; and more or less stars may, in later days, have been assigned to particular groups. But some must always have been the same—the Pleiades, the Hyades, Castor and Pollux, Capella and her Kids; the Three Kings of Oriōn, and the Great Bear; and to each of these groups, the idea of unity must have been attached.

Comets were no doubt considered to be flaming bodies, different in that respect from the stars and planets, which, without flame, emitted only light, visiting the heavens at intervals. There is, I think, no allusion to them

in the Vedas. Seneca says that neither Eudoxus nor Conon, both of whom had diligently studied the astronomy of the Egyptians and collected such accounts of eclipses as had been preserved by that people, makes any mention of comets; but that Epigenes and Apollonius of Myndus, who had studied among the Chaldæans, did speak of those bodies; one of them saying that they were considered as bodies kindled in the air, and the other, that they were of the number of planets, or wandering stars. There is not a word in Ptolemy regarding comets. The Pythagoreans held them to be nothing more than planets, reappearing after long intervals, and approaching the sun as near as the planet Mercury does. A thousand years after the time of Pythagoras, Olympiodorus considered a comet to be a sublunary body, consisting of dry vapours set on fire by the sun. In the Vedic age, it is not likely that any speculation as to their nature was indulged in.

In the writings of the ancients, we find no hint that comets then inspired any of the terror with which they were afterwards viewed.

Meteors, shooting with a brilliant light athwart the sky, were, like the lightning, to the Vedic people, a manifestation of the celestial fire. The Aurora, with its brilliant and many-coloured streamers and banners of light unrolled over the Northern sky, was another of these manifestations, of the cause whereof, if they ever thought of causes, they were profoundly ignorant. They had no means of ascertaining the causes of anything, and undoubtedly accepted each phenomenon as a sufficient cause of itself. They were all manifestations of Agni, like the parti-coloured, brilliant flames of the domestic and sacrificial fire.

The rainbow with its seven colours, with vast and beautiful arch spanning the sky, was a phenomenon for which they could account as little as the Hebrews, whose books taught that it was set in the heavens as the token of a covenant made with men, that He would not again destroy the earth by a flood.

It is asserted in the ancient poems entitled the Chaldæan Oracles, that the universe was divided into seven distinct spaces or worlds. The Father, it is said in the Poem on the Heavens,

> made seven worlds, including them under a globular form: he made the great host of inerratic stars: he also placed the earth in the centre, the waters within its bosom, and the air above it.

Psellus, the commentator, considered these worlds as concentric spheres, which he defines, the first, or the exterior of the universe, being the pure empyreal fire, the next three ethereal, and the last three the spheres of the fixed stars, the seven planetary spheres, and the sublunary region.

THE VEDIC GODS.

The Vedic Gods resolve themselves into a mere collection of terms, all denoting at first different aspects of the same idea. (*Cox, ii.* 110.)

The consciousness that all the Deities are but different names of one and the same Godhead breaks forth, indeed, here and there in the Veda; but it is far from being general. One Poet, for instance, says (*Rig-V. i.* 164. 46),

> They call him Indra, Mitra, Varuṇa, Agni; then he is the beautiful-winged heavenly Garutmat; that which is one, the wise call it in different manners; they call it Agni, Yama, Mâtariswain.

And again (*Rig-V. x.* 114. 5):

> Wise Poets make the beautiful-winged, though he is one, manifold by names. (*Müller: Chips: i.* 29.)

That *One*, of which Müller and the hymns that he quotes, speak, is not *God* or the *Godhead*, in any sense that we now attach to either word. There is no trace in the Veda of any conception of a God, existing by himself before the universe became, and of that universe the generator, maker or creator. The Vedic Poets never rose to the idea of such a God, or of a being like the Zarathustrian Ahura Mazda. Their intellectual vision never reached beyond the universe, or sought a First Cause for it, independent of it.

Agni was *fire*, the *actual* fire, produced by attrition, of which *flame*, *light* and *heat* were manifestations; the animal heat that was vitality; the celestial fire, manifested in the lightning, the Aurora, the rainbow, the comets, the light and heat emitted from the sun, and the light alone from the luminaries of the night; and all these luminaries were but embodied forms of Agni.

But also Agni is the invisible Spirit of Fire, and as such invested with personality and intelligence, with power, wisdom and beneficence. In a single hymn (*ii.* 6), he is besought to accept a log as an offering. He is the youngest of the Gods, as the earthly fire. He is the messenger of the Gods (bringing down the celestial fire, and mediator, because by him sacrifice is effected). He is also son of strength, conqueror of horses, high-born, loving songs, delighting in riches, lord and giver of wealth, wise and powerful, giving rain, invincible strength, and food; the sage, who goes wisely between heaven and earth, like a friendly messenger between two hamlets. He is intelligent, and is asked to perform the sacrifice, and sit down on the consecrated grass. Such is Müller's translation (*Chips i.* 34).

But only a paraphrase or commentary can express the real meaning of the text, and be indeed a translation. The phrase "high-born" evidently means, originating above the earth, and passing to and fro between the earth and sky. I doubt whether the words "wise" and "intelligent" correctly reproduce the original. "Son of strength" may mean that the strength of the hands produces it by attrition of two pieces of wood, of which the Veda often speaks. He grants riches, because his light and heat, flowing from the sun, cause the earth to produce food for men and animals. He delights in riches, because he delights to cause the earth to produce riches, and, by thus furnishing food, the cattle and horses that were then the chief wealth. Manifested as lightning, he shatters the clouds and produces rain. His warmth, and the food whose production he causes, and which he cooks, give strength; and as the material fire he performs the sacrifice and becomes manifest and visible on the grass. How he is conqueror of horses, is more difficult to say. Probably the phrase should be subduer or driver of the horses of the chariots of the luminaries.

The sun, in the Veda, is frequently called the "racer," the "runner," or simply the "horse," and is often represented as standing on his car, drawn by two, seven or ten horses. These are called *Haritas*, and are always feminine. Various epithets are applied to them, as, joyful, many-coloured, bathed in dew, beautifully-stepping, with lovely backs, etc.

In the Ninth Ashṭaka we read,

> The sun has yoked the *ten* Harits for his journey:

in the First,

> the *seven* Harits bring thee, O bright sun, on thy cart;

and in the Fourth,

> The *seven* Harits bring him, the sun, the spy of the world.

These Harits also are sometimes called the *seven sisters* (*vii.* 66. 15), and in one passage they appear (*ix.* 86. 37) as

> the Harits with beautiful wings.

In fact, *Ârvat*, meaning, "quick, running, vehement," is often applied to the sun, in the Veda, so that sometimes it stands as the name of the sun, and sometimes, as a noun means a horse or his rider. It originally means the *swift* sun, but it set other ideas vibrating, which gradually caused the sun to be called a horse or horseman. One of the Poets (*i.* 163. 2) praises the bright Vasus, because

> out of the sun they have wrought a horse.

In *i.* 163. 3, the Poet tells the sun,

> Thou, O Ârvat (*horse*) art Aditya (the sun);

and in *vi.* 12. 6, Agni is invoked by the same name:

> Thou, O Ârvat, keep us from evil report! O Agni, lighted with all the fires! Thou givest treasures.

Sometimes the horses (Müller thinks, the rays of the sun) are called not only *haritas*, but *rohîtas* or *rôhitâs*, and *ârushîs* or *arushâs*.

> Yoke the Arushis to thy cart, O bright Agni! The Harîts, the Rohîts. With them, bring the Gods to us.

These may originally have been mere adjectives, meaning "white," "bright" and "brown," but they soon grew to be the names of certain animals, belonging to certain Gods. Thus we read (*ii.* 10. 2),

> Hear thou, the brilliant Agni! My prayer; whether the two black horses bring thy cart, or the two brown (*rôhitâ*), or the two white horses (*arushâ*); [and, *vii.* 42. 2]: Yoke the Harits and the Rohîtas or the Arushâs which are in thy stable.

Ârushî, by itself, means "cow," and the Arushîs or bright cows belong more particularly to the dawn. Instead of saying "The day dawns," the old Poets of the Veda frequently say, "The bright cows return." The Arushîs, like the Harits, were sometimes termed *the Seven Sisters* (*x.* 5. 5),

> He brought the Seven Sisters, the Arushîs.

Arushâ, a masculine, is, in the Veda, one of the most frequent epithets or names of the sun. It is used in the sense of *bright* (*vii.* 75. 6):

> The red bright horses are seen, bringing to us the brilliant dawn.

Ârushâ is always the young sun, in the Veda, who drives away the dark night (*vii.* 71. 1):

> Night goes away from her sister, the Dawn, the dark one opens the path for Arushâ.

Once he is called the bright Sun with beautiful wings.

> *iv.* 15. 6. Him, the God Agni, they adorn and purify every day like a horse that has run his race; like Arushâ, the bright Sun, the young child of Dyaus.
>
> *vi.* 49. 2. Let us worship Agni, the child of heaven, the son of strength, Arushâ, the bright light of the sacrifice.
>
> *ii.* 38. 6. Before the night has half finished her weaving, the sun rises again. Then Agni goes to all men and all houses; his light is powerful, and his mother, the Dawn, gives him the best share, the first worship among men.

Mr. Cox says (*i. Mythol.* 48):

> The root *vah*, to "convey" (the Latin *veho*), gave a name to the horse, to the flame of fire, and to the rays of the sun. Metaphor, without which there can be no growth or expansion of language, soon changed the rays of the sun into horses. But these horses, *Vahni*, had yet another epithet, *Harit*, which signified at first the brilliance produced by fat and ointment. "Glittering with fat" became a title for the horses, or flames, of Agni. By a like process of metaphor, the rays of the sun were changed into golden hair, spears and lances, and rays of light.

But if it is the *rays* of the sun, that are the Harits, his horses, why are they of a definite number, seven or ten?

The writers of Aitareya-brahmana could still say,

Agni, is all the Deities, Vishṇu is all the Deities.

Light and heat manifest themselves in all.

We are all familiar with the philosophical doctrine that God is all his manifestations, the whole Deity manifesting itself limitedly and in one particular phase: but no manifestation is all of Deity, nor gives any cognizance of the Very Deity. It is the whole soul of a man that thinks a thought; but no one thought nor any number of thoughts are the whole soul.

The root of this doctrine is in the old Aryan fire-worship. All light and heat and all luminaries and meteors and luminous appearances, the lightning, the Zodiacal light and the Aurora, the Galaxy, the dawn, are manifestations of Agni, the fire, the essential, unmanifested principle, which manifests itself in flame, light and heat, including the vital warmth, which to them was life itself. Fire was not, to the Aryans, the symbol of the First Cause. To say that, as Narrien does, is to impute to those simple herdsmen the idea of a much later age.

Rig-V. ii. 1. 3. Thou, Agni, art Indra, bountiful to the excellent: Thou art Vishṇu, the wide-stepping, the adorable.

vii. 20. 2. All divine power, like that of the sky, was completely communicated to thee, Indra, by the Gods, when thou, O impetuous Deity, associated with Vishṇu, didst slay Vṛitra Ahi, who shut up the waters.

The "divine power, like that of the sky," here spoken of, is plainly the energy of the celestial fire, as it manifests and displays itself in action, as the lightning. Its effects must often have been seen, upon trees and other objects struck by it; and it was supposed, by shattering the dark clouds, to set loose the imprisoned rain.

v. 3. 1. Thou, Agni, art Varuṇa, when thou art born [i. e., manifested outwardly, thou art Varuṇa]; thou art Mitra, when thou art kindled [i. e., Mitra is fire burning, blazing, flaming]; son of strength, in thee reside all the Gods [i. e., thou art the essence and principle of all of them, and they are all manifestations of thee]: Thou art Indra, to the man who sacrifices [i. e., Indra, when manifested as the sacrificial fire].

Thou art Aryaman, when thou, self-controlled, possessest the secret name of the maidens. [When self-limited and so by limitation manifested, thou art called by the mystic name of the maidens. These, whatever luminaries they are, are in some way connected with the luminary called Aryaman.]

Satapatha Brahmana xi. I. 6.

The man who became Prajâpati is the same as this Agni who is kindled on the altar. [What *man* became Prajâpati? There is no deification of men in the Veda. The meaning must be that it is the same Agni that burns on the altar, which exercises specific functions and is invested with individuality and a person, as Prajâpati.]

Prajâpati is *Daksha*. He is also, Mr. Cox says, time and death.

The Gods were afraid of this ender, Death, the year which is Prajâpati, lest he should by days and nights bring on the end of our life.

It is *light* that in one sense constitutes time; for without light there would be no measurement of time, no days and years. Prajâpati was, probably, this measure of time, light, fulfilling this office. Time is indeed the ender. The returning days at last bring with them death; and thus light, making the days, becomes, as it were, the author of death.

He is Rudra, he is Siva, he is Agni, he is Saivâ, the all-conquering; he is Indra, he is Vayu, he is the Aṣwins, he is the lightning, he is the moon, he is Iswara, he is Sûrya, he is Varuṇa, he is death the ender, he is time; he is darkness and night and the days; he is the months and the half-months of the seasons, the morning and evening twilight, and the year.

If we collect from the Veda, and group together under different heads, what the hymns contain in respect to the characteristics of Agni and his relations to the sacrifices, to men, and to the other Deities, we may learn what it was, that, as him, they worshipped, and be prepared to make, more intelligently, the same inquiry as to the other Gods.

As *simply* fire, he is termed the radiant,

the constant illuminator of truth, increasing thine own dwelling.

This, Wilson thinks, is the *chamber* in which fire-worship is performed. The phrase "illuminator of truth" he does not endeavour to explain. As an English phrase, it has simply no meaning. May not the phrase rendered by it, have meant, whose light makes visible the *reality* of things, the material objects, by which men are surrounded, and which, but for the light which reveals them, would have for them, as it were, no real existence? I think that the word "truth" should be "the real" or "the actual," i. e., "material nature."

The phrase "increasing thine own dwelling," is easily explained by comparison with other passages, where the *habitation* of Agni is spoken of. Agni is *all* fire, wherever manifested. When kindled, by attrition or otherwise, he localizes himself, and *dwells* where he burns, as he does in a star or dawn; and spreading and extending, he increases continually the size of the place or space in which he manifests himself and dwells. I see no reference to the "fire-chamber." The sacrifice was generally in the open air; and a chamber would not be increased in size by the fire kindled in it.

Agni is generated by attrition, resplendent, ever young (for he never changes nor grows feeble, nor decays), and wise, radiant, remover of disease, bright, the purifier, shining with pure radiance. (Whether the word "wise" is a correct interpretation, I doubt. Knowledge of the actualities of the world, comes by means of the light which makes them visible to us; and it was a natural idea that the fire knew and saw all things which the light made visible. It searches and penetrates into the most secret corners and intricate ways, and may be said to know all things.)

He abides in the waters, for he illuminates them also, so that the eye can look into the depths of the streams and lakes; and in them the stars seem to dwell at night, and the sun by day.

> Lord of Sustenance [the Poet says], assume thy vestments, and offer this our sacrifice.

His vestments are the visible shape which he assumes, of flame, to manifest himself withal: and he is Lord of Sustenance, because his light and heat cause the earth to produce, and by his heat, what is produced is cooked for the support of life. Moreover, his heat is the vital force, the life and sustainer of life of all living beings.

He is vast, illimitable, smoke-bannered, of variant splendour, brilliant-rayed, distributer of riches as the waves of a river are parted by interjacent isles; the word rendered "riches" probably meaning his wealth of light, divided into different portions and manifestations, and among the various luminaries.

He is manifold, for the benefit of all the world, intelligent, the offspring of two mothers, and reposing in various ways for the use of man; pre-eminent over the world, become manifest to the worshipper. He is sapient and intelligent, because he explores everywhere, and sees all that is and all that is done. For the benefit of the world, he is manifested in many ways and by many orbs, as flame, light and heat, and the vital force. He is the offspring of the heavens and the earth, and becomes fixed and stationary in various ways for the use of man. From above the world, from the skies, he is asked to come down, and become manifest in flame to the sacrifice.

"It announced Heaven to man;" i. e., it enabled him to discern the sky. It enables the herdsman who has followed the wrong path, to retrace his steps, and find the true way. It sustains life, by furnishing food, and by cooking many things otherwise unfit to be eaten.

Irreproachable, a vigilant God, in the proximity of thy parents. For nothing is so pure, so free from the grossness of matter, so immaculate, stainless, taintless, of such tenuity and subtility, as fire and flame. It is watchful, vigilant to gain an advantage, to evade men's watchfulness, and extend and encroach, is open-eyed and wary. "In the proximity of thy parents," must mean, in intimate connection with, latent and inherent in, the heavens or sky, and the earth.

He is styled "four-eyed" Agni, blazing as the protection of the worshipper: and the meaning of the expression "four-eyed," must allude to something that belongs to the ordinary fire of the sacrifice; perhaps to the different colours of the flame; or perhaps four fires were lighted, at the cardinal points.

> All-wise [i. e., all-beholding and knowing], he instructs the disciple, and defines the limits of the horizon.

"Instructing the disciple," probably meant showing the way over the plains or through the forests, to one who had not yet learned the features of the country, or to the young herdsman.

> The flames of thee, who art mighty and eternal, spread around thy rays, and reach to the heavens.

Nothing is more irresistible than fire, and not being subject to decay, there are no limits to its existence. When it consumes the forests, it seems to flame upward to the sky.

> The good and durable actions which the Gods perform, are all aggregated in thee [i. e., are manifestations of thyself].

From Agni emanate, through the luminaries of the sky, all the beneficent influences of light and heat, by which those luminaries act upon the earth and living beings.

> Bright with thine own radiance [i. e., thy brightness being thine own manifestation]; sit on the sacred grass: shine forth: emit the curling and graceful smoke. Agni, with the burning rays; whose rays pre-eminently shine [i. e., shine far above us, in the sky].
>
> Manu detained thee, Agni, light to the various races of mankind.

Denizen of the sky, he was domiciled on earth by Manu, as Prometheus gave men the fire from heaven. His flames are luminous, potent, fear-inspiring, and not to be trusted.

He is "the immortal sustainer of the universe;" for the fire, light and heat are the very life of Nature. He is *associated* with Ushas and the Aṣwins; for it is his light that they manifest.

He is "the radiant-haired, whose flames give delight;" "strength-generated," "son of strength," because produced by attrition: "quick-hearing, widely-renowned;" quick, perhaps, to hear the coming wind; and "widely-renowned," probably, meant celebrated and adored everywhere.

"By suitable paths he has made the firmament:" an expression which, taken literally, has little or no meaning. How could it be imagined that fire had made the firmament? The meaning must have been that, manifesting himself in light, at such points, in such directions, and by such movements as pleased him, he made the array of luminaries in the sky, without which there would be no visible sky, but only intense impenetrable darkness.

> "Armed with the flame, and vivified by the wind, with all his might, in a volume of fire, he rushes triumphant through the forest: swiftly devouring it, he climbs the dry wood: his blaze, consuming, runs like a race-horse, and his roaring sounds as if high in the air.

He is asked to be "a shelter to those who praise him;" to "protect his worshipper from sin;" by which word, rendered sin, was probably meant being lost in the plain or forest.

He is "rich with righteous acts," and is therefore asked to come early in the morning. The phrase, "righteous acts" applied to fire or light, is simple nonsense: but with light and heat, Agni abounds with effects that are good and excellent and beneficial to men.

> All other fires are branchings of Agni. In him, being immortal, they rejoice. He is manifested as Vaiswânara, the navel of men, supporting them like a column deeply planted. Treasures [i. e., potencies, powers, the manifestations of Agni], were deposited in him. He slew the stealer of the waters, and sent these down on the earth. All the Gods engendered him, in the form of night, for the venerable sage: and, as him, Agni, the head of heaven and navel of the earth, became ruler over both earth and heaven. Vaiśwánara by his greatness is all men, and is to be worshipped as the diffuser of manifold light.

What was intended by the Agni Vaiśwánara, can only be conjectured. He is "engendered by all the nocturnal luminaries, for the venerable sage," a meaningless phrase. He is "the navel of *men*," which is nonsense, "supporting them like a column." The word rendered "*men*" we have noticed elsewhere, means simply individuals, and in that sense is applied to luminaries. The navel of these luminaries was probably that through which they were imagined to receive their sustenance of light. Agni is styled the head of the heavens, perhaps because the luminaries of heaven are its eyes, and the navel of the earth, because fire and light are its life.

Vaiṣwânara was supposed to have some direct agency in causing rains. He lighted both earth and heaven, by his magnitude equalled all the luminaries together, and diffused manifold light. By him must have been intended, either the lightning, or the Aurora, or else Agni in his character and office of manifester of light in the darkness; i. e., Agni as light alone.

Agni is

> the kind kinsman of the waters . . . . he breathes amid the waters like a sitting swan . . . . Awakened at the dawn [it is said in this connexion], he restores consciousness to men. Born from the waters, like an animal with coiled-up limbs, he became enlarged, and his light flowed afar.

This is evidently a description of day coming from the ocean. Neither fire, light nor heat can be said to come from the water or be in it, or be kinsman of it, except in the sense that day and the sun rise out of it.

> He tosses about his rays, like streams of water. The rays commingle, visible in the sky. He is born in the woods, and hides in the hollows. He upholds the earth and sky, and *props up* heaven with true *prayers*.

It is not likely that this phraseology in the least degree reproduces the real meaning of the original. How fire *props up* the sky with *prayers*, the most vivid imagination would find it difficult to conceive. The fire, which seemed inherent like a soul, in all Nature, was regarded as its principle and source of life, activity and movement. The spheres were fed by it, and from them the earth received nourishment and sustenance. But it would be hard to find any meaning in the phrase, "Like the *unborn*, he *props up* the heaven with true *prayers*." "Like the unborn" probably means (or at least the words thus rendered mean), that Agni, not being anything produced by the earth or sky, but existing before them, or independent of them, gives them life and sustenance, by sending up to them the smoke and flame of the sacrifices.

> Radiant among the Gods, and in his single self comprehending the potencies of all of them. Born living in the dry wood, he who delights in the sacrificial chamber, has studded the sky with constellations. He assumes all celestial natures; is white-shining, extinguisher of the dawn, illuminator, is possessed of manifold light, and while filling the all with radiance, gives homes to men, and enables them to descry the forms of the objects that surround them.

In his essence, he is not perceptible by the senses, but is cognizable by the intellect alone. He is manifested as light. He is in everything, and everywhere, exercising beneficent influences; he rules the night, and is all-knowing, knowing the origin of Gods and men; for he is the source and origin of all the Gods, and all men owe to him their vitality. He was before any of these were, and therefore could be said to know their origin.

Invested with actuality, as a visible fire, everything augments him. The air makes him bright, and to shine in every mansion. He bestows light on his daughter, Ushas, the dawn.

It is the golden-haired Agni who shakes the clouds, when the rain is poured down. As the lightning, he nourishes the world with the milk of the rain.

He is localized as the digestive agent in the human body, as the vital principle: then among the *seven conspicuous mothers;* and, thirdly, the associated generate him, delighting in the ten quarters of space, to produce rain, or to send down light upon the earth.

His radiance is undecaying, his rays are everywhere visible and bright, penetrating and pervading everywhere. He is three-headed and seven-rayed. For he is flame, light and heat. These are his manifestations or heads; and passing through a prism, his light is of seven colours. He is

> the living breath of three-fold Nature, co-extensive with the sky, perennial heat.

When Professor Wilson speaks of "producing by attrition the far-seeing, single-minded, intelligent, immortal, radiant-limbed Agni," we plainly enough see that these English epithets are ludicrously inapplicable to a fire kindled in the woods by rubbing two sticks together. We suspect at once that "far-seeing" should be "shining to a distance," that "single-minded" should be "acting for, or applied to, a single purpose;" and that the words "intelligent" and "immortal" probably express ideas to us, which nothing suggested to the makers of these hymns. Nothing shows that they had any idea of endless existence: and I do not believe that they meant to ascribe the human intelligence to Agni, or wisdom or truth, in the meaning that these words have to *us.*

Latent in the dry wood, produced by attrition from it, and manifested in the sky, distinct names were given to Agni.

Strong-toothed, he attacks and devours the forest; unimpeded, he traverses the sky and earth. He causes the rivers to flow, by producing rains. Men have cognizance of him as white, in the chief place of his manifestation. That is, he is manifested as light, and not as flame, in the firmament. As such, he is Vaiṣwânara Agni, in worshipping whom, air, earth and sky unite. Shining as such with never diminishing splendour, he pours light over both the heavens and the earth. It is he also, who shines resplendent as the sun. He shines before the dawn comes; he is latent in the waters, and enters into the nascent plants.

As possessed of various faculties, and performing many functions, Agni is, further, the high priest of the sacrifice, because it is the fire that consumes the offering. He is the ministrant, who presents the oblation; the invoker of the Gods. He is the messenger of the Gods, because his light and heat come from them to the earth, and he conveys to them the smoke and smell of the sacrifice. He is the bearer of offerings, beloved by many. He is the possessor of wealth, because he is the bestower of it. He removes disease by drying up and dispersing its causes. He is the giver of rewards, i. e., of benefits and the returns of labour; the benefactor of the universe; the giver of strength, children and long life. He is like a loving father to a son, a kinsman to a kinsman, a friend to a friend. He is the lord of men, the gracious, the chosen, the first of the immortals, the friend of the Deities; the giver of delight, the domestic guardian of mankind. He is the permanent sustainer of the universe, exempt from death, preserver.

He is the protector in villages, the associate of man, placed in the East; the provider of dwellings, i. e., who supplies the wants of the household. He is the guest at sacrifices, to be valued as an affectionate friend. He is the friend of man, holding in his hand all wealth. He appropriates the prayers addressed to the eternal creator: i. e., he may be appropriately addressed as the eternal author of all life, since there is no other creator than he.

He has a visible existence as (is *like*, *Wilson*) the divine sun, who discerns all the material world (*all that is true*). He preserves by his influences in all encounters (or emergencies); manifested in Nature he is unchangeable; and in his essence, is the source of all comfort and enjoyment. In him is all existence.

> He is, as it were, the generator of men, as well as of heaven and earth. From him, creation has drunken in life; and yet he becomes manifested, in place and by limitation, where his glories are. It is he who, entering into the womb, procreates.

In this expression we catch the first glimpse of that which led to the Phallic worship. The instrument by which Agni, the vital principle, was conveyed into the womb, naturally enough became the symbol of that principle.

> He is the first of the Gods, and their nourisher, also, when he is kindled by man upon the altar.

He is the most wise, the creator, the son of strength, whose chariot is the lightning, his hair, flame, and his glory manifested on the earth. He is like a great ocean, everywhere. He goes to the vapours in the heavens; congregates the Divinities that are the vital airs; animates the waters, in the bright region above the sun, and in the atmosphere below. Like a horse, he conveys men's supplications to the Gods, and like a benefactor is affectionate and propitious, ministering at the sacrifices. He is the mediator between men and the Deities, the earth and the heavens. As the sun, he is the lover of the dawn. Enabling men to find their way, he preserves them from error and wandering astray, i. e., from sin. He consumes the foes of his worshippers, by which may perhaps be meant cold and storm.

He bestows faculties; because in perpetual darkness, men would have none, or the use of none. He is the guide of those who conciliate him by devotion. He is brilliant, beautiful, auspicious, righteous, and also destroyer: the enduring maker, the beholder of men; the purifier, and the king of men. Knowing the ascents of the sky, he travels between earth and heaven.

As connected with or related to particular Divinities, he is Deva (bright, shining, radiant). He is invoked to bring with him to the sacrifice, all the Divinities that awake with the dawn—Indra, Vayu, and the glories of Mitra, with them to drink the Soma, to arrange them and decorate them.

He is invoked to come with the Maruts (the winds), Divinities abiding in the radiant heaven above the sun.

He is invoked,

> that he may give us to the great Aditi, and that I may behold again my father and my mother.

The meaning of this we can only conjecture. The great Aditi may have been the great Nature Goddess, like the Egyptian Isis; and the whole may have been the expression of or longing to know to what powers, of generation and production, the universe owed its existence. For surely those old Poets must sometimes have thought that the material world must have had a beginning, and if a beginning, a cause or causes.

Agni was the first Angiras, Ṛishi, or Divinity. Thou, Vasu, it is said to him, hast worshipped the venerable Gods.

> The Deities Varuṇa, Mitra and Aryaman kindle thee, their messenger from of old.

Meaning, probably that the luminaries Varuña, Mitra and Aryaman light up in themselves, or blaze and shine with the light of Agni, which they have always sent down to the earth.

That Agni, whose rays Kanwa made more brilliant than the sun, is the blazing sacrificial fire. This the context shows.

Agni is "associated with Ushas and the Aṣwins." He is Vaiśwánara the lightning. As Yama, he is all that is and that will be born. Ushas, the dawn, is his daughter. He is chief of the Angirasas, and with him, Mitra and Varuṇa, the two kings, are invoked, to worship for the sacrificer.

> When Agni refreshes the world with rain, then Mitra, Aryaman, Varuṇa and the Encompassers, pierce through the envelope into the womb of the cloud. He abides with the seven conspicuous mothers; and the associated generate him, revelling in the ten quarters of space.
>
> By him, Mitra, Varuṇa and Aryaman are animated, for at his origin, they were all comprehended in him [in their wholeness, in all their functions]: he encompassing them as the felly of a wheel does the spokes.
>
> They have styled the sun, Indra, Mitra, Varuṇa, Agni. Agni is all the Divinities.
>
> He is Indra, the adorable Vishṇu. Thou Brahmaṇaspati art Brahmâ. He is the royal Varuṇa, the adorable Mitra, Aryaman. He is Rudra, the divine Savitṛi; and, to the offerer of the oblation, Aditi.
>
> Agni, Varuṇa, Mitra, Maruts, grant happiness, Gods!

It is impossible to doubt what Agni was, to the Aryan Poets. He was the Universal Fire, and as such the vital principle of the universe. And it is equally impossible to doubt that all the other Deities were but manifestations of him, phenomena or orbs of light.

Neither heaven nor earth could measure his greatness. He was *all* the fire, *all* the flame, *all* the light, and *all* the heat, in the earth and upon it, in the expanse, in its luminaries, and in the sky; and beyond them all in every direction.

And this all was regarded as *One*, as a unit, of which all portions were the outflowings or emanations, and the orbs were manifestations, each of them Agni himself, manifested and limited, in place and form.

From these ideas of self-limitation, of manifestation in place and form, by the luminaries, and of the invisible fire-essence or universal, the fire-spirit, becoming visible by manifestation, giving and preserving life, and blessing men with benefits, creating, preserving, and also consuming and destroying, came not only the idea of the Hindû Triad, and the emanation doctrines of the Kabbalah and the Gnostics, but all the great philosophical and religious doctrines of the later days, and of this day of ours.

It was the old Aryan thought that spoke, by the mouth of one of another race, in the sentences which became the creed of Christendom: Ἐν αὐτῷ ζωὴ ἦν, καὶ ἡ ζωὴ ἦν τὸ φῶς τῶν ανθρώπων; καὶ τὸ φῶς ἐν τῇ σκοτία φαίνει, καὶ ἡ σκοτία αὐτὸ οὐ καέλαβεν . . . . Ἦν τὸ φῶς τὸ ἀληθινὸν, ὃ φωτίζει πάντα ἄνθρωπον ἐξχόμενον εἰς τὸν κόσμον. . . .

> In him life was, and the life was the light of men; and the light shines in the darkness; and the darkness does not limit [or contain] it. . . . . It was the true light, which illuminates every man who comes into the world.

Plato, of that Greek race which seems to have been more purely Aryan than any other branch of the great family, or else to have intermixed with aboriginal races more nearly equal to itself, than the others did, says,

> The primary God must be free from works, and a king; but the Demiourgos must exercise government, going through the heavens. Through him comes this our condition; through him reason being sent down in efflux, holds communion with all who are prepared for it; God then looking down, and turning himself to each of us, it comes to pass, that our bodies live and are nourished, receiving strength from the outer rays which come from him.

And Philo, the Alexandrian Jew, born before, and living after, Christ, after recounting the four chief potencies of God, says:

> So that the Word is, as it were, the charioteer of the potencies, and he who utters it is the rider, who directs the charioteer how to proceed with a view to the proper guidance of the universe.

And, borrowing his ideas from the Greeks, he takes us at once back to the early Vedic thought. He says:

> And the invisible divine Reason, perceptible only by intellect, he calls the image of God. And the image of this image, is that light, perceptible only by the intellect, which is the image of the divine Reason, which had explained its generation. . . . . If any one were to call it universal light, he would not be very wrong; since it is from it that the sun and the moon, and all the other planets and fixed stars derive their due light, in proportion as each has power given to it; that immingled and pure light being obscured when it begins to change, according to the change from that which is perceptible by the intellect only, to that which is perceptible by the external senses.
>
> Even before the creation, God saw [Philo says], using himself as light . . . . When the beams of the light-giving God, immingled as they are, and entirely pure, and visible at the greatest distance, shone upon the eye of the soul, being comprehensible only by the intellect, then the eye of the soul could see nothing else.

Agni is *wise;* and Philo says,

> It is owing to wisdom that what is wise is contemplated; but not only is wisdom *like* light, the instrument of seeing; but it also beholds itself. Thus, in God, is the archetypal model of the sun, and the sun itself is only its image and copy; and he who shews all things, is the only all-knowing being.
>
> He to whom all things are known, who illuminates the universe by the most brilliant of all lights, Himself.
>
> We must understand that the expression, Yehŭah was seen by Abraham, has not the meaning that the Cause of all things shone forth and became visible; but that some one of the potencies that are of him, viz., the regal potency [Malakoth], became visible to the light.

It will be easy for any one familiar with the ancient philosophies to find passages in abundance, in which the ideas of the Aryan hymns are developed into doctrines, and became articles of faith or tenets of philosophy. We need not cite them here.

As the *Zend-Avesta* contains the development of an advance in the Aryan religion, earlier than the Veda, and retained the adoration of fire and light, with that of the creator, Ahura Mazda, we may naturally expect to find in it ideas corresponding with those of the Veda. In *Fargard xviii.* we find:

> 43. For the first third of the night, the fire of Ahura Mazda asks the master of the house for protection: 'Stand up, O master of the house!'
>
> 44. 'Put on thy clothes, wash thy hands, seek fire-wood and bring it hither to me, make me shining with the pure fire-wood, with washed hands.'
>
> 45. 'To me might the Azis, created by the Dævas come, who appears, to snatch me from the world.'
>
> 46. For the second third of the night, the fire of Ahura Mazda asks the husbandman for protection: 'O active husbandman, lift thyself up!'
>
> 47. 'Put on thy clothes, wash thine hands, seek fire-wood, bring it hither to me, make me shining with the pure fire-wood, with washed hands, else the Azis created by the Dævas might come, who appears to snatch me from the world.'
>
> 48. For the third third of the night, the fire asks the holy Çraosha for protection: 'O holy Çraosha, beautiful!'
>
> 49. 'Then he brings me to the fire-wood of the corporeal world, to the purified with washed hands.'
>
> 50. 'Else might Azis created by the Dævas come hither, who appears to snatch me from the world.'
>
> 56. 'Whoso brings pure fire-wood to the fire of Ahura Mazda, with washed hands,'
>
> 57. 'Him will the fire bless, contented without hate and satisfied.'

And, *Vispered viii.:*

> 21. Thee, the Fire, the son of Ahura Mazda, the pure, lord of purity, we praise.

Yaçna lxi. is an invocation to Fire, vowing to it offering and praise, as son of Ahura Mazda.

> Give me, O Fire, son of Ahura Mazda [it cries], swift brightness, swift nourishment, swift blessings of life, greatness in holiness, fluency for the tongue, but for the soul, sense and understanding . . . . then manly courage . . . . well nourished, heavenly posterity, ... which grows up, is enduring, pure from crime and manly . . . . May I attain good reward, good renown, good sanctification for the soul . . . . We praise the holy fire, the strong, the warrior.

PHILOSOPHICAL DEFINITIONS.

I have spoken of Agni as being, according to the Aryan idea, a "universal," and of his "hypostases" or "persons;" of "emanations" and "manifestations." It may not be amiss, for general readers, to mark more definitely the meanings, in philosophy, of these and some other terms; since I may thus enable them to gain a clearer conception of my understanding of the Vedic ideas.

I understand them to have conceived of Agni as a *substance*, in the philosophical meaning of that term, and as a *Universal* substance, everywhere diffused and existing, and nowhere manifested except partially.

Spinoza says,

> I understand by *substance*, that which is in itself and is conceived of by itself; that is to say, that the conception whereof can be formed, without there being need of the conception of another thing.

Substance is defined to be, "that which *is* and abides." It may be derived from *subsistens* (*ens per se subsistens*), that which subsists of or by itself; or from *substans* (*id quod sub-stat*), that which *lies under* qualities. But in Greek, "substance" is denoted by *οὐσία*, *being:* so that that which truly *is*, or "essence," seems to be the proper meaning of *substance*.

Locke says,

> The idea, then, we have, to which we give the name of 'substance,' being nothing but the supposed but unknown support of these qualities we find existing, which we imagine cannot subsist, *sine re substante*, without something to support them, we call that support, *substantra*, which, according to the true import of the word is, in plain English, standing under or upholding.

Dr. Hampden has said,

> Substance, in its logical and metaphysical sense, is that nature of a thing which may be conceived to remain, when every other nature is removed or abstracted from it—the ultimate point in analyzing the complex idea of any object.

I do not propose to enter into the subtleties of metaphysics, in regard to substance, considered by itself, with all its accidents, attributes and qualities abstracted or eliminated. I wish only to find a word, by which I may express the Aryan idea.

Conceive of a soul or spirit, not resident in a body, but indefinitely extended, a veritable, intelligent, but immaterial, being, of which, in itself, we can have no cognition. Conceive it thinking, and that the utterances of its thoughts are not sounds or words, but fire, flame, light and heat, and that are all manifestations and visible revealings of its Self. *It*, the substance that is behind them, *is* each and all of them. Before manifestation they have no separate existence, but only exist as indivisible parts of its Self. They are, in metaphysical language, "subsistences;" *subsistentia* being "a substantial *mode*, added to a singular nature, and constituting a *suppositum* along with it. It means (*i.*) the thing *itself*, the *suppositum;* hence we call the three Persons of the Trinity three *hypostases* or *subsistences;* (*ii.*) the *mode*, added to the singular nature, to complete its existence; this is the metaphysical sense." *Fire*, as perceptible by the senses, *flame*, *light* and *heat*, are subsistences or hypostases of the invisible Substance or Soul, and, before manifested, are in and parts of its unity.

This is identically the idea of Philo and the Gnostics, according to which, the Supreme Being is the Primitive Light, or Archetype of Light, source from which the rays emanate, which illuminate souls. The Logos or Word, is his image, a form more brilliant than fire, which is not pure light. This Word abides in God, and is the vehicle by which God acts in the universe. The potencies of God were the ideas of Plato hypostasized; and so the visible manifestations of Agni were his potencies constituted into Persons or Deities.

According to the *Zend-Avesta*, the Supreme Being was so enveloped in his own glory, and his nature and attributes were so inaccessible to human intelligence, that he was, for it, only the object of a silent veneration. The first emanation from the eternal was the primitive light. From the Persian ideas those of the Kabbalah were borrowed; and its Ancient of Days or King of the Light, was the Archetype of Light of Persians, and the Brahm of the Hindūs, unapproachable by the intellect. In the Kabbalah, the universe is his revelation, and his holy splendour; and the Sephiroth or Ten Emanations, were his out-shinings, the first including all the others, and *being* all the others, and Ain-Soph, of whose Very Self no cognizance can be had, manifesting himself by each of them.

> The holy and blessed Being is the space in which the universe is contained, and not the universe the space in which he is contained—for God is not comprehended in anything; but he comprehendeth all things.—*Philo Judæus.*

The Gnostics adopted most of the doctrines of Philo, and especially these:

> that the Supreme Being is a Source of Lights, whose rays or emanations permeate the universe; that the lights and shadows, in all time hostile principles, dispute with each other the empire of the world; that the world has been created, not by the Supreme Being, but by a secondary agent, who is but his Word, and according to types that are but his Ideas, assisted by an Intelligence, a Sophia [wisdom],

> which is but one of his Attributes; that the visible world is the image of the invisible world; that the essence of the human soul is the image of God, and it existed before the body, etc. (*Matter: Histoire du Gnosticisme, i.* 75.)

All these ideas are to be found, in substance, in the Veda or the *Zend-Avesta.*

So, in the later Egyptian religion, the same Aryan ideas were incorporated. Amon was the Pleroma, comprehending all things in himself, and the Light, for he was the God-Sun. He created nothing, for all things emanated from him. His image was necessarily the representation of the principal attributes of the Divinity, attributes which the other Gods possessed only in part, being themselves only so many manifestations of the Supreme Being. (*Matter: Hist. du Gnost. i.* 84.)

Saint Ignatius said, in his Epistle to the Magnesians,

> There is one single God, who has manifested himself by his Son, which is the eternal Word, which has not issued forth from silence; and which has fully satisfied him who sent him.

In all the Gnostic systems, the Eternal Nameless Deity at first kept contained and concealed in himself the plenitude of his perfections, and when he displayed and manifested them, there resulted therefrom as many particular existences, all analogous to himself, *and all himself still:* and these developments did not change his manner of being. He remained unchangeable at their head. These ideas, conceptions, manifestations of the Divinity were so many *creations,* so many *beings,* who were all *God,* who were nothing without him, but were far more than what we call *ideas.* They emanated from and re-entered into God. (*Matter: Hist. du Gnost. i.* 409.)

So the Christian Tertullian held, that God was concealed and inaccessible, and did not reveal Himself to man in the plenitude of his Divinity, but according to the strength of the human intelligence, being revealed by his Son; as we cannot see the sun in its proper substance but only in its rays:

> *ut invisibilem patrem intelligamus pro plenitudine majestatis, visibilem vero filium agnoscamus pro modulo derivationis; sicut nec solem nobis contemplari licet, quantium ad ipsam substantiam summam quæ est in cœlis, radium ejus toleramus oculis pro temperaturâ portionis, quæ in terram unde porrigitur.* (*Adv. Marc. ii.* 27.)

The Word of God he considered as a result, an ulterior consequence of the divine Reason (*quia non sermonalis a principis, sed rationalis Deus*). But both were in the beginning with God, the Word being included in the

Reason, and this soon to be spoken by the Word (*quæ per sermonem moxerat dicturus*). (*Adv. Prax.* 7.)

And Origen, though he calls the Word a creature of God, yet describes the production of it as a natural outflowing from God: and if we admit an eternal manifestation of God in his revelation, as Origen held, it follows that the Force emanated from him must be considered as an eternal essence, different from God, the Father of this Force: for the Wisdom of God, which regulates all creation, does not consist in pure representations; it establishes a true Being, an essential Substance; it is a Creative Power, the Word-Creator, or the Son of God. (*Ritter: Hist. de la Philosophie Chretienne, translated by Trullard, i.* 443.)

Sabellius endeavoured to reconcile the doctrine of the Trinity with the Unity of God, by considering the differences of the Father, Son and Holy Spirit as differences of manifestation, and not of individual substance. (*Id. ii.* 12.)

The word "God," Leibnitz says, means sometimes the divine *substance*, sometimes a *Person* of the Divinity. (*Disc. de la Conformitè de la foi.* 22.)

The Emperor Julian, in his *Discourse on the Sun-King*, says that the material world has existed always, and will always exist,

> under the direction and immediate conservation of the fifth body, or solar principle, whence it emanates as a ray; then, ascending a degree, under the mediate influence of the intellectual world [the universe existing in idea, in the divine mind, and not yet revealed in actuality of existence]: and, finally, under that of a third cause, more ancient or more remote, which is the King of all beings, around which the vast whole adheres. This ulterior Cause, or Principle, which may be called the Being above our intelligence, or, if you please, the Prototype of all that is, or, still better, the Single Being, or the *One* (for this *One* must precede all the others, as being the Most Ancient); or, in fine, what Plato was accustomed to style 'The Being Supremely Good,' or 'The Supreme Good'—this Cause, I say, being the simple and unique model of what all beings can contain, of beauty, perfection, harmony and power, produced from itself, by its permanent and primordial energy, the Being like in everything unto Itself, the God-Sun, midway between the intellectual causes and the active intermediary principles.

This, he says, is Plato's Intelligent Reason, produced from the Supreme Good, engendered supremely good, and like unto this principle, because proceeding immediately from it. This Intelligent Reason, Plato says (*Republic, Book vi.*), sets the sun in place to preside over the visible world, as it, itself, presides in the intellectual space, over all that is of the domain of the spirit and thought.

> This first Universal Product [Julian continues], which I say emanated from the form of the primary and sovereign Good, because it was, from all eternity, in the proper substance of the latter, has received from it domination over all the intelligent

> Gods . . . . This second and Great Sun communicates and distributes to the immaterial or intelligent beings, the same benefits which it has received from the first, the Supreme Good, by which it has been set over them to rule them, though they have been produced like itself, and simultaneously with itself . . . . And a third sun is visible, that luminous disk which is, for all things, the Principle of Health or Conservation, and which communicates to visible beings all that we have said the Great Sun distributed to the intelligent and immaterial Gods . . . . Is not the light of our sun the incorporeal and divine form of that which is actively transparent? For that which is diaphanous or transparent, though having in itself all the elements, whereof it is the immediate form, is nevertheless neither corporeal nor mixed, and has none of the properties of bodies . . . .

Proclus says:

> The Gods themselves are beyond all beings, and are the measures of existence, because every being is contained in them, precisely as number is in monads. But beings proceed from them, some indeed [at the same time that they proceed from] abiding in them; but others, through their manifold nature, falling off from the unity of the Gods, in consequence of a diminution of essence.

Plotinus says,

> Fire emits heat; snow, cold, fragrant bodies, odours; and every organic thing, so far as it is perfect, begets something like itself. In the same way, the All-Perfect and Eternal, in the overflowing of his perfection, sends out from himself that which is also eternal, and, after him, the best, viz., the Reason or World-Intelligence, which is the immediate reflection and image of the Primal One . . . . This Reason contains in itself the whole ideal world, and the whole of true and changeless being . . . . As Reason flows from the Primal One, so the World-Soul eternally emanates from Reason, though the latter incurs no change thereby. The World-Soul, is the copy of Reason, permeated by it, and actualizing it in an outer world.

It is impossible not to see that the source and origin of all these philosophic ideas are in the Veda; and that they are essentially the same as those of the Aryan Poets in regard to Agni, his attributes, subsistences and manifestations. And, however unreal and merely nominal this invisible Fire-Power and Spirit may seem to be, like matter or substance conceived of as deprived of all its qualities, yet it was indeed the Deity, imperfectly conceived of, and not yet removed beyond the reach of all cognition of the intellect. It was God, wise, intelligent, powerful, beneficent, rewarder of the good and punisher of the evil, but not yet conceived of as First Cause, as creator, generator or producer of Nature and the universe. Eliminate from substance or matter all its qualities, and you have only what is called an intelligible, a *somewhat* not cognizable otherwise than by the intellect, and which has to our conception none of the reality of *being*, and is, in fact, but a hypothesis. God, considered as beyond the reach of all cognition, seems indeed to be but little more; and is, in essence, precisely what Agni was to our Aryan ancestors.

We do not find in the Veda any trace of the Zarathustrian doctrine of the twin principles of Good and Evil, Light and Darkness. The only powers of evil are those that hold back the rains, and against whom Indra contends. There is no trace of any worship of the Devil; nor does it seem that the Poets were in the least troubled by the great enigma of the existence of evil, under the dominion of a beneficent and omnipotent Deity. All the Deities of the Veda are beneficent ones; and the hymns breathe a singularly profound trust and confidence in their beneficent good will.

VEDIC THEOSOPHY.

All the expressions in the Veda, we see, I think, that have been supposed to indicate a conception in the minds of the Poets, of a single Supreme God, refer only to the One Universal, Fire. To this one principle or being, they certainly ascribe, not only energies and potencies, but also intelligence and benevolence. Otherwise, they could not have addressed prayers to him and invoked his aid and favour. They do not assign to him any form: and of *what* he was, they had, no doubt, as vague an idea as we have of what God or our soul, or even electricity, light or heat *is*. They knew him by his powers and effects; and in his essence he was to them what spirit is to us—a *somewhat*, this is *not* matter.

We still persist in ascribing *sex* to the Deity; and although philosophy tells us, and religion admits, that we can have no conception at all of the Deity itself, and cannot rightfully ascribe to it any of our own moral or intellectual qualities or powers, any more than we can our physical ones, we *do* ascribe them to him, and only admit that we can have no conception of his mode of being, and his nature as a spirit. We do unconsciously invest him with a human personality, in our own minds, with vague notions of shape and form, clinging there in spite of ourselves, connected with him, and morally and intellectually we make of him, and he is for us, only a being possessed of human faculties, infinite and perfect.

The Aryans so conceived of fire. It had for them the attributes of human personality and human energies and powers, affections, temper, and qualities.

They ascribed what we consider divine attributes, qualities and faculties, to this One Universal. Therefore it was veritably a God for them. It was immaterial and formless, it was omnipresent, not in our sense of infinite extension and presence everywhere in infinitive space, but as pervading the world and even extending beyond it. When their descendants in India, as Zarathustra had done in Bactria, conceived of a Deity superior to the fire and its manifestations, they only transferred to this ideal Being, of which they had no conception, the attributes of Aryan Agni.

Is it certain that their ideas of Agni as Deity were not nearer a belief in the true God, than the ideas of the Hebrews who worshipped Yehūah, as we find their anthropomorphic conceptions of him in their old books? Their real idea of God was expressed in the statement that he made man after his own image: and his characteristics in the Psalms and Prophets are those of Indra wielding the thunderbolt and punishing rebellious or Godless nations.

Müller protests against the imputation of polytheism, in the ordinary sense of the word, to our Aryan ancestors. And, as to their principal Deities, all Fire-Gods and Light-Gods, their faith was no more polytheism, than the emanation doctrines of the Gnostic or Kabbalah; or than the doctrine of the Logos and the Holy Spirit, as Persons, distinct from God the Father, and yet one with him.

The Aryan Poets had not attained to the conception of an anthropomorphic God; but they had invested Agni with the character of personality, and with the attributes of mind and spirit. They did not view him as creator and generator of the material universe, or as supreme mind entirely distinct from materiality. When the human mind had attained to that conception, it soon became discontented with the investiture of God with the attributes of humanity, and, removing him to an inconceivable distance, as in himself wholly beyond the reach of human cognition, they interposed between him and the universe, and even between him and the work of creation or generation, his emanations or manifestations, the Elohim or Demiourgos, the Only-Begotten or the creative Logos. *He*, thus, became but a name, and the potencies of himself that were in reality deified, were not more divine than the Vedic Gods were.

The *name* by which the Deity is called, is of no importance. Whether we worship the True Deity or a false and unreal one, depends altogether upon what we conceive it to be, and what attributes we ascribe to it. Among the ancients a different name made a different God, though the attributes and characteristics of the two might be identical. Names of Deity may sometimes have been merely arbitrary combinations of letters, without particular meaning, as the name "God" is, to *us*, but generally they have been either the signs or actual expressions and designations of certain qualities, faculties or powers. Mackay (*Progress of the Intellect*, *i.* 109) very truly says,

> We speak of things, but we know only impressions. Our knowledge of existence is purely hypothetical; and when we speak of matter, of electricity, or of mind, we only give a name to the unknown cause of a particular class of phenomena. The circle of our real knowledge is confined to phenomenal succession, and its laws . . . . If we know nothing of the essence of matter, still less are we able to penetrate the constitution of mind. Why, then, attempt to confine the idea of the Supreme Mind within an arbitrary barrier, or exclude from the limits of veracity any conception of the Deity, which, if imperfect and inadequate, may only be a little more so than our own?

The *negative* notion of God (we quote, condensing, from the same author), consists in the abstraction of the inferior and finite; and is the only way in which, according to Philo, it is possible for man to apprehend worthily the nature of God.

> When we attempt to investigate the essence of the Absolute Being, we fall into an abyss of perplexity, and the only benefit to be derived from such researches is the conviction of their absurdity. This negative view contrasts the divine greatness with human littleness, and often employs expressions apparently affirmative, such as Almighty, All-Wise, Omnipresent, Eternal, etc., but which, in reality, amount only to the negation in regard to God, of those limits which confine the faculties of man. We arrive at this negative and cautious mode of expression only when, having exhausted the varieties of symbolism, we remain content with a Name, which is a mere conventional sign or confession of our ignorance . . . . In the immaturity of the intellect, names and signs are undistinguished from things, and mislead the inquirer by inducing him to confound a negative cypher with a positive idea. Hence arises the positive or sensuous mode of representation, which, comparing the Deity with something either within or without, confounds the sign with the thing signified, and blends them in some idolatrous form. The character of the worship varies with the elevation or triviality of the comparison. God was first recognized in the heavenly bodies, and in the elements; each and all of which were worshipped in their turn . . . . The religious sentiment, originally derived from the contemplation of Nature, was, under peculiar local circumstances, directed exclusively, or nearly so, to certain selected natural agencies. When man attains a consciousness of the dignity of his own being, and reflects upon himself, his idea of Deity becomes proportionably modified. The fire or water assumes the human form, and becomes Osiris or Vishṇu, Ormuzd or Apollo.

But there was with the Aryan race an intermediate stage, during which the Vedic hymns were composed, when the heavenly bodies and elements were no longer worshipped, but the ideal Beings and Existences, of which Fire, Flame, Light and Heat, and the Luminaries of Heaven, the Dawn and the Winds were the manifestations: and it was but a step easily taken, from this to

> the last stage of religious development [which] is the matured consciousness of intellectuality, when, convinced that the internal faculty of thought must be something more subtle than even the most subtle elements, he transfers his new conceptions to the object of his worship, and deifies a mental principle, instead of a physical one.
>
> He is, however, unable to remain long in the regions of abstraction, and being experimentally acquainted with no spiritual existences distinct from his fellow men, his imagination cannot picture anything more exalted than a being similar to himself, though more perfect . . . . Do what we will, the highest efforts of human thought can conceive nothing higher than the supremacy of intellect; and this, subjected to the realizing and plastic power of the imagination, forever brings us back to some familiar type of exalted humanity . . . . Man at first deifies Nature, afterwards, himself. (*Progress of the Intellect*, *i.* 111. 112. 113.)

Unquestionably, the Aryans had advanced so far as to deify intelligence and a mental principle in their Gods, since they ascribed to them intelligence and beneficence, and the moral sense which tells us that virtuous acts deserve reward. Nor did they ascribe to them any of the repulsive and odious features of human nature. They tempt no one to sin, they harden no heart, and punish because of the hardening. They read men no lessons of cruelty or rapacity. They subdue and slay the Dasyus, but it is on account of their good will to the Aryans, and of the merits and deserts of these their favourites. They are just and wise and intelligent, bestowers of good, the benefactors of man.

It is true, they are not the creators of the visible universe, nor did they exist before it. Neither, in the Hebrew book Genesis, is Elohim represented as creating matter, but only as brooding on its chaotic mass, to beget the universe.

> One of the earliest and noblest forms under which the religious sentiment found a distinct expression, was the worship of the heavenly bodies, or of the elements; and if the changes of the seasons and aspect of the sky form a prominent topic of modern conversation, the same phenomena exercised a yet stronger influence over the uncultivated minds to which they were objects of superstitious fear, as well as of curious speculation. The beam of the celestial luminaries might be justly said to have penetrated the intellect, as having first awakened the idea of a Supreme Being; and it was long before the primitive veneration in which they were held, was superseded by a colder and less poetical philosophy.

"The glorious images of Divinity" which formed the Hosts of Heaven, and from the early worship of which by their ancestors, the Hebrews called their God, *Yehuah-Tsabaoth*, God of the Heavenly Armies, or, truly and correctly rendering it, "The Life and Being of the Hosts of Heaven,"

> were the divine dynasty, or real theocracy which governed the early world; and the men of the Golden Age, whose looks held commerce with the skies, and who watched the radiant rulers bringing winter and summer to mortals, might be said, with poetic truth, to live in immediate communication with heaven, and like the Hebrew patriarchs, to see God face to face. (*Prog. of the Intellect, i.* 116. 117.)

Advanced beyond that, and worshipping, not the luminaries themselves, but that of which they were but the organs or manifestations, the religion of the Aryans was neither idolatrous nor degrading. The advance which Brahmanism made, the first step whereof was to recognize an intelligent and creative power, beyond or above the universe, ended by plunging into the most monstrous idolatry, into the very lunacy of incredible beliefs, defiled by the most detestable obscenities.

> As the language of philosophy itself is only a more refined symbolism, so the most abstract expression for Deity, which language could supply, was only a sign for an object unknown, one which could be called more truthful and adequate than the terms 'Osiris' or 'Vishṇu,' only as being less sensuous and explicit. Those

> symbols of Deity are the most appropriate and durable, which, vague metaphysically, have a positive significance, only in a moral or relative sense. (*Id.* 135.)
>
> We often hear complacent self-congratulations on the recognition of a personal God, as being the conception most suited to human sympathies, and exempt from the mystifications of Pantheism. But the Divinity remains still a mystery, notwithstanding all the devices which symbolism, either from the organic or inorganic creation, can supply; and personification is a symbol liable to misapprehension as much, if not more so, than any other, since it is apt to degenerate into a mere reflection of our own infirmities, and to suggest to our minds in regard to the Deity, the same unreasonable expectations which cause such frequent disappointment in regard to our own familiar acquaintance and kindred. (*Id.* 150.)

As Dr. Mansel admits (*Limits of Religious Thought Examined,* 106), which it is our duty to think of God as personal, and to believe that he is infinite,

> we cannot reconcile these two representations with each other; as our conception of personality involves attributes apparently contradictory to the notion of infinity. . . . . To speak of an absolute and infinite Person [he says (103)] is simply to use language to which, however true it may be in a superhuman sense, no mode of human thought can possibly attach itself. [It is true that] it does not follow that this contradiction exists anywhere, but in our own minds; it does not follow that it implies any impossibility in the absolute nature of God . . . . It proves that there are limits to man's power of thought, and it proves no more.

But one of two consequences of this always has followed, and always will follow. Either, as is the case now, God will be to us a *person* neither infinite or absolute, as we habitually think of him, how-much-soever we may theoretically profess to consider him both, and men will take refuge from distressing doubts and contradictions in the nebulous haziness of a sleepy vagueness of notion about God's nature, which is not either conviction or belief; or else, as was the case in India, the questions how, after an eternity of inactive and solitary existence, he proceeded to create, or to generate and produce the universe; and the immense variety of his seemingly conflicting attributes, made utterly contradictory and irreconcilable by considering each as infinite, will lead to the creation in the mind of intermediate and subordinate Deities, at first his various emanations, personifications, and potencies in action; and to endeavour to express the union of his many attributes by symbols that at last become idols; until the whole Hindū or Egyptian pantheon exists, and the most degrading superstitions brutalize the people. The Amesha-Çpentas of the Persians, and the Archangelic Hierarchy of the Hebrews, become mediators between man and God: the existence of evil, under the rule of a God *infinitely good,* wise and just, is explained by a twin God, Aṅra Maiṅyus or Shaitan; Tuphōn and Indra, originally Light-Gods, become demons, and the Dævas evil spirits; as the angels rebel and become devils.

From all this, at least, the Aryan faith was free; and it contains only the germs of the true, and not of the false, in the later religions. It did not endeavour to go beyond the limits set to human thought; nor, in the words of Dr. Mansel, "babble about nothing, under the name of the 'infinite.'"

INDRA.

Indra is *"apprehended by the understanding, and appreciated by the wise;"* i. e., in his *essence* and *very self*, he is not cognizable by the senses, but is perceptible by the intellect only. He is therefore neither the firmament, nor an orb or luminary, nor any phenomenon of visible appearance; and must of necessity be something that is existent in the Universal Fire, emanating from it, and then by itself acting outwardly and visibly.

The commentators speak of *Dyaus* as a Vedic Deity, and as it became the *Zeus* of the Greeks, and Δῖος, and the *Deus* of the Latins, they ascribe to it the character and attribute of the Supreme Deity. Dyaus or Dyu was, to the Vedic Poets, the sky, and Prithivi, the expanse or space between the sky and earth. Both were personified, but neither is invoked as a God. Powers only, potencies, universals possessed of active energies, or their manifestations exercising those energies, are the Deities of the Vedas, or at least the principal ones; and not the earth or firmament or sky, or anything else that is motionless and inactive.

Agni *is*, or *includes* as a component part of his essence, Indra. They are "associated" together. They ride in the same car. Sometimes one of them, sometimes the other, and sometimes both jointly slay Vṛitra and Ahi, rend the imprisoning clouds and set free the fertilizing and refreshing rains. Agni does in the Veda all that Indra does; as all that the Logos, the Son or the Demiourgos does, is done by the Father; but Indra does not do all that Agni is adored for. Nothing is ascribed to him, I think, which belongs or which the imagination can ascribe to fire, but which cannot be imputed to light.

The word "associated," I am convinced, does not adequately express the meaning that belonged, when the hymns were composed, to the original Aryan word which is represented by it. If it does not mean "identical with," it expresses a much more intimate connection than the word "associated" expresses. It means, as I think the passages show, where it occurs, "united," "acting with one action to produce one effect;" precisely that which was meant by the phrase, "and the Word was *with* God (*πρὸς τον θεὸν*), and God was the Word."

Indra and Agni, together, are pious ministers, present at the Holy Rite. For Indra, the light, is in and of the fire, and emanates from it; but Indra alone is never the minister, the messenger or the invoker of the Gods. He and Agni are "kinsmen" and "relations," conceived of as such by the intellect. What can that mean, except that they are generated in the same womb (of the dry wood or elsewhere) together, and are of one essence, as human kinsmen are of one blood? Really, unless it was supposed that the Poets had no coherent ideas, I do not see how it was ever imagined that Indra was the firmament.

> Those stationed around [i. e., the various orbs, in their places], associated with Indra, the mighty, the indestructible—the moving [πλάνηται, the wanderers, the planets], and the lights (fixed stars) that shine in the sky.
>
> These harness to his car, side by side, his two bay (or red) horses. To him mortals owe their daily birth from sleep,

for he, with the radiance of the morning, gives them the use of their senses and by making things visible invests them with forms.

He is the wielder of the thunderbolt, and his most noted function is, by shattering the clouds, to free from its bonds the rain, and send it upon the earth. Thus destroying Vṛitra or Ahi, he is invested with the characteristics of a great warrior, victorious over all foes.

He is "the blender of all things," i. e., he mingles and blends *with* all things in Nature; and is richly decorated, i. e., splendidly coloured. He, to make things visible, set the sun in the sky, and filled the cloud with waters. He dwells in an eternal mansion, being always a denizen of the sky or heavens.

"From his ancient abode, he visits many worshippers;" and is therefore not the firmament, as has been absurdly supposed; 1st, because the firmament is his habitat, and 2nd, because he passes from it to the earth and men. He is called "The Man," who visits them; i. e., the individuality, the being. He is sovereign of all that is, mobile or stationary (perhaps the planets, including the sun and moon, and the stars; but more probably, earth and heaven, and all that moves on or in either). He abides the Monarch of men, i. e., becoming localized by form, limitation and place, he is the essence of all light-beings or orbs, and includes in himself all these individual manifestations, as the felly of a wheel does the spokes: as Jehovah does the Elohim; and as the Very Deity, Ain-Soph, does the ten Sephiroth or emanations, of the Hebrew Kabbalah.

"Thou enjoyest both heaven and earth, investing the universe with thy greatness:" i. e., thou possessest thyself of both sky and earth, thy amplitude clothing both with light. "The ram who makes heaven known:" since without light it would never be visible to mortals or its existence known to them. "Extended throughout the region of dew:" spreading and flowing through and filling the air. "Replenished in the sky by the libations sprinkled on the sacred grass, as its kindred rivers hastening to it fill the ocean." For the vapour exhaling from the Soma juice sprinkled on the grass, like that from the dew, rises, invisible, and as part of the flame and light of the fire, towards the sky.

"He abides in his might," i. e., potentially or in his essence and energy unmanifested, "beyond the limits of the sky or atmosphere." "Thou hast framed the earth for our preservation:" i. e., probably, has communicated to the earth the capability of producing food. "Thou hast been the type of vigour:" i. e., to thee is owing the virile energy, or power of generation: "Thou hast encompassed (pervaded and enwrapped), the air and sky, to the very utmost heavens."

He is "the counter-measure of the wide-extended earth:" i. e., he is co-extensive with it: "Thou art the Lord of the vast God-frequented:" holding and possessing the great vast of the air and sky, peopled with the celestial luminaries. "Thy bulk fills the firmament: and no other being," no luminary, "is equal unto thee."

> The heavens and earth, and the waters of the heavens are less in extension than Indra . . . . Thou, alone, hast made every other thing dependent on thee.

Alone, that is, by thyself, of thine own virtue and essence, independently of other existences or powers; and by "every other thing" was probably meant every other being of light, all being mere organs or instruments of Indra, through which his light emanates: or it may mean that, for us, everything in the universe depends for its actuality to us as an object of our senses on Indra.

His "foe-prostrating *associate*," "and brightly-gleaming spear," is the lightning: the word "associate" meaning that which, being a manifestation of himself, is used by him as an instrument, organ or weapon. He

> *purifies* the heavens and earth with his irresistible might, sends showers, and by his bounty gratifies our desires.

"Purifies" may mean to make clearly visible, or to purge of clouds and mist. "He is the firmament-inhabiting, the Haughty One, taking precedence of all Gods," i. e., of all luminaries, on account of his exploits, i. e., his powers and influences, and the great results of which he is the cause.

> He is quick in action and puissant. His perfect and unfailing power to destroy shines in the conflict of the elements, as a mountain peak, snow-covered, glitters in the sunlight. He subjugates the malignant clouds, and with resolute vigour opposes the encroachments of night and darkness. In his essence, and as his own, is all potency. He pervades the universe, is potent, rapid, mighty and resistless, and hurls the thunderbolt. He is self-irradiating in his dwelling;

i. e., wherever manifested in place, by whatever orb or phenomenon, it is his own radiance that shines forth. "It is he that with the dawn and the rays of the sun scatters the darkness. He makes straight" (or smooth) by lightening them and driving from them the darkness, "the elevations of the earth." "He strengthens the foundations of the ethereal regions:" i. e., he gifted them with potency and energy, by manifesting himself therein as the luminaries of heaven, to which all life and production are owing. "He divided in twain the eternal and united," the unity of darkness that would otherwise have been perpetual, making day and night: and "he cherished [fed with energy and vigour and life] the heavens and the earth, like [as, manifested as] the sun in the brilliant and beautiful sky."

> Indra, the Mighty One [the potency and energy], becoming manifest in *alarm*, did, by his energy exerted and in action, sustain heaven and earth. Then, through fear of thee, all creatures, and the mountains, and all other vast and solid things trembled, like the rays of the sun.

Becoming "manifest in alarm," evidently means appearing as a terror, to Vṛitra, or the Cloud-God, in the forked lightning, and with the hoarse reverberations of the thunder causing even the solid mountains to tremble.

He has "fixed the constellations:" by permanently manifesting himself as the bright points which compose them. "No one has ever been born, or ever will be born, Indra, like unto thee." For the human mind cannot conceive that anything will ever exist, comparable to the light. It is promised in a much later religion that there shall be light there, direct from the Deity, without sun, moon or stars to give it: and that is the Essential Light, conceived of by these old Poets.

Often we hear them say that he sustains and upholds earth and heaven and the firmament. The Aryan ideas are probably badly expressed by the words "heaven" and "firmament." Indeed, unless each means the sky, they have little or no meaning to us. We do not now suppose that above the sky is the locality or heaven, to which souls are to ascend after death, or that there is any firmament, in the old sense of the word, i. e., of a solid sky. It seems that the Aryans thought that the celestial luminaries were in the open space *below* the sky; and it is not made at all probable, by anything in the Veda, that they conceived of anything above the sky.

As to the sustaining or upholding power of Indra, they probably regarded heat as a mere effect of light, or at least considered them inseparable; and undoubtedly they ascribed to the lightning the power to burn and consume. They knew that heat caused expansion and ascension, and might naturally think, knowing no other forces of Nature, that the force which produced the bubble was competent to raise and to sustain the hemispherical vault of the sky. Nor do we know why it might not, since that would be no more an extraordinary effect, than those produced by other equally immaterial and imponderable forces, such as attraction and magnetism.

"He has begotten the sun and the dawn": For they are but manifestations of the Light. "Born in the highest heaven, he pervades heaven and earth, and became the first Artificer." What this means, can only be conjectured. Probably, that light, manifesting itself, was the origin of the heavenly bodies. It is not in the least likely that the word "artificer" expresses their real idea.

> He overspreads the day with his radiance. He generates the day: he illumines for man the banner of the days: he obtained light for the great conflict. He animates the dawns and makes great their radiance. He gave the sun, bestowed plants and days, gave trees and the firmament, and shattered the cloud. His horses pasture in the two azure spheres of heaven and earth:
>
> He is the azure-coloured showerer, who as soon as he is manifested, the whole luminous region [i. e., as the lightning, he illumines the whole sky and air].
>
> He is the master of the tawny steeds, that are harnessed to his car. He holds the yellow thunderbolt. He is fleet and of wonderful splendour. [And he is] apprehended by the understanding, and appreciated by the wise.

These words seem to have been selected for their peculiar unfitness to express the evident meaning. That meaning is, that Indra, as a *being*, is cognizable by the intellect only, becoming visible only by his manifestations. Such is, according to *our* ideas, the soul of man, as *unreal* to our conceptions, as the invisible Indra. Such also, after all, is the philosophical idea of God. For what is he, to us, but That Unknown, invisible, appreciable by the intellect only, of which the manifestations only are known?

"Indra is the parent of the Sun." He is "clothed at night" ["with gloom," the commentator adds]. But this addition does not at all express the meaning, which is, clothed with *form*, i. e., manifested within definite dimensions, as the celestial luminaries. In the Kabbalah, the limits of the manifested are termed envelopes and garments, and were imagined to be like the shell that contains the egg. Such is the meaning of the word "clothed," here.

> Indra and Agni sit together in their wonderful car, which illuminates all beings.

This car was undoubtedly the sun, which seems a great globe of fire and flame, pouring upon sky and earth both heat and light.

Their names are "associated," and they are "allied" as slayers of Vṛitra. The word "associated" as appears by its use elsewhere, very faintly expresses the meaning of the original. Agni was the fire, and Indra the light, one of the manifestations of fire. Agni *is* Indra: for fire *is* light, heat and flame. This is the association of their names, i. e., of their personalities. The lightning appears to be a flame, as well as a diffuser of light, and in it Agni and Indra were united, to slay Vṛitra. They are "the two *seated* together:" i. e., flame and light limited by form, manifested and in place, as the lightning. "I consider you in my mind as kinsmen and relations": i. e., the intellect conceives of you as one the progeny of the other, as parent and child: precisely as God and the Logos were conceived of long afterwards by the Greeks, inheritors of the Aryan intellect: The word was in the beginning near unto God, and the Word was God.

> They are the discomfiters of foes, the destroyers of Vṛitra; the pious ministers present at sacrifices; and the illuminators of heaven.

The moral and intellectual attributes ascribed to Indra are like those of Agni.

He is wise, whom nothing can harm, bestower of good gifts, protector of wealth, mighty, accomplisher of good deeds, friend of the sacrifice. He is mighty, the averter of violence, always gracious, of boundless wealth, showerer of blessings, handsome, victorious, vast and most powerful, praise-deserving, graceful, performer of great deeds, fleet, magnificent, etc., etc.

In one Sûkta he is addressed jointly with Varuña: in one with Vishṇu; and in one with Soma. And in one place it is said, "The seven worlds praise Sudás as if he were Indra." What the translator supposed the idea of the Poet to be, we have no means of knowing. What were *the seven worlds*, that praised Sudás? The Aryans knew nothing about any other "worlds" than this which they inhabited. They knew nothing about the seven *planets* or wanderers.

The Pleiades and Ursa Major were the only two groups, of seven stars each, that were anciently regarded with reverence and watched with interest. The Pleiades, led by Aldebarán, opened the spring at the Vernal Equinox, three thousand years before Christ, rising a little before the sun; and the great Arctic constellation never set, but always kept its unvarying circuit around the Pole-Star. As to praising:

> The morning stars sung together with joy.

The notions of Mr. Cox, in regard to Agni, are for the most part correct, except his general and most important conclusion (*ii.* 354), that to the Aryan Poets,

> Indra, Dyu, Agni, Vishṇu, Varuṇa were but names for one and the same divine Being, who alone was to them the maker and preserver of all things.

That is precisely the same as if one were to say that the Father, the Son or Word, and the Holy Spirit, of the Trinitarian Christians, are but names for one and the same divine Being, to them the maker and preserver of all things. Indra, Mitra, Varuṇa and Aryaman were as *really* distinct from Agni, to the Aryan mind, as the Logos was, to Plato and Philo, from God the Father: and to them as much entities, as the Sephiroth were to the Kabbalists, or the Demiourgos and Sophia Achamōth to the Gnostics.

By this brief sentence, Mr. Cox substitutes another religion for that of the Aryan Poets. It is no doubt true that the attributes imputed to Agni, his Oneness, the cognition of him by the intellect only, his identity in all his manifestations, his sustaining and upholding the universe, led Zarathustra to the higher conception of an intellectual God, superior to fire and light, older than the earth and heavens; and the maker and preserver of them, a moral being, author of the law of morals and righteousness for all mankind. But that conception first appeared in the Zarathustrian teachings, and is not even remotely hinted at in the Veda.

It is true, as Mr. Cox says, that the enemies of mankind were manifestly physical; and that nothing in their hymns leads us to the notion of any evil power or principle having an existence independent of the Great Cause of all things. For the only adversaries mentioned in the Vedas, are the Asuras, the dark clouds that imprisoned the beneficent rains, and Vṛitra or Ahi, the spirit or being of which these clouds were the manifestations.

When the old Vedic faith, Mr. Cox says (*ii.* 190), had been long overlaid by an elaborate sacerdotal ceremonialism, Agni still remained, as it had been from the first, a name for light or heat, as pervading all things, or as concentrated in the flame of fire. (But there was in the old Vedic hymns nothing of the uncertainty and indefiniteness which this sentence imputes to them. Agni was the Fire, the fire essence or principle, of which Light and Heat were but manifestations or emanations. In the Hebrew Kabbalah, all the emanations or Sephiroth are *contained in* and *produced from*, and *depend from* the Very Deity, Ain-Soph; and the nine emanations that succeed the first, Kether, are all contained in it; in each the Deity is, but neither one of them is, nor all of them are, the Deity. The Aryan idea was not equally as profound, but it was the same: and in the Kabbalah, too, the Very Deity, before creation, was universally diffused Light.)

In the Satapatha Brâhmana, Mr. Cox continues, Svetaketu tells King Janaka that he sacrifices to two Heats in one another, which are ever shining, and filling the world with their splendour. When the King asks how this may be, the answer is,

> Aditya (the sun) is heat; to him I sacrifice in the evening in the fire (Agni). Agni is heat; to him I sacrifice in the morning, in the sun (Aditya).

When to Somasushma, who says that he sacrifices to Light in light, the king puts the same question, the Brahman replies,

> Aditya is light: to him I sacrifice in the evening, in Agni. Agni is light; to him I sacrifice in the morning, in Aditya.
>
> Thus Agni, like Indra, is sometimes addressed as the one great God who makes all things, sometimes as the light which fills the heavens, sometimes as the blazing lightning [Agni Vaiṣwânara] or as the clear flame of earthly fire. The Poets pass from one application of the word to another, with perfect ease, as conscious that in each case they are using a mere name, which may denote similar qualities in many objects.

But though this sounds well, and is pronounced with confidence, it is not in the least true. The Aryan sages and thinkers had intellects as acute as the later philosophers of India and Greece. They had perfectly definite ideas in regard to their Deifications, and, correctly understood, they never confounded one Deity with the other. Agni is all of them. They all emanate from him and are his manifestations; but no one of them is the whole Agni. He is the farthest possible from being a mere name, that may denote similar qualities in many objects.

There is, Mr. Cox truly says,

> no rivalry or antagonism between these Deities. Agni is greatest, Varuṇa is greatest, and Indra is greatest: but when the one is so described, the others are for the time unnoticed, or else are placed in a subordinate position. Thus Agni is said to comprehend all other Gods within himself, as the circumference of a wheel embraces its spokes; and not unfrequently Indra is said to be Agni, and Agni is said to be Indra; while both alike are Skambha, the supporter of the universe.

But Agni is never placed in a subordinate position. No other God is ever said to comprehend *him*, or to be greater than him. It is true, the sacrificial and domestic fire is Agni. So is the lightning, and so is the spark of the glow-worm. But each is Agni limited, self-manifested in form: and if in each the God, the whole God, acts in partial self-manifestation, do we not now so conceive of the manifestations of the Deity? The creative Logos is not the Very Deity. We imagine God as acting directly in Nature. Is the whole Deity manifested in every minor act? Is the whole omnipotence of God exerted to hold up the falling sparrow? If light were, as all the ancients imagined it to be, an Emanation from the Deity, himself the light-principle, God would be present in the least ray and in the faintest earthly spark, as completely as in the ocean of it that flows over earth and sky with the rising of the sun.

Hence, Mr. Cox says,

> the character of Agni, as we might expect, is almost wholly physical. The blessings which his worshippers pray for, are commonly temporal, and very rarely is he asked, like Varuṇa, to forgive sin.

We do not believe that that prayer is addressed to any God, in the Vedic hymns. They prayed to the Fire- and Light-Gods to enable them by their light to find the true way again, when lost and wandering in the woods and forest; and they did ascribe to Agni the power and will to do that. It was natural they should appeal more directly to the special luminary whose light they wished for, than to the universal Fire shining by it. So the Catholic appeals more earnestly to the Saints and the Virgin, and the Protestant to Christ, than either does to God, the All-Father.

In the following sentences, Mr. Cox speaks both truly and eloquently:

> In the earlier hymns, he is generally addressed as the fire, which to mortal men is an indispensable boon: in the more developed ceremonialism of later times, he is chiefly concerned with the ordering of the sacrifice. As bearing up the offerings on the flames which mount to the sky, he stands in the place of Hermes, as the messenger between Gods and men. Like Phoibos and Indra, he is full of a secret wisdom. He is the tongue (of fire), through which Gods and men receive each their share of the victims offered on the altar. Nay, so clearly is his mythical character still understood, that although he is sometimes the originator of all things, at others he is said to have been kindled by Manu (man); and the expression at once carries us to the legends of Prometheus, Hermes and Phorôneus, who is himself the Vedic God Bhuranyu. The very sticks which Manu rubbed together, are called the parents of Agni, who is said to have destroyed them, as Oidipous, and Perseus, Kuros and Romulus are said to have destroyed their fathers. The hymns describe simply the phenomena of fire.
>
> As the special guardian and regulator of sacrifices, Agni assumes the character of the Hellenic Hestia, and almost attains the majesty of the Roman Vesta. He is the lord and protector of every house, and the father, mother, brother, and son of every one of the worshippers. He is the keeper of hidden treasures, and all blessings proceed from him as the giver. He is Vasu, the Lord of Light. During life he shields men from harm. But in every phase of his character, the appellative force of his name remains discernible.

But, we cannot agree with Mr. Cox, that

> at death he becomes the Psuchopompos, as conveying the unborn part of the dead to the unseen world.

We find nothing of that in the Veda. Nor do we find any "plain assertions that Agni is but one of many titles for the one Great Cause of all things."

Mr. Cox also says,

Like Ushas and Eōs, Agni never grows old. He is emphatically the youngest of all the Gods, not as being the latest born, but as never losing his strength and might: and in this name Yavishtha, which is never given to any other Vedic God, we may recognize the Hellenic Hephaistos.

Agni is distinctly called "first Divinity of the immortals;" "the first Angiras;" all other fires are but branchings of him; and he comprehends in himself the potencies of all the Gods: he assumes all celestial natures. He was originated, comprehending in himself Mitra, Varuṇa and Aryaman, and he animates them all. He is all the Divinities: he is the first of the Gods:

He is called, also, it is true, the youngest of the Gods, *who shines when kindled in his own abode:* for he is then the latest manifestation of himself. As the domestic and sacrificial fire, he is continually called young: for each new fire is a new manifestation or birth; and thus he is ever-young, ever renewing his youth.

Indra, we are told by Mr. Cox (*i.* 388) was the son of Dyu.

Dyaus [he says], the glistening ether, became to the Hindū, as Zeus was to the Greek, the name for the Supreme God: but although some mythical feature entered gradually into the conception of this Deity, the name retained its original significance too clearly, to hold its ground in Hindū theology.

The root *dyu*, he says, means to *shine:* and

Dyu, in the land of the Five Streams, was at once a name for the sky, and a name for God; *Dyaus Pitâr*, Dyaus the Father, answering to the *Zeus Patēr* of the Greeks, and the Jupiter and Janus Pater of the Latins. As such, he was *Visvakarwan*, the great architect of the universe, who knows all spheres and worlds, *janita* (γενετήρ), the parent of all things; Prithivi or the broad earth, being the mother of his children. The Maruts, or storms, go about in Dyu, the sky, while their worshippers on earth invoke the mercy of Dyaus, Prithivi and Agni. But the Indian land, under its scorching sun, depends wholly on the bounty of the benignant rain-God; and hence Indra, who is the child of Dyu, and from Dyu receives his might, becomes more immediately the fertilizer of the earth, and is regarded as more powerful than his father. But Dyu, although his greatness is obscured by that of his son, still wields the thunderbolt; and the original meaning of the name appears in the myth which represents him as the father of the dawn, who is invincible by all but Indra.

Thus [he continues], Dyaus is to Prithivî, what Ouranos is to Gaia in the Hesiodic theogony; the Greek myth differing from the former, only in deciding that Gaia herself produced Ouranos, to be co-extensive with herself. The Hindū had not so far solved the difficulty, and the doubt expressed on this subject shows the peculiar attitude of the Indian mind to the problems of the sensible universe. Heaven and earth, it would seem, are in the earliest hymns alike self-existent; but Dr. Muir remarks that we are not told which of the two is the older. On the contrary, he

> says, one of the ancient Poets seems to have been perplexed by the difficulty of this question, as at the beginning of one of the hymns (*i.* 185) he exclaims, 'which of you twain was the first, and which the last? How were they produced? Sages, who knows?' And of Indra it is said, 'Thy father was the parent of a most heroic son: the maker of Indra, who produced the celestial and invincible thunderer, was a most skilful workman. (*Rig-V. iv.* 17. 4.) But it was obvious that the abstract conception of Dyu as the father of Indra could not stand against the overwhelming weight of the myths which were continually springing up from phrases not originally antagonistic with the monotheistic belief or conviction.'

"*Was* obvious!" To whom? When Tecumseh, the Shawano Indian, said to the American commander,

> The Sun is my father, and the Earth is my mother, I will sit on her bosom,

did he express an "abstract conception" of his parentage? Where are the Vedic texts that express a monotheistic belief or conviction? We shall never know what the original Aryan belief was, if such are to be the only commentaries upon them.

Mr. Cox continues:

> The Hindū, ever dwelling on the thought of an unseen world, strove to gain some insight into the nature of things, and to unlock secrets for which the material world could never furnish a key. While [he says], the Greek was at once contented with answers suggested by the old mythical phrases, or by the phenomena which he might be describing.

The *Hindū* mind, after Brahmanism arose, dwelt on the thought of an unseen world; but the *Vedic* mind never did. But Mr. Cox sadly mixes up the later Hindū faith and the old Vedic notions. For he continues to say:

> Hence *Dyu* was for him sometimes the Supreme God, sometimes the heaven which with the earth had been fashioned by the Gods, and strengthened with undecaying supports, and which trembled and bowed down in the presence of the Deities. Sometimes he was the all-pervading spirit, sometimes a material and tangible firmament; and thus again the question of matter.

It would be impossible to crowd more errors into the same number of words, if this is at all meant to apply to the Poets of the Vedas. It imputes to them conceptions that they never entertained. They never thought of Dyu as a Supreme God, or that earth and heaven had been fashioned by the Gods; and the only trembling and bowing down of which they spoke was produced by the thunder. They never thought of Dyu as the all-pervading spirit: and though it can hardly be supposed that they did not sometimes wonder how the heaven and earth came to be where they were, we find no speculation upon the subject; at most, only a brief reference to it. What Mr. Cox immediately adds, is much more consistent with the facts.

> Of his own ignorance, the Hindû was perfectly conscious, and he had already begun to think that this ignorance extended even to the Gods themselves. Who can tell whence this creation arose? *The Gods are subsequent to its production.* Who then knows whence it sprung.

It is quite unnecessary to say that the words "creation" and "production," their accepted and narrow meanings being such as they are among us, were not in the least fit to be used in translating the Vedic words. For the Vedic Poets had no idea of any creator of the earth and sky, or of any producer of them; and without a creator there can be no creation, and without a producer no production.

> He who in the highest heaven is its ruler, he knows, or perhaps not even he. [This ruler was Sûryâ, the sun, or Indra, the light.]
>
> So far [Mr. Cox continues] as this question was answered at all, it was answered, as Dr. Muir has well remarked, by Greek and Hindû in the same way. In the Hesiodic theogony, Chaos, Gaia and Tartaros *are beings apparently self-existent;* or, at the least, the scheme *begins with Chaos,* and *no parents are assigned* to Gaia and Tartaros. The Hellenic Poet had brought with him from his primeval home the tradition which he shared with the Hindû; but having given utterance to it, *he bestowed no further thought upon it.*

The truth is that it never was anything more than a poetic idea of the days when Zeus was worshipped, that Chaos had, ages before, been a God. It was never really conceived of as such. And Ouranos, Gaia and Tartaros were but *names* for sky, earth and hell; and no people ever worshipped heaven, earth and hell as Gods, or any Gods by those names. They were merely imagined poetically as having been Deities in the earlier ages. There were no traditions to that effect.

We have copied all the extracts from the Vedas cited by Mr. Cox in support of these notions. It would have been much more satisfactory if he had given us the texts of the Veda, that sustain his conclusions. The last sentences which we have cited, state the simple truth. The Veda deemed that the sky and earth, Dyu and Prithivi, existed before any of the Gods. The visible and material universe was to them apparently self-existent. It was a long while before the human mind entertained the idea that this universe was created, or had a beginning or a maker. Do *we* inquire, satisfied as we are that there *is* a God, who made him, or when he began to exist? Is his existence without beginning any more easily conceived of, than that of the material sky and earth? Fire and light were deemed to have their origin *in* the sky, not to be *begotten* or *created by* the sky. Hence the sky was poetically termed their father. Venus was said to be born of the waves, because she emerged from them. If the sea was therefore called her mother, the idea was not conveyed that she was really produced by it. The earth nourishes the fire, furnishes it with food to consume, and the flame, so fed, rises towards the sky. Naturally, therefore, it was poetically called the mother of fire and the light. It is quite certain that the Vedic hymns never address heaven (the sky) and the earth as Gods, or impute to them creative powers.

After quoting passages of the Vedas addressed to Varuṇa, Mr. Cox says,

> These simple utterances of the Vedic Poets show that the genuine belief in one Almighty Being, who is at once our Father, our Teacher and our Judge, had its home first in the Ancient Aryan land.

Deferring reply to this until we inquire what *was* meant by Varuṇa, we continue to quote:

> It was a conviction to which they were guided by all that they saw or could apprehend of outward phenomena, as well as by the irrepressible yearnings which stirred their hearts. For such yearnings and such a consciousness in the Hebrew tribes, we look in vain, before the Babylonish captivity.

How then were the Aryans guided to this conviction? The Hebrews saw the same phenomena as they. Why should they not have had the same yearnings? They *did* conceive of the world as generated, created or made, out of chaos, by the Alohim or Yehovah-Alohim: while the Aryans never inquired whether it had a beginning or a creator at all.

Mr. Cox then says of another name found in the Veda:

> The process which converted the physical Varuṇa into a spiritual God, is carried to its extreme results, in the conception of Aditi, *the unbound, the unbounded*, or even, as being expressed by the negation of *Diti*, a *bond*, the Absolute. This indefinite term was naturally used to denote the Source from which all life, even the life of the Gods, springs; and thus Aditi, the Infinite, become the mother of all the Gods. The fact is startling; but in Professor Müller's words, the thoughts of primitive humanity were not only different from our thoughts, but different also from what we think their thoughts ought to have been. The Poets of the Veda indulged freely in theogonic speculations, without being frightened by any contradictions. They knew of Indra as the greatest of Gods, they knew of Agni as the God of Gods, they knew of Varuṇa as the ruler of all, but they were by no means startled at the idea that their Indra had a mother, or that their Agni was born like a babe from the friction of two fire-sticks, or that Varuṇa and his brother Mitra were nursed in the lap of Aditi. Hence 'Aditi' was contrasted with 'Diti,' the unbounded with the definite, while it became more and more a name for the distant East from which all the bright Gods seem to come, and for the boundless space beyond the East, drawing a sharp distinction between 'what is yonder and what is here.' The Gods had been called *Dâksha-pitar*, he says afterwards, *the fathers of*

> *strength*, the *mighty;* and the epithet *Dâksha* was converted into *the father of the Gods.* It followed that Aditi was sprung from Dâksha, or Dâksha from Aditi, who also owed his existence to *Bhu, being;* and the conclusion was reached that not being and being are in the highest heaven, in the birthplace of Dâksha, in the lap of Aditi. But more especially, Aditi became the mother of the bright Gods, of Varuṇa, Mitra, Aryaman, and in fact of the seven Adityas, although their names are not definitely given in the Rig-Veda.

What is said above in regard to Dâksha and Bhu, belongs to a much later period than that of the Veda. As to the rest, we remark:

That the words "infinite," "unbounded," have a different meaning to us, from that which these old Poets attached to the words rendered by them. Their *infinite* was merely the indefinite; their *unbounded*, that space whose bounds were beyond measurement; their *limitless*, Aditi, not that which had *no* limits, but that which was so vast that its limits were beyond their reach. The mistranslation is the same as is effected in the vulgar translation of the Hebrew books, by the use of the word *eternal*. As to the idea that Aditi, to the Aryans, meant what Sir William Hamilton meant by *the Absolute*, it is simple nonsense.

Mr. Cox needs often enough to be reminded of that which he quotes from Müller, that the thoughts of these ancients were not what we think they should have thought. The Vedic Poets were not frightened by any contradictions, because they did not involve themselves in any. We firmly believe that they only *seem* to do so, because they have been misunderstood; and because, while continually telling us of the childishness of their thoughts, the new commentators will insist on imputing to them the notion of one incomprehensible First Cause, author and creator of the material universe, a notion or idea to which they never attained, even more absurdly making them to have regarded Varuṇa as that immaterial and undefined First Cause and creator; which at the same time ignoring their evident possession of other ideas, too philosophical not to prove that we derive our philosophical and metaphysical intellect legitimately from them; and that, in that respect, they were the farthest possible from being children in mind or intellect.

אור פשוט *Aūr Pasūt*, say the "Kabbalistic Commonplaces," *Lux Simplicissima*, is called אין סוף *Ain-Soph*, or the Infinite before any emanation: for then there was no space or vacant place; but *the All* was (*omnia erant*) infinite light. All things (*the All*) says the *Introductio in Librum Sohar*, "were then full of the Light of His Substance." Ain-Soph is called light, because there is no other name that can be given it. Of this infinite light, the light of the substance, the unmanifested, the manifested light of the universe, the *Aur Peni-El* (*light of the countenance of God*), the *Tehirū* (*splendour*), was but a point.

The "*Porta Cœlorum*" of Rabbi Abraham Cohen Irira says,

> God produced (put forth outwardly) all things, by his intellect and will and of his free determination; and although he could have produced all things immediately, he preferred to produce them mediately, through his Sephiroth and persons, which, although principiated are yet not his *creatures*, but his *rays*, whereby he can as perfectly as possible be manifested.

The Supreme Light of all lights, the most exalted and limitless (says *Tractatus i. Libri Druschim*, of Rabbi Jitzchak Lorjensis), and which is called the Infinite, can be attained unto by no cogitation or speculation, and its substance (*fundamentum*) is entirely abstracted and remote from all intellection. From this Infinite afterward descended the existence of that great light, produced by emanation, which is called Adam Kadmon, and in like manner from him descend the lights down-hanging (*dependentra*) from him, which are many, and go forth from him, and emit the rays of his splendour out from him.

This idea, of the invisible light manifesting itself by emanation or outflow, not by creation—by the mediation of Sephiroth or persons, that are not creatures of it, but rays, was wholly borrowed by the Kabbalists from the Persians, and had its root in the old Aryan faith. From the same source came the idea of the self-limitation and manifestation of God, the infinite, as the Word, the Monogenes, the Logos Demiürgos, of Plato, Philo and Saint John or the unknown author of the book that bears his name.

The Aryan Poets were not startled at the idea that Indra had a mother: any more than it would have startled them to hear it said that the dew was born of the air, or that vapour was born of the water and had the sun for father. We personify the objects of Nature every moment in our daily and common speech, and are not *startled* at it. We make the old and new year, the days, the nights, joy and sorrow, hope and faith, poverty and power, to be things and persons whenever we speak of them. The sky *smiles* for us; the sea is *cruel*, *treacherous*, *sleeps* in the calm, and *wakes* when stirred by the winds. The stars watch over us; spring comes to us with her delicate fingers full of flowers, and time and death have all the attributes of personality. The "Hail, heaven-born light," of Milton, precisely expresses the Aryan idea of the *birth* of Indra. It is the local manifestation of the all-pervading Agni, that is born by attrition; and Varuṇa and Mitra were nursed in the lap of Aditi, mother of the Adityas; because she is the vast open space between earth and sky, in which the celestial luminaries dwell and move, and wherein they had their origin. Aditi was *not* an indefinite term, nor did it denote the *source* from which all life, even the life of the Gods, springs; but only the *space* in which the luminaries existed, moved and originated. Agni was the universal fire, of which Indra was the light. Both were manifested in all the luminaries and in the lightning; and yet Agni, manifested and limited as the sacrificial fire was the messenger and invoker of these Gods that were but his other manifestations. There is no contradiction in this, but it is profoundly philosophical; and from it have flowed all the speculations of Plato, of Philo and of the Kabbalah and the Gnostics.

Of Indra, specially, Mr. Cox says (*i.* 336):

> The picture which the oldest Vedic hymns present to us, of this God, has a special value, as enabling us to determine the measure in which religion and mythology affected each other. That a moral or spiritual element may be discerned in some of the characteristics of this Deity, is beyond question . . . . Dyaus and Indra, Varuṇa and Agni, are each in his turn spoken of as knowing no superior, and the objects of their chief care are not the children of men, but the winds, the storms, the clouds and the thunder, which are constantly rising in rebellion against them.

The looseness of Mr. Cox's writing, and his frequent disregard of accuracy, as if that were a consideration inferior to the construction of sounding sentences, is curiously apparent here. The lightning is *always* a manifestation of Indra, his weapon or lance, and never rises in rebellion against him; nor, we think, are the Maruts (winds) ever represented as doing so.

> No sooner is one conflict ended than another is begun, or rather the same conflict is repeated as the days and seasons come round. Whenever the rain is shut up in the clouds, the dark power is in revolt against Dyaus and Indra. In the rumblings of the thunder, while the drought still sucks out the life of the earth, are heard the mutterings of their hateful enemy. In the lightning flashes which precede the outburst of the pent-up waters, are seen the irresistible spears of the God, who is attacking the throttling serpent in his den, and in the serene heaven which shone out when the deluging clouds had passed away, men beheld the face of the mighty Deity.

This is "fine writing," but it does not reproduce the Vedic hymns to Indra. The dark power is not spoken of as in revolt against *Dyaus and Indra,* whenever the rain is shut up in the clouds. The hymns are addressed to Indra *alone,* as wielder of the thunderbolt, and slayer of Vṛitra. And the blue sky, which men saw when the storm passed away, was not, to the Vedic Poets, the face of a mighty Deity.

> In the Vedic Indra [Mr. Cox continues], there is this further peculiarity, that although his name ceased, like that of Dyaus, to be chiefly a name for the sky [it could not *cease* to be that which it never was], and although the struggle in which he is constantly [at intervals] engaged, has indefinitely affected the faith of Christendom, yet the Deity himself has but little of a *purely* moral or spiritual element in his character. [He has nothing at all of a spiritual element, in *our* sense of the word

> *spiritual*, and nothing moral, except figuratively.] It is true that he is sometimes invoked as witnessing all the deeds of men, and thus taking cognizance of their sins [of their wanderings, when lost, on the plains or in the forests]; but the warfare which he has to wage is purely a physical conflict, and it is chiefly in the phrases by which his adversary is described, that we find the germs of the dualistic creed which bears the name of Zoroaster. Nowhere, then, in the oldest monuments of Hindū thought, is the real character of Indra lost sight of. His home is in the bright heaven [his *origin* is there; his *home* both in heaven and on the earth: he fills both and out-measures both]; but as his name denotes, he is specially the bringer of the most precious of all boons to a thirsty and gaping land. He is the giver of the rain which falls on the earth, when the tyranny of the scorching wind is overpast.
>
> Vyansa, exulting and striking hard blows, smote thee, Maghavan, upon the jaw; whereupon, being so smitten, thou provedst the stronger, and didst crush the head of the slave with the thunderbolt.
>
> Like Herakles and Phoibos, again, he has to go in search of lost or stolen cattle. With the conveying Maruts, 'the traversers of places difficult of access,' he discovers the cows hidden in their caves.

We need not repeat the quotations from the Veda that follow. In one, Indra, manifested as the wielder of the lightning, is designated by the epithet *Maghavan;* and in another, as the "rain-bringer," by that of *Parjanya.*

Nor need we follow much further the lucubrations of Mr. Cox as to Indra. They may be summed up thus:

> He is called wanderer at times, and is therefore the solar God [he is *wanderer*, as *every* celestial luminary by which he manifests himself]: He is the Lord of Heaven, omnipotent and all-seeing: he is younger than the sky; but however sharply his personality may be defined, the meaning of the name is never forgotten. The clouds sometimes move in Indra, the sky, as the Maruts or winds are said sometimes to course through Dyaus, the heaven.

What *was* the *heaven*, but the *sky*, to the Vedic Poets? If Indra was Lord of Heaven, how was he the sky? If Dyaus, his father, was also Lord of Heaven, how was he heaven itself, or Lord of the Sky, if it and the heaven were not one and the same? Commentaries like this plunge the Vedas into a maze of confusion, and represent the Poets or worshippers as having no definite ideas as what their Gods were. There is in reality no such confusion and uncertainty. The winds move through the air or open space between the sky and earth; the clouds swim in the light and are tinged and coloured by it. When the words *heaven*, *sky* and *firmament* are used in a translation, in what senses we are not informed, confusion is the necessary result.

> In all the phrases which describe this God, the local colouring arising from the climate of northern India may be plainly discerned [Mr. Cox informs us] . . . . He has golden locks, and a quiver of arrows: he holds a golden whip: his arrows

have a hundred points and are winged with a thousand feathers [for they are the rays of the Light]: he rides in a flaming chariot, drawn by the tawny or glistening steeds called the Harits: his beard flashes like lightning, as he rides. He is possessed of an inscrutable wisdom. He chases the dawn, of whom he is sometimes said to be the father, sometimes the son, and sometimes the husband. [If Mr. Cox had but opened his eyes wide enough to see that the name Indra is applied equally to the universal light as a whole, and to itself as manifested in the luminaries and otherwise, he would have wandered about less helplessly in his disquisitions. But he gets glimpses of *some* of the truth.] The prayers addressed to this God [he says], show that the chief idea associated with him was that of an irresistible material power. The prayer of the heart is addressed to Varuṇa. The cry for mercy from those who have sinned is never sent up to Indra [Mr. Cox says, from those who have broken the law of God, no such law is spoken of in the Vedas]; though he engages in many conflicts for the good of men, with overwhelming power. The great work for which he may be said to exist was to battle for life or death with the hateful monster who imprisons the rain-clouds in his dungeons.

It will be easy for the reader to satisfy himself, by looking back to what we have quoted from the Veda in regard to Indra, that "the great work for which he might be said to exist, was to fight the clouds and produce rain," is simply ludicrous. That is but one of his many beneficent functions. Nor does he fight against a monster who imprisons the rain-clouds in dungeons. He fights against the clouds, the Asuras. They are not imprisoned; they imprison the rain. He does liberate them from their dungeons: he shatters and rends them, and sets free the imprisoned waters, in rains. Nor is it a battle for life or death. It is never represented as doubtful.

This battle [Mr. Cox says], is presented under a thousand forms. His great enemy, Vṛitra, the hiding thief, is also Ahi, the strangling snake, or Pani the marauder. He appears again as Atri: he is Namuka and Sambara, both of whom he slays with his bolt. He grinds the head of the deceiver Namuki, like [in the shape of, or as], a sounding and *rolling* cloud. In the same way he slays Bala, Chumuri, Dhuni, Pipou, Sushna, and many others; and against him the strength of the Rakshasas is concentrated in vain. The religious instinct found little scope in the phrases which described the offices of Indra, and most assuredly had nothing to do with suggesting them.

The clouds of the thunderstorm assume a thousand shapes, monstrous, portentous and gloomy. Nothing in Nature is more terrible than this coming of a mighty storm, typhoon or tornado. The fearful masses change at every instant; and these changing phases suggested to the imaginative Aryan mind as many descriptive epithets, which became names of the monsters whose shapes the clouds seemed to assume. As the lightning darted in its zigzag or serpentine course, it seemed to follow up and disclose the track of a huge serpent.

How nearly Mr. Cox is right in saying that the Vedic hymns never send up a cry for mercy from those who have sinned, to Indra, may be seen by the following extracts:

> O God (Indra) have mercy! Give me my daily bread! Sharpen my mind, like the edge of iron. Whatever I now may utter, longing for thee, do thou accept it; make me possessed of thee. (*Rig-V. vi.* 47. 10.)
>
> Let us meditate on the adorable light of the divine Maker: may he rouse our minds.
>
> Destroy not our future offspring, O Indra; for we have believed in thy great power.

It is true that such invocations to Indra are not common. They are chiefly addressed to Varuṇa, one of his manifestations.

> Wise Poets [it is said (*Rig-V. x.* 114. 5)], make the beautiful-winged, though he is one, manifold by words, i. e., by names.

The epithet "beautiful-winged" applied to one made manifold by names or words, is most fit to be used to characterize the many-coloured light. And it is Indra, the light, that is thus made manifold.

The following hymn (*Rig-V. x.* 121) obviously is addressed to the light:

> 1. In the beginning there arose the golden child. He was born the one Lord of all that is. He stablished the earth and this sky—who is the God to whom we shall offer our sacrifice?
>
> 2. He who gives life; he who gives strength; whose command all the bright Gods [the sun, moon, stars and planets] revere; whose shadow is immortality [i. e., whose disappearance from the universe would make unending darkness], whose shadow is death— who is the God to whom we shall offer our sacrifice?
>
> 3. He who, through his power, is the one King of the breathing and awakening world—he who governs all, man and beast—who is the God to whom we shall offer our sacrifice?
>
> 4. He whose greatness the snowy mountains, whose greatness the sea proclaims, with the distant river; he, whose these regions are, as it were his two arms—who is the God to whom we shall offer our sacrifice?
>
> 5. He, through whom the sky is bright and the earth firm—he through whom the heaven was stablished—nay, the highest heaven—he who measured out [manifested by limitations, within limits] the light in the air—who is the God to whom we shall offer our sacrifice?
>
> 6. He to whom heaven and earth, standing firm by his will, look up, trembling inwardly—he, over whom the rising sun shines forth—who is the God to whom we shall offer our sacrifice?
>
> 7. Wherever the mighty water-clouds went, where they placed the seed and lit the fire, thence he arose, who is the Sole Life of the bright Gods—who is the God to whom we shall offer our sacrifice?

8. He who by his might looked even over the water-clouds [i. e., who, manifested and potently acting, displaying and exerting his force and influences, is visible above the clouds], the clouds which gave strength, and lit the sacrifice; he who alone is God above all Gods [is that of which the celestial luminaries are the partial manifestations]—who is the God to whom we shall offer our sacrifice?

9. May he not destroy us—he, the Creator of the Earth; or he, the righteous, who created the heaven; he also created the bright and mighty waters—who is the God to whom we shall offer our sacrifice?

The mention of the sea in this hymn, is sufficient proof that it was composed after the Aryans had passed from the land of the Five Rivers, into India, and reached the sea-coast.

What but the flame or light arises when it is lighted? And what else than light is the life of the bright luminaries of the sky? All the bright Gods revere his command, i. e., all these luminaries are his dependents, receiving their light from the Universal Light. "Arose the golden child," i. e., the golden light, beginning to exist, soared upward, and became the life and strength of all that is. His opposite, the shadow or darkness, is death, and the annihilation of all measured time. By its influence and power, the light has dominion over all that breathes, i. e., lives, in the world, when awaking in the morning. The snowy mountains, flooded with light, the sea and rivers that reflect the light, disclose its magnitude. By it the sky is bright, and the earth firm, and the heaven established, to its utmost height: for without light, what would the earth be of real and actual to man? And it is by the light that the expanse between earth and sky, even unto the sky, the utmost limit of the expanse, is made known.

Heaven and earth stand firm by his will; because if light were annihilated both would disappear for us, and be as though they were not. Wherefore they do honour to the light, trembling for fear lest it should cease to be. Light is life; it is with the clouds, with the planted seed, with the flame of the fire. What the clouds are "which gave strength and lit the sacrifice," it would be hard to say. Corruption of the original text or mis-translation, is evident; for everywhere it is Agni who lights the sacrifice. The clouds do not do it, nor do they give strength.

Light or the fire, Indra or Agni, is the life of the heavens, earth and waters. It is vitality, and therefore these are said to owe to it their being, and it to be their creator. For darkness, utter and entire, was deemed to be non-existence: and there was no contradiction between this idea and the distinct assertion elsewhere, that before any of the Gods, the sky and the earth were. The account of the Cosmogony in the Hebrew book Barasith, represents chaos, enveloped in utter darkness, as existing before the "beginning." Then the breath of Elohim moved or brooded, on the surface of this oceanic chaos, and the generation of things commenced. So, when

Elohim had formed man of the dust of the earth, it breathed into him the breath of life, and man became a living being. Heaven and earth *were*, but had no real *existence* for any save themselves, until light flashed forth and filled the great expanse.

In the hymn, *Rig-V. i.* 53, as translated by Müller (*I Chips.* 31),

> Indra is the giver of horses, cows and corn; having the disposal of wealth, the old guide of man, disappointing no desires [i. e., probably, enabling him with certainty to find his way], a friend to friends, achiever of many works [i. e., the cause and producer of a multitude of effects]; gracious by day, and at night keeping the enemy from the cows and horses. With his help they 'tear the fiend' night after night.

Wilson renders it, "subduing our adversary;" and we imagine it would have been difficult to express to the Aryans, by any number of words of their language, that which the word "fiend" expresses to us. To use such words is not to *translate.* With just as much propriety might the *Devil, Satan*, or *the fallen Angel*, have been used. The word *electric* might just as well be used to render a term applied to Indra, as the word *righteous*, and *Purgatory* as *Heaven* as different from the sky. It is a wonder the phrase *saving grace* has not found its way into the translation, or Plato's ideas been represented as familiar to the old herdsmen-poets of Bokhara or the Punjab. Under cover of darkness, thieves or predatory bands could approach, unseen, the herds, and drive them away; but if the night were lighted by moon or stars, their approach could be descried. Hence Indra keeps off the hated ones, and with his help they are defeated and foiled, night after night: and the Poet could well say,

> Let us rejoice that we have preserved our food, and have received no injury from those who hate us.

Indra is besought to rejoice his invoker, with treasure and food, with "wealth of manifold delight and splendour;" a phrase which, as the "wealth" and "treasure" desired consisted of cattle and horses, probably does not very accurately reproduce the sense of the original. He is asked for "the blessing of the Gods, which gives us the strength of offspring," i. e., for the virile energy which gives many children; and by which energy also, cows and horses are given.

He is represented as irresistibly striking down ten thousands of enemies, as advancing bravely from battle to battle, destroying from town to town; and with Namî as friend, striking down *from afar* the deceiver Namuki: as slaying Karaṇga and Parnaya, with the brightest spear of Atithigva; as demolishing without a helper the hundred cities of Vaṇgrida, which were besieged by Rigisvan; as felling down with the chariot-wheel the twenty kings of men who had attacked the friendless Susravas, and glorious by the sixty thousand and ninety-nine forts; as thus succouring Susravas and Tûrvayâṇa, and making Kutsa, Atithigva and Ayu subject [i. e., giving their services to] this mighty, youthful king.

> The sun and moon go on in regular succession, that we may see, Indra, and believe. (*Rig-V. i.* 102. 2.)

Believe *what?* Is not the meaning, to enable us to see, and act confidently and without uncertainty and doubt?

> When Indra hurls again and again his thunderbolt, then they believe in the brilliant God. (*Rig-V. i.* 55. 5.)

The cloud-monsters, perhaps, learn his presence by the lightning. Müller thinks that *men* are meant, and says,

> a similar sentiment, namely that men only believe in the Gods when they see their signs and wonders in the sky, is expressed by another Poet. (*Rig-V. viii.* 21. 14):
>
> Thou, Indra, never findest a rich man to be thy friend; wine-swillers despise thee. But when thou thunderest, when thou gatherest, then thou art called, like a father.

Max Müller is a great authority, and one should distrust an opinion contrary to his. But I can not think that this expresses any "belief in God." It seems to me that the meaning is, that rich men in their houses care nothing for the light, as manifested by the brilliant luminaries of the night, care not to view the splendid beauties of the heavens, or even to look casually at the stars, much less to sleep under them, as the herdsmen do: and the swillers of wine, passing nights and days in revelry, despise alike the daylight and the starry splendours. But when the pealing thunder-voice of Indra rouses them, when he gathers and concentrates his energies, then they cry to him, as scared children do to an angry father.

> With this belief in God [Professor Müller thinks], is coupled that doubt, that true scepticism, if we may so call it, which is meant to give to faith its real strength. [In proof of this, he cites *Rig-V. viii.* 89. 3]: "If you wish for strength, offer to Indra a hymn of praise, a true hymn, if Indra truly exists, for some one says, Indra does not exist; who has seen him? Whom shall we praise?"
>
> And Indra answers, through the Poet:—"Here I am, O worshipper! Behold me here, in might I surpass all things."

It seems to me that Professor Müller sees here what is not to be seen. I think the hymn shows the very reverse of doubt or scepticism, on the part of the Poet. It is some one else who expresses a doubt whether Indra exists, whether there is a God, the Light-Principle of whom the visible light is the manifestation, a real intelligence, possessing power, and replying by protection and benefits to the invocations of the worshipper.

Indra is certainly not an orb or luminary. He is as evidently a pervading principle, not only co-extensive with the world, but extending beyond it and not limited by it. He is not flame; because he fills the *whole* expanse, and is manifested by *all* the luminaries; and in none of these except the sun, is there any appearance of flame. The moon and planets and stars do not seem to *blaze*, but only to *shine*.

Indra, then, is Light, or the Light-God.

Professor Wilson thinks that in *Asht. i. Anuv. xi. Sûkta ii.*, Vaiṣwânara is identified with Indra. He is so identified, precisely as Agni is, of whom Vaiṣwânara is merely a name.

I cannot see any colour for the remark of Professor Wilson, that the Vaidic theogony resolves all the Divinities into three, *Fire*, *Air*, and the *Sun;* and these three again into the Sun. Many of the Deities are manifestations of Agni; but others are not; and the sun is but a creature or organ of Agni and Indra.

The scholiast says that Vaiṣwânara, in *v.* 6, of the Sûkta above referred to, is the Agni of the firmament, the Vaioyuta, lightning, or electric force. But it is not the force—it *exerts* the force, being the fire, of which the lightning is one manifestation.

In *Sûkta i. Anuv. ii. Adhy. i. of Asht. i.*, we find, addressed to Indra, this phrase,

> We recognize thee in the midst of the right-minded, who are nearest to thee.

Undoubtedly the original had some meaning. I am quite sure that the composers of the hymns always knew what they wished to say, and how to say it, and that they had no confusion of ideas about their Gods, and never merely babbled and jabbered, in words that were entirely barren of ideas.

There is certainly no sense in the translation of the phrase; and I venture to submit this, as its real meaning:

> We recognize thee, Indra [the Universal Light], in the light-giving orbs that are thy immediate manifestations. Come to us, and do not pass by us, unseen, invisible,

unmanifested, to manifest thyself elsewhere. [The last clause is rendered by Professor Wilson, 'Come to us, pass us not by to reveal.']

Indra is termed "the pervader." That epithet could not have been appropriately applied either to the firmament, or to any luminous body or orb. It is as inconsistent with the idea of shape and form, as the words "mind," "soul," or "spirit" are.

Elsewhere he is styled, "expanded like the ocean." This is equally inconsistent with the idea that he is the sun or any other orb. He is represented as having "engendered" the sun, the dawn and the firmament. It is not at all likely that in the word translated engendered there was any sexual meaning. But the Logos, also, is styled "the only begotten" Son of God. Evidently the meaning is that he manifests himself as the sun and dawn, and makes visible the firmament, which, but for light, would certainly be as though it did not exist for men.

He irradiates the firmament: he is the pervader of the universe, the All-Pervading, in whom "the Gods have concentrated riches and worship and power, manifesting his own sovereignty." "His own sovereignty" is manifested by "the Gods": the sovereignty which is his, peculiar to him; as Paul, writing to the Christians at Rome, said,

> "For since the making of the world, the invisible nature of God is clearly seen, being cognizable in that which has been created; even his Eternal Potency and Divine Sovereignty [Godhead].

As he is said in the Kabbalah to manifest himself by each of the Sephiroth, the tenth being his sovereignty [Malakoth], although no Sephirah or emanation is the Very God, because emanation or manifestation is the limitation of the infinite, and therefore not the unlimited infinite, so the sovereignty of Indra is manifested in and as every one of the luminaries of the sky. It is *he* that shines as each of them; and in him are concentrated all the potencies of all of them: they have their control of wealth, and power of bestowing it, their worshipfulness, or all those faculties and attributes whereby they deserve adoration, and their puissant influences concentrated in him. He is the source and origin of all.

> If, Indra [it is said in *Mandala viii.*], a hundred skies and a hundred earths were thine, a thousand suns could not equal thee, Thunderer, nor could the two worlds attain to thee, when thou hadst been born. [*Muir: Orig. Sansk. Texts. iv.* 91.]
>
> When thou, O unrivalled Maghavan, wast born for the destruction of Vṛitra, then thou didst spread out the earth, and then thou didst establish the sky. Then was thy sacrifice produced, then thy hymn and thy song of praise. Then thou didst transcend all things that have been born and shall be born.
>
> Thou, Indra, art the most powerful: thou hast kindled the sun; thou art great, the architect of all things, and the lord of all.

x. 134. 1. When thou, Indra, like the dawn [*as* the dawn, or wearing the form of the dawn, i. e., manifested as the dawn], didst fill both the worlds [the sky and earth, with light], a divine mother bore thee, the Mighty Monarch of mighty creatures [sovereign and light principle of the luminaries]; a gracious mother bore thee.

In *Sûkta x. Anuv. xv. Adhy. vii. of Asht. i.*, we find,

1. The sages have formerly been possessed of this thy supreme power, Indra, as if it were present with them [*parachais*, which is equivocal. It means, literally, *inverse, averted*]; one light of whom shines upon the earth, the other in heaven, and both are in combination with each other, as banner in battle [i. e., I think, the light of the fire on earth and that which fills the expanse, unite to form one body of light, a single battle-flag, as it were, for the Warrior-God, Indra].

Indra is said, in *Sûkta i. Anuv. ii. Adhy. vi. of Asht. ii.*, to have fixed firm the moving earth, to have tranquilized the incensed mountains, spread the spacious expanse and consolidated the sky. He generated fire in the clouds, and made all the perishable. He gave birth to the sun and the dawn; he rendered earth visible to heaven, and generated the various luminaries of heaven, and being of vast bulk comprehends in himself the Vast. He fixed the heaven in the unsupported, and filled the spacious firmament, and heaven and earth. He has upheld the earth and made it renowned; and has done all this in the exhilaration of the Soma. Without him, all this were nothing: all powers whatever are aggregated in him. Sustaining heaven and earth, he overspread them with effulgence, and scattering the malignant glooms, ensouled the all. It is he who gives birth to the light of the morning.

"Make the universe truth," it is said to him; "be concentred in thee." The scholiast reads, "the abode of truth;" and "let such power be concentred." But, "make the universe *truth*" means, "make all things real, by making them visible;" and the other phrase contains nothing to indicate that the addition to it is correct. The whole more probably means, "make the universe, revealed and visible, be enwrapped, encompassed, enveloped, by thee."

The victorious associated perceived a great light issuing from the darkness. The dawns recognizing him, arose, and Indra was the sole sovereign of the rays . . . . The radiant Indra, with the leaders, generated the sun, the dawn, the earth and fire [i. e., the light of the luminaries of the dawn was all his, manifested by them; he supplied light to the sun and dawn, and thus created them; and by him the earth and fire itself became visible]. Born in the highest heaven, he pervaded heaven and earth, and became the primary artificer. From him many [luminaries] are born, and heaven contains him not.

Copiously drinking the libation (the Soma), he exults, and this generates the efficient seven, from heaven, which, being glorified, have made the objects of perception by day. When the vast luminous heaven, manifested by the rays, is displayed, then are the Deities resplendent, according to abode

(i. e., each in his place); the Chief of Leaders in his approach has scattered the thick glooms so that men may see, and filled both heaven and earth by his magnitude. The phrase rendered by the scholiast, "which being glorified, have made (manifest) the objects of (human) perception by day," is obscure. But the general meaning is clear enough. "The seven efficient" are the rays of the sun or of light, and these are "glorified" when their glory is displayed: and these, thus glorified, make the daylight, and re-create, as it were, the objects of perception.

Another expression in regard to Indra is,

> Having person in the proximity of the sun, thy form becomes redolent of ambrosia; . . . . and thou art like the cervine elephant, consuming the strength, and art like a terrible lion, when wielding thy weapons.

Indra and Agni go together in one chariot, to recover the cows and destroy Vṛitra. Indra made the indistinct, wide-spreading darkness distinct, with the sun. By his magnitude, that of heaven and earth are exceeded, as the axle by the wheels. No limit has been set to his strength: heaven and earth are intimidated by its greatness: he surpasses heaven and earth: a mere portion of him is equal to both earth and heaven. By him the sun was made daily visible, and he spread out the spacious regions. By him the worlds have been rendered stationary. (It is strange that it should ever have been imagined that Indra was the firmament.)

> This Soma, Indra, has lighted up the unlustrous nights, and days and nights, and years: those of old established it as the ensign of days, and it has made the dawns generated in light. This radiant one (Indra) has illumed the non-radiant, and pervaded many dawns with true lustre.
>
> Indra, the prototype, has assumed various forms [i. e., has manifested himself by various limitations, by bodies having form and limited dimensions], and such is his form as that which for his manifestation, Indra, multiform by his illusions proceeds; for the horses yoked to his car are a thousand.

Professor Wilson's note to this is, that Indra presents himself as Agni, Vishṇu or Rudra, or any other Deity who is the actual object of worship, and is really the Deity to be adored, being identifiable with each. His chariots and horses are multiplied according to the forms in which he manifests himself, and he is here identified with Parameṣwara, the Supreme First Cause, identical with creation.

All that is, it seems to me, mere Hindū speculation. I read the passage thus: Indra, the universal principle or essence of light, the very light, invisible until manifested, has limited and manifested himself by means of, or *as*, various luminaries the form or body of each of which is his manifestation; each is he, manifested in that form of each. He is thus multiform, by his out-shining, and thus emanates or flows forth, the horses yoked to his car (the stars), being a thousand.

Your greatness, Indra and Agni [it is said in *Sûkta x. Anuv. v. Adhy. viii., of Ashṭ. iv.*], is after this fashion, and is most deserving of praise: your progenitor is one and the same: you are twin brothers, whose mother is here and there.

By Indra [*Sûkta ii. Anuv. iii. Adhy. i. Ashṭ. v.*], the constellations were made stable and firm and stationary, so that they could not be moved by any . . . . The vast strength of whom, powerful in both, has sustained the heaven and earth, and by its vigour the swift clouds and flowing waters . . . . The rays of the ever-recurring mornings, favoured, Indra, by thy vigour, confer consciousness as they shine. ['Favoured by thy vigour,' i. e., owing their light to thee] . . . . Indra with his greatness rules over the leaders: as the atmosphere encompasses the earth, so he encompasses, and being the master of the rain, he upholds the sky as well as the earth and the firmament . . . . Defend (Indra) like a lion, the untamed, quick-moving Agni, that he may abide in his dwelling, fulfilling his functions . . . . Sage Indra, who art the Lord, thou hast carried off by thy strength one wheel of the sun.

So, *Sûkta xv. Anuv. ii. Adhy. i. of Ashṭ. iv.*:

Thou hast formerly detached one wheel of Sûrya: another thou hast given to Kutsa, wherewith to acquire wealth.

And, *Sûkta xvii.* of same,

He, Indra, has formerly arrested in battle the rapid chariot of the sun: Etaşa has borne away the wheel, and demolishes.

The meaning of the original is uncertain. Professor Wilson says,

Bharach chakram Etaşah: according to the comment, *Etaşah* is put for *Etaşaya*, he, Indra, has taken the wheel for Etaşa.

In *Sûkta i. Anuv. xviii. Adhy. viii. Ashṭ i.*, we find (13)

Stop, Sura, your yellow horses, for this Etaşa, Indra, drags the wheel.

Elsewhere we read,

He has hurled the wheel of the sun, and has stopped Etaşa going forth to (battle) . . . . In which (conflicts), for the sake of Kutsa and his allies, thou hast stolen, Indra, the sun. In which thou hast, for the sake of a mortal, discomfited the sun, and hast protected Etaşa by exploits. [Elsewhere it is Agni who 'blazed forth in the contest, in defense of Etaşa:' and, finally (*Sûkta i. Anuv. i. Adhy. vii. Ashṭ. v.*)] When Sûrya harassed Etaşa, Satakratu conveyed Kutsa, the son of Arjunî, with his two prancing horses (swift) as the wind, and stealthily approached the irresistible Gandharva. [In *Sûkta iv. Anuv. xi. Adhy. iv. Ashṭ. i.*, we find], Indra has defended the pious Sacrificer Etaşa, when contending with Sûrya, the son of Swaşwa.

The real meaning of all this, it is probably impossible to discover: but the coincidence is curious, between Indra detaching a wheel of the chariot of the sun to assist Etaṣa, a Ṛishi, and Joshua stopping the course of the sun to enable the Beni-Isräl to win a battle. So, *Exod. xiv.* 25, Yahūah took off the chariot wheels of the Egyptians, that they drove them heavily. Perhaps all these allusions are to some partial or total eclipse of the sun, by calculating and predicting which, Etaṣa' triumphed over and became the superior of another Ṛishi.

A frequent name of Indra is *Maghavan*, especially applied to him as warring against Vṛitra and the Asuras. It is perhaps from the same root as *Mahatvan*, "grandeur, power;" Greek, *μέγεθος*; Latin, *Majestas;* Gothic, *Mahts;* German, *Machts;* English, *Might*, *Mighty;* Lithuanian, *Macis;* Russian, *Mocz;* Gaelic, *Mead;* Keltic, *Maint*. Or it may be from *Magh*, to "move, agitate, etc."

He is also called *Ṣakra*, "a common synonym of Indra, but which is used as an epithet, implying the *powerful*, from *ṣak*, to be able."—*Wilson*. Elsewhere he says, "Indra, as Ṣakra, is one of the twelve Âdityas." But this is not found in the Veda. Wherever the name Ṣakra occurs in the hymns, it is as a synonym of Indra, as the slayer of Vṛitra, dispenser of benefits, etc.

Ṣatakratu, as we have already said, is also a name of Indra. It means, it is said, "he to whom many rites are addressed, or by whom many acts are performed." Neither it nor Ṣakra designates Indra in any special character or manifestation.

Parjanya is said to be Indra, in his character of the sender of rain. This name first occurs in the fourth *Ashṭaka, Adhy. iv. Anuv. vi. Sûkta xi.*, which, in ten stanzas, is wholly addressed to him. The derivations of the name, cited by Sâyaṇa from Yaska, Nirukta 10. 10. are merely fanciful. He is, in this hymn, the mighty Parjanya, the thunderer, the showerer, the bountiful, who impregnates the vegetable creation with rain. He strikes down the trees; he destroys the Râkshasas, he terrifies the whole world by his mighty weapon; even the innocent man flies from the sender of rain, when Parjanya, thundering, slays the wicked. Driving the clouds before him, he makes manifest the messengers of the rain; the roaring of the lion proclaims from afar that Parjanya overspreads the sky with rainy clouds. He fertilizes the ground with showers: through his function the earth is bowed down (submits to be impregnated), through it hoofed cattle increase; and plants assume all kinds of forms (i. e., the vegetable world develops itself in every species and variety of growth). Through him the rivers flow unimpeded and sky and earth are saturated with water. He rains, he pours down water. He makes the deserts passable, he is the author of comforts for men, and he checks the rain in season. Elsewhere, Parjanya and Vata are showerers of rain, sending water from the firmament. They are granters of food, and Parjanya, through the vegetable world, a giver of happiness.

In the fifth *Ashṭaka,* the large celestial arrow is called the growth of Parjanya. Its point is anointed with venom, its blade is iron.

Sûktas xii. and *xiii. Anuv. vi. Adhy. vii. Ashṭ. v.*, are addressed to Parjanya. He is, there, the augmenter of plants, the increaser of the waters, the showerer, who loudly roars, engendering the infant, the embryo of the plants. He grants the desired light at the three seasons. One form of him is like a barren cow, he takes whichever form he pleases: the mother receives the milk from the father, thence the father, thence the son is nourished. In him all beings exist, the three worlds abide in him. From him the waters flow in three directions; the three water-shedding masses of clouds pour the waters round the Mighty One. He is self-irradiating. He, the *bull,* is the impregnator of the ever-renewed vegetable world. In him is the vitality of both stationary and moveable things. He is the cause of the impregnation of plants, of cows, of mares, and of women. The frogs utter praises that are agreeable to him, when he sends down the rain upon them.

Sûkta i. Anuv. ii. Adhy. viii. of Ashṭ. v., says:

> Indra, who is great in might, *like* Parjanya the distributor of rain.

I am quite sure that here, as in many other passages, "like" should be "as" or "in his character of."

Parjanya is, unquestionably, Indra, as the supplier of rain to the earth, and thence as its impregnator, the generator, procreator, vivifier, to whom all pregnancy and parturience, of vegetation and the animals and women, is owing. He is the prototype of Priapus; and in these characteristics we have the germ of the worship of the Phallus and the Lingam. *Jan* means, to "bring forth," to "produce," and *Jani* is a "female." *Janas* is a "man," a "begetter." The allusion to the *bull,* also, is not without interest, since that animal subsequently became the symbol of the generative divine power.

Rijishin is once used as a name of epithet of Indra. Its meaning is uncertain. It probably means "partaker of the oblation," or "receiver of the juice" of the Soma plant, which he is invited to come and drink.

"Uṣanas the Son of Kavi," is said, *Sûkta i. Anuv. xviii. Adhy. viii. Asht. i.*, to have given Indra the thunderbolt, with which to destroy Vṛitra. And, *Sûkta i. Anuv. x. Adhy. iv. Asht. i.*, it is said to Indra,

> If Uṣanas should sharpen thy vigour by his own, then would thy might terrify by its intensity both heaven and earth.

In *Sûkta v. Anuv. iii. Adhy. vi. Asht. iii.*, Indra says,

> I have been Manu and Sûrya: I am the wise Ṛishi, Kakshivat: I have befriended Kutsa, the son of Arjuni; I am the far-seeing Uṣanas, So behold me.

Indra and Uṣanas went, with vigourous and rapid coursers, to the dwelling of Kutsa, and destroyed his foes: and then, in one chariot with Kutsa and the Gods, he slew Ṣushṇa—

> Thou, Indra [it is said elsewhere], hast been an ancient benefactor of Uṣanas the son of Kavi: having slain Navavástwa, thou hast given back to his own grandson, who was to be restored to the grandfather.

These passages, and many others like them, referring to wars among men, between the Aryas and Dasyus, the fair-skinned and warlike race, and the dark barbarians, and to rivalries and strifes between princes and rivals, in which Indra fought on the side of his worshippers may be altogether mythical, or may have related to real occurrences, far even then in the past: and remind us of the Olympian Gods of the Iliad, not only aiding their favourites on either side, but themselves engaging in actual battle, as

> the stars in their courses fought against Sisera.

Sûkta i. Anuv. xv. Adhy. vi. Asht. i., is a hymn by the Ṛishi *Kutsa*, son of *Angiras*. Elsewhere, Indra is represented as having espoused his quarrel and fought for him when he slew Ṣushṇa. He is called the son of Arjuna, and was protected by the Aṣwins. Indra bears him in his chariot, to the ceremony. To him, his charioteer, Indra subjected Ṣushṇa, Asusha and Kuyava. Kutsa, the son of *Ruru*, was eager for Indra's friendship. The two alighted in his habitation, and being entirely similar in form, the truthful woman was perplexed (Indra's wife, Sachi, the Hindūs say). Indra and Kutsa rode in the same chariot, and Indra defended him, and enabled him to win through his trouble, slaying Ṣushṇa, Kuyava and the Dasyus for him.

Marutwat is another name applied to Indra. It means, "attended by the winds."

We find "Indra and *Parvata*" named together, in a few places, and Professor Wilson says that the latter is "another name of Indra, as regulating the *Parvas*, the *joints* or periods of the day or year." In *Sûkta ii. Anuv. xviii. Adhy. i. Ashṭ. ii.*, we read, after an invocation to morning and night, to the dawn, to the circumambient Divinity who invests himself with many forms, and to the wind,

> Do you, Indra and Parvata, sharpen our (intellects), and may all the Gods show us favour. Whenever I, the son of Usij, worship with my offerings those two, who eat and drink at (the season) of the world-whitening (dawn).

And in *Sûkta vi. Anuv. xix.* of the same

> Indra and Parvata, who are foremost in battles, slay every one who is arrayed against us . . . .

And here Professor Wilson says,

> Parvata is said to mean a cloud, or the Deity presiding over clouds, another form of Indra.

In *Sûkta i. Anuv. iii. Adhy. vii. of Ashṭ. ii.*,

> When Bṛihaspati . . . . for thy glory, Parvata, had concealed the herd of kine, thou didst set them free, and with thine associate Indra, didst send down the ocean of water . . . .

In *Sûkta xv. Anuv. iv. Adhy. iii. Ashṭ. iii.*, Indra and Parvata are invoked, as distinct Deities, to come together in a spacious car; and in *Sûkta vi. Anuv. iv. Adhy. viii. Ashṭ. iv.*, Parvata and *Saviṭri* are jointly invoked to give food and water. With them, Ahirludhnya is invoked. Elsewhere, Parvata is invoked in the same stanza with Saviṭri, as a bestower of riches.

The passages in which this name occurs do not contain anything that can enable us to determine what was intended by this Deity.

In *Sûktas xx.* and *xxi. Anuv. iii. Adhy. iv. Ashṭ. v.*, *Vâshtospati* is addressed. *Vâstu* is the *foundation* of a *house*, and is said to be put for the house itself, and came to mean "protector of the dwelling." An excellent, comfortable, opulent, delightful abode is prayed for, blessings, protection of property, bestowal of wealth. The Deity invoked is styled, "remover of disease, assuming all forms;" and the second stanza of *Sûkta xx.* reads,

> Protector of the dwelling, be our preserver and the augmenter of our wealth; possessed of cattle and horses, Indra, may we, through thy friendship, be exempt from decay.

The name *Vâshtospati* is evidently only an epithet of Indra. It occurs nowhere else.

VAYU.

Agni is the Universal Fire, and all its manifestations:

Indra is the Universal Light, and all its manifestations and emanations:

Parjanya is the fructifying or generative Potency of Light; light as generator, prototype of Priapus.

Flame and Heat, it is natural to suppose, were not overlooked, when Light, an emanation from Agni, was deified.

In seeking to ascertain, not from the commentaries or later Brahmanic books, what was represented in the Veda by Vayu, and what by Arushâ and the Ârushîs, I found but few passages that could serve to resolve my doubts, in regard to the former.

Mr. Cox says,

> The God of the bright heaven, who is known as Dyu, Indra and Agni, is also called Vayu, a name denoting, it would seem, the gentler movements of the air, which are expressed by the pipings of the Greek Pan, and the soft breathings of the Latin Favonius.

I am at a loss to know whether by "the God of the bright heaven," he means the firmament itself, or the sky, or some ideal Deity who presided over and had in charge the firmament or sky; or whether he means the heaven when illuminated with light, as contradistinguished from the darkened sky: and what he adds, makes the uncertainty more distressing.

> *As such* [he says], he comes early in the morning [who or what *comes?* the God, or the bright heaven?], to chase away the demons; and the dawns weave for him golden raiment. He is drawn by the nights and has Indra for his charioteer. There are only three Deities, according to the etymologists, Agni, whose place is on earth, Vayu or Indra, whose place is in the atmosphere; and Sûrya, whose place is in the sky.

In *Sâtapatha Brâhmana, xi.* 2. 3. 1 (*p.* 838), Brahma (in the neuter), is introduced as being the original Source of all things:

> In the beginning, Brahma was all this: He created the Gods. Having created the Gods, he placed them in these worlds; in this world, Agni; Vayu in the atmosphere, and Sûrya in the sky. (*Muir: Orig. Sansk. Texts*, 25.)

In the *Nirukta, vii.* 5, it is said,

> There are only three Deities, according to the Nairuktas (etymologists), Agni, whose place is on earth, Vayu or Indra, whose place is in the atmosphere, and

> Sûrya, whose place is in the sky. And Sâkapûṇi thinks that these are the triple manifestations [the three steps], of Vishṇu, in the form of fire on earth, of lightning in the atmosphere, and of the solar light in the sky. (*Muir: iv.* 56. 57.)

We attach no importance to these Brahmanic notions. According to them, every Vedic God is at different times everything, and at no time anything in particular. All knowledge of what Vayu, Vishṇu and other Gods originally were, had been lost for at least a score of centuries.

Vayu, in the Veda, yokes two *red* or *purple* horses to his car. He is invoked to cause "intelligent beings" to arise, as a lover arouses her whom he loves, from her sleep; to summon sky and earth, and to light up the dawn.

> For thee [it is said], by means of thee, the brilliant Dawns, from afar, display their welcome garmenting, in variegated and splendid radiance.

And Vayu and Indra are conveyed together, in a chariot drawn by the Niyuts.

His horses are strong-limbed, youthful and full of vigour. They bear him through the space between heaven and earth, *growing in bulk*, and strong as oxen. They are not lost in the expanse, but continue on unretarded, with undiminished speed, difficult to be arrested, as the beams of the sun.

In *Sûkta ii. Anuv. i. Adhy. i. Asht. i.*, we find,

> Vayu, pleasant to behold, approach . . . . Indra and Vayu, abiding in the sacrificial fire.

The same attributes, powers and faculties are so continually ascribed in the Vedas to different Gods, as to have sadly perplexed all the modern commentators, and in resorting to the Hindū interpreters of the Vedas, they have found only confusion worse confounded. But I am very strongly inclined to believe that in the Vedas themselves, at least in the older hymns of the Rig-Veda, the confusion is only apparent, and entirely owing to our uncertainty as to the personalities of their Gods. Many of the phrases used in invoking Agni and Indra, seem as exaggerated, strained and far-fetched, as any that are used in speaking of other Deities; but when we succeed in identifying ourselves, to some extent, for the time, with these Poets, and become familiar with their processes of thought, we find the phrases to be deductions as to the effects and action of fire and light, that are singularly ingenious, and evincive of acute and profound thought. And we also find that plain and direct expressions as to the nature or office or relations of a particular God, are never loosely made, but always mean exactly what the words import.

And when it is said that Indra and Vayu "abide in the fire of the sacrifice," this is not a mere meaningless expression, nor is it anywhere contradicted by any other expression inconsistent with it. To "*abide*" in the fire, is to be *in* it and *of* it, as a component part of it. Light is so, and emanates from it. So are and so do, flame and heat. But heat has no colours, and drives no red or purple horses, as the flame of the fire, the flashings of the Auroras, and the blazing orb of the sun may be said to do.

In *Sûkta vi. Anuv. v.*, of the same, we read:

> We invoke both the Divinities abiding in heaven, Indra and Vayu, to drink of this Soma juice: the wise invoke for their preservation Indra and Vayu, who are swift as thought, have a thousand eyes, and are protectors of pious acts [acts of worship].

As component parts of the fire, they are ministers of sacrifices, and so are protectors of acts of worship. This function hardly seems to belong to "the gentler movements of the air, expressed by the pipings of Pan."

Professor Wilson says that Vayu is invoked in a visible form, as the Deity presiding over the wind. He doubts whether Vedic expressions intimating personality, are to be understood as indicating actual figures or idols, and thinks that the personification is probably only poetical.

Certainly a visible form, or rather a visible *appearance*, is assigned to Vayu. He is not represented as limited, as the luminaries are, in place or by definite shape and outlines. He is visible as flame is visible, and rides in the same car with Indra, the light, and his horses are of the principal colours of flames, red and purple. He is not represented as presiding over the winds, but as the producer of them. Professor Wilson is unquestionably right in thinking the Poets of the Veda did not include figure or form or limitation, in the idea of personality. But their personifications are as real as our personifications of the soul and of Deity are, which also include no idea of form or figure.

> For thee [it is said], the cow that yields ambrosia, milks all kinds of treasure.

The original word, rendered "ambrosia" (which is a word without definite meaning), is *Sarardughâ, explained* by the scholiast, by *Amṛita*, a *supposed* drink of the Brahmanic Gods. What *Sarardughâ was*, we are not told. It was some liquid, we imagine, that was poured upon the flames of the sacrifice, perhaps mead, the beverage of the Norse Gods: for honey is mentioned in the Veda. "Treasure" or "wealth," to the Gods, was what was sacrificed to them. The "cow" is, of course, merely figurative, whatever the beverage was. The hymn continues:

> Thou begettest the Maruts [whose father Rudra is often said to be] of the Expanse [their mother, Priṣni?], for showering rain, the rivers . . . . Thou defendest from all beings: thou protectest us from the fear of evil spirits . . . . Thou, Vayu, who art preceded by none [because an emanation from Agni, and being to him

> as the Logos to the Father, or Agni manifested]: . . . . Vayu with thousand steeds . . . . the Gods hold back for thee, as the Deity first to drink [because the beverage of the sacrifice must be poured upon and become part of the flame, before it can reach and be imbibed by the other Deities].

As Proclus says,

> Fire dissolves the elements of that which it burns, and transmutes them into itself.

The horses of Vayu, which bear him through the space between earth and the sky, "grow in bulk" because it is of the nature of flame to spread and expand. Every one who has seen great fires in the open air has noted how rapidly the flames flash from place to place, and seem, as it were, to revel in a delirious ecstacy. The steadiest flame, of even the household fire, is restless and unquiet; and to one who has seen herds of wild horses on the American plains, as the Aryans saw them on their native steppes, free as the wind, full of life and action, with luxuriant manes and tails floating in the morning breeze as they careered swiftly, and "terrible as an army with banners" over the grassy ridges that stretched between the delighted observer and the glowing sunrise—to one who has seen the wild horse in his pride, it seems natural that to them, thus seen, the streaming glories of the rising sun and of the Northern Aurora should have been likened.

The horses of Vayu are young and vigourous, and strong as oxen:

> They are not lost in the expanse, but hold on their speed, having no dwelling by speech [no fixed place by expression in form]. They are difficult to be arrested as the beams of the sun: they are difficult to be arrested by force.

In *Sûkta ix. Anuv. iv. Adhy. viii. Asht. ii.*:

> Vayu, whose are a thousand chariots, and the Niyut steeds . . . . Leaders Indra and Vayu, Lords of the Niyut steeds . . . .

In *Sûkta i. Anuv. v. Adhy. vii. of Asht. iii.*:

> Vayu, who art drawn by the Niyuts, and hast Indra for charioteer . . . . [and in the other five verses, Indra and Vayu are invoked together]: so also they are in the next Sûkta; as 'Lords of Strength, vigourous, and drawn by the Niyut steeds, in the same car: and in the third we read, 'Vayu, the terrifier of foes, come with thy brilliant car . . . . Vayu, who art the *niryurvâno aşastih* [which Professor Wilson cannot translate], who art drawn by the Niyuts, and hast Indra for thy charioteer . . . . The dark nurses of wealth [*Qu.* the Maruts?], the universal forms attend upon thee . . . . May the ninety-nine steeds harnessed together, that are as swift as thought, convey thee . . . . three-fold Vayu, and Agni, concurring in satisfaction with heaven.
>
> Vayu, the divine, the fulfiller of desires, the adorable . . . . the two Lords of People, Vayu with the Niyut steeds, and Pushan . . . .

Asht. v. Adhy. vi. Anuv. vi. Sûkta i. The Hero Vayu: . . . . harness thy Niyut steeds . . . . the white-complexioned dispenser of wealth, Vayu whom heaven and earth bore for the sake of riches, whom the divine language of praise sustains as a Deity, for the sake of riches . . . . Those munificent princes who confer on us prosperity, by gifts of cattle, horses, treasure, gold, Indra and Vayu, overcome . . . .

Sûkta ii. Preservers of mankind, Indra and Vayu . . . . the white-complexioned Vayu, intelligent, glorious with the Niyut steeds . . . . Harnessing the Niyuts, come, Indra and Vayu, hither . . . . [Twice more, in the same hymn, they are addressed jointly.]

Sûkta iii. [Addressed to Vayu, and to Indra and Vayu. The latter is prayed to bestow riches and male progeny, and to come with hundreds and thousands of Niyut steeds.]

Such are the data for deciding as to Vayu.

It is true that Eichhoff gives us the root वा to "move" or "breathe," or "blow;" whence the Greek *άω, ἀάω, ἀέω* and *ἄημι*, "breathe, blow," whence *ἄημα, flatus, spiritus;* Gothic, *waja;* German, *wehe;* Lithuanian, *wēju;* Russian, *wieiu;* from which root is *vâyus*, "air;" Greek, *ἀήρ*; Latin, *aer;* and *vâtas, vâtis*, "wind." The root वह also means, to "move," and so does the root वज. The original meaning of the root, we may conclude, was to "move, fluctuate, waver, etc.," and that to "blow," as the wind does, was a secondary or derivative meaning: and that *vayus* meant the "air," as "moving, inconstant, wavering," and the like, all which peculiarly apply to flame, easily conceived of as air made visible by the heat. It is quite certain that the epithets applied and the attributes ascribed, to Vayu, are not fitting or appropriate, when applied to the invisible colourless air.

The air might be termed the mother of the Maruts, but could not be said to "beget" them. How could the *air* be said to arouse men in the morning? It is the daylight that does that, and the light is emitted by flame. How does the air "summon sky and earth, and light up the dawn"? How could it, with red and purple steeds, be said to ride in the same car with Indra; and to cause the brilliant dawns to display their garmenting "in variegated and splendid radiance"? How is the air "pleasant to behold"? And how does it "abide in the sacrificial fire"? How could the invisible air be properly styled "white-complexioned"?

Vayu is styled "intelligent and glorious," and the word translated "glorious" seems always to have reference to radiance and brilliance, and could not be properly applied to the air.

The appellation *Niyut* is several times applied to the horses of Vayu. The only root to which I can refer it is *Ni* or *Nay*, meaning to "move, direct, govern or control;" whence *Nayas*, "tendency," and *Nayanan*, "intelligence."

It would be very presumptuous in me to even endeavour to conjecture the meaning of many of the expressions used in the Veda. Professor Wilson often declines to attempt it, and gives merely what he considers the equivalent *words*, whether the sentence, thus formed, makes any sense or not. Mr. Bleeck feared that parts of his translation from the German of Spiegel, of the Gâthâs and Yashts would, to English readers, "be almost as unintelligible in their present form, as in the Zend itself;" and much of every translation of the Veda is so.

Thus, it is said to Vayu,

> The dark nurses of wealth, the Universal Forms, attend upon thee.

I have no doubt that the "Universal Forms" are the celestial luminaries; the universal or essence, Agni or Indra, or Agni containing Indra and Vayu, limited and manifested in place, by form, and thus dependent upon and subordinates of Vayu as part of Agni. But I can not conjecture what is meant, if the translation is correct, by the "dark nurses of wealth." The word rendered "dark" may mean the night, and if so, the phrase is intelligible, for it would mean "the night's nurses," i. e., the luminaries of the night, or which shine in the darkness, and in which is stored up, as milk is in the bosom of the nursing mother, the wealth of light, or the light which is the cause and source of the wealth of the herdsman and husbandman.

The "ninety-nine steeds harnessed together, that are as swift as thought," which convey Vayu, are beyond the reach of conjecture: and the addition of the phrase, "three-fold Vayu, and Agni, concurring in satisfaction with heaven," throws no light upon it. The word "three-fold" indicates that "ninety-nine" is used as being thrice thirty-three, a number that is mentioned elsewhere, and so *explained* by the commentators as to be utterly incomprehensible.

The air could not, in any sense, be said to be "three-fold." As applied to Vayu, its meaning can only be conjectured. It may be supposed to mean the flame of the ordinary fire, on earth; the flame of the sun, and that of the Aurora or lightning, at night: or the three colours of flame; or, as I am inclined to think from the peculiar idea entertained of fire in the hymns, the flame itself, and the light and heat contained in it as an integral part of it. These and Agni, which contains them and manifests them all, "Concur in satisfaction with heaven," i. e., they rejoice and are glad as the heavens and their Gods are, with the ascending sacrifice. This, at least, is not nonsense.

Vayu and Pushan are "the two Lords of People," i. e., men are dependent upon them, for their welfare and comfort, perhaps.

Heaven and earth bore Vayu, "for the sake of riches," and he is the "dispenser of wealth, whom the divine language [utterance or expression] of praise sustains as a Deity, for the sake of prayer." The praise or adoration uttered or expressed by means of the fire of sacrifice, sends upward toward the sky the flame manifested separately, and thus a distinct Deity. It is itself the utterance of praise: and it is so for the sake of the riches prayed for; for the sake of which, also, it is generated, produced or manifested in heaven and earth, in each of which it blesses men. "The *divine* language of praise" is the adoration by sacrifice; for it is Agni, a Deity and Divine, who is the invoker of the celestial Gods.

Indra and Vayu are the preservers of mankind, since without flame and light men could not exist: and they are the munificent princes [superior to their manifestations, the luminaries], "who confer on men prosperity, by gifts," of various kinds. Once, Vayu is invoked to come with hundreds and thousands of Niyut steeds: for the Sun's rays of flame, flashing forth, are innumerable.

I conclude that Vayu is unquestionably the *flame*, or Agni manifested, as an emanation.

The Aryan emigrants carried with them everywhere, this worship of fire, flame and light. Æschylus, in Agamemnon, says,

> And the altars of all our city-guarding Gods, of those above, and those below, Gods of heaven and Gods of the Forum, are blazing with offerings; and in different directions, different flames are streaming upward, high as heaven, drugged with the mild unadulterated cordials of pure unguent, with the royal cake brought from the inmost cells.

We hear in this passage the Vedic Poet exclaiming,

> Agni, thine offering, and thy glory, and thy flames beam high.

Euripides, in *Antigone* (1010) says,

> I essayed straightway the divination by fire, on the sacred altars; [and (1020)], And the Gods no longer accept from us the sacrificial prayer, nor the flame of the thighs.

Sophocles says, in *Œdipus Tyrannus*,

> O give, our sire, blast by thy thunderbolt. Thine invincible arrows also, O Lord of Light, from the golden-twisted horns of thy bow.

The Emperor Julian said,

> He uttered out from Himself the sun, the Greatest God, in all things like Himself.
>
> Zeus [it is said in the Orphic Fragments], is the rushing of indefatigable fire . . . . He is the sun and moon . . . . his eyes the sun and the opposing moon; his unfallacious mind the royal and incorruptible Æther. [And *Orphic Hymn v.*], O thou that hast the might on high always untired, of Zeus, a portion of the stars and sun and moon, all-subduer, fire-breathing, that kindles all that live: Æther, that givest light from on high, best rudiment of the world: O shining growth, light-bringing, star-radiant, calling on I beseech thee, tempered, to be serene.

In Nonnus (*Dionus. xl.* 378) we read,

> When dewy Sélēnē milkṣ the resisting fire of thy parturient beam, drawing together her bent-forward cow-horn.

Orpheus is represented as saying:

> Light broke through the Æther. The light was the Demiurgos, a being Supreme above all others, and its name is Metis, Phanēs, Erikapseus. These three powers are the three names of the One Power and Strength of the Only God, whom no one ever beheld. By this power, all things were produced, both the incorporeal beginnings (*archai*), and the sun and moon and their influences.

The Hindūs applied the Vedic idea of manifestation to Brahma.

> Brahma, through whom all things are illumined, who with his light lets the sun and the stars shine, but who is not revealed by their light. (*Sankhara, Atma-Bodha.* 61.)

And so the Persian or Zend Scripture says,

> when I made the wide-ruling Mithra, I created him just like myself in the divine nature and dignity, I who am Ahura Mazda. Go up, shining sun, with thy swift horses, rise above Mount Berezaiti, and shine to the creatures on the way which Ahura Mazda has made in the air, which the Gods have created. Praise to the sun, who drives on with four horses, and works purity.

We cite these passages, not to show what the later ideas were, but as explanatory of the meanings of the Veda. It was only necessary to attain to the conception of a supreme creative mind, and the Veda furnished the rest. From it came all the doctrine of emanation and manifestation, which, applied to Brahma, Ahura Mazda and Zeus, made the three Great Religions: from it the idea of the divine Triads, of three divine *Hypostasēs* or persons in the Divine Unity; and Athēnē issuing, completely armed, from the brain of Zeus was but the symbolic expression of the idea of the emanation of the divine creative wisdom or intelligence.

The Poet Shelley says,

Men scarcely know how beautiful fire is;

and surely nothing is so beautiful as flame. It seems composed of all gems, of every hue and colour, rarefied into most beautiful and brilliant vapour; and as it leaps and frolics, as if in exuberance of delight, one easily invests it with the characteristics of a living creature. Beautiful exceedingly on the earth, it is even more beautiful in the heavens; and as the diffuser of grateful warmth, the best friend of man during the harsh winter's cold. It gives him the warmth of the sun; it is the destroyer of the forests, the purifier, free of all the grossness of matter; and it would have been very strange if the Aryan Poets had not deified, or at least personified, it.

As manifested by the flashing, coruscating glories of the Aurora, it could well be said that the Seven Sisters (the stars of Ursa Major), nursed Ârushâ, the flaming radiance of the sky. As coming with the dawn, manifested by the glowing flames that herald the rising of the sun, and seem to blaze among the clouds, he might be associated with the Pleiades.

This brings us to consider what Ârushâ was: for Vayu was unquestionably flame, as a hypostasis of Agni.

ÂRUSHÂ.

We have quoted, on a preceding page, what Müller says, etymologically and otherwise of *Ârushî*, *Ârushâ* and the *Ârushîs*.

The horses of Indra, of Agni, of Bṛihaspati, as quick as the wind and as bright as Suns, who lick the udder of the dark cow, the night, are called *Ârushâ;* the smoke which rises from the burning sun at day-break, the limbs of the sun, with which he climbs the sky, the thunderbolt which Indra throws, the fire which is seen by day and by night, all are called *Ârushâ.*

He who fills heaven and earth with light, who runs across the darkness along the sky, who is seen among the black cows of the night, is called *Arushô Vṛishâ, arushâ* or the bright bull. (*Müller: Chips. ii.* 135.)

Arushô, here, is evidently not a name, but an adjective.

But this very Ârushâ is, in the Veda, as in Greek Mythology, represented as a child, as a Solar Agni:

Rig-V. iii. 1. 4. The Seven Sisters have nursed him, the joyful, the white one, as he was born, the Ârushâ, with great might; as horses go to the foal that is born, so did the Gods bring up the sun, when he was born. (*Id.* 135. 6.)

The reader will remember that *Ârushâ*, masculine, and *Ârushî,* feminine, are from the participial form *Arvas*, nominative, *Arvân;* and that *Ârushâ* is used in the sense of "bright," as (*Rig-V. vii.* 75. 6),

The red, bright horses are seen, bringing to us the brilliant dawn.

Mr. Cox says *Arvân* is a horse. It may be: I find in Eichhoff that *Açvan* is:

Ârushâ is always the young Sun, in the Veda; the Sun who drives away the dark night, and sends his first ray to awaken the world. (*Rig-V. vii.* 71. 1.) Night goes away from her sister, the Dawn; the Dark One opens the path for Ârushâ. (*Id.* 136.)

Though in some of his names there is an unintentional allusion to his animal character, he soon takes a purely human form. He is called *Nṛikakshâs* (*iii.* 15. 3), having the eyes of a man; and even his wings have commenced to grow in the Veda, where, once at least, he is called *Arushâh Suparnas,* 'the bright Sun with beautiful wings.' As Eros is the child of Zeus, Ârushâ is called the child of Dyaus (*Divâh sisus*).

Rig-V. iv. 15. 6. Him, the God Agni, they adorn and purify every day, like a horse that has run his race, like Ârushâ, the bright Sun, the young child of Dyaus (heaven).

Rig-V. vi. 49. 2. Let us worship Agni, the child of heaven, the son of strength, Ârushâ, the bright light of the sacrifice. (*Müller: Chips. ii.* 136.)

In the phrase "the bright sun," the word "sun" is supposed to be *understood* in the original, the only word for the phrase being *Ârushâ*. I suspect that the word "light" also, in the phrase "the bright light," is understood.

This child is the first of the Gods, for he comes (*v.* 1. 5), *agre ahnâm*, 'at the point of the days,' *ushasâm agre*, 'at the beginning of the dawns'; but in one passage two daughters are ascribed to him, different in appearance—the one decked with the stars, the other brilliant by the light of the sun—Day and Night, who are elsewhere called the daughters of the Sun. As the God of Love, in the Greek sense of the word (*Eros*), Ârushâ does not occur in the Veda. (*Id.* 136. 137.)

'Âruṣhâ born at the beginning of all the days;' Ârushâ, the child, the son of Dyaus; he yokes the Harits, and is, if not the son, at least the beloved, of the Dawn. (*Id.* 138.)

Professor Curtius, quoted by Müller in a note (*ii.* 138. 9), says

that the root *ar* means 'going, running, striving;' that in Sanskrit, the meaning of 'horse' or 'solar horse' was assigned to *Arvat;*

and that, in India, *arvat*, "running," and *harit*, "bright," had each assumed a secondary or idiomatic meaning, becoming recognized names for *horse*, is said by Professor Müller, in the same note, who adds that,

as *arvat* was also applied to the sun, the heavenly runner, the conception of the sun as a horse became almost inevitable, and required no poetic effort on the part of people speaking Sanskrit.

In his notes on the Rig-Veda Sanhita (*Vol.* I. *p.* 11), Müller, noting the objections made to some of his interpretations of passages in which the word Ârushâ occurs, on the ground that in them the word is an epithet of Agni, or Sûrya remarks,

that this objection would apply to many other names, originally intended for these conceptions, but which, nevertheless, in the course of time, become independent names of independent Deities.

These are his views in full as to Ârushâ, and they leave us entirely in doubt as to the real character of that Deity; or whether the word was the name of a Deity at all. Let us sum up what he says:

Ârushâ brings us as near to the Greek Eros (Love), as we can expect. It is used in the sense of bright, and applied to the horses of Indra, Agni and Bṛihaspati; to the smoke rising from the morning sun; to the sun's limbs; to the thunderbolt,

> and to fire. All these are called *Ârushâ.* He who fills heaven and earth with light, runs across the *darkness* of the sky, is seen among the black cows of the *night*, is called the bright (*Arushô*) bull.

He is a joyful and white one, and he is nursed, when born, by the Seven Sisters. He is of great might. Is he a luminary that "fills the heaven with light?" Is it in the day or night, that he "runs across the *darkness* of the sky?" Surely it is in the night that he is "seen among the dark cows of the night." He is at once the young sun, a luminary of the night, or the lightning; the "Dark One opens a path for him." He has the eyes of a man, and wings. He is the child of Dyaus: he is the bright sun, and the Bright Light of the Sacrifice: he comes at the early dawns, the beginnings of the days; and he has two daughters, one decked with stars, and the other brilliant by the light of the sun; and these children are Day and Night.

From all this, can any one say what Ârushâ *is?* Is the young Sun the father of Day and Night? Does *he* have the eyes of a man, and wings? Above all, is *he* visible among the dark clouds of the night; and does he traverse the sky through the darkness? And yet, if the translation is correct, he is *both* the bright sun, and the bright, i. e., the shining light, or flame, of the sacrifice; and he was nursed, when first manifested, by the Seven Sisters.

He is also "The child of the expanse, or heaven," "The Son of Strength," an epithet applied to Agni, because he is produced by attrition, by means of muscular strength. He is called the Sun, and he is also called Agni. He yokes the Harits. And we read, also, that "when the sun flew up, the Arushîs refreshed their bodies in water." Who are these? Mr. Cox says, the horses of the sun. Do *they* refresh their bodies in water, when the sun has risen? Also, he says, they are said to mean "the bright cows."

I do not clearly comprehend how *Arvas* or *Ârushâ* obtains the signification of "bright." The root *AR*, it is said, means to "go," to "run," whence, a *horse*, and, as the sun *runs*, the *sun*. Thence, as the sun is bright (*Ârushâ*), *Ârushâ* means "bright." Without much knowledge, or indeed any, of Sanskrit, one may doubt the soundness of this derivation, when the data are thus all placed before him.

What are we to conclude, from the fact that *Ârushâ* is an adjective, applied to horses, and also to the sun; that it also is a noun, the name of a Deity who is the Son of Strength; that he is identical with Agni, as the bright light of the sacrifice; and that traversing the sky at night, he is the father of two daughters, one decked with the stars, the other brilliant by the sun?

But I do not think *he* is called "the Son of Strength." I think that this phrase is applied to Agni, and not to Ârushâ; that Ârushâ *is* Agni, as he is, and as Vayu is—that is, that he is a person or hypostasis of Agni, the fire. I think that the verse addresses *Agni* as child of heaven and Son of Strength, and, as Ârushâ, only as the *brilliant* Light, that is, the *radiant*, coruscating splendour of the Flame of the sacrificial fire; and here, I think, we have a clue to the individuality of this subordinate Deity.

Again, the phrase, "he runs across" the darkness of the sky, may not mean that he *traverses* it, as the luminaries are said to do. It rather indicates that he leaps or flashes across it; and its "darkness" may mean, not night, but that caused by storm. As the gleaming, blinding radiance of the electric flame, he may be

> seen among the dark cows [clouds] of the night, or that make day to be like night. As the radiant splendour of the flames of the sun, he is seen at the beginnings of the days.

There may be light, and is light, without appearance of flame and without heat. The light of the moon has no appearance of fire or flame. The glow-worm gives light: and light begins to come in the morning, and continues in the evening, when all appearance of flame or radiant splendour has disappeared.

The same imagination that could conceive of light as latent and invisible in the latent fire, and manifested outwardly by the fire when kindled, could conceive of the flame and blaze as also existing when unmanifested, having in itself the splendour and radiance and coruscation also unmanifested; so that these are a manifestation of the flame or blaze. They may be seen flashing forth from the flame, glittering, darting, flickering, quick-moving, flashing from the sun as his rays; coruscating from the lightning, and magnificently displayed by the Aurora.

I think that Vayu is *flame*, and Ârushâ the coruscating *radiance*, *effulgence* and *beams* of the flame, which send their light far forth beyond themselves, and with it fill heaven and earth.

We are so familiar with the phenomena of fire as to see nothing marvellous in them. For us, the universe has no surprises. The performances of Deity in the physical world (I speak in no lack of reverence of Him, but little reverencing an age that itself reverences nothing, except money and rank and success) have lost the charm and gloss of novelty, the perpetual miracles of the natural world are like a play of which audiences are weary, and which no longer, draws; and we, miserable atoms of intelligence that we are, having invented names that have no sort of meaning to us, for the unknown powers and inexplicable phenomena, fancy that we know what they are, and what the natural causes that produce effects; and having substituted words and names for things, and made the universe still more incomprehensible, look smirkingly around upon its thousand marvels, imagine in our self-conceit that we know its processes, and can afford to dispense with God, whom we have also made a mere name, as a Cause, altogether; and no more really *reverence* Him than we do an ingenious mechanic who has succeeded in obtaining a patent for some new labour-saving invention.

If one could imagine himself in utter darkness, not an infant, but a man, and that, after so remaining for a time he sees the light of dawn faint in the eastern sky, growing and extending, until it makes all the material world visible; that he sees the glories flashing many-coloured upward, that herald the rising of the sun, sees his brilliant orb on which the eye cannot look, rise above the hills or the horizon of the plain and begin his majestic march, and feels the warmth of his beams in which his chilled frame and all Nature rejoices, he would be able to comprehend the Aryan ideas of the light and heat and splendour of the Sun.

If, chilled with cold that continues to increase in intensity and threatens certain death, he could for the first time see fire, and feel and know its effects; if he could see attrition of the dry wood produce, first heat and smoke, and at length flame, and that flame evolving heat, feeding upon the wood of which it was born, and at last leaping, flashing, exulting in its terrible and destructive energy and might, he would know how the most ancient men came to worship Fire as a God.

And we can easily understand how light and heat, and flame and the radiant splendour darting and flashing from the flame, would seem to him to be different things, yet all included in the unity of fire; and each would, by degrees, become to him a Deity.

What are light and heat to us? It was enough for the old Aryans to know that they *were: what* they were, they do not enquire. Do we, any more than they did, know *what* they are? They were actual, visible existences, to them, more real, because visible, than soul, spirit and God are to us. Other beings and things than matter were *real*, to *them*. So electricity and magnetism are real and actual entities to us, invested by our imagination with the characteristics of substantial things; and yet we no more know *what* either is, in its Very Self, than these ancients knew what fire and light and heat were. We know each only by its manifestations, its display of its powers, by its *effects*.

There have been two theories as to the physical nature of light. That of Descartes was, that it consists of small particles of matter, which he compared to balls, emitted by the luminous body. His theory was extensively accepted, and it became the generally received opinion that these inconceivably minute particles, light-dust, as it were, projected by some inconceivable force, with almost inconceivable velocity, from the heavenly bodies, never diverted in their course from a straight line, traversed the vast distances of space, to reach this earth in a few moments, an hour, a day, a year, or centuries, according to the distance of the orb from which they were shot forth—to reach this earth, or lose their light and become dark atoms in the void, as they soon became after reaching the earth. How they retained their heat in the journey, it was not attempted to explain. The light, it is evident, was not these particles, but only a quality or attribute of them, which they could part with, and it then ceased to exist: so that what light was, remained as completely unknown as ever.

In 1664 Hooke propounded the rival theory of *undulations*, which Huyghens developed in 1690. He asserted light to consist in a "quick, short, vibrating motion," and that it is propagated in a homogeneous medium, in such a way, that

> every pulse or vibration of the luminous body will generate a sphere, which will continually increase and grow bigger, just after the same manner (though indefinitely swifter), as the waves or rings on the surface of water do swell into bigger and bigger circles, about a point in it.

But this theory obtained little credit. Newton adopted the theory of emission, and gave it a currency among his followers, which kept down the undulation theory for above a century.

Euler embraced the undulation theory, urging various objections against the other, among them, that the passage of particles through transparent substances was inconceivable. These were answered by urging the exceeding minuteness and velocity of the matter of light. How the force of particles could be increased in proportion to their velocity, was not explained.

Revived by Young, at the close of the eighteenth century, and taken up by Fresnel, the undulation theory is now generally accepted. It is now generally agreed that light "consists in the vibrations of a peculiar fluid;" in undulations or waves. There is believed to be a *transverse* vibration, the motion of the particles being oblique to the direction of the ray.

If light be thus produced by the undulations of æther, and if this æther is only luminous when undulating, we are as far as ever from knowing what light *is*. The æther itself is not light, but matter, and not even luminous matter, unless we go back to the Aryan idea, and hold that light is *in* the æther, and of it, unmanifested, until it is revealed and flashed forth from it by its undulations. But how conceive of light not luminous? Or of *rays*, refracted and reflected, of an *effect* of undulation, that is *but* an effect or phenomenon, and not matter.

Upon this theory, light is either a manifestation of the invisible æther, or a product from it; or the undulations *are* the light. The waves of the æther are simply the æther assuming particular forms, and in motion. To say that this *motion* is light, is as absurd as the discussion by Proclus and Plato of the dissolution into triangles of bodies burned, and of triangles being dissolved by fire; and as the notion of Proclus, that *place*

> is the most pure and genuine light which is in bodies.

If light is the *product* of the æther, generated by undulation, then it is a thing or a *somewhat*, no more the æther itself, than sound *is* the undulations of the atmosphere, or the atmosphere itself. And if light is the manifestation outwardly of that which, in and of the æther, is invisible, what is this but the old Aryan idea?

In either case, how will the theory explain the light evidently *resident* in the glow-worm or fire-fly, and in the phosphorus contained in a bottle, and which is perfectly visible, how near soever the object is placed to the eye. And how explain the continued progress of the light, after the æther ends, and the atmosphere, and even the water begins, so that there is light for the fishes, in the depths of the sea?

Who *knows* that throughout space there exists an æther, composed of inconceivably minute particles of *somewhat*, "with finite intervals between them"? And how, upon this theory, is the sun the source of light, and how is light a consequence or effect or product of fire?

And what, again, *is* heat? *How* does it expand substances, increase the intervals between particles or atoms, and rarefy the air and transmute water into invisible vapour? *What* is it, that does all this? Until recently it was held to be material, and propagated by emission. Latent in bodies, and thus not heat, but the heat-principle, becoming heat by manifestation, it was to us what it was to the old Aryan philosophers (for such the Poets were). The most eminent modern French mathematicians have extended and asserted the hypothesis of a material caloric: but now that theory is ruined, and heat is held to "consist in transverse vibrations." Now, bodies are imagined to "consist of solid molecules or atoms, arranged at intervals in a very rare æther; and that the vibrations of the molecules, causing vibrations of the æther, and caused by them, constitute heat." Another theory is, that "heat itself *is* motion," and that "motion may be converted into heat, and heat into motion."

So that, after all, we know as little about light and heat, as the old Aryans did; and the jargon of science in regard to them is as unintelligible to us, as the jargon of alchemy or the Kabbalah. Our ancestors said,

> Agni, the Fire, is the universal, the all-pervader: He contains and is, Indra the Light, Vayu the Flame, Vishṇu the Heat, Ârushâ the radiating splendour of the

> Sun and Fire, the Aurora and the Lightning; and they, outflowing, are the manifestations of Himself. [And their immediate descendants said], There is a Supreme Mind above all these, the Light-Principle, and light is the Deity manifested.

Is it so certain as we think, that we are wiser than they? What theory explains the chemical action of light, its absorption, its connection with heat, and with the colours of bodies, and the many-coloured composition of its rays; whose seven colours, three primary and four secondary, are perhaps the Seven Sisters that nursed the young Ârushâ, immediately upon his manifestation by the sun or fire.

I pass to other Aryan ideas, which, if I am not mistaken, will sustain my conclusions.

VISHṆU.

What Vishṇu became in the Hindū mythology is known to all. There, he was one of the twelve Adityas, and became the preserver, in the Great Triad, Trimurti or Trinity, of Brahma, Vishṇu and Siva. In the Veda, he is not named as one of the Adityas.

I take the following passages of the Veda, in regard to Vishṇu, from the *Original Sanskrit Texts* of Dr. Muir (*iv.* 54 *et seq.*):

> *Rig-V. i.* 22. May the Gods preserve us from the place from which Vishṇu strode through the seven regions of the earth. Vishṇu strode over this; in three places he planted his step: enveloped in his dust. ['The World, or his step, was' is here supplied, before the word 'enveloped.' Benfey thinks that the meaning of the expression is, that the World is *subjected* to him. In his *Orient and Occident*, he explains it thus, 'He is so mighty that the dust which his tread raises, fills the whole earth.' And Dr. Muir asks, 'Can this dust be understood of the dazzling brightness of the sun's rays, surrounding his progress, and obscuring his disk from the view of the observer?'] Vishṇu, the unconquerable preserver, strode three steps, bearing from thence fixed observances. Behold the acts of Vishṇu, through which this fitting (or intimate) friend of Indra perceived religious ceremonies. Sages constantly behold that highest position of Vishṇu, like an eye fixed in the sky. Wise men, singing praises, and ever wakeful, light up that which is the highest station of Vishṇu.
>
> *Rig-V. i.* 85. 7. They (the Maruts) strong in themselves, increased in greatness; they ascended to heaven, and have made a spacious abode. When Vishṇu assisted the hero, who humbles pride, they sat down like birds on the sacrificial grass which they love.
>
> *Rig-V. i.* 90. 5. 9. Pushan, Vishṇu, swift-goer, make our prayers to bring us cattle as their principal fruit. Make us prosperous . . . . 9. May Mitra, may Varuṇa, may Aryaman, may Indra, may Bṛihaspati, may the wide-striding Vishṇu, all grant us prosperity.
>
> *Rig-V. i.* 154. 1. I declare the valourous deeds of Vishṇu, who measured the mundane regions, who established the upper world, striding thrice, the wide-stepping. 2. Therefore is Vishṇu celebrated for his prowess, terrible like a wild beast, destructive, abiding in the mountains; he within whose three vast paces all the worlds abide. 3. Let the hymn proceed, strength to Vishṇu, the dweller in the aërial mountains, the wide-stepping, the vigourous, who alone measured with three steps this wide, stable firmament. 4. Whose three stations, replenished with honey, imperishable, gladden us spontaneously; who alone sustained the triple universe, the earth and the sky, all the worlds. 5. May I attain to that beloved heaven of his, where men devoted to the Gods rejoice; for there is a spring of honey in the highest abode of the wide-stepping Vishṇu. 6. We desire to attain to those abodes of you two, where the many-horned and swiftly-moving cows abide. Here that supreme abode of the wide-stepping vigourous, shines intensely forth.

The original phrase, in *Verse i.*, rendered "measured the mundane regions," is *pârthivâni vimame rajamsi*. *Pârthivâni*, rendered "mundane," means "connected with Pṛithivi." Whether it is correctly rendered, depends on what *Pṛithivi* was; and I do not believe she was the earth; but, on the contrary, the expanse, between earth and sky. *Rig-V. i.* 108. 9, says,

> whether, Indra and Agni, ye are in the lowest Pṛithivi, in the middle, or in the highest;

and there is not the least ground to believe that the old Poets imagined there were three earths.

Yaska says, "Worlds are called *rajâinsi*:" and the Nirukta says that *rajas* is derived from the root *raj;* and that water is called *rajas*, and the worlds *rajamsi;* and it quotes *Rig-V. v.* 63. 5, "Brilliant and resounding (the Maruts) sweep over the worlds (*rajamsi*)." In *Rig-V. i.* 164. 6, it is said, "who established these six *rajamsi*." In *Rig-V. iii.* 26. 7, Agni says of himself that he is *arkas tridhâtû rajaso vimânah*, "the three-fold light, the measure of *rajas*," rendered "the *World*."

Dr. Muir thinks that the verb *vimame* cannot have the meaning of "constructing." It not only occurs in *Verse i.*, but in *Verse iii.*, of the above hymn, and in the latter, must have the sense of "measuring" or "traversing." The phrase *râjaso vimânah*, rendered "measure of the world," occurs in the hymn (*Rig-V. x.* 121. 5) to Hiraṇyagarbhah; and *Rig-V. x.* 139. 5. Also it seems that the participle *mimânah* has the same sense, as, in *Rig-V. i.* 50. 7, *vi dyâm eshi râjas, pṛithvaha mimânô aktubhih*, rendered "Sun, thou traversest the sky, measuring the broad space [*rajas*]": and this clearly shows what is meant by "measuring," and that *rajas* does not mean the *world;* unless there were no fixed or definite meanings to the words used by the Poets of the Veda.

Eichhoff gives the root *raj*, as meaning to "animate," or "colour:" Greek, ῥαγω; Latin, *rabro*, *rubeo;* French *rage*, *rengis;* German *rase*, *rothe:* and from it, *rajas*, "passion;" *raktas*, "coloured;" and *rajat*, *rajatan*, "silver."

From *râj*, to "excel, shine," come *râj*, "king," *râjas*, *râjan*, "sovereign."

We find the phrase *yah pârthivâni vimame sa etaṣo rajamsi*, in *Rig-V. v.* 81. 3, where the function of measuring Pṛithivi is ascribed to Savitṛi.

Roth renders *Verse vi.*, of the above hymn:

> May we arrive [Mitra and Varuṇa], at your abodes, where the many-horned, moving cattle are; for thence shines brilliantly down the highest place of the far-striding showerer.

How can a *place*, in our sense of the word, *shine down?* It is quite evident that the "showerer" is here represented as manifested and limited, in place;

and the word rendered "place" means the luminary, having form and shape in place, by which he is there manifested.

Rig-V. i. 155. 1. Sing praises to the great Hero who desires the draught of your Soma, and to Vishṇu, who both stood, great and invincible, on the summit of the mountains, as if on an excellent steed. 2. Indra and Vishṇu, the drinker of the libation escapes the assault, so fierce, of you two who are energetic . . . . 3. These (libations) augment his virility; he conducts the parents to receive the fertilizing seed; the son has the inferior name, the superior belongs to the father, the third is above the light of heaven. 4. We celebrate this virility of him, the strong, the deliverer, the uninjuring, the fecundator, who with three steps traversed far and wide the mundane regions (*parthivani*), for the sake of a wide-stepping existence. 5. A mortal, contemplating, can approach two of the steps of this heavenly; but no one dare attempt his third step, not even the soaring, winged birds. 6. He has set in motion, like a rolling wheel, the revolutions of time (?) with their four times (?) ninety names. Conceived by those who adore him to be vast in body, the youthful, full-grown, advances to the combat.

"Conceived by his adorers to be vast in body:" i. e., conceived of by the intellect of the worshippers, as indefinitely extended, and not as a mere luminary, of limited dimensions; "the youthful, full-grown," he, recently manifested, yet of full stature, "advances to the combat."

He and Indra stand together, great and invincible; together they attack, and together avert from man the bolt of the Archer Kṛiṣânu, aimed at him. There is, therefore, similitude and analogy between them; and one is not a Principle or Universal, and the other a luminary or manifestation.

No explanation is attempted of the assignment of the "inferior name" to the sun, and of the superior to the father; while the third is above the light of heaven (*adhi rochane divaḥ*). Virility, the generative and fertilizing power, is ascribed to Vishṇu. "He conducts the *parents* to receive the fertilizing seed," cannot mean that he "conducts" the father and mother; for he is himself the generator and father. The word "parents" must mean the mothers, those that receive his seed, are impregnated and produce. The son, the product, is on the earth; Vishṇu, as generator, is in the expanse. In another and higher character, he is above the region in which the birds fly, above, perhaps, the celestial luminaries.

Rig-V. i. 156. Be to us beneficent, like a friend (or like Mitra), worshipped with butter, greatly-renowned, swiftly-moving, broadly-diffused. Truly, Vishṇu, thy praise is to be celebrated by the sage, and sacrifice is to be performed to thee by the worshipper. He who worships Vishṇu, the ancient, the disposer, the recent, the with-the-noble-spouse, he who extols the birth of this mighty being, shall excel his rival in (renown). [But there is no certainty that the translation here is correct. *Sumaj-janaye*, which is rendered 'the with-the-noble-spouse,' may mean that, Sayana says, or 'born by his own power,' which would be to say that he was self-manifested, and not a luminary, which is the manifestation of that self as a distinct and inferior personality. After the word 'birth' we find, 'or, offspring:' and 'excel his rival in renown' is but a guess at the meaning.] Adorers, strive to the utmost of your skill to please him who, by his nature [i. e., in his essence], is the primeval Source of sacred rites [i. e., is Agni, or included in Agni, as a part is in the whole]. Knowing his name [i. e., the name given him as an emanation, as manifested, as 'born' of Agni], declare, 'Vishṇu, we seek the good will of thee, the Mighty One.' ['Mighty One,' is the principle that communicates its energy and potency to other Deities, and manifests itself through them.] 4. King Varuṇa and the Aṣwins wait on the decree of this Ruler, attended by the Maruts. [Varuṇa and the Aṣwins are luminaries, as I shall endeavour to show; and as they 'wait on the decree,' are obsequious to the will, of Vishṇu, and display such potencies only as he is pleased to assign to them, he must be, like Agni, an essential principle, universal like Agni and Indra]: Vishṇu possesses excellent wisdom [as Agni is constantly said to do], which knows the proper day, and with his friend [Indra] opens up the cloud. 5. The divine Vishṇu, who has chosen companionship with the beneficent Indra (himself) more beneficent: [what could be imagined to be more beneficent than light, except warmth and heat?]; this wise God, occupying three stations, has gratified the Aryya, and renders the worshipper a share in the sacred ceremony. [This he could only do as included in Agni, the messenger and mediator between the adorers and the Gods.]

Rig-V. 164. 36. Seven half children (?), the prolific sources of the world, abide by the command of Vishṇu in the function of supporting. They by thought and by mind, they intelligent, circling, revolve in every direction.

Dr. Muir says that he attempts no explanation "of this obscure and mystical utterance;" and his note of interrogation after "half-children" shows that he doubts whether the original means that. If it does, the idea intended to be expressed must have been that the Seven were manifestations of Vishṇu and of some other principle or father, jointly. The seven rays of the sun are manifestations of both Light and Heat, of Indra and Vishṇu: but the residue of the description will not permit its application to them. They "*abide*, by the command of Vishṇu;" i. e., they are *in place*, limited and defined, and having a permanent home in the heavens; and they so abide as manifestations of Vishṇu. They are the prolific sources of something which, by conjecture, is rendered "world:" and they are invested by Vishṇu with the function of "supporting," if the original means that. They circle, and revolve in every direction. No stars do so, but those of the constellation Ursa Major. No doubt, if we certainly knew what was intended to be designated by the "Seven," the epithets, and the functions ascribed to them would cease to be obscure. Unfortunately, instead of being able so to explain the phrases of Veda, we have, by means of the phrases, obscure and very often apparently unmeaning and inapplicable, to ascertain the character and individuality of the Deity in regard to whom they are used; and this when, by themselves, there is no certainty as to their interpretation.

ii. 1. 3. Thou Agni, art Indra . . . . thou art Vishṇu, the wide-stepping, the adorable: thou Brahmaṇaspati, art a priest . . . . thou, sustainer, art associated with devotion. [Indra, as we have shown, and Brahmaṇaspati, as we shall show, are hypostases of Agni, or components of him and emanations from him. Vishṇu, named between them, and thus 'associated with devotion,' the sacrifice, must also be in Agni, and emanate from him.]

iii. 6. 4. The Great, firm, seated in his abode, aspires to between the mighty sky and earth, the two cows [producers], joint-wives [both fertilized and made prolific] of the wide-stepping; aggressive [or, according to Roth, united], undecaying, inviolable, dispensers of waters [the expanse, from the clouds, the earth, by its springs and rivers].

iii. 54. 14. . . . . Vishṇu, the worker of many wonders, ... the wide-stepping, the exalted, whose primeval created wives are indefatigable.

iii. 55. 10. Vishṇu, a protector, preserves the highest heaven [the lofty arch of the sky], sustaining the vast, undecaying regions. Agni knows all these worlds [*bhuvanani*]: great and incomparable is the divine nature of the Gods.

Bhuvanani is from *bhu*, to "be born," to "exist:" whence *bhûs, bhûtis*, "creation;" *bhûs, bhavat*, "being;" *bhutas, fœtus; bhavitar*, "hereafter to be born;" *bhutan*, "creature;" *bhûs, bhûmis*, "ground;" *bhuman, bhaumas*, "productive, of the earth." As no derivative of this root could mean "the world," except because it means something born or produced, or existing, it is very evident that *bhuvanani*, with the Poets of the Veda, may as probably have meant the stars or existences, as worlds; of which, in our sense of the word they knew nothing. For them, there was but one world. Meanwhile, this verse treats Agni and Vishṇu as identical, or at least as of like nature: and it is certain that no *luminary* is ever spoken of in the Veda as preserving, sustaining or upholding the sky. That function is ascribed only to Agni and his hypostases.

iv. 2. 4. [Indra and Vishṇu are associated; as they habitually are.]

iv. 18. 11. And his mother asked the Mighty, 'My son, do those Gods forsake thee?' Then Indra, being about to slay Vṛitra, said 'Friend Vishṇu, do thou stride vastly.'

viii. 89. 12. 'Friend Vishṇu, stride vastly; sky, give room for the thunderbolt to strike: let us slay Vṛitra and let loose the waters; let them when released flow in the path, Indra.'

iv. 55. 4. . . . . Indra and Vishṇu, when they are praised, according to human ability, bestow on us prosperity and strong protection.

v. 3. 3. . . . . Agni . . . . through that which has been fixed as the highest abode of Vishṇu, thou possessest the mysterious name of the cows.

v. 51. 9. . . . . Associated with Soma and Vishṇu, come Agni, and rejoice in our libation . . . .

v. 87. 4. 8. . . . . The wide-striding strode forth, from the great common abode [from Agni, the universal, in and of whom he was, and abode in him, as the Logos in the Father], ... when by himself [manifested outwardly and separately, as Heat, Vishṇu], he has yoked his emulous and vigourous (ones), he issues from his own [he emanates from Agni, who is Vishṇu also, his Self, his Source], with his swift heroes, augmenting our felicity . . . . Maruts, ... of the same mind with the great Vishṇu . . . .

vi. 17. 11. For thee, Indra, ... Pushan and Vishṇu cooked a hundred buffaloes [we shall, hereafter, see how fitly Pushan is associated with Vishṇu, in *cooking*].

vi. 48. 14. . . . . Conferring extended enjoyment, like Vishṇu . . . .

vi. 49. 13. May we, ourselves and our offspring, be gladdened by wealth, in the home given by thee, that Vishṇu who thrice measured the mundane regions for Manu, when he was oppressed: [*Yo rajamsi vimame parthivanitris chid Vishṇu.*]

vi. 50. 12. [Vishṇu and Vayu are invoked together.]

Hymn lxix. of Mandala vi., is addressed to "Indra-Vishṇu," repeated in seven verses, and in the eighth, Indrascha-Vishṇo.

v. 1. Indra-Vishṇu are stimulated with the rite and oblation, and besought to 'accept our sacrifice, and grant us wealth, conducting us to our goal by secure paths.'

2. Indra and Vishṇu, ye who are the generators of all prayers, and the bowls which hold the Soma-juice.

3. Indra-Vishṇu, ye two lords of exhilarating draughts, come to the Soma-juice, bringing with you wealth . . . .

4. Indra-Vishṇu, may your steeds, vanquishing foes, and sharing in your triumph, bear you hither . . . .

5. Indra-Vishṇu, this deed of you twain is worthy of celebration, that, in the exhilaration of the Soma-juice, you took vast strides; you made the atmosphere wide, and stretched out the worlds [*rajamsi*], for our existence.

6. Indra-Vishṇu, growing by our oblation [increasing and enlarging by the additional energy given to the fire, by the offerings, of butter, and other things, thrown into it]. Swallowers of the essence of the Soma, ye who are worshipped with reverence . . . . bring us wealth, for ye are the receptacle, the bowl, in which the Soma is held.

7. Indra and Vishṇu, workers of wonders.

8. Ye two have both conquered, and are not vanquished. Neither of these two has been overcome. Vishṇu, when thou and Indra fought, ye scattered thrice a thousand.

vii. 36. 9. . . . . Vishṇu, the preserver of embryos.

vii. 40. 5. Branches of this bountiful and rapid (?) Deity Vishṇu, with oblations in the sacrifice.

vii. 99. 1. Thou who, with thy body, growest beyond our measure, do not attain to thy greatness [do not become excessive]: we know both thy two regions of the earth [*rajasî pṛithivyâh*]; thou, divine Vishṇu, knowest the remotest.

2. No one, O divine Vishṇu, who is being born, or who has been born, knows the furthest limit of thy greatness: [I think that this does not mean human beings, but celestial orbs, rising or risen. Vishṇu, a universal, extends beyond the ken

of all the stars]: thou didst prop up the lofty and vast sky; thou didst uphold the Eastern pinnacle of the earth.

3. . . . . Vishṇu, thou didst prop asunder these two worlds; thou didst envelop the earth [*pṛithivim*] on every side with light.

4. Ye (Indra and Vishṇu), have provided ample room for the sacrifice, producing the sun, the dawn, and fire: [of what could that be said, but of Agni, or his hypostases, light and heat?]: Ye, O heroes, destroyed in the battles . . . .

5. Indra-Vishṇu, ye smote the ninety-nine strong cities of Sambara: together ye slew, unopposed, a thousand and a hundred heroes of the Asura-Varchin.

6. This great hymn magnifies you two, the great, the wide-striding, the powerful: Vishṇu and Indra, I present to you two a hymn . . . . 7. Vishṇu, I utter to thee this invocation . . . . Ṣipivishta, receive this my oblation . . . .

vii. 100. 1. That man never repents, who, seeking, brings offerings to Vishṇu, the wide-stepping, who worships him with his whole heart, and propitiates one so powerful.

2. Vouchsafe to us, swiftly-moving Vishṇu, thy benevolence, which embraces all mankind, thy unpreoccupied regard: that thou mayest grant us abundant good, and brilliant wealth, with horses.

3. Thrice this God, by his greatness, has traversed this earth [*pṛithivim*] with its hundred lights. [Which fitly applies to the expanse, with its stars; but not at all to the earth.] May Vishṇu be the strongest of the strong; for awful is the name of that Immovable.

4. This Vishṇu traversed the earth [*pṛithivim*], to bestow for a habitation on Manu. The men who praise him are secure: of exalted birth has given them an ample abode.

5. I, a Master (*Aryah*), who know the sacred rites, to-day celebrate this thy name, Ṣipivishta. I, who am weak, laud thee who art strong, and, afar off, reignest over this lower world.

6. What, Vishṇu, hadst thou to conceal, that thou declared, 'I am Ṣipivishta'? Do not conceal from us this form, since thou didst assume another shape in the battle.

viii. 9. 12. When, Aṣwins, ye ride in the same car with Indra . . . . or when ye abide in the strides of Vishṇu.

viii. 12. 27. When (Indra) by thy force Vishṇu strode three steps, then thy dear steeds grew.

viii. 15. 9. . . . . Vishṇu, the high ruler . . . .

viii. 25. 12. 14. . . . . the innocuous and beautiful Vishṇu . . . . Vishṇu, the beneficent . . . .

viii. 29. 7. Another, wide-stepping, strode three, where the Gods rejoice [the luminaries].

viii. 31. 10. . . . . the mountains, the rivers, and Vishṇu, who is associated with them.

viii. 66. 10. The wide-striding Vishṇu, urged by thee, O Indra, carried off all, a hundred buffaloes, broth cooked with milk, and a fierce hog.

x. 1. 3. Vishṇu, the great Being, knowing thus his (Agni's) highest, protects his third. Men unanimously worship him here, when they offer him their libation, face to face.

x. 184. Let Vishṇu form the womb [*yonim*]; let Tvashtṛi mould the forms; let Prajapati infuse; let Dhatri form the embryo.

Dr. Muir, after quoting these and other passages (which, containing merely mention of the name of Vishṇu, or, at least, of no importance, I omit), remarks, that

> the attributes ascribed to Vishṇu in some of these passages are such, that, if these hymns stood alone in the Rig-Veda, they might lead us to suppose that this Deity was regarded by the Vedic Ṛishis as the Chief of all the Gods. [And still, he says] Indra is associated with Vishṇu even in some of those texts in which the latter is most highly magnified; in one place the power by which Vishṇu takes his three strides, is described as being derived from Indra; in two other texts, Vishṇu is represented as celebrating Indra's praises; while in one, Vishṇu is said to have been generated by Soma.

He also remarks that the hymns addressed to him are comparatively few, and that he is often mentioned among a great crowd of other Divinities, from whom he is there in no way distinguished as being in any respect superior. Hence he concludes that Vishṇu was on a footing of equality with the others.

But Dr. Muir errs. Agni and Indra are often named among a great number of other Divinities, with nothing to distinguish them as superior: and in most instances where Vishṇu is so mentioned, he *is* distinguished from the rest, by being named with Indra.

Further Dr. Muir says,

> the Rig-Veda contains numerous texts in which the Ṛishis ascribe to Indra, Varuṇa, and other Gods, the same high and awful attributes and functions, which are spoken of in the hymns before cited, as belonging to Vishṇu. [And he concludes that he] occupied a somewhat subordinate place in the estimation and affections of the ancient Ṛishis.

Certainly, so far as the Vedic Deities have heretofore been defined, by the Hindū or English commentators, all is lamentable confusion and uncertainty. Agni is agreed to be Fire, the Maruts, Winds, and Sûrya the Sun; and as to all the rest, everything is chaos. *Why* the same powers and functions are ascribed to different Deities, and what seem to be contradictory functions sometimes to the same Deity, no one endeavours to explain; but all the modern commentators stare helplessly at the muddle which the Hindū blind guides have made of the whole matter.

Certainly such is not the character of the Veda; and the notions of the Ṛishis as to their Deities *could* not have been thus confused, misty and unintelligible. There must be some key by which the meaning can be laid open. It seems to me that I have, at least in part, that key; and that it is this: Agni is Fire, as a Universal Substance, invisible, extending everywhere, and including in and of his unity, the fire, flame, light and heat, in no wise distinct or separate from himself or each other, until manifested by emanation from him. Then they become subsistences, persons or hypostases of the Universal Substance, and each, as well as the substance itself, is deified. Each being Agni, though manifested but partially and limitedly as the particular hypostasis, the functions of Agni, so far as they are not inconsistent with the nature of the particular subsistence, are sometimes assigned to it; and they are represented as equals, associated and sometimes acting together, and exercising their powers jointly.

And, if we add that this substance, Agni, and its subsistences, Indra, Vishṇu and Vayu, are also conceived of and represented as by self-limitation manifesting themselves in form and place, as the celestial luminaries, and out-shining by them, we shall find, I think, no other unintelligibility or confusion in the Veda, than so much as arises from ignorance of the true meaning of words and phrases, in a great measure caused by Hindū interpretations.

Vishṇu is particularly designated as the *generator*, to whom production and fruitfulness are owing; and hence as the preserver, or perpetuator. The sages continually contemplate his supreme station, as the eye ranges over the sky—the highest or greatest orb, whereby he fixes himself in place and by the outflowing heat manifests himself most potently—the Sun. Professor Wilson's translation is, in many places, different from that of Dr. Muir. Here, for example, the latter translates,

> Sages constantly behold that highest position of Vishṇu, like an eye fixed in the sky;

which even more clearly shows the meaning to be as I have supposed it, above. And again, in Dr. Muir's translation we find the same idea, in the phrase,

> Here that supreme abode of the wide-stepping vigourous shines intensely forth;

the word "vigourous" meaning that he is the source of the energy, the heat, which he manifests by the sun.

For Vishṇu is elsewhere described as not only "swiftly-moving," but as "broadly diffused"—an epithet that could not be applied to any luminary, but only to a substance.

Where Dr. Muir reads "the disposer" Wilson translates by "the creator;" and *sumaj-janaye*, "the self-born," which Dr. Muir translates,

"He with the noble spouse." Sâyana says it may mean "born by his own power;" and in this sense, or that of "self-born," it is fitly applied to a substance, of which the luminaries are the hypostases. He is "the primeval source of sacred rites," which could not be said of a luminary; but fitly of Agni or any one of his first manifestations, Flame, Light or Heat. He is even more beneficent than Indra, the Light; for he is the generator. All production is due to warmth or heat, all that grows upon and from the earth, the bird from the egg, and the child from the womb.

Agni is declared to be Indra and Vishṇu; and Vishṇu to be "associated" with the sacrifice, i. e., to bear a part in it, to aid in offering it. "The great, firm, seated in his abode," i. e., the heat of the fire, kindled upon the earth, "aspires to between the sky and earth," i. e., rises and ascends into the expanse. He is "the worker of many wonders," i. e., he is manifested and thereby produces great and astonishing effects. Indra and Vishṇu, when adored by the worshipper according to his means, bestow prosperity and give protection.

Indra and Vishṇu are the generators of prayers. This has a definite meaning, and can have no other. It can apply to and mean, only that by means of which the adoration of the worshippers is enabled to reach the Gods, i. e., to the sacrificial fire or that which ascends from [it]. The flames of it *are* prayers, *are* adoration; and they are generated by the heat, which causes them to ascend. The light and the heat, Indra and Vishṇu, ascend together. And they "grow by the oblations," and "swallow the essence of the Soma," which the fire consumes. They are the receptacle of the Soma, for changed into vapour by the heat, it is by them taken and conveyed upward toward the stars.

Vishṇu is the preserver of embryos; because it is warmth only that enables them to retain vitality, and attain perfection. With his body, he grows beyond men's measure: i. e., when developed substantively as actual heat, he becomes too intense, in the hot days of summer in that latitude, for men to endure.

Nothing created, limited and in form and place, knows how far heat extends. And Indra and Vishṇu, Light and Heat, have produced the sun, the dawn and the flame of fire. Together they rend the clouds and send down rain; and together they shatter cities. Both are great, wide-striding and powerful. The benevolence of swiftly-moving Vishṇu embraces all mankind. He is the strongest of the strong. "Awful is the name of that Immovable"—a phrase that must be badly translated; for Vishṇu, swiftly-moving, cannot be immovable. This word probably means the vast fixed source of all manifested heat, of whose intensity they judged from that poured forth by the sun, an orb of apparently so moderate a size.

Afar off, Vishṇu, called Ṣipivishta, reigns over the earth, by his manifestation in the sun. Knowing his highest, i. e., present in the heights of the sky, he protects his third, the earth; and men offer him their libations face to face, when he is in and of the sacrificial fire.

Thus clearly a subsistence of Agni, Vishṇu *is never characterized as radiant or bright, shining or lighting up the sky.* What else, then, *can* he be, but *heat,* which, as it expands all things, and causes smoke and vapour to ascend, could easily be imagined to have raised up the sky like a bubble, and to hold and support it there above the earth.

Mr. Cox says, that in strictness of speech, the Vedic Vishṇu is nothing but a name. The writers of the Aitaeya-Brâhmana could still say,

> Agni is all the Deities, Vishṇu is all the Deities.

It must at once be admitted that he is not a luminary, a body. He is Agni, as Indra, the Light is, i. e., he is a manifestation of Agni. He and Indra are united, in shattering the clouds with the lightning. He is the worthy friend (the *equal,* in dignity and rank) of Indra. Wherever the eye ranges over the sky, it sees the dwelling-place of Vishṇu. He is not confined to one spot, or gathered into one orb or body. He and Indra are the two invincible Deities, and they ride together above the clouds.

Sometimes, Mr. Cox says, Vishṇu rises to a dignity greater even than that of Dyaus and Indra, while at others he is spoken of as subordinate to them (we do not find that), or is regarded as simply another form of the three Deities Agni, Vayu and Sûrya. Nothing could be more wide of the truth. He is not "another form" of either, nor is Sûrya the same as Agni or as Vayu. They are manifested by him, as God by the Logos, as the soul is by thought.

Then Mr. Cox, to get as far as possible from the truth and utterly incapacitate himself to understand the Veda, hazards this sonorous proposition:

> In truth, it may almost without exaggeration be said, that the whole Vedic theology may be resolved into a series of equations, the result being one quite consistent with a real monotheism. Thus Vishṇu is himself Agni and Indra.

It would be just as sensible to say that the Hindû Trinity was an "equation" or that the Christian Trinity is one.

But Mr. Cox imagines that the whole is clear to him. He says,

> It is scarcely necessary, then, to say, that in all the phrases which describe the attributes of Vishṇu, the origin of each conception is plainly discernible. He is especially the God who traverses the heaven in three strides, these strides being taken by some commentators to denote his manifestations as fire on the earth, as

> lightning in the atmosphere, and as the sun in the heaven; or, in other words, his identity with Agni, Vayu and Sûrya. By others they are regarded as setting forth the rising culmination and setting of the sun; *and there can be little doubt* that the latter idea was at the first most closely associated with the thought of Vishṇu.

There is no doubt that "the latter idea" never was associated with him, at all.

In the Ramayana, a work of a later age, we get a glimpse of the real meaning of Vishṇu and his strides. It is, no doubt, the old myth, with additions. Vishṇu, manifesting himself as a *dwarf*, obtains from the Asuras a gift of as much space as he can lie upon, or as much as he can cover in three strides. Thus Bali, the great enemy of the Gods, is overcome. Having conquered the three worlds (earth, expanse and sky), he terrifies Indra, who, with the other Deities beseeches Vishṇu to take the shape of a dwarf and deceive their conqueror. In that shape he approaches the son of Virochana, and obtains the boon of the three paces; and then, "the thrice-stepping" Vishṇu assumed a miraculous form, and with three paces took possession of the worlds. For, with one step he occupied the whole earth, with a second the eternal atmosphere, and with a third the sky. Then he gave the empire of the three worlds to Indra.

Mr. Cox thus concludes:

> The personality of the mythical Vishṇu is, in short, as transparent as that of Helios or Sělēnē. He dwells in the aërial mountains, in a gleaming palace, where the many-horned and swiftly-moving cows abide. Here that Supreme Abode of the wide-stepping vigourous God shines intensely forth. These cows are in some places the clouds, in others, the rays that stream from the body of the sun. But on the whole it must be admitted that the place of Vishṇu in the Rig-Veda, as compared with the other great Deities, is in the background; and the institutional legends of later Brahmanic literature, throw but little light on the mythical idea of this Deity, and perhaps none on the mythology of any other people.

How far, in all this, Mr. Cox is right and how far in error, the reader must determine. It is clear that he is entirely at a loss to determine what Vishṇu really was, among the Vedic Gods, although he speaks with so apparent a confidence.

The three steps or strides of Vishṇu remain an inscrutable enigma; and whatever he is concluded to have been, the enigma remains the same.

I group together here all the passages that relate to them:

> Vishṇu strode through the seven regions of the earth [*Vishṇur vichakrame pṛithivyâḥ sapta dhâmabhiḥ*].

Kram, a verbal root, means to "go," to "move." Dr. Muir renders *kramaṇâch*, in the Mahabharata Santi-Parva, "striding." *Dhaman* is a "mass" or "body." *Pṛithivi* is rendered "*earth*," by Bopp, and Muir and Müller: and we find *dyâvâ-pṛithivî*, in which the Vedic dual termination is added to *dyâu*, rendered, "heaven and earth;" and *dyâvâ-pṛithivî-bhyâm*, "to the heaven and to the earth," by Bopp. The derivation of *pṛithivî* is clear. It is the same as *parthvî*, from *parth* to "spread out, display," meaning something *extended*, *spread out;* and *parthus* means "vast," from the same.

> Vishṇu strode [*vichakrame*] over this: in three places he planted his step [*tredha nidadhe padam*]: enveloped in his dust . . . . Vishṇu strode three steps [*trîni padâ vichakrame Vishṇur*], bearing from thence fixed observations.
>
> Vishṇu strides over this [*tad vikramate Vishṇuh*] whatever exists: he plants his step in a three-fold manner [*tredha nidhatte padain*]: for a three-fold existence [*tredhâ-bhâvayâ*], on earth, in the atmosphere, and in the sky [it is said in the Nirukta, where the last-cited verse is quoted; and that explanation is ascribed to Ṣâkapûṇi, while Aurṇavâbha says it means] on the hill where he rises, on the meridian and on the hill where he sets. [*See Muir, Orig. Sansk. Texts, iv.* 55. 56. 57. for all the conflicting Hindū opinions as to these steps.]

Vishṇu is several times called wide-striding [*urukramah*, *urugayah*], without other words.

> Vishṇu, who measured the mundane regions [*pârthivâni vimame rajâṁsi*].

Here the word *pârthivâni*, rendered "mundane," is clearly from the root *parth*, *repondre*, *deployer* (*Eichhoff*), and, according to its derivation means "extended, spread out, expanded." If the earth is called *pṛithivi*, which we see is from the same root, it is because it is spread out and extended: and I believe that in the Vedic times, whatever it may have come to mean afterwards, *pṛithivi* meant the *expanse* between the earth and the sky. . . . .

> Striding thrice, the wide-stepping [*vichakramâṇas tredhâ urugâyah*] . . . . He within whose three vast paces [*trishu vikramaṇeshu*], all the worlds [*bhuvanani*] abide. [*Bhu, to be born, to exist: bhûs, bhûtis, creation, that which exists*]: . . . . Vishṇu, the wide-stepping [*urugâyâya*], who alone measured with three steps this wide stable firmament . . . . Whose three stations [*trî padâni*], gladden us . . . . who alone sustained the triple Universe, the earth and the sky [*tridhâtu pṛithivîm uta dyam*], all the worlds [*bhuvanâni*].

His three "stations" are "replenished with honey," and "there is a spring of honey in the highest abode of the wide-stepping [*urukramasra*] Vishṇu." *Pade parame*, highest *step* or *abode;* for his *steps* are elsewhere *padam*. The words rendered "*honey*" are *madhuna* and *madhva*.

> *Pad*, *padas*, is "foot," from *pad*, to "go," to "march" [*Eichhoff*].

Sâyana, in a single passage, renders *rajamsi*, "regions," and then says,

> the term *rajas* denotes a *world*, since Yaska says, worlds are called *rajamsi*.

Pṛithivi, he says is the *earth*, and yet all the three *worlds* are intended to be designated by it. The Nirukta says,

> Light is called *rajas;* day and night are called *rajasi:*

and *Eichhoff* defines the root *raj*, *animer*, "colourer." In *Rig-V. i.* 50. 7; we have

> Sun, thou traversest the sky, measuring the broad space [*vi dyam eshi rajas pṛithv* *rajas* being rendered 'space,' and *pṛithv*, 'broad'].

Is not this *rajas pṛithv*, broad or expanded space or region, *Pṛithivi?* When words had more nearly the original meanings of their roots, *pṛithivi* meant, no doubt, "space or expanse," the *spacious* or *extended*, merely: and the derivatives of *raj* must have had meanings more closely connected with that of the root, to *animate*, or *colour*.

The "*abode*" of Indra and Vishṇu is where the many-horned (*bhûri-ṣringâ*) and swiftly-moving "cows" abide. The word rendered "cows" is *gâvo*. *Gaus* is a "cow," from *ga*, to "create, produce:" and *sarnis*, *sarngan*, or *çarnis ÇARNGAN*, is a "point," "sharp-pointed" thing, or "horn," from *sar* or *çar*, to "pierce," to "penetrate." All rays, the Nirukta says, are called *gāvah*. I can not see why *gâvo* should be rendered "cows" here, or (*bhûri-ṣṛiṇgâḥ*), "many-horned," especially when the *gâvo* are "swiftly-moving" (*ayasah*), from *ay*, to "go, pass." The rendering, "where the many-pointed, flashing or darting rays are," seems to me far more likely to be correct.

> The sun has the inferior [lower] name: the higher belongs to the father: the third is above the light of heaven [*dadhâti putro avaram param pitur nama tṛitîyam adhi rochane divaḥ*].

> Who with three steps traversed far and wide the mundane regions [*pârthivâni*] . . . . A mortal, contemplating, can approach two of his steps; but no one dare attempt his third step, not even the birds who fly highest.

Does this mean that the height and distance are too great for them to soar to? What, then, is meant by the phrase that mortals *contemplating*, can reach two of the steps? The thought or intellect could reach the third. Or does it mean that the eye cannot attain it, because the third station or step is in the sun, which no mortal eye can see, on account of its brilliance, nor even the birds can gaze at it?

(The world or his step—or something else), enveloped in his dust [*samulham asya pâṁsure;* which, the Nirukta says, may mean, 'his place is not seen in the atmosphere,' or 'enveloped in the dust, as it were, his place is not seen'].

Vishṇu, stride vastly [*vitaraṁ vikramasva* which may quite as well mean 'extend or expand thyself indefinitely'].

Vishṇu who thrice measured *rajâṁsi pârthivâni* for Manu.

Indra and Vishṇu are both addressed as *urukrama;* and it is said to them,

Ye took vast strides [*akṛinutam*], you made the atmosphere (?) wide, and stretched out *rajâṁsi* (translated 'the worlds').

We know thy two regions (*rajasî*) of earth (*pṛithivyâh*). He 'props asunder *rodasi*,' rendered 'the two worlds, and envelop the earth (*pṛithivim*), on every side with light.' 'Thrice this God has traversed this earth [*pṛithivim*] with its hundred lights, by his greatness [*mahitva*, from *mah*, to *grow*, to *increase*, to *overcome*. Why not, 'by expanding?'].

When, Aṣwins, you abide in the strides [*vikramaneshu*] of Vishṇu . . . . When Vishṇu strode three steps [*trini pada vichakrame*].

In *viii.*, 15. 8, where Indra and Vishṇu are named alternately, we find

Indra, the sky *dyaus* increases thy virility [*pauṁsyam*], and *pṛithivi* increases thy renown;

Vishṇu is called *ḅrihan xayo*, "lofty ruler or king;" and the generative power is ascribed to Indra.

Another, wide-stepping [*urugayo*], strode three [*trini vi chakrame*], where the Gods [*devaso*] rejoice. [The *devaso* are simply, 'those in the sky.']

Vishṇu, the great Being [*itthâparamam*] knowing thus his highest [*bṛihanu*], protects his third [*tṛitîyam*].

Extension, to extend and spread itself, is a peculiar and striking faculty of heat. It penetrates every thing. From the small fire, kindled in a room, it extends into and warms the remote corners of the apartment. When the summer sun rises in the morning, the heat seems at once to diffuse itself through the whole expanse. It is omnipresent: It is in the thermal springs, and in the earth below the mud volcanoes of the Caspian. It is in the bodies and blood of all living creatures, as the vital heat. It may be produced by friction, and is manifested before the flame, when fire is obtained by attrition. The herdsman, driving his wooden axled cart, had often seen the axles heated, and at last taking fire, as he journeyed. Volcanoes long since extinct, informed the Aryans that it was in the bosom of the earth, and it filled the expanse, and came from the sun in his station.

It came to men in the enervating winds of the summer, and in the spring it melted the snows and ice, and put an end to the rule of frost.

When it was supposed to have been first manifested, it stepped, as it were, upon the earth, and took possession of its entirety. Where it came, the earth dried up, and clouds of dust arose on the desert steppes. It stepped, extended or expanded, into the space between earth and sky, and filled it. It stepped upon or extended to the sun, and he became the great Source of heat and cause of generation. Each of the three was but his single foot-step, or halting-place.

It went where light did not. It is not inseparable from it. There is light without heat, and abundant heat, everywhere, without light: but they reside together in the sun, as they do in the fire, and flow from him together in inexhaustible profusion. Thus they are often associated. The lightning had often been seen to set fire to what it shattered, and therefore Vishṇu was associated with Indra as wielder of the thunderbolt and slayer of Vṛitra. In the dark, yet heated metal, in the human body, in the summer air at night, heat exists without light, and in the moon and planets and stars it is not the associate of Indra. And, according to the later myth, when Bali had conquered the light, the soul of the universe, Indra called upon the Heat, its Potency and Vigour, to reconquer for him the three realms.

As generator, Vishṇu was the preserver and perpetuator; and as the vigour and potency of the universe, also, he sustained, supported and preserved it. And thus, singularly enough, when the Hindū descendants of the Aryans had forgotten what Vishṇu originally was, they knew him as the Preserver: and when the Brahmanic reformer conceived of Brahma as the creative power of the universe, and invented Siva as the destructive power, he retained Vishṇu as the preserving power, because he had from of old been called the preserver.

Mand. i. 194. 6, which I have given above, as translated by Dr. Muir, is thus translated by Professor Wilson:

> He causes, by his gyrations, ninety-four periodical revolutions, like a circular wheel, vast of body, and evolving in many forms, through the praises: ever young, though not infantine, he comes at our invocations.

Professor Wilson says,

> Vishṇu is here identified with *time*, comprising ninety-four periods—the year, two solstices, five seasons, twelve months, twenty-four half-months, thirty days, eight watches and twelve zodiacal signs.

Why not the two equinoxes, also? I think the Vedic Poets knew very little about all that. Are *these* "like a circular wheel, vast of body, and evolving in many forms," or are *these* "forms"? A word that invariably means bodies, having form and limited dimensions. What is meant by the number ninety-four, I cannot even conjecture, unless it is used to express a merely indefinite number. The rest seems to have this meaning—that Vishṇu, by his gyrations, causes periodical revolutions, i. e., revolves, as a vast spherical mass, from which portions are detached, and from it many luminaries are evolved. One is reminded of the theory of some modern astronomers, of a mass of nebulous matter, throwing off portions, which by degrees become spherical, and are condensed into planets.

Dr. Muir attempts no explanation of this passage. That of Professor Wilson is a Hindū interpretation, simply arbitrary, and not even rising to the dignity of a conjecture. Which interpretation is the more correct, I am not competent to decide.

Another passage is thus translated by Professor Wilson:

> That Ancient Vishṇu . . . . You know him as born as one with sacrifice;

by which is clearly meant that his primal existence is as an unmanifested subsistence or hypostasis of Agni; that he and Agni are one, as the Logos and Father are said to be.

Mand. i. 156. 5, given above, as translated by Dr. Muir, is thus translated by Professor Wilson:

> The divine Vishṇu, the best of the doers of good deeds, *Sachathâya Indrâya* [translated, 'who came to the pious institutor of the rite,' a Brahmanic interpretation—*Sachathâya* being explained 'for giving assistance at the ceremony,' and *Indrâya* to apply to the Yajamana, a sacrificer; on the strength of one of Yaska's many etymologies of Indra. But the phrase evidently connects Vishṇu with Indra, as his intimate associate, Heat with the Light of the Fire; *sac* meaning to 'join,' to 'adhere;' whence *sakha, sakhyas*, 'a friend']; to assist, knowing, and present at the three connected periods, shows favour to the Arya . . . .

Another text is translated by Professor Wilson, as follows:

> The Seven, the embryo for half a year, abide by appointment in the various functions of Vishṇu [i. e., he has delegated to them his functions, and they exercise them, being manifested in place. During half the year they are embryotic; i. e., as we know by the same expression applied to Agni, they are not seen at night, during half of the year: and during the other half they make the world fruitful], the fecundating of the world [or, it may mean that during half the year they do not exercise their generative and fecundating influence]. By intelligence they pervade in thought all around, for they are intelligent and diffusive [i. e., radiant, light-giving, and 'intelligent' as Agni is often said to be].

Mand. viii. 100. 6, given above as translated by Dr. Muir, is thus translated by Professor Wilson:

> What is to be proclaimed, Vishṇu, of thee, when thou sayest, I am Ṣipivishṭa? Conceal not from us thy real form, although thou hast engaged under a different form in battle. [And, Stanza 7] Be pleased, Ṣipivishṭa, with my offering.

This name is *explained*, "penetrated," or "clothed," "with rays of light," but in common use it means a man naturally without prepuce. It is used once elsewhere, as an appellation of Vishṇu. Professor Wilson thinks it is to be understood here in that sense. The expression, he says, is *curious*. It is curious that in the Kabbalah the retraction of the prepuce is spoken of in describing the Ṣephirothic generation. No doubt it is used here to show the exceeding great virile power of Vishṇu and his readiness at all times to cause production. And it is certainly very curious, if the Aryan linga and phallus worship in India and Greece grew out of the ascription in the Veda, of the generative function and virile energy to Vishṇu, and the employment of an epithet expressive of it by a symbol, that generative power being the energy of warmth and heat, in producing gestation and production.

The reader thus has all that the Veda contains in regard to Vishṇu. These quotations from the translation of Professor Wilson, compared with those of the same passages by Dr. Muir, will show how very uncertain it is whether difficult and obscure passages, and many that are not so, are correctly translated. I doubt whether there is really any confused thought or inconsistency in the original; but I do not believe that any *literal* rendering of the Veda will ever make it intelligible for modern readers. Certainly no translation that renders each word by what is supposed to be an equivalent English word, will reproduce its meaning. No very ancient language can be so translated.

Nor is there any doubt that to the correct understanding of very many texts, a true and correct idea of what was meant by the Deity addressed or spoken of, is absolutely essential. For, if there be a wrong idea of the Deity in the given case, and the text be doubtful and will admit of more than one rendering, that will naturally be preferred that best suits the preconceived theory: and it may, indeed, be often impossible to ascertain the true and exact meaning of a passage, unless it is known what the Deity was, to whom or of whom it speaks.

And when it is once certain that the theosophic ideas of the Ṛishis were eminently philosophical, a much more philosophical meaning will at once appear in a multitude of texts, which must be rendered in philosophical language, or the true meaning will escape in the process of translation.

BRAHMAṆASPATI.

BṚIHASPATI.

These are supposed by the commentators to be mere names or synonyms of Agni. I think that it can be plainly shown that they are Deities, and that the inquiry in regard to them will in a singular and striking manner confirm my conjectures in regard to the other Deities already spoken of.

Asht. i. Adhy. i. Anuv. v. Sûkta i.

1. Brahmaṇaspati, make the offerer of the libation illustrious among the Gods. . . . .

3. Protect us, Brahmaṇaspati . . . .

4. The liberal man, whom Indra, Brahmaṇaspati and Soma protect. . . . .

Adhy. iii. Anuv. viii. Sûkta iii.

13. Praise Brahmaṇaspati, Agni, and the beautiful Mitra.

Sûkta v.

1. Rise up, Brahmaṇaspati, devoted to the Gods. . . . . [Meaning, rather, as we shall see, 'ascend, adorer of the Deities'].

3. May Brahmaṇaspati approach us . . . .

5. Brahmaṇaspati proclaims the sacred prayer, in which the Divinities Indra, Varuṇa, Mitra and Aryaman have made their abode.

It seems absurd to say that Deities "have made their abode" in prayer. But I think we may comprehend the Aryan idea. Indra is Light; Varuṇa, Mitra and Aryaman, as well as Indra, "abide" in Agni, he being the *substance*, of which Indra is a *subsistence* or *hypostasis*, and they are emanations or manifestations—in later language, the archangelic images of the Deity, and in the Kabbalistic idea, apertures, windows or eyes, through which a ray of the Primal Light flows forth, as a rivulet from the ocean. Then, if the Aryan conceived of prayer, at the sacrifice, *coalescing* and becoming one with the flame, becoming Agni, and ascending to the skies, we may understand how they could say that Indra, and the Deities named had been included in prayer; but I am inclined to think that "in" should be "by" or "with," meaning that they are prayer, as they are Agni, manifested and fixed in place.

8. Let Brahmaṇaspati concentrate his strength. Associated with the Regal [Indra], he slays: in the time of danger he maintains his station, armed with the

thunderbolt, there is no encourager or discourager of him in the battle, great or small.

Asht. ii. *Adhy. vi.* *Anuv. iii.* *Sûkta i.*

[In this hymn, he is invoked as 'Chief Leader of the Hosts,' a Sage of Sages, abounding beyond measure in nourishment, *best Lord of Prayer;* as a protector, and invoked to 'sit down in the Chamber of Sacrifices. A kind Protector, he defends men.']

11. Thou, Brahmaṇaspati, who hast no requiter [men cannot sacrifice to Prayer itself]: Showerer, repairer to combat, the Consumer of foes, the Victor in battles.

19. Brahmaṇaspati, who art the regulator of this [sacrifice]; understander of hymn, and grant us posterity; for all is prosperous that the Gods protect.

Adhy. vii. *Anuv. iii.* *Sûkta ii.*

2. That Brahmaṇaspati, who by his might has humbled those who deserved humiliation; who in his wrath rent asunder the clouds, who sent down the undescending, and made way into the mountain opulent.

3. . . . . who set the cows at liberty: who *by the sacred prayer* destroyed Bala: who dispersed the darkness and displayed the light.

4. That stone-like, solid, down-hanging, water-laden (cloud), which Brahmaṇaspati has with his strength divided, the universal solar rays have drunk up.

5. For you, the Constant and Manifold through months and through years, set open the gates of the future rains . . . .

8. Whatever Brahmaṇaspati aims at, with the truth-strung, quick-darting bow, that he surely hits: holy are its arrows with which he shoots, for the eyes of men, and having their abode in the ear. [The bow is the mouth or tongue. Words, the arrows.]

9. He, Brahmaṇaspati is the aggregator and subjugator, *the family priest,* and the renowned in battle: the beholder, who bestows food and coveted treasures, whence the radiant sun shines without exertion.

11. He who is all-pervading and delighting . . . . greatly is that Brahmaṇaspati renowned among the Gods, and therefore is he verily Supreme above all.

14. The purpose of Brahmaṇaspati, engaging in a great work, has been successful . . . . for it was he who recovered cattle for heaven, and distributed them; so that of their own power they took different directions, like a mighty river.

12. All truth, Lords of Wealth (Indra and Brahmaṇaspati), is in you both . . . . Come to our presence, our oblations, like a pair of steeds to their provender.

Sûkta iv.

4. Brahmaṇaspati leads by a straight path the worshipper . . . . he guards him against sin, he protects him from foes and from distress . . . .

3. He who with a believing mind worships Brahmaṇaspati, the father of the Gods [*Devânâm pitaram*], with oblations, he verily receives food.

Professor Wilson says, of Brahmaṇaspati, that the scholiast furnishes us with no account of the station of functions of this Divinity.

> The etymology will justify Dr. Roth's definition of him, as the Deity of sacred prayer, or rather, perhaps, of the text of the Veda; but whether he is to be considered as a distinct personification, or as a modified form of one of those already recognized, and especially of Agni, is doubtful. . . . . His being associated with Indra and Soma, whilst it makes him distinct from them, leaves him Agni as his prototype.

He is a protector, a dispenser of wealth; devoted to the Gods, the father of the luminaries [*devânâm pitaram*]. He "proclaims the sacred prayer," in which Indra, Mitra, Varuṇa and Aryaman "have made their abode," which, to mean *any* thing, must mean that he is the visible flowing forth or utterance of the fire of sacrifice, in which as a Universal, those Divinities are contained. He is strong, and, like Indra, with whom he is associated in more than one hymn, is armed with the thunderbolt. He is the leader of the starry hosts, sage of sages, beyond measure abounding in nourishment [light?], and best lord of prayer [essential, therefore, as flame is, to the sacrifice]. Come, it is said, "with thy protectors" [i. e., with thy subordinates, who are protectors]. He protects and defends, combats, consumes foes, is victor in battles; he rends the clouds, and sends down the rain, follows the bright clouds of the morning and releases them from their imprisonment; in all which and in slaying Bala, he *seems* identical with Indra. He is the constant and manifold, through months and years; i. e., being one and unchanging, like fire or light, he is variously manifested by the celestial bodies that mark the recurrence of the months and years. He shoots arrows from the bow, arrows "holy for the eyes of men, and which have their abode in the ear;" which would seem to indicate that he is praise or adoration by uttered words, which are imagined to mingle with and become a part of, and be invested with the powers and energies of, the sacrificial flame. This is to impute to prayer an immense power; but such power will be found expressly imputed to it in some of the hymns. And if the Poets deemed, as they certainly did, prayer to be a force, it was natural to impute to it the virtues and energies of Agni, in producing rain and otherwise, and so to represent it as a component part of Agni, and the associate of, and co-actor with, Indra.

He is "the aggregator and subjugator," a phrase, the meaning of which can only be conjectured. What does he aggregate, collect together or condense? Perhaps the vapours into rain. He subjugates Bala. He is the family priest, the family prayer, perhaps, offered up, not by a priest, but by the father of the family, in the privacy of home. He is "renowned in battle," as Indra is; is the beholder [who looks, through the stars, that are his eyes, upon the earth]. He bestows food and wealth, as Agni and

Indra do; for these primitive men believed in the actual efficacy of prayer: and hence the sun shines with radiance, without exertion, i. e., lavishly and freely, it being of his nature to do so, and the light being manifested by him, without action of his own. He pervades and delights all. Prayer reaches everywhere: and is renowned among the Gods, i. e., the celestial luminaries, and may therefore be said to be supreme over all, because all concede what is asked by prayer. Dawn comes, and the bright cows are released, return to the east, and thence roam at will, when the return of day is prayed for. In him is all visible reality, for but for prayer, the light would not displace the darkness, and return to make visible the objects of Nature. He leads the worshipper by a straight path, guards him against error, protects him from enemies and distress.

Asht. i. *Adhy. v.* *Anuv. xi.* *Sûkta v.*

3. When the search was set on foot by Indra and the Angirasas Saramâ secured food for her young; then Brihaspati slew the devourer and rescued the kine, and the Gods, with the cattle, proclaimed their joy aloud.

Angiras is, in Hymn *i.* of the Veda, a name applied to Agni. In Manu and all the Purâṇas it is the name of a Ṛishi, and is used, Professor Wilson says, in that sense, frequently, in the text of the Veda, as the designation of the founder of a family or school. Angâra is a live coal; and the Aitareya Brâhmana says, "the coals became the Angirasas." In *Sûkta i. Anuv. x. Adhy. iv. of Asht. i.*, Indra is said to have opened the cloud for the Angirasas (the descendants of Angiras). In *Sûkta v. Anuv. xi. Adhy. v. of Asht. i.*, "We meditate, like Angiras, an acceptable address to that powerful and praise-deserving Indra." In *Sûkta vii. Anuv. xii.* of the same, we find,

> our forefathers, the Angirasas, by their praises terrified the strong and daring devourer; they made for us a path to the vast Heaven, and obtained accessible day, *Aryah*, and the cows. They secured him, they made his worship the source of wealth, whence opulent votaries preserve his fires and practice his rites.

"Accessible day," thus means fire or light, of which men could have possession. *Aryah* is explained *dhanasya swâminah*, the "ensign of day." Of course this is a mere guess. But it is clear that the *Angirasas* are men, deified; and that to them was ascribed the origin of worship by fire.

Accordingly, in *Sûkta x. Anuv. xiii. Adhy. vi. of Asht. i.*, it is said, "The Angirasas first prepared the sacrificial food, and then with kindled fire, with a most holy rite." And they are called "The institutors." In *Sûkta i. Anuv. xviii. Adhy. viii. of Asht. i.*, Indra is invoked to listen to the praises of the Angirasas, devoted to the Gods. Elsewhere, Agni is called "The eldest of the Angirasas." The Chief of the Angirasas discovered the hiding place of the cows. Indra opened the cloud for the Angirasas, restoring them their cows.

Indra is propitiated by the hymns of the Angirasas, and permits them to recover their cattle. In *Sûkta ii. Anuv. iii. Adhy. i. Ashṭ. iii.*, they are called the "Seven intelligent Sages," who ascertained that the bright cows of the dawn were hid in the cavern, and by sacrifice persuaded Indra to recover them. Then Angiras became his worshipper; and the Angirasas, with hymns, "followed the road to immortality."

We shall recur again to the *Angirasas.*

The *Asuras*, named *Panis*, stole in the night the cows of the Gods, or of the Angirasas, i. e.,

> the clouds that glow with the golden and purple colourings of the Dawn and Evening, and which, unseen, until then, often appear just at the Dawn, in the East;

and hid them in a cave, where the bitch Saramâ sent in search of them, discovered them. Who or what was meant by Saramâ, we will inquire hereafter. We return to Bṛihaspati.

> *Sûkta vi. Anuv. xiv. Adhy. vi. Ashṭ. i.* May Indra and Bṛihaspati be propitious to us.
>
> *Sûkta xii.* (17). *Anuv. xv. Adhy. vii. Ashṭ. i.* Bṛihaspati, who liberates many from sin, heard.
>
> *Ashṭ. ii. Adhy. v. Anuv. xxiv. Sûkta xi.*
>
> 1. Augment by your hymns Bṛihaspati, who deserts not, the showerer, the pleasant-tongued, the adorable; of whom, resplendent, Gods and men, of the institutor of the sacrifice, emulous in sacred songs proclaim.
>
> 2. The hymns of the (rainy) season [*Ritwiyâ*] are addressed to him, who is verily the creator (of rain), and has granted it (to the prayers of) the devout; for that Bṛihaspati is the manifester, the expansive wind [air] that (dispensing) blessings has been produced for the diffusion of water.

The additions in parentheses are but guesses, of those whose preconceived notions completely incapacitated them to underṣtand the Vedas. Here, the phrase "the expansive wind" makes it probable that the guesses approximate to the truth; but it is uncertain.

Bṛihaspati bestows wealth, and his glory spreads through heaven and earth like the sun. He receives worship and gives intelligence. His weapons fall daily on the workers of guile. He is wise, and "greedy," and stationary in the midst, contemplates both. The explanation is, that he is greedy of rain, and contemplates the ferry and the water. But these are forced and fanciful, the fruits of preconceived notions of this Divinity, all knowledge of whose original character had been lost. "Both," it is much more likely, mean the sky and the earth; and "greedy," that he forces or finds his way everywhere, through the smallest crevices.

He is mighty, beneficent, powerful, the showerer, the divine, in whose gift are progeny and cattle.

Asht. ii. *Adhy. vi.* *Anuv. iii.* *Sûkta i.*

2. Bṛihaspati, destroyer of the Asuras, through thee the intelligent Gods have obtained the sacrificial portion. In like manner as the adorable sun generates the rays by his radiance, so art thou *the generator of all prayers.*

3. Having repelled revilers and darkness, thou standest, Bṛihaspati, *on the radiant chariot of Sacrifice*, formidable, the humiliator of enemies, the destroyer of evil spirits, the cleaver of the clouds, the attainer of heaven.

4. Thou leadest men, Bṛihaspati, by virtuous instructions [correct indications]: thou preservest them. Sin will never overtake him who presents to thee: thou art the afflictor of him who hates prayers: thou art the punisher of anger: such is thy great mightiness.

6. Thou, Bṛihaspati, art our protector, and the guide of our path, the discerner.

7. Turn aside from the path, Bṛihaspati, the arrogant and savage man who advances to injure us . . . . and keep us in the right way. . . . .

8. Bṛihaspati, defender, we invoke thee, the protector of our persons, the speaker of encouraging words, and well disposed towards us. Destroy the revilers of the Gods: let not the malevolent attain supreme felicity.

10. . . . . Fulfiller of our desires, pure and associated.

13. Bṛihaspati is to be invoked in battles: he is to be approached with reverence: he who moves amidst combats, the distributor of repeated wealth: the Lord Bṛihaspati has verily overthrown all the assailing malignants, like chariots.

14. Consume with thy brightest the Rakshasas, who have held thy witnessed prowess in disdain: manifest, Bṛihaspati, thy glorified, such as it was, and destroy those who speak against thee. ['Thy glorified': thyself manifested in fire and light].

15. Bṛihaspati, born of truth, grant us that wonderful treasure, wherewith the pious man may worship exceedingly; that which shines among men; which is endowed with lustre, the means of rites, and invigorates with strength: [the art of song].

18. When Bṛihaspati, descendant of Angiras, for thy glory Parvata had concealed the herd of kine, thou didst set them free, and with thine associate Indra didst send down the Ocean of water, which had been enveloped by darkness.

Of this Sûkta, verses 1, 5, 9, 11, 17 and 19 are addressed to Brahmaṇaspati; and Professor Wilson says that there is no marked distinction between the two Deities in any of the stanzas.

The former is, perhaps, something of a more martia. character, and his protection is sought for against enemies in a more especial manner, but there is nothing very precise in the passages addressed to him, to assign to him any particular office or character.

The etymological explanations of these names, by Sâyaṇa and Mahîdhara are of no value. Brahmaṇaspati is explained by Sâyaṇa to mean "protector or cherisher of food, or of any great or solemn acts of devotion": and Mahîdhara explains Bṛihaspati as meaning "cherisher or protector of the Vedas": but in the next Sûkta, Sâyaṇa interprets *bṛihat* by *mantra*, a "hymn," or "formula of devotion."

Adhy. vii. Anuv. iii. Sûkta ii.

1. Inasmuch, Bṛihaspati, as thou rulest. . . . .

10. Expansive, vast and excellent riches are the attainable of Bṛihaspati, the sender of the rain; these are the gifts of the adorable giver of food . . . .

[Of the sixteen stanzas of this Sûkta, all the others are addressed to Brahmaṇaspati.]

Sûkta viii.

9. Pierce him, Bṛihaspati, with thy sharp (thunderbolt) [for which we see no warrant], and overthrow our enemies with thy weapons. Hurl, Monarch, thy destroying (shaft), against the oppressor.

Ashṭ. iii. Adhy. iv. Anuv. v. Sûkta ix.

4. Bṛihaspati, friend of all the Gods, accept our oblations: grant precious treasures to the offerer.

"Friend of the Gods," i. e., of the luminaries, means that they owe to him somewhat which they manifest, or something of their energy and power. This is evident from other passages.

5. Adore the pure Bṛihaspati at sacrifices, with hymns. I solicit of him unsurpassable strength.

6. The Showerer on men, the omniform, the irreproachable, the excellent Bṛihaspati.

"*Omniform*" means that his manifestations as, by or through luminous bodies having form, are very many. "Pure" means such purity as that of fire and light. "Irreproachable" means spotless, unalloyed, unmixed with grosser matter: and "excellent" does not relate to moral excellence, but the sense would be better expressed by "excelling."

Sûkta iv. Anuv. v. Adhy. vii. Ashṭ. iii. is addressed to Indra and Bṛihaspati, as *Sûkta i.* and *ii.*, of the same are to Indra and Vayu, jointly. In each of the six stanzas they are jointly invoked. They are entreated to come and drink Soma, and be exhilarated; and to grant horses and cattle.

Asht. iii. Adhy. vii. Anuv. v. Sûkta v.

[In nine of the eleven stanzas, Bṛihaspati is invoked alone; in the tenth and eleventh, with Indra.]

1. . . . . the *pleasing-tongued* Bṛihaspati, who propped up by strength the ends of the earth, and who *abides with noise* in the three regions.

2. Bṛihaspati, protect the fruit-yielding, progressive, uninjured, ample sacrifice of this—they who are the Terrifiers, the Delighters of thee, who art possessed of great wisdom, glorify in our behalf.

3. Those, Bṛihaspati which had come from that distant, the Best, have sat down in connection with the ceremony, and to thee the Soma juices, expressed by the stones flow copiously, by the sounds of praise, like deep wells that supply water.

4. Bṛihaspati, when first being born in the highest heaven of Supreme Light, seven-mouthed, multiform, with sound, and seven-rayed, has subdued the darkness.

[The seven metres or measures, in which the Vedas were composed, are said to be his mouths. *Wilson.*]

Of the phrase "seven-rayed," Professor Wilson does not attempt an explanation. Bṛihaspati is prayer or praise or adoration, hymned in words, in poetry, and perhaps sung or chaunted. This, like the prayer expressed by sacrifice and the ascending flame, is imagined to unite and coalesce and become one with, the flame and fire, and so to be invested with the attributes of Agni. This is shown by the epithet, "pleasing-tongued," applied to Bṛihaspati, and by the phrases, "who abides with [not 'noise'], sound, resonance," on earth, in the air and in the sky, "the three regions;" "the sounds of praise," "multiform with sound."

Thus identified with Agni and Indra, with fire, flame and light, he is represented as "seven-rayed," as the light of the sun is, and it may be that the expression "seven-mouthed" refers to the seven notes of the musical octave, or scale. If it does not, and that scale was unknown, the coincidence is at least a singular and interesting one.

5. By *the praised and brilliant troop* he destroyed *with sound* the mischievous Bala: Bṛihaspati *shouting aloud,* set free the boon-bestowing, oblation-supplying kine.

6. The paternal universal Deity [*Viçwadevâya*] . . . . Bṛihaspati.

7, 8, 9. [These represent as surely prosperous, the prince who liberally cherishes, glorifies and honours Bṛihaspati, and who extends hospitality to the Brahman, and bestows gifts upon him.]

It is useless to consult the Sanskrit books for the original meaning of the word "Brahman." *Brahm* and *Brahma*, as names of Deity, were clearly derived from this word, but the Sanskrit books represent *it* as derived from *them*, making the Brahmans sons of Brahma, and giving various fanciful accounts of their creation. The Jâtimâlâ says,

> In the first creation by Brăhmâ, Brâhmănas proceeded, with the Veda, from the mouth of Brahmâ. The Pŭrŭsha Sûkta, the oldest account (*Rig-V. x.* 90), represents the Brahman as the mouth of the victim Pŭrŭsha, when he was cut into pieces; Indra and Agni also as coming from his mouth, and Vayu from his breath. All the accounts may be found in Muir's *Original Sanskrit Texts, Part i.*

The Vedic or Vaidic hymns were called *Mantras*. The *Brahmanas* (so called by the Hindŭs) are the liturgical institutes in which the ceremonial application of these hymns is prescribed, and the Aranyakas and Upanishads, or theological treatises, in which the spiritual aspirations are preserved, that were gradually developed in the minds of the more devout of the Indian Sages. (*Muir: Part iii. i.*)

The hymns, prayers or praises uttered by the Ṛishis, are called by a great variety of names, among which is *brahman*. (*Muir: Part iii.* 121.) And in *Rig-V. iii.* 29. 15, we find *brahmano* and *brahma* meaning "prayer," (*dyumnad-ad brahma Kuṣikâsa*, the Kusikas have uttered a prayer).

The names we are considering are both compounds of *patis*, a "chief, husband, master, etc.," which we find in *Divaspatis*, "Chief or God of heaven or the sky," whence Δις πατηρ Ζευς πατηρ, and the Latin *Diespiter;* and also in *Dyupatis*, which means the same, from *Div*, "sky," and *Patis*, "master."

These names are Brahmaṇas-pati, and Bṛihas-pati. *Brahma* and *Brahman* are probably from *barh*, to "resound or echo," or from the root of *bhraje*, "I burn or shine." From the former are the Greek βραχω, βρυχω.

And *Bṛihas* is from *bru*, "resound, enunciate, speak;" whence also βρυω, and in French, *bruit*, "noise, sound." As *sṛiṇu* is a contracted form of *ṣruṇu*, and from *ṣru*, an irregular root, comes *sṛiṇômi*, so *Bṛihas* is from *bru*.

The termination *as* does not indicate the plural. *Châkṣhas* means "the seeing;" *tapas*, "the burning;" *tavas*, "the growing," from the root *tu;* and *mahas* (greatness), "the growing," from *mah*, to "grow."

Brahmaṇas means, therefore, "the praying" (ones), those who offer up prayer or praise, the adorers, perhaps by means of the sacrificial flame; i. e., the priests or sacrificers; and *Bṛihas*, those who *audibly* praise the Gods, the praisers by the voice, the Poets.

In *Sûkta iii., Anuv. iii. Adhy. i. of Asht. i.*, we find,

The chaunters hymn thee, *Ṣatakratu;* the reciters of the Richas praise thee, who art worthy of praise; the Brâhmaṇas raise thee on high.

In *Sûkta iv. of Anuv. iv.*, of the same,

Drink the Soma juice, Indra, from the precious vase of the Brâhmaṇa [*Brâhmaṇâdradhasah*].

In *Sûkta viii. Adhy. iii. Anuv. xxii. Ashṭ. ii.*,

This altar is the uttermost end of the earth; this sacrifice is the navel of the world; this Soma juice is the fecundating power of the rain-shedding steed; this Brahmâ is the highest heaven of speech . . . . Four are the definite grades of speech: these Brahmans who are wise know them [*Brâhmaṇa ye manîshiṇah*]: Three, deposited in secret, indicate no meaning: men speak the fourth grade of speech.

Sâyaṇa says that "the speech which is in Heaven, with Âditya, is Bṛihatí, or the thunder." This confirms the derivation of *Bṛihas* from *bṛu*.

In *Sûkta ii. Anuv. iv. Adhy. vii., of Ashṭ. iv.*,

I invoke with hymns Indra, our friend, who is Brahma, who is attracted by prayer and entitled to adoration.

In *Sûkta ix. Anuv. i. Adhy. v. Ashṭ. iii.*,

Agni may be the officiating priest, or the master of the house in the sacrificial chamber, or he sits down as the Brahman.

In the Fifth and Sixth Ashṭakas are these passages:

May the Brahmans, the progenitors, presenters of the Soma, the observers of truth, protect us . . . . May the Brâhmanas, the Angirasas, be everywhere present . . . . Like Brahmans at the Soma libation, at the Atirâtra sacrifice . . . . They utter a loud cry like Brahmans when bearing the Soma libation, and reciting the year-long prayer . . . . You (Aṣwins) who always carefully protect Brahmâ (the great praise) among men . . . . Indra is Brahma, Indra is the Ṛishi [i. e., he is the hymn and its author, the Poet].

Bopp (*Comparative Grammar, iii.* 1335) is of opinion that Bṛihaspati means Lord of Greatness. It is true that *bhar* or *bri* means to "bear, support or nourish," and thence, to "make great." But I think that the Veda itself shows the real derivation to be from *Bru:* and that the *literal* meaning of Brahmaṇaspati is "Lord or chief, of prayer, praise or adoration;" and of Bṛihas-pati, "Lord or chief of speech or sound." The former is prayer, praise or adoration, as a universal, as that of which each individual or particular prayer or act of praise or adoration, is an emanation or manifestation, like a ray from the splendour of the sun, a beam of the universal light; and the latter is praise, prayer and adoration uttered and spoken aloud, universal speech of praise, devotional poetry, of which each hymn is an emanation, like a rivulet that flows out of an ocean, or the manifestation of Agni by a spark or a star. Perhaps the former meant that of which *acts* of adoration, whether by sacrificial or liturgical ceremonial, were the manifestations, through the Brahmans, who were priests; and the latter the hymns chaunted aloud by the Poets, who were the prototypes of the Keltic and Gaelic Bards.

Asht. iv. Adhy. ii. Anuv. iii. Sûkta x.

7. Glorify the first donor of precious treasures, Bṛihaspati, the distributor of riches, the bestower of great happiness on him who recites or chaunts; who comes laden with ample wealth for his invoker.

Sûkta xi. 12. Place the mighty Bṛihaspati, whose back is dark blue, in the chamber. Let us worship him who is seated in the interior of the mansion, everywhere shining, golden-hued, resplendent.

Here the sacrificial hymn assumes the characteristics of the sacrificial flame, issuing out of the dark blue smoke, resplendent and of the hue of gold. The sacrifice itself, and the ascending flame of the sacrifice are regarded as the praise and adoration of the worshipper, expressed in them as if they were his utterances; and the words that he chaunted were regarded as an integral part of that praise and adoration.

Asht. v. Adhy. i. Anuv. vi. Sûkta xii.

1. Bṛihaspati, who is the render of the mountain, the first-born, the observer of truth, the descendant of Angiras, the partaker of the oblation, the traverser of two worlds, abiding in the region of light, is to us as a father: he, the showerer, thunders loud in heaven and earth.

2. Bṛihaspati, who has appointed a region for the man who attends diligently at divine worship, destroying impediments, conquering foes, overcoming enemies, demolishing various cities.

3. This divine Bṛihaspati has conquered the treasures, and the spacious pastures with the cattle; purposing to appropriate the waters, he destroys *with sacred prayers* the adversary of heaven.

Asht. v. Adhy. vi. Anuv. vi. Sûkta viii.

2. . . . . Bṛihaspati . . . . that showerer, who is our benefactor from afar, as a father.

4. May that best beloved Bṛihaspati, who is the desired of all, sit down in our hall of sacrifice. May he gratify our desire of riches, and of male posterity . . . .

5. The unresisted Bṛihaspati, to whom pure praises are addressed, the adorable of houses.

['Pure' praises are praises by fire. *Pū*, to 'purify,' is the verbal parent of both wind and fire, which are always characterized as 'pure.' *Pavana* is wind, and *pavaka*, fire.]

6. May his powerful, brilliant horses, wearing a lustrous form like the sun, acting together, bring that Bṛihaspati, to whom strength belongs, and whose friendship bestows a dwelling.

7. He verily is pure, borne by numerous conveyances, he is the purifier, he whose speech is benevolent, the object of desire, the enjoyer of heaven: he, Bṛihaspati, is well domiciled, of goodly aspect, a most bountiful giver of ample food to his friends.

8. The divine heaven and earth, the generatrices of the Deity, have, by their might, given growth to Bṛihaspati . . . .

9 and 10. [Brahmaṅaspati and Indra, and Bṛihaspati and Indra, are invoked. The two latter are addressed as Lords of both celestial and terrestrial treasure, and riches and blessings are asked of them.]

No one who reads the hymns that ascribe the powers and faculties of Agni, Indra and all the Gods, to that power of intoxicating and exhilarating contained or rather manifested in the juice of the Soma plant, will wonder at the efficacy, powers and faculties ascribed to prayer and to praise and adoration, in worship and poetry. In *Sūkta xi. Anuv. i. Adhy. vi. of Ashṭ. ii.*, Indra is told that his brilliant strength is invigorated by the praises of the worshipper, and the thunderbolt placed in his hands by them. Professor Wilson says (*Introduction to Vol. i. p. xxv.*):

> The main objects of the prayers are benefits of a mere worldly and physical character. The tone in which these are requested indicates a quiet confidence in their being granted, as a return for the benefits which the Gods are supposed to derive from the offerings made to them, in gratifying their bodily wants, and from the praises which impart to them enhanced energy and augmented power.

Twice, at least, we have found Bṛihaspati called "Descendant of Angiras." The Angirasas themselves, were like their ancestor Angiras, ancient Ṛishis, represented as having been translated to the skies, for their great devotion to the Gods; and there are, I think, sufficient evidences in the Veda, that they were supposed to have become stars. In later ages, the stars of the Great Bear were called "The Seven Ṛishis or Sages." A name of this kind, for such a constellation, known to all the people, and in common use, would outlive traditions and remain in use for ages. The Angirasas were, it is certainly probable, these seven stars.

Bṛihaspati was called the descendant or progeny of Angiras, that which was born of him or produced by him, or which issued from him, because Angiras was a most ancient Ṛishi, perhaps, traditionally, the earliest Poet.

We shall find the great deeds of Indra ascribed to the Soma juice used at the sacrifices; and it is generally supposed that this is because of its intoxicating and exhilarating effects. Undoubtedly, in part, but the ideas of the Ṛishis in regard to it are very inadequately conceived, if we suppose that to have been the *whole* reason. We shall find even the fuel that feeds the fire to be a Deity, as entering into the fire and becoming of its essence. And the *great* reason for ascribing to Soma its potencies was, that being poured upon the fire, it became incorporated in Agni, an indivisible part of the unity of the fire, adding to it exhilarating effects. Silent praise, expressed by the sacrifice, and perhaps the mere liturgical worship, if there was any, was not Brahmaṇaspati's Self, for he was the *Whole*, the *Universal* of adoration, conceived of as a unit and a being; and every act of adoration and praise, whether uttered in words, or expressed by the fire and ascending essence and savour of the butter and the Soma, or whether merely silent in the thankful and grateful heart, was an emanation from Brahmaṇaspati; word, as it were, of his thought. He was not the aggregate of all prayers and adoration, but that of which they were the outflowing, a unity, a being, the spirit of prayer and adoration; *Principium undè fit manifestatio;* and, as is said in the Commentary on the Sephra de Zeniutha, *Est Principium istius quod manifestatur vel tunc quando manifestatur; et non dicitur, Principium quod manifestatur:* He is the Principle of that which is manifested, or then when it is manifested; and not the Principle which is manifested.

And Bṛihaspati is the Principle, of which all hymns of adoration are emanations—*The Spirit of the Poetry of Adoration, sung or spoken aloud.*

And each is considered an indivisible part of the divine unity of Agni, because the prayer, uttered or silent, and the words of the hymn of adoration, sung or spoken, unite and coalesce with the sacrificial fire, and all forms one act of adoration, which ascends to the skies.

VANASPATI.

Vanaspati, supposed, so far as I find any opinion expressed, to mean "Forest-Lord," and thus a tree, or a post, is also invoked as a Deity.

Pati, like *Pitar* (*Father*), is from the root *pa*, to "nourish" or "sustain" or "support," and became the name of the begetter of children, designating his relationship to them, not because he *begat* them, but because, after they were born, he cared for, protected and fed them. Here, as in Brahmañas-pati and Bṛihas-pati, *pati* means the principle from which the *Vanas*, whatever that means, proceeds or proceed.

The texts of the Veda, in which Vanaspati is named, are subjoined, and will enable us to determine what was worshipped under that name.

Ashṭ. i. Adhy. i. Anuv. iv. Sûkta ii.

11. Present, divine Vanaspati, our oblation to the Gods, and may true knowledge be of the giver.

Adhy. vi. Anuv. xiv. Sûkta vi.

8. May Vanaspati be possessed of sweetness towards us . . . .

Ashṭ. ii. Adhy. ii. Anuv. xxi. Sûkta iii.

11. Vanaspati, here present of your own accord, convey our offerings to the Gods: the divine and intelligent Agni accepts for the Deities.

Adhy. v. Anuv. xxiv. Sûkta ix.

10. Vanaspati, deliver of thyself the victim to the Gods, so that Agni may taste the oblation . . . .

Ashṭ. ii. Adhy. v. Anuv. i. Sûkta iii.

10. May Agni, who is Vanaspati, approach, and by his especial acts well cook the victim . . . .

Adhy. viii. Anuv. i. Sûkta iv.

10. Vanaspati, bring the Gods nigh: May Agni the Immolator prepare the victim.

Ashṭ. iii. Adhy. i. Anuv. i. Sûkta viii.

1. Vanaspati, the devout anoint thee with sacred butter at the sacrifice, and whether thou standest erect, or thine abode be on the lap of this thy mother, grant us riches.

2. Standing on the east of the kindled, dispensing food, of undecaying, and excellent progeny, keeping off our enemy at a distance, stand up for great auspiciousness.

3. Be exalted, Vanaspati, upon this sacred spot of earth, being measured with careful measurement, and bestow food upon the offerer of the sacrifice.

4. Well clad and hung with wreaths comes the youthful: it is most excellent as soon as generated: steadfast and wise venerators of the Gods, raise it up.

5. Born, and beautified in the sacrifice celebrated by men, it is engendered for the sanctification of the day. . . . .

6. May those which devout men have cut down, or which, Vanaspati, the axe has trimmed, may they, standing resplendent with all their parts, bestow upon us wealth with progeny.

7. May those posts which have been cut down, upon the earth, and which have been fabricated by the priests, those which are the accomplishers of the sacrifice, convey our acceptable (offering) to the Gods.

9. Arrayed in bright, entire, these pillars ranging in rows like swans, have come to us, erected by pious sages on the east; they proceed resplendent on the path of the Gods.

10. Entire in all parts, and girded with rings, they appear upon the earth like the horns of horned cattle; hearing by the priests; may they protect us in battles.

11. Vanaspati, mount up with a hundred branches, that we may mount with a thousand, thou whom the sharpened hatchet has brought for great auspiciousness.

In a note to this hymn, Professor Wilson says:

Vanaspati, literally, Forest-Lord, is here said to mean the post of wood to which the victim is tied.

If that were all for which it served, it would be difficult to see how any human creature, not a born idiot, could pray to it, the post, to bestow wealth and progeny, to protect the worshipper in battles, and convey his offering to the Gods.

In his note to the first hymn from which we have quoted a verse to Vanaspati, Professor Wilson says,

Vanaspati, Lord of the Woods; usually, a large tree, here said to be an Agni, as if the fuel and the burning of it were identified.

Asht. iii. Adhy. viii. Anuv. i. Sûkta v.

10. Wherever thou knowest, Vanaspati, the secret forms of the Gods to be, thither convey the oblations.

Asht. iv. Adhy. iv. Anuv. vi. Sûkta vi.

5. Open, Vanaspati, like the womb of a parturient female.

Here, Sâyaṇa says, according to the ancient chroniclers, Vanaspati was a large basket, in which the Ṛishi was shut up. He first addresses the basket, and then invokes the Aṣwins to set him free, begging them, in the next stanza also, to sunder by their devices the wicker-work, and set him free. In Stanzas 8 and 9, the birth of "the boy who has reposed for ten months in the bosom of his mother," is prayed for, that he may come forth alive, unharmed, living, from a living (parent). In Stanza 7, we have, "As the wind ruffles the lake on every side, so may thy womb be stimulated, and the conception of the months come forth."

The legend repeated by Sâyaṇa, is one of the many tales invented when the Veda had become to the Brahmans, for the most part, a confused mass of enigmas, to explain expressions no longer understood, as the Greek Poets invented their myths.

I find in Eichhoff the verbal root *van*, with the meaning of "serve" or "cherish." He derives from it the Greek ὀνεω, ονημι, "assist, benefit, be useful to;" the Latin *veneru;* and the Gothic *unna*. *Vanas* may be an adjective, meaning "nourishing, feeding, sustaining;" or a noun, meaning "that which nourishes, cherishes or sustains, food, fuel." And I do not see how it could have come to mean *tree* or *forest*, except because *wood feeds* and *keeps up* the fire.

The fire of the sacrifice seems habitually to have been obtained by attrition of two pieces of dry wood, the primitive method used still among savage tribes. Of course it could no longer have been necessary, but it was no doubt preserved as the ancient mode of procuring fire, used by the ancestors of the Aryans, and because, so obtained, it was deemed more pure and holy.

The mode of procuring it was, to lay a flat piece of dry wood upon the ground, and to twirl rapidly, with the hands or a cord, a stick held upright, with its pointed end upon the piece below. Naturally, this pointed stick was imagined to generate, and the flat piece to produce, the heat first, and finally the fire and flame; and these, until produced, were deemed to be "in embryo," latent, in the wood.

Agni and all his subsistences, in him, were thus deemed to be, and conceived of as, in the wood or tree; and this conception was of the same nature as ours, that the invisible soul is within the body, and acts upon it; and as to us the soul is the Very Self of the man, so, it seems, Agni, in the wood or tree, was its soul and self, its life, and it could fitly be said, "Thou, Agni, are Vanaspati."

And as the fire, latent in the wood, issued from it, and is produced by it, generated by the strength that causes the stick to revolve, so, also, the wood consumed by the fire, and disappearing, was deemed to be changed into and *become* the light, heat and flame, manifestations of Agni. As the glowing coals, the wood emitted all these, and was therefore invested with the characteristics and powers of Agni, and came at last to be considered as merely one of his names or an epithet.

Vanaspati was, therefore, unmistakably the principle of the food of the fire, its feeder with aliment, its nourisher and sustainer. He is the tree with the hundred branches, the trimmed trunk, prostrate on the ground, the posts of the sacrifice, and the fuel prepared for feeding the fire.

Thus he presents the oblation to the Gods, for he becomes the flame, light and heat that bears it upward, the divine and intelligent Agni accepting for the celestial Deities. He delivers the victim to the Gods, by becoming the fire that consumes it. "By his *especial* acts," that is, by exercising that particular function, "Agni who is," i. e., Agni *as*, "Vanaspati," "well cooks the victim." He is invoked to grant riches, whether he "stands erect," as tree or post, or "his abode is on the lap of *this* thy mother," i. e., whether, felled, he lies recumbent upon the ground. He is of "undecaying and excellent progeny," flame, light and heat, often termed "undecaying" being produced from him as he burns. He dispenses the food, cooked by him; and by the light that he produces "keeps off the enemy at a distance," the wild animal or the stealthy and cunning aboriginal savage. He is "exalted," set upright, "on this sacred spot of earth." "Well clad and hung with wreaths comes the youthful" tree or sapling. It is "most excellent as soon as generated: born, and beautified in the sacrifice celebrated by men, it is engendered for the sanctification of the days." Does this allude to some particular tree, of rapid growth (as the fig and banana are, in the warm climate of the Punjab), specially devoted to the sacrifices, "engendered for the sanctification of the days," i. e., of the fixed sacrificial days of particular seasons of the year; beautified by being trimmed, or decorated? or is "the youthful, well clad and hung with wreaths," a young branch thus ornamented? or is it possible that we have here the origin of the Druidic veneration of the mistletoe?

The posts, cut down, and trimmed and shaped ("fabricated") by the priests, are "the accomplishers of the sacrifice;" and must therefore finally have been placed with pomp and ceremony upon the fire, to feed it. Until then, they were "arrayed in bright, entire, and stood in rows like swans." Not cut or split up into pieces, like the ordinary fuel, they were hung, perhaps, with wreaths of gay colours; but were finally used to convey to the Gods the acceptable offering. Then they "proceed resplendent on the path of the Gods," i. e., the flame which they become ascends towards the celestial luminaries, the *Devaso*, or denizens of the sky. They were numerous; for, "girded with rings" they seemed like the horns of a herd of cattle; and were supposed to hear the invocations of the priests.

He, "whom the sharpened hatchet has brought for great auspiciousness," to obtain great favours from the *Devaso* by feeding the fire of sacrifice, is invoked to "mount up with a thousand branches," to ascend skyward with a thousand tongues of flame, "that we may mount with a thousand," i. e., that our prayers may ascend with the flames produced by *all* the fuel. He is invoked to convey the oblations wherever he knows "the secret forms of the Gods to be." The forms of the Gods, are their visible orbs; and he is asked to convey the oblations to such of them as have not risen or as have set, and are no longer in the sky.

Finally, Vanaspati, who produces the food of the fire, is invoked to "open like the womb of a parturient female;" the Aṣwins are invoked to sunder the "wicker-work;" and it is prayed that the child "who has reposed for ten months in the bosom of his mother, may come forth alive, unharmed, living, from a living." It is prayed that the womb of Vanaspati may be stimulated, and the conception of the months come forth.

I dismiss as absurd the idea that Vanaspati was a basket in which a Ṛishi was confined. The issue to come from Vanaspati, to permit which to be born he is invoked to open like a womb, one would at once say was the fire, latent in the wood, and with difficulty and labour caused to issue from it, were it not that it is a child that has reposed ten months in the bosom of his mother, and the conception of the months.

That it is a prayer for the safe delivery of the wife of the Ṛishi or Prince, is inconsistent with the express invocation to Vanaspati himself to open. It may be that the same piece of wood was used for producing the fire for the sacrifice, at successive festivals, and religiously preserved in the interim; for any thing considered sacred would become more so, the longer it was kept, and would hardly be flung away as worthless (though it might be burned), after it had been used. To keep it from year to year may have seemed equivalent to keeping unextinguished the fire itself.

I shall hereafter inquire whether there is not evidence that the festivals and ceremonies of sacrifice were held annually, at a particular season of the year. For the present I will only say that I think they were; and if they were continued, as they may have been, during two months, while the same stars rose at the dawn, with the Morning Star, and ten months elapsed from their close to the beginning of the next annual sacrifices, the fire then lighted anew would have reposed in the bosom of its mother during ten months, and would have been the conception of the months.

This is but a conjecture; but it is not improbable nor unreasonable; and, unfortunately, there are absolutely no means of attaining certainty as to the meaning of these obscure passages of the Veda. Neither can we be certain that the sense of the original is reproduced in the translation. What *is* certain, is, that Vanaspati is the principle of nourishment of the fire, indispensable to its existence and continuance. Produced from the wood, the fire is fed by it, and it becomes, by the energy developed by itself, that which consumes itself.

VAIṢWÂNARA.

The name *Vaiṣwânara* occurs frequently, applied to Agni, the two names often forming, as it were, one.

Asht. i. *Adhy. iv.* *Anuv. xi.* *Sûkta ii.*

1. Whatever other fires there may be, they are but ramifications, Agni, of thee: but they all rejoice, being immortal, in thee. Thou, Vaiṣwânara, art the navel of men, and supportest them like a deep-planted column.

2. Agni, the head of heaven . . . . became the ruler over both earth and heaven: all the Gods engendered thee, Vaiṣwânara, in the form of light.

Professor Wilson says, in notes on these stanzas, that this "is a very unusual appellative of Agni, and is a common synonym of Indra, although, in its proper sense of a *possessor* of *riches*, it may be applied to either." But then he gives this derivation of it: *Vaiṣwânara*, from *viswa*, "all," and *nara*, a "man;" a fire common to all mankind; or, as here indicated, the fire or natural heat of the stomach, which is a principal element of digestion.

3. *Treasures* were deposited in thee, Agni, Vaiṣwânara, like the permanent rays in the sun; thou art the sovereign of all the *treasures* that exist in the mountains, in the herbs, in the waters, or amongst men.

4. Heaven and earth expanded, as it were for their son . . . . praises addressed to the graceful-moving, truly-vigourous, and all-guiding Vaiṣwânara.

5. Vaiṣwânara, who knowest all that are born, thy magnitude has exceeded that of the spacious heaven; thou art the Monarch of Manu-descended men; thou hast regained for the Gods in the battle, the wealth.

6. . . . . The Agni, Vaiṣwânara, slew the stealer (of the waters), and sent them down, and clove the cloud.

7. Vaiṣwânara by his magnitude is all men, and is to be worshipped as the diffuser of manifold light.

Asht. i. *Adhy. vii.* *Anuv. xv.* *Sûkta v.*

1. . . . . Vaiṣwânara . . . . the august sovereign of all beings: as soon as generated from this, he surveys the universe: he accompanies the rising sun.

2. Agni, who is present in the sky, and present on earth, and who, present, has pervaded all vegetation: may the Agni Vaiṣwânara, who is present in vigour [as the vital force or energy], guard us night and day against our enemies.

Asht. ii. *Adhy. viii.* *Anuv. i.* *Sûkta ii.*

1. . . . . Agni, who is Vaiṣwânara, the augmenter of water . . . .

11. . . . . Vaiṣwânara, the resplendent, the immortal, giving precious treasures to the donor . . . .

12. . . . . Vaiṣwânara of old ascended to the sky that is above the expanse, bestowing upon his worshipper wealth, as he did in former times; he travels, ever vigilant, the common path.

Sûkta iii.

1. Intelligent, offer to the powerful Vaiṣwânara precious things at holy rites, that they may go; for the immortal Agni worships the Gods; therefore let no one violate eternal duties.

5. The Gods have placed in this world the delightful Agni in a delightful chariot, the tawny-hued Vaiṣwânara, the sitter in the waters, the all-knowing, the all-pervading, the endowed with energies, the cherisher, the illustrious.

10. Vaiṣwânara, I celebrate thy energies, whereby, O Sage, thou hast become all-knowing; as soon as born, Agni, thou hast occupied the realms and heaven and earth, and hast comprehended all these with thyself.

Vaiṣwânara is styled "divine, observer of truth, cognizant of heaven, bountiful, charioteer, the radiant Agni, Vaiṣwânara, the illuminator of the firmament, the adorable lord of sacred rites, the wise, the hearer, the guest, the quick-moving, kindled in every age by the Kuṣikas; who, bright with great lustre, sustains the heavens with his entire vast and insupportable, as a pillar." "Agni, who is wise, immortal, discriminating, Vaiṣwânara, chief conductor, the mighty:" "Agni, who art the protector of the good, most wise, powerful and opulent; Vaiṣwânara:" "Drink, Vaiṣwânara, who art identified with the ancient emblem" [flame].

In *Sûkta vii. Anuv. i. Adhy. v. of Asht. iv.*, we read,

The priests [or Gods, *Devâ*] have generated Vaiṣwânara, Agni, as the brow of heaven, the unceasing pervader of earth, born for sacrifice, wise, imperial, the guest of men, in whose mouth is the vessel [that conveys the oblation]. Immortal Agni, when born like an infant; when thou shinest, Vaiṣwânara, between the parental (heaven and earth). Agni Vaiṣwânara, these thy mighty deeds no one can resist: when born on the lap of thy parents, thou hast stationed the banner of the days on the paths of the firmament. The summits of the firmament are measured by the light of Vaiṣwânara, the manifester of ambrosial; all the regions are overspread on his brow, and the seven gliding spring from thence like branches.

"Ambrosial," in the translation, is followed by "rain," and "overspread," by "vapour," while the seven gliding are made to be "rivers." I see no reason for this, and think the allusion is to light, and the Seven Luminaries. The next stanza is, Vaiṣwânara, the performer of sacred acts, is he who made the regions, fireseeing, the luminaries of the sky, and has spread throughout all worlds, the irresistible guardian, the protector of ambrosial.

In the next Sûkta (*viii.*) we read:

New, pure and graceful praise issues to Agni Vaiṣwânara: Agni has made the manifold firmament; Vaiṣwânara, the performer of good deeds has attained heaven by his greatness . . . . Vaiṣwânara comprehends all creative energy; [and in this and the next Sûkta 'Agni Vaiṣwânara' is addressed]. Manifested like a prince, he dispels darkness by his lustre.' [Then], This Vaiṣwânara is the first offerer of burnt-offerings: behold him! this is the light immortal among mortals: he has been born in a bodily shape, immovable, all-pervading, immortal, ever-increasing: a steady light, swifter than thought, stationed among moving beings [the revolving Hosts of Heaven], to show the way to happiness. All the Gods, being of one mind, and of like wisdom, proceed respectfully to the presence of the one agent.

Sûkta ix. Anuv. i. Adhy. v. Asht. iv. (6) Mine ears are turned, mine eyes; this light that is placed in the heart; my mind, the receptacle of distant, hastens. What shall I declare? How shall I comprehend him? (7) All the Gods, alarmed, venerate thee, Agni, abiding in darkness. May Vaiṣwânara preserve us with his protection! May the immortal Agni preserve us with his protection.

This must mean that Vaiṣwânara is not the visible fire that the eye can see, and whose roaring the ear can hear; but that the intellect endeavours to obtain perception of him, and cannot succeed in doing so, or at least cannot succeed in expressing its conception. So we in vain endeavour to conceive of *Spirit*, and to express, affirmatively our imperfect and inadequate conceptions of it. The Gods, which, while enveloped in darkness, are alarmed, and worship Agni, are the heavenly bodies, which shine only when he manifests himself in them. The ancient Aryans had no idea of any other "Gods."

Sûkta v. Anuv. i. Adhy. ii. Asht. v. is addressed to Agni as Vaiṣwânara. We read in it:

1. Offer praise to the strong Agni, traversing without hindrance heaven and earth; he, who, Vaiṣwânara, prospers at the sacrifices of all the immortals, being *associated* with the awaking Deities [manifested by the Luminaries of the Morning].

2. . . . . Vaiṣwânara shines upon human beings.

4. Vaiṣwânara Agni, the firmament, the earth, the heaven, combine in thy worship: shining with undecaying splendour, thou overspreadest heaven and earth with light.

5. The lord of men, the conveyer of riches, the Vaiṣwânara of dawns, the manifester of days.

9. Grant us, Agni Vaiṣwânara, infinite happiness.

Sûkta vi.

6. Agni Vaiṣwânara has come to the excellent station between heaven and earth.

7. The divine Agni Vaiṣwânara has removed from the firmament the investing glooms, at the rising of the sun.

And in a subsequent Sûkta, Agni Vaiṣwânara is said to enter into the sacrificial food.

What is ascribed as peculiar, to Agni Vaiṣwânara, or to Vaiṣwânara alone, may be summed up thus:

He is the "navel" of men, supporting them as firmly as a column; all the Gods engendered him in the form of light. "Treasures" were deposited in him, like the permanent rays in the sun; and he is sovereign of all the "treasures" that exist in the mountains, in the vegetable creation, in the waters, and among men. He is graceful-moving, truly vigourous and all-guiding. He knows all that are born, and is greater than the expanse of space. He regained the "wealth" for the Gods, in the battle, slew the stealer, rent the clouds and sent down the rain. By his magnitude *he is all men*, and is to be worshipped as the diffusion of manifold light. He has *pervaded all vegetation*. He is present in the sky, and present on earth, and he is present in vigour.

Here we catch a gleam of light to guide us, and the idea is at once suggested that Agni, as Vaiṣwânara, is the vital heat, force, or vitality, life or the cause of being and existing, not only for living creatures and all that the earth produces, but for the celestial orbs, and all that exists in the wide universe. We look back to see if any phrase or expression conflicts with this, and we find none. Does anything confirm it? As vitality, he is the "navel" of men; for the child in the womb is supposed to receive the nourishment by which it grows, by the navel; and he sustains men, maintaining their existence, as firmly and steadfastly as a column upholds a roof. The Gods engendered him in the form of light, for light is the life of the celestial orbs.

What are the "treasures" that are "deposited" in him, as the unmanifested rays are in the sun? the "treasures" of which he is the sovereign? They are not cattle and horses nor gold; for they exist in the vegetable creation and even among men. They are "deposited" in him, but "exist" in these. What does this mean but that he is the principle of these "treasures," which are revealed in actual being, in men and animals, the vegetation, the waters and the mountains. They are life, health, strength, all that vitality gives, of enjoyment and of energy. He is all-guiding, for vitality upholds and sustains all, and is movement, action, energy.

He "knows" all that are born; he is with and in all; he is omnipresent, and the monarch of men. Warring for the Gods (the luminaries) he regained wealth for them, i. e., renewed their life and vigour, when they had been eclipsed or obscured. By his magnitude he is all men, i. e., he extends to and is present with all men. As vitality and vigour, he slew Vṛitra. He is to be adored as the diffuser of manifold light. [Compare, "In him was life, and the life was the light of men."] He is the august sovereign of all beings: for he is the life of all: and as soon as generated from the wood, he "surveys," pervades and becomes present in, the whole universe. He accompanies the rising sun; and by his light gives life and fertilizes the earth.

Thus it is that he is present "in vigour," i. e., in action and energy, everywhere, and pervades all vegetation. He is the all-knowing, all-pervading, the *cherisher*, the illustrious. "*Vaiṣwânara comprehends all creative energy.*" He is the light immortal among mortals; has been born in a bodily shape, immovable, all-pervading, and immortal, and ever increasing. All the Gods proceed respectfully to the presence of the one agent.

We find him also invested with the characteristics of the light-principle, or Indra, which is simply the identification of light and vitality; which once conceived, the poetic imagination soon enlarged and developed, and ascribed to vitality all the functions of light. Light *was*, indeed, to them, the life of the sun, stars and planets; for they knew its nature no more than they knew that of vitality; and ascribed all its energies to it as the Cause of Life. It is the same to us; and what else it is, in its real nature, we know as little as they did.

Vaiṣwânara is Agni in his special capacity, character and function as vitality or the vital principle, the life-principle of all being; and he is not anywhere regarded as a distinct individuality or as a subsistence of Agni. He is light, also, and Indra, as such, and might, therefore, from detached passages be regarded as the same.

VAHNI.

Asht. ii. *Adhy. viii.* *Anuv. i.* *Sûkta v.*

1. The sagacious Agni, cognizant of the dawn, is awakened to the paths of the sages; the luminous Vahni, kindled by the devout, has thrown open the gates of darkness.

Agni, here, the sacrificial fire, kindled, and beginning to blaze, at the first glancings of the dawn, which he represented as descrying in the east. He is awakened, he shines, on the paths by which the priests come to the sacrifice. Kindled by them, be penetrates into the body of the darkness, as one enters a city, forcing open its gates.

Vahni is but an epithet, probably from the root *vah*, to "move, bring," whence *vâhas*, "wagon," *vahanan*, "vehicle;" Latin, *veho*, "carry, convey;" *vahis*, "far;" *vâhas*, "road, route;" *vâḍhas*, "transported;" *vahitran*, "transportation;" *vanḍhar*, "conductor." Bopp says that Vahni, sometimes, in the Vedas, is *horse*, from *bearing, drawing;* which is to derive it from the same root. I take it, as an epithet applied to Agni, to mean conveyor or carrier, i. e., of the oblation, to the Deities.

SÛRYA.

The Sun is adored in the Veda, under the name of Sûrya, from the roots *Sur*, to "dart, shine," whence *Sûris*, *Sûryas*, "Sun;" Greek, *σειρ*, *σειριος*; Latin, *Sirius;* Gothic, *Sauil;* Lithuanian, *Saute;* and *su* or *sû*, to "dart forth, produce;" whence *savas*, "birth," *sutis*, "emission," *Sunus*, "Sun."

Asht. i. *Adhy. ii.* *Anuv. ix.* *Sûkta vii.* (*L.*)

1. The divine, all-knowing sun, the all-illuminating sun . . . .

4. Thou, Sûrya, out-strippest all in speed. Thou art visible to all. Thou art the source of light. Thou shinest throughout the entire expanse.

8. Divine and light-diffusing Sûrya, thy seven coursers bear thee, bright-haired, in thy car.

9. The sun has yoked the seven mares that draw his chariot safely.

10. We approach the divine sun among the Gods [the luminaries of heaven], the excellent light.

Bopp (*Comparative Grammar*, *iii.* 1279, *note*) discusses the derivation of Sûrya. He says that the Indian grammarians *assume* a root *sur*, to "shine," which he regards as a contraction of *svar*, contained entire in the radical word *svar*, "Heaven" (as "*shining*"), on which is based the Zend *hvarĕ*, "the Sun;" according to which, in *Sûrya*, the syllable *va* or its lengthened form *vâ* would be contracted to *û*. The name, it seems, should be pronounced "*Sûr-ya.*" *Svar* means to "shine." He does not think it is from the root *su*, to "produce."

We take the following texts from Muir (*Sansk. Texts*, *iv.* 96, the references are to the Mandalas):

Rig-V. i. 50, 7. Thou traversest the sky, the broad expanse [*Vi dyam eshi rajas prithv*], measuring the days with thy rays, beholding created things, Sûrya. [And here we see that *prithv* does not mean the earth; nor *rajas prithv*, the mundane regions.]

i. 160. 4. He, the most active of the active Gods [*devanam apasam*], who *produced* the heaven and earth [*rodasi*] which are beneficent to all; who, from a desire to benefit, measured the worlds [*mame rajasi*] . . . . [The 'active Gods' are the revolving or swiftly moving luminaries.]

viii. 90. 11, 12. Verily, Sûrya, thou art great: verily, Aditya, thou art great. The majesty of thee who art great is celebrated: certainly, God [*Deva*], thou art great. Verily, Sûrya, thou art great in renown: O God [*Deva*], thou art very great:

through thy greatness thou art the divine leader of the Gods [*devanam asuryah*], the pervading, irresistible luminary.

It is unnecessary to multiply quotations in regard to Sûrya, about whose character and individuality there is no manner of doubt. And I only note here, that he is an Aditya, and chief or leader of the *devanam*, a word applied exclusively to the celestial luminaries, in the Veda.

SAVITṚI.

Asht. i. *Adhy. ii.* *Anuv. v.* *Sûkta v.*

5. I invoke Savitṛi, the golden-handed, to protect me. . . . .

6. Glorify Savitṛi, son of the waters [*apamnapat*], for our protection . . . .

7, 8. We invoke Savitṛi, the enlightener of men [i. e., who gives light to men], the dispenser of various home-insuring wealth . . . . the giver of riches . . . .

Anuv. vi. *Sûkta i.*

3. Ever-protecting Savitṛi . . . . who art the lord of opulence . . . .

Adhy. iii. *Anuv. vii.* *Sûkta v.*

2. Revolving through the darkened expanse, arousing mortal and immortal, the divine Savitṛi travels in his golden chariot, beholding the worlds [shining upon them].

3. The divine Savitṛi travels by an upward and by a downward path; deserving adoration, he journeys with two white horses: he comes hither from a distance, removing all sins.

4. The many-rayed, adorable Savitṛi, having power (to drive) darkness from the world, has ascended his high-standing chariot, decorated with many kinds of golden ornaments, and furnished with golden yokes.

5. His white-footed coursers [but the word rendered 'white-footed,' is *syava*, 'brown'], harnessed to his car with a golden yoke, have manifested light to mankind. Men and all the regions are ever in the presence of the divine Savitṛi.

6. The spheres are three; two are in the proximity of Savitṛi, one leads men to the dwelling of Yama. The immortals depend upon Savitṛi as a car upon the pin of the axle; let him who knows declare it.

7. The well-winged, deep-quivering, life-bestowing, well-directed, has illuminated the three regions. Where is Sûrya now? Who knows to what sphere his rays have extended [gone]?

8. He has lighted up the eight points of the horizon, the three regions of living beings, the seven rivers: may the golden-eyed Savitṛi come hither, bestowing upon the offerer of the oblation desirable riches.

9. The gold-handed, all beholding Savitṛi travels between the two regions of heaven and earth, dispels diseases, approaches the sun, and overspreads the sky with gloom, alternating radiance.

This must mean that the luminary Savitṛi leaves the sky, by alternation, covered with darkness, it not shining, and then again appears and gives light. The scholiast endeavours to explain the expression that he "approaches the sun," by saying that although Savitṛi and Sûrya are the same as regards their *divinity* (each being the sun), yet they are two different *forms*, and therefore one may go to the other. The explanation is not philosophical. Of the question "where is Sûrya now," it explains, that it is said of the sun before dawn, while he is absent. But it seems rather to be said of him after he has set.

> 10. May the golden-handed, life-bestowing, well-guiding, exhilarating and affluent Savitṛi be present: for the Deity, if worshipped in the evening, is at hand, driving away Râkshasas and Yâtudhânas.
>
> 11. Thy paths, Savitṛi, are prepared of old, are free from dust, and well-placed in the firmament. . . . .

Asht. ii. Adhy. viii. Anuv. iv. Sûkta vi.

> 1. In truth, the divine Savitṛi, the bearer, has perpetually been present for the generation; for such is his office: verily he grants wealth to the pious . . . .
>
> 2. The divine, vast-handed, having risen, stretches forth his arms for the delight of all; the purifying waters for his rites, and this circumambient air sports . . . .
>
> 3. The moving is liberated by his rapid rays: verily he has stopped the goer from going; he restrains the desires of warriors for combat, for night follows the function of Savitṛi.
>
> 4. She enwraps the extended, like weaving: the prudent man lays aside the work he is able, in the midst; but all spring up when the divine unwearied sun, who has divided the seasons, again appears.

I leave out the interpolations of the scholiast. One of them is, in Stanza 3, "the cessation of," which was deemed necessary to sustain the theory that Savitṛi was the sun.

> 5. The engendered domestic radiance of Agni spreads through various dwellings, and presides over all food: the mother has assigned to her son the best portion, which is the manifestation of him, imparted by Savitṛi.

No explanation is attempted of this stanza, except that the Agnihotra rite was to be performed at dawn, and therefore might be considered as enjoined or instigated by the rising sun. But "the manifestation of him imparted by Savitṛi" is the light of Agni that is manifested by and shines from that luminary. "The engendered domestic radiance of Agni" may mean the lights lighted in the houses, or fires built in them: and this radiance, presiding over all food, may mean that by the lights so burning, the inmates eat; or that by the fires so kindled, they cook. The meaning of the mother giving the son the best portion, may mean that, to insure her child good fortune or health, the mother placed it in the moonlight, if Savitṛi is the moon.

> 6. The warrior, eager for victory, who has gone forth, turns back: home is the desire of all moving beings [i. e., all who are abroad seek their homes]: abandon-

ing his half-wrought toil [half-finished work], the labourer returns, when the function of the divine Savitṛi. [The scholiast adds 'is suspended.' It is strange that if this belongs there, it, as well as 'cessation of' should be omitted in the original. I should incline to read the phrase, when the office of Savitṛi begins.]

7. The animals search in dry places for the watery element which has been collected in the expanse by thee; the woods are assigned to the birds. [I think that the meaning is that the animals seek dry places for their beds, and the birds repair to their places of rest in the woods.] No one obstructs these functions of the divine Savitṛi.

8. The ever-going Varuṇa (the Evening Star) grants a cool, accessible and agreeable place to all moving, on the closing of the eyes; and every bird and every beast repairs to its lair, when Savitṛi has dispersed beings in various directions.

9. . . . . that divine Savitṛi, whose functions neither Indra nor Varuṇa, nor Mitra, nor Aryaman nor Rudra, nor the enemies, impede.

Asht. iii. Adhy. iv. Anuv. v. Sûkta iii.

6. Savitṛi, descended from heaven, bestow upon us blessings thrice every day.

Asht. iii. Adhy. viii. Anuv. v. Sûkta viii.

1. . . . . The divine, powerful and intelligent Savitṛi . . . .

2. The supporter of heaven, the protector of the world, the wise, puts on his golden armour; discriminator, filling, Savitṛi has engendered great and laudable felicity.

3. The divine fills the celestial and terrestrial regions, and boasts of his own functions; Savitṛi puts forth his rays for production, regulating the world, and animating it with light.

4. The divine Savitṛi, unrestrained, illuminating the regions, protects the righteous acts; he extends his arms for the people of the earth; observant of obligations, he rules over the whole earth.

5. Savitṛi, encompassing them by his magnitude, pervades the three (fold) firmament, the three worlds, the three brilliant spheres, the three heavens, the three-fold earth; may he by his three functions, of his own (pleasure) protect us.

The interpretations of this stanza by the scholiast are not worth repeating. It is at least a curious coincidence that among the Greek and Latin Aryans, the Moon, Σεληνη, Luna, or Diana, and 'Εκατη, was *triformis,* and some of her statues represented her with three heads, those of a horse, dog and boar. Diana was armed with a bow and quiver, and drawn by *two white stags.* The following verse expressed her three-fold powers and functions:

Tenet, lustrat, agit, Proserpina, Luna, Diana,
Sura, Suprema, feras, sceptro, fulgure, sagittâ.

Hecaté was called "*Diva triformis, tergemina, triceps.*" Nations and kings supposed themselves indebted to her for their prosperity.

If Savitṛi was the moon, we should find here, in the Veda, the origin of all the Greek and Latin notions in regard to the triple character and functions of Diana, Proserpina and Hecaṭê.

And, for the origin of the Vedic idea of the triple form and functions of the moon, we should be wise to look to those changes and phenomena, which would be apparent to and noticeable by the simplest herdsmen, and not to the conceits and vagaries of the Brahmans. At the season of the new moon, when she had not been seen at all for two or three days, she would appear as a thin crescent low in the western sky, at the evening twilight. At the full, she would appear, a huge red orb "in golden armour," upon the eastern horizon, among other stars than before, rising majestically to shine during the whole night; and before disappearing from the heavens during both day and night, she would be seen rising at or a little before dawn, among still another train of stars. These would be three divisions or portions of the firmament and heavens, and the three worlds, and the three forms of the moon would naturally be represented as three different luminaries or spheres, and Savitṛi, as each, would exercise different functions. "The three-fold earth," even the Brahmanic ingenuity has not endeavoured to explain: but as the moon, at new and full, and at the end of her last quarter would view the earth in a different aspect, the term three-fold, applied to the earth, would be no *more* inappropriate, to say the least, than many others used in the Veda. I have no idea that "earth" is correct.

6. May that divine Savitṛi, who is the source of great happiness, the engenderer, the comprehender, the regulator of both the movable and the stationary [the planets and fixed stars, perhaps], grant us happiness in the three worlds, and be to us for the destruction of sin. [The original of 'the three worlds' evidently did not mean worlds in the Brahmanic sense or in our sense of that word. The old Poets prayed for happiness in this life and world, not in other worlds. The real meaning probably was, 'during those three seasons'.]

7. May the divine Savitṛi, approach along with the Ṛitus [*ṛitu* means 'season'], prosper our dwelling, and bestow upon us good progeny and food; may he be favourable to us by night and by day . . . .

Sûkta ix.

1. The divine Savitṛi has been manifested.

2. First thou bringest forth for the adorable Gods, the best portion, immortality: then, Savitṛi, thou spreadest abroad thy rays, and excitest among men the consequent offices of vitality.

There is no certainty that this interpretation is correct. It is that of Mahîdhara. Wilson follows the scholiast, which is, "then settest open (the day) to the donor (of the oblation), and grantest successive existences to men." The "adorable Gods" are the planets and great stars. For them

Savitṛi produces lengthened existence, by the emanation through them of his light. Then he displays all things to the worshipper, and renews or continues his existences by making the world visible to him.

4\. . . . . The divine Savitṛi, he upholds the whole world, whereby his gracious hand spreads fertility over the whole earth, and the magnitude of the heaven: such is but true.

5\. Thou elevatest those of whom Indra is chief, above the vast clouds: for these thou providest dwelling filled with habitations: as when advancing they detained thee, so in like manner at thy command they stayed [became fixed in their places].

In *Sûkta v. Anuv. iv. Adhy. iii. of Ashṭ. iv.*, Savitṛi and Bhaga are invoked together, as distributors of wealth among men. "Worship," it is said, "the divine Savitṛi with holy hymns. May the irreproachable Savitṛi give us that desirable" . . . .

Ashṭ. iv. Adhy. iv. Anuv. vi. Sûkta ix.

1\. . . . . the intelligent, great, adorable Savitṛi . . . . great is the praise of the divine Savitṛi.

2\. The wise Savitṛi comprehends all forms, he has brought forth what is good for biped and quadruped: the adorable Savitṛi has illumed the heaven, and shines in sequence to the passage of the dawn [where the word rendered 'dawn,' it is quite likely, as will be seen, means the evening twilight].

3\. After the passage of which divine, the other Deities proceed to majesty with power. [These must be the planets and stars, because by day one luminary only shines—the sun]: he who by his greatness has measured out the terrestrial regions, the divine Savitṛi, resplendent.

4\. Either thou traversest, Savitṛi, the three regions, or combinest with the rays of Sûrya [according to Sâyaṇa, Savitṛi is especially the sun before rising; Sûrya is the sun in general. It is strange, then, that we have, so far, found Savitṛi mentioned once only in connection with the *Sun*—(I do not know what the original word there is)—and then as approaching him; and once with Sûrya, and then as combining with his rays, which could very appropriately be said of the moon]; or thou passest between the night on either hand [and certainly the sun does not go through a lane cut, as it were, in the darkness that forms on either side of it]: or thou, divine Savitṛi art Mitra [takest the place of the Evening Star] through thy functions [appearing in the west where Venus does, and performing her offices].

5\. Thou alone rulest over living beings: thou art Pushan, divine, by thy movements; thou art sovereign over the whole world.

Sûkta x.

We solicit of the divine Savitṛi the enjoyable; may we receive from Bhaga that which is excellent . . . . Nothing impairs the sovereignty of this Savitṛi, which is most especially renowned and beloved . . . . That Savitṛi, who is Bhaga, bestows precious treasure on the donor of the offering . . . . Grant us today, divine Savitṛi, affluence with progeny, and drive away evil dreams . . . . Remove from us, divine Savitṛi, all misfortunes: . . . . Savitṛi, the protector of the good, the observer of truth . . . . The divine object of meditation, Savitṛi, who ever vigilant, precedes both night and day [for in the short winter days, the moon rises before sunrise, and is in the west in the evening, as the new moon] . . . . Savitṛi, who proclaims his glory to all these living beings [the stars], and gives them life.

Ashṭ. v. Adhy. i. Anuv. vi. Sûkta x.

1. The divine and benevolent Savitṛi puts forth his golden arms [*Qu.* the horns of the crescent?], for donations: the adorable, youthful, sagacious, stretches out his hands, filled with water, in the various service of the world. [The Indians judge whether the moon is to be a rainy or a dry one, by the manner in which the new moon lies.]

2. . . . . Thou art he who art in the procreation and perpetuation of many, bipeds and quadrupeds.

3, 4. . . . . Thou who art golden-tongued. . . . . May the divine, munificent, golden-handed, golden-jawed, adorable, sweet-spoken Savitṛi, rise regularly [in due time], at the close of night, when he bestows abundant and desirable upon the donor of the oblation.

5. May Savitṛi put forth like an orator his golden well-formed arms: from the ends of the earth he ascends to the summit of the sky, and moving along, delights everything that is.

Ashṭ. v. Adhy. iv. Anuv. iii. Sûkta v.

1. The divine Savitṛi has diffused the golden radiance on high, of which he is the asylum; verily Bhaga is to be adored . . . .

2. Rise up, Savitṛi: hear, upon the celebration of this ceremony, diffusing light over the spacious earth, and bestowing human enjoyments upon men.

3. Glorified be the divine Savitṛi, whom all the Gods praise . . . .

4. Whom the divine Aditi, delighting at the birth of the divine Savitṛi, glorifies; whom the supreme sovereigns, Varuṇa, Mitra, Aryaman, consentaneously adore.

Sûkta xii.

1. Borne by his steeds, may the divine Savitṛi, who is possessed of precious treasure, and filling the firmament, come hither, holding in his hands many things good for man, and tranquillizing and animating human beings.

2, 3, 4. May the outspread, vast and golden arms of Savitṛi extend to the ends of the sky . . . . *May the sun impart energy unto him:* [*Sûraschid asmâ anudâd apasyam:* which is explained, *Sûryo asmin Savitṛe Karmechchâm anudadâtu*, May Sûrya subsequently give to that Savitṛi the desire for acts.—Wilson, note].

Here, for the *third* time only, Savitṛi and Sûrya, the sun, are mentioned together. The passage clearly shows that the two were not the same. Whether the Ṛishi knew that the moon shone only by the reflected light of the sun, is very doubtful; but it is equally clear that he thought that she received her energy from him.

3. . . . . the divine Savitṛi, who is endowed with energy, the lord of treasures

4. . . . . the eloquent-tongued, dextrous-handed, whose hands are full . . . .

Elsewhere it is said, "when the dawns arise, the divine Savitṛi casts his splendours on high." But this does not necessarily show him to be the sun, because the moon, rising at or near midnight, would be high in heaven at "the rising of the dawn," and the sun's rays would not then be cast on high . . . . The eye of the Gods (of the stars and planets) has been manifested for religious rites: the clause immediately preceding reads, "The divine Savitṛi, the leader of all, sends upwards the immortal, all benefiting light:" then "the eye of the Gods has been manifested for religious rites: the dawn has made all creatures visible."

2. The paths that lead to the Gods are beheld by me, innocuous and glorious with light: the banner of Ushas is displayed in the east, she comes to the west, rising above high places.

3. Many are the days that have dawned before the rising of the sun, in which thou, Ushas, hast been beheld, like a wife repairing to an inconstant husband, and not like one deserting him.

In *Sûkta ix.* it is said,

Thy rays, Ushas, annihilate the darkness; they diffuse light, as Savitṛi his arms.

And, in *Sûkta vi. Anuv. iii. Adhy. i. of Ashṭaka vi.*, Savitṛi, Bhaga, Varuṇa, Mitra and Aryaman are addressed as the *Adityas:* which the sun certainly is not classed among.

If Savitṛi was, in these ancient days, what it became among the Brahmans, ages afterward, a name of the sun, it is extraordinary that it is not once used as a synonym for Sûrya.

Sûrya's chariot is drawn by seven mares, called in one hymn "seven bay steeds," and once his glorious white horses are spoken of. Savitṛi has but two. There are three hymns of Sûrya, in one of which several of his names are mentioned; but Savitṛi is not among them. It is not possible to doubt that Sûrya is the sun. That is explicitly said, again and again, and is made plainer still, by the epithets and descriptive phrases applied to him, and used in addressing him, in the hymns. If Savitṛi also is the sun, it is strange that the two names are never used together, and that they *appear* to be as distinct from each other as Agni and Indra.

Mr. Cox gives the following quotations, with others, from the Veda:

Shining forth, he rises from the lap of the dawn, praised by singers: he, my God Savitar, stepped forth, who never misses the same place.

He steps forth, the splendour of the sky, the wide seeing, the far shining, the shining wanderer: surely, enlivened by the sun, do men go to their tasks and do their work.

May the golden-handed, life-bestowing, well-guarding, exhilarating, and affluent Savitṛi be present at the sacrifice.

Mr. Cox says that Sûrya or Savitṛi occupies the place in the Veda, which is filled by Hēlios in the Greek mythology, as the dweller in the globe of the sun, or by Nereus as the actual inhabitant of the sea. Of Savitṛi he says:

Savitar, the inspirer, from the root *su*, to 'drive' or 'stimulate,' is especially the glistening or golden God. He is golden-eyed, golden-tongued, and golden-handed. The story went that once, when Savitar cut off his hand at a sacrifice, the priests gave him, instead, a hand of gold.

This is ages later than the Veda, and in the same spirit the commentators interpreted the epithet as denoting, not the splendour of the sun, but the gold which he carried in his hand to lavish on his worshippers.

The full moon, rising in the east, very well deserves to be designated as golden. The far-stronger reason for identifying Savitar or Savitṛi with the sun, is, that he is said to rise from the lap of the dawn: but the festival may have been held a few days before the new moon, when the Queen of Night rose just before the dawn; but it is added, immediately afterward, that, enlivened by the sun, men go to their work. And if there were expressions equally clear; forbidding the identification of the two, there would be no reason to doubt their identity.

Mr. Cox continues:

The power and strength of Savitṛi are naturally represented as irresistible. Not even Indra or Varuṇa, or any other being, can resist his will; and the verse which is regarded as the holiest in the Veda, is addressed to Savitar. He is a Tithōnus who waxes not old.

But we find this, also, in the Veda, and it "gives us pause":

Either thou traversest, Savitṛi, the three regions, or combinest with the rays of Sûrya, or performance of the functions of Mitra.

How could this be said of Sûrya himself? It could well be asked where the moon was, when she had disappeared from the sky, and it could well be imagined that her light was merged in that of the sun; but it could not be said that perhaps Savitṛi, the sun, was combining with the rays of Sûrya, the sun. If this was said at sunset, when the moon, just changed, had not yet shown her crescent in the west, and if she had not set, was invisible in the glowing radiance of the sunset; and if the Evening Star then shone out, it might well be asked if this was really the moon, performing the functions of that planet. When and how does the sun play the part of Mitra; whatever Mitra may be?

Again, the sun *always* "traverses the three regions;" for every day he goes from the east, by the mid-station of the south, to the west, in the sight of men. The moon does so, during part of the nights only; but from new to full she is not seen to travel the whole journey: and at the new moon, *her* rays do combine with those of the sun.

Savitṛi had established *pṛithivi* by supports: and fixed the sky in unsupported space; has milked the atmosphere, restless as a horse. He is called the son of the waters, and is said to know the place where the ocean, supported, issued forth. All this, applied to the sun, is as hard to be understood, as it is if applied to the moon.

The wise Savitṛi "comprehends all forms." The sun does not assume different forms, nor manifest himself under the forms of other luminaries. The moon is continually changing her form, and of course comprehends in herself all the forms she assumes.

The adorable Savitṛi, it is said, "has illuminated the heavens, and shines in sequence to the passage of the dawn." She does that, when in midheaven at the break of day, and, having illuminated the expanse before daylight, she continues to shine for a time, as the dawn is passing away, and until the rising of the sun.

> I invoke night [it is said] who brings rest to the world. I invoke the divine Savitṛi, for my preservation. *Revolving through the darkened firmament,* arousing mortal and immortal, the divine Savitṛi travels in his golden chariot, beholding the worlds.
>
> He is golden-haired, but he ascends and descends with two *white* horses. He is many-rayed, with power to disperse darkness. [It is Ushas who disperses it for the sun, who therefore never comes into the darkened expanse, or disperses the darkness.]
>
> His white-footed coursers are harnessed to his car with a golden yoke. They manifest light to mankind. Men and all the regions are ever in his presence.

The spheres are three. Two are in the proximity of Savitṛi. One leads men to the dwelling of Yama. As I do not know the meaning of the word translated "spheres," I can only conjecture the meaning of this passage. A "sphere" that leads anywhere, must be a luminary, an orb: and therefore the three spheres may be the three planets, Jupiter, Venus and Mars. Two of these are the Morning and Evening Stars, and therefore often in the neighbourhood of the new moon. I do not know what is meant by the dwelling of Yama. But, if the three spheres mean the three planets, they are much more naturally associated with the moon than with the sun.

Sûrya, it is said, has lighted up the eight points of the horizon, the three regions of living beings, the seven rivers. "Where is he now?" it had just been asked: "who knows to what sphere his rays have extended?" And then the golden-eyed Savitṛi is invoked to come hither. This *seems* to be an invocation to the full moon to rise, after the sun had set.

> The paths of Savitṛi are prepared from of old, are free from dust, are well placed in the expanse. They are easy to be traversed.
>
> The divine Savitṛi diffuses his light on high, dispersing the dew. Then Varuṇa and Mitra and others hasten to their offices, to lead up the sun in the sky.

If Savitṛi is the sun, it is not easy to comprehend how, when he is shining on high, the Morning Star should hasten to fulfill his office, by leading the sun up into the sky. If Savitṛi is the moon, the sense is clear.

The chariot of Sûrya, the sun, is drawn by seven mares. That of Savitṛi, as we have seen, by two white horses. What could be more appropriate to the moon, golden at first, when rising at the full, and when swimming higher in the heavens, seeming like an orb of liquid silver?

I cannot but believe that Savitṛi was the moon. If one or two verses, as translated, seems to be inconsistent with this hypothesis, there are much greater difficulties to be encountered in interpreting it to mean the sun: and it was certainly one or the other of these luminaries.

At that day all the luminaries seem to have been regarded as of one sex; and it is no objection to my views that Venus and the moon afterwards became feminine.

In one passage of the Fifth Ashṭaka, it clearly appears, I think, that Savitṛi is not the sun, and is the moon. We have on a previous page, under the head of Ushas, quoted the entire passage.

> The divine Savitṛi, the leader of all [i. e., of all the luminaries of the night], sends upward her light. The eye of the Gods [i. e., of the luminaries] has been manifested, for religious rites. The dawn has made all creatures visible. The ways to the stars are seen, glorious with light. The Banner of Ushas is displayed in the east. She extends to the west, spreading over the sky.

Of course the sun had not risen; for his rising is the death of the dawn, according to the Veda. The hymn fixes the time of the sacrifice at daylight, before sunrise, when the moon was high in heaven, and the dawn, Ushas, was in her full glory.

I do not believe that there were either confusion or contradictions in the ideas of the Vedic Poets, in regard to their Deities. Wherever contradictions or confused notions appear, I believe them to be only apparent, and owing to the difficulty of now ascertaining the real meaning of their language. They were not the inventors of their mythology. It had come to them from their remote ancestors, and in shapes perfectly definite and distinct. What they meant by Agni and Indra, Savitṛi and Sûrya, they perfectly well understood; and if the two last had both been names of the sun, they would somewhere have been used together as such.

They called Savitṛi, ruler by himself, or of himself, over living creatures: sovereign over the whole world, divine saviour, protector of the good; observer of truth; and all the Devas. He is the enlightener of man and the giver of riches. He is unfriendly to waters. "Youthful Agni," it is said, "bring hither for our protection the wives of the Devas." Is this an invocation to the new-born crescent moon, young manifestation of Agni, to cause the stars and planets to shine out?

I know that all the commentators, ancient and modern, take Savitṛi to be the sun. I feel the great weight of their authority. Dr. Muir takes him to be so, in quoting *Rig-V. v.* 81. 3, where it is said that *Devah Savita Mahitvana* measured out the regions of the expanse by his power, *pârthivâni vimame sa etasô rajamsi;* and that the other luminaries (*deva*) have followed his course and might with vigour. There Savitṛi, or Savitar, is called a steed.

In *Rig-V. ii.* 38. 9, it is said that neither Indra, Varuṇa, Mitra, Aryaman nor Rudra can resist the purpose of Deva Savitar. This could as properly be said of one orb as of another. The moon "measures," i. e., traverses, the expanse, as well as the sun, is apparently of the size of the sun, and at the same distance from us; and the planets could be more appropriately said to follow *her* course, than that of the sun.

With many of the ancient nations, the moon was at first designated as male. Everywhere, and among every other people, she was worshipped. It is not to be believed that those who adored the sun and planets did not also adore the empress of the night, who above all other of the heavenly bodies, measured for them by her regular changes, the weeks and months; and if not so brilliant as the sun, her changes of shape made her more a subject of admiration and wonder, and her soft and beautiful light could not but give an idea of beneficence and kind protection.

On all these grounds, I conclude that Savitṛi, Savita, or Savitar, was the moon.

The common Sanskrit name of the moon is *mâs*, from *mâ*, to "measure," whence *masas*, "month," and *manan*, to "measure, divide out." She was therefore, really, *The Measurer*.

Bopp says (*Comparative Grammar*, *iii*. 1280, *Germ. Ed.* 1319, *note*):

> The opinion that *Sûra-s*, 'sun,' springs from *sû* or *su*, to 'bear,' to 'produce,' finds confirmation in the fact, that another appellation of the sun, viz.: *Sav-i-târ* (*-tṛi*), has decidedly arisen from the root *su* or *sû*. This word occurs frequently in the Vedic hymns: I would not, however, from the circumstance that the Vedic Poets delight in extolling the Sun-God as producer (of the produce of the fields), as also as supporter (*Pûṣhan*), deduce the inference that the proper designation of the sun, which existed so early as the time of the unity of the languages, must have pointed towards this image; for it certainly approximates more to the primary view of people, to designate the sun as lighting, or shining, than as producing or nourishing. . . . . Might we assume, together with *svar*, *sur*, to 'shine,' a root *su*, of the same meaning, I should derive from it the appellation of ye moon, *tio*, *sô-mâ-s*, ... while another *Soma* (the Soma-plant) belongs to a different root *su*, which signifies to 'express.'

In *Rig-V*. *x*. [*Mand.*] 149. 1, the hymns of which are chiefly of later date, we find:

> Savitâ has established *pṛithivim* [trans. 'the earth'] by supports: Savitâ has fixed *dyam* [trans. 'the sky'] in unsupported space: Savitâ has milked the atmosphere, restless as a horse [*asvam*], or, Savitâ has extracted from the atmosphere the ocean, etc., restless as a horse—the ocean fastened in the impassable expanse. Savitâ, the son of the waters, knows where the ocean, supported, issued forth. From him the earth, from him the atmosphere arose: from him the heaven and earth [*dyâvâ-pṛithivî*] extended.

Yaska says that the Savitṛi here mentioned is the "intermediate" one (i. e., the Deity residing in the atmosphere) and adds, "The sun also whose place is in the sky" [*Adityo*], is called Savitṛi.

Professor Roth translates this verse thus:

> Savitṛi has fixed the earth with supports; he has fastened the heaven in unsupported space; he has milked the atmosphere, shaking itself like a horse; the stream that is confined within limits which cannot be overpassed. (*Muir, Orig. Sansk. Texts, iv.* 98.)

All this is quite inconsistent with the character of Savitṛi, and as much so with that of Sûrya, in the earlier hymns. No *luminary* could be said to have established the earth with supports, or fixed the heaven in space; and it is only of interest as showing that long before the era of the Brahmanas, Savitṛi was misunderstood. At last the name became but a synonym of Sûrya.

YAMA.

Yama is not often named in the Rig-Veda. In one passage, three paths are spoken of, one of which leads "to the dwelling of Yama." And I find also the following passages:

Asht. i. Adhy. v. Anuv. xii. Sûkta ii.

4. Agni, as Yama, is all that is born; as Yama, all that will be born.

Asht. ii. Adhy. iii. Anuv. xxii. Sûkta vii.

2. Trita harnessed the horse that was given by Yama. Indra first mounted him, and Gandharba seized the reins. Vasus, you fabricated the horse for the sun.

3. Thou, horse, art Yama: Thou art Trita, by a mysterious act.

Asht. v. Adhy. iii. Anuv. ii. Sûkta xvi.

9. .... The Apsarasas sit down, wearing the vesture spread out by Yama.

The *Sama-Veda* says,

> Garuda, the Messenger of Varuṇa, bird that producest in the womb of Yama, the all-controlling [and], Those who from their hearts desire union with the Divine Being, in the Heavens, in the bosom of Yama, look with steady vision to thee.

Wuttke gives this quotation, "Yama, of Sun-like glory."

In the *Atharva-Veda, vi.* 93. 1, it is said, "May Yama, death, who brings dire destruction, may the tawny hell, etc."

Mr. Cox thinks Yama to be the sun after he has set. He says, after defining *Yama* as meaning "twin,"

> In this Yama we have probably the Hindū God of the Dead, whose two dogs, with four eyes and wide nostrils go about among men as his messengers. .... The twin who represented the evening, would naturally become the lord or judge or guide of the departed. As from the east came all life, so in the west lay the land of the dead, the Elysian fields, the regions of Sutala; and thither the sun hastens, as he sinks down from heaven. [Thus], Yama is said to have crossed the rapid waters, to have shown the way to many, to have first known the path on which our fathers crossed over. .... But although a darker side is not wanting to his character, Yama remains in the Veda chiefly the God of the blessed, in the paradise where he dwells with Varuṇa. (*Mythol. i.* 392.)

He does not remain that in the Rig-Veda. These are notions of a much later growth, founded on two or three ambiguous and obscure phrases in the ancient hymns.

Dunlap says (*Spirit History of Man*), referring to Weber (*Indian Studies*),

> Yama is the sun, the source of the souls, and of all life; later, he becomes, like Osiris, King of the Dead. The Earth-Goddess, Niniti, is his wife.

In India, in the later times, Vivaswat was one of the forms of the sun, and the father of Yama. In Ancient Persia (Burnouf thinks) these names became *Vivanghvat* and *Yima*.

I think it is quite clear that he was not the sun, in the Rig-Veda. He was Agni, in some special character or function, and as such, was all that are and that will be born. This could be said only of a principle, and not of a luminary. It is doubtful whether it will ever be possible to learn what is meant by the horse given by Yama, which Tṛita harnessed; the horse "fabricated by the Vasus for the sun." "Thou horse," it is said, "art Yama." And "by a mysterious act," he was also the horse of Tṛita. These, and the "dwelling of Yama" will probably always remain enigmas, as will Yama himself, as a Vedic Deity. The *Sama-Veda* is modern; and what it says of Yama is of no value. He is neither King of the Dead, nor Lord of the Blessed, in the Rig-Veda.

Equally enigmatical is "the vesture spread out by Yama," which the Apsarasas wear.

Eichhoff gives us the root, *yam*, to "hold, enclose, clasp, contain, lock up, etc." [*tenir, sener*]; whence *yaman*, a "couple;" *yamas*, *yâmanas*, a "twin;" Latin, *geminus; yâmis*, "daughter-in-law;" Greek, *γαμετις*; *yâmâtṛi*, "son-in-law;" Greek, *γαμρος*.

Only one solution of this enigma occurs to me as possible; and that I offer to the reader as a mere conjecture, for his consideration.

It is that Yama is the God of bodies formed of flesh, and of the earth; the God of bodily forms. As such, he is also flesh and the earth. He gave men the horse, and the horse so given is flesh, furnished with the bodily organs and senses, and as flesh and body, is Yama. It is a "mysterious act" that gives to a body composed of matter, the faculty of sensation and the powers and senses that are the consequence of organization. The Vasus (*ουσια*, "existence, vitality") fabricated the horse for the sun.

Flesh, or meat, offered in sacrifice, becomes an integral part of the flame and thus it is Agni, as all other fuel is; and Agni, as flesh, is all mankind. The body, which when buried combines with the earth, has always been said to be formed of the earth; and thus the earth is the dwelling of Yama. The bosom of the earth is the womb of Yama, "the all-controlling," to which all bodies return. Flesh is the vesture spread out by Yama, with which the Apsarasas are clothed. Union with the Divine is effected when the breath of life ascends to the sky, and the body goes into the bosom of Yama. And Yama, the grave, is fitly coupled with death and the tawny hell. The body *encloses* the soul; and is the twin of the soul, the mind or the intellect.

The reader must decide.

SOMA.

It would be profitless to quote all the passages in which Soma is named. There is no room for doubt as to the meaning of this Deity.

Asht. i. Adhy. vi. Anuv. xiv. Sûkta vii.

1. Thou, Soma, art thoroughly appreciated by our intellect. Thou leadest us along a straight path. [It is the principle of intoxication or exhilaration, manifested in the Soma juice, that is adored.]

2. Thou, Soma, art the doer of good by holy acts; thou art powerful by thine energies, and knowest all things: thou art the showerer by thy bounties, and by thy greatness: thou, the guide of men, hast been well nourished by sacrificial offerings.

3. Thy acts are of the royal Varuṇa: thy glory, Soma, is great and profound; thou art the purifier, like the beloved Mitra: thou art the augmenter of all, like Aryaman.

4. Endowed with all the glories by thee in heaven, on earth, in the mountains, in the plants, in the waters.

5, 6, 7. Thou, Soma, art the protector, the sovereign of the pious, ... thou art holy sacrifice . . . . Thou, Soma, fond of praise, the lord of plants, art life to us: if thou wilt, we shall not die. Thou bestowest wealth . . . .

8, 9. Defend us, royal Soma, from every one seeking to harm us. . . . . Soma, be our protector. . . . .

12. . . . . Soma, the bestower of riches, the remover of disease, the cognizant of riches, the augmenter of nutriment, an excellent friend.

13, 15, 18. Soma, dwell happy in our hearts, ... Protect us, Soma, from calumny, preserve us from sin . . . . be our friend . . . . Being fully nourished, do thou provide, Soma, excellent viands in heaven for our immortality.

21. Soma . . . . invincible in battle, triumphant among hosts, the granter of heaven, the giver of rain, the preserver of strength, born amidst sacrifices, occupying a brilliant dwelling, renowned and victorious.

22. Thou, Soma, hast generated all these herbs, the water and the kine; thou hast spread out the spacious firmament; thou hast scattered darkness with light.

23. Divine and potent Soma, bestow upon us, with thy brilliant mind, a portion of wealth.

Professor Wilson thinks

> there is evidently great confusion in this hymn, between Soma the moon, and Soma the acid Asclepias;

though few passages indicate the former distinctly, except perhaps the twenty-second stanza, which alludes to the function of scattering darkness by light. Does the moon "spread out the spacious firmament"? I see no allusion to the moon. The exhilarating principle of the Soma is invested with the characteristics of all the Deities, unto whom, imbibed, it enters. It becomes a part of them; and it is they, and they are it—that is all.

But the attributes ascribed to this principle, as a Deity, enable us to understand better the force of the same expressions, when applied to other Deities.

Dr. Windischmann, "on the Soma-Worship of the Aryans," as quoted in Dr. Muir's "*Sanskrit Texts*" 469, *etc.*, says that the Soma of the Veda and the Haŏma of the *Zend-Avesta* are named etymologically identical. Both come from the root *su*, in Zend *hu*, signifying to "beget," but also, especially in the Vedic dialect, to "drop" or to "press out" juice. It is only in *later* Indian mythology, that it means the *moon*. It is the *Asclepias acida* or *sarcostema viminalis*, the expressed juice of which produces a peculiarly astringent, narcotic and intoxicating effect. It was unquestionably the greatest and holiest offering of the ancient Indian worship. The Gods drink it, they long for it, they are nourished by it, and thrown into a joyous intoxication. Indra performs his great deeds under its influence. It is divine, it purifies, it is a water of life, protects and nourishes, gives health and long life, prepares the way to heaven, destroys enemies, etc.

As Soma is a God in the Veda, so is Haŏma, the juice of (it seems) the same plant, in the Bactrian Gathas and the Yaçnas.

The hymns of the ninth book of the Rig-Veda, one hundred and fourteen in number, are all addressed to Soma. Soma and Rudra are also invoked together, to cure diseases; and there are indications that the juice of the plant was supposed to increase virility.

> The ambrosial Soma [it is said], destined for Indra, flowed forth, and thou, Indra, didst manifest thy virility.

The Haŏma grew on the mountains, and was supposed to possess a healing virtue. In *Yaçna x.* of the *Zend-Avesta*, the invoker says:

> I praise the lofty mountains, where thou, O Haŏma growest. . . . . I praise the tracts where thou growest, sweet-smelling over the wide field. As a good growth of Mazda growest thou upon the mountains. . . . . Wherever one brings in, wherever one praises the healing Haŏma. . . . . To his body Haŏma devotes himself for healing. O Haŏma, give me of thy remedies . . . . There growest thou upon these mountains, of many kinds, O Haŏma, sweet and golden. To thee flow the healing powers, through the wisdom of Vohu-Manô. . . . . Praise be to the Haŏma, for he makes the soul of the poor in greatness like that of the richest. Praise be to the Haŏma, who makes the mind of the poor so large in greatness, that it soars on high with wisdom. Many men makest thou very holy, and clothed with much wisdom.

The hymns to Soma are perhaps the most singular of all. The ninth book of the Rig-Veda is composed wholly of these hymns. They praise him as the source of life and vigour, of mental power and bodily strength, both to Gods and men, as the generator of the principal Gods; and yet it is perfectly evident, all the time, that nothing more is meant than the intoxicating quality of the Soma juice, the power inherent in it to exhilarate and to give energy, activity and strength. This power is generalized, and supposed to exist everywhere, acting on Gods as well as men, and thus it became itself divine, a life-giving and strength-giving force. Soma gives Indra the power that enables him to conquer Vṛitra, and like Indra he conquers demons and cities. He rules over Gods and men, and upholds heaven and earth, and his powers exceed, if that is possible, those attributed to Varuṇa, Indra and Vishṇu. He is Indu, the sap that flows for Indra, the stream which is purity itself, and the cleanser of all defilement: for *Indu* like *Indra*, is from the root *Idh* or *Indh*, to "shine, blaze or burn."

Thus we read in the hymns:

> Soma purifies; the generator of hymns, the generator of the sky, the generator of the earth, the generator of Agni, the generator of Sûrya, the generator of Indra, and the generator of Vishṇu.

He is the beatific vision which men walking on the earth desire to have. He can transport men to the world where there is always light, where the sun is, the world that does not perish: where there is happiness and delight and joy and pleasure: and there he can give long life, or, as Professor Wilson translates, make men immortal. (*Rig-V. ix.* 113. 7, *Müller*, *Chips*, *i.* 47.) Müller thinks that this and other hymns express a real belief in immortality. So does Professor Roth, whom he quotes.

In the Veda Müller says,

> passages occur, where immortality of the soul, personal immortality, and personal responsibility after death, are clearly proclaimed. Thus we read: 'He who gives alms goes to the highest place in heaven: he goes to the Gods.' (*Rig-V. i.* 125. 56.)

Another Poet, after rebuking those who are rich and do not communicate, says:

> The kind mortal is greater than the great in heaven.

One Poet prays that he may see again his father and mother after death (*Rig-V. i.* 24. *i.*); and the fathers (*pitṛis*) are invoked almost like Gods; oblations are offered to them, and they are believed to enjoy, in company with the Gods, a life of never-ending felicity.

Then he gives the hymn to Soma, already cited, wherein four verses end with the phrase, "there make me immortal." He thinks also that there are allusions to punishment after death. Professor Roth says,

> after quoting several passages from the Veda, in which a belief in immortality is expressed . . . . we here find, not without astonishment, beautiful conceptions on immortality expressed in unadorned language, with child-like conviction. If it were necessary, we might here find the most powerful weapons against the view which has lately been revived, and proclaimed as new, that Persia was the only birth-place of the idea of immortality, and that even the nations of Europe had derived it from that quarter. As if the religious spirit of every gifted race was not able to arrive at it by its own strength.

Nevertheless, it seems singular that an intoxicating liquor, or that potency which produces intoxication, should be invoked to give a real immortality. The hymn to Soma rather resembles the rhapsodies of an opium-eater or of one in the habit of using hashish, than a devout prayer for immortality after death. "The great in heaven" more probably mean the celestial luminaries: but still it is probable that these Poets had a vague idea of a life after this life, to be passed among the stars.

In some hymns of the Veda, all creatures are said to spring from the divine seed of Soma: and as he is styled the generator, it is probable that the juice of the Soma was an aphrodisiac, and supposed to contain a generative potency, a portion of a universal generative power, supposed to pervade the universe, and to have caused the existence of Gods and men.

> 'This divine Soma, with Indra for his ally, crushed, as soon as generated, Paṇi by force.' He baffled the devices and weapons of that hider of stolen cattle. He is purified for the Gods, in the filter which is the support of the world. - The Usijas first gathered him. In him all worlds are contained. (*Rig-V. ix.* 86.)
>
> The Soma flowed into the vessel, for Indra, for Vishṇu. May it be honied for Vayu! (*Rig-V. ix.* 63. 3.) It hastens to them, to Varuṇa and the Maruts. (*Rig-V. ix.* 65. 20.)
>
> 'Indu, do thou flow sweet to Indra, to Vishṇu. Preserve from sin the men who praise thee.' (*Rig-V. ix.* 56. 4.)
>
> 'Soma, Indu, purified, thou exhilaratest Varuṇa. So he exhilarates Mitra, Indra, Vishṇu, the Maruts, the Gods and the great Indra, that they may be merry.' (*Rig-V. ix.* 90. 5.)

How free a rein these old Poets gave to their imaginations, may also be seen in these verses, addressed to the winds:

'Lances gleam, Maruts, upon your shoulders, anklets on your feet, golden cuirasses on your breasts, and pure (waters shine) on your chariots; lightnings blazing with fire glow in your hands, and golden tiaras are towering on your heads.

'Adorned with armlets, the Maruts have shone like the skies with their stars; they have glittered like showers from the clouds, at the time when the prolific Rudra generated you, Maruts, with jewels on your breasts, from the shining udder of Pṛisni.' (*Rig-V. ii.* 34. 2.)

At a later day, the Aryan mind took another step forward, and conceived of a life-principle, cause of the origin of all that is. This was almost attained by their vague ideas as to the life-giving potency of Soma. It clearly appears in the celebrated hymn known as the Pŭrŭsha Sûkta, found in the *Rig-V. x.* 90, and in two other later Vedic Sanhitas.

The hymn is addressed to Pŭrŭsha. Mâhîdhăra the commentator says that Pŭrŭsha is the source of the universe, the supreme spirit. Wuttke considers him as Brahma. In another hymn, in a later work, the Bhâgăvăta Purâna, it is said that at the end of many thousand years, the living soul (*jîva*), which resides in time, action and natural quality, gave life to the lifeless egg sleeping on the water; and Pŭrŭsha, having divided the egg, issued from it. The Brahman was his mouth, and the worlds were fashioned from him.

These later vagaries of Hindū thought are as nonsensical as the Kabbalah. The old hymn is still much later than those of the Punjab, but the true original meaning of Pŭrŭsha can be descried in it.

He has a thousand heads, eyes and feet. Everywhere he pervades the earth. He alone is *the whole*, that has been and is to be. He is the lord of immortality, that which expands by nutriment: (i. e., to whom is owing length of life, obtained by means of abundant food). *All* creatures make a fourth of him; three-fourths of him are immortality in the sky. With these three parts he ascended. A fourth of him was again produced here. Then he diffused himself everywhere, among things animate and inanimate (i. e., living creatures and the vegetable and mineral creation. The life-principle or spirit is all the vitality and life that there is on earth; but this is no more than a fourth of the whole. With three times as much it animates and ensouls the celestial luminaries).

From him sprung Viraj. Over Viraj was Pŭrŭsha. Being originated, he extended himself, and produced the earth and corporeal forms.

The Gods offered up Pŭrŭsha as a sacrifice. Spring was the clarified butter of the sacrifice, summer the wood, and autumn the oblation. This victim, Pŭrŭsha, primevally born, they immolated on the sacrificial grass.

With him as their oblation, the Gods, Sadhyas and Ṛishis sacrificed. From that universal oblation were produced curds and clarified butter. He produced the animals, wild and tame, of which Vayu is the Deity. From that universal sacrifice were produced certain hymns and metres, horses and other ruminants, cows, goats and sheep. From his various parts came the four races or castes of Hindūs: the moon from his mind, the sun from his eye, Indra and Agni from his mouth, and Vayu from his breath: the atmosphere from his navel, the sky from his head, the earth from his feet, the four quarters from his ear. So they formed the worlds. When they bound him as victim, there were seven trenches, and seven times three pieces of fuel. With sacrifice the Gods worshipped the sacrifice. These were the first rites. These great beings attained to the heaven where the Gods, the ancient Sadhyas reside.

Manu says that when Brahma had divided his own being into two parts, male and female, he created (begot) *Viraj* in the female, and Viraj created Manu, and he the All. The *Viraj* was a species of Vedic metre, known to the Brahman Vasishṭha, son of Mitra and Varuṇa. (*Muir: Sansk. Texts, Part i.* 78.)

It is perfectly useless to undertake to interpret any of the Brahmanic myths in regard to the creation of things or men; as much so as it would be to endeavour to make comprehensible the astounding vagaries and confused babblings of the Kabbalah and the Kabbalistic commentators in respect to the combinations of letters, the manipulations of the divine light and its vestiges, and the features and members of Macroprosopos and Microprosopos.

If Pŭrŭsha was the life-principle, by the sacrifice of it is probably meant that it originally belonged to the Gods alone, nothing else as yet existing, and that they gave up, sacrificed, a portion of it, in order that, by means of the portion so surrendered, creation of men and things might be effected. The details of the creation are merely fanciful and arbitrary.

VARUṆA. MITRA. ARYAMAN.

Varuṇa is in many hymns of the Veda, as has been seen, invoked alone: Mitra is so invoked in a few: Aryaman in none. But the three are very often invoked together; and they evidently constituted a Triad. None of the commentators give us any definite and certain information as to what they really were; nor, in fact, has any attempt been made to ascertain that, by a comparison of the texts of the Veda in which they are mentioned, so far as I have the means of knowing.

It may at once be said, with entire confidence, that neither of them is ever addressed as a principle or substance, having subsistences, hypostases or manifestations. They are themselves not *hypostases* of Agni or Indra, but *bodies*, having *form*, and limited dimensions, and being in *place;* by which Agni manifests himself and Indra lights the world.

It needs no argument to prove that the adoration of substances and principles, of the personal spirits, intelligent and beneficent, of fire and light, could not have been the *first* phase of religious adoration, of any people: for, at the beginning, no people, however highly gifted by Nature, can philosophize.

And the fact that the worship of the sun and moon still lingered among the Aryans, ages after they had left the steppes of Turkistan, the country bordering on the immense sea that covered what are now the Caspian and Black Seas and perhaps the Sea of Aral, and certainly a vast extent of what are now low, flat lands, on all sides of the two great inland seas—the fact that, in the valleys of Cashmere and on the plains of the Punjab, they still, though rarely addressed their hymns to Sûrya and Savitṛi as Gods, prove that these and other luminaries had been adored by their ancestors, and had by degrees become subordinate to Agni and Indra.

How can we doubt, then, that, originally, the planets also, and the principal stars and most brilliant and noteworthy constellations were also adored? They were, in fact, still called *Devas*, in the Punjab; and that word simply means those of the sky or heavens. From the root *div*, to "shine" or "emit radiance," came the Greek διs, Ζευs, and Θευs, each meaning "Deity;" and the Sanskrit words, *div, dyaus*, the "sky;" *divas*, "day" or "daylight;" and the Latin *dies* and Gothic *dags* and English *day*, as well as the Latin *Deus*, and French *Dieu*. From it also came, in the Sanskrit, *divyas*, "of the sky," or "heavenly;" *divatanas*, "daily;" *Daivas*, "Deity;" Lithuanian, *diewas; Daivi*, "Goddess;" *Dâivas*, "divine;" *daivikas*, "divine;" Lithuanian, *diewiszkas; Daivatâ*, "divinity;" and the Latin *Divus*, an appellation of the Roman emperors; as well as our own words *Deity* and *divine*.

Without any previous theory or notion to that effect, I have become satisfied, from studying the hymns, that they were sung and the sacrifices held, at particular times and seasons; not only at the early dawn, but when certain planets occupied particular places, and when particular stars rose in the east before the dawn and led the way for the sun to ascend into the heavens. And it was not until after I had become convinced of that, that I read the following passage in the *Chips from a German Workshop* of Max Müller, *i.* 115. He quotes as follows, from Dr. Haug:

> 'The proper time of commencing and ending their sacrifices, principally the so-called Sattras or sacrificial sessions, could not be known without an accurate knowledge of the time of the sun's northern and southern progress. The knowledge of the calendar forms such an essential part of the ritual, that many important conditions of the latter cannot be carried out without the former. The sacrifices are allowed to commence only *at certain lucky constellations*, and in certain *months*. So, for instance, as a rule, no great sacrifice can commence during the sun's southern progress; for this is regarded up to the present day, as an unlucky period, by the Brahmans, in which even to die is believed to be a misfortune. The great sacrifices generally take place in spring, in the months of Ḳaitra and Vaisakha (April and May).'

And Müller says,

> This argument of Dr. Haug's seems correct, as far as the date of the establishment of the ceremonial is concerned [i. e., of Brahmanas, which Dr. Haug places at between 1400 and 1200 before Christ]; and it is curious that several scholars, who have lately written on the origin of the Vedic Calendar, and the possibility of its foreign origin, should not have perceived the intimate relation between that calendar, and the whole ceremonial system of the Bṛahmâns.
>
> Since the perceptible influences of the two great luminaries in the heavens, seemed to depend, in a great measure, upon their situations, which were distinguished by the neighbourhood of particular clusters of stars, it was a natural supposition that these influences, as well as those of the planets, should be produced by the action of the heavens themselves; that is, probably, by the energies of the Deities imagined to be there residing. In fact, we find that certain divisions of the heavens lying near the apparent paths of the sun, moon and planets, were supposed to be the causes of heat or cold, dryness or moisture, on the earth; and that the conjunctions of planets in those divisions were conceived to be indications of the physical effects to be produced by such powers in the heavens. The Chaldæans, we learn from Diodorus Siculus, ascribed the greatest efficacy to the five planets, or as they called them, interpreters, which, by their risings, settings and conjunctions announce to men the will of the Gods. (*Narrien, Astron.* 4.)

Bailey computed that, in the latitude of the place where Job (Ayub) is supposed to have lived, the rising of the Pleiades with the sun coincided with the arrival of the sun at the vernal equinox, about the year 3900 B.C.;

and that is the approximate date assigned by Bunsen to the settlement of the Aryans in the Punjab.

In the time of Hesiod, corn was reaped at the heliacal rising of the Pleiades, and the ground was ploughed at their heliacal setting. This was about 900 years before Christ. The heliacal rising of the Pleiades must then have taken place about forty-three days after the vernal equinox. The season of the vintage was when Orion and Sirius were in the mid-heaven, at sunrise, and Arcturus rose with the sun, i. e., about eighteen days before the autumnal equinox. When the Pleiades rose as the sun set, i. e., acronycally, sailing was dangerous, on account of violent winds and rain. This was, in Hesiod's time, about fourteen days after the autumnal equinox.

Virgil directs that the soil should be prepared for corn, when the Pleiades set in the morning, and the bright star in the Northern Crown rose with the sun. Tares and pulse were sown when Sirius and when Arcturus set with the sun. Then the heliacal risings of Orion and the Pleiades indicated approaching tempests and rains. Some of these indications, as well as those mentioned by Columella, belong to an earlier age, and had ceased to correspond with the actual state of the heavens, in consequence of the changes produced in the times of their occurrence by the slow displacement of the equinoctial points.

In the earlier Aryan ages, few circumstances required a knowledge of the celestial phenomena, and the observations were such as one not an astronomer could make. We may safely conclude that they consisted in noticing, at night and morning, the risings and settings of such stars as I have mentioned, and a few others.

The vernal equinox was naturally, to all the ancients, as it is to us, the most interesting and important epoch of the year. For then the winter closed, and the spring commenced; the sun began again to be sovereign, and to exert his power of generation. Nature then awoke from her lethargy, and prepared to clothe herself in living green. Animals perpetuated their kind, the life of the world seemed renewed. Accordingly, the great festivals of the ancient nations; and because the sun entered the sign of the Bull at this period, 2,500 years before our era, that animal became thesymbolof the generative potency of Nature, of the sun and of the Deity, worshipped as Apis in Egypt, upholding the brazen laver in the temple builded by Solomon, and standing, winged and human-headed, as sentinels at the broad entrances to the temples of the Assyrians. So, more than two thousand years afterwards, when, by the precession of the equinoxes, the sun had come to enter Aries at that season, the Ram or Lamb, which had for some centuries rivalled the Bull, as the symbol of the divine power, succeeded to his honours. Two thousand years or more before the sun entered the sign of

Taurus, at the vernal equinox, he entered that of the Twins, and the two stars of that constellation, the Horsemen, were deified.

But besides the stars, there were other celestial bodies, of greater magnitude, and which by their movements as well as by their appearance, were soon and easily distinguished from them. Three of the planets, the ancient herdsmen must soon have noticed. Two, especially, would soon become as noticeable as the moon—the great planets, Jupiter and Venus.

I think it will appear that invocations were addressed to these, only when one or the other of them was the Morning Star; and hence the hymns might seem to be addressed to some luminary that at all seasons of the year was in the same place at the same hour.

It can hardly be believed that these brilliant stars were not adored as Gods in the infancy of the Aryan race, even if they had ceased to be so, before the immigration of the Indian Aryans into the Punjab. For they were deified by all the ancient nations; and while among the Greeks and Romans, the sun was only Apollo, son of Zeus or Jove, the largest of the planets was named for the Father of the Gods himself. Even among the later Hindūs he bore the name of Bṛihaspati.

Mitra and Varuṇa are invoked to be present with Ritu, at the sacrifice.

They are Lords of the Twilight, Divinities abiding (bodies having a local habitation and a name, in the sky) in heaven.

They and Aryaman *kindle* Agni: i. e., they are his manifestations, burning with a flame, or pouring forth light.

Mitra and Varuṇa, *with true speech*, are the encouragers of pious acts, and are Lords of True Light. "True speech" is meaningless. Truth is, Horne Tooke says, that which one *troweth*. It is that which is steady, sure, real, fixed, and may be relied on. Speech, applied to a luminary, or to any phenomenon of light, fire, flame or heat, must mean, not Words, but the utterance of Something, as Logos and the Word do. It is out-flowing, emanation, expression. Mitra and Varuṇa, shining with steady light, ever returning to shine in due season, and never deceiving or deluding their expectant worshippers, encourage acts of adoration of themselves, warranting them and being entitled to them; and are possessed of and do control a light that belongs to themselves, and is true and real, and not reflected. They are not like the images of the stars in the water.

At the sacrifice of Manu, they sat down together on the sacred grass.

Mitra of pure vigour, and Varuṇa, devourer of foes, *are joint accomplishers of the act of bestowing water*. Can they, then, be either the sun and moon, or day and night, or the sky or firmament in any aspect?

> Today at sunrise we solicit you with hymns, for (wealth) which, Varuṇa, Mitra, Aryaman, bearers of water, you convey. . . . . Unconquerable, resplendent Mitra and Varuṇa, ... gentle Mitra and Varuṇa, destroyers of foes, come from heaven with your glories . . . . Come, Mitra and Varuṇa, leaders of rites . . . . augmenters of the sacred rite . . . . Accepters of rites, generated for rites, augmenters of rites, fierce enemies of the neglecter of rites. . . . .

In *Ashṭ. vi. Adhy. i. Anuv. iii. Sûkta vii.*, we find,

> Agni . . . . we adore that of thine, by which Varuṇa, Mitra, Aryaman, the Nâsatyas and Bhaga shine.

In *Ashṭ. v. Adhy. vi. Anuv. v. Sûkta xvii.*:

> 1. Varuṇa prepared a path for the sun: he set free the waters of the rivers generated in the expanse: hastening, as a horse let loose rushes to mares, he divided the great nights from the days.

Professor Wilson says, "Varuṇa is here said to imply the setting sun, by whose departure day ends and night begins." Thus it is that the Hindū commentators make the Aryan Deities to be sometimes one thing and sometimes another, and make a confused and senseless medley of the whole.

> 2. The wind is thy breath [*atmâhtevâtah*]: he sends abroad the waters; he, the cherisher of the world, is the feeder on food, like an animal upon fodder. All thy glories, Varuṇa, manifested between the vast and spacious sky and earth, give delight.
>
> 3. The thronging rays [*spaṣâh smadishṭâh*] of Varuṇa behold the beautiful sky and earth, as well as those who, celebrators of rites, constant in sacrifice, wise and intelligent, address praise.
>
> 5. In him are deposited the three heavens; the three earths, with their six seasons, are sown in him: the most adorable royal Varuṇa has made this golden sun undulating in the sky, he has made it to diffuse light.

The original of the last phrase is *Subhe Kam, diptyartham.* Professor Wilson refers, in the note giving this, and telling us how the scholiast explains *Kam*, to *Sûkta xiii. St. 2. Anuv. vi. Adhy. iv. of Ashṭ. iv.*, which is,

> He (Varuṇa) has extended the firmament over the tops of the trees, ... he has placed fire in the waters, the sun in heaven. [*St. i.* had said] The imperial and renowned Varuṇa has spread the firmament as a bed for the sun, as the immolator the skin of the victim. [And here he refers to *Sûkta i. Anuv. vi. Adhy. ii. Ashṭ. i.*], The regal Varuṇa verily made wide the path of the sun; [and, in the stanza preceding], The regal Varuṇa, of pure vigour, in the baseless, sustains on high a mass of light, the rays (whereof) are pointed downwards, while their base is above; [of which he says], The attributes here assigned to Varuṇa, his abiding in the

Antarîksha, and his holding a bundle of rays, would rather identify him with the sun, or, at least, refer to him in his character of an Âditya.

6. As the sun, Varuṇa placed the ocean, white as a drop, vigourous as an antelope, object of profound praise, distributor of water, the powerful transporter beyond sin, the ruler of this existing.

In these two stanzas, as translated, we have merely the conjectures of the Hindū interpreters. By them, it seems from the fourth stanza, "the wise and intelligent Varuṇa," giving instruction to his worthy disciple, has declared the mysteries of the place (of Brahma, the scholiast adds, which is but an adaptation of the text, by the Brahmans, to their own later creed).

Sûkta v. Anuv. iii. Adhy. vii. Asht. ii. had said, of Mitra and Varuṇa (and perhaps of Aryaman), "They uphold three worlds" (or spheres), [*tisrobhûmir dharayan*], of which Professor Wilson says,

bhûmi is here said to mean *loka*, "world" or "sphere, earth, firmament, and heaven," which the *Adityas* support, by supplying them with rain. That is, the Hindū commentators *substitute loka* for *bhûmi*, to make the phrase square with their notions about a number of worlds.

I do not believe, nor find any evidence, that the Aryans had any idea of *three* worlds, or of *any* other world than the visible one, which they saw by means of the light. The whole sentence is, as translated:

They uphold the three worlds, the three heavens, and in their sacrifices (are) three ceremonies: by truth, Adityas, has your great might (been produced), such as is most excellent; Aryaman, Mitra and Varuṇa. [I believe that it means]: They maintain on high the three orbs (their own, the three celestial bodies, and though their essence and principle is one, and they only different manifestations of it, they are addressed and sacrificed to by three separate ceremonies, as being three separate orbs and Deities). Your brilliant outshining and potent influences are the emanations of the one great universal light, which is truth, because it *makes* things real and true, realities and not illusions, by making them visible to men.

The root *bhu* means to "be born," to "exist," whence *bhus*, "being, existence;" *bhutas*, "fœtus;" *bhutan*, "creature;" *bhutis*, "creation;" *bhus*, *bhumis*, the "sun," *bhûman*, *bhâumas*, "productive, terrestrial." *Bhûmi* means the "world," only because the world is that which was *created*. It means a *being*, an existence, an entity, a body that exists, has form and is *in place*.

So, in the principal texts, "the mysteries of the place" mean the mysteries of the manifestation, as bodies in space, in place, having form and locality, of that universal principle of which they are the emanations. Varuṇa is spoken of as that of which he is the manifestation limited and in form. He is Agni and Indra, as the Monogenēs, the Demiūrgos, the Logos, the Word, the Son, is called God, and invested with the characteristics of the Very God, and spoken of as possessing the plenitude of his powers. He contains in himself, as such, the three orbs, they are "deposited" in him; the three bodies, with their six seasons (each being alternately the stars of morning and of evening): he has made the sun and enabled it to diffuse light, for the Morning Star precedes it, and so could be imagined to *cause* it to rise: and, manifested as the sun, he placed the ocean in its bed (if the original is rightly translated, which Professor Wilson shows to be wholly uncertain).

> By thee, Agni [it is said in *Sûkta ii. Anuv. xxi. Adhy. ii. Asht. ii.*], Varuṇa, observant of his duties, and Mitra and Aryaman, bountiful Divinities, are animated, so that thou didst begin to exist, comprehending them all in thyself, in all their functions, and encompassing them all, as the felly encompasses the spokes . . . . He who is one with light, Agni.

And in *Sûkta xiii.* of the same,

> we behold the lover of the maidens, ever in movement, never resting for an instant, wearing inseparable and diffusive (radiance), the beloved abode of Mitra and Varuṇa.

The scholiast or Professor Wilson deems this the sun: but the restlessness and fluctuation described, never resting for an instant, better suits flame. The *inseparable* and diffusive, means that which coheres together and remains one, while diffused and spreading. Nor is the sun the *abode* of Mitra and Varuṇa; but the flashing, flaming glories of morning and evening, the lambent, fluctuating, restless splendours, like flame, of the sky and clouds, before sunrise and after sunset, are the abode of Jupiter and Venus, as the Morning and Evening Stars.

> Without steeds, without stay, borne swift-moving and loud-sounding,

the next stanza says; and this describes the formless, bodiless flame, swiftly flashing and spreading, scorning all bounds and limits, and never stationary, and loudly roaring as it moves.

> It travels, ascending higher and higher, connecting *the unconceivable mystery* [a mere guess at the meaning of *achittam brahma yuvânah*, which is, Wilson says, obscure. *Yuvan* is "young," and *yuva, yauvanan*, "youth," from *yu*, to "join, increase." *Brahma* is "praise, adoration;" and *achittam* is explained to be not an object of the mind or thought, the meaning of the phrase probably being the manifested or visible praise or adoration (manifested by the sacrificial flame, which utters what is in the heart), young, new or fresh], 'with the radiance in Mitra and Varuṇa, eulogising glorify.' The sacrificial flame ascends, as praise, glorifying Mitra and Varuṇa, and becomes a part of their own radiance. For the offering, the flame

fed by it and formed of it, and the praise and adoration expressed by it, were deemed to *feed* the luminary adored, and to supply him with new light, energy and power.]

Sympathizing in satisfaction with Varuṇa, drink, Indra, the Soma juice [it is said in *Sûkta ii. Anuv. iv. Adhy. vii. of Asht. iii.*: and in *Sûkta ix. Anuv. iii. Adhy. ii. of Asht. iv.*], who, Mitra and Varuṇa, desiring to sacrifice to you (is able to do so)? Do you, whether in the region of heaven, or of the vast earth, or of the firmament, protect us, ... [As the light of the Morning Star is Indra manifested, Varuṇa, it is supposed, will share the pleasure which the Soma gives to Indra, and so shine with a more vivid light; as the eye shines when the Soul is glad.]

In "the sacred prayer," the Divinities Indra, Varuṇa, Mitra and Aryaman have made their abode. "The sacred prayer" must mean the fire of the sacrifice, ascending heavenward.

Varuṇa, Mitra and Aryaman protect men, and enable them to subdue their enemies. Great is their glory. Varuṇa, Mitra and Aryaman lead them by straight paths. Aryaman, doing so, rejoices with the others.

The acts of Soma are those of the royal Varuṇa. He is the purifier, like the beloved Mitra; the augmenter of all, like Aryaman.

A very significant passage is the following:

The wonderful host of rays has risen; *the Eye of Mitra, Varuṇa and Agni; the Sun, the Soul (Life) of all that moves or is stationary has filled the sky, the earth and the expanse between.*

This idea, that the Sun is the Soul or Life, of the planets and fixed stars, i. e., that they receive from him the light by which they shine, may explain, if Varuṇa, Mitra and Aryaman were planets, the meaning of the expression that he is their eye. If they were Venus, Jupiter and Mars, they always disappeared when the day had fairly come, and as they could not be supposed not still to shine, it was a natural idea that their light mingled with the light of the sun, it being really his own light distributed to him, so that during the day, he was the eye through which they looked upon the earth.

So we find it said that the sun, *in the sight of* Mitra and Varuṇa, displays his form midway the universe.

Mitra and Varuṇa are addressed as, "you who traverse the sky," an expression applicable only to moving *bodies*. "Let your spacious and bright-rayed chariot," it is said, "Mitra and Varuṇa, blaze like the sun." "Those two Deities," it is said, "have existed from of old." The sky is the brilliant mansion of Mitra, Aryaman and Varuṇa.

They are sons of Aditi (the expanse). They are Lords of Munificence. They are all the animators of mankind, i. e., they supply light which is the life of men.

Mitra and Varuṇa, it is said, bestow abundantly that unenduring water which you obtain from the sun: through *your own* energy, through the energy of the vigourous. What is meant by the "unenduring water," it is difficult to say. If it is vapour or rain, how do they obtain it from the sun? It is plainly enough indicated that their energy and that of the sun are one and the same. Is it meant that they, by means of the sun, or of his energy acting through them and exerted by them, draw upward the water which disappears from the earth in the shape of vapour?

Mitra and Varuṇa wear vestments of light. Therefore, it would seem, they are bodies, invested or clothed with light.

> Mitra and Varuṇa, it is your doing that the footless dawn (having no form or shape or limits) is the precursor of footed beings (of luminaries having form), and that your progeny (the sun) sustains the burthen of the world, diffuses truth and disperses falsehood.

Light is truth, or the reality, and darkness is falsehood, or the unreal, because without light all things would be as if they were not. And if Mitra and Varuṇa are the Morning Star (sometimes Venus and sometimes Jupiter), we can understand how they *cause* the dawn to precede the coming of the sun; for even philosophers hold that we have no other idea of cause and effect than that one always precedes the other. What always precedes, is readily imagined to cause. And the word progeny is probably a mistranslation, though it may be literal, the meaning being that the Morning Star *leads up* the sun: or that the sun *succeeds* the Morning Star, and shines in part with his brightness.

The inseparable and diffusive radiance is the abode of Mitra and Varuṇa —the radiance that is in them. This is only consistent with the idea that they are bodies. I think the meaning to be that they have a place or places in the expanse, an abode; and in that have a radiance inseparable from each, belonging to each, and which *is* each, and which it diffuses abroad.

Agni, flaming, is Mitra, and as Mitra, is the invoker. Varuṇa is Jâtavedas. Mitra is the ministering priest; Mitra, associate of rivers and mountains, i. e., perhaps, reflected in the rivers, and sometimes resting on the crests of the mountains, like a fire burning there. Mitra and Varuṇa may have been associated with sacrifices at night or earliest dawn; for the light of either may sometimes be seen in a long line of silver, on still water, on the grass, and on the ways through the woods.

The child of two mothers (the sun) sleeps in the west; but the single infant (one of two) goes on: these are the functions of Mitra and Varuṇa. An infant sun must needs be a heavenly body; and I think it is impossible to doubt that the meaning here is, that when the sun sinks to sleep in the west, the Evening Star, whether Venus or Jupiter, which has kept him company during the day, keeps on his way. The sun, it is said, proceeds thenceforward: he abides. Literally taken this is contradictory and nonsense. But if it means that, being the "Soul" of Mitra or Varuṇa, and his light shining through and by them, he, by the Evening Star proceeds onward, or by both, while himself sleeping stationary, then the sense is clear.

Ushas, the dawn, is "the golden light, as it were, of Mitra and Varuṇa:" for when either Venus or Jupiter is the Morning Star, the light-bearer, it continues to shine in the sea of the dawn which flushes and glows over the sky.

The divine Savitṛi diffuses his light on high; i. e., the moon, far up in the sky, pours forth light from herself; "dispersing the dew. Then Varuṇa and Mitra and others [the other planets and stars] hasten to their offices" [to perform the duties and service which they owe], where they *elevate* the sun in the sky [where they go in advance of him and lead him up].

It is not meant that both do it together; but that one or the other does it, and sometimes both. Each takes the office alternately, being alternately the Morning and the Evening Star, Lucifer and Hesperus or Vesper.

> Thou, Agni, art born Varuṇa [hast existence as, art, Varuṇa, as a body formed by self-limitation, a manifestation or revealing of himself in form, as a planet]. Thou becomest Mitra, when kindled [manifested in flame and light—shining]. Thou art Aryaman, in relation to maidens. [What this means, I cannot pretend even to conjecture. If the translation is correct, it must have reference to the energy of generation.]

Indra is said to be Mitra and the royal Varuṇa. For, if they are planets, each is the out-shining of a part of the universal light.

By the *greatness* of Mitra and Varuṇa, the sun constrains the rain to fall. They augment all his rays. At the break of dawn, at sunrise, they ascend their golden-bodied, iron-pillared car, and thence behold the earth and its inhabitants. The meaning is the same as that of the expression that the sun is their eye.

They are the protectors of the universe, imperial rulers of the world. They shine at sacrifices, *the beholders of heaven*. Their *forms* traverse earth and heaven. They are therefore bodies, having forms; orbs, luminaries, revolving between earth and sky, and looking down on the earth like eyes, from on high. They approach with variegated clouds, i. e., when dawn fills the clouds with many colours.

> Your *dence* is manifest in heaven, when the light that is the sun, your wonderful weapon, moves. You invest him in the sky with cloud and rain. You illumine

the whole world with water, you sustain the sun, the adorable chariot, in the sky: [by contributing their light to him. What the dence is intended to mean, I do not know, unless it be their *action*, as givers of light, which they do through the sun, when he begins and advances on his daily march. The light is their weapon, i. e., their energy, that by which they produce effects and achieve results, their instrument. And, at times, they invest him with cloud and rain, when, after he has risen, the clouds shut down in the east, and a day of rain follows].

Mitra, Varuṇa and Aryaman are divine sons of Aditi (the expanse), omniscient, all associated at the sacrifice, i. e., all shining at once upon the earth. They are observers of truth, i. e., viewers of material things, realities; distributors of water, protectors of the holy rites among men, guides in the right way, i. e., preventing men from becoming lost, liberal givers and benefactors.

Mitra and Varuṇa are eminent Deities among the Gods, i. e., large and distinguishable luminaries. They are upholders of heaven and earth. The immortal Gods do not impair their eternal works. That is, they are permanent; and Agni and Indra do not withdraw their light from them. They are two divine Adityas. Agni "*sympathizes in satisfaction*" with them; which means, I suppose, either that with and by them he receives gratification from the sacrifice; or that he acts with them in conferring benefits.

The two royal Divinities, Mitra and Varuṇa. The radiance of the sun is grateful to them [for they were supposed to shine by it]. Varuṇa is called the multi-present, meaning, perhaps that he is continually changing his place, rising every night at a different hour. Mitra, Aryaman, Varuṇa are of equal exploits, i. e., are bodies of like nature and action. They are Adityas, luminous, purified by showers. Their guidance is invoked to enable the worshipper to escape the sins that are like pitfalls; or, accidents in the shape of pitfalls. They are asked to lead him by the path that is easy, free from thorns and pleasant.

Sûrya, again, is the divine eye of Mitra and Varuṇa; and they are worshipped when the sun has risen. They are the two leaders of the sky, presiders over the world. At dawn, they scatter the glooms. They come to the sacrifice with their bright splendour, and light up the lustre of their car, emitting vast and infinite radiance. They drive their horses over deserts, with water.

They are called the eldest of existing things, perhaps because they are the largest of the stars. They are two, though not the same, i. e., twins, as it were, but not united and moving together; they manifest vigour daily, for daily they shine: they support the arch of the sky, as with a pillar.

Together they emitted the semen, of which Vasishṭha the Brahman was born, and Mana arose.

The three wheels of the Aṣwins, which were invisible, have become manifest. [This would seem to indicate that the reference was to three distinct celestial orbs.] Do you two, who are cognizant of the past, come by the paths of truth, to the presence of living beings [rising after the others]?

Mitra is said to look on men with unclosing eyes. He and Varuṇa are "cognizant of the past," because they have from the beginning looked calmly upon the earth. To come "by the paths of truth" is to become manifest and visible, and thus actually to exist for men. The "paths" or "ways of truth" mean actuality or reality. To the Aryans, the *visible* was the only *real*. Is anything else real to *us?* What would an unmanifested God be to men?

Mitra is styled adorable, entitled to worship, sovereign, endowed with vigour, creator, divine, renowned, victorious, and bestower of food as the reward of sacrifice.

Varuṇa, of *pure vigour*, i. e., whose energy and force are his own and not borrowed, the radiant or regal, keeps fixed on high, in the *baseless*, i. e., in the open immaterial expanse between earth and sky, a mass of light, which sends downwards its rays, while their base is above. Certainly this is the description of a celestial *body*, and not of a phenomenon or principle. The word rendered by "mass" evidently meant a body, with shape and form, the base or source of the rays that flowed from it. These rays, concentrated in men, are the sources of existence, i. e., supply the vital energy and force.

Varuṇa, the radiant or royal, *makes broad the path of the sun*, to travel in his daily course, a path to travel in the pathless. (As the pioneer or settler cuts a way through the woods, or as men, traveling it in advance of others make plain and broad a road over the plain, so Jupiter or Venus, when the Morning Star, going westward, though unseen during the day, in advance of the sun, "makes broad" his path.)

Varuṇa prevents misfortune that produces sorrow; is wise and irresistible, the doer of good deeds, prolongs life, and is the protector of men.

The constellations that are set on high, visible by night and going elsewhere by day, are the "undisturbed holy acts," i. e., the permanent light-manifestations of Varuṇa; and it is he that causes the moon to move resplendent by night. Varuṇa, therefore, is not the moon, and the idea that he and Mitra are the old moon in the lap of the new, or the new and full moon, must be abandoned.

And it is, we confess, difficult to comprehend how the planet Jupiter could be imagined to be the source of light to the constellations, and regent of the moon. "By his command" may mean "following his guidance," and the phrase "undisturbed holy acts" may only mean that he is the chief and leader of the stars, of which he is by far the largest and brightest; so that, they obeying him, their acts or influences are his.

If *Ṛikshâh*, translated "*constellations*," designates the Seven *Ṛishis*, and these are *Ursa Major*, it is hard to see what connection there is or could be imagined to be, between them and the planet Jupiter, or any other orb, or anything else except fire and light. A connection would more readily be imagined to exist between the Pleiades and Jupiter, the Morning Star, since they are often together.

Probably the true explanation is, that Varuṇa being the chief and prince of the stars, and regarded as Agni and Indra manifested as such chief and prince, their characteristics and powers were ascribed to that planet, and he was, in a measure regarded as Agni himself, in the full exercise of his universal powers. At all events, if we suppose Varuṇa to be the Morning Star, the difficulties are no greater than if we suppose him to be some other orb, phenomenon or principle; and if he was not the Morning Star, we cannot even conjecture what he really was.

He knows the path of the birds flying through the air; and, abiding in the ocean, he knows the course of the ships. This, therefore, is a later hymn; for in the Punjab, nothing could have been known of the ocean or of vessels navigating it. Jupiter *abides* in the ocean, because he rises from it and is reflected in it. The hymn can hardly date from the residence near the Caspian.

He knows the twelve months, and their productions, and the intercalary month. And this again proves the modern origin of this hymn, and accounts for the enlarged ideas which it contains in regard to Varuṇa. When it was composed, the original character and significance of this Deity had probably been forgotten.

He has seated himself among his progeny, to exercise supreme dominion. The *prince* or *chief* was in those days peculiarly the *father* of his people. In the Semitic tongues, the same word meant *father*, *chief*, *master*, *leader*. And the stars, led and ruled by Jupiter, and under his "supreme dominion," were appropriately styled his "progeny."

Through him the sage beholds all the marvels that have been or will be wrought. For under his leadership the starry hosts make visible the wondrous beauty of the heavens. The idea of leadership, chieftainship, royalty, soon caused the ascription to Varuṇa, the planet Jupiter, of all the attributes and characteristics that are imagined to belong to royalty. To the Greeks, he became Zeus, the King of the Gods; to the Romans, Jupiter and Jovis, Head and Sovereign of the Hierarchy of Olympus. Melchizedek (*Malaki-Isadoc*) was King and Priest of *Isadoc* or *Sydyk*, the same planet; as Astarte or Ashtarat, the Queen of Heaven, was Venus, the Evening Star.

The *person* of Varuṇa is *clothed:* he wears golden *armour*, and from *it* the rays of light flash around. This clearly shows that he is a *body*, with form and shape, and an orb from around which the rays of his light flash forth. Ushas, the dawn, is his sister. Very appropriately she is called the sister of the Morning Star. The *irreproachable* precede his course. This was probably said at a season when a particular constellation, rising earlier than Jupiter, preceded him in the heavens in the early morning. The epithet "irreproachable" does not enable us to identify the constellation; but the Three Kings in the belt of Orion were more likely to attract attention in connection with the Morning Star, than any other group of stars, as being more noticeable, and often preceding him.

Varuṇa is the sage, the self-radiant; the chief guide, the upholder; the supreme monarch, endowed with truth. He is called the brother of Agni, the ruler of the water, the Aditya, the sustainer of men, the sovereign venerated by mankind. Agni is prayed to avert from the worshipper his anger. He spread the expanse as a *bed* for the sun, extending it over the tops of the trees (for if there were no light in the heavens, the darkness would rest upon the tree-tops): he gives strength to horses and milk to cows, and determination to the heart. And, finally, he has placed fire in the waters (perhaps when reflected there), and the sun in the sky (perhaps when he leads the sun upward into the sky in the morning). That Jupiter was much less in size than the sun, was probably no reason why the Poet, knowing the superiority of intellect over mere strength, and the influence of the wise counsellor over the strong ruler, should not have fancied the Morning Star, chief and general, director and controller of the hosts of heaven, to be the guide and advisor, and thus the controller and leader, of the sun, investing more and more with the characteristics of Agni, and imputing to him the exercise of the powers of Agni, as the exercise of the plenitude of the powers of God was by other minds imputed to the Logos or Word.

He is monarch of all the world, and waters earth, the expanse, and the sky. He is the destroyer of the Asuras, and, stationed in the expanse, measures the sky by the sun, as by a measure.

We cannot find that *Mitra* is, in its ordinary sense, a name of the sun: and when Professor Wilson tells us that Varuṇa is a name of the regent of the waters, we are none the wiser for the information.

Indra and Varuṇa are the sovereign rulers, the guardians of mankind, the givers of riches and victory, and happiness. They are royal and sovereign, and the guardians of heaven. Here, probably, Indra, the Light, is spoken of as the sun, which is his principal manifestation, not his instrument or organ, but himself manifested and in action.

It would require much that was seemingly inconsistent with the identification of Varuṇa and Mitra as the Morning and Evening Stars, to outweigh the expressions, "lords of the *twilight*, Divinities *abiding* in heaven," for it connects them with the morning and evening twilight, and as having local habitations: and the word "Divinities" has a meaning to us, which the word rendered by it could not have had to the Aryans. By the word rendered by it was probably meant divine beings or orbs, i. e., luminaries, so that it also identified Mitra and Varuṇa as planets.

The Deities, Mitra, Varuṇa and Aryaman *kindle* Agni, their messenger from of old. They *manifest* the Fire (Agni), in the light with which they shine: and he is their messenger, because, as Light, he comes from them to the earth, and returns to them in the flame of the sacrifice.

The sun displays his form in the expanse, in sight of Mitra and Varuṇa. On one hand (when he rises, and the Morning Star, Varuṇa, preceding him still shines, and shining sees him), his rays extend afar his infinite and brilliant energy: and on the other (when he sets, and the Evening Star, Mitra, following him shines, and shining sees him), he brings on (i. e., is, is followed by) the darkness of night.

They are the loyal bestowers of delight, and they traverse sky, and are therefore luminaries.

It is, I think, quite probable, that Varuṇa was originally the Morning Star, whether Jupiter or Venus; and that Mitra was originally the Evening Star. At first, probably, they supposed the Morning Star to be always the same star. Afterwards, they must by observation, have learned otherwise, and the name Varuṇa then became the designation of Jupiter, but of Jupiter as the Morning Star; and Mitra of Venus, as the Evening Star. This will explain why Varuṇa was more often invoked than Mitra, and more associated with the dawn and the rising sun: while Mars, having no peculiar office to fulfil, and being merely their companion, as the only other known planet, was, as Aryaman, never invoked alone. In the Greek name of Mars, "Αρης, *Arēs*, we perhaps have Aryaman reproduced.

Mr. Cox thinks Varuṇa was "the veiling heaven," and Mitra, "the light-illumined sky." If the veiling heaven and light-illumined sky traverse the heavens in the *car*, riding side by side, and have their *mansion* in the heavens or expanse, and are *lords of the twilight*, and if the veiling heaven is a body of light, pouring downward its rays, which have their base on high, then this may be so: and if it be so, then the Veda is such a mass of contradictory nonsense as not to be worth studying, and the Vedic Gods had no fixed individuality or identity; but each was every thing at once, and nothing certain.

Varuṇa, Mr. Cox says,

> as the solid heaven, which is spread over the earth [how could the solid heaven be invoked to come down with Mitra and Aryaman, and sit on the grass at the sacrifice?] is strictly a creation of mythical speech, and is embodied in a visible form. He sits on his throne, clothed with golden armour [he strengthens the summit of the sky, as with a pillar], and along with Mitra dwells in a palace which, like that of Helios is supported by a thousand columns, while his messengers stand around [him] to do his bidding. [When Savitṛi diffuses his light on high, this veiled heaven and Mitra run to perform their service, while they lead up the sun into the sky.] But his mythical characteristics are, in the Rig-Veda, perpetually suggesting the idea of an *unseen* and *almighty* being, who has made all things, and upholds them by his will. [We find no passage where the characteristics of Varuṇa suggest an *unseen* being. He is continually addressed as visible and radiant. He is a body, an orb, that in a chariot traverses the sky.]

In many of the Vedic hymns, Mr. Cox continues,

> *we are carried altogether out of the region of mythology, and we see only the man communing directly with his Maker.*

The authority of Mr. Cox for this, is the following passage from Dr. Muir's "*Principal Deities of the Veda*," and the quotations from the Vedas, which he copies from Müller.

> Dr. Muir says, Varuṇa, in the hymns, dwells in all the worlds as sovereign: indeed, the three worlds are embraced within him. [The passage referred to, we suppose, is this, as given by Prof. Wilson (*Asht. iv. Adhy. iv. Anuv. v. Sûkta xiii.*): 'Mitra and Varuṇa, you uphold the three realms of light, the three heavens, the three regions of earth. The immortal Gods impair not your eternal works. You two divine Adityas, upholders of celestial and terrestrial worlds.' What is meant by the three heavens and three regions of earth, we do not know; but we *are* certain that it is *not* 'the veiling heaven' which upholds them.] The wind which resounds through the firmament, is his breath. He has placed the sun in the heaven, and opened up for it a boundless path to traverse. He has hollowed out the channels of the rivers. [We do not find this, nor that the wind is his breath.] It is by his wise contrivance, that, though all the rivers pour out their waters into the sea, the sea is never filled. [If this were in the Veda, it would be an evident interpolation, of a date long subsequent to the exodus from the land of the Five Rivers.] By his ordinance the moon shines in the sky, and the stars which are visible by night, disappear on the approach of daylight. Neither the birds flying in the air, nor the rivers in their sleepless flow, can attain a knowledge of his power or his wrath. His spies (or angels) behold both worlds. He himself has a thousand eyes. He knows the flight of birds in the sky, the path of ships on the sea, the course of the farsweeping wind, and perceives all the hidden things that have been or shall be done.

I have already given my understanding of the passages here referred to, so far as I have found them in the Veda. Even as they literally read, Dr.

Muir strains, exaggerates and *paints* them. I think he is mistaken as to their meaning, and that none of them in the least convey the idea of a *God*, in *our* sense of the word.

I do not doubt that, by means of such phrases, Varuṇa came by degrees to be regarded as a moral and intellectual being. So did Agni and Indra. An orb or luminary would more readily become that, than fire, flame or light, which had no bodily shape, form or limits. The ancient men more readily ascribed individuality to beings that they saw, and whose influences and effect upon themselves were immediate. Nobody wonders that the sun, moon and planets became Gods everywhere. Kronos, Ouranos and Gaia never were *real* Deities, but only poetic ones. Agni never became really a God, and his name soon disappeared; and that of Indra was preserved, only because he became something other than the light.

We find the idea of the sovereignty and power of Varuṇa more enlarged and developed in the later hymns. Once addressed as leader, ruler and king of the starry hosts, all the attributes of power and sovereignty were soon assigned to him. Thus, *Rig-V. vii.* 86. 1, we read (*Müller*, *Chips*, *i.* 38):

> Varuṇa *stemmed* asunder the wide firmaments; he lifted on high the bright and glorious heaven; he stretched out apart the starry sky and the earth.

That the explanation I have attempted to give to the passages that seem to ascribe these powers to Varuṇa, is probably correct, and that they do not mean what literally, *in English*, they seem to mean, seems to me manifest from two other passages, quoted by Müller, which are these:

> 'Who has seen the first-born [that which was the origin or beginning]? Where was the life, the blood, the soul of the world [i. e., whence, from what, did these come]? Who went to ask this from any that knew it?' *Rig-V. i.* 164. 4.
>
> 'What was the forest, what was the tree [i. e., the material], out of which they shaped the heaven and earth? Sages, ask this indeed in your mind, on what he stood, when he held the worlds.'

The Deities of the Veda are all of subsequent origin to the sky and earth. Not one of them is conceived of as existing before the world.

But Varuṇa soon came to be regarded as really a God, a being, moral and intellectual. Originally he was not so, and the language that ascribed to him moral and intellectual powers, was merely figurative and fanciful. Afterwards it became, as it had already in a measure become in the Punjab, to be regarded as truly descriptive of his nature. And it is undoubtedly true, that such has been the process of formation and development of all mythology, everywhere.

For, if Varuṇa was the Morning Star, and originally worshipped by the Aryans, as, being such, he must have been, a thousand years had elapsed, if not more, from the time when he was adored on the steppes, to the time when the Poets composed hymns to him in the Punjab, and it would not have been at all surprising if, in that long succession of centuries, the knowledge of what he originally was and meant had been entirely lost. It *would* have been extraordinary if his personal attributes had not been continually added to, and magnified, until it had become almost impossible to discover in the God Varuṇa, the ancient Planet-God, the God of the Morning Star of the herdsmen of Sogdiana. Thus Apollo almost ceased to be himself the sun, and the Huntress Diana was but vaguely conceived of as the moon. So in Phœnicia the moon became the Goddess Astarat, and in Egypt Osiris almost lost his identity with the sun, as Mithras did in ancient Persia.

The very antiquity, therefore, of the worship of the planets and stars, would cause the Deities which at first they were, to become more and more unlike themselves, and the attributes and functions ascribed to them, to become more and more difficult to reconcile with their original characters.

Thus we find powers and functions ascribed to Osiris and Apollo, which seem to have no connection with their original character of Sun-Gods. Old epithets and phrases, misunderstood, became the parents of new and contradictory ones; until we have Diönusos-Bakchos, of forgotten origin.

The following hymn (*Rig-V. vii.* 89), copied from Müller (*Chips, i.* 39) shows to what stature Varuṇa had grown:

1. Let me not yet, O Varuṇa, enter into the house of clay: have mercy, Almighty, have mercy!

2. If I go along trembling, like a cloud driven by the wind: have mercy, Almighty, have mercy!

3. Through want of strength, thou strong and bright God, I have gone wrong: have mercy, Almighty, have mercy!

4. Thirst came upon the worshipper, though he stood in the midst of the waters: have mercy, Almighty, have mercy!

5. Whenever we men, O Varuṇa, commit an offence before the Heavenly Host, whenever we break the law through thoughtlessness: have mercy, Almighty, have mercy!

The following hymn (*Rig-V. vii.* 86) is also translated by Professor Müller, in the same volume, at page 40:

1. Wise and mighty are the works of him who stemmed asunder the wide firmaments (heaven and earth). He lifted on high the bright and glorious heaven: he stretched out apart the starry sky and the earth.

2. Do I say this to my own self? How can I get unto Varuṇa? Will he accept my offering without displeasure? When shall I, quieted in mind, see him propitiated?

3. I ask, O Varuṇa, wishing to know this my sin: I go to ask the sages. The sages all tell me the same; it is Varuṇa who is angry with thee.

4. Was it an old sin, O Varuṇa, that thou wishest to destroy thy friend, who always praises thee? Tell me, thou unconquerable lord, and I will quickly turn to thee with praise, freed from sin.

5. Absolve us from the sins of our fathers, and from those which we committed with our own bodies. Release Vasishṭha, O king, like a thief who has feasted on stolen oxen; release him like a calf from the rope.

6. It was not our own doing, O Varuṇa; it was necessity (or temptation), an intoxicating draught, passion, dice, thoughtlessness. The old is there to mislead the young. Even sleep brings unrighteousness.

7. Let me without sin give satisfaction to the angry God, like a slave to the bounteous lord. The Lord-God enlightened the foolish; he, the wisest, leads his worshipper to wealth.

8. O Lord Varuṇa, may this song go well to thy heart! May we prosper in keeping and acquiring! Protect us, O Gods, always, with your blessings!

The following is from the *Atharva-Veda* (*iv.* 16):

1. The great Lord of these worlds sees as if he were near. If a man thinks he is walking by stealth, the Gods know it all.

2. If a man stands or walks or hides, if he goes to lie down or to get up, what two people sitting together whisper, King Varuṇa knows it, he is there as the third.

3. This earth, too, belongs to Varuṇa, the king, and this wide sky with its ends far apart. The two seas (the sky and the ocean) are Varuṇa's loins; he is also contained in this small drop of water.

4. He who should flee far beyond the sky, even he would not be rid of Varuṇa, the king. His spies proceed from heaven towards this world: with thousand eyes they overlook this earth.

5. King Varuṇa sees all this, what it is between heaven and earth, and what is beyond. He has counted the twinklings of the eyes of men. As a player throws the dice, he settles all things.

6. May all thy fatal nooses, which stand spread out, seven by seven and threefold, catch the man who tells a lie, may they pass by him who tells the truth.

The following is *Rig-V. i.* 25:

1. However we break thy laws from day to day, men as we are, O God Varuṇa.

2. Do not deliver us unto death, nor to the blow of the furious; nor to the wrath of the spiteful.

3. To propitiate thee, O Varuṇa, we unbend thy mind with songs, as the charioteer a weary horse.

4. Away from me they flee, dispirited, intent only on gaining wealth; as birds to their nests.

5. When shall we bring hither the man, who is victory to the warriors? When shall we bring Varuṇa, the wide-seeing, to be propitiated?

6. [This they (Mitra and Varuṇa) take in common; gracious, they never fail the faithful giver.]

7. He who knows the place of the birds that fly through the sky, who on the waters knows the ships;

8. He, the upholder of order, who knows the twelve months, with the offspring of each, and knows the month that is engendered afterwards;—

9. He who knows the track of the wind, of the wide, the bright, the mighty; and knows those who reside on high;—

10. He, the upholder of order, Varuṇa, sits down among his people; he, the wise, sits there to govern. [His 'people' are his subject stars, surrounded by whom the Morning Star governs all.]

11. From thence perceiving all wondrous things, he sees what has been and what will be done.

12. May he, the wise Aditya, make our paths straight all our days! May he prolong our lives!

13. Varuṇa, wearing golden mail, has put on his shining cloak; the spies [out-lookers, stars] sat down around him.

14. The God whom the scoffers do not provoke, nor the tormentors of men, nor the plotters of mischief;

15. He who gives to men glory, and not half-glory; who gives it even to our own selves;—

16. Yearning for him, the far-seeing, my thoughts move onwards, as kine move to their pastures.

17. Let us speak together again, because my honey has been brought: that thou mayst eat what thou likest, like a friend.

18. Did I see the God, who may be seen by all? Did I see the chariot above the earth? He must have accepted my prayers.

19. O hear this my calling, Varuṇa! Be gracious now! Longing for help, I have called upon thee.

20. Thou, O wise God, art lord of all, of heaven and earth. Listen on thy way!

21. That I may live, take from me the upper rope, loose the middle, and remove the lowest.

How unmistakably the eighteenth verse sets before us the ancient worshipper, before day, his fire lighted and his offering ready, in the open air, repeating his invocation, and waiting for the rising of the Morning Star, to whom his hyperbolical language is addressed! If he imagined Jupiter to be a God, and invested him with truly divine attributes, was it the planet that he worshipped? or was it not rather those attributes and the ideal personality to which he imagined them to belong? Did he not then worship God, the Very Deity? For what can man know of the Deity, *except* his attributes? We know only the attributes of matter itself; and what we love and admire in another man is not his soul *itself*, but only its *attributes*, which we say, are part of its *nature*. To separate those attributes of Varuṇa from the planet, those of Agni from the fire, and those of Indra from the light, and imagine an unknown being possessing them, and call him Ahura Mazda, was but what some one else would soon have done, if Zarathustra had not done it, for it was but the natural progress of the intellect.

A very cursory glance at the ideas and phrases common, and familiar to the Aryan mind at a later day, will help us to understand how the attributes of power and intelligence could, without any sense of incongruity, be ascribed to the King of the Planets.

He is said to *see* all that passes on the earth; and in Homer (*Iliad iii.*) we read,

> *Thou, O Sun, who beholdest all things.*

And, *Oduss. xix.* 275,

> *For Zeus and the Sun were angry with him.*

In Æschylus (*Choephoræ*, 990),

> *The Father, he that beholdeth these things, the Sun.*

Julian says,

> The Sun, the Greatest God, *he has caused to appear out of himself, in all things like himself.*

And the Orphic hymn to the sun, *xi. Ed. Hermann*, reads as follows:

> Titan of golden lustre, moving above, Heavenly Light, self-produced, ... fiery, food-bringing, fruitful Paian: glowing, pure, Father of Time, immortal Zeus, serene, visible to all, *the circumambient eye of the world, eye of righteousness, Light of Life.*

Macrobius says,

> Physicians have called Bakchos the *mind* of Zeus, because they said the sun was the mind of the world.

Sophocles, in *Antigone*, 1149, says,

> O Leader of the Choir of Flame-breathing Stars, director of the voices that sound by night, youthful God! son of Jove!
>
> The creative power [Philo said], *is God;* for it is by this that he made and arranged the universe.
>
> The soul of the world, *in the person of the sun* [says the *Sama-Veda*], enlightens the heaven and the earth.

What was afterwards said of Brahma, expressed the Vedic idea of the manifestations of Agni.

> Brahma, through whom all things are illumined, who *with his light lets the sun and the stars shine*, but who *is not revealed* by their light' (*Sankhara, Atma-Bodha.* 61).

Landseer, in his "*Sabæan Researches*," says:

> The sun was, in the primitive superstition, King, Lord or Ruler of the diurnal heavens. In some countries, the planet Jupiter gradually became so, of the nocturnal heavens, being 'the most refulgent of its stars; and at a later period was venerated as Jove the Thunderer, the Supreme Deity of the symbolical ages, the poetical and popular ruler of the upper regions of the air.'

He inquires whether the Grecian Zeus

> was not generated between the supposed astral effluence of the planet Jupiter, and the attributes of the vernal sun.

Macrobius speaks of certain symbols held by a statue at Baal-bec, "denoting the consociate powers of Jupiter and the sun;" and there is no doubt that much of that which, in the Grecian mythology, is represented as belonging to the sun, really related to the planet Jupiter, the king of the starry armies of heaven. Sagittarius has always been the proper domicil or station of power, of that planet; and Landseer finds, on a Babylonian cylinder, Jupiter brandishing his arrows or the thunder, in his peculiar mansion of might and dignity.

Ptolemy and Manilius term Jupiter and Venus, "the two Benevolent Fortunes;" and each of them, Jupiter rising in the east as the Morning Star, and Venus smiling in the west as Hesperus, seems to look encouragingly and beneficently upon man.

On the title page of the "Sabæan Researches" is an engraving of a Babylonian cylinder, on which is a female figure having on her breast five globes, one, three times as large as the others, in the centre, one above it, and three in a line below, one of these held in each hand, and the one between them being the smallest of all. These in the hands are equal in size to each other. These no doubt represented the sun in the centre, the moon above him, and the three known planets, Jupiter, Venus and Mars, below.

The very fact that the planet Jupiter bore among the Romans the name of the King of the Gods, while among them and the Greeks, Apollo and Bakchos or Dionusos were the sun, shows what ideas of power and supremacy attached originally to the most brilliant of all the starry Host of Heaven. If the ancient Aryans worshipped the celestial luminaries at all, it is not credible that they did not adore and invoke the Morning and Evening Stars. And this is especially incredible, when we know that they regarded all the luminaries as manifestations localized and limited, of Agni and Indra.

And, if they adored Jupiter, Venus and Mars at all, they adored them under the names of Varuṇa, Mitra and Aryaman. If not so worshipped, they are neither noticed nor even named at all.

> "We have also a more sure word of prophecy; whereunto ye do well that ye take heed, as unto a light that shineth in a dark place, until the day dawn, and the day star arise in your hearts."

Nothing could more forcibly show, than this verse does, the veneration which the ancient nations had for the Morning Star, "Lucifer, son of the Morning" or Dawn—Hesperos, the most beautiful star of the heavens, who appears as the herald of Eos in the morning, and is again seen by her side in the evening. The Hellenic Heosphoros, the Latin Lucifer, the Light-bringer, who is Phosphoros, son of Astraios and Eos, the starlit skies of dawn.

If I am wholly in error in thinking that Varuṇa, Mitra and Aryaman were Jupiter, Venus and Mars, it is impossible to conceive what triad of similar beings it was that the Poets addressed under those names. In naming them, sometimes one and sometimes another of them is named, first, second or last; as if the worshipper carefully avoided even the appearance of ascribing superior dignity to either. And I cannot but believe that if the original Sanskrit texts that speak to or of these Deities are carefully analyzed, and the ancient meaning of the words diligently sought for, with a willingness, if not a desire to see disappear whatever seems in the translations to be inconsistent with the theory that these three planets were intended, my views would be confirmed. I regret that I am utterly incompetent to do it, and hope that what I have so imperfectly said may seem reasonable enough to some intelligent and thorough Sanskrit scholar, to induce him to undertake the task.

"King Varuṇa" or "Royal Varuṇa," is in the original, "*Raja Varuṇas.*" "Thou, divine Varuṇa, art King," is "*Tvaṁ viṣveshâṁ Varuṇâsi raja.*" It is *dyava-pṛithivi*, that are "held asunder by the support" of Varuṇa.

Dr. Muir, *Orig. Sansk. Texts*, *iv.* 95, translates thus:

> *Rig-V. vii.* 86. 1. Wise are his creations who by his power propped asunder the two vast worlds [*rodasi*]. He raised up the high and wide firmament, and spread out apart the stars and the earth.
>
> *vii.* 87. 1. Varuṇa has opened out paths for the sun [*radat patho Varuṇah Sûryâya*]. Like a troop of horses let loose, following the mares, he has made great channels for the days. The wind [*âtmâ*] which has agitated the atmosphere, like an impetuous beast grazing in a pasture. Within are these two great and vast worlds [*antar mahî bṛihatî rodasîme*]: all thy realms, O Varuṇa, are beloved (or, unlimited).
>
> *viii.* 42. 1. The omniscient [*visvaveda*, all-seeing] Asura has propped up the sky [*dyam*]: he has measured [*amimîta*] the expanse [*varimâṇam*] of the earth [*pṛithivyâḥ*]; he has pervaded all the worlds [*bhuvanâni*], the monarch; all these are the achievements of Varuṇa. Reverence, then, the mighty Varuṇa [*Varuṇaṁ bṛihantaṁ*]: bow down before the wise guardian of immortality [amritasya]. May he impart to us triple prosperity.

It is evident that much yet remains to be done, before any certainty of correctness can be attained in translating the Veda. Upon the hypothesis that Varuṇa was a planet, many of the words used in regard to him and his functions would take upon themselves meanings very different from that which they appear to have when they are to be so understood as to correspond with a different hypothesis. The great difficulty undoubtedly is, from the modern meanings of the Sanskrit words, to get back to those more ancient than them by at least two thousand years: and this, for the most part, without a guide. Müller says (*Chips*, *i.* 76),

> The Brâhmanas, though nearest in time to the hymns of the Rig-Veda, indulge in the most frivolous and ill-judged interpretations. When the ancient Ṛishi exclaims, with a troubled heart, 'who is the greatest of the Gods? who shall first be praised by our songs?' the author of the Brâhmana sees in the interrogative pronoun

> 'who,' some divine name, a place is allotted in the sacrificial invocations to a God 'who,' and hymns addressed to him are called 'whoish' hymns.

He remarks that, "to know what a passage *cannot* mean, is frequently the key to its real meaning:" and we may of course always be sure that when the translation makes nonsense, it is because the original is not understood.

That Mitra and Varuṇa are Adityas is proof that they are luminaries. That Varuṇa is styled "Raja" proves the same. They never slumber nor close their eyelids: they are decorated with golden ornaments: they are to be worshipped at the dawning of the day: they excel in radiance: Varuṇa, whose *form* is water, shows, whatever the word rendered *water* really means, that Varuṇa is an *orb*, having definite *form*. The "spacious and much frequented kingdom" of Mitra and Varuṇa, is the starry firmament, in which they rule. Sûrya, Mitra and Varuṇa have one common dwelling-place, and are therefore all orbs alike. Mitra, Varuṇa and Aryaman are the unconquered sons of Aditi. They animate with energies the unconscious [arousing them before the dawn, from sleep, "the twin-sister of death," and restoring to them their energies; or, by their influences arousing them; as the Morning Star, shining upon the eyes of the herdsman sleeping in the open air, would naturally do].

The eyes of the three are "unclosing;" and they "conduct the ignorant man." They do not wink or twinkle like the fixed stars, but shine always open-eyed and steadily; and by them a wayfarer in an unknown region may know the direction in which to go.

"The association of these is of mysterious lustre:" "by their secret strength they overcome:" which probably means, that each of them being a manifestation of Indra, ensouled with light, as it were, by him, they are cognates, as it were, of one blood, three persons of one substance, perhaps; at all events, three out-flowings of the same light from one source, itself hidden and mysterious; and by that unseen essence they have their power over the elements and the fortunes of men.

> Spreading around the beautiful light, Mitra and Varuṇa, of you two Divinities, Sûrya rises.

The phrase "spreading around," is clearly not a correct translation, if Mitra and Varuṇa are planets. If they were *principles*, or *substances*, by whose light Sûrya shone, such as Agni and Indra, then he could be said to "spread around" the light so received: but certainly he spreads around no other light than his own.

It must always be uncertain, not only what the ancient meanings of many Sanskrit words were; but also what the original roots and their primitive meanings were. We find, for example, *rodasi*, *bhuvana* and *jagata*, are all rendered "worlds," and we have, resident in Parjanya, "*viṣvani bhuvânani*," "all the worlds;" and "*tisro dyavas*," "the three heavens;" as the same "*viṣvā bhuvânani*" are "contained" in Soma. It is probably impossible to ascertain the exact meaning of any of the apparent synonyms. Time wears away the shades of difference between words, whether of *kindred* original meaning, or whether of original meanings very different, but applied to the same object, and as appellatives, coming by degrees to mean the same thing: while, again, a single word in time assumes many meanings, some of them the exact opposites of each other—a striking instance of which is, in the Hebrew, that *Kadosh* or *Kodesh*, means both "holy, holiness," and a female "prostitute;" and proves that at *some* time it was a religious duty, among the Hebrews or their ancestors, for women to prostitute themselves.

And as to the blendings of the shades of difference of words, until the pure distinctions between them are lost, by being disregarded in speech and by inaccurate writers, it is enough to look into any book of synonyms. In our language we have many real synonyms, because it is a composite one; but it is hardly to be believed that in any *original* language there were many pairs of triads of words having precisely the same meaning.

When what may be called the boundaries between the meanings of words are effaced, one word will be used in different senses by different persons, until its exact meaning becomes uncertain; and from this cause more than one religious schism has grown up, and been the prolific source of persecutions and bloody wars.

But I think that languages have in their infancy and youth, at least this advantage, which by and by they lose, as ours has, that they have no words which mean nothing at all. Such a word is "worlds," in the translation of the Veda, and such are "heaven" and "firmament" in the same.

The *roots* of Sanskrit words are, necessarily, to a great extent conjectural, both as to the letters that composed them, and as to their original meanings. Disused for a score of centuries, it must be impossible to determine with certainty exactly what either they or their meanings were, in very many cases. Originating long before the earliest Aryan emigration, they are undoubtedly softened down in the Hindū reproduction of them, and were originally more nasal or gutteral, as, to be the parents of Keltic, Sclavonic and Gothic or Germanic words, they must have been.

If, "what a phrase *cannot* mean, is often the key to its true meaning," we ought to be able to find the meaning of the phrase, "spreading around the beautiful light of your two Divinities:" and we might, if we had the root of the word rendered "spreading around," find it meaning to envelop or wrap up, and thence to cover, obscure or hide; and the meaning of the expression may be that the sun, when he rises, overwhelms and surrounds, envelops and merges in itself the lesser splendour of the Morning Star.

Mitra and Varuṇa are said to be "vaster" than earth or heaven; to maintain beauty in plants and people, and to keep heaven and earth asunder. This their "strength by its mightiness effects," and for it their "splendour" is praised. Their light, diffused everywhere, may here be taken for themselves; and it keeps earth and sky asunder, because, in profound darkness, they would seem to be one.

They rule the waters, are preservers of waters, and powerful lords of rivers; and we need not be surprised at these epithets when we remember that the Greeks fancied that the Hyades caused the spring rains, and named them accordingly. They, Mitra and Varuṇa, are asked to bedew with water "him who fabricated your chariot in his mind." This English phrase is mere nonsense. The original, undoubtedly, once had a meaning. What is meant by their "chariot" cognizable by the intellect, I do not pretend to understand.

Varuṇa, Mitra, Aryaman and others are designated as *Adityas*, or sons of Aditi; as the Morning Star was, by those of a different race, styled "Lucifer, son of the Morning."

In *Rig-V. ix.* [*Mand.*] 72. 8. 9, we find the number of the Adityas stated at seven:

> The seven points of the compass, with their respective suns [*nânâ-sûryâh*], the seven *Hotri* priests [*hotâra ritvijah*], and the seven Gods, the *Adityas* [*Devâ Âdityâ ye Sapta*].

In *Rig-V. x.* 72. 8. 9, it is said that eight sons were born from the body of Aditi; with seven she approached the Gods, but cast away Marttanda.

> With seven Aditer approached the former age.

The hymn, evidently modern, celebrates the birth of the Gods [*devanam*]. Brahmaṇaspati blew them forth. Bhû was born from Uttanapad, and the regions sprang from Bhû, the Earth: or, as Roth translates it,

> Bhû (the world) was born, and from her opened womb (*Uttanapad*), spring the spaces.

Daxa sprang from Aditi, and Aditi forth from Daxa. So Aditi was produced, daughter of Daxa, and then the Gods [*Deva*].

Six Adityas only are *named* in the Veda, of whom Vishṅu is not one. Afterwards, the number was increased to twelve; all of which, the Satapatha Brâhmaṇa says, were placed in the sky. In *Rig-V. ii.* 27. 1, six Adityas, who have been Rajas always, are named, Mitra, Aryaman, Bhaga, the Mighty Varuṇa, Daxa and Ansa.

Eichhoff derives *Aryas*, with the meaning of "valiant," from the root AR, and gives it also the meaning of "*excellent*," a remote and later meaning, referable to the time when the institution of castes was established.

Man is a Sanskrit suffix, I learn from Bopp (*Comp. Grammar, iii.* 1073), the original form of which appears to be *mân*, which has remained in the strong cases. The words formed with it have, like the kindred participles, either an active or a passive signification. Some are abstract substantives. But few masculines in *man* remain to us in Sanskrit, and these, too, are, for the most part, but rarely used. The following are examples: *sûshman*, "fire," as that which dries; *ûshman*, the hot time of the year, as "the burning;" *pâpman*, "sin," as that which is sinned; and others given by Bopp (1074). The masculine bases in *man* all have the accent on the last syllable, and express partly a passive, partly an active relation, or are abstracts; as *dhâman*, a "house," as that which is made or built, from *dha*, to "place" (*vi-dha*, to "make"); *vârtman*, "way," as that which is gone upon, from *vart, vṛit*, to "go;" *jânman*, "birth," from *jan*, to "bear;" *prêman*, from *prî*, to "love, etc." (1075); *ahman*, "spirit," from *ahya*, "I think," is another (1079).

Also, the suffix *man* also forms abstract substantive or adjective bases; as *prath-i-mân*, "breadth," from *pṛithû*, "broad," *kṛishṇ-i-mân*, "blackness," from *kṛishṇâ*, "black" (1080).

Arya-man, accordingly, is "valour, bravery, daring, audacity, prowess," from *arya*, "valiant, brave, etc." It has, therefore, precisely the same meaning as "Αρης, Mars, the God of War and Battle of the Greeks.

I find in Eichhoff, *mitras*, "amicable," from *maith*, to "unite;" whence also *mithas*, "aggregate, union;" and Latin *mitis* and *mutuus*.

Varyas, also, means "excellent," from *var*, to "love, prefer;" whence, Latin, *verus*, "true;" French, *vrai*, "true;" English, *very* and *verily;* Lithuanian, *wiernas;* Russian, *wiernyi;* Gaelic, *feavy;* Keltic, *gwir;* German, *werth;* English, *worth;* Lithuanian, *wertas*.

Daksha or *Daxa* is from *daks*, to "attain," to "succeed;" whence *dakṣas*, *dakṣiṇas*, "skilful, straight, right;" Greek, δεξιος; Latin, *dexter*, "right, the right hand."

Ansa is from *anç*, to "traverse, penetrate;" whence *anças*, "friction;" *ançus*, a "ray."

PHRASES APPLIED TO USHAS, ETC.

Sûrya is unquestionably the sun; and *Ushas* as unquestionably the dawn. The *Maruts* are the winds. *Soma* is the intoxicating and exhilarating, strength- and courage-giving power and principle that manifests itself in the juice of the plant called by that name. A reference to the hymns to these Divinities may serve to shed some light on the apparent contradictions of those to Varuṇa, Mitra, Aryaman, Ârusha, Savitṛi, Vayu and Vishṇu.

Rig-V. i. 39 (as translated by Müller, *i. Chips,* 34) is addressed to the Maruts and Rudras. They from afar cast forward their measure like a blast of fire. [The meaning must be that they hurl onward their whole vast bulk and mass, as a body of flame hurls itself forward in the forests.] They have no real foe, in heaven or earth; i. e., there is nothing in the expanse or on the earth that can withstand them. They make the rocks tremble, and rend the kings of the forest. They are Gods, who have harnessed the spotted deer to their chariots, a red deer drawing as leader. The earth listens to hear their coming. Their help is invoked, for the human race, to free them from every adversary. They are worshipful and wise, bounteous givers, possessing all strength, all power.

Ushas [in *Rig-V. vii. 77. Müller, i. Chips,* 36], shines on men like a young wife, rousing them to go to their work. She makes the light, by striking down darkness. She rises up, spreading far and wide, moving everywhere. She wears her brilliant garment. She is the mother of the cows, the leader of the days, gold coloured, lovely to behold. She, fortunate, brings the eye of the Gods, who leads the white and lively horse; the dawn was seen, revealed by her rays, with brilliant treasures, following every one. She is a blessing, when near; she drives away the unfriendly, makes the pasture wide, gives men safety. She disperses the enemies and brings riches, and raises up wealth to the worshipper. She lengthens life, gives food, gives wealth of cows, horses and chariots. She is the daughter of the sky, and high-born: i. e., she becomes visible and so has her origin, above the earth and in the sky.

To the Poets of all countries and ages, the phenomena of morning and evening have been fruitful sources of imagery, as of old they were of myths born of the figurative language of the Poets. To the Vedic Poets, the sun was the lover of the dawn, but his glance was fatal to her. She faded and died in the greater glories of his risen light. He looks upon the tender dew, and under his fervent gaze the trembling, sparkling drops vanish away. The evening turns to look longingly after the sinking sun, and as her life commences, his is seen to end. They can remain together only on the condition that one shall not see the face or form of the other. From the fading away of the violet hues of the morning, upon the rising of the sun, came the phrases, growing afterwards into myths, that Indra or Phoibos or Orpheus had fixed their eyes on Dahaña or Daphnē or Euridikē, and that their loved one had passed away from them like the fleeting colours of a dream.

Ushas is the image of undying youth, for day after day she appears, in unfading beauty, although they who daily look upon her, do daily grow older, and at last die.

Therefore she is said to conduct all transient creatures to decay. She is divine and ancient, born again and again, with unchanging hues, and she wastes away the life of a mortal, like the wife of a hunter, cutting up the birds.

We see in this how, with these Poets, sequences became causes and effects. As the dawns come and go, and the days pass, our life is taken, piece by piece, as it were, away; and the dawn is conceived of as causing these daily losses for which there is no reparation. Precisely thus the light *creates* what it enables us to *see* and *know*, and upholds the sky which in the darkness would, as it were, be close above us.

She is "endowed with truth," also, like Agni and Indra. She is visible and real to men, not an invisible principle, but an actual phenomenon, her return certain and unfailing. The word *truth* is but a false translation. She is the sister of Bhava and of Varuṇa, and hymned first of the Gods: i. e., first invoked in the morning.

Unimpeding divine rites, though wearing away the ages of mankind, she shines, the likeness of the mornings that have passed, etc. Night, her sister prepares a birth-place for her elder sister, and having made it known to her, departs. Of all the sisters that have gone before, a successor daily follows the one that has preceded.

She reveals mysteries, and opens the ends of heaven, where the Paṇis had hidden away the cows (the bright clouds), of which she is the mother. She tells the Angiras where they are to be found, and as she lightens the sky, she is said to drive her own herds to their pastures.

The Sanskrit *budh* (Mr. Cox says) means both to "make" and to "know," and *vayunâ* has the double meaning of *light* and *knowledge*, just as the notions of knowledge and creative power are both expressed by the root *jan*, and the English *can* and *ken*. Hence Ushas is said to enable men to cross the frontier of darkness, and, as the seer, to give light far and wide. Thus, as the day, she is the mother of the divine night, who reveals all her splendour after she has driven away her sister, the twilight.

Once the word *Ahanâ* occurs in the Veda:

Ahanâ comes near to every house, she who makes every day to be known.

The *flexibility* of the old mythology, Mr. Cox thinks, justifies us in attributing to Ahanâ all that is told us of Ushas and Saramâ. So he applies to Ahanâ certain phrases used in regard to Ushas, as pursued by the sun, who slays, though he loves her, or as dying in his arms, and gets the origin of the myths of Daphnē and Prokris. We do not see why it was necessary to make Ushas and Ahanâ identical, to get that "offshoot from the parent stem:" and we do not see how the double meanings of *budh*, *vayunâ*, *jan* and *can* or *ken* show that

> in Ushas we have the germ of the idea that found its most graceful expression in the Hellenic Athēnē, and its most majestic development in the Latin Minerva.

All the Vedic Gods are said to see and know and are revealers of truth: and the Veda does not represent Ushas "as sprung from the forehead of Dyaus the Sky," but only as originating in the expanse.

In the same hymn which mentions *Ahanâ* (*the burning light*), *Rig-V. i.* 123. 4, it is said that *Dyotana* (the dawn), the active maiden, comes back continually; she enjoys always the first of all goods. Dyotana is probably an epithet only, applied to Ushas.

It is a quaint idea that Indra did a strong and manly deed in striking the daughter of the sky (Dyaus), a woman difficult to overcome; which is said in *Rig-V. iv.* 30.

> He, a great hero, grinds to pieces the daughter of the sky (Dyaus), the magnified, the dawn.

She rushes off from her crushed car, fearing that Indra, the Bull, might strike her. The car lay there, wholly ground to pieces, and she went far away.

This is somewhat injurious to the pretty fancies that the sun is the lover of the dawn; for it is Indra, the light, manifested through the sun, that puts an end to the brilliant and gorgeous colours of gold and purple and the half-light of the dawn. But it required some stretch of imagination to conceive of light, as a bull, crushing with horn and hoof the car of Ushas, and heroically compelling her to flee far away, lest she too should be ground to powder, like the crushed car. And yet, as the broad daylight blazing from the sun does end the dawn, the idea of its conquering her was not unnatural. And that he did so as a bull, proves that when this hymn was composed, the sun was in Taurus at the vernal equinox, and the Stars of the Celestial Bull rose heliacally.

THE AṢWINS.

The *Aṣwins* or *Aṣvins* have vastly perplexed the commentators. Mr. Cox says (*i.* 390):

> These Aṣvins have been made the subject of a lengthened controversy. Their features are not very definite, but in the oldest hymns they are worshipped with a peculiar reverence, as able not merely to heal sicknesses, but to restore the aged to youth. [This feat the Poets of the Veda never imagined possible.] Speaking of them, the commentator Yaska says, that their sphere is the heaven, and remarks, that some regard them as *heaven* and *earth*, as *day* and *night*, or as *sun* and *moon:* while they who anticipated the method of Euemeros affirmed that they were two deified kings. But when he adds that their time is after midnight, whilst the break of day is yet delayed, all room for doubt seems taken away. [Strange, then, that there should have been so lengthened a controversy; for the Veda tells us *that*, plainly enough, and again and again.] The *two* Ahans, or Dawns, Day and Night, are born, it is said, when the Aṣvins yoke their horses to their car. The twins are born, when the Night leaves her sister, the Dawn, when the dark one gives way to the bright. After them comes Ushas, the Greek *Ἐως*, who is followed first by Sûryâ, a feminine, a sister of Sûrya, the Sun, then by Vrishakapayi, then by Saranyu, and lastly by Savitar. They are *ihehajate*, born here and there, *either* as appearing in the east *or* west, or as springing up on the earth and in the air; and this epithet may explain the alternate manifestations of the Dioskouroi, who stand to Helen in the same relation which the Aṣvins bear to Saramâ or Ushas.
>
> The Aṣvins are thus the conquerors of darkness [thus! how?], the Lords of Light; ever youthful, swift as thought, and possessed, like Indra, Agni and Phoibos, of a profound wisdom . . . . They are adored at morning and evening tide as Rudran, the terrible lords of wealth . . . . The twin pair adopt various forms. One of them shines brightly, the other is black; twin sisters are they, the one black, the other white.

We omit what "this brings before us," as we do the information as to whom the Poet must give them for father and mother; and we wonder *what* Mr. Cox supposes the Aṣvins *were*. For his "whirl of words" is very far from removing doubt, and rather makes confusion worse confounded.

At page 426, he makes another effort:

> So too, the morning and the evening, the gloaming and the dawn, became, as we have seen, twin steeds—the Aṣvins—joined together in a mysterious bond which made it impossible to draw a line between the approach of the one and the vanishing of the other.

Really, one wearies of this bald, loose, disjointed chatter.

By referring to the citations which I have in previous pages made from the Veda as to the Aṣwins, we shall find as follows:

They are the two leaders of the sky, the presiders over this world. This is language only applicable to *luminaries*, of some importance, and not to morning and evening, or day and night, or heaven and earth. At the dawn, they scatter the investing glooms to the ends of the earth. For that office, again, they must be luminaries.

They are but two, having only the joint name of *Aṣwins*, *Aṣvins*, or, as Eichhoff prints it, *Açvins*. They are also addressed by the appellatives, *Naṣatyas* and *Dasras*.

The word *Aṣvin* is from the root *as*, to "traverse" or "penetrate;" whence *Açvas*, a "horse," and *Açvin*, a "horseman," and *Açvîyas*, "equestrian."—*Eichhoff*. They are evidently inseparable and indissolubly united. One of them is not, in any particular, distinguished from the other; and, in fact a single Aṣvin is nowhere mentioned. Their union is like that of the shining and the dewy [of sky and air, or light and air]. They come to the sacrifice together, lighting up the lustre of their car, emitting vast and limitless radiance. Over the deserts, with water, they drive their horses. When the beloved Ushas, "until now unseen," scatters the darkness from the sky, the worshipper with profound veneration invoked the Aṣwins, called them divine [children of the sky], children of the sea, whose appearing causes rejoicing. Even before the dawn, Savitṛi sends their car to the sacrifice. Their chariot, harnessed for both alike is imperishable, and travels through the air. It is said to them,

> may Ushas *follow* the lustre of your approach, circumambient Aṣwins: may you both drink, and bestow upon us happiness.

They are "good-looking," and from the expanse or the sky beyond it, they bring riches. "Come to us in your well-constructed car, with the rays of the sun, with your sun-clad chariot;" but "the steeds awakened at dawn" bring them. They cannot, at that hour, be sun-clad, or come with the rays of the sun. In the Ramayana I find,

> That region, though sunless [*visûryyo*] . . . . is recognizable by a sun-like splendour, as if the sun were shining.

So that "sun-clad," and "rays of the sun" may refer only to the nature and splendour of the light of the Aṣwins, and may not mean that they actually shine by the light of the sun. They "send adorable light from the sky to men;" and they are invoked to harness their chariot, and come, that Savitṛi may animate all beings, when Agni is awakened on earth, when the sun is about to rise, and the dawn has dispersed the darkness.

Their car is laden with honey, and filled with treasure. They sustain the germ in all moving creatures, are in the interior of all beings, and supply fire, water, and the trees of the forest. They are physicians, with medicaments [compare "with healing in his wings"].

They are showerers of blessings. They are creators, and are invoked to hear the hymn, whether they are moving or resting. Their resplendent forms, in the halls of sacrifice, bring prosperity. If they are also called Dasras, they are called Rudras, too; and are said to repair to heaven, their horses conveying them on their heavenward journey, in a golden, three-shafted chariot, going by an easy road.

> May this hymn [it is said] be associated with your forms, and do you unite with the dawn [shine together with it, with mingling light].

That they have "forms," unmistakably indicates that they are luminaries; and they were, it is equally evident, worshipped when they had risen in the east, and ascended some distance into the sky.

> We invoke you two today [it is said]; the same on any other day, when the morning dawns.

The morning dawns every day; and probably the meaning is that they are invoked on those days when they have risen at the beginning of the dawn. At any rate, it is at the dawn, that they are invoked. They are Nasatyas, and grandsons of heaven. There is no untruth in them. "Like arrows to acquire glory, and to carry off Sûrya" is unmeaning to us.

> Aṣwins [it is said], we cross over the limit of darkness; which must mean that it is just as the dawn commences, that they are invoked to come, by the path traversed by the Devas.

They are styled "The two husbands:" they are invoked to descend like the falling stars, like the Brahmans repeating hymns, and to come like messengers in the land. They move at dawn, like two heroes in a car, like a pair of goats, like two women lovely in form, or, like husband and wife; and are invoked to come like a pair of horns, or of hoofs, like a pair of chakravâkas, awaiting day; to bear the worshipper across, like two vessels, like two poles of a car; to be like two dogs, averting harm, and like two coats of mail.

To what stars can these expressions apply? To what constellation more fitly than Gemini, the Twins? The parent of the Twins (the very meaning of *Gemini*), brings forth the Twins: they two, dispersers of darkness, combine

(i. e., shine side by side), assuming bodies as a pair (light manifesting itself by the two stars), *at the origin of day.* The praiser awakes the Aşwins, preceding [preceders of] the dawn.

Their car is the "Associator" of the solar rays; and bears the daughter of the sun (Sûryâ:—but may not this word simply mean sunlike, i. e., splendour?). They are grandsons of heaven, again; not Devas, i. e., planets, but stars, yet they are Divinities.

The following texts clearly and fully explain some on which I have already commented:

> Your chariots appear *at the opening* of the dawn, scattering the surrounding darkness *like* the sun, spreading bright radiance over the firmament . . . . Wakers at dawn. Praise the united Aşwins at the break of day.

Ushas is "the friend" of the Aşwins. They are swift of speed, gentle, unrefractory (having no irregular movements), golden-winged, "bearers.".

It is when "the extremities of darkness are seen nigh at hand," and the beginnings of the daylight are perceptible in the east, that the priest chaunts hymns to the Aşwins, the Nasatyas. They are called *Mâdhwîs*, and invoked as protectors. (*Mad,* to "intoxicate:" *madhu, madhus,* "honey, nectar." And *maḍ* is to "conciliate, adapt," whence *madhyas,* "central;" Latin, *medius; madhyai,* "in the middle;" *madhyan,* "middle." Also, *maid* or *maidh,* is to "observe, conceive;" whence, Latin, *meditor; maidhas,* "sentiment.")

Their devoted worshipper, waking before the dawn, praises them with hymns. The daughter of Sûrya is their spouse, and rides with them in their chariot, selected by her at the approach of night. Its two wheels form the extremities of the sky; and they come to the sacrifice at the dawn of day. Their chariot comes at the approach of dawn. It is the precursor of the day. Praises waken them and the celestial dawns, and they are praised when the dawns arise.

The Nasatyas are invoked to come from the west and east; the Aşwins from the south and north, from every quarter (which must have been before they had risen, and it was not known in what quarter of the heaven they might be). Of goodly aspect, the Aşwins *accompany the dawn,* like *leaders,* with their mighty chariot, when, advancing from afar, she brightens the sky, and spreads light on all sides. They are "Bringers of the Day;" and are said in three days and three nights to traverse from afar all the brilliant. (We can imagine nothing, luminary or phenomenon, substance or subsistence, of which that could literally be said.) Ushas is invoked to wake them; and when she shines, they go to the hall of sacrifice. Wherever they may be, they are invoked—whether in the sacrificial hall, in the expanse or above it, in the west or the east; whether traversing the expanse, or passing along *Dyava-prithivi*, heaven and earth (?).

"The Aṣwins preceding the dawn," are endowed with power, and ever young, unwearied, munificent, and free of untruth. By their chariot they become Lords of Sûryâ, who is borne on it. She is said to be the daughter of the sun; and I can understand this in no other way than as showing that the Poets had an idea that it was the splendour of Sûryâ, the sun, after he had disappeared, that during the night shone from the stars; and that by Sûryâ, his daughter, they meant that splendour furnished by him to them.

Thus it is said that the sun rises, and the chariot of the Aṣwins, traversing, is associated with the Divine, on the summit (i. e., being in mid-heaven, when the sun rises): and also, that when Sûrya ascends the chariot, bright-waving, resplendent rays encompass the Aṣwins.

They are guardians of heaven, and lords of water; invincible, and showerers of wealth. They are the two who come first at dawn (at the particular season of the festival, probably the vernal equinox). They claim the morning sacrifice;

> the ancient sages praised them at dawn: worship the Aṣwins at early dawn.

They are invoked to alight like two swans, like two deer, like two wild cattle in a pasture. They are "the two leaders of heaven," presiders over the world, who at dawn dispel the darkness. And they are the magnificent lords of good fortune, showerers of wealth, swift-moving and good-looking. Lords of men, and adorable Deities.

There is one peculiarity of the Aṣwins, which seems hopelessly enigmatical: and yet it is so frequently and distinctly repeated as to convince us that it had allusion to some notable peculiarity of the Aṣwins, whatever they were, by which they were distinguished.

Though they were but *two*, the wheels of their chariot are *three* in number: the columns placed upon it for support, are three; and in it the Aṣwins journey "three times by night, and three times by day." They are invoked to come three times, with the seven mother-streams. They are told that the three rivers are ready (the three vessels of Soma juice), and the triple oblation prepared. The car is triangular, and has three fastenings and props; and when it is asked where all these are, it is also asked, "when will be the harnessing of the powerful ass?" They have one wheel, it is elsewhere said, "on the top of the solid, while the other revolves in the sky." This "three-columned, triangular, three-wheeled car, three canopied," is drawn by swift horses. It is golden, and three-shafted.

A "three-fold hymn" is addressed to the Aṣwins. The car has three "benches" and three wheels, and is quick as thought; and it is embellished with three metals. It traverses "The Seven Flowing." It is renowned among the "five orders of beings;" it furrows with two wheels the extremities of the sky.

The three wheels of the Aṣwins, which were invisible, have become manifest

and consequently, this triad must be of stars, which become visible when they rise, or when, night coming, they appear. Once the chariot is said to "traverse as their all-pervading form: but a *form*, in the Vedic sense, is a body, a limited manifestation. It *journeys* and *traverses;* but it does not *pervade.* The chariot is harnessed "at a thought;" the horses are rapid and like falcons, and with it, in three days and three nights, they traverse from afar all the brilliant. It is plated with gold, honey-tinted, water-shedding, laden with ambrosia, quick as thought, rapid as the wind. Finally, the translation makes the Aṣwins rise "above the three worlds." But this has no connection with or reference to the three wheels.

There is a meaning to all this, if it could but be found out. So far, no one has attempted a rational explanation. We do not even know what exact idea was attached by the Poets, to the *chariots* of Agni, Indra, Sûrya and the other Gods, with their horses of different colours and sometimes of particular number. Did they mean by the chariot of the sun or of Agni, the sun himself or the fire itself, or the splendour surrounding them, in which they might be fancied to ride, the rays being the horses? At the beginning, to speak of the chariot of the sun, must have conveyed some distinct idea, not unnatural nor absurd, but which would strike those who heard it as natural and sensible. If there had not been an obvious fitness in the figure, it would not have been so universally accepted as appropriate, graphic, and not expressing a supposed resemblance that was wholly unreal. If the clouds were compared to and termed "cows," it was not because they *looked like* cows, or herded together like them, or moved like them; but because they yielded rain, as cows do milk. The body of the sun is enveloped by a splendour, which could well be conceived of as a vehicle, conveying him; and the rays, shooting from this splendour, and which we can even see in fine lines of light close to us in the air, seemed drawing him onward; and by the horses of the sun, these, no doubt, were meant. We know that this figurative language commended itself very generally to the ancient imagination; for we find the idea in many mythologies; and every school-boy knows the legend of Phaëthon, son of Phœbus, who undertook to drive the chariot and horses of his father, the Sun.

The chariot of the Aṣwins is laden with "treasure;" because the light is the most precious of all human possessions: but it is also laden with honey, which is more difficult to understand, although we learn from the Vedas that the Soma juice, offered at the sacrifice, was made sweet with much honey, *madhumattamaḥ*. It must have been imagined that the honey so offered, entered into flame, and with the Soma juice *fed* the Deities, and became a part of their light and splendour.

But why the chariot is represented as *three*-wheeled, *three*-columned, etc., is a greater enigma; and it is made more difficult by the fact that, though the Aṣwins were but *two*, the effusions of Soma juice to them were *three*, and the oblation *triple;* as if they were *three* devas.

I can conceive of but one explanation; and if the arrow I shoot goes wide of the truth, it may possibly still serve to point out to some one far more competent than I am, the way that will lead to the true interpretation.

I believe that the Aṣwins were two great and noticeable stars, closely united to each other in the popular mind, and, at that remote day, having a peculiar significance, as fulfilling peculiar functions or marking the recurrence of a particular season; and that, in the same constellation with them, near them in the heavens, was a third star, never associated with them in the popular mind as in close and intimate union; but still noticeable with them, and always accompanying them.

All the texts that seem inconsistent with this conjecture may need only to be more perfectly understood, to make them consistent with it. In Professor Wilson's translation, the Aṣwins rise or ascend "above the three worlds." The Vedic Poets knew nothing about what we call "worlds," meaning thereby heaven, earth and hell, or three realms or states of being. I imagine it would be difficult for even Professor Wilson, if living, to tell us what *he* understood by the phrase, when he used it. If he understood by it, the earth, the expanse or firmament, and the sky, it should have occurred to him that whatever the Aṣwins were, they could not have been conceived of as ascending above and getting outside of the sky, in their chariot. *Bhûvana*, everywhere translated "*worlds*," does not mean that, in our sense of the word; and I am satisfied that the Aryans had no word that can be honestly rendered "world," other than those that meant this *earth* of ours, or the visible universe. *Jagat*, from *ga*, to "create, produce;" *janata*, from *jan*, to "give birth to, produce;" and *bhûs*, *bhûtis*, from *bhû*, to "be born, exist," are all translated, "world," or, in French, *monde*, *gâus*, "earth," is from *gâ*, to "create, produce;" *irâ*, "earth," is from *îr*, to "produce, push forth;" *dharar*, "earth," is from *dhar*, to "fix, hold;" *talan*, "soil, foundation," is from *tal*, to "found, hold;" and *ditis*, "earth or Goddess of the earth," is from *dai*, to "give sustenance to, nourish." I do not know what word is rendered *worlds*, in the passage on which I am commenting, but it is more likely to mean regions than worlds; and it may mean three regions of the earth, perhaps the mountains, the plains, and the forests or the sea.

Professor Müller frankly says that he does not understand many of the hymns, and cannot translate them at all. Professor Wilson conscientiously and creditably did all that was in his power, and where he could not understand, he reproduced the literal later meanings of the words, as nearly as he could, and left it for future students to discover the meaning. Already, Müller and Muir and Roth know much more of the real meaning of the Veda, than the Hindû commentators; but much is still left to conjecture, even in regard to the meanings of words whose *modern* sense is well known.

The Aşwins are said "to defend the sun in the sky;" for they act as a vanguard for him, rising in advance of his rising, to clear the way for him, as it were, that he may ascend into the sky.

The car of the Aşwins is the associate of that which bears the sun; for if the Aşwins were what I have supposed, the festivals were held at a later time when they rose before dawn. The times of their rising, long observed, marked times and seasons, and especially the return of spring, and its great festivals; and when they rose in the morning, they were naturally regarded as attendants upon, and outriders, as it were, of the sun.

By their quick-moving chariot they become the lords of Sûrya—not his superiors and rulers, but his princes, nobles or courtiers.

The sun rises, their chariot, moving westward, is associated with him, on the summit, that is, high in the sky, while he is as yet close to the horizon. When his daughter (Sûryâ, his splendour) has ascended their car (has overtaken them, and mingles with their light), his rays encompass them (i. e., they are enveloped and hidden, by his superior brilliancy).

Mandala x. of the Rig-Veda contains hymns that are manifestly much more modern than those of the other Mandalas. But all are not so. In 61. 4, of that Mandala, is this:

> When the night stands among the tawny cows [*goshu aruṇishâ*, rays of the dawn, Dr. Muir says], I invoke you two, Aşwins, sons of the sky.

And this agrees with what is elsewhere said, that when the three wheels of the Aşwins, which were invisible, have become manifest, then Mitra and Varuṇa are invoked to rise, and to come, "by the paths of truth," to the presence of living beings.

It is to me a very persuasive fact, that, unless the Aṣwins were stars, none of these bodies were regarded as Deities by the Aryans. I find it difficult to believe this possible, when every imaginable hypostasis of Agni was worshipped, and when he and Indra were manifested by all the stars; and all of them were the Great Universal Principle, in action, limited in form and place. Worshipping Agni and Indra, they must have revered the stars.

It is scarcely an admissible hypothesis, that this race of men alone, in its youth, attached no ideas of potency and influence to particular luminaries and groups, that were then worshipped by all other races, and were afterwards the origin or source of much of the mythology of their own decendants. The evidences that the planets and stars were adored by the early Greeks and Latins, Goths, Sclaves, Kelts and Germans, are ample. And the sacred Zend books not only show that this was the worship of the ancient Persians, but, in doing so prove that the ancestors of both the Bactrian Zends and of the Aryans of the Punjab worshipped the stars. They are still invoked in all the books—Tistrya, with beautiful eyes, the stars pertaining to Tistra, the Star Vanant—*all* the "Lights without a beginning."

Mr. Prescott (*Mexico, i.* 121) says,

> As the eye of the simple child of Nature watches through the long nights the stately march of the heavenly bodies, and sees the bright host coming up, one after another, and changing with the changing seasons of the year, he naturally associates them with those seasons as the periods over which they hold a mysterious influence.

Æschylus says (*Prometheus Bound,* 454. 7),

> And they had no sure sign, either of winter, or of flowery spring; or of fruitful summer, but they used to do everything without judgment, until I showed to them the risings of the stars, and their settings, hard to be discerned.

So, in the opening of his *Agamemnon:*

> I have beheld the gathering of the nightly stars, both those that bring winter and summer to mortals, brilliant lords, stars conspicuous in the æther.

Spring was the season for rejoicing; and Plutarch tells us that the common time for the solemnization of the sacred rites (among the Greek descendants of the Aryans) was within that month in which the Pleiades appear. These were long esteemed the leading stars of the Sabæan year, long after the colure of the vernal equinox had quitted Aldebarán and the Hyades.

The periodical ascension and departure of certain groups of stars, could not but have been found (long before the immigration into the Land of the Five Rivers, thousands, perhaps, of years before that, and long before the first wave of Aryan emigration flowed out to the west and northwest, to become the northern races of Europe) to be the invariable forerunners, and those of other groups the never-failing concomitants, of the changes of the seasons; and adoration of the stars, brilliant in their appearance, at an immense distance, infinite in number, and constant and unerring in their courses, appears to have been the earliest religious movement of the human mind. The stars became celestial oracles, announcing the approach of those changes, on which the prosperity of men, if not their existence, depended.

By the precession of the equinoxes, the equinoctial point is continually, but very slowly, moving along the ecliptic, in a direction contrary to that of the sun's proper motion. This regression of the equinoctial points on the plane of the ecliptic, a constant shifting of the intersection of the ecliptic and equator, causes the annual arrival of the sun in either of the equinoxes to be a little earlier than it would otherwise be. The amount of the precession is a little over 50 seconds of longitude annually, or, exactly, 50″. 1.

The equinoctial colure now passes through the constellation Pisces: 390 years before Christ, it passed through the principal star (γ) in the constellation Aries; about 2,500 years before Christ, it passed through the Hyades, in Taurus. Sirius then rose heliacally (with the sun, at the summer solstice); and the Hyades rose with the sun at the vernal equinox. As the Bull then opened the spring, the sun being then in Taurus at that equinox, the Bull became to the ancient nations the symbol of the generative power, being supplanted by Aries about 390 years before Christ. About 4,500 years before Christ, the sun was in Gemini or the Twins, at the vernal equinox, and the two great stars of that constellation then led the heavenly host, preceded by the constellations Taurus and Orion.

The constellation Aries is followed, in the east by Taurus, the most westerly group of stars in which is the Pleiades, in the shoulder. Southeast of these, in the forehead, are the Hyades, and east of these is a star at the extremity of each horn. East of Taurus, opposite the horns, is Gemini, the Twins, in the northeastern part of which, not far apart, are the bright stars α and β, Castor and Pollux.

Between Taurus and Gemini, but to the south of both, is Orion, the most splendid constellation in the heavens, with a bright star in each shoulder and each leg, and three in a line on the belt. Below Orion, to the southeast is Sirius, the most brilliant star in the heavens. The bright star Aldebarân is one of the Hyades, and when he rose with the sun at the vernal equinox, he was called the Leader of the Celestial Hosts; and his name, which is Arabic, means "The Leader." When the Pleiades rose just before the sun, the ancients knew that the spring season had returned, and therefore their heliacal rising was hailed by the orientals, with grateful and glad acknowledgment of their sweet influences, and their promises of genial abundance. They were emphatically "The Seven," and were, I think, the "Seven Mother-Streams;" for their heliacal rising announced the coming of the rains of the vernal equinox.

In the Hindū astronomical work, Sûrya-Siddhânta (*translation of Rev. E. Burgess,* 183), the stars Castor and Pollux are called *Punarvasu,* from *punar,* "again," and *vasu,* "good, brilliant." In all the more ancient lists, the name appears as a dual, *punarvasû—Burgess.* (But *vasu* is "being, existence," ουσια.)

The Greek legend as to these stars, and as to the Demigods that became the constellation Gemini, may, if we examine it, be found to have grown or been fashioned out of the old and much simpler Vedic notions in regard to these stars.

Castor and Pollux were called by the Greeks the Dioscuri [Διοσκουροι], children of Dios or Zeus. They were the children of Leda, to seduce whom Jupiter became a swan. Pausanias mentions the great regard paid to them, particularly by the people of the Island of Cephalonia, who "styled them by way of eminence, the Great Gods." There are altars extant, which are inscribed *Castori et Polluci Diis Magnis;* and in Grüter is a Greek inscription, which designates them, in the genitive, as Θεων Μεγαλων Διοσκορων Καβειρων, "the Great Gods," *Dioscuri Kabeiri.* Their Greek names were Καστωρ and Πολυδεύκης, *Kastŏr* and *Poludeukēs.* Castor, in another account, was reputed, though born of the same mother, and at the same time, with Pollux, to be the son of Tyndarus, Leda's husband, and mortal, while Pollux was immortal. They went with Jason in quest of the fleece of gold, and Castor was distinguished in the management of horses, while Pollux was the God and patron of boxing and wrestling. Afterwards, they cleared the Hellespont and the neighbouring seas of pirates. Castor being killed, Pollux entreated Jupiter to restore him to life, or relieve himself of his immortality, which Jupiter permitted Castor to share; and consequently, as long as one was upon earth, the other was detained in the infernal regions; and each alternately lived and died every day, or, according to others, every six months. Jupiter rewarded them for their fraternal affection, by transferring them to the heavens, as the two great stars of the constellation Gemini. They are said to have been initiated into the sacred mysteries of the Kabiri, and are also called by that name. They had many surnames, indeed, and were generally represented mounted on white horses, armed with spears, and riding side by side, their heads covered with bonnets, with a star glistening on the top of each.

They were styled the health-giving Divinities, or Divine Saviours, and especially protected sailors against shipwreck.

There are very striking resemblances between these stars, as mythologically represented, and the Aşwins. The close and intimate union between the two Aşwins, so distinctly and emphatically stated and reiterated in the Veda, indicates much more than mere proximity; and the Aryan expressions of it were but developed in the Greek myth.

Another point of resemblance is even more suggestive. In the Sanskrit, *Aşvan*, or *Açvan* is a "horse," and *Aşvin* or *Açvin* a "horseman, rider" or "cavalier." The *Aşwins* or *Aşvins*, then, are the *Horsemen*, as the Greek Dioskouroi were—the Kabeiroi, riding their white horses, side by side.

The stars of the constellation Gemini opened the vernal year 4,500 years before Christ. The Dioscuri were then the most noticeable of all the stars, for their rising marked the recurrence of the vernal equinox. When, 2,000 or more years later, they were supplanted by the Hyades, Aldebarán became the Leader, in their stead, and continued so, long after the Hyades had ceased to be the heralds of the spring, and the Pleiades had taken their places.

Now, we find, in the same astronomical work, the Sûrya-Siddhânta, which is among the earliest textbooks of the Indian science, that about the year 570 after Christ, or somewhat earlier, the star ζ of the constellation Pisces coincided in position with the vernal equinox, that star being the principal one of the asterism Revati, which ends where the asterism Aşvini or Açvini begins. The latter is composed of either two stars (β and γ) in Aries, or of three, or Arietis being included with them. The beginning of Açvini became the initial point of the fixed Hindū sphere, from which longitudes are reckoned, about the year 570 A.D., in consequence of its coincidence, then, with the vernal equinox.

In the older lists, as also often elsewhere, we find, instead of *Açvini*, the dual *açvinâu*, *açvayajâu*, the "two horsemen," or "*Açvins*." Mr. Burgess says,

> The Açvins are personages in the ancient Hindū mythology, somewhat nearly corresponding to the Castor and Pollux of the Greeks. They are the Divinities of the asterism which is named from them. The group is figured as a horse's head, doubtless in allusion to its presiding Deities, and not from any imagined resemblance. The dual name leads us to expect to find it composed of two stars; and that is the number allotted to the asterism by the Çakalya and Khaṇḍa-Kaṭaka.

The later authorities state the number of the stars in the asterism at three.

Now, the two largest stars in Aries are only of the third magnitude, and the third is still smaller. The two are in no way noticeable, simply as stars, though easily enough recognized; and they never could have been of any importance, or have attracted particular attention, until after Aries had come, about 350 or 390 years B.C., to be the sign into which the sun entered at the vernal equinox, when, insignificant as they were, they became the Leaders, in the place of Aldebarân, who had, more than two thousand years before (about 2455 B.C.) supplanted Castor and Pollux.

And Mr. Burgess says,

> In the most ancient recorded lists of the Hindū asterisms (in the texts of the Black Yajur-Veda and of the Atharva-Veda), Kṛttikâ, now the third, appears as the first. The time when the beginning of that asterism coincided with the vernal equinox, would be nearly two thousand years earlier than that given above, for the coincidence with it of the first point of Açvini.

My conclusions are, that when the sun was in Gemini, at the vernal equinox (from 5500 B.C. to 2000 B.C.), the two stars, Castor and Pollux, leading upward the heavenly hosts, were the celestial riders, or horsemen and leaders, the Açvins, and were called Açvini. Kṛttika is the Pleiades. After the sun had reached that asterism at the vernal equinox, about 2000 B.C., Aldebarân had not lost his place as leader, and the Açvini may have continued to be Castor and Pollux, or the name have been transferred to the two stars of the horns of Taurus, or to Betelgeux and Bellatrix in Orion. If either, probably the former pair received the name, since, being on the same meridian, they rise and set together, while the others are on an east and west line. However, as to this we have no further information than that the Pleiades were, some two thousand years before the stars of Aries became so, the first asterism and initial point of the Indian sphere, Alcyone being the junction star.

The two small stars in Aries could not have been called the Aṣwins, in the Punjab. For then, being west of Taurus, they were high in heaven, and insignificant, when the Twins opened the year, and Castor and Pollux were invested with the characteristics and attributes that were afterwards developed into the Grecian myths. They must have been called by the Aryans, "The Horsemen" and "The Twins," or, if not called by the latter name, have been described as intimately united, as they are in the Veda, before that stream of emigration flowed off, which made Greece an Aryan colony.

And when we see that in Greece these stars became emphatically the Great Gods, the Kabeiroi, protectors of sailors, Gods of health and salvation, we shall not wonder at the terms in which the Aṣwins are spoken of in the Veda.

These are the relative positions of the principal stars of the constellation Gemini:

and south of them is their "triangular, three-wheeled, three-benched, three-columned" car. For the Açvini in Aries, that car could only be themselves and the small third star, by later astronomers included in the asterism.

If the two stars at the extremities of the horns of Taurus ever were the Aṣwins, the triangular car may have been themselves and Aldebarân, which form a triangle, thus:

and if Betelgeux and Bellatrix ever became the Aṣwins, the car was formed by themselves and β, of the horns of Taurus, thus:

but the language of the Vedas applies to none of these asterisms so well, as to that of Gemini; and it can confidently be said, that either the name Açvini was not applied to *any* asterism, until the equinoctial colure passed between Pisces and Aries, about the year 570 of our era, or that it was before then applied to a different asterism, further to the east. In the Vedic times, and afterwards while Aldebarân was the leader, there was nothing to cause the application of the name to the small stars of Aries.

I conclude, therefore, that the Aṣwins of the Vedic Poets were the two stars, Castor and Pollux.

It has always seemed strange to me that the Pleiades should have received the name of "The Seven," when to the naked eye they are but six in number. I never believed that originally there were seven, and that one had disappeared; and I did believe that the legend of the lost Pleiad was a mere invention, for what purpose conceived of, I had no idea. If "The Seven" were originally another group of stars, whose place the Pleiades took, when Taurus succeeded Gemini as opener of the spring, this, otherwise inexplicable, becomes clear; and there are seven bright stars, besides Castor and Pollux, and below them, in the constellation Gemini. These were perhaps the original seven "shedders," or "mothers of water."

It is noteworthy, in this connection, that all the Divinities to whom the regency of the Hindū asterisms is assigned, are from the Vedic pantheon. The popular Divinities of later times are not to be found among them, and, on the other hand, more than one whose consequence is lost, and whose names almost are forgotten, even in the epic period of Hindū history, appears in the list. Prajapati, "the lord of created beings," is regent of the Hyades, and Yama, Indr-Agni, Mitra, Soma, Rudra, Bṛihaspati, Bhaga, Aryaman, Savitar, Tvashtar, Indra, Vishṇu, Pushan, the Vasus and Varuṇa, are regents of other constellations. The name Aṣvini is as old as they, and in the Vedic period designated *some* two stars: and these could not have been the same that now bear the name. They must have been those that 4,500 years ago marked by their heliacal rising, as the stars of Aries did 1,200 years ago, the advent of the vernal equinox. And, though it is, perhaps, only a slight coincidence, the Aṣwins are invited to alight like two *swans;* and, in the Greek myth, Castor and Pollux, begotten by Jupiter in the shape of a swan, were born from an egg.

Mr. Cox (*Mythol. ii.* 67) says,

> The presence of the Dioskouroi, the bright Aṣvins or Horsemen, complicates the story, of Theseus.

Of the Kabeiroi, he says (*ii.* 314) that

> they have a protecting and soothing power, and hence are nourishers of the earth and its fruits, and the givers of wine to the Argonautai.

Again, speaking of Herakles, he says,

> Kastor, who shows him how to fight in heavy armour, is the twin brother of Polydeukēs, these Twins answering to the Vedic Aṣvins or horsemen.

Here, Mr. Cox had a glimpse of the truth; but looking back, I find him saying (*i.* 426),

> so, too, the Morning and the Evening, the Gloaming and the Dawn, became, as we have seen, twin steeds, the Aṣwins, joined together in a mysterious bond which made it impossible to draw a line between the approach of the one and the vanishing of the other;

and I close the book in despair. The Vedic Gods are only vague, shifting shadows, to Mr. Cox.

The subjoined sketch or diagram of the stars and constellations of which we have spoken, will assist the reader, perhaps, in judging of the value of my suggestions. He must remember that the upper side of the page is north; but that the left hand and not the right, is east. If he will turn over the leaf, *keeping the upper side to the north,* and holding it *above* his head, look *up at it* he will see the stars in their true positions, and will understand that Gemini rises *after* Orion, and Orion after Taurus after Aries; so that when The Twins rose at dawn at the vernal equinox, the *present* Aṣwins had ascended far into the sky, and Orion, the Hyades and Pleiades were far below the horizon; and that when all had risen, seven great brilliant stars could be seen at once in the eastern and southeastern sky, Castor, Procyon, Sirius, Rigel, Betelgeux, Capella and Aldebarân.

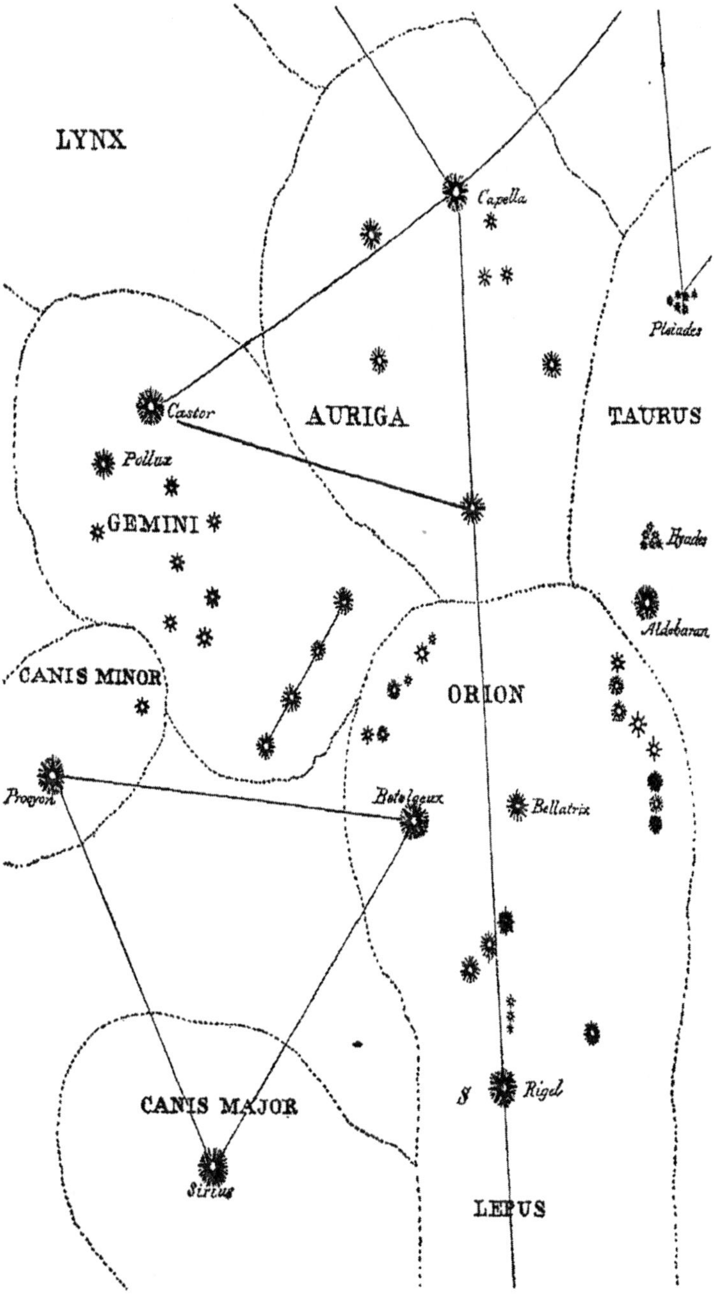
LYNX
Capella
Pleiades
Castor
AURIGA
TAURUS
Pollux
GEMINI
Hyades
Aldebaran
CANIS MINOR
ORION
Procyon
Betelgeux
Bellatrix
Rigel
CANIS MAJOR
Sirius
LEPUS

OTHER DEITIES OF THE VEDA.

The Deities of the Veda are very numerous, and of many of them it will always be impossible to know more than the names, inasmuch as either their names are merely mentioned once, twice or a few times, without more; or, in what is said of them or addressed to them, there is nothing to identify them with any visible or intellectual object of worship.

In one hymn (*ii. of Anuv. iii. Adhy. iii. of Ashṭ. v.*), the following are named: Indra, Agni, Varuṇa, Somas, Pushan, Bhaga, Sansas, Purandhi, Aryaman, Mitra, the Aṣwins, the Vasus, Rudra, the Rudras, Twashtṛi, Aditi, the Maruts, Vishṇu, Vayu, Savitṛi, Parjanya, Sambhu, Saraswatî, the Ribhus, Aja-ekapad, Ahirbudhnya, Pṛisṇi, and the Adityas.

And, in other hymns, besides these, Vṛihaspati, Bṛihaspati, Brahmaṇaspati, Ritu, Neshṭri, Daksha or Daxa, Ansa, Asridh, Tarkshya, Trita, Yama, Ribukshin, Sûrya, Swar, Vibhwan, Atri, Vaja, Vidhâtri, and Vata and yet others, are named.

In addition to these are the Goddesses, Ila, Sûryâ, Indrani, Agnâyî, the Aṣwinî, Rodasî, Varunânî, Râkâ, Sînîvâlî, Gangu, Mahi, Iḷita, Gna, Pṛithivi, Dhishana, Varutri, Bharati, Hotra, Urvasi, Nivṛiti, Suna, Sua and Sita.

I shall not particularly inquire as to any other of all these, in addition to those already considered, than Pushan, Bhaga, Twaṣhtṛi, Rudra, Saraswati, Saramâ, Pitu and Vasu. Of the others, only a few words can be or need be said.

Many of the names are perhaps merely epithetical, appellatives of Agni, Indra and other Gods; and some are certainly the names of deified men, supposed to have been anciently translated to the stars.

Gandharva or *Gandharba* is named two or three times, and said, in Professor Wilson's note to one passage where it occurs, to be a name of the sun. In another note, it is said to be a synonym of one or the other of two other Divinities.

In *Mand. x.* 139. 5, is this passage:

> The divine Gandharva [*Divyo Gandharvo*], measurer of space [*rajaso vimânaḥ*]. [Dr. Muir translates *rajaso, "the world."*]

In the Udyoga-parva, a mountain Gandhamadana is mentioned. In the Brahmanic books, a people named Gandhârvas are mentioned, of whom

Nagnajit was king, and whom Krishṇa destroyed. The appellation *Divyo* shows that some luminary, probably a star, bore this name.

Trita, "the son of the waters," is several times mentioned. He harnessed the horse given by Yama; slew the mutilated Vṛitṛa: he is named with Vayu and Agni; and is supposed in one note to be a name of Indṛa, in another, of Yama, and in other places is evidently a Ṛishi.

In *Mand. viii.* 12. 16, we find,

> whether, Indra, thou enjoyest Soma, along with Vishṇu, or with Trita Aptya, or with the Maruts. . . . .

Dadhikra ordinarily means a horse. In one hymn of *Ashṭ. iii.*, it occurs as the name of a Divinity. In two others, as a horse, he is extravagantly lauded, and said to be as brilliant as Agni, to be Hansas, dwelling in light, Vasu, dwelling in the firmament, and Agni on the altar and elsewhere, even in the rays of light and the sky.

At first blush, all this seems to be simply nonsensical; but it is not. The hymn is the composition of a time when, probably on the steppes, horses were sacrificed to the Gods. The flesh, burned in the sacrificial fire, fed it, became part of it, was transmuted into the flame, and so becoming of the very substance of Agni manifested, ascended to the skies, and, as light, became Hansas and Vasu, as, at and on the altar, it became Agni.

Ansa is named as one of the Adityas, with Varuṇa, Mitra and Aryaman. In the Linga-Purana, Vishṇu is represented as calling himself *Hansa*, the swan. I think *Ansa* was a name of the moon.

Tishya, the commentators say, is the eighth lunar mansion. That is no Vedic idea. Sâyaṇa calls him an Aditya. He was probably some star. What he became in later ages, it is of no interest to know. The Gandhârvas, after the Vedic period, became evil spirits of some sort; as the Devas became the evil Daevas of the Persians, and gave to the devil of the Christian religion his name.

Ribukshin is two or three times said in the notes of Professor Wilson, to be an ordinary name of Indra; but unfortunately, in a hymn of *Ashṭ. iv.* it occurs in the same stanza with Indra—Ribukshin, Vaja and Purandhi forming a triad.

In *Mand. i.* 186. 10, we have, by Dr. Muir's translation,

> Vishṇu is free from malice, and so is Vata, and Ribhuxan [*Vishṇu, Vâtaḥ, Ṛibhuxâḥ*].

Dr. Muir parenthesizes "Vayu," after Vata.

And in *Mand. ii.* 1. 3, it is said, to Agni, "Thou, sustainer, art associated with Purandhi," which Dr. Muir parenthesizes as "devotion;" and in the preceding clause, Agni had been addressed as Brahmaṇaspati. In a note on p. 14 (*Orig. Sansk. Texts, iv.*) Dr. Muir quotes from *Mand. x.* 168. 4,

> Soul of the Gods [*atmâ devânâm*], and Source of the World [*bhuvansya*], this Deity [*deva*] marches at his will. His sounds are heard, but not his form: to this Vata [*Vâtâya*] let us offer our oblations: [and Dr. Muir renders *Vata* by 'wind'].

Vibhwan was the artificer of Varuṇa, as Vaja was of all the Gods, and Ribukshin of Indra. (*Sûkta i. Anuv. iv. Adhy. vii. Asht. iii.*) One note of Professor Wilson says that he was the second of the Ribhus, a skilful artist. Ribhu, Vibhwa and Vaja are, in *Asht. ii.*, said to be sons of Ṡudhanwan. They were the Ribhus; and were men deified. I do not doubt that by them some group of three stars was indicated. For "the Seven Ṛishis" were the constellation Ursa Major; and it is a reasonable presumption that other brilliant and notable stars were assigned to other Ṛishis as their domicils. Apamvatsa is the Hindū name of Spiça Virginis, and it means "child of the waters." That is what Trita is called. Tishya was probably Sirius.

Aja-Ekapad occurs three times, as the name of a Divinity, and *Ahirbudhnya* six times. The texts give no clue to the character of either. The latter is said to mean "a Deity presiding over the firmament." I cannot find such meanings for its parts.

"The adorable *Umas*, who come when they are invoked," are mentioned once. The Veda gives no clue to the meaning of the name. In the Hindū books, *Umâ* or *Umâ Haimavati*, was the wife of Siva—knowledge [*Vidya*], in the form of Umâ, very resplendent, the daughter of Himavat; and it is said, "Uma is divine knowledge." No doubt the Umas were a group of stars.

The brilliant *Râkâ* is mentioned once. There is nothing to show what he was.

Sindhu is once or twice named as a Divinity, and several times as a river. It is the true name of the Indus.

Iḷita is said to be an appellation of Agni, meaning "adored," "worshipped."

Agni is once invoked to bring with him the divine *Gna;* and this name is said to be a synonym of *Stri*, a "woman," a "wife."

Gangu is invoked, "who is *Siñivali*, who is *Râkâ*, who is *Saraswati.*" Gangu is said to be a synonym of *Kuhu*, the day of conjunction, when the moon rises invisible. How that *day* is Siñivali, Râkâ and Saraswati, the

River Goddess, we do not learn. In the Ramayana, Ganga is the Ganges. She was the sister of Umâ, daughter of Himavat, king of the mountains.

Hotra is called the wife of Agni; and Bhârati of Bharata, who is said to be an Aditya.

Dhishaṅâ is said to be the Goddess of Speech. Its root is probably *dhai*, to "observe, meditate;" whence *dhis*, "thought, reflection."

Indrani, *Varunâṇi* and *Agnâyî* are named two or three times, and are wives of Indra, Varuṇa and Agni: what they were, or with what identified, it is not possible to know. If we *could* know, an entirely new angle of Vedic ideas might be open to us. Neither of these Deities is represented as having progeny; and, unless these feminine words were mere names and no more, without any real idea of personality connected with them, they may be evidence of the existence of an idea largely developed afterwards, to-wit, that each of these Deities was of a double nature, masculine and feminine; and that so, for example, Agni was both the generator and producer of fire. In that idea we should have the germ of the Hindū myth, of the self-division of Brahm, by the sexual impulse, and the production of the universe by Maya, his feminine self.

Rodasi is said to be the wife of Rudra. Once she is bride of the Maruts.

Varutri is named but once. It is doubtful whether the word is the name of a Goddess, or an epithet of one having another name.

Ila, "the mother of the herd," is said to be the earth. In one place, she is styled the instructress of Manu (father of the race of Aryans); and to her is ascribed the first institution of sacrifices. She is said to have been the daughter of Manu. "For him we worship Ila," it is said in *Asht. i.*; "on the most sacred spot of earth, upon the foot-mark of Ila," in *Asht. ii.* The scholiast says she made that foot-mark, when in the shape of a cow. She is said by Sayana to be the Goddess presiding over the earth, Bhârati over the heaven, and Saraswati over the firmament; but all are special manifestations of the majesty of the sun. There is nothing in the Veda to warrant this. Saraswati has nothing to do with the firmament; for she is a river and a river Goddess. What is the *meaning* of the phrase "special *manifestations* of the *majesty* of the sun?" Does it mean that these Goddesses are the light, the heat, the fertilizing energy, his melting, drying or tanning power, or other potencies or energies, manifested on earth, in the expanse and in the sky? I do not find any reason to believe that either of these Deities was any such manifestation. Nor do I suppose that Sâyaṇa meant that either of them was any thing specifically. The phrase is one of those that neither expresses nor conveys any idea.

In the Third Ashṭakâ, this Goddess is "Ila, daughter of Daksha," and is said to be earth, or the altar. "Offerer of the oblation," it is said in

Asht. iv., "sit down on the foot-mark of Ila." The texts do not enable us to even conjecture what Ila was. Certainly no manifestation or subsistence of Agni, because it is impossible to imagine any one of these making a foot-mark, in which a Deity could be supposed to sit down. When named with Saraswati and Mahi or Bhárati, we have nothing more than the names.

The root *Il* meant to "move, hasten;" whence the Greek ἐλαω, "agitate," and ιαλλω, "send, emit, utter;" and Sanskrit *Ilat*, "mobile." But this gives us no assistance in determining what Ila was.

That *Bhárati* is one of the above-mentioned triad, is all that we learn in regard to her. The *Bháratas* were a race or family among the Aryans, the descendants of Bhárata, who was the son (according to tradition) of Ṣakuntalâ, the daughter of the celebrated mythical sage. Vaṣishtha was their family priest.

Urvasi is named twice. In *Asht. iv.*, with Ila, as

> Urvasi with the rivers, the bright-shining Urvasi, investing the worshipper with light.

In the Fifth Ashṭaka it is said that Vaṣishtha is the son of Mitra and Varuṇa, born of the will of Urvasi, after the seminal effusion. Who or what she was, does not appear. The root *ur* means to "move, extend;" whence, Greek, ὀρω, to "excite, arouse," and, passive, to "be aroused," to "arise;" Latin, *orior*, to "rise;" and Sanskrit, *urus*, "vast;" *uras*, *urvî*, "body, extension."

As Saraswati is certainly a river and a river Goddess, and Ila, Mahi and Bhárati are associated with her, I believe that all, as well as Urvasi were water Goddesses. Saraswati was a particular river, as Sindhu was the Indus and Gangu the Ganges or some river in the Punjab, after which the Ganga was subsequently named. Ila, I think, was a Goddess of springs or fountains, of water springing up, agitated and bubbling, from the earth, near the places of sacrifice and elsewhere; and "mothers of the herds" because of them the horses and cattle drank. Urvasi, I believe, was the Goddess of the clear, smooth, bright lakes, from which the rivers ran. There were several such in the higher country of the Punjab.

Ṣuna, *Sûra* and *Sîta* are invoked but once—in *Sûkta xii. Anuv. v. Adhy. viii. of Asht. iii.*, a hymn relating to field-work, and evidently intended to be sung in the spring, at the ploughing time. The imbecility of Hindū interpretation is peculiarly manifest in relation to these Goddesses. Ṣuna and Sûra are asked to sprinkle the earth with the water they have created in heaven; which of course is rain; and Sîta is prayed to be present, to be propitious, that she may yield the worshipper abundant fruit. Indra is invoked to "take hold" of Sîta, Pushan to guide; and the Poet adds, "may she, well stored with water, yield it as milk, year after year."

Ṣuna and Sîra are, in the original, *Sunâ-sîrau*, in the dual. One authority makes Ṣuna the Deity of the sky, that is, Indra; and, according to Sâyaṇa, Sîra is then Vayu. Another authority considers Ṣuna to be Vayu, and Sîra, Aditya. In ordinary acceptance, Professor Wilson says, Ṣûna-Sîra is a name of Indra.

Sîtâ, it is said, is usually a *furrow*, and as such occurs as a personification of "the Deity" in the Yajush. Sâyaṇa *explains* it, "the wood supporting the furrow," which Indra is to "take hold of;" and, says Professor Wilson, "Sîta may mean the sky." In the Hindū books she is daughter of Janaka and wife of Rama an incarnation of Vishṇu. Accused by her husband of unchastity, she threw herself into the fire.

Sîra, from *si*, to "tie or bind together, join, unite," is, in Sanskrit, a "nerve." From *su* or *sû*, to "dart, hurl, fling, throw, cast, produce, emit, etc.," come *sûtas*, "emitted," *sûtis*, "emission," *sûnas*, *sûnus*, a "son:" and the root *sur* is to "dart, hurl or shine." *Sura* also was wine, an intoxicating liquor.

Mahi, with Ila and Saraswati forms a triad. The word is said to be a synonym of Bhârati. The scholiast says that the three are personifications of Agni. Mahi is not named alone, nor is there a word in the Veda by which to identify her, nor any clue to aid us, except that she is named and connected with Saraswati.

Nirṛiti (calamity) is named two or three times as an evil Goddess, against whom protection is invoked. She is styled "powerful and indestructible." Once, she seems to be the Deity of poverty and misfortune. In another hymn she is divine, and acknowledges Indra as ruler; and there the note thinks she is the earth: and once she is invoked to sustain the body with food, and preserve it from decay.

Pṛiṣni is the mother of the Maruts, who are styled, in one hymn, *Pṛiṣni-matârah* (who have Pṛiṣni for mother). Sâyaṇa says that Pṛiṣni is the many-coloured earth. How *it* is the mother of the storm-winds, he does not explain. In the Nighantu, the word is a synonym of sky or heaven in general, we are told; and Rosen shows, Professor Wilson says, that in some texts it occurs as a name of the sun. Truly an admirably defined Deity—at once earth, sky, heaven and sun, and mother of the storm-winds also, whose father is Rudra! In another place, where the Maruts are called *Pṛiṣni-matârah*, the scholiast explains *pṛiṣni* by *dhenu*, a "milch-cow."

The phrase, "sons of Pṛiṣni," without more, occurs three times in *Ashṭ. i.* Pṛiṣni is named as mother of the Maruts, the phrase, the second time, being, "golden-breasted Maruts, the vigourous begot you of the pure womb of Pṛiṣni." In *Ashṭ. v.*, Pṛiṣni is distinctly said to have received the germ of the Maruts from Rudra, and to give milk from her bright udder. The Gods (*Deva*, the luminaries) are her guardians, and she grants happiness. "The vast Pṛiṣni" bore the Maruts at her udder (*udho babhana*). Udhas, it is said, may mean the firmament or womb. In *Ashṭ. iv.*, the Maruts are styled "offspring of the maternal cow." In *Ashṭ. iv.*, it is said, that the Maruts "have declared Pṛiṣni mother; the mighty ones have declared the food-bestowing Rudra, father;" and three times more in that Ashṭaka, they are declared to be the sons of Pṛiṣni. Dr. Muir translates *Mand. ii.* 34. 2,

> at the time when the prophet Rudra generated you, O Maruts, with jewels on your breasts, from the shining udder of Pṛiṣni.

And *Mand. v.* 52. 16,

> These wise and powerful Maruts, who, when I was seeking with my friends, declared to me that the earth, Pṛiṣni, was their mother, and that the rapid Rudra was their father. I do not find any word meaning 'earth,' in *'vochanta Sûrayaḥ pṛisṇim vochanta mâtaram.'*

I think that Pṛiṣni is the atmosphere. *We* know that the winds are the air in motion; but this the Aryans did not know. They could have conceived of the wind only as an immense power or force, vast, irresistible, mysterious, generated by some potent agency in the expanse, and sweeping, mighty though invisible, over the face of the earth. They could not have conceived of it as the same in substance as the soft breathings of the summer air; or if they did, the force and power, manifested by the winds, and not the masses of air themselves, were the Maruts whom they adored; and this force and power had, according to their ideas, to be generated by something, and produced from something. Therefore the Maruts were born from "the prolific womb of Pṛiṣni;" certainly either the expanse or open space, or the air that covered the earth.

Pṛithivi is said everywhere to be the earth. It is so rendered wherever it occurs. To many of these passages I have already referred, and need only say here that the word simply means "extended" or "expanded," and that, in my opinion its oldest or older meaning in the Veda, was that immediately derived from the root, "the extended," "the expanse." Its confinement to the earth, as spread out or extended, was a later appropriation.

There is one hymn of three stanzas as addressed to her (*Sûkta xii. Anuv. vi. Adhy. iv. Ashṭ. iv.*), in which, by Professor Wilson's translation, she is said to "sustain the fracture of the mountains," and, "mighty and most excellent, to delight the earth with her greatness." I do not see how she can *be* the earth, which she delights. She is termed "wanderer in various ways;" which the earth certainly was not, to the Aryans, who thought it solidly fixed.

> Bright-hued,' she tosses the swollen, like a neighing horse. . . . . With solid earth, she sustains by her strength the forest lords, when the showers of her cloud fall from the shining sky.

She cannot *be* the earth, when she unites with the earth, to nourish with the rain from her clouds the lords of the forest. So Sâyaṇa, always equal to the emergency, says that here Pṛithivi has a *two-fold* meaning, and applies *also* to the firmament. That is, being *one* thing, the earth, it is *two*, the earth and the expanse. *Dyava-Pṛithivi* often occurs, the conjunction "and" being omitted; and it is always rendered "heaven and earth." I think it is, "sky and expanse." In *Sûkta iii. Anuv. xxii. Adhy. iii. of Ashṭ. ii.*, which is addressed to Dyava-Pṛithivi, they are called

> the benevolent father, and the mother, who with kindness have secured by their excellent protections, the vast and manifold immortality of their progeny: [the luminaries, I think, of heaven].

They are styled "*Dyau voh Pitâ, Pṛithivî mâtâ.*" But Yaska explains *mata* to denote the *antariksha*, "the firmament." Of the children, "the progeny, whether stationary or moving" (fixed stars or planets), Stanza 4 says,

> Those provident and intelligent sisters, conceived of the same womb, united, and dwelling in the same abode, mete out [times and seasons?]: knowing and bright-shining, they spread in ever new [i. e., diffuse ever fresh and undiminished radiance], throughout the radiant expanse.

Was the earth conceived of as mother of the stars?

Ayu is several times named as an Aryan prince, aided in war by Indra; once it is said that Indra made the planets manifest to Ayu and Manu; and twice Ayu is named as a Deity—once with Mitra, Varuṇa, Aryaman and Indra, where, the commentators Sâyaṇa and Mahidhara say, the name is synonymous with Vayu; and again, with the same, in a hymn in which Vayu also is named twice. Nothing is said by which it can be known what Ayu was.

> Wide-hipped *Sinîvâli*, protectress of mankind, who has beautiful arms, beautiful fingers, and is the parent of many children,

is said by the Hindû commentators to be the new moon, on the first day of its appearance. The next stanza says:

I invoke her who is Gangu, who is Sinîvâlî, who is Râkâ, who is Saraswati, Indrâṇî for protection, Varunâṇî for welfare.

She is named nowhere else.

The two great rivers of India, the Indus and the Ganges, have their principal sources in valleys parallel to the line of greatest elevation of the Himalayas, and are found in the closest connection, and interlacing, as it were, with each other, between the Meridians of 77° and 82° east longitude. In longitude 81° 30′ is Lake *Tso Mapham* or *Manasarowar*, the confluence of the highest sources of the Jumna, the principal branch and real main river of the Ganges. So the sources of the Indus and its own tributary, the Sutlej overlap each other, having their rise in close proximity to those of the Ganges and Jumna. Lake *Manasarowar* is about 15,200 feet above the sea level, and the scenery upon it is magnificent. It is of circular shape, with rocky coasts, and about fifteen miles in diameter. The elevation of the sources of the streams that fall into it is not less than 16,000 feet. North of it is a mountain 22,000 feet above the sea; west of it, one of the height of 20,000, and immediately south of it, one of the height of 25,200. From this lake a stream flows into a neighbouring lake, *Tso Lanak*, or *Rakas Tal*, about five miles distant. This lake is of more irregular form, with several islands in its southern extremity, where it spreads considerably to the east and west. Its length is about twenty miles, and its greatest breadth at the south fifteen. From it flows the main stream of the Sutlej, which, like the Indus, runs to the westward, and then, through a pass or gap in the mountains, to the south, running a long distance through an immense ravine, and falling 7,000 feet in two hundred miles.

Yaska calls the Sutlej the *Sutudri*, and speaks of its junction with the *Vipas*. It was the river next in importance to the Indus, to the men of the Punjab; and the name of the Indus at that day we know to have been *Sindhu*. The *Saraswati* was honored above all other rivers by the Vedic Poets; and therefore I thought it was the Sutlej. The name *Râkâ* still survives, in *Râkâs Tal*, that of the lake out of which the Sutlej flows; *Sinîvâlî* is *Gangu*, *Râkâ* and *Saraswati*, and may have been the Lake *Manasarowar*, a stream from which runs into Lake *Rakas Tal*, while from itself go out the head waters of the Jumna. She is "wide-hipped," and Lake Manasarowar is circular. She has many children, and these and her beautiful arms and fingers may mean the streams that run from the lake, and the mountain brooks and rivulets and larger streams that run into it.

Vasu, addressed as a God, is said to be a synonym of Indra in the character of original donor or cause of habitations, from the root *vas*, to "dwell." The name occurs once in *Ashṭaka i.*, and once in *Ashṭaka iii.*, where the phrase is, "Vasu, dwelling in the expanse:" there the scholiast interpolates "wind:" and it occurs once in *Ashṭaka vi.*, as a synonym or name of Agni.

In later ages, *Vasu-deva* (Vasu the divine) was a name of Krishna. In the Sabhâ-parva, it is said,

> He is to be known as *Vasudeva*, from his dwelling [*vasanât*] in all beings, from his issuing as a *Vasu* from a divine womb. [There, he] possesses the nature of all principles:

he is not generated by a father, is unborn, and is absolute existence. He is the source and destruction of all things, the existent as well as the non-existent. In the Anujāsana-parva, he is the Supreme Spirit, omniscient and omnipresent, source of all things; the four-armed son of Sura, one with Brahma.

From *vas*, to "be, exist," comes *Vasu*, "being, substance;" Greek *ουσια*; Gothic, *wisan;* German, *wesen;* Russian, *weszcz.*

Agni, we know, was as well the vital warmth of the body and of Nature, as he was the household fire. One or two of the Poets, it seems, had conceived of him as abstract being or existence, the principle or substance of which each individual existence is a ray or spark. It was the first germ of a vast religious development. It was precisely the idea that was embodied in the Hebrew name of Deity, יהוה; the vague undeveloped idea of absolute, abstract existence, of course eternal, without being or end, because its nature is to be, and it cannot not be. It was but a little step from it to the conception of it as the source of all existences, the creative God, which it afterwards became, as Vasudeva. But in the Veda, the second step had not been taken. Agni was Vasu—the Fire-Principle was the cause of existence, was that in which existence consisted.

In *Mandala x.* we find *dhatūr dyutānāt*, the shining *dhâtṛi*, named, with Savitṛi and Vishṇu, three times in three stanzas of one hymn; and in another we find,

> Let Vishṇu form the womb; let Tvashtṛi mould the forms; let Prajapati infuse; let Dhâtṛi form the embryo. [In the original, *Dhâtâ*.]

Sâyaṇa makes Dhâtṛi (*Dhâtâ*) an Aditya. From *dha*, to "put down, found, effectuate," are *dhâtus*, "base" or "foundation;" *dhâtar*, "founder;" *dhaman*, "structure;" Greek, *δωμα*, "house." *Dhâtṛi* seems to have been the Deity of conception; and was clearly a luminary, probably one of the planets. The hymns are late ones, like many others of this Mandala, and new Gods are named in them.

In *Mandala x.* 92. 11, "the four-limbed *Naraṣansa*" is named, with Yama, Aditi and others.

In *Mandala v.* 46. 3, *Saṁsa* is named with Brahmaṇaspati, Bhaga and Savitṛi. Manu says that the waters are called *Nârâ*, because they are the offspring of *Nârâ*. In the Mahābhārata, Nârâ and Nârâyaṇa are called venerable Ṛishis: and in another passage of the same, they are Krishna and Arjuna. Narasansa is, in the original, *Narasamsas.*

Skambha, in *Mandala x.* 7 and 8, is "he on whom Prajapati has supported and established all the worlds." He established earth and sky, the atmosphere, the six wide regions, and pervaded the universe. He is "all this which has Soul, which breathes, which winks:" and the name is said to mean "supporter" or "propper." The hymns are evidently, from other names contained in them, of a date much later than the Vedic times; and this new God is but the personification of the function of propping up the sky, ascribed in the Veda to Indra and the other principal Deities. It is one example, of many, of the manufacture of new Gods, out of misunderstood expressions of the Veda.

Ṣaru is once named (*Ṣarave bṛihatyai*, the great Ṣaru), in *Mandala iv.* Dr. Muir thinks that the name is a synonym of Nivṛiti. That is entirely uncertain. Agni is asked why he should declare the worshipper's sin to Pushan, Vishṇu, Rudra or Ṣaru. Nivṛiti, calamity, would hardly be associated with them. The root *sar* means to "go, move."

In *Rig-V. vi.* 50. 12, we find *Vaja* and *Vata* named.

> May Ribhuxan, Vaja, the divine disposer, Parjanya and Vata increase our energy! [*Ribhuxâḥ Vajo, daivyo vidhâtâ Parjanyavata pipyatâm isham naḥ.*]

Vidhâtâ may also be a name, though rendered "disposer." Vata is also named with Ribhuxan, *Mandala i.* 186. 10: and with Vishṇu, as free from malice; and in *Mandala x.* 168, where it is rendered "wind." These are probably names of stars, as they are all *Devas.*

I have mentioned these, not to explain them, but because they unmistakably show that the Aryans worshipped as Deities many of the stars, and the Gods of the streams and lakes, as well as the better-known Vedic Deities; and that many of these were afterwards invested with higher attributes, their original characters being forgotten, in the Hindū pantheon. And we see that the Greeks and Latins also legitimately inherited their adoration of deified men, of the Deities of the stars, and of the Gods of the rivers; while the Vedic ideas were at a still later day developed into the highest truths and most profound ideas of philosophy and religion.

There are also, in the Veda, classes and families of Deities.

The *Viṣwadevas* were *all* the Deities, of all classes. The word first occurs in *Sûkta iii.* of *Mandala i.*, and is translated by Wilson "universal Gods." Literally it means "all the Deities," *Viṣva* or *Viṣwa* meaning "all."

The principal classes and families are the Adityas, Vasus, Ribhus, Rudras, Nasatyas; and the Umas, and Ribukshins or Ribuxhans are also mentioned.

The *Adityas* are the children of Aditi. I have already spoken of them. It is said that Sûrya is not named as one of them in the Veda; but that is an error. For in *Mandala viii.* 90. 11, we find

> Verily, Sûrya, thou art great: verily, Aditya, thou art great;

and Aditya is never an individual *name*. And in *Mandala x.* 88. 11, Sûrya is called *Âditeya*. The Adityas, Mitra, Aryaman, Bhaga, Varuṇa, Daxa, Ansas, it is said, "have been *rajas* always." In *Mandala ix.* 114. 3, the Adityas are said to be seven. The *number* corresponds with the seven orbs anciently considered planets, the Sun, Moon, Mercury, Venus, Mars, Jupiter and Saturn. I shall cite hereafter the texts in which Bhaga is mentioned. Daxa or Daksha is probably Mercury. From *daks*, to "attain, succeed," we have *daksas*, *dakshinas*, "skilful, adroit;" the Greek δεξιος, the Latin *dexter*, and the English *dextrous;* as well as the Gothic *taihswa*, and the Lithuanian *desszinis*. Mercury, as we know, was the most cunning, dextrous and adroit of the Gods, and as such became the patron of thieves. He was emphatically the rogue-God. The Hindū names for this planet are *jna* and *budoha*, "wise, knowing." For Venus, one Hindū name is *bhṛgu*, and another is *bhargava*. I think the Adityas were these seven planets; Ansa (swan) being a name of the moon.

The *Vasus* "fabricated the horse from the sun." They may be, Professor Wilson says, "the particular Gods before specified" (in the text) "or Demigods so named, the personified solar rays." In one hymn, they are praised with the Rudras and Adityas. In another, Agni is honoured by the Rudras and Vasus. They are several times addressed and spoken of, in *Ashṭakas iii.* and *iv.*, and styled "divine" and "adorable." Once we find "celestial Adityas, terrestrial Vasus" in the translation; but in the original the words "Vasus" and "Adityas" are not found, only the epithets *divyah* and *parthivâsah* being used, and meaning, "of the sky," and "of the expanse." They "have concentrated vigour" in Agni, i. e., it is he who is their potency and light, which are manifested by them: and Agni is associated with them and the Rudras. They are named with Indra, and dwell among the devas. In one Sûkta, the name *seems* to be a synonym of Maruts. They know the hearts of men, and are invoked to convey the worshippers, in their vessel, beyond the reach of calamities.

In *Mandala* x. 66. 4, we find,

> we invoke Aditi, *dyâvâ-prithivî*, the great rite [*ṛitam mahad*], Indra and Vishṇu, the Maruts, the great sky [*svarbṛihad*], the divine Adityas [*devan Adityan*] to our succour.

Another God, *Sarasvat*, is also named. And in *Mandala* x. 141. 3, the Adityas are invoked, with Soma, Vishṇu, Sûrya and Bṛihaspati, and also with *Saravati*. At a much later day, *Aditya* became the name of an individual Deity.

The *Ṛibuxhans* [*Ṛibuxhaṇaḥ*] are named in *Mandala* x. 92. 11; *devas Tvashṭa, Draviṇoda, Ṛibuxaṇaḥ, pra rodasî, Maruts Vishṇur.*

The *Nasatyas* are the two Aşvins.

The *Rudras* I will speak of with *Rudra;* and the *Ribhus*, hereafter.

A striking confirmation of the truth of what I had concluded as to Vasu, was not seen by me until after I had written what I had to say upon that subject; and I prefer to cite it here, as evidence of what I am sure is true, that a competent Sanskrit scholar may find in the original, by careful study and comparison, many words and phrases that will throw great light upon these questions; and that the Veda will never be correctly translated, until it is ascertained what was meant and represented by each of the principal Gods.

I have concluded that Vasu was abstract existence—not individual life, but that Universal, from which all life proceeds. And in *Mandala* v. 51. 13, I find,

> May all the Gods, may Agni, the Vasu common to all men [*Vaiṣvaṇaro vasur Agnih*] . . . . preserve us for our welfare.

PITU.

Sûkta viii. Anuv. xxiv. Adhy. v. Asht. ii. is addressed to Pitu. We condense as follows:

> Pitu, the great, the upholder, the strong, by whose invigorating power Trita slew the mutilated Vṛitra. Savoury Pitu! Sweet Pitu! We worship thee; become our Protector! Come to us, Pitu, auspicious, with auspicious aids; not unpalatable; a friend well respected. Thy flavours, Pitu! are diffused thro' the regions, as the winds are spread through the sky.
>
> 'The thoughts of the Mighty Gods are fixed, Pitu, on thee: by thy kind and intelligent assistance, Indra slew Ahi. We extract from thee, Pitu, who art exhilarating to the Gods.'

It is perfectly evident that Pitu is food, or meat, and especially the meat burned in the fire as a sacrifice, and, thus transmuted into fire and flame, ascending to the Gods. There being no doubt whatever as to this, these expressions become peculiarly valuable, as keys to the meaning of others, similar or dissimilar, employed in speaking of other Deities, and as specimens of mistranslation, by which (*expede Herculem*) we may judge of the whole.

Carried to the Deities, as part of the invisible effluence of the sacrificial fire, the food so consumed is imagined to feed and strengthen the Gods, as the Soma juice exhilarates them. Pitu is therefore the sustainer or nourisher (upholder). It is food that supports the life of the worshipper, also, and therefore Pitu is the preserver or maintainer of life (protector); and is invoked, as a benefactor (auspicious) to come with gainful nutriment or succour (auspicious aids). He is "a friend well-respected," i. e., a helper, affording sustenance inestimable; and the winds carry to different quarters the saviour of the sacrifice. The Deities desire this invigoration. By the strength which it communicated, Indra was enabled to slay Ahi; but how this assistance was not only kind, but "intelligent," is not easily understood; and this word is, of course, no representation of the original. So the concluding phrase, being nonsense, cannot be a correct translation; and the meaning probably is,

> we extract from the food sacrificed, the essence of it, which gives confidence and strength to the Gods.

PUSHAN.

Asht. i. Adhy. ii. Anuv. v. Súkta vi.

8. Divine Maruts, of whom Indra is the chief, and Pushan the benefactor [*Púsharâtayah*, of whom Pushan is donor or benefactor].

Adhy. iii. Anuv. viii. Súkta vii.

This hymn is addressed to Pushan. It invokes the protection on the road, against enemies, robbers and evil men, thieves and deceivers; asks for riches and food, and a pleasant journey. He is styled "son of the cloud, Deity," sagacious and handsome, possessed of all prosperity and well equipped with golden weapons, and good-looking.

Adhy. vi. Anuv. xiv. Súkta vi.

Pushan is named with Indra: 'we invoke that lord of living beings. . . . . Indra . . . . as Pushan has always been our defender, for the increase of our riches, so may he be the unmolested guardian of our welfare!

Elsewhere he is glorified as "the bountiful Pushan," with the Aṣwins.

Asht. ii. Adhy. ii. Anuv. xx. Súkta v.

[Addressed to Pushan only.]

1. The greatness of the strength of the many-worshipped Pushan is universally praised. . . . . I adore him whose protection is ever nigh, who is the source of felicity; who, when devoutly worshipped, blends with the thoughts of all; who, a Deity, is united with the sacrifice.

The interpretation of this by the scholiast is mere nonsense. "United with the sacrifice" it is probable, merely means that Pushan, a Deva, when worshipped, receives and unites with himself the sacrifice carried up to him by the fire.

2. . . . . Divine bestower of happiness . . . . render our invocations productive: render them productive in battles [i. e., let them avail us, gaining your aid].

3, 4. . . . . as consequent upon thy recent favour, we solicit infinite riches. Free from anger, and entitled to ample praise, be our leader in every encounter. . . . . Free from anger, and liberal of gifts, be nigh to us, Ajâṣwa . . . . be nigh to those, Ajâṣwa, who solicit food . . . . Pushan, accepter of offerings.

Asht. ii. Adhy. iii. Anuv. xxii. Súkta vi.

2, 3. . . . . the parti-coloured goat . . . . becomes an acceptable offering to Indra and Pushan. This goat, the portion of Pushan.

Adhy. viii. Anuv. iv. Súkta viii.

1. Soma and Pushan, you two are the generators of riches, the generators of heaven, the generators of earth: as soon as born, you are the guardians of the whole world: the Gods have made you the source of immortality [*Akṛiṇavan Amṛitasya nâbhim*, the cause or source of not dying, i. e., the means of sustaining life].

2. These two Divinities . . . . drive away the disagreeable glooms: with these two, Soma and Pushan, Indra generates the mature in the immature heifers. [This cannot mean to make them pregnant, but to cause them to grow to maturity.]

3. Soma and Pushan, showerers, direct towards us the seven-wheeled car, the measure [traverser] of the spheres, indistinguishable from the Universe, everywhere existing, by five reins, and to be harnessed by the mind.

Sâyaṇa thinks that this refers to the year, consisting of seven seasons, reckoning the intercalary month as an additional *ritu* or season. The scholiast thinks that the five reins mean the solar year, reduced by amalgamation of the cold and dewy seasons, into five. If we can ascertain what Pushan was, it may be possible to determine what the car and reins were.

4. One of them has made his dwelling above, in the heaven; the other, upon earth and in the expanse.

5. One of you has generated all beings: the other proceeds, looking upon the Universe: Soma and Pushan, protect my rite. . . . .

6. May Pushan, who is the benefactor of all, be propitious . . . . May Soma, the lord of wealth, grant us affluence.

Elsewhere we read,

Ribhus, associated with Pushan, make us joyful . . . . Divine, resplendent Pushan . . . . that Pushan who looks upon all the worlds, who thoroughly contemplates them . . . . Thou, divine Savitṛi, art Mitra, through thy functions . . . . Thou art Pushan, divine one, by thy movements. For thee, Indra, for thee may Pushan and Sudra dress an hundred buffaloes . . . . Hasten, Pushan, to me: (repel) bright Deity, deadly assailing foes . . . . Uproot not, Pushan, the Forest Lord, with its progeny of crows: utterly destroy those who are my revilers . . . . Thou art supreme above mortals: thou art equal in glory to the Gods: therefore, Pushan, regard us in battles . . . . Pushan the rewarder.

Asht. iv. Adhy. viii. Anuv. v. Sûkta iv.

1. Pushan, Lord of Paths [*Pathas-pati*. In another hymn he is called *Pathas pathahparipatim*, 'Protector of all paths'], we attach thee to us like a chariot for bringing food.

According to the tenor of this and another hymn already quoted, Pushan is the Deity presiding especially over roads or journeyings. The scholiast describes him as presiding Deity of the earth, also as cherisher of the world, from *pûsh*, to "nourish." And in this hymn he is further invoked to guide the traveller to a hospitable host, to soften the hearts of the avaricious, instigate the niggard to liberality, solicit good roads and drive enemies from them, etc. And he bears the goad and drives the cattle.

The next Sûkta, also, is addressed to Pushan. He is invoked to give guides who know the roads, and can direct the traveller aright; to protect the horses of the worshippers, and their cattle; to give riches and avert poverty, and bring back cattle that have strayed.

Sûktas vi. vii. and *ix.* are addressed to Pushan, and *viii.* to Indra and Pushan. In these, Pushan is the chief of charioteers, the wearer of a "braid" (of hair), the lord of infinite wealth. He is a torrent of riches. For steed, he has a goat, and is the rider of a goat, the giver of food, him who is called the gallant of his sister, the husband of his mother, the brother of Indra. With him as ally, Indra destroys his foes.

> He, the impeller, the chief of charioteers, ever urges on that golden wheel, the shining one who revolves [so rendered, in note, by Professor Wilson; or, perhaps, who revolves periodically or regularly]. Of Indra and Pushan, one drinks the Soma, the other desires the buttered meal. Goats are the bearers of one; two horses, of the other. When Indra sends down the waters, Pushan is along with him.

He is also called, as we have seen, "son of the cloud."

> *ix.* 1. One of thy forms is luminous, one is venerable, so that the day is variously complexioned; for thou art like the sun.
>
> 2. The rider of the goat, the protector of animals . . . . who has been placed over the whole, the divine Pushan, brandishing his loosened goad, proceeds, contemplating all beings.
>
> 3. With these thy golden vessels, which navigate within the ocean-firmament, thou dischargest the office of messenger of the sun.
>
> 4. Pushan is the kind kinsman of heaven and earth, the lord of food . . . . of goodly form; whom the Gods gave to Sûrya, vigourous, well-moving.

In *Sûkta vi. Anuv. iii. Adhy. iv. of Asht. v.*, it is said,

> Pushan, invoked before the dawn, upon the close of night, appear now in the firmament, for the welfare of mankind.

Invoked before the dawn, appearing in the firmament at the close of night, given by the Devas to Sûrya (the sun), vigourous and well-moving [i. e., regularly revolving?], of goodly form, navigating the sea of the expanse with golden vessels, performing the functions of messenger of the sun;

kind kinsman of heaven and earth; one of his forms luminous, and one venerable, so that the day is variously complexioned, for he is like the sun; the impeller, chief of charioteers, urging on his golden wheel, that, shining, revolves; guiding travellers aright; looking upon and contemplating the world; whom Savitṛi is, by his movements; supreme above mortals, and equal in glory to the Devas; divine (i. e., habitant of the sky), resplendent; all these expressions seem applicable only to some one of the celestial luminaries.

But, on the other hand, Pushan is benefactor of the Maruts, as Indra is the chief of them; he is the "son of the cloud." When devoutly worshipped, he blends with the thoughts of all, and, a Deity, is united with the sacrifice. He is particularly addressed jointly with Indra and with Soma; and he and Soma are styled generators of riches, of heaven and of earth; and, as soon as born, guardians of the whole world. The Devas have made both the means of sustaining life. Both drive away "disagreeable glooms," and with them Indra generates the mature in the immature heifers. They are showerers, and they direct (or drive) the seven-wheeled car, the measure of the spheres, indistinguishable from the universe, everywhere existing, by five reins, and to be harnessed by the mind. One of them has made his dwelling above, in the sky; the other, on earth and in the expanse. One has generated all beings; the other journeys looking upon the universe.

Is there anything in these expressions, absolutely inconsistent with the hypothesis that Pushan is a luminary? The last two sentences are quoted with the others, because they exclude the conclusion that might otherwise seem necessary to be drawn from the coupling together Soma and Pushan. For we conclude that it is Pushan, who has his *dwelling* above in the sky (which is appropriately said of the heavenly bodies), and Soma, who has his as a plant on the earth, and, mingled with the fire, in the air. And it is Soma, we think, who is considered as the generator of beings, and Pushan who revolves in the sky.

It is difficult to understand how a star or a planet could be called benefactor of the Maruts, or "son of the cloud;" how it could blend with the thoughts of all, or be generator of heaven and earth; or, as soon as born, guardian of the whole world, with Soma. How is a star or planet the means, like Soma, of sustaining life? How does it drive away disagreeable glooms, as Soma does, if these are anxieties and cares? How does it, with Indra and Soma, or how does Indra, with it and Soma, generate the mature in the immature heifers? What, indeed, does that expression mean? Is it that, by means of these, as nourishment, Indra causes the growth to maturity of cattle?

Principles or substances, and luminaries, alike, have chariots, in the Vedas. What the seven-wheeled chariot of Soma and Pushan can be, is hard to say. It is "the measure of the spheres;" but the Vedic Poets knew nothing about the "spheres." It traverses the whole semicircle of the arch of the sky: and this would indicate a celestial body. How is it "indistinguishable from the universe, everywhere existing;" and what does this phrase mean?—What are the five reins, and how is the car to be "harnessed by the mind?"

And still, that he protects and guides travellers, against enemies and robbers, and those who would lead them astray, seems to define him as some luminary by which men can direct their course. If he is "son of the cloud," he is also a Deva, a denizen of the sky, is sagacious and handsome, well-equipped with golden weapons (rays), and good-looking (i. e., shining brilliantly). That, as a Deity, he is "*united with* the sacrifice," does not mean that he is a part of it, as a subsistence of Agni, or anything that becomes part of the flame, because he is also called "the *accepter* of offerings." The parti-coloured goat is offered to him and Indra. The goat is "the portion" of Pushan, and he rides upon a goat. The golden wheel that revolves regularly must, it seems, be his orb, traversing the sky. That Soma acts by, with, and through him, is not significant. The Soma spirit of exhilaration is credited with the deeds and potencies of more than one God; and could well be said to travel in the same chariot with any of them. That Pushan looks upon and contemplates all visible things, indicates that he is an orb, one of the eyes of Agni and Indra.

How is Savitṛi (whether sun or moon), Pushan by his movements? How is it that Pushan dresses buffaloes for Indra? What is he, that he is asked not to uproot the forest lord, with its progeny of crows?

He is equal in glory to the Gods, and supreme above mortals. Is he, then, not himself a God, or Deva? If a subsistence of Agni, how is he the lover of his sister, husband of his mother, and brother of Indra; and, yet, if he be a luminary, how can he be brother of Indra, and his ally in battle against his foes?

He not only rides a goat and is lord of paths, and protects horses and cattle, but he carries the goad, and driving the cattle proceeds, contemplating (looking down upon) all beings.

What are his two forms, one luminous, and the other venerable, making the day variously complexioned? and how is that so because he is like the sun? What are those golden vessels, sailing in the ocean of air, with which he fulfils the office of messenger of the sun? How did the Gods give him to Sûrya; and how is he the beneficent kinsman of heaven and earth? of goodly form, vigourous and well-moving. I have fancied that this indicated that he was Mercury, who is never seen far above the earth, and is always a close attendant on the sun. The Mercury or Hermes of the Greeks and Romans was the messenger of the Gods, and the patron of travellers and shepherds; and in the wars of the giants against the Gods, he showed himself spirited, brave and active. Always within the sun's rays, he could well be said to associate with Indra, and with Soma, the associate of Indra. But his orb is no guide for travellers, and it is not possible to see how he was rider of a goat, or had a seven-wheeled chariot and five reins, or two forms, one luminous and the other venerable; though he could be said to have been given by the Gods to Sûrya, and to be kinsman of heaven and earth.

On the other hand, how could a God not a luminary be invoked, before the dawn, upon the close of night, to appear in the firmament, for the welfare of mankind? But what luminary could be lover of his sister, and husband of his mother? Nothing but the new moon, with the old moon in its lap, one of the forms luminous and the other venerable, would suit this description; but many things said of Pushan could not be said of the moon. She is divine and resplendent, and can be said to guide and protect travellers; but she is not invoked before the dawn, nor is associated with goats, and what can be *her* seven-wheeled car and five reins? How, too, can she, brandishing a goad, be the driver of cattle?

This suggested to me Boötes, the herdsman, and the great star Arcturus, with the seven stars of Ursa Major as his seven-wheeled chariot, and the four stars of Ursa Major that form a square, with the bright star between them and Ursa Major, for the reins.

The goat suggested to me Capella (the she-goat), the bright star in Auriga, the charioteer; but I do not find there the car and the reins.

If Pushan were the constellation Taurus, Aldebarán would have his seven-wheeled car, the Pleiades, and the Hyades as the five reins, or from which the five reins are imagined ("harnessed by the mind") to extend to the Pleiades. This constellation, rising at the dawn, announced the vernal equinox, was deemed to possess, as the bull was the symbol of the generative power. We would have here the golden vessels navigating the ocean of air, and the guide for travellers; and Aldebarán, rousing the herdsman at dawn, might be said to drive the cattle.

If Pushan is not a star or planet, what is it possible to imagine him to be? There are expressions that seem to show that he is of the same nature as Soma, i. e., a nourishing and generative potency. But the constellation Taurus, opening the spring, was appropriately called the generator, of heaven and of earth, or, rather, the fructifier. It could be called the showerer, also, as the vernal equinox brought rains, the change of the monsoons occurring at the equinoxes. As showerer, this constellation was fitly associated with Indra, in warring against Vṛitra; and it could be called the benefactor or aider or encourager and inciter of the storm-winds, the Maruts. So, at that stormy season, the Pleiades and Hyades could well be styled "son of the cloud;" and Aldebarán could be imagined as a herdsman, brandishing his goad, and driving the stars before him like cattle. What is meant by his wearing a braid (of hair) I do not know. But, rising before the sun, he could well be called the messenger of the sun, and the stars led by him, his golden vessels.

The expression, "devoutly worshipped, he blends with the thoughts of all," must mean, I think, that, gratified by such worship, he sympathizes with, and shares the feelings and wishes of the worshipper. By its supposed influences, this constellation was made by the Devas the means of sustaining life, by making the earth to produce, impregnating and fructifying it with rains and the sweet influences of spring. And it not only drove away the glooms of the night, but those of winter, whose close it announces. Overlooking, looking down upon, contemplating the world, these stars could fitly be said to be the guardians of it; and the young cows then beginning to give milk, they could be said to make mature the immature heifers.

That their car is "indistinguishable from the universe everywhere existing," and is "harnessed by the mind," may mean that the stars composing the constellation are not larger or brighter, or particularly distinguishable in any way, from the others in every part of the heavens; and that it is only by means of the imagination that they are conceived of as forming a unit, a single constellation—that it is the intellect only, which conceives of them as connected together and forming one.

But what is meant by the parti-coloured goat being offered to him; by his riding the goat, being drawn by goats, the goat being his portion?

Pushya is still the name of one of the twenty asterisms or groups of stars, established and designated by the Hindū astronomy, about 560 A.D., at which time the observations were made that undertook to fix the latitude and longitude of the junction star of each group. These asterisms are called *Makshatras*. Though there are twenty-eight of these, the ecliptic is divided into only twenty-seven lunar mansions, or asterisms, each occupying 13° 20′ or 800′ of the extent of the ecliptic, Abhijit, one of the asterisms, being omitted. And the twenty-eight are very unequally distributed along the ecliptic, and at greatly varying distances from it. To divide the ecliptic into twenty-eight parts, and assign these to the twenty-eight asterisms, would cause sixteen asterisms to fall within the limits of portions bearing different names, four portions (of the ecliptic) would have no asterisms at all, and four others would contain two each.

Therefore, the system of asterisms was not founded, originally, on the division of the ecliptic into twenty-seven equal parts, and the selection of a star or constellation to mark each portion, and be, as it were, its ruler; but the series of twenty-eight asterisms is of greater antiquity than any division of the ecliptic into equal arcs, and one system was only artificially brought into connection with the other, complete harmony between them being altogether impossible.

The Parsis, Arabs and Chinese have a similar system of division of the heavens into twenty-eight portions, marked or separated by as many single stars or constellations. The Arabs call their divisions *Manâzil-alkamar*, lunar mansions, or stations of the moon. And this division into twenty-eight parts everywhere had a special connection with the moon's revolution.

The native tradition of Indra has, for centuries past, been of no decisive authority as regards the position and composition of the groups of stars constituting the asterisms. These, Mr. Burgess says, must be determined upon the evidence of the more ancient data handed down in the astronomical treatises.

The primitive identity of the Chinese and Hindū asterisms has been demonstrated by Biot. And the Chinese system does not commence, as the Hindū system has commenced since 560 A.D., with the stars of Aries, but with the Pleiades, *as the Hindū system anciently did—Burgess, viii.* 9.

It will at once occur to any one that all these asterisms were probably, at the beginning, such stars or groups of stars as were notable and remarkable for their magnitude, brilliancy, position or relations. The most notable of all the stars, in all ages, have been the Great Bear, and whatever stars or constellation at the time marked the recurrence of the vernal equinox. And it will at once occur to the student, that it is singular there should be, among the Hindū asterisms, any that are entirely unimportant and unnoteworthy.

The first Hindū asterism, since A.D. 560, at least, has been Açvini, two stars in Aries: only notable because, at that time, the sun was in that constellation at the vernal equinox. The second is Bharaṇŷi or Bharaṇyas, three little stars (3rd or 4th magnitude) in Aries. The third is Kṛttikâ, the Pleiades, called also, in the plural Kṛttikâs. The appellative meaning of this word is doubtful. Mr. Burgess thinks it *may* be from the verbal root *kart*, to "cut," because one may fancy he sees in the asterism a knife with its handle. It is more probably from *kar*, to "do, make, act," whence the Greek κρεω, "create" and χειρ, "hand," and the Sanskrit, *karas*, "doing;" *karas*, "hand;" *kriya*, "affair;" *kart*, "effectuating;" *kartis*, "action;" etc.

The fourth asterism is Rohini, "ruddy," the Hyades, in the face of Taurus, the junction star of it being Aldebarân. The Arabs call it *Aḷ-dabarân*, the "follower" (of the Pleiades), which shows that the Arab system also commenced originally with the Pleiades, and that the Hyades were the second of the system.

Mr. Burgess remarks that

> it is contrary to all the analogies of the system, that a faint star should have been selected, to form by itself an asterism.

He says this with reference to Ârdrâ ("moist"), of which I will speak shortly. Regulus in Leo is the junction star of the tenth asterism; Spica, in Virgo, is by itself the fourteenth; Çitra, "brilliant;" Arcturus, in Boötes, is by itself the fifteenth; Antares, in Scorpio, is by the junction star of the eighteenth; Vega, in Lyra, is the junction star of the twenty-second; the four large stars in Pegasus and Andromeda form the twenty-sixth and twenty-seventh. The great stars Canopus, in the ship, Sirius and β Tauri, are not in any of the asterisms. Of the asterisms containing more than one star, there are but two whose junction stars are selected as the most brilliant; and several of the asterisms, besides those already mentioned, are composed of very insignificant stars.

Mr. Burgess remarks,

> Perhaps we have here only the scattered and disconnected fragments of a more complete and shapely system of stellar astronomy, which flourished in India before the scientific reconstruction of the Hindū astronomy transferred the field of labour of the astronomer from the skies to his text-books and his tables of calculation.

There are many discrepancies between the *actual* positions of stars of the asterisms, and their positions, by latitude and longitude, as given by the astronomers: and it is unquestionably true that some, perhaps many, of the asterisms are not now, in place or composition, what they anciently were. Insignificant stars and groups have taken the places of more brilliant and noteworthy ones, in consequence of the changes of characteristics and of relation to the seasons, produced by the precession of the equinoxes. It is plain that Castor and Pollux were the Aṣwins, when Gemini opened the year. There is great uncertainty as to the identity of the stars designated as Bhâdrapadrâs, and composing the twenty-sixth and twenty-seventh asterisms, supposed to be the four that compose "the Square of Pegasus." The latitudes and longitudes given do not suit the junction stars. It is impossible to tell what thirty-two stars compose Aevatî, the twenty-eighth. There is great confusion in regard to Ârdrâ, the sixth, which is a single star, and the Hindūs cannot explain it. Tauri 135 is the only star that answers at all nearly to the definition of its position; and it is a faint star of the sixth magnitude. The great bright star, α, Orionis, it cannot possibly be doubted, Mr. Burgess says, was Ârdrâ; but the longitude does not correspond, by more than seven degrees, nor the latitude, by nearly three.

Castor and Pollux are now the seventh asterism, Punarvasu (again good or brilliant), the reason of which designation is not apparent; and Pushya is the eighth, composed of three little stars in Cancer. Âçleshâ, the ninth (*entwiner, embracer*), of five stars, is of necessity deemed to be in the head of Hydra, but the longitude does not suit by nearly five degrees.

Without remarking upon the uncertainty as to others, let us see what has become of Oriōn, one of the most magnificent of the constellations, and one of those that has longest attracted the admiration of mankind, in which are seventy stars plainly visible to the naked eye, two of them being of the first magnitude, four of the second, and three of the third. Betelgeux and Rigel are of the first; Bellatrix and the three stars of the Belt, of the second, and three below the girdle, in a line inclined to it, and at greater distances from each other, are of the third. Oriōn lies below, south, of the horns of Taurus, north of which is Capella. Aldebarân, the belt of Oriōn, and Sirius are nearly in the same straight line. Capella, the Hyades and Oriōn all come to the meridian together.

The Pleiades rose heliacally (with the sun or a little before sunrise) as early as 3,900 years B.C. Ulysses, in his bark, on leaving Calypso, is made by Homer, in the fifth book of the Odyssey, to observe, "the Pleiades and Boötes, the Hyades and bold Oriōn, and the Bear which is called the Wain." Virgil calls Oriōn *Aquosus*, because his rising, about the ninth of March, was accompanied with storms and rain.

When figured in human form, Oriōn has on each shoulder a star, on his belt three, and on each knee one, all of nearly the same magnitude (1st and 2nd), composing the mystic number 3, 5, and 7, and forming a figure which could easily be fancied to resemble a wain or car.

Now, although this is the most splendid group of stars in the heavens, and, rising nearly at the same time with Capella, Aldebarân and the Pleiades, must always have been imagined to exercise the same influences as they on the seasons; and though, at any season, they would serve as guides to the herdsman or traveller on the plains, and could never have been unnoticed by any manner of men, we find that none of its great stars are included in any asterism of the Hindūs.

For the fifth, Mrigaçirsha or Mrigaçiras, *whose divinity is Soma*, contains only the faint cluster of three little stars (4th magnitude) in the head of Oriōn; and the Arab Marizil *Al-hak'ah* is composed of the same stars; and the third Chinese *Sieu*, named *Tse* is the Hindū junction star, λ, Orionis.

And though Mr. Burgess says that α, Orionis (Betelgeux), *must* be Ârdrâ, the sixth asterism, the position of Ârdrâ does not at all correspond with that star, but only with 135 Tauri, a little star of the sixth magnitude.

And the Chinese have, for the fourth Sieu, Tsan, the upper star, δ, in the Belt of Oriōn, while the Arabs have their sixth station, in the feet of Pollux. And Pushya, as we have seen, has become two little stars in Cancer. It is also called *Tishya*, "conspicuous," and *Sidhya*, "prosperous."

Mṛigaçîrsha means "the antelope's head," and the figure assigned to that asterism corresponds with the name, but, Mr. Burgess says, "the reason for the designation we have not been able to discover." An antelope is but a species of goat; and it may be that the origin of this figure is to be found in the Vedic expressions which connect the goat and Pushan together: and Pushan brandishing his goad and driving the cattle, the protector and guide of travellers, and the showerer, messenger or avant-courier of the sun at the vernal equinox, 4000 B.C., may have been Oriōn, who with the Greeks became the Great Huntsman—the seven great stars of his shoulders, belt and knees being his seven-wheeled car.

With us, as with the herdsmen of the Asiatic steppes, Oriōn was so low in the heavens as to be in a measure obscured by the mists of the horizon, and might therefore be termed "son of the cloud;" and the expression, that he has two forms, one luminous and the other "venerable," so that the day is variously complexioned, he being like the sun, may have meant, simply, that sometimes, when he rose before the sun, at or before the dawn, he shone clearly and brightly, and sometimes was obscured and dimmed by the gray haze and vapourous mist, and that the day which followed was in like manner either clear or bright, or cloudy, the sun shining brightly or being obscured, according as his avant-courier was one or the other.

It was natural that the constellation which to the Greeks became a giant and a huntsman, brandishing a club studded with stars, should have been, to a race of herdsmen on the Scythic plains, a herdsman like themselves, brandishing his goad. And as, when Auriga, the charioteer, composed of Capella and the Hædi, the she-goat and the kids, rises heliacally, the sun enters Taurus: and, as the Greeks made Seirios the hound of Oriōn, the Indian Aryans may have fancied the stars of Auriga to be his goats, driven by five invisible reins. And, if Oriōn was Pushan, it was natural they should say to him, when he rose, announcing the coming of the sun, at the time of the vernal equinox,

> **Pushan, invoked before the dawn, upon the close of night, appear now in the firmament for the welfare of mankind.**

I have only to add, that as we know how completely the Greeks and Latins had forgotten the original significations of the Aryan Gods, and how they imputed to them, calling them by other names or those radically the same, entirely different and contradictory characteristics, it is natural to believe that this was also to some extent the case with the Indian Aryans of the Punjab; and that it would be strange if we did *not* find expressions in regard to them, hard to reconcile, and even utterly irreconcilable with, their original characters and personalities. It is, indeed, to be wondered at, and is most fortunate, that in the free compositions, rich in figurative phrases and expressions, of a long succession of Poets, we should be able to trace with so much certainty the original outlines of most of the Deities, and gain so much and clear insight into the workings of that Aryan intellect, which shines, clear as a star, through all the haze and splendid colourings of the poetic imagination and phraseology.

And with this, and all our doubts and conjectures, we submit it to the reader to decide what Pushan truly and originally was.

BHAGA.

Ushas is called the sister of *Bhaga* and Varuṇa: and Bhaga is often mentioned in connection with Mitra, Varuṇa and Aryaman. In *Sûkta iii. Anuv. xx. Adhy. i. Ashṭ. ii.*, it is said,

> 2. The most excellent dawn has been seen proceeding to the comprehensive, the path of the revolving has been lighted up by rays: the eyes of men, by the rays of Bhaga: the brilliant mansion of Mitra, of Aryaman, of Varuṇa . . . .

Elsewhere it is said,

> Thou, Agni, art Draviṇodas . . . . thou art the divine Savitṛi . . . . Protector of men, thou art Bhaga, and rulest over wealth . . . . May Mitra, Aryaman, Bhaga, the multi-present Varuṇa, the powerful Ansa, hear us. Bhaga, Saviour, grant us thrice a day riches of three elements [here he is named after Savitṛi] . . . . How can we offer praise to the mighty posterity of Rudra, or to the all-knowing Bhaga? . . . . May our . . . . praise . . . . attain Varuṇa, Mitra, Bhaga and Aditi . . . . I approach today the divine Savitṛi and Bhaga, the distributors of precious among men . . . . Pushan, Bhaga, Aditi, bestow excellent viands . . . . we solicit of the divine Savitṛi . . . . may we receive from Bhaga that which is excellent. May the divine Savitṛi and Bhaga, and the grandson of the waters, ... preserve us . . . . I praise you, protectors of the solemn sacrifice, the well-born Aditi, Mitra and Varuṇa and Aryaman and Bhaga . . . . May the divine Savitṛi, Bhaga and Diti give us wealth. [Elsewhere he is named with Sansa and Purandhi; with Pushan and Vaja] . . . . Verily Bhaga is to be adored by men, who, abounding in wealth, distribute treasures . . . . The ardent repeatedly invokes Bhaga for protection; the less ardent solicits Bhaga for wealth . . . . The swift Bhaga, the Nasatyas and Purandhi . . . . Riches that Vayu and Bhaga may always preserve in our keeping.

In *Sûkta viii. Anuv. iii. Adhy. iv. Ashṭ. v.*:

> 3. Bhaga, chief leader of rites, Bhaga, faithful promiser of wealth, Bhaga, granting, make fruitful this ceremony . . . .
>
> 4. May we now have Bhaga, whether in the forenoon or at midday or at sunrise . . . .
>
> 6. . . . . as rapid steeds convey a chariot, so may the dawns bring to us Bhaga, down-descending.

Elsewhere, we find named together,

> Agni, Bhaga, Indra, Vishṇu, Pûshan, Brahmaṇaspati . . . . Mitra, Aryaman, Savitṛi, Bhaga, bestow today at sunrise . . . . May Savitṛi, Bhaga, Varuṇa,

> Mitra and Aryaman bestow upon us . . . . these sons of Aditi know how to drive away enemies.

And, finally,

> Protected by Indra, well knowing the path that through thy power (Agni) we should follow, we adore that of thine, by which Varuṇa, Mitra, Aryaman, the Násatyas and Bhaga shine.

The Nasatyas are the Aṣwins (I think, Castor and Pollux); and Bhaga is certainly a luminary, either planet or star—possibly the planet Mercury or Saturn. The data are not sufficient to enable us to decide.

TWASHṬRI.

i. i. iv. ii.

10. I invoke the chief and multiform Twashṭri: may he be solely ours . . . .

i. ii. v. iii.

6. The Ribhus have divided into four, the new ladle, the work of the divine Twashṭri.

v.

9. Agni, bring hither the loving wives of the Gods, and Twashṭri, to drink the Soma juice.

Twashṭri sharpened the far-whirling thunderbolt of Indra. So he augmented Indra's vigour . . . . They found, on this occasion, the light of Twashṭri verily concealed in the mansion of the moving moon . . . . The skillful Twashṭri formed the thunderbolt for Indra. He is implored to send down water [and is said (note) to be the electric fire]. When Twashṭri observed the one ladle become four, *gnâsu antar nyânaje* [he became invisible among the females]. When Twashṭri said, Let us slay those who have profaned the ladle . . . . Twashṭri, who is the master (of) the forms, has made all animals distinct . . . . Thou Agni, art Twashṭri, of great wealth to worshipper . . . . May Twashṭri prolong for us a continuous line of progeny. . . . Twashṭri engendered thee (Bṛihas-pati), amongst all beings: thou art the reciter of many a holy hymn. May the divine Twashṭri, the defender of the world, together with the wives, well pleased, urge on the chariot . . . . Divine Twashṭri. . . . give issue to our procreative vigour . . . . The divine Twashṭri, the able artificer, the dextrous-handed, the possessor of wealth, the observer of truth—Twashṭri, the lord of foundations, ... Indra, the prototype, has assumed many forms, ... Indra, multiform by his illusions, proceeds; . . . . yoking his horses to his car, Twashṭri shines in many places here in the three worlds. . . . . Twashṭri, the first divider (of forms), the renowned, the giver of food, the well-handed [skillful], the vast, the adored of men living in houses, the readily invoked . . . . Mitra, with Twashṭri and Aryaman, accept our praise . . . . Divine Twashṭri . . . . give issue to our procreative vigour . . . . When the wives come before us, may the dextrous Twashṭri grant us male progeny . . . . May Twashṭri be propitiated by this our praise; may he who is of comprehensive understanding, be inclined to give us wealth. May the generous Twashṭri be our sure refuge: may he give us riches . . . . May Twashṭri, with the wives of the Gods, be for our happiness, and hear us.

Only by means of the heat of fire, could the metals, and especially iron, be wrought into shape and form, into weapons of war and the chase, implements of husbandry, and tools for the artificer, and implements for household use. The iron must glow and blaze with splendour, at a white heat, before it can be hammered into shape, and especially before it can be welded.

It *feeds* the fire, also, being consumed by it, by degrees. It glitters and scintillates, and by applying it to dry materials, new birth may be given to Agni, by the constant creation of blazing flame.

Twashṭṛi is the original of Mulciber or Vulcan. He is the artificer of the Gods, the creator of forms. Without the heat of the fire, the silver and copper could not be extracted from the ore, nor the materials of bronze be made to combine, nor the gold or silver be worked into ornaments, nor the bronze or lead be melted and moulded into forms. As producer of these effects, Agni is Twashṭṛi. Naturally, to these were conjoined the effects of Agni, as the warmth of the sun, and the vital and animal heat, by which the varied forms of vegetation are produced, and the germ in the seed develops and grows into the herb, the grain, the shrub, the trees, the leaf and flower and fruit, and the formless seed in the womb into the animal or child, born with form and features and life. As producing these effects, also, Agni is Twashṭṛi, who gives issue to men's procreative vigour, and who also forges or sharpens the glittering, keen-edged, solid thunderbolt of Indra.

Twashṭṛi comes with the wives of the Gods: and perhaps we have here the germ which afterwards developed into the idea of the Sole Deity, Brahm, dividing himself into male and female, and of that worship of the generative energy which degenerated into that of the lingam and priapos.

RUDRA.

These passages relating to Rudra, are found in the Veda:

The brilliant and vigourous Maruts, who are of (or belonging to) Rudra .... The wise, the most bountiful and mighty Rudra, who is in our hearts. By which (hymn) Aditi may grant the gifts of Rudra [*Rudriya*] to our cattle, our people, our cows and our progeny. By which Mitra and Varuṇa and Rudra and all the Gods, being gratified, may show us (favour) .... Rudra, the encourager of hymns, the protector of sacrifices, possessed of medicaments that confer happiness.

The Maruts are gliders, the sons of Rudra .... the sons of Pṛiṣni.

i. viii. xvi. ix.

1. We offer these praises to the mighty Rudra, with the braided hair [*kapardine*], the father of imperial heroes.

3. Rudra, showerer .... come to our posterity, with purpose to promote their happiness ....

4. The illustrious Rudra, the accomplisher of sacrifices, he who goes crookedly, the wise ....

5. We invoke from heaven, with reverence, him who has excellent food, who is radiant, and has braided hair, who is brilliant, and is to be ascertained ....

6. This praise .... is addressed to Rudra, the father of the Maruts, immortal Rudra ....

10. Of whom the imperial heroes are the sons, ... brilliant hero .... thou who art mighty over the two ....

11. .... May Rudra, with the Maruts, hear our invocation ....

Elsewhere we find:

The reward showering Rudra .... who, with his heroic, as from a quiver, expelled from heaven .... the Maruts between heaven and earth .... the self-glorifying Rudra .... Thou Agni, art Rudra, the expeller from the expanse of heaven; thou art the strength of the Maruts .... Father of the Maruts, thou art the chiefest of beings in glory; thou, wielder of the thunderbolt, art the mightiest of the mighty .... Invigorate our sons by thy medical plants, for I hear that thou art a chief physician among physicians .... Rudra, who is soft-bellied, of a tawny hue, and handsome chin .... May the showerer of benefits, the lord of the Maruts, gratify me, his suppliant, with invigorating food: .... Where, Rudra, is thy joy-dispensing hand, which is the healer and delighter? .... who art the dispeller of the sins of the Gods .... The showerer, the cherisher, the white-complexioned, the consumer: we glorify the illustrious name of Rudra .... With strong limbs, assuming many forms, fierce, and tawny-coloured, he shines with brilliant golden ornaments: vigour is inseparable from Rudra, the supreme ruler and lord of this world . . . . Thou bearest arrows and a bow . . . . thou wearest an adorable and uniform necklace [*nishka*, so interpreted (*hâra*) by the scholiast]. The renowned Rudra, riding in his car, ever youthful, destructive, fierce, like a formidable wild beast . . . . Giver of much, protector of the virtuous, bestow healing herbs upon me . . . . May the javelin of Rudra avoid us: may the great displeasure of the radiant Deity pass away: . . . . Cherisher of the world, omniscient and divine, ... Golden-breasted Maruts, the vigourous one begot you of the pure womb of Pṛiṣni . . . . The man-destroying Rudra . . . . the object of worship, the giver of the oblation.

Praise him who has the sure arrow, the strong bow, who presides over all sanitary drugs; worship Rudra, for a comprehensive and sound understanding.

Exalt Rudra with these hymns, by day, the parent of the world: . . . . animated by the far-seeing, we invoke him, mighty, of pleasing aspect, undecaying, endowed with felicity, prosperity.

May Rudra and Saraswati, alike well-pleased, and Vishṇu and Vayu make us happy, sending rain . . . .

Asht. v. Adhy. i. Anuv. vi. Sûkta xiii.

1. Soma and Rudra . . . . possessors of the seven precious things [Qu. rays?].

4. Sharp-weaponed, sharp-arrowed, profoundly honoured Soma and Rudra, grant us happiness in this world.

Elsewhere, again,

Agni, associated with the Rudras, with the Vasus . . . .

Adhy. iv. Anuv. iii. Sûkta xiii.

1. Offer these praises to the divine Rudra, armed with the strong bow and fast-flying arrows, the bestower of food, the invincible, the conqueror, the creator, the wielder of sharp weapons . . . .

2. He is known by his rule over those of terrestrial birth, by his sovereignty over those of celestial . . . . Come to our dwellings, and be to them a guardian against disease.

3. May thy blazing, which, discharged from heaven, traverses the earth, miss us: thine, appeaser of the wind, are a thousand medicaments . . . .

Elsewhere,

these resplendent chiefs, the dwellers in one abode, the sons of Rudra . . . . those white-complexioned beings, whom the vast Pṛiṣni bore at her udder.

Dr. Muir (*Orig. Sansk. Texts, 252 et seq.*) gives the originals and translations of all the Sanskrit texts of the Rig-Veda, in which Rudra is addressed or spoken of. I quote such passages, phrases and expressions as, by different interpretation or otherwise, may afford additional data for determining what Rudra was. The references are always to *Mandala*, *Hymn* and *Verse*.

i. 27. 10. Agni is termed *Rudrâya:* and in *x.* 70. 2, 3 and *viii.* 26. 5, the same epithet is applied to Mitra and Varuṇa and to the Aṣvins, respectively.

The root *rud* means to "resound," to "groan;" and *rudh*, to "care for, defend." *Ruh* is to "grow, increase;" whence *rûḍhis*, "growth." From one or the other of these, probably, *Rudra* is derived. In the place first cited, it is rendered "terrible."

i. 43. What can we utter to Rudra, the intelligent, the most bountiful, the strong, which shall be most pleasant to his heart? That so Aditi may bring Rudra's healing to our cattle and men and kine and children? . . . . We seek from Rudra, the lord of songs, the lord of sacrifices, who possesses healing remedies, his auspicious favour. Who is brilliant as the sun, who shines like gold, who is the best and the brightest of the Gods. He grants prosperity and welfare to our horses, rams, ewes, men, women, and cows.

In *i.* 64. 2, the Maruts are styled *Rudrasya*, the sons and offspring of Rudra, produced from the sky (*diva*): and, *i.* 85. 1, we find, "The Maruts" (*Marutaṣ*), energetic sons of Rudra (*Rudrâya*).

i. 114. In this hymn, Rudra (*Rudrâya*) is the strong, with braided hair (*karparddin*), ruling over heroes. He is invoked to the end that there may be prosperity for man and beast in the village, and that everything in it may be well-fed, and free from disease. He is invoked to be gracious and cause happiness. He is ruler over heroes, and beneficent. He is impetuous, the fulfiller of sacrifice, the crooked-goer, the wise. "The dark-hued celestial boar (cloud?) with braided hair, a brilliant form" (*divo varaham, arusham kaparddinam twesham rupam*), is invoked with obeisance. He is besought to be gracious, and not to slay the worshipper or those near to him, nor to injure them or theirs.

Like a keeper of cattle, I have prepared for thee hymns [it is said]: Far from us be thy cow-slaying and man-slaying [weapon]: Be gracious to us, *deva*, and intercede for us, and bestow on us prosperity, lord of both worlds [*yachha dvi-barhâḥ*].

i. 122. 1. The bountiful Rudra: . . . . The praise of the divine Marut [*divo Maruto*] is celebrated in heaven and earth [*rodasayah—rodasi* being taken always to mean both].

i. 129. 3. Indra, I have uttered this at length to thee, and to the sky, and to Rudra *svâ-yasase* [who derives his renown from himself], and to Mitra and to Varuṇa.

ii. 1. 6. Thou, Agni, art Rudra, the Deity of the great sky [*Rudro asuro maho divas*]. Thou art the host of the Maruts . . . . Thou, Pushan, by thyself protectest those who worship thee.

ii. 33. In this hymn the worshipper asks Rudra for kindness and increase of offspring, and for long life (a hundred winters) through the remedies conferred by him. He is invoked to drive away enmities, sins and diseases. He is styled vigourous, and the greatest physician of physicians, and is asked to cure the sick. He is mild, easily invoked, tawny, with a beautiful chin, fair-complexioned, fiery, of glorious name; firm of limbs, multiform, fierce, tawny, invested with bright golden ornaments. He gladdens the suppliant with invigorating nourishment. His hand is healing and restorative, and removes the evil that comes from the Gods. Divine power is ever inseparable from Rudra, the lord of this vast world. Governing, he holds arrows and a bow, and a glorious bracelet of every form. Nothing is more powerful than he. He is renowned and youthful, mounted on his chariot like a terrible wild beast, destructive and fierce: and yet he can be gracious, and is the giver of much, and lord of the excellent. The worshipper prays for the pure, auspicious, beneficent remedies of the Maruts, and for the blessing and favour of Rudra.

> May the *bolt* of Rudra [it is said], avoid us! May the great malevolence of the fiery depart far from us. Unbend thy strong bows . . . . Dispenser of good, be gracious to our children and descendants. Tawny and vigourous, intelligent God, Rudra.

I do not doubt that if we can but ascertain exactly what was personified as Rudra, all these enigmatical phrases and contradictory attributes will become clear, consistent and harmonious. It is positively certain, since Agni is declared to be Rudra, that the latter is some manifestation of the former, certain potencies of Agni in action, Agni performing or possessing certain functions, and producing certain effects. He is a subsistence of the substance which is Agni. He can be wild, fierce, destructive. He wields the thunderbolt, bends the bow, and hurls the arrows; and yet he is gracious, easily propitiated, dispenses benefits, heals the sick and gives long life. He is the most eminent of beings, vigourous, energetic, source of his own renown; he slays, and he lengthens life. He has divine power, and is lord of the universe, governs, and possesses all the vast. Nothing is more powerful than he: he is renowned and youthful. Physically, he is tawny, and yet white-complexioned, fiery, strong-limbed, many-formed, with a beautiful chin, with braided hair; and he wears bright golden ornaments and a golden bracelet.

Pushan and the Tritsus are also spoken of, elsewhere [*vi.* 55. 2: *ix.* 67. 11: *vii.* 83. 8], as wearing or adorned with braided hair (*kaparddin*). And the Maruts, also, are adorned with armlets, and wear jewels on their breasts: and yet they are invisible. And Rudra is said to be a brilliant form, brilliant as the sun, shining like gold, the best and brightest of the Gods. He is impetuous, wise, dark-hued, celestial, a crooked goer, and fulfiller of sacrifice: i. e., he performs the last and final office of the sacrificial fire, in conveying the oblation to the Gods.

When we find what there is among the phenomena of fire, that in appearance, action and effect fulfills all these conditions, we shall have found out what Rudra was. It is clear that he was not a luminary, and he was not light; nor does flame fulfill *all* these conditions. These conditions, I say—but there is one other—that this subsistence or hypostasis of Agni must be that which could naturally appear to the Poets to be the cause of great movements of the air, and thus to be the generator of the winds.

In *Mand. iii.* 2. 5, the sacrificial fire, burning upon the grass, Agni the brilliant, acceptable to all the Gods (*viṣva-devyaṁ*), is termed *rudra*, which is translated "terrible." Certainly that epithet is not applicable to Agni as the fire of the sacrifice. I think that *rudra* is from the root *ruh*, meaning to "rise, ascend, swell up, grow, expand, increase."

In *Mand. iv.* 3. 1. 6. 7, we have *Agne-Rudrâya*, and *Agnim Rudram* (translated *Agni the terrible*); and Rudra is styled "the man-slaying," "the adored, the giver of oblations."

In *Mand. v.* 42. 11, the worshippers are urged to adore with prostrations Rudra, "the spiritual Deity" (*devam asuram.* "Spiritual" is a sublimated rendering of *Asura*).

In *Mand. v.* 52. 16, he is called the *rapid* Rudra; and in *v.* 60. 5, "young and energetic."

In *Mand. vi.* 49. 10, he is called *Bhuvanasya pitaraṁ*, "father of the exist ing," or the "world," the mighty, the exalted, the undecaying, the blessed.

In *Mand. vi.* 74, Soma and Rudra are invoked, bearing with them seven jewels, to favour man and beast and drive away disease, by their remedies; and their weapons are said to be sharp and their bolts piercing.

In *vii.* 46, he is called "Rudra with the strong bow and swift arrows, the self-dependent, unassailable, the assailant, the disposer, armed with sharp weapons." *Devaya svadhavne* is the original here, of "self-dependent." Professor Roth considers *svadhâvat* to mean "independent," "whose glory is inherent;" and elsewhere gives to *svadhâ* the sense of "according to one's own determination," "according to pleasure." I think the meaning here, clearly is, that the potencies and energies of Rudra are inherent in him as a subsistence of Agni, as distinguished from those which the luminaries receive from Agni, of whom they are not subsistences or hypostases, but only instruments and organs. In the same Mandala and Hymn, it is said, "By his potency he perceives the terrestrial race, and by his universal dominion that of the sky (*divyasya*, which Dr. Muir translates "divine").

In *Mand. viii.* 20. 17, is the phrase, "Rudra, the Deity of the sky." In *viii.* 22. 14, the Aṣwins are called *rudrau*, lords of wealth; and in *viii.* 61. 3, we have the same adjective, in each place rendered "terrible." And, *x.* 64. 8, we have *Rudraṁ Rudeshu rudriyaṁ*, "Rudra, terrible among the Rudras." In *x.* 66. 3, *Rudro Rudrebhir devo*, "divine Rudra with the Rudras."

In *Mand. x.* 92. 5,

> The waters flow, by the moving Rudra . . . . with them the circumambient, roaring God, who moves round the wide expanse, fertilizes all contained in its womb . . . . the mighty Rudra, the ruler of heroes, ... those rapid and ardent Deities, with whom the gracious and opulent, who derives his renown from himself, comes down from the sky.

Professor Wilson remarks that the name *Rudra* is unequivocally applied to Agni; and that although the scholiast renders it "terrible," there is no warrant for this in the text; and he says,

> we may be content, therefore, with the latter, to regard Rudra as a *form* or *denomination* of fire.

In the later ages of the Hindū mythology, Rudra became identified with Mahadeva or Siva and elevated to the highest rank in the Indian pantheon. Dr. Muir gives the texts of several of the Hindū books, and traces "the successive mutations which the conception of this Deity undergoes, in the later, as compared with the earlier passages." Writing for the Hindūs themselves, he sought to show them the real source of all their mythological nonsense; and has admirably executed his work. All the later myths, legends and fables about Rudra are the fruits of passages, phrases and words of the Veda, in regard to him, misunderstood. So it is that the figures and hyperboles of the Poet, the word-paintings of the poetic imagination, literally understood in after ages, became the germs of monstrous fables and a grotesque idolatry, until we have the linga infinite in its dimensions, as God the creator, and all the abominations of the phallic and priapian worship. The symbols of the sages and the figures of the Poets always become the idols of the vulgar.

Professor Weber remarks that

> the epithet *kapardddin seems* to have some relation to a characteristic attribute of Siva, the wearing of his hair in a peculiar manner; but, he says, the term has probably in the Veda a very different signification—one now forgotten—although it may have suggested in aftertime the appearance of Siva in such a head-dress, as identified with Agni. [It may have meant, he says, that Rudra's head was surrounded with a radiating flame.]

Professor Wilson, quoted by Dr. Muir (*Orig. Sansk. Texts, iv.* 334), thinks that *Rudra* originally signified, generally, the "howler," "and can consequently stand as well for an epithet of the crackling fire as of the raging storm." In the earliest period, he thinks, the word had been used to denote the latter signification. The unbridled fury of the storms, their roaring and fearful effects must, he says, have produced a strong and overpowering effect on the Aryan Indians, in the high mountain valleys in which they then lived.

But I find little in what is said of Rudra in the Veda, to give countenance to the idea that his name had the signification of "roaring." In fact, he is but once spoken of as "roaring" or as making a noise of any kind. *Rûḍhis* means *growth* and *vigour;* and I doubt whether *rudra* even means "terrible." It is true that *rud* is to "resound," to "groan;" and *raudat, ruditan*, a "cry" or "murmur;" but if the name were derived from that root, one would expect to find in the epithets applied to Rudra, and the phrases used in speaking of him and to him, some allusion to that meaning of his name.

Professor Weber remarks that it was natural that the Aryans should connect everything terrible and horrible with the idea of the God of storms, and regard him as the lord and the cause of every evil.

But Rudra is not so regarded in the Veda. It is true, Professor Weber says,

> that Rudra is also appealed to as wise and bountiful, author of fertility and giver of happiness; but it is only indirectly that he is so addressed, and merely because he departs, and directs his destroying arrows towards some other quarter, against the enemies of the suppliant, and leaves the latter himself in peace.

The worshipper, he thinks, is merely cajoling the God, with insincere words. True, he heals diseases, but he is only beneficent so far as he chases away clouds and vapours and purifies the atmosphere; and he carries diseases and contagions as arrows in his quiver, and with them slays men and cattle. Dr. Muir thinks these "ingenious and interesting speculations." They utterly misrepresent the Veda. Professor Wilson much more truly says, of the Vedic Rudra,

> He is termed the slayer of heroes, but so is Indra: the effects of his anger upon men and animals are deprecated; but . . . . his peculiar characteristics are evidently his presiding over medicinal plants and removal of disease, attributes of a beneficent, not of a malignant and irascible Deity.

In truth, he is essentially and in the highest degree a beneficent, bountiful dispenser of good, gracious, easily propitiated, kind and mild in his benevolence. As the storms are rare and occasional, so is his anger and fierceness. He is the father of the winds, and they furnish his attributes. He is the "healing Rudra," and "men making obeisance in their own place of sacrifice, seek by worship his friendship, and life." Lauded by men, he has distributed food amongst them. This reverence is most dear to Rudra: and hymn 169. *v.* 1, of the Tenth Mandala expresses the Aryan appreciation of him and of the wind:

> may the wind, causing prosperity, blow upon the cows. Let them consume invigorating herbage; let them drink, being fat and life-sustaining: Rudra, be gracious to our moving sources of food.

After summing up what is said of Rudra in the Veda, Dr. Muir says that

> in most places Rudra has no clearly defined function [such, for instance, as is ascribed to Indra and Agni, or even to Vishṇu] as an agent in producing the great phenomena of the physical world. [He thinks that] it would be difficult to make out, from the larger portion of the texts cited, to what region of the universe his activity should be referred.

As father of the Maruts, he thinks, it might be expected

> that he would be described as, even more eminently than they, the generator of tempest and chaser of clouds;

but that except in a small number of texts, there are few distinct traces of any such agency being ascribed to him. The numerous vague epithets applied to him, Dr. Muir thinks, would not suffice to fix the particular sphere of his operation, or even to define his personality, as most of them are equally applied to other Deities. But Dr. Muir regards him as principally a malevolent Deity, who heals when he ceases to destroy, only, and whom the worshipper flatters and cajoles, fearing to excite his jealousy by calling in any other Deity, to provide a remedy. I do not read the Veda in that sense, at all. If we can conceive of God as the author of both good and evil, I do not see why our remote ancestor could not conceive of a Deity generally beneficent, and occasionally fierce and destructive. That is the nature of the winds: and one can surely conceive of the possibility of what he actually sees and feels.

In the lower country of the Punjab, intersected by rivers, and alluvial, and covered with a rank vegetation—in which the fruits of the tropics grew and the summer heat was oppressive, the same diseases must have been common, as prevail in the southern part of the United States, bilious and typhoid fevers, and chills. When the south winds ceased to blow, and the cool northern breezes came down from the summits of the mountains, they came with healing in their wings to the sick, even when they were preceded by elemental commotions and thunderstorms. Even the monsoons purified the air, and healthful winds, the beneficent Maruts, succeeded them. And I wonder it did not occur to Dr. Muir and Professor Weber, that the Maruts, the direct authors of the storms, are continually represented and invoked as most beneficent Deities.

Two effects of fire, no one could fail at once to notice. It expands water into vapour, and causes the vapour and its smoke to ascend. A little observation would show that it caused an ascending movement of the air, because the observer would see small things of little weight, leaves and chaff, carried upward by the current so created. Above the flame he would see a visible rippling of a thin transparent substance; and this he could discern even in the warm sunshine. In the case of a great conflagration of the grassy plains or of the woods, he would find the fire, if long continued, causing wind and rain.

He would see the smoke and rarefied vapours eddy and whirl in the air, and whatever they took up with them carried in spiral circles higher and higher up, until they disappeared. He would soon attribute to a like agency the little whirls of wind that dance, of a summer day, across the plains and along the roads. And he would not long delay, after personifying the light, the heat and the flame, and deifying the softening and melting potency of the fire and heat, to consider the power of expanding, of causing upward currents of air, and whirls, and even winds and rain, as a distinct function of Agni, if not as a subsistence of his substance, an hypostasis, and so to deify it, as he deified Tvashṭṛi. He could call the personification white-complexioned, because the rippling in the air caused by the heat is colourless and diaphanous, as one may imagine that silver, vapourized, would be. And, when the smoke ascended with it, he could call it dark-hued and tawny. The spiral curls of vapour would suggest an epithet that would compare them to ringlets, and which might by and by be taken to mean that the God who in action and manifested was this potency and energy, wore braided hair.

Once the conception of this immeasurable potency and force was attained, and Rudra became father of the winds, generated by him in the expanse, the imagination and fancy of the Poet would have a vast field in which to display their powers. As the heat from the sun fills the whole expanse, so would Rudra be deemed to exercise his powers everywhere; and as there would be no known limits to the powers, so there would none imaginable to their effects. The mode of action of the powers being unknown, the Poets' conceptions of Rudra would be vague and indefinite.

Father of the storm-winds as well as of the zephyrs of spring and the mountain breezes of the summer, and carrying the clouds hither and thither, the lightnings would be deemed his arrows, and the rains his gift. Issuing from the flame, he would still wear its colours as his golden ornaments, and be justly styled beautiful and brilliant. The Sanskrit terms that designate the features of the face and parts of the body are from roots that have general meanings; as, for example, *pad*, *padas*, *foot*, "that which goes or steps," from *pad*, to "go" or "march;" *nas*, *nâsâ*, *nose*, "that which projects," from *nas*, to "jut out, spring, leap forth." The epithets that in later ages had come to mean "soft-bellied," and "with a beautiful chin," had, it is very probable, in the Vedic age a meaning much nearer to those of the original roots, and less ridiculous as applied to a Deity. The Maruts are called "bright as suns," "brightly arrayed like women," "adorned with jewels;" and therefore Rudra, a fire-spirit, could well be styled "best and brightest of the Gods." He would naturally and aptly be called mobile, rapid, circumambient, the crooked-goer. He is *xayad-viraya*, which is translated "ruler over heroes." *Var* means to "cover, shield, defend, prevent;" whence *varas*, *viras*, a "male, husband;" *varas*, "obstacle, effort;" *varahas*, a "wild boar;" as well as *viras* and *vairin*, a "warrior, combatant." *Xayad* or *ksayad*, from *kṣi*, to "break, destroy," may mean "ruler," but it may also have meant "breaker, subduer, overcomer:" and the compound word may as well have meant "overcomer of obstacles," as "ruler of heroes." He is called *divo varāham arushaṁ*, which Dr. Muir translates, "the dark-hued celestial boar," with a query whether *varahaṁ* may not mean "cloud." *Varahas* came to mean a "wild boar," but its root meant to "cover, defend."

I do not find that the quiver of Rudra is represented as filled with contagion and disease, for arrows. He is represented as slaying men and cows, and his "cow-slaying weapon" is spoken of. It was not uncommon, I imagine, for men and cows to be killed by lightning. He could well be called "lord of songs," "lord of sacrifices," "lord of the sacrificial food," and the "fulfiller of the objects of sacrifices and rites," *Agne-Rudraya*, king of the sacrifice, for it is he that bears the oblation upward to the Gods.

What else can Rudra be, than I have said?

USHAS.

Asht. i. Adhy. i. Anuv. vi. Sûkta vii. (xxx.).

20. Ushas who art pleased by praise, what mortal enjoyeth thee, immortal?

21. Diffusive, many-tinted, brilliant. Daughter of heaven.

Adhy. iv. Anuv. ix. Sûkta v.

1. Ushas, daughter of heaven, dawn upon us with riches! . . . . Diffuser of light . . . . Bountiful Goddess.

4. Ushas, at thy comings wise men turn their minds to benefactions.

5. Ushas, nourishing all, comes daily like a matron.

6. She animates the diligent, and sends clients . . . . Shedder of dews, knows not delay. Bestower of food.

8. Bringer of good, she lights up the world. Affluent daughter of heaven.

13. Ushas, whose bright auspicious rays are visible all around.

14. Adorable Ushas, radiant with pure light.

15. Ushas, thou hast today set open the two gates of heaven with light.

Sûkta vi. (xlix.).

4. Thou, Ushas, dispersing the darkness, illuminest the shining universe with thy rays.

Adhy. vi. Anuv. xiv. Sûkta viii. (xcii.).

The Divinities of the morning [*Ushasah*, in the plural] have diffused light; they make manifest the light in the eastern portion of the firmament, brightening all things—the radiant and progressing mothers.

The Deities of the dawn, bright-rayed, have attended on the glorious sun. The female leaders illuminate with their inherent radiance the remotest parts.

Ushas cuts off the accumulated (glooms): she bares her bosom as a cow yields her udder: and as cattle hasten to their pastures, she speeds to the east, and shedding light upon all the world, dissipates the darkness. Bright-shining she smiles, lovely in all her radiance.

The divine and ancient Ushas, born again and again, and bright with unchanging hues . . . . wearing away the ages of the human race, she shines with light like the bride of the sun.

Adhy. viii. Anuv. xvi. Sûkta viii.

Mother of the Gods, rival of Aditi, illuminator of the sacrifice, mighty Ushas, shine forth.

Asht. ii. Adhy. i. Anuv. xviii. Sûkta iii.

The self-illumined dawn, is born, white-shining, out of the gloom.

Sûkta iv.

She, the daughter of heaven, is beheld in the east, gracious, and arrayed in lights . . . . Born in the eastern quarter of the spacious firmament, she displays a banner of rays of light.

8. Ushas, dispersing the darkness with the rays of the sun, illumines the world, like congregated lightnings.

11. This youthful (Ushas) approaches from the east. She harnesses her team of purple oxen.

Asht. iii. Adhy. iii. Anuv. v. Sûkta viii.

Affluent, giver of sustenance, possessed of intelligence . . . . divine, ancient, yet young. Divine, immortal. Ensign of the immortal (sun), opulent: bride of the far-darting sun. Auspicious, promoting sacred acts. Possessor of truth.

7. Mighty Ushas, the golden light, as it were, of Mitra and Varuṇa, diffuses her lustre in different directions.

Asht. v. Adhy. v. Anuv. v. Sûkta v.

The dawn, the daughter of heaven, has risen; she comes, manifesting her magnificence in light: she scatters our foes, as well as the odious darkness, and relumes the paths that are to be trodden . . . . The bride of Sûrya . . . . The light and wondrous steeds, conveying the resplendent Ushas, are visible. She advances, radiant in her every-way-moving chariot.

Sûkta vi.

The divine Savitṛi, the leader of all, sends upward the immortal, all-benefitting light: the eye of the Gods has been manifested, for religious rites: the dawn has made all creatures visible. The paths that lead to the Gods are beheld by me, innocuous, and glorious with light; the banner of Ushas is displayed in the east; she comes to the west, rising above high places.

Those ancient sages, our ancestors, observant of truth, rejoicing together with the Gods, discovered the hidden light, and, reciters of sincere prayers, they generated the dawn.

Sûkta vii.

Ushas shines radiant, in the proximity of the sun. Agni is to be kindled for the good of men. The dawn has risen: clothed in pure and brilliant vesture, she expands. Of golden colour and of lovely radiance, she shines, the parent of sounds, the leader of days.

The auspicious Ushas, bearing the eye of the Gods, leading her white and beautiful courser, is beheld, manifested by her rays.

SARASWATÎ.

The passages in which Saraswatî is mentioned are the following:

Asht. i. Adhy. i. Anuv. i. Sûkta iii.

10. May Saraswatî, the purifier, the bestower of food, the recompenser of worship with wealth, be attracted by our offered viands to our rite.

11. Saraswatî, the inspirer of those who delight in truth, the instructress of the right-minded, has accepted our sacrifice.

12. Saraswatî makes manifest by her acts a mighty river, and enlightens all understandings.

Anuv. iv. Sûkta ii.

May the three undecaying Goddesses [rivers, that never run dry], givers of delight, Ilâ, Saraswatî, and Mahî, sit down upon the sacred grass.

Adhy. vi. Anuv. xiv. Sûkta v.

3. We invoke them with an ancient text, Bhaga, Mitra, Aditi, Daksha, Asṛidh, Aryaman, Varuṇa, Soma, the Aṣwins; and may the gracious Saraswatî grant us happiness.

Asht. ii. Adhy. iii. Anuv. xxii. Sûkta viii.

49. Saraswatî, that retiring breast, which is the source of delight, with which thou bestowest all good things, which is the container of wealth, the distributor of riches, the giver of good; that do thou lay open at this season, for our nourishment.

Adhy. vii. Anuv. iii. Sûkta viii.

8. Saraswatî, do thou protect us! Associated with the Maruts, and firm, overcome our foes, whilst Indra slays the chief of the Saṇdikas, defying him and confiding in his strength.

Adhy. viii. Anuv. iv. Sûkta ix.

16. Saraswatî, best of mothers, best of rivers, best of Goddesses, ... grant us distinction.

17. In thee, Saraswatî, who art divine, all existences are collected; rejoice, Goddess, among the Sunahotras; grant us, Goddess, progeny.

18. Saraswatî, abounding in food, abounding in water, be propitiated . . . .

Anuv. i. Sûkta iv.

8. May Bhâratî, associated with the Bhâratîs; Ilâ, with the Gods and men; and Agni; and Saraswatî with the Sarawatas: may the three Goddesses sit down upon the sacred grass before them.

Asht. ii. Adhy. v. Anuv. i. Sûkta iii.

8. May the three Goddesses, Saraswatî, perfecting our understanding, the divine Ilâ, and all-impressive Bhâratî, having come to our dwelling, protect this faultless rite.

In *Sûkta i.* of the same,

Thou, divine Agni . . . . thou lord of wealth, art Aditi . . . . thou art Hotra and Bhâratî . . . . thou art Ilâ, of a hundred winters, to him who makes thee gifts; thou art the destroying Vritra, Saraswatî.

Thus Agni is either represented as bounteous as these rivers; or as *being* each, because he sends down the rains that feed them, melts the snows, and thaws the winter ice, in the spring.

Asht. iii. Adhy. i. Anuv. ii. Sûkta xi.

4. . . . . Do thou, Agni, shine on the frequented (banks) of the Drishadvatî, Âpayâ and Saraşwatî, rivers.

Elsewhere, Saraswatî and Râkâ are called "illustrious grantors of desires:" and in *Sûkta xi. Anuv. iii. Adhy. ii. of Asht. iv.*,

May the radiant Saraswatî come to the sacrifice from the heavens or the spacious firmament: may the Goddess, the showerer of water . . . . hear.

Rudra and Saraswatî, with Vishņu and Vayu, are invoked to send rain. Elsewhere she is called "Saraswatî, dwelling with rivers."

Asht. iv. Adhy. viii. Anuv. v. Sûkta xii., is addressed to Saraswatî.

1. She gave the donor of the oblations . . . . a son, endowed with speed, ... she who destroyed the churlish niggard . . . . such are thy great bounties, Saraswatî.

2. With impetuous and mighty waves she breaks down the precipices of the mountains, like a digger for the lotus fibres. We adore for our protection, with praises and with sacred rites, Saraswatî, the underminer of both her banks.

3. Destroy, Saraswatî, the revilers of the Gods, ... giver of sustenance, thou hast acquired for men the lands, and hast showered water upon them.

She is called in this hymn, the divine Saraswatî, the protectress of her worshippers; the fierce Saraswatî, riding in a golden chariot, the destructress of enemies; she whose might, infinite, undeviating, splendid, progressive, water-shedding, proceeds loud-sounding; dearest among those dear to us; filling the vast expanse of earth and heaven; abiding in the three worlds, comprising seven elements, cherishing the five races, ever to be invoked in battle. She is distinguished among them, as eminent in greatness and in her glories. She is the most impetuous of all streams: she has been created vast in capacity as a chariot.

And she is invoked to sustain the worshipper with viands, to protect him engaged in conflict for the sake of wealth; to

> overcome all our adversaries, and bring to us her other water-laden sisters, as the ever-rolling sun, the days.

She has seven sisters, and is ever adorable: and she is invoked not to overwhelm with water.

In *Sûkta iii. Anuv. iii. Adhy. iv. Asht. iv.* we read:

> 6. May the seventh, Saraswatî, the mother of the Sindhu, and those rivers that flow copious and fertilizing, bestowing abundance of food, and nourishing, by their waters, come at once together.

Sûkta vi. Anuv. vi. Adhy. vi. Asht. v. is addressed to Saraswatî. We condense it as follows:

> This Saraswatî, firm as a city made of iron, flows rapidly with sustaining water, sweeping away in its might all other waters, as a charioteer. Saraswatî, chief and purest of rivers, flowing from the mountains to the ocean, understood the request of Nârusha, and distributing riches among the many existing beings, milked for him butter and water. [The third stanza is addressed to the Showerer Saraswat, friend of man, who, even while a child, increases among his adorable wives; and bestows upon the affluent a vigourous son; and purifies their person, for the reception.]
>
> The auspicious and gracious Saraswatî .... White-complexioned, be magnified: bestow food on him who glorifies thee, and ever cherish us with blessings.

Sûkta vii. is also to Saraswatî:

> Saraswatî, who is both in heaven and earth [because the rains that *are* the river come from the expanse, and the springs rise out of the earth]. Beautiful Saraswatî, inasmuch as by this might men obtain both kinds of food .... friend of the Maruts, bestow riches .... the auspicious Saraswatî, ... the faultless-moving, food-conferring .... [In the three last stanzas, Saraswat is invoked, the fifth and sixth being]: with these thy waves, Saraswat, which are sweet-tasted, the distributors of water, be our protector. May we recline upon the protuberant breast of Saraswat, which is visible to all, that we may possess progeny and food.

Twice, Ilâ, Saraswatî and Mahî are invoked, as Goddesses, together, in the whole Veda.

It is quite evident that Saraswatî is more than the river of that name. She is also the river Goddess, the prototype of the Goddesses of the Grecian mythology. Saraswat must have been the male Deity of the same river, the water God. These were probably later conceptions of the Aryan mind; and yet the conception of Saraswatî *may* have been a very early one; and it is akin to the idea formed of Agni and his manifestations. This plainly appears, in the first text that we have quoted—from the First Ashṭaka. In that, Saraswatî is first addressed as a Deity, propitiated by worship, and rewarding it, inspirer of those who delight in truth, and instructress of the right-minded; if these phrases at all reproduce the real sense of the original. And immediately afterwards, she is said to "make manifest by her acts a mighty river," by which I understand that she, the invisible spirit or substance, manifests herself in act, outwardly and visibly, as an actual river, as, in more modern idea, the Deity manifests Himself, by utterance, in the visible and material universe. But how, by thus becoming embodied, and invested with actuality as a river, she "enlightens all understandings," I must leave to others to explain; certain, only, that this phrase, which is mere nonsense, does *not* reproduce the sense of the original.

Her "retiring breast" that is the source of delight, is probably the river's hidden source in the high mountains in which it rises. The "existences," all of which are "collected" in her, are, probably, all streams, characterized as actualities, and which are included in her, as, in later philosophies the universe exists in idea in the Deity, before it is uttered outwardly, and *becomes*, as the manifold of existence. Her seven sisters may be the seven rivers of the Punjab, or the Pleiades, as shedders of rain. She is said to fill the vast expanse of earth and heaven, and abide in the three worlds, comprising seven elements, and cherishing the five races: and, in the same breath, she is declared to be the most impetuous of all the streams. That these enigmatical phrases are applied to her, of whose personality there is no doubt, and that they seem utterly inappropriate, proves that they are not correct renderings of the originals, and also contents us with like phrases that seem equally inconsistent with the character and personality that we have ascribed to other Deities, where there was no such certainty. No doubt, if we knew their real meaning, the apparent inappropriateness and incongruity would disappear.

The seven "elements" "comprised" by her, may mean the seven parts or branches, that unite to form the one river; and this would indicate that Saraswatî was the Indus. What the five races were, it is impossible to tell. Probably, five different tribes or peoples, through whose countries the river or rivers ran. The three regions in which she abides may be earth, expanse and sky, in which she was supposed to be present as the spirit or invisible substance or essential principle of water; or they may be the mountains, the forests and the alluvial plains.

She fills the great expanse, as the vapour that forms the clouds and falls in rain.

In the Fifth Ashṭaka, as we have seen, she is expressly called the seventh, the mother of the Sindhu, and is invoked to come to the sacrifice.

As a river, therefore, she is the Sindhu or Indus. She may at first have been the Oxus; and long afterwards the Jumna or Yamuna. But it is clear that to the Ṛishis of the Country of the Seven Rivers, she was, as a river, the Indus, flowing from the mountains, impetuous, regardless of obstacles, and tearing huge masses from its banks, when, overflowing it devastated by inundation the alluvial lands.

In the Hindū mythology, she became the wife of Brahma, Goddess of harmony, arrangement, and the creative acts; of learning, music and poetry. And she also became a sacred and mythical river, which, rising in the mountains, flowed underground, to fall into the Ganges at Allahabad, where the Yamuna united with it. This meeting of the three sacred rivers is called *Triveni*, or "the three-plaited locks."—*Moor*, *Oriental Fragm.* 251. Allahabad is the modern Mohammedan name of the city. The Hindūs call it *Prayaga*, "the Union," and *Devi-Prayaga*, "the Union of the Goddesses."

This seems to indicate that after the Indian Aryans crossed the Ganges, Saraswatī was the Yamuna, and afterwards assumed a mythical character, because there was no stream except that, to which the language of the Veda in regard to Saraswatī could apply.

Whether the Aryans of the Punjab, before crossing the Sutlej, knew anything about the ocean into which the Indus falls, and meant that by the sea to which Saraswatī runs from the mountains; or whether it indicates that she was originally the Oxus, receiving seven streams from the mountains in Bactria, and pouring the aggregated waters into the great Caspian Sea, no one can decide.

THE RIBHUS.

The Ribhus, it is said (protecting and fostering), hastened to the presence of Indra, and by them, encouraging words were uttered. Professor Wilson remarks that here they are the Maruts. Elsewhere he says that a text of the Veda identifies them with the solar rays; and they are indeed said to be the rays of the sun. In *Sûkta v. Anuv. xvi. Adhy. vii. Asht. i.* they are said to have been among the ancestors of the worshipper, and that they were the sons of Sudhanwan (who was a descendant of the Angiras). Savitṛi bestowed on them immortality. Brilliant as the sun, they became associated with the ceremony. Associated with Indra, they also builded a car for the Aṣwins, and framed the vigourous horses for Indra. In the Third Ashṭaka, also, they are called grandsons of a man, sons of Sudhanwan;

> swift as the wind, the doers of good works, they were borne quickly across the expanse by rapid steeds. When, reposing for twelve days, they remained in the hospitality of the unconcealable, they rendered the fields fertile, they led forth the rivers, plants sprung upon the waste, and waters covered the low places. They were the artificers of the Gods, and formed the all-impelling, multiform milch-cow. They made the ladle four-fold. They soar aloft in the sky like falcons. Vâja, Ribhu and Vibhwan are named among them: and they are called Vâjins and Ribhukshans, and Vâjas. They are sons of strength, possessors of wealth, and givers of precious things; and Indra and the Ribhus overcame all foes.

It is not easy to see how some of these expressions apply to either the winds or the rays of the sun. If the Ribhus were the winds, it would not be said of them that "swift as the wind" they were borne anywhere. How could the winds be said to build chariots and form horses, for the Aṣwins and Indra? If they are the rays of the sun, would it be said that they are "brilliant as the sun"? How could either the wind or the rays of the sun be associated with the ceremony? What meaning is there in the phrase "reposing for twelve days, they remained in the hospitality of the unconcealable," as applied either to the winds, or the rays of the sun? What are the meanings of their being artificers of the Gods, forming the all-impelling, many-formed milch-cow, and making the ladle four-fold?

They are men, Ṛishis, sons of Sudhanwan, descendants of the Angiras, on whom Savitṛi bestowed immortality, by transferring them to the skies, wherein they soar aloft like falcons. Three of them are named—Vâja, Ribhu and Vibhwan. That they hastened to the presence of Indra and uttered encouraging words, means that they were ministers of the sacrifices to Indra, and offered up prayer and adoration to him.

The Seven Ṛishis, translated in like manner to heaven, became the Seven Stars of Ursa Major, and that constellation received the name of "The Seven Ṛishis;" and these stars were, in all likelihood, originally the Amĕsha-Çpĕntas of the Gâthâs of Zarathustra. The probability is that all Ṛishis thus reputed to have been invested with immortality, and translated to heaven, became stars—and stars forming a particular group or constellation were, I believe, the Ribhus. They were therefore said to be brilliant as the sun, and associated with the ceremony (the sacrifice), and with Indra (the light). Traversing the sky, they are swift as the winds, and borne quickly across it by rapid steeds. That they are "doers of good works," means that they exert beneficial influences; and what these are, we learn elsewhere: they, at a particular season [during the twelve days], fertilize the land, lead forth the waters, cause vegetation to spring up, and the water to cover the cow grounds. Thus they possess wealth and bestow benefits. They are sons of strength because of these potencies.

The formation of the all-impelling, multiform milch-cow unquestionably has some meaning. If we refer to the Gâthâs, we shall find the primeval bull invoked, the ideal progenitor of all cattle; and it is evident, I think, that the "all-impelling" cow is the universal, containing in its unity, and *being*, all the manifold of cattle, as the ideal unit, humanity contains and is, all the individuals of the human race. "All-*impelling*," is, I think, all-*producing*: for to "produce" is but to "put forth, push out, emit."

And this induces me to conclude that they were a group of stars which, 4,000 years before Christ, rose with the sun at the vernal equinox, or did so at some period not later than 2,500 years before our era. During the latter portion of these two periods, the sun was in the constellation Taurus at that period; and the celestial bull then opened the year, and caused fertility and productiveness, vegetable and animal. The twelve days during which they reposed, remaining in the hospitality of the unconcealable, were perhaps the days during which they continued to rise not long before the sun, in the glow and glory of the dawn; and as they caused the rains to fall and the rivers to rise and overflow, I think they were the Hyades. The appellation, "*artificers of the Devas*," is immediately followed, and is explained, by the phrase "and formed, etc., the cow": and thus the word "artificers" appears to mean creators or generators, among the Devas; as in the Hebrew, the word *bara* means to "form, fashion, beget, produce, create." They invest with forms and the actuality of existence the individuals that exist in idea in the universal.

I do not think that it is possible to know what is meant by their making the ladle fourfold; but whatever the Ribhus are supposed to be, that enigma will remain the same.

Nor, perhaps, will it ever be possible to ascertain what is meant by their building the car for the Aṣwins, and framing the horses for Indra; but this enigma, also, will remain the same, whatever they may be supposed to be.

SARAMÂ.

Allusion is frequently made, Professor Wilson remarks,

> to a legend of the Asuras named Paṇis having stolen the cows of the Gods, or, according to some versions, of the Angirasas, and hidden them in a cave, where they were discovered by Indra, with the help of the bitch Saramâ.

What we find in the Veda about her, is as follows:

> When the search (for the cattle stolen from the Angirasas, 'our forefathers'), was made, and they, 'knowing the foot-marks,' recovered them, it 'was set on foot by Indra, and the Angirasas' and 'Saramâ secured food for her young; then Bṛihaspati slew the devourer, and rescued the kine.'
>
> For thee (Agni), Saramâ discovered the abundant milk of the kine, with which man, the progeny of Manu, still is nourished.
>
> The seven intelligent Sages [(the Angirasas): *Qu.* the seven stars of Ursa Major?], having ascertained that the cows were concealed in the strong, propitiated by mental devotion. They recovered them all by the path of sacrifice; for Indra, knowing, and yielding to their wishes, entered.
>
> When Saramâ discovered the cleft of the mountain, then Indra made great and ample for her young, as previously: then the sure-footed, first recognizing their lowing, proceeded, and came to the presence of the imperishable kine.

Indra, aided by the Maruts, recovered the kine from the cave, and Angiras became his worshipper: and the Angirasas,

> contemplating their own giving milk to their former progeny, were delighted; their shouts spread through heaven and earth: they replaced the recovered kine in their places, and stationed guards over the cows.
>
> Invoked of many (Indra), when thou hadst divided the cloud for the waters, Saramâ appeared before thee.
>
> Saramâ, going to the ceremony, discovered the cattle, and Angiras rendered all the rites effective. [The Poet or Priest has invited those with him, to 'celebrate that solemn rite' which was effectual in setting open the stalls of the cattle; at this sacrifice, it is said, the stone, by the hands, makes a noise, whereby the nine-month ministrants celebrated the ten months' worship; when Saramâ, etc.]

When all the Angirasas, on the opening of this adorable dawn, came in contact with the cattle, then milk and the rest were offered in the august assembly; for Saramâ had found the cows by the path of truth (by following the track by which they had been taken, and which the light enabled her to see).

Sûkta xxii. Anuv. iii. Adhy. iv. Asht. v. is an enigma. The First Stanza invokes the protector of the dwelling and remover of disease, assuming all forms, to be a friend and grantor of happiness. The next three stanzas chide the white offspring of Saramâ (Sarameya), with tawny limbs, for barking and showing his teeth at the worshippers of Indra, to intimidate them, instead of attacking the thief or robber; and order him to go to sleep. "Do thou rend the hog;" stanza four says:

> Let the hog rend thee! Why dost thou assail the worshippers of Indra? Why dost thou intimidate us? Go quietly to sleep.

Then follows this:

> Let the mother sleep, let the father sleep, let the dog sleep, let the son-in-law sleep, let all the kindred sleep, let the people around sleep. The man who sits, or he who walks, or he who sees us, of these we shut up the eyes, so that they may be as unconscious as the house. We put men to sleep through the irresistible might of the bull with a thousand horns, who rises out of the ocean: [explained as the sun with a thousand rays; but how does the sun put men to sleep at night?].

I do not find these cows connected in the Veda, with Ushas, or the dawn, except by the interpolations of the commentators, and nothing to warrant the identification of them with the bright clouds of dawn, brought back from captivity in some cave or cleft of a mountain, by the aid of Saramâ, the messenger of Ushas.

The language is figurative, but the legend seems to me a very simple one. The sons of Angiras, forefathers of the Ṛishis for whom the Poet speaks, lost their cattle, "lifted" by some predatory band, whose name, Paṇis, has been preserved. Taken in the night, they were driven to a distance, and hidden in a valley of the mountains, from whose fastnesses these Highland Caterans of the Caucasus had descended. The plundered owners cried aloud in prayer, to Indra, for light, that they might see to follow the robbers; and Bṛihaspati, the spirit of prayer, prevailed with Indra. Daylight came, and they found and followed the trail. Saramâ, going to the ceremony, discovered the cattle, she discovered the cleft of the mountain, and the Seven Sages (the Angirasas), having ascertained that the cows were concealed in the fastness, prayed mentally to Indra, and the sure-footed (sure followers of the trail?) aware of the proximity of the cattle by their lowing, effected an entrance, and came to where the kine, destined not to be then slaughtered, were confined. It was owing to their sacrifice to Indra that they recovered them, for he, informed of their wishes, and complying with them, entered with them into the fastness. In this he was aided by the Maruts. It was Angiras, the father, who officiated at the sacrifice, which proved effectual to open the stronghold in which the cattle were confined.

When the cattle were recovered, Angiras worshipped Indra, and the Angirasas, seeing their cattle giving suck to their calves, were delighted, and their joyful exclamations resounded far abroad and high towards heaven. And they restored the cattle to their wonted folds, and after that had them guarded at night.

Saramâ discovered for Agni the abundant milk of the kine, with which Man, the progeny of Manu, still is nourished. This *may* mean that she first taught men to milk their cows, and so caused the sacrifices to be fed with butter: or, more probably, that, by enabling the Angirasas to recover the kine, which she found for them, she enabled them to supply themselves with milk and butter, for the fire of the sacrifice.

When the robbers' stronghold was carried by assault, Saramâ found food there for her young. Indra, by whose light the cattle were tracked and followed, furnished this food, great and ample, for her young, as he had done before; and it was prayer, Bṛihaspati, to whom it was owing that the robbers who would have slain and eaten the cattle, were killed, and the kine recovered.

As the kine were recovered "by the path of sacrifice," so Saramâ found them "by the path of truth," by means of the daylight. She appeared before Indra, when he had divided the cloud, to cause rain: going to the ceremony, she discovered the cattle. What the significance of her appearing before Indra is, we do not discover. After the return of the cattle to their homes, the Angirasas, at the opening of the dawn, offered milk and other things as a sacrifice, in an assembly of all their people, returning thanks because Saramâ had found the cattle, by pursuing them in the true direction.

It seems that some particular day of the year was celebrated as the anniversary of this recovery, at which the Soma juice was expressed, and "the nine-month ministrants celebrated the ten months' worship," an obscure phrase which it is useless to endeavour to explain.

Saramâ is not invoked or sacrificed to as a Deity. Her white offspring, with tawny limbs, Sarameya is plainly a watch-dog, without sufficient discretion not to know the worshippers of Indra from robbers, and therefore chidden for barking at them.

Mr. Cox says (*Mythol. i. 417*), that Ushas

> reveals mysteries, and opens the ends of Heaven, where the Paṇis had hidden away the cows of which she is the mother. She tells the Angiras where they are to be

found, and as she lightens the sky, she is said to drive her own herds to the pastures. [But we do not find her playing that part in the Veda.]

Again Mr. Cox says,

It is to the phrases which speak of the dawn under the name of Saramâ, that we must look for the germ of the great epics of the Western Aryans . . . . Whatever may be the precise meaning of the name, whether Saramâ or Saranya is taken to denote the storm cloud or the morning, there is no doubt that the root of the word is *sar*, to "creep," or "go," which we find in *serpent*, as well as in the Greek Erinys and Sarpêdôn.

Saramâ is certainly not a name for the dawn. On the contrary, she is, in the legend, a bitch that has young, for whom she secures food. *Sarpas* or *sarpin*, in Sanskrit, is a "reptile," from *sær*, to "go" or "creep:" and *ahis*, *agas*, is a "serpent," from *ag*, to "approach," to "infold;" but how this tends to prove that Saramâ is Ushas, the dawn, we utterly fail to see. If Saramâ *is* from the root *sær*, its meaning much more probably was a messenger, a goer of errands; and, perhaps, from the other meaning of the root (to *creep*), a *stealthy* messenger. Eichhoff gives, as the root of *sarpas*, *sarp*, to "go, creep, crawl;" and the meaning of the root *sar* to "be," to "go," to "move;" and of "*çar*," to "pierce, penetrate." From *sar* we have *saras*, "fluid, milk."

Mr. Cox continues,

In the Rig-Veda, Saramâ is especially the guardian of the cows of Indra, and as his messenger she goes to the Paṇis, who have stolen them away. [We do not find her to be such guardian, or to go as his messenger.] She, too, like Ushas, is said to be the first to spy out the cleft in the rock, where the Paṇis, like Cacus, had hid the plundered cattle, and like Herakles, she is the first to hear their lowings. [It is not said that she heard them at all; but that the Angirasas did.] Like Ushas, also, she walks in a straight path [which she does not do like Uṣhas, but as a dog following a trail]: but when she comes to the stronghold of the Paṇis, a conference follows, in which we see unmistakably the dawn peering about through the sky in search of the bright clouds, and restoring them in all their brilliance and beauty to the broad pastures of the Heaven.

Mr. Cox then quotes as follows:

The Paṇis said, 'with what intention did Saramâ reach this place? for the way is far, and leads tortuously away. What was your wish with us? How was the night? How did you cross the waters of the Râsa?'

The Paṇis—'What kind of man is Indra, O Saramâ, what is his look, he as whose messenger thou comest from afar? Let him come hither, and we will make friends with him, and then he may be the cow-herd of our cows.'

Saramâ—'I do not know that he is to be subdued, for it is he himself that subdues, he as whose messenger I came hither from afar. Deep streams do not overwhelm him; you, Paṇis, will he prostrate, killed by Indra.'

The Paṇis—'Those cows, O Saramâ, which thou desirest, fly about the ends of the sky, O darling. Who would give them up to thee without fighting? for our weapons too are sharp.'

Saramâ—'Though your words, O Paṇis, are unconquerable, though your wretched bodies be arrow-proof, though the way to you be hard to go, Bṛihaspati will not bless you for either.'

The Paṇis—'That store, O Saramâ, is fastened to the rock, furnished with cows, horses and treasures. Paṇis watch it who are good watchers; thou art come in vain to this bright place.'

Saramâ—'Let the Ṛishis come here fired with Soma, Ahasya (Indra), and the ninefold Angiras: they will divide the stable of cows; then the Paṇis will vomit out this speech.'

The Paṇis—'Even thus, O Saramâ, thou art come hither, driven by the violence of the Gods; let us make thee our sister: do not go away again: we will give thee part of the cows, O darling.'

Saramâ—'I know nothing of brotherhood or sisterhood: Indra knows it, and the awful Angiras. They seemed to me anxious for their cows when I came: therefore get away from here, Paṇis, far away.'

'Go far away, Paṇis, far away; let the cows come out straight; the cows which Bṛihaspati, Soma, the Stones and the wise Ṛishis found, hidden away.'

And on this, Mr. Cox says:

This hymn, seemingly so transparent in its meaning, becomes unintelligible if interpreted of any other being than the dawn, in her struggle with the powers of darkness; and hence it seems a superfluous task to show that all the essential features of Ushas reappear in Saramâ: that like Ushas, Saramâ is followed by Indra, and that walking first she reveals the treasures which had been hidden away; that both alike go to the uttermost ends of heaven; that both break the stronghold of the Paṇis; both are the mothers and deliverers of the cows; 'both drive forth their cattle to the pastures; both walk in the right path, and bestow wealth and blessings upon men.' [Saramâ is not mother of the cows. She does not deliver them or break the stronghold. She guides the Angirasas to it, and they break it. She does not drive forth the cattle to the pasture. The Angirasas drive them home. She does not bestow wealth or blessings on men, and is not invoked at all.]

Every phrase [he continues] tells us of some change in the heaven, from the time when the sun sinks to sleep in the west, to the moment when his face is first seen again in the east. As the light of evening dies away, the power of the darkness is restored, and the Paṇis extinguish the bright-coloured clouds which have looked down on the death of the sun, or in other words, they steal the cows of Indra. [All of this that is to be found in the Veda is, that the cows, not of Indra, but of the seven sons of Angiras, are stolen and driven off by the Paṇis, and that it must have been in the night, as they were recovered at dawn.]

During the weary hours of night, they are shut up in the demon's prison-house; but at length the messenger of the day comes to reclaim her children. [The dog Saramâ leads the Angirasas to the place where the cows are concealed and confined.]

> With a faint flush she starts slowly from the doors of the east. Her light, creeping along the dark face of the sky, seems to ebb and flow like the sea-tide; and so might Saramâ be said to hold parley with the Paṇis who refuse to yield up their plunder. But the dawn is only the messenger of one far mightier than herself, and if they will not yield to her, they shall feel the force of the arm of Indra; and the conference with the Paṇis, which answers to the spreading of the dawn, ends in their overthrow, as soon as Indra appears in his chariot—in other words, when the sun is risen. [And then, the Angirasas forcing the stronghold, Saramâ obtains plenty of meat, with which to feed her young.]

If the stolen cows were the bright clouds, how were they found by Bṛihaspati (the spirit of prayer), Soma, the stones that crushed and ground the Soma, and the wise Ṛishis? What had prayer to do with the return of the clouds? The sons of Angiras, finding their cows gone, sacrificed and prayed to Indra, and their prayer and sacrifice, and the light granted them by Indra, enabled them, finding their footprints and led by Saramâ, to discover the hiding-place. And they said, "Indra found the kine, and Bṛihaspati killed the robbers;" because they enabled the Angirasas to do both.

Indra is not the sun; nor were the cattle released by him, or when he rose. They were released at the opening of the dawn.

In the very hymn which Mr. Cox quotes, Saramâ tells the Paṇis that when the Ṛishis come, exhilarated or strengthened by Soma, with Ahasya and the nine-fold Angiras, they will force open the place of confinement of the cows; and then the Paṇis will eat their words.

The road by which Saramâ reached the stronghold ran tortuously away, a crooked road or path in the rugged mountains. She came there in the night, too; and crossed the waters of the Râsa. If there *are* rocks and mountains in the sky or heavens, in which the bright clouds are shut up at night, is there a *river* also, which those going after the cattle have to cross?

Do the bright clouds leave "foot-marks," by which they can be followed? Did the Angirasas recover the bright clouds, "concealed in the stronghold," by "the path of sacrifice"? Did they recognize them by their lowing? Did they "contemplate their own bright clouds, giving milk to their former progeny"? Did they "replace the recovered bright clouds in their stalls, and station guards over them"? To what ceremony was Ushas going, when she discovered the cattle?

What is meant by Indra feeding the cows, is made plain by the saying, that Bṛihaspati, Soma, the stones and the Ṛishis found them. To the stones used to crush the Soma, as well as to the Soma itself, the success of the Ṛishis was owing. It was the Angirasas who "seemed anxious for their cows." And the place in which the robbers kept them, was not only "fastened to the rock," but it contained horses, cows and treasure.

One expression, only, gives any colour of plausibility to the notion that the stolen cattle were the bright clouds. The Paṇis are made by the translation to say to Saramâ, that the cows which she desires "fly about the ends of the sky." This cannot mean that the Paṇis pretended not to have the cattle, and that they were wandering somewhere afar off; for they immediately say that their weapons are sharp, and they will not give them up without fighting; and in the next breath they expressly say that they have them shut up, and that they are in force sufficient to hold them. The phrase may have meant that the cows were high up in the mountains, towards where the sky and the mountain ridges seemed to meet. I am slow to believe, indeed, that the Vedic Poets ever used a phrase of which "the *cows* that *fly* about the ends of the *sky*" is a correct translation.

The Paṇis are made to say to Saramâ, that she comes, "driven by the violence of the Gods." They would hardly be represented as telling her that, when she came as their messenger; and the phrase probably means, merely, "obedient to the will of the Aryan Deities."

Now, the hymn first cited, is an invitation by the Poet, to his companions, to celebrate with him that solemn rite (that fixed and appointed ceremony of sacrifice), that had anciently proved effectual to procure the release and return of the stolen cattle of the Angirasas. The hymns are laudatory of Indra and Bṛihaspati, in proof of whose power and beneficence the old legend is recited, how by prayer and sacrifice their favour was secured and the cattle recovered.

Of the verses in which Sarameya, the watch-dog is chided, Mr. Cox remarks, that "it makes but little difference" whether Sarameya is "definitely the son of Saramâ, or whether the word remained a mere epithet for any one of the Gods who might denote the morning." I see nothing in the poem which indicates that by the barking watch-dog, the morning was meant. Professor Müller says that Vashtoshpati is here called Sarameya; and adds, that this Deity would thus denote "the peep of day conceived as a person, watching unseen at the doors of Heaven, during the night, and giving his first bark in the morning."

But I cannot find any such overstrained allegories as that, in the Veda: and I think that the song is but a simple and primitive ballad, with no allegorical or figurative meaning at all; and certainly in no sense religious. The fanciful interpretation of Professor Müller is as strained and groundless, I think, as the exploded misinterpretations of the amatory "Song of Solomon." No imagination could have been so diseased and feverish, as to conceive of morning as a white dog with tawny limbs, showing his teeth and barking at the worshippers of Indra, as if they were thieves or robbers.

Could the worshippers of Indra have been conceived of as saying, to the *morning*,

> Do thou rend the hog [the wild-boar]: let [or, may] the hog rend thee! Why dost thou scare us? Go quietly to sleep!

And, if this dog was the *morning* giving "his first *bark*," to awaken the inmates of the house, how could the worshippers of Indra have been anxious that all in the house should *sleep* "as unconscious as the house?"

Dr. Mommsen (*History of Rome, i.* 18) says:

> The divine grey-hound, Saramâ, who guards for the lord of heaven the golden herd of stars and sunbeams, and for him collects the nourishing rain-clouds of heaven for the milking, and who moreover faithfully conducts the pious dead unto the world of the blessed, becomes in the hands of the Greeks, the son of Saramâ, Sarameyas or Hermeias.

Why not Seirios, the dog-star, the barking dog or Caleb Anubis of the Egyptians? Dr. Kuhn finds in Saramâ a name identical with the Teutonic *storm*, and the Greek *Hormē* (*impetus, appetite of the mind*). And Professor Müller says that *Saramâ* and the Greek *Helēnē* are "phonetically identical, not only in every consonant and vowel, but even in their accent."

And Mr. Cox concludes that Saramâ, as going before Indra, like Ushas, is the dawn, and Sarameya or Hermeias is the dawn-child. He says that we find no divine grey-hound Saramâ in the Veda. But Saramâ is assuredly a bitch, in the Veda, if not a grey-hound, though not divine, and one that has progeny, and feeds them on the food taken from the Paṇis, who were, beyond doubt, some predatory band who lived in the hills and did not worship Indra, nor know who he was. Mr. Cox thinks that Professor Müller himself supplies the clue that may lead us through the labyrinth in regard to the Greek *Hermes*, and *Saramâ*, and their identity when he tells us, that Hermes is born in the morning,

> as Sarameya would be the son of the twilight, or, it may be, the first breeze of the dawn.

> The idea which lies at the root [Mr. Cox says (*ii.* 231)] of the Vedic Saramâ and Sarameya, is that of *brightness;* which idea, he thinks, is involved in the root *sar*, that means only *motion.*

No one can more highly appreciate the labours and acuteness of Professor Müller, than I do, or be more grateful to him for the light which his writings have shed upon ancient Aryan history, than I am. But I can find no warrant for these fancies in the Veda, and I think them calculated utterly to lead us astray, and to create notions radically incorrect in regard to the philosophical ideas and very mode of thought of the Vedic Poets. They seem to me to be as illusory and far-fetched as the etymological feats of Godfrey Higgins, and as baseless as many of the chronological conclusions of Baron Bunsen.

I find no evidence in the Veda that Saramâ was the dawn, or Sarameya the first whispering breeze of the dawn; nor any that the Aryan Saramâ became the Greek Hermes or Hermeias, or was regarded as a Deity at all. No doubt the legend of the robbery of the cattle of the sons of Angiras, and of their being found by the aid of the bitch Saramâ, was old enough to be known to the Greek Aryans, and to become the stock from which many of their myths branched. I cannot find any evidence in the Veda that the cows were Indra's, or that they were the bright clouds.

The Seven Angirasas, translated to heaven, became the seven stars of the Great Bear, the seven Ṛishis or Sages, and the originals, probably, of the Zarathustrian Amĕsha-Çpĕntas (Amshaspands), but I cannot find that Saramâ became a star, or any other than the mother of dogs. She may, at a later day, have become the Dog-Star, Seirios, or the Planet Mercury or Hermes: but the name is not found in the Hindū astronomy.

NUMBERS.

I have said that I believe that certain numbers, in the Veda, always refer to stars or constellations.

> Come, Aṣwins, *thrice* [it is said in the First Ashṭaka], with the *seven* mother-streams . . . . The *three* rivers are ready [*three* vessels of Soma juice]: the *triple* oblation is prepared. Rising above the *three* worlds, you defend the sun in the sky.

In the Second Ashṭaka,

> I have beheld the lord of men, with *seven* sons; of which delightful and benevolent, who is the object of our invocations, there is an all-pervading middle brother, and a third brother, well fed with ghee.

They yoke the *Seven* to the *one*-wheeled car: *one horse, named seven*, bears it along; the *three-axled* wheel is undecaying, never loosened, and in it all these regions of the universe abide.

The *Seven* who preside over this *seven*-wheeled chariot are the *seven* horses who draw it: *seven* sisters ride in it together, and in it are deposited the *seven* forms of utterance.

This *Sûkta viii. Anuv. xxii. Adhy. iii. of Asht. ii.* containing fifty-two stanzas, is of late composition, all its stanzas being found in the Atharva Veda, with the general style of which it best agrees. The hymn itself deals largely in numbers, applying to the year and its divisions. There is a twelve-spoked, and also a six-spoked and five-spoked wheel; a five-footed and twelve-formed parent, seven hundred and twenty children in pairs, abiding in the twelve-spoked wheel. There are *six* that are twins, and movable, and born of the Gods, and a *seventh, single-born*. A cow, holding her calf underneath with her forefeet, and then above with her hindfeet, which rises up, and then is gone, turning back halfway, has greatly puzzled the commentators. *Two* birds, associated together, take refuge in the same tree. One eats the sweet fig, the other merely looks on.

All this is very alien to the simplicity of the old hymns, and does not help us to understand them. These phrases may be descriptive of various groups of stars.

In *Adhy. viii. of Ashṭaka ii.* we find Soma and Pushan invoked to bring the seven-wheeled car, the measure of the spheres, indistinguishable from the universe, everywhere existing, by five reins, and to be harnessed by the mind.

In the First Ashṭaka, the *five shedders*, who abide in the centre of the expanded heavens, are invoked to convey the worshipper's prayers to the Gods, and return. No doubt these are the Hyades, the shedders of rain.

And in *Mandala viii*. 41. 2 (3 *Muir*, 126) we find,

> He (Varuṇa), who dwells at the birth-place of the streams, the lord of the Seven Sisters, abides in the Centre.

As the Soma juice in the pitchers is called "streams" and "rivers," it is nothing strange if the Pleiades are called so, which brings the season of rains; and it was perhaps from the term *sisters* thus applied to them, that the Greek mythology made them sisters, Atlantidæ, daughters of Atlas.

THE MARUTS.

It will assist the student, perhaps, in judging of the correctness of the conclusions to which his attention is hereinafter invited to have grouped together some of the epithets applied in the hymns to the *Maruts*, which were beyond any dispute merely the *winds*, or, generally, the storm winds.

To these, invisible as they are, the following epithets are, among many others, applied:

Ever youthful: wise: adorable: valiant: powerful: benevolent: riding in a chariot devoid of wickedness: resplendent: brilliant: white-complexioned: richly decorated with ornaments: invested with beauty: with unrelenting minds: self-irradiators of their persons: pure: purifying: of pure worth: with bright ornaments on their shoulders: with shining pendants on their breasts: wide radiating: shining with brilliant weapons and persons: irreproachable: glorified: high-spirited: protectors of the pious man: opulent: at whose violence the heaven seeks to rise higher, abandoning the firmament: well-born: whose is the glory over armies: curers of sickness: restorers of the enfeebled.

The monsoons extend into the Punjab, producing violent storms and accompanied with terrific lightning and thunder. In mountainous regions, electrical disturbances are more violent than elsewhere, and vehement winds and sudden changes of temperature are common. Storms are grander there than elsewhere, and all the powers of Nature seem to assume larger proportions. Probably they did not conceive of the storm winds as mere movements of masses of air; and it is quite sure that they had no knowledge of the means by which a body of air could be invested with powers so tremendous as are exhibited in the tornado and the whirlwind. No doubt the winds were a wonder and a marvel to them, and their imagination invested them with a thousand fanciful attributes.

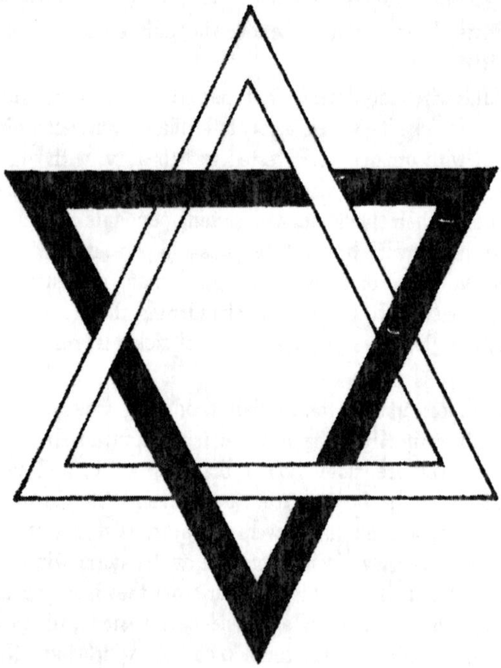

ZARATHUSTRA.

I propose to look a little way into the *Zend-Avesta*, to see whether it contains anything to confirm or conflict with the suggestions that I have made in regard to the nature and character of the Vedic Deities.

It is the sacred record and Holy Scriptures of the ancient Persians and of the Zarathustrian faith and creed.

Of Zarathustra (ordinarily called Zoroaster) Baron Bunsen speaks as follows [*Egypt's Place in Universal History, iii.* 472]:

> The old songs of the *Zend-Avesta* described him as follows: 'He it is who offers words in songs, who promotes purity by his praise: he, upon whom Ahura Mazda conferred the good gift of eloquence—he was the first in the world who made the tongue subservient to the understanding: he is the only one who understood the doctrines of the Supreme God, and was in a condition to transmit them.' The king, Kava Vîstâspa, patronized him. He was a Priest of the Fire-worshippers, and found the doctrine of a duality of good and evil already in vogue. Nevertheless, the name of Ahriman [*Añra-Mainyus*] does not occur as yet in the oldest records. What is understood by evil, is evil thought (*akô manô*) or falsehood; and this is contrasted with good thought, which is identical with the Good Principle. An absolute personification of the Good Principle is hardly to be found in the songs of Zarathustra. Zoroaster opposed the faith in the Gods of Nature, as the highest beings. He found in existence the faith in good spirits, *Ahuras*, the living, who are also called 'the dispensers of wisdom' (*Mazdas*). At their head he placed the One Holy God, '*Ahura Mazda*,' *Ormuzd*, 'The Highest Spirit.' He is the lord of all the Powers of Nature, creator and sustainer of all existence. He rules over earthly and spiritual life, by which latter Zoroaster understands a better state on this earth. His great axiom, so full of intelligence, was, that 'The Highest Trinity (*drigu*) is *thought, word, deed.*' These three he considers to be pure in the Pure, evil in the Evil: from the thought emanates the word; from the two together, the deed.

I doubt if Baron Bunsen penetrated into the inmost meaning of Zarathustra; and the whole paragraph is singularly unsatisfactory.

It was long ago supposed that Vîstâspa, who is mentioned in the books of the *Zend-Avesta*, as the royal patron of Zarathustra, was the father of King Darius Hystaspes. But philological and historical criticism, Baron Bunsen declares, has long ago set this unfortunate theory at rest.

The name of Zoroaster is known to us as that of the Median conqueror of Babylon, who vanquished the realm and city of the Chaldæans, and founded the Second Babylonian Dynasty, in the year 2234 B.C. This is known from the Armenian edition of Eusebius, in the Chaldæan lists of Berosus.

This king, Bunsen says,

> can only have received this title from being a follower of Zarathustra, and professing the religion of the Prophet . . . . But he was preceded by a series of eighty-four Median kings: and Media was not the historical birth-place of the religion and language of the Zend books; but Bactria, the seat of a primeval kingdom.

Considering the First Fargard of the Vendidad as a record of the wanderings and dispersion of the Aryan race,

> as a reminiscence of the early conquest of Asia, as far as the land of the Indus—a record which has been preserved for us by the followers of the founders of the religion of the Aryan East;

Baron Bunsen, considering *Sogdiana* as the original home of the race, finds the next settlement in *Margiana*, a fruitful province of Khorassan, to the southwest of, and across the Oxus, from the original home; and the next to that, in *Bactria*, to the east of Margiana. The fourteenth settlement was in *Hapta Hindū*, the Punjab. The eleventh settlement was in northeastern Media. What we call the Zend language, was the Bactrian: and says Baron Bunsen,

> there cannot be a more unfortunate theory than that which makes Persia the original seat of Zoroaster and his disciples.

Taking all the circumstances into consideration, Bunsen thinks, the date of Zoroaster, as fixed by Aristotle, cannot be said to be so very irrational. He and Eudoxus, according to Pliny, place him 6,000 years before the death of Plato; and Hermippus, who had translated his writings, placed him 5,000 years before the Trojan War.

> We may consider the latter date as derived from the same source as that of Aristotle and Eudoxus, who were men of the greatest learning and the keenest investigators of any age.
>
> The two dates essentially agree, for 6,000 years before the death of Plato (*Olymp. 108. 1: B.C. 348*) brings us to about 6,350; and the date of Hermippus is about 6,300, according to the common Alexandrian Chronology of the Trojan War, 407 or 408 before *Olymp. 1 = 1184 B.C.*

Avesta, Bunsen says, means "direct higher knowledge, divine revelation:" *Zend* means the *explanation* of this; and *Pazend* the *supplements* to the Zend, a further explanation of the Zend doctrine. The Avesta is the original groundwork of the code, which, although of very ancient date, is still almost all of it post-Zarathustrian. The Zend was compiled long afterward, and the Pazend long after that. All these three steps exist in the present *Zend-Avesta*, or, more properly, Avesta-Zend.

The Avesta, translated by Professor Spiegel into German, and by Mr. Bleeck into English, consists of (1) The *Vendidad*, containing 22 Fargards; (2) of the *Vispered* and *Yaçna;* and (3) of the *Khordah-Avesta*. The Vispered and Yaçna constitute what may be called the Mazdayaçnian Liturgy. The former, which is short, consists merely of liturgical additions to the Yaçna, and can never be recited alone. It appears to mean invocations to all the lords.

Yaçna signifies "offering with prayers." It is divided into two parts, the latter of which, written in a different dialect, contains the *Gâthâs* or *Gâhs*, ancient religious hymns, somewhat resembling those of the Vedas.

The Vendidad consists of supposed replies made by Ahura Mazda to Zarathustra, and supposed communications from him not in answer to questions. Of these there are but a few, the First Fargard being one of them, and commencing

> Ahura Mazda spake to the holy Zarathustra.

This Fargard, Bunsen thinks, was borrowed from some old work of the Avesta period, perhaps an early Iranian history (as also was the second chapter), and incorporated into the general text by either the author of the Zend or of the Pazend. The original text, he holds, has been added to, but it is itself

> unquestionably of great antiquity, and one of the oldest compositions of which the present Vendidad consists. But in its present shape, even after eliminating the later additions, it is decidedly after the time of Zarathustra, and posterior to the so-called *Gâthâs* or Songs, in which the greater part of the genuine maxims and doctrines of Zarathustra have been transmitted.

The reasons for this conclusion are given by Baron Bunsen in the work above cited, *iii.* 476. He thinks, however, that the First Fargard is very old, certainly older than the foundation of the Median Empire by Deioces (708 B.C.), and when the Aryans had probably only begun to spread through Media, and when Bactria was the centre of an empire.

It is, at all events, rendered quite certain by the *Zend-Avesta*, that the separation of the two great branches of the Aryan family, the Zend or Persian and the Indian, had taken place ages before either the Vedas or Gâthâs were composed. The two languages in which they are written are so much one, radically, as almost to deserve to be called dialects of the original older language. In each, the people among whom the songs were composed, are called "Arya," but the names of the Deities and stars are totally different, and the multitude of these names (the objects of which are now, for the most part, undiscoverable), is, in the *Zend-Avesta*, very great. These differences of names, almost without exception, could only have become so after an immense lapse of time.

That the stars, Tistrya and others, still continued to be adored by the Persians, is sufficient to prove, what I have already said, that this worship was more ancient among the Aryans, than the Vedas themselves, and had, when they were composed, in a great measure died out.

FIRE IN THE ZEND-AVESTA.

In *Fargard xii.* of the Vendidad, Ahura Mazda informs Zarathustra how dwellings are to be purified after death therein of particular inmates. In each case, the clothes and body are to be washed, and the Gâthâs recited. And then,

> Let them praise the *fire*, let them bind the *Bareçma*, let them bring *Zaŏthra* to the good water.

The *Zaŏthra* was the concentrated water; and the *Bareçma* a bundle of sacred twigs, both of which the priest had to hold in his hand during the offering.

In *Yaçna ii.* these are invoked to be present at the sacrifice, with praise. Then Ahura Mazda and the Amĕsha-Çpĕntas are invoked to be present; then Hâvani, Cavañhi and Viçya, the pure, lords of purity; then Mithra, Rama-qâçtra, Rapithwina, Frâdaṭ-fshu and Zantuma; and then (*v.* 18),

> Here, with Zaŏthra and Bareçma, I wish hither with praise: Asha-Vahista, the fire, the son of Ahura Mazda. [Then are invoked to be present, Uzayêirina, Frâdat-vîra and Daçyuma; then] the great lords, possessing women, shining, the navel of the waters, possessing swift horses. [Invocations follow to the water created by Mazda, to Aiwiçruthrema Aibigaya, the Frâdaṭ-viçpanm hujyâiti and the Zarathustrôtema], the good, strong Fravashis of the pure; . . . . the women who have an assembly of men, ... the yearly good dwelling, the powers, the well-formed, beautiful, the Verethraghna, created by Ahura, the Vanainti which descends from on high, Ushahina, Berejya, Nmânya, the holy Çraŏsha, Rashnu the most just, Arstat who advances and creates the world, the monthly feasts and new moons, the full moon, Vîshaptatha, and Maidhyô-Zaremaya, Maidhyôshĕma, Paitishahya, Ayâthrĕma, the advancer, who distributes strength, Maidhyâirya, Hamaçpathmaêdaya, the pure years; and all the lords of purity, which are the lords of purity, the three and thirty nearest, which are round about Hâvani, which belong to the best purity, which Ahura Mazda has taught, Zarathustra announced; the stars, the moon, the sun, trees, etc.; and 'thee, the fire, the son of Ahura Mazda, the pure, lord of purity, together with all fires.'

The Fire is also addressed and praised in *Vispered viii.*:

> We praise the shining heaven, the first brought forth, first-created earthly, of the earthly creation. Thee, the fire, the son of Ahura Mazda, the pure, lord of purity, we praise. [So], *Yaç. i.* I invite and announce to thee, the fire, son of Ahura Mazda, together with all fires. *Yaç. iii.* The wood wish I hither with praise, together with fragrance, for thy satisfaction, fire, the son of Ahura Mazda, the pure, possessing a renowned name, worthy of honour. *Yaç. xxii.* For the satisfaction of Ahura

Mazda and the Amĕsha-Çpĕntas, and the holy Çraôsha, the fire, the son of Ahura Mazda, the great lord of purity. *Khordah-Avesta xi.* Satisfaction for Ahura Mazda. Praise be to thee, fire (son) of Ahura Mazda, to the fire, son of Ahura Mazda—[the phrase, 'fire, son of Ahura Mazda' being several times repeated].

One would almost believe that the Fourth Stanza was taken from the Veda:

Offering and praise, good nourishment, fortunate nourishment, helpful nourishment, vow I to thee, O fire, son of Ahura Mazda! To thee it is to be offered, thou art to be praised, mayest thou ever be provided with offering and praise, in the dwellings of mankind. Prosperity be to the man who continually offers to thee, holding firewood in the hand, holding Barĕçma in the hand, holding flesh in the hand, holding the mortar in the hand. Mayest thou ever obtain right firewood, right perfume, right nourishment, right augmentation . . . . Mayest thou burn in this dwelling, mayest thou continually burn in this dwelling, mayest thou be in brightness in this dwelling, mayest thou be in increase in this dwelling, throughout the long time until the complete resurrection, the perfect good resurrection included. Give to me, O fire, son of Ahura Mazda, swift brightness, swift nourishment, much brightness, much nourishment, many blessings of life, greatness in holiness, fluency for the tongues, but for the soul, sense and understanding, which afterwards increases itself, and does not diminish, then manly courage, activity, wakefulness the third part of the night, easy going, increase, well-nourished, heavenly offspring, which forms a circle, gathers itself together, increases, enduring, free from debt, and manly, which can advance for me the house, the clan, the confederacy, the region, the district.

Give to me, O fire, son of Ahura Mazda, that which teaches me now and for all times, concerning the best place of the pure, the shining, very brilliant. May I attain good reward, good fame, good holiness for the soul. With all speaks the fire of Ahura Mazda, for whom throughout the night it gives light and cooks food: from all, it desires good nourishment, wholesome nourishment, helpful nourishment. To all who come, the fire looks at their hands (saying), 'What does the friend bring to the friend, the Entering in to the Sitting alone?'

We praise the holy fire, the strong, the warrior. If one brings for the same, wood brought in purity, Bareçma bound together in holiness, or the tree *hadhânaêpata*, then blesses the fire, of Ahura Mazda, contented, without hatred, satisfied: . . . . May there rise round about thee herds of cattle, fullness of men; may it happen according to the wish of thy mind, according to the wish of thy soul. Be cheerful; live thy life the whole time which thou wilt live. . . . . This is the blessing of the fire, for him who brings it dry wood, sought for burning, purified with the wish for purity.

Satisfaction to Ahura Mazda. Praise to thee, fire, son of Ahura Mazda, giver of good, greatest Yazata. *Ashem Vohû.*

Kh.-Av. xii.—Praise to thee, O fire, son of Ahura Mazda, giver of good, greatest Yazata, Ashem Vohû. I confess myself, etc. To the fire, the son of Ahura Mazda; to thee, fire, son of Ahura Mazda.

Ashem Vohû—Thee, the fire, lay I hold on with the offering of good thought. Thee, the fire, lay I hold on with the offering of good words. Thee, the fire, lay I hold on, with the offering of good works, for the enlightenment of thoughts, words and works.

Praise to thee, Ahura Mazda . . . . For thy fire, the offerings of a good mind, as far as I can and think . . . . To him belongs brightness, etc.

Yaçna xxxvi.—We approach ourselves first to thee, Mazda Ahura, through the service of the fire.

To thee, holiest spirit, who requitest the torment upon him who decrees it.

Happy is the man to whom thou comest mightily, fire, son of Ahura Mazda.

More friendly than the most friendly, more worthy of adoration than the most worthy of honour.

Mayest thou come helpfully to us, at the greatest business.

Fire, thou art acquainted with Ahura Mazda, acquainted with the heavenly.

Thou art the holiest of the same (fire), that bears the name Vâzista.

O fire, son of Ahura Mazda, we draw near to thee, with good mind, good purity, with deeds and words of good wisdom, draw we near to thee . . . .

This thy body, the fairest of all bodies, we invite, Mazda Ahura, the greatest among the great lights, that which they call the sun.

The hymn that is quoted before this last, also forms *Yaçna lxi.*

Yaçna lvii.—In prayer we rejoice, Ahura Mazda, in prayer we desire . . . . As you created us, O Amĕsha Çpĕnta, so support us . . . . All the creatures of the creator would we, together with the created lights of Ahura Mazda, keep. Praise to thee, fire, of Ahura Mazda; mayest thou come hither to the greatest of affairs . . . . with the highest prayer inform we thy body, the fairest among bodies, Mazda Ahura, among these lights the highest of the uplifted, that which is called the sun.

Yaçna xlv.—Whom has Mazda appointed as protector for my fellows, if the wicked chooses me for vengeance? What other than thee, the fire and the spirit, through both of whose deeds purity is increased.

The domestic and sacrificial fire, we see, was the *son* (i. e., the manifestation of or emanation from Ahura Mazda, in whose name we find the same mystic letters, A.·. U.·. M.·. which are the initials of the names of so many of the Vedic Gods). And the sun was his body, i. e., he is the soul of the sun, the radiance being his manifestation.

Ahura Mazda, therefore, is but the Vedic fire-substance, or principle, invested with higher and creative attributes: and we find the same Aryan worship of Agni under another name, among these Bactrian Aryans. The sacrifices to the fire God were of the same kind. The juice expressed from the Haŏma (the Bactrian name for the Soma) was used, as we shall more fully see hereafter; flesh was burned, and the Manthras (the Vedic "Mantras") were sung, and invested with the same mystic powers as in the Veda.

Indra had become an evil Deity. In *Fargard x.* of the Vendidad, we find Ahura Mazda dictating to the worshipper these words:

> I combat Indra, I combat Çauru, I combat the Daeva Nâoñhaiti, away from the dwelling, the clan, the tribe, the region . . . . I combat the Daeva Aeshma, the very evil; I combat the Daeva Akatasha, etc.

AHURA MAZDA.

Ahura Mazda is "the heavenly, the holy, creator of the corporeal world, the pure." Yima, the fair, the beautiful, son of Vivanhâo, was the first of all mankind with whom be conversed. The creator, Ahura Mazda, twin brother of Añra-Mainyus, produced a congregation, the heavenly *Yazatas* (commonly known heretofore, to us, as *Izeds*),

> the renowned in Airyana-Vaêjâ, the good creation. There Yima produced a congregation of the best men, renowned; and Ahura Mazda came there to him with the Yazatas.

Añra-Mainyus, the evil one, created the *Daevas;* but Ahura Mazda is the creator of all corporeal things,

> of the pure creation, of the wind, of the earth, the water, and the trees. He created Vĕrĕthraghna, the carrier of light, the air, and this abode, the beautiful, brilliant, admirable.

In the Yaçnas we read,

> The creator Ahura Mazda, the brilliant, majestic, greatest, best, most beautiful, the strongest, most intellectual, of the best body, the highest through holiness; who is very wise, who rejoices afar; who created us, who formed us, who keeps us, the holiest among the heavenly.

He created the Kingly Majesty; and, in *Yaçna xxxi.*, we find,

> when thou, Mazda Ahura, the heavenly, createdst ways for her, ... when thou, Mazda, first created the world for us, and the laws, and the understanding, through thy spirit, when thou clothedst the vital powers with bodies, and createdst deeds and teaching, to satisfy the wish for the world to come.

But it is not my purpose now to examine all the texts that would enable us to ascertain what was the Zarathustrian idea in regard to Ahura Mazda. It would be an interesting inquiry. The Deities of the *Zend-Avesta* might perhaps be found to be as little understood as those of the Veda.

For we find in the Vendidad (*Farg. xix.*),

> Let Vohu-Manô invoke the lofty created lights, that the stars created by the Baghas may shine on it; [and, in the same Fargard], I praise the lights *without a beginning, the self-created* . . . . I praise the mid-world, the self-created. [And in *Farg. ii.*]:

Then answered Ahura Mazda; *self-created lights*, and created in rows. Of a single kind and course are seen the Stars, the Moon and the Sun. [In *Farg. xi.*]: pure the stars, pure the moon, pure the sun, pure the lights *without beginning*, pure all the good things which were created by Ahura Mazda, and have a pure origin. [This is repeated, in substance, four times in this Fargard. In *Farg. xix.*], Praise thou, O Zarathustra, the *self-created* firmament, the infinite time, the air, which winks on high. Praise thou, O Zarathustra, the swift wind, created by Ahura Mazda; Çpĕnta Ârmaiti, the fair daughter of Ahura Mazda . . . . I praise the heaven, *the self-created*, the never-ending time, the air which winks above.

In *Yaçna i.* the stars are termed "the creatures of Çpĕnta-Mainyus;" and Çpĕnta-Mainyus (in parenthesis, Ahura Mazda, is elsewhere termed "creator of creatures").

Ahura Mazda is "the shining, the majestic": Ahura and Mithra (*Yaçna i.*) are both great, imperishable and pure, and the shining sun with the swift horses is the eye of Ahura Mazda and Mithra. In *Yaçna iii.* Ahura Mazda is the shining, the brilliant. In *Yaçna iv.*, "the creator, the brilliant, majestic, the heavenly spirit." Mithra and Ahura are praised together, as "both great, imperishable, pure." In a note to *Yaçna i.* where they are thus coupled together, it is said,

Ahura here signifies the planet Jupiter, which was called by the Armenians, Ahura Mazda. Mithra is probably the Sun.

Aṅra-Mainyus (Ahriman) is also a creator, but not of corporeal things as Çpĕnta-Mainyus creates

the dog with the prickly back and woolly muzzle, Vaṅhâpâra, upon whom evil-speaking men impose the name Dujaka; which every morning at the rising of the sun comes forth, as a thousand slayer of Aṅra-Mainyus; [so Aṅra-Mainyus creates] the Daeva Zairimyaṅura, upon whom evil-speaking men impose the name Zairimyâka, which every morning at the rising of the sun comes forth, as a thousand slayer of Çpĕnta-Mainyus.

And, in *Yaçna xxx.*, Ahura Mazda and Aṅra-Mainyus are styled

These heavenly beings, the twins. [They] gave first of themselves to understand both, the good and the evil, in thoughts, words and works: rightly do the wise distinguish between them, not so the imprudent. [And it is said], when both these heavenly beings come together, in order to create at first life and perishability, and as the world should be at last . . . . [And in Note 2, it is said], In naming Ahura Mazda and Aṅra-Mainyus 'Twins,' this description agrees with that contained in the Armenian writers, Esnik, for example, where they are both considered as 'the sons of time.'

In *Yaçna xxxi.*, it is said,

> To Mazda belongs the kingdom, so far as it prospers to him through Vohu-Manô. He came as the first fashioner (when) brightness mingled itself with the lights; he (fashioned) the pure creation, he upholds the best soul with his understanding; thou causest both to increase in heavenly way, O Mazda Ahura, thou who art also now the lord. Thee have I thought, O Mazda, as the first to praise with the soul, as the father of Vohu-Manô, since I saw thee with eyes, the active creator of purity, the lord of the world in deeds.

Ahura Mazda was originally one of the Amĕsha-Çpĕntas. In *Visp. xxii.*, we read,

> Holy! (*çpentem*), we praise Ahura Mazda. Holy! we praise the Amĕsha-Çpĕnta. Holy! we praise the pure man . . . . Holy! we praise the good Çpĕnta-Ârmaiti. The creatures created by the holy one, the pure, we praise. The first after the understanding among the pure creatures, we praise. The omniscient understanding praise we, Ahura Mazda. The sun, the highest among those on high, praise we. The sun's light praise we. Together with the sun, we praise the Amĕsha-Çpĕntas.

Yaçna i. after an invocation to "the creator Ahura Mazda, the brilliant, majestic, greatest, best, most beautiful, etc.," invokes the Amĕsha-Çpĕntas. As these are praised together with the sun, the highest among those on high (i. e., the celestial luminaries), it seems that the Amĕsha-Çpĕntas were originally seven of the heavenly bodies.

They are, 1. *Vohu-Manô* (incorrectly called, long afterwards, *Bahman*), the protector of all living creatures; whose especial adversary is Akô-Manô. Though he is the highest of the creatures of Ahura Mazda, it is nowhere said that he himself has the power of creating.

2. *Asha-Vahista* (*Ardibehest*), the genius of fire, whose opponent is Andar.

3. *Khshathra-Vairya* (*Shahrĕvar*) is the lord and protector of metals. His opponent is Çaurva.

4. *Çpĕnta-Ârmaiti* (*Sapandomat*) is a female genius, the Goddess of the earth. In the older writings, she is expressly the Goddess of wisdom. Her opponent is Nâoṅhaithi.

5. *Haurvat*, lord of the waters, whose opponent is Taric: (formerly *Khordad*).

6. *Ameretât* is the lord of trees. His opponent is Zaric: (formerly *Amerdad*).

7. *Ahura Mazda* was originally counted as one of the Amĕsha-Çpĕntas; but in the later mythology he is no longer reckoned so, and Çraŏsha is the Seventh. His especial duty was to watch over the world, and above all, to protect it in the night-time, during which he was to traverse the whole

world three times, and combat the Daeva Aêshma seven times. Morning and evening prayers were addressed to him, and the cock was sacred to him.

As Ahura Mazda was originally an Amĕsha-Çpĕnta, he was one of the seven celestial bodies, known at that time. The sun was not one of them, and therefore they were not the seven planets, as afterwards known. What they *were*, it may be very difficult to ascertain.

The note to *Yaçna ix. v. i.* says,

> with regard to the personality of Haŏma, it must be particularly borne in mind, that in this, as well as in many other cases in the Avesta, the same word is at once a *genius*, and the *thing* which is under the special protection of the genius. Thus Vohu-Manô may stand for either an Amĕsha-Çpĕnta, or the living creation; while Khshthra-Vairya is either a genius or metal in general. In like manner, Haŏma is sometimes a Yazata, and sometimes the juice of a plant.

And so, in the Veda, Agni is both a Deity, the genius or invisible substance, of fire, and the domestic or sacrificial fire itself; as Soma is both a Deity, the principle of intoxication and exhilaration, and the Soma plant and juice.

In *Yaçna iv.* we find:

> We make them known: to the Amĕsha-Çpĕntas, possessed of good lordship, wise, ever-living, ever-profitable, which live together with Vohu-Manô . . . . to the creator Ahura Mazda, the brilliant, majestic, the heavenly spirit, to the Amĕsha-Çpĕntas, for praise, for adoration, satisfaction and laud.

The Yasht (invocation) of the seven Amshaspands (*Khordah-Avesta xviii.*) begins thus:

> To Ahura Mazda, the shining, majestic, to the Amĕsha-Çpĕntas, to Vohu-Manô, to the peace which smites victoriously, which is placed over other creatures, to the heavenly understanding heard with the ears, created by Mazda.

Asha-Vahista is styled the fairest, and Khshthra-Vairya, the metal. All are called "the good wise kings."

The *Zamyad Yasht: Kh.-Av. xxxv.:*

> The strong kingly majesty, etc. [often said to have been created by Ahura Mazda], which belongs to the Amĕsha-Çpĕntas, the shining, having efficacious eyes, great, helpful, strong, Ahurian—who are imperishable and pure, which are all seven of like mind, like speech, all doing alike, like is their mind, like their word, like is their action, like their father and ruler, namely the creator Ahura Mazda.
>
> Of whom one sees the soul of the other, how it thinks on good thoughts, how it thinks on good words, how it thinks on good deeds, thinking on Garo-Nĕmâna.

Their ways are shining, when they come hither to the offering gifts [i. e., to the sacrifice]. Which are there the creators and the destroyers of the creatures of Ahura Mazda, their creators and overseers, their protectors and rulers. They it is who further the world at will, so that it does not grow old and die . . . . Ever-living, ever-profiting, a kingdom as one wishes it, that the dead may arise, and immortality for the living may come.

The *Gâthâ Çpěnta Mainyû*, and the *Gâthâ Vohu Khshthra* are written in the oldest dialect of the Avesta, as all the Gâthâs (composing the second part of the Yaçna), are. They may be even older than the Veda, which they resemble. I quote these verses:

So will I praise you with laud, Mazda Ahura,
Together with Asha and Vohu-Manô,
And Khshathra, that he may stand on the way of the desiring . . . .
With these Yaçnas I offer you praise;
Mazda, Asha, with the deeds of Vohu-Manô . . . .
I do that which others have done before,
What appears worthy in the eyes, through Vohu-Manô,
By the Light, by the Sun, the day of the Morning . . . .
To your praise, Asha, Mazda Ahura!
Thy praise will I proclaim, O Mazda, with the mouth,
So long as I, O Asha, can and am able;
Let the Creator of the world bestow through Vohu-Manô,
What is best for the wish of those working openly.

We see, in these ideas in regard to Ahura Mazda and the Aměsha-Çpěntas, a striking resemblance to those of the Kabbalah in regard to the Sephiroth, emanations from Ainsoph, and by each of which the Very Deity, the most hidden of the hidden, manifested himself in action. May not the Alohim or creative powers have been considered as similar emanations. Quite certainly, the Aměsha-Çpěntas were the prototypes of the seven archangels of the later Hebrews, presiding over the seven planets.

And in Agni and his various manifestations, we find the origin of all these philosophic ideas.

The Yasht *Ardibihest* (*Kh.-Av. xix.*) is a hymn of adoration to Asha-Vahista, the genius of fire and most powerful of the Aměsha-Çpěntas.

We quote the second verse:

Then spake Zarathustra: Speak the words, the true words, O Ahura Mazda, how are the succours of Asha-Vahista become as singer, Zaôta, praiser, reader, offerer, lauder, celebrator of good, effecting that the good lights may shine to the praise and adoration of you, Aměsha-Çpěntas?

We find here the Vedic ideas, of Agni as the messenger and invoker of the Gods, conveying to them the praises and prayers of the worshippers; and manifesting himself by the bright luminaries of the sky.

We find also in the *Zend-Avesta* a Deity answering to Brahmaṅaspati and Bṛihaspati of the Veda, in Manthra-Çpĕnta, the holiness of hymn, prayer or praise. Thus, *Yaçna xxv.:*

> The most righteous wisdom, created by Mazda, pure, praise we, the good Mazdayaçnian law praise we. The Manthra-Çpĕnta, the very brilliant, ... the spreading abroad of the Manthra-Çpĕnta . . . . the knowledge of the Manthra-Çpĕnta . . . . the heavenly wisdom created by Mazda . . . . the wisdom heard with the ears, created by Mazda, praise we.

Prayer, and the recitation of the sacred writings are considered in the Avesta to have the same efficacy as in the Veda. The recitation of the Yaçna-haptanhaiti, is

> great, strong, victorious, without adversary, before all victorious prayers. *Visp. xviii.*

In *Yaçna xix.*, a certain portion of the Ahuna-Vairya (one of the three principal prayers), is said by Ahura Mazda to Zarathustra, to have been spoken,

> before the creation of this heaven, before the water, before the earth, before the trees, before the creation of the four-footed bull, before the birth of the pure man, the two-legged, before the body of this sun was created according to the wish of the Amĕsha-Çpĕntas. I have spoken it out of heavenly holiness, ... as an example of the works in the world of Mazda . . . . All the words which are uttered, every word springs from Ahura Mazda. The best Ahura Mazda has spoken the Ahuna-Vairya, the best has made it perfect . . . . This speech which Ahura Mazda has spoken contains three heads . . . . which are the heads? To think, speak and do good.

In *Fargard xix.*,

> Him answered Aṅra-Mainyus, who has created the evil creatures, 'by whose word wilt thou smite, by whose word wilt thou annihilate . . . . my creatures?' Him answered the holy Zarathustra: . . . . 'the words which Ahura Mazda has spoken . . . . which Çpĕnta-Mainyus (i. e., Ahura Mazda) created; he created in the Infinite Time (*Zrvâna-akarana*); which the Amĕsha-Çpĕntas created, the good rulers, the wise. Zarathustra pronounced the Ahuna-Vairya; *Yatha Ahu Vairyo.*'

In the Gatha *Ahunavaiti* (*Yaçna xxviii.*) we find,

> Teach thou me, Mazda Ahura, from out thyself, from heaven through thy mouth, whereby the world first arose.

And here we find the origin of the Platonic, Alexandrian and Christian idea of creation by the *Word* or Logos.

In *Fargard xxi.* we find the phrase, "The way which Ahura Mazda has created, the air which the Baghas (*Baghô*) have created: then, before that Manthra Çpĕnta." It is said in the note to this, that *Baghô* means "God," seldom used in the Avesta, though frequent in the Cuneiform inscriptions. But the *baghas* are the *divisions* of each of the principal prayers (see *notes* 1 *and* 4 *to Yaçna xix.*), and why should it mean "God" elsewhere? The meaning clearly is that Ahura Mazda exercised his creative power by means of these sacred formulas of words, *Yathâ-Ahu Vairyo; Ashem vôhû vahistem açtî, etc.*

"The holy Gâthâs [songs], the rulers of the times, the pure," were also adored—the Gâthâ *Ahunavaiti*, the Gâthâ *Çpĕnta Mainyu*, etc., all of which are hymns of the Yaçnas. The different prayers and Yaçnas are styled, "the pure lords of purity," and the Gâthâs, "the pure mistresses of purity." Çpĕnta-Ârmaiti is styled "the Manthra of the profiting, through whose deeds the worlds of the pure increase." In the note it is said that Çpĕnta-Ârmaiti is perfect wisdom, as well as the genius of the earth.

In the *Ormazd Yasht*, Ahura Mazda says:

> Here is Vohu-Manô, my creature, O Zarathustra; Asha-Vahista, my creature, O Zarathustra; Khshathra-Vairya, my creature, O Zarathustra; Çpĕnta-Ârmaiti, my creature, O Zarathustra; here are Haurvaţ and Amĕrĕtâţ [Khordad and Amerdad], my creatures, O Zarathustra, which are a reward for the pure who attain to incorporeality . . . . Through my wisdom, through which was the beginning of the world, so also its end shall be . . . . Then spake Zarathustra: 'I come to you, the eyes of Çpĕnta-Ârmaiti, who annihilate what is desert in the earth, to hunt the wicked.'

In *Fargard xxii.* of the Vendidad, Ahura Mazda applies to "Manthra-Çpĕnta, the Very Brilliant," to heal his creatures, whom Añra-Mainyus had afflicted with much sickness. Then, it seems, he addresses him by the name of "Çsaoka, the good, created by Ahura Mazda, pure," which is often repeated. Manthra-Çpĕnta replies, and Nairyo-çañha "the Assembler," is sent to the dwelling of Airyama, to ask him in the name of Ahura Mazda, to heal his sick. He styles him, "the desirable Airyama," "the lusty Airyama;" who hastened forth to the mountain on which the holy questions take place, carrying with him horses, cattle, camels, and willows; and drew nine circles. Here the Vendidad abruptly ends. The annotator thinks that Airyama is unquestionably identical with Aryaman. It is exceedingly to be doubted whether he is a Deity at all.

Çraðsha is "the victorious." He is "bound with the fulness of purity." He is, in the Sirozah of the Khordah-Avesta, "the holy, strong, who has the Manthra as a body, the Ahurian, with strong weapons."

The *Çrosh-Yasht-Hadôkht*, of the *Khordah-Avesta* [*xxvii.*], is in praise of

> the holy Çraðsha, the firm, whose body is the Manthra, whose weapons are terrible, the holy, beautiful, victorious, promoting the world, pure, lord of purity, he who most nourishes the poor, who most slays the Drujas. [He smites wicked men and wicked women. It is he], who watches over the treaties of peace and the compacts of the Druja, and is the holiest in regard to the Amĕsha-Çpĕntas over the earth consisting of seven Kareshvares; who is the lawgiver for the law. To him has Ahura Mazda the pure, taught the law.
>
> He is the strong, the protector, who possesses strength in the arms, the warrior who smites the heart of the Daevas, gives victorious strokes, grants victorious strokes to the pure . . . . All dwellings protected by Çraðsha we praise, where Çraðsha, beloved as a friend, receives, where the pure man especially thinks purity, especially speaks purity, especially does purity.

So, in the *Çrosh-Yasht* [*Yaçna lvi.*], one of the ancient Gâthâs, he is "the holy, strong, whose body is the Manthra, whose weapon is uplifted, the Ahurian;" as, in *Yaçna iv.* he is "the holy, strong, whose body is the Manthra, who has a strong weapon, who originates from Ahura, as Khshnaðthra, for praise, for adoration, satisfaction and laud." Fire also is "the son of Ahura Mazda, as Khshnaðthra." This is the technical expression for a particular kind of prayer.

Çraðsha, his body being the Manthra, seems to be the spirit of prayer, or prayer as a universal, as humanity is the universal of all individual men. First among the creatures of Ahura Mazda, he bound together the Bareçma (the holy sacrificial twigs of a particular wood, date, pomegranate or tamarisk), and offered sacrifice to Ahura Mazda and the Amĕsha-Çpĕntas, and to the Yazatas. He bound together *three, five, seven* or *nine* twigs. He first sang the five Gâthâs of Zarathustra. Sleepless, he protects and preserves with watchfulness the creatures of Ahura Mazda, with upraised weapon the whole corporeal world, after the rising of the sun; and no longer softly sleeps, since the two heavenly beings, Çpĕnta-Mainyus and Añra-Mainyus have created the world. He is a firm, well-chambered dwelling for the poor men and women, after the rising of the sun. He smites down Aeshma, who despises his strength. He is strong, swift, mighty, terrible, heroic, very deadly, and victorious in all combats, holy, beautiful, and furtherer of the world. The man in whose dwelling he receives nourishment, is pure, and thinks, speaks and does much good. He smites the Daevas, warring with them night and day, and they bow affrighted before him, and hasten to darkness. He is praised by Haôma, is the healer, fair, kingly, having golden eyes. He, on the highest summit of the high mountain, speaks well, speaks protecting words, at the right time. He possesses greatness of all kinds, and perfect wisdom. His victorious dwelling is formed with a thousand pillars, on the highest summit of the great mountain, and shines inwardly with its own light, and outwardly like a star. Through his strength and victory, his wisdom and knowledge, the Amĕsha-Çpĕntas are over the earth. He is the lawgiver for the laws, and as unbounded ruler steps along over the corporeal world. Through this law, Ahura Mazda, Vohu-Manô and the other Amĕsha-Çpĕntas are gracious to him, the Ahurian Question, the Ahurian Custom, in both worlds, the corporeal and spiritual.

Four horses carry him, spotless, bright-shining, beautiful, holy, wise, swift, obeying heavenly commands, their hoofs of lead, with gold wrought therein. They are swifter than horses, wind, storm, the clouds, the birds, the arrow. Great, high-girt, he abides among the creatures of Mazda. Thrice each day and each night, he descends on the Kareshvare Qaniratha, holding the axe of a wood-cutter, to smite Añra-Mainyus, Aêshma, and the Mazanian Daevas.

All these are functions of Indra, in the Veda. Originally, it seems, Ahura Mazda was the first of the Amĕsha-Çpĕntas, the Çpĕnta-Mainyus, the fountain from which they flowed, in which they were all contained, as in the first Sephirah of the Kabbalah, the other nine Sephiroth were contained. Çraôsha seems then to have been the visible light; but when higher conceptions of Ahura Mazda came to be entertained, and he came to be regarded as above and not one of the Amĕsha-Çpĕntas, Çraôsha also came to be what the Vedic Indra was, the light-spirit, i. e., the invisible of which light is the visible manifestation. Then he became, in the stead of Ahura, the first of the Amĕsha-Çpĕntas, or, at any rate, the equivalent in the Bactrian faith, of Indra, the light-god, of the Veda.

That the soul of man survives the body is taught in many places in the Avesta. In Fargard *xix.* Ahura Mazda informs Zarathustra, where the soul, after death, accompanied by a dog (his children, labour and good actions in that shape), at the end of the third night, comes to the bridge Chinvat, where the consciousness and the soul are interrogated as to the man's conduct in the corporeal world. The souls of the pure are then led away over the Haraberezaiti (*Alborj*):

> over the bridge Chinvat it brings the host of the heavenly Yazatas. Vohu-Manô rises from his golden throne. Vohu-Manô speaks: how hast thou, O pure,

come hither? From the perishable world to the imperishable world? The pure souls go contented to the golden thrones of Ahura Mazda, of the Amĕsha-Çpĕntas, to Garo-Nemâna, the dwelling of Ahura Mazda, the dwelling of the Amĕsha-Çpĕntas, the dwelling of the other pure.

We shall better understand the Zarathustrian ideas of the soul, when we refer to the passages in regard to the Fravashis.

In Yaçna *xxvi.*, which is a hymn to all the Fravashis, the "earlier" Fravashis are first invoked and praised—those of Ahura Mazda, the greatest, best, fairest, the strongest, most intelligent, best-formed, the highest on account of his purity; and of the Amĕsha-Çpĕntas, the kings, the eyes or fountains (emanations), the great, mighty, strong, proceeding (going or flowing forth) from Ahura, who are imperishable, the pure of the first faith, the first disciples (like Hakemah and Bainah, wisdom and understanding, the second and third Sephiroth, the first spiritual forms, as it were, or bodies, ensouled or filled with the Divine wisdom).

THE YAZATAS.

According to the Second Fargard of the Vendidad, after Yima, the first of mankind with whom Ahura Mazda conversed, had three times enlarged the earth, that there might be room for the men and animals crowded upon it to move forward (a figurative description of the increase and multiplication of the Aryan race in its original home, and of three great waves of emigration from it), it is said that

> The creator, Ahura Mazda, produced a congregation, the heavenly *Yazatas*, the renowned in Airyana-Vaêjâ, of the good creation . . . . Yima, the shining, the possessor of a good flock, produced a congregation of the best men, the renowned in Airyana-Vaêjâ, of the good creation. To this congregation came the creator, Ahura Mazda, with the heavenly Yazatas;

and Yima came with his congregation of the best men, the renowned ones. Then Ahura Mazda informed him that winter would come upon the earth, frost and snow, and clouds over all the inhabited regions, and advised him to make a new abode, "in the everlasting golden-hued, whose food never fails," and there to make an enclosure, walled around, and with a window to give light within, and therein to place the seeds of men and women, of cattle, beasts of burden, dogs, birds and the red-burning fires, and trees and everything that grows for food, all in pairs and inexhaustible; where there should be no strife or vexation, aversion or enmity, poverty or deceit, beggary or sickness, nor any other tokens of Añra-Mainyus. In this enclosure are self-created lights, the stars, moon and sun. There men lead a delightful life: the bird Karshipta there promulgated to Mazdayaçnian law, and Urvataṭ-Narô and Zarathustra are master and overseer.

Yazata, in Sanskrit, *Yajata*, "worthy of honour," is the modern Persian *Ized*, pl. *yezdam*.

The legend, Bunsen thinks, has a historical background: that originally Airyana-Vaêjâ, the primitive Iranian land and cradle of the Aryans, enjoyed a mild and delightful climate, and was a Paradise of fruitfulness; but that by some convulsion of Nature or climatic change, it became a land of ten months of winter and two of summer; from which a favoured few, under Yima, the Yemshed of the later Persian legends, emigrated southward to lands in a more temperate latitude. The "enclosure" may have meant the mountains that walled in the fertile valleys, perhaps of Cashmere, where the Aryans had their fabled golden age. The mythical character of the legend most strikingly appears from the creation of the heavenly Yazatas being subsequent to the creation of men and animals, and during the lifetime of Yima, the son of Vivanhâo, who refused to be the recorder and bearer of the law, but consented to enlarge the world and make it fruitful, and to obey Ahura Mazda as protector, nourisher and overseer of the world.

It is said the Yima is identical with the Yama of the Veda, but the two have nothing in common except similarity of name, like Airyama and Aryaman. It is a merely idle notion.

But we are only concerned to inquire what the Yazatas were.

In *Yaçnas iii.* and *iv.* we find

> all good created Yazatas [invoked], the heavenly and the earthly, who are worthy of praise and worthy of adoration, on account of the best purity [and]: all-wise Yazatas, the heavenly and earthly, to whom is to be offered, who are to be praised on account of the best purity.

In the *Ashi-Yasht* [*Kh.-Av. xxxiii.*] a hymn to Ashis-Vañuhi, the daughter of Ahura Mazda and sister of the Amĕsha-Çpĕntas, it is said to her:

> Thy father is Ahura Mazda, the greatest of the Yazatas, the best of the Yazatas. Thy mother is Çpĕnta-Ârmaiti. Thy brother, the good Çraŏsha, the holy, and Rashnus the high, strong, and Mithra who possesses wide pastures, who watches with ten thousand eyes, and has a thousand ears.
>
> *Visp. ix.* . . . . Ahura Mazda, the pure, together with the good Yazatas, the Amĕsha-Çpĕntas, who have a good empire, good wisdom. *x.:* for the strong Yazatas. . . . . *xix.:* the descendants of the fire, the Yazatas we praise, the descendants of the fire, those sojourning in the (dwelling) of Rashnu, we praise.
>
> *Yaçna xxvi.:* 23. 24: All pure heavenly Yazatas praise we. All pure earthly Yazatas praise we.
>
> *Kh.-Av. ix.* 6.: Yazatas, endowed with much brightness, Yazatas, very health-bringing! May greatness be manifest from you, manifest from you the profit which follows the invocation. Great! be ye manifest, in reference to splendour for the officers.
>
> *Qarshet Yasht* [*Kh.-Av. xxii.*]: . . . . When the sun shines in brightness, when the sunshine beams, then stand the heavenly Yazatas, hundreds, thousands. They bring brightness together, they spread abroad brightness, they portion out brightness on the earth created by Ahura, and advance the world of the pure, and advance the body of the pure, and advance the sun, the immortal, shining, having swift horses . . . . For if the sun does not rise, then the Daevas slay all which live in the seven Kareshvars. Not a heavenly Yazata in the corporeal world would find our defence nor withstanding . . . . The sun . . . . gives satisfaction to all heavenly and earthly Yazatas.

MITHRA AND THE SUN.

Both the sun and Mithra are adored in the *Zend-Avesta.* It is universally supposed that they were the same. That the sun was adored, simply *as* a luminary, is certain.

In *Visp. xxii., v.* 6, we read,

> The omniscient understanding praise we, Ahura Mazda. The sun's light praise we. The sun, the highest among those on high, praise we. Together with the sun, we praise the Amĕsha-Çpĕntas.
>
> *Yaç. i.*—I invite and announce to: Ahura and Mithra, both great, imperishable, pure; and to the stars, the creatures of Çpĕnta-Mainyus. And the star Tistrya, shining, brilliant, and the moon, which contains the seed of earth, and the shining sun with the swift horses, the eye of Ahura Mazda and Mithra, the lord of the region.
>
> *Yaç. iii.*—And for the sun, the shining, possessing swift horses, the eye of Ahura Mazda, the lord of the regions: I wish hither with praise: for Ahura Mazda, the shining, brilliant.
>
> *Yaç. xxii.*—For the satisfaction of Ahura Mazda, the brilliant, majestic—of the Amĕsha-Çpĕntas, of Mithra, possessing many pastures, and of Râma-Qâçtra, of the sun, the immortal, brilliant, with swift horses.
>
> *Yaç. xxv.*—Ahura Mazda, the brilliant, majestic, praise we. The Amĕsha-Çpĕntas, the good rulers, the wise, praise we. Mithra, who has a wide territory, praise we: Râma-Qâçtra praise we. The sun, the immortal, shining with swift horses, praise we.
>
> *Yaç. lxvii.*—Praise to Mithra, who possesses many pastures. Praise to the sun, who is endowed with swift horses. Praise to the two eyes of Ahura Mazda.
>
> *Quarset Nyâyis [Kh.-Av. vii.]*—Praise to thee, Ahura Mazda, three-fold before other creatures. Praise to you, Amĕsha-Çpĕntas, who have all like wills with the sun.
>
> Praise be to Ahura Mazda. Praise to the Amĕsha-Çpĕntas, praise to Mithra who possesses wide pastures, praise to the sun with swift steeds, praise to the eyes of Ahura Mazda, praise to the bull.
>
> The immortal sun, shining, with swift steeds, we praise. Mithra, possessing wide pastures, we honour—the truth-speaking gatherer, the thousand-eared, well-shaped, with ten thousand eyes, great, endowed with far-watching, the strong, not sleeping, wakeful. Mithra, the lord of all regions, we praise, *whom Ahura Mazda has created as the most brilliant of the heavenly Yazatas.* Therefore come to our assistance, *Mithra and Ahura the great.* The immortal brilliant sun, with swift steeds, we praise . . . . All pure heavenly Yazatas we praise, all earthly Yazatas we praise . . . . The immortal brilliant sun, with strong steeds, we praise [this five times repeated]: Offering, praise, might, strength, implore I for the sun, immortal, brilliant, with swift horses. The Ahurian pastures of Ahura praise I.

I think we may pause here, and, finding the sun and Mithra invoked and praised, again and again separately in the same passages, the sun always spoken of as having swift horses, and Mithra possessing wide pastures, as if specially and pointedly to designate each as distinct from the other, may with some confidence conclude that Mithra was not the sun. And, further, that as Ahura was the planet Jupiter, and Mithra was the most brilliant of the heavenly Yazatas, that these were the planets and stars, and Mithra the Morning Star, as he was with the Vedic Poets. Therefore it is that "Mithra and Ahura, the Great," are invoked to come together.

In the next Yasht, *Mihr-Nyâyis*, Mithra is several times praised as possessing wide pastures; and the same phrase is often repeated elsewhere. It must therefore have had some peculiar significance, as applied to him. It may be possible to discover its meaning, by the aid of other expressions.

In this Yasht, he is

> the truth-speaking, gathering, thousand-eared, well-formed, provided with ten thousand eyes, great, possessing a wide watch, strong, not sleeping, vigilant.

He is set over the "regions," is within them, with them, below them, before and behind them, lord of all regions. "Mithra and Ahura, both great, immortal, pure, praise we. The stars, the moon and sun praise we." He is praised for his brightness and majesty, He comes to the worshipper for protection, joy, profit, benevolence, healing, victory, purifying and sanctification. He is strong and mighty, deserving of offerings, praiseworthy, not to be lied to in the whole corporeal world, mighty, worthy of honour, most profitable Mithra of created beings, and he has "a named name, a well-known name."

Here, again, we find Mithra and Ahura named together, and distinguished from the sun. If Mithra was Venus, the revolutions of that planet and its being sometimes the Morning, and sometimes the Evening Star, may explain its different positions in regard to the "regions." As chief of the stars, they may be its ten thousand eyes; and its thousand ears to hear the adoration of its worshippers.

It is "well-formed," which indicates that it is not a principle or substance, without form or limit, but a body, an orb or luminary. To be in different places, with personality in each, it must be a body. That it has a named or well-known name, indicates the same thing. It possesses a wide watch, since its light flows over the whole earth, and over all the plains wherein the cattle are pastured. It is vigilant and sleepless, shining with a broad, steady, abundant light, and may well be characterized as brilliant and majestic. What is meant by its being the gatherer, we do not yet see.

In the *Ormazd-Yasht*, Ahura Mazda calls himself "The Gatherer;" which is, says a note, because he created mankind and animals and plants, and gathered them together upon the face of the earth. Did Mithra also do this?

The *Mihr-Yasht* (*Kh.-Av. xxvi.*) is in praise of Mithra. The phrases already quoted are continually repeated in it. Here, as elsewhere also, he is coupled in praise with Râma-Qâçtra. He is "the Yazata with named name." "When I created Mithra," Ahura Mazda says to Zarathustra, "I created him as worthy of honour, as worthy of praise, as I myself." He bestows swift horses, if one does not tie to him. He is the great, with wide watch-towers, the strong, sleepless, increasing. The lords of the regions praise him at early dawn, the warriors on horseback, praying for his aid. He

> as the first heavenly Yazata, rises over Hara before the sun, the immortal, with swift steeds, who first, with golden form, seizes the fair summits, then surrounds the whole Aryan-place, the most profitable.

In the note to this, it is said,

> From this passage it appears that Mithra was typified as the first sunbeams which illumine the mountain-tops, and that he then became separated from the sun, and hastened in front of him, like the Indian Açvins.

But how, then, *is* he the sun? It seems to me that it far more appears that Mithras was the Morning Star, rising over the Eastern Himalayas before the sun, before the dawn, and worshipped by the princes and warriors before or at, the early dawn.

Over this ancient land, lying under the mountains, with broad rivers, canals for irrigation, and great herds of cattle, from which the rivers flow north and south—into all the Kareshvares or quarters of it, Mithra the health-bringing goes round, marches into all "as a heavenly Yazata bestowing brightness" and rule, increasing the victory of those who sacrifice to him piously, knowingly and in purity. How could it be more plainly said that he is one of the luminaries of the sky?

If lied to, he is wrathful and offended, and destroys those who so offend. Not lied to, he gives strength and victory. He is the bestower of profit, the gatherer. His body is the Manthra. He upholds the dwellings of men, but where he is angered, he destroys them. And yet it is immediately said,

> Thou art alike to the bad and the best, O Mithra; to the regions thou art alike, to the bad and the best; to men, thou, O Mithra, art lord over peace and discord, for the regions.

He is the debt-paying, host desiring, gifted with a thousand strengths, ruling, mighty, all-wise. His dwelling, as broad as the earth, is fast-set in the corporeal world, large, unlimitedly high, broad, affording wide space. His eight friends sit spying for him on all heights, on all watch-towers, spying out those who lie to him. His famous golden horses, with broad hoofs, carry him to the hostile hosts.

Ahura Mazda has made him a dwelling on Haraběrězaiti, the far-reaching and lofty, where there is neither night nor darkness, cold wind nor hot, nor sickness, nor dust, nor mist.

Then, as if to make the enigma inexplicable, we find Mithra, with uplifted hands, weeping to Ahura Mazda, complaining that though he is the protector of all creatures, the skilful, the ruler of all, men do not sacrifice to him by name, as they do to the other Yazatas. *It is a demand for the restoration of the old worship.*

Then again, his fame, body and praise are good, and he guards the working peasant against oppressors, and is the upright-standing, watchful watcher, the mighty gatherer, who advances the water, listens to the call, makes the water to run, the trees to grow, etc.

He rides in a chariot made in heavenly way, with high wheels, and with the majesty and victory created by Ahura. (These remind us of the Sephiroth of the Kabbalah, Magnificence, Victory, Glory and Dominion.) Ashis-Vanuhi guides his chariot; the Mazdayaçnian law accompanies it, horses draw him with heavenly will, light, shining, fair, holy, wise. Before him goes Věrěthraghna in the shape of a boar.

Again he complains to Ahura Mazda, saying that if men would offer to him as they do to the other Yazatas, he would come to the pure men at the set time and times, at the set time of his own shining, heavenly life. He

> advances at sunrise, broad as the earth, and sweeps both ends of it, surrounding all that is between heaven and earth.

Through all this accumulated nonsense of the later "Minnesingers," to whom phrases were of more value than ideas, a keen eye can pierce to the old original Aryan idea of Mitra, the Morning Star, lord of light and truth, rising before the dawn over the snowy summits of the Bolor Tagh or Asiatic Caucasus, restoring life to the darkened world, and rousing the herdsmen and the peasants, from the unconsciousness of death's sister, sleep, and urging the one to prepare to drive his herds afield, and the other to prepare to till his ground, the good housewife to kindle the domestic fire, and the Priest and Bard to prepare for the morning sacrifice. Kingly, majestic, brilliant, he drove before him like a routed host, the gloomy and reluctant shadows, in which the men of humanity's childhood saw, gloomy and menacing, the spirits of mischief and malice. With him came the cool, healthy, invigorating mountain-breezes, the peculiar freshness and sweetness of the early morning, the exhilarating and inspiring influences of the return of day; and, "healthful and fair, ruling with golden eyes," in a sky from which a thousand twinkling eyes looked down upon the earth, "on the highest summit of the high mountain which bears the name Hukairya," he took possession with his light of the wide Aryan pastures, and by that light the herdsmen on the steppes gathered together their scattered herds.

So we see, through the cumbrous drapery of the later notions, the original idea of Ahura, the Varuṇa of the Veda, the kingly planet Jupiter; and the Amĕsha-Çpĕntas, the same as the Seven Ṛishis, the stars which revolving round the North Star never set—the Amĕsha-Çpĕntas,

> whose bodies are beautiful, to whom the sun with swift steeds announces praise from afar.

To Mithra,

> Ahura Mazda, the well-working, brings rule over the worlds which behold him as Lord and Master among the creatures of the world, as the best purifier among these creatures [i. e., translated from this foreign tongue into intelligible English], Ahura Mazda, the author of benefits, has given him potency and influence [to benefit and bless] all of the material world that by his light sees him as the chief among the stars and planets, in brightness and the light diffused by him, excelling them all.

So it is that, when sunrise is at hand, he rises and pours his light over all the earth, flooding with it both the horizons, and filling with it the whole space between sky and earth.

And, remembering that in the Greek mythology, it was not Zeus or Diespiter, the Jupiter and Jove of the Roman Aryans, who was the divinity of the sun, but Apollo; and that the planet Jupiter bore the name of the sovereign of Olympus, we shall not wonder that in these two branches of the Aryan faith, nearer the cradle of the race, Varuṇa, Ahura and Mitra, the planets are oftener and more earnestly invoked than the sun, and that Ahura became the God-Creator of the Zarathustrian protest against Nature-worship. For it is certain that Ahura was originally a Yazata, as the fire and all the stars were; and that when the songs of the Avesta were composed, the old worship of the lights of the sky had not died out, though new and more abstract and spiritual ideas had grown up, and the luminaries were both orbs and veritable Gods.

Thus Mithra, the mightiest, strongest, most famous, swiftest and most victorious of the Yazatas, "stands with wide pastures, on this earth," when, pausing on the mountain-summit, he flashes his light in one great flood, over all the sleeping plains. Thus he "marches forward," possessing himself of the wide pastures, "to the very end of the broad, circular, far-to-traverse earth;" Çraôsha, the good and holy, marching on his right hand, and Rashnus the great and powerful, on his left.

Imagining him a warrior, routing the serried phalanxes of the embattled glooms, the poetic imagination pictured him "with shining steeds, sharp lance, long hilt, arrows flashing to their mark," himself "the far-seeing bold warrior."

And, when in the still night moving in serene majesty upon his path high in the heavens, it was easy for the imagination to say of him,

> whom Ahura Mazda created as ruler and overseer of all living Nature, who, sleepless, watchfully protects the creatures of Ahura Mazda. [High in the heavens and filling the whole expanse with light, it could be said of him], whose long arms grasp forward here with Mithra-strength; that which is in Eastern India he seizes, and that which is in the western he smites, and what is on the steppes of Rañha [the Jaxartes], and what is at the ends of this earth [the shores of the Indian Ocean].

No man, with a hundred-fold strength, thinks, speaks or does so much evil, as Mithra with heavenly strength, thinks, speaks and does good.

> Mightily Mithra goes forward, powerful in rule marches onward, and shining in the distance gives to the eyes power to see far and wide . . . . Manifest are the ways of Mithra, when he comes to the region where, well-honoured, he makes the deep plains into pastures . . . . With uplifted arms, Mithra, with wide pastures, marches to immortality; from Garo-Nemana, the shining, he rides on a beautiful chariot, one alike strong, of all shapes, golden. To this chariot are yoked four white horses of like colour, who eat heavenly food, and are immortal. Their fore-hoofs are shod with gold, their hind-hoofs with silver. Then they are all harnessed to the same pole, which is curved above, bound with split, firm, inlaid clasps of metal.

On his right rides Rashnu, the rightest wisdom, white robed; on his left, near by, a boar; and

> outside of this flies along the fire which has kindled the strong kingly brightness . . . . Mithra, who, as the first announcer promotes strength among the creatures of Çpĕnta-Mainyus, he, the well-created, greatest Yazata, when he illumines the body, as the self-illumining moon, shines.

Originally the Morning Star itself, Mithra had become, before these Yashts were composed, the ideal and spiritual being, the invisible archangel, the soul, of that planet, which had become to him as a body. And the meaning of this verse seems plainly enough to be, that he, the greatest of the stars and planets, when he rose before the dawn, announcing the approaching day and arousing and invigorating awakened men, manifested himself in shape and form as the visible luminary, shining as the moon was deemed to do, by his own and no borrowed light.

And in the next verse (143), we find that his

> countenance shines like that of the Star Tistrya [Sirius], whose chariot, the undeceiving seizes, first, O Holy, namely, among the fairest of creatures, created with sunshine for the shining Yazatas, the star-shining created by Ahura Mazda. [That is, I think], whose orb is radiant like that of Sirius, whose car he who never misleads or deceives men, takes possession of—he, namely, O Mithras, Holy one, who is chief among the most beautiful of created things, of those created with light like the light of the sun, to be radiantly visible as the stars that shine—he shines as a star, created by Ahura Mazda, to traverse the sky.

The last verse (145) is,

> Mithra and Ahura, both great, imperishable, pure, we praise. The stars, the moon the sun, in the Bareçma-bearing trees, Mithra, the sovereign of all regions, we praise

A single passage is enough to show that Mithra was not the Sun: in *Fargard xix.* of the Vendidad, *v.* 91, 2 and 3:

> In the third night, at the coming and lighting of the dawn, and when the victorious Mithra places himself on the mountains with pure splendour, and the brilliant sun arises.

And that the Yazatas are luminaries is apparent from *v.* 6 of the *Mâh Nyâyis* (*Kh.-Av. x.*):

> Yazatas, endowed with much brightness, Yazatas, very health-bringing! May greatness be manifest from you, manifest from you the profit which follows the invocation. Great! be ye manifest in reference to splendour, for the offerers.

Fire, also, because the luminaries are its manifestations, is also styled a Yazata, in the Khordah-Avesta:

> Holy Fire, warrior, Yazata with much majesty, Yazata with many healing remedies! . . . . Praise to thee, fire, son of Ahura Mazda, giver of good, greatest Yazata!

This is the visible fire. It is Asha or Asha-Vahista, the spirit of the fire, the second Amĕsha-Çpĕnta, that is the Agni of the Veda, and to whom, with Ahura Mazda and Vohu-Manô, the first Amĕsha-Çpĕnta, the first Gâthâ (*Ahunavaiti*, *Yaç. xxviii.*) is addressed. To these three, almost entirely, the Gâthâs are addressed, the other Amĕsha-Çpĕntas being only occasionally invoked, Çraŏsha at more length than any of these; and Mithra is very briefly spoken of, only five times in all. I infer that these hymns contain the true Zarathustrian teachings and ideas, the creed taught in opposition to the original Nature-worship; and that those who composed the later invocation returned, in a measure, to the adoration of fire and the heavenly orbs, its manifestations; although, as a natural consequence of the struggle between the new creed and the old, the beneficent Devas of the Veda, the divine, had become the evil Daevas, creatures of Aṅra-Mainyus, or his manifestations, hypostases or subsistences, and Indra, the great Deity of light, had become their coadjutor and the enemy of Ahura Mazda or Çpĕnta-Mainyus.

THE STARS.

Unquestionably, the stars continued to be adored, as the following passages will show:

> *Vend. Farg. xix.* I praise the shining heaven: I praise the lights without a beginning, the self-created: I praise Vĕrĕthraghna created by Ahura Mazda, the carrier of light, created by Ahura Mazda. I praise the good Çaŏka, who possesses many eyes. I praise the Star Tistar, the shining, brilliant, who has the body of a bull, and golden hoofs. I praise Haetumat, the beaming, shining.

> *Tistar-Yasht, Kh.-Av. xxiv.*—I confess, etc., for the Star Tistrya, the brilliant, majestic; for Çatavaeça, the distributor of water, the strong, created by Mazda; for the stars which contain the seed of the water, contain the seed of the earth, contain the seed of the trees, created by Mazda; for Vanaṇt, the star created by Mazda; for the stars which are the Haptô-Iriñga, the brilliant, healthful Khshnaŏthra, etc. Yatha Ahu Viryo.

> In order to protect sovereignty, the supreme rule, the moon, the dwelling, we will praise the Myazda, that my stars, the brilliant, may unite themselves and give light to the moon. Praise thou the distributor of the field, the Star Tistrya, with offering.

The whole hymn purports to be spoken by Ahura Mazda to Zarathustra, and commands praise and adoration to be offered to the Star Tistrya, the shining, majestic, great, going round about from afar with shining beams, the name of the bull created by Mazda. The stars mentioned in the first verse, it is said in the note, are the watchers in the four quarters of the heavens—Tistrya in the east, Çatavaêça in the west, Vanaṇt in the south, and Haptô-Iriñga in the north. And elsewhere, Tistrya is said to be Sirius. I condense from the Yasht the following phrases:

> The Star Tistrya, which contains the seed of the water, working on high, renowned from this height, shining from the navel of the waters . . . . The Star Tistrya, who glides so softly to the Sea Vôuru Kasha, like an arrow, who comes from the damp mountain to the shining mountain . . . . who torments the Pairikas, seeks to overthrow the Pairikas, which fly about like fish-stars between heaven and earth . . . . The Çatavaêça causes the water to go down . . . . The Star Tistrya spake to Ahura Mazda, saying, when men will offer to me with offerings by name, as they offer to the other Yazatas with offerings by name, then will I shine to the pure man at the appointed time . . . . I praise the Stars Haptô-Iriñga for resisting the sorcerers and Pairikas. [The *Haptô-Iriñga*, therefore, is a constellation of seven stars, i. e., Ursa Major] . . . . Tistrya, who has healthful eyes . . . . The first ten nights, Tistrya unites himself with a body, going forth in the bright space, with the body of a youth of fifteen years, a shining one, with bright eyes, large, arrived at his strength, powerful, nimble: the second ten nights, with the body of a

> bull, with golden hoofs: the third ten nights, with the body of a horse, a shining, beautiful one, with yellow ears, with a golden housing: coming out against him runs out the Daeva Apaŏsha, in the form of a horse, a black one, and they fight. Tistrya fights against all the evil ones, created by Aṅra-Mainyus, as opponents of all constellations that contain the seed of the waters. He overcomes them, and the clouds gather, and rains refresh the land, and all lakes, running waters and springs praise Tistrya, 'whom Ahura Mazda has created as Lord and Overseer over all constellations' . . . . And Ahura Mazda says, 'I have created, O Holy Zarathustra, this Star Tistrya, as worthy of praise, as worthy of adoration, as worthy to be satisfied [sacrificed to], as rightly created, as I myself, Ahura Mazda. Offering shall the Aryan regions offer him, Bareçma shall the Aryan regions strew for him, cattle shall the Aryan regions cook for him, and the Haŏma, of whatever colour.'

Drvâçpa is a female Deity, praised in the *Gosh-Yasht, Kh.-Av. xxv.* She is the strong, created by Mazda, who gives health to the cattle and beasts of burden, the friends and minors, and "keeps much watch, stepping from afar, the shining, long-friendly." In the Parsee prayer (modern) which precedes the Yasht, she is called *Géus-Urva* Drvâçpa, *Géus-Urva* meaning *the soul of the bull*, the especial protector of cattle. The appellation *Drvâçpa*, it is said in the note, signifies, "possessing sound horses." She

> has harnessed horses, armed chariots, sparkling wheels, is fat, pure, the strong, beautiful, profitable of herself, the firm-standing, strongly-armed for protection to the pure men.

Zarathustra is said to have sacrificed to her in Airyana-Vaêja, and others to have sacrificed to her thousand upon thousands of cattle, and horses by hundreds. She has brightness and majesty, and is strong and pure, and enables her worshippers to conquer the snake Dahâka and the Drukhs and their Turanian enemies.

In the *Rashnu-Yasht*, the Ized or Yazata *Rashnu* is praised and invoked—

> Rashnu the most first, with Arstât who furthers the world. [He is] the truly-created of the Maṅthra-Çpěntas, the surpassing, distinguishing, healing, shining, powerful, placed higher than other creatures; the Maṅthra, the very majestic, the truly created Maṅthra-Çpěnta, the eminent. Invoked at the third part of the night, toward the east, he will come to help the worshipper, he, the great, mighty, pure, most just, holy and wise, most chosen, most far-seeing, helping to victory, whether he is in any quarter of the land, at the waters or steppes of Raṅha, at the ends of the earth, or at the Star Tistrya or Vanant, or the Stars Haptô-Iringa, or at other stars, at the moon or sun: at all of which he seems to be deemed to be at the same time.

The *Farvardin-Yasht, Kh.-Av. xxix.*, is addressed to the Fravashis (*Frohars*, in Parsee). These are the Genii or Spirits, of men and Gods. For

Ahura Mazda himself has his Fravashi. They are of the dead, and of those yet unborn; of dwellings, clans, confederacies, regions and priests; and in *Yaçna xxvi.*, these are praised, with "all the earlier Fravashis," the Fravashi of Ahura Mazda, those of the pure, of the Amĕsha-Çpĕntas, of "the pure men and women here," of "the well-created cow, who was the protectress of Purity," and those of Zarathustra, of Kavi-Victâçpa, of Içat-Vâçtra, of the Nabâzdistas, of the deceased pure, the living pure, the yet unborn; the last verse being, "the Souls of the deceased praise we, which are the Fravashis of the pure."

> *Fravashi* [it is said in the note], which is usually applied to the power which holds body and soul together, seems here to be equivalent to the conscience.

Professor Guigniant, in his edition of Creuzer, *Religions de l' Antiquité, ii. 326,* says of the Fervers (*Fravashis*), that they are

> the ideas, the prototypes, the models, of all beings, formed of the essence of Ormuzd, and the most pure emanations of that essence. They exist by the living Word of the Creator, wherefore they are immortal, and by them everything lives in Nature. They are placed in heaven as regular sentinels against Ahriman, and bear to Ormuzd the prayers of pious men whom they protect, and purify from all evil. Upon the earth, united to bodies, they incessantly combat with evil spirits. They are as numerous, and as diversified in their kinds, as the beings themselves. Even Ormuzd has his Ferver, because the Eternal contemplates himself in the omnipotent word, and this image of the Ineffable Being is the Ferver of Ormuzd. The Law (the Word) has its Ferver, which is the spirit and life of the Law, the Living Word, such as God conceived it. The Ferver of Zerdusht (Zoroaster) is one of the finest, because this prophet published the law. Thus the Fervers constitute the ideal world; all the rest is the real or created world . . . . Every Parsee has his ideal prototype, his pure model, which he must endeavour to express and realize, who inspires and directs him in all his actions, and serves as his guide in the pilgrimage of life.

The *Farvardin-Yasht, Kh.-Av. xxix.*, recites at great length the infinitely diversified potencies of the Fravashis. It is through their brightness and majesty that Ahura Mazda upholds the heavens and supplies water to the world. Every possible potency is ascribed to the Fravashis of the pure. The sun, moon and stars journey through their brightness and majesty. They give victory, and, wearing their armour, they fight in battle;

> For they are the most active of the creatures of both the heavenlies, the good, strong, holy, Fravashis of the pure, who at that time stood on high, when the two heavenly ones created the creatures—the holy spirit and the evil.

The Amĕsha-Çpĕntas have their Fravashis; and so has the shining heaven.

The *Bahram-Yasht, Kh.-Av. xxx.*, contains invocation of and praise to Vĕrĕthraghna, the best armed of the heavenly Yazatas. He is the strongest, most victorious, most majestic, the most beneficent and liberal, and the most healing, praised for his brightness and majesty. He comes as a bull, a horse, a camel, a boar, a youth of fifteen, a bird, a ram, a goat and a man. He decks the world with majesty through his arms. He is a warrior, the comrade of Mithra and Rashnu. He is sacrificed to, with flesh and the Haŏma.

The *Ashi-Yasht, Kh.-Av. xxxiii.*, is in praise of *Ashis-Vanuhi,*

> the shining, great, beautiful, very worthy of honour, with her shining wheel, strong, bestower of profitable gifts, the healing. She is the daughter of Ahura Mazda, and the sister of the Amĕsha-Çpĕntas; is fair and beaming, giving much brightness to the men whom she follows. She comes to men's dwellings, attaching herself to the inmates. Her mother is Çpĕnta-Ârmaiti (the earth). Çraŏsha, Rashnus and Mithra are her brothers, and the Mazdayaçnian law, her sister. Zarathustra and Yima made offerings to her, the high, and she ran round and came up. Others sacrificed to her; and she aided them to smite the Daevas and Turanians. [And the last verse (62) is]: Offering, praise, strength, might, I vow to Ashis-Vanuhi, to the good wisdom, the good justice, the good equity, the brightness, the profit, created by Mazda. Ashem-Vohû.

Ahura Mazda tells her not to ascend to heaven, nor to creep on the earth, but to go to the dwelling of a fair king; and in the next Yasht (*Astâd*), she goes to the abode, into the midst of the dwelling of the handsome, who has collected himself a kingdom.

In the *Râm-Yasht, Kh.-Av. xxxi.*, the waters and the air are invoked. In the *Din-Yasht xxxii.*, the rightest wisdom, created by Mazda, the good Mazdayaçnian law. In the *Astâd-Yasht* and *Zamyâd-Yasht xxxiv.* and *xxxv.*, the majesty of the Aryans, created by Mazda, the various mountains, and the strong kingly majesty, created by Mazda, that belongs to Ahura Mazda, to the Amĕsha-Çpĕntas and the heavenly and earthly Yazatas, and united itself with Yima and other great and valiant men, as manly courage, and attached itself to Zarathustra, for thinking, speaking and fulfilling the law; and attached itself to the victorious Çaŏshyanç that he might make the worlds progressive and immortal, that the dead might rise, and immortality come for the living. It is at last to be possessed by Açtvat-ĕrĕto, or messenger of Ahura Mazda, son of Viçpa-taurvi, who purifies the victorious wisdom, who is to make the whole corporeal world immortal, who is to smite the wicked Drukhs, and

> Vohu-Manô will smite Akô-Manô, the truth smites the lie, Haurvatâț and Amĕrĕtaț subdue hunger and thirst, and the evil-doer Aňra-Mainyu bows himself, robbed of rule.

The Star Vanant is praised in the *Vanaṇt-Yasht*, of only three verses; the prayer *Ashem-Vohû*, in a fragment; and in the *Afrigân-Rapithwin*, the Lord *Rapithwina*, *Frâdatfshu* and *Zantuma*, lords of purity. These three are also praised in the *Gâh Rapitan* (*Kh.-Av. xvi.*), where, in note, it is said,

> The protectors of the time Rapithwina are Asha-Vahista, the fire, Fradâṭfshu, the increaser of cattle, and Zantuma, the protector of confederacies: and in the text, 'That assembly and meeting of the Amĕsha-Çpĕntas we praise, which is prepared in the height of heaven, for the praise and adoration of Zantuma the lord.' Rapithwina is said to be from mid-day until the commencement of twilight.

The *Abân-Yasht* (*xxi.*), 132 verses, is devoted to the praise of Ardvi-çura

> the strong, brilliant, great, beautiful, whose flowing waters come hither by day as by night, namely, all the waters which flow along on the earth, which hasten away mightily.

She drives her chariot, drawn by four white draught-cattle, gives women good child-birth and brings them fitting and proper milk. Chiefs and leaders are represented as invoking her effectual assistance against the Daevas, the snake Dahâka, sorcerers, Pairikas, and other enemies, and obtaining it; and these foes as praying first and being refused. Men pray to her for horses and the majesty that comes from above, and maidens for good husbands, and women in child-bed, for fortunate delivery. And she flows down from the lofty Hukairya, and supplies all the Aryan world with water. She has a thousand basins and a thousand channels, and

> in greatness of majesty is as mighty as all the waters that flow on the earth. Ahura Mazda created for her the wind, the clouds, the rain and the hail, and all these she pours down.

And she is described as a woman, a fair maiden, beautiful, with brilliant face, holding the Bareçma, wearing ear-rings, and a golden necklace, with full bosom, a diadem on her head, set with a hundred stars, wearing garments of beaver-skin.

The *Yasht Nyâyis Ardviçur* (*x.*) is also addressed to her; and, in part, the *Farvardin-Yasht* (*xxix.*), where she is said to purify the seed of men, and the bodies of all women for a good delivery, to bestow good delivery, and give fit and suitable milk to all women; and her waters to flow from Hukairya the high to the Sea Vôuru-Kasha, and thence by a thousand canals and channels, into the Seven Kareshvares of the Aryan land.

The description of this Goddess of the waters is strikingly like that of Ardhanari, the Hindū Goddess of water, who became at last a hermaphrodite, conceiving to be in face and figure a female, but representing Siva-Mahadeva and Parvati-Bhavani, seated in a full-blown lotus, above a tiger and ox, between whom the Ganges flowed forth. The origin of both was perhaps the Vedic Saraswati.

The Prayer *Usahin* (*Kh.-Av. xvi.* 5), is addressed to Çraðsha, Rashnu and others, and to Ushahina, the dawn, the Ushas of the Veda.

> Ushahina, the pure, lord of purity, we praise. The fair morning-dawn we praise. The dawn we praise, the brilliant, with brilliant horses, which thinks of men, which thinks of heroes, which is provided with brightness, with dwellings. The dawn we praise, the rejoicing, provided with swift steeds, which floats over the earth, consisting of Seven Kareshvares.

The *Haôma*, the *Soma* of the Vedas, was used in the sacrifice, its juice being expressed in a consecrated mortar. In *Yaçna ix.*, Haôma comes at dawn, as a man, to Zarathustra, appearing to him "as the most beautiful in the whole corporeal world," endued with his own life, majestic and immortal. He is the pure, the far from death, and demanded to be praised by Zarathustra, as others had praised him. Yima first prepared him, and to him owed all his glory. Next, Athwya prepared him, the father of Thraetaonô, and then Thrita, and then the father of Zarathustra. Zarathustra then praises him, for wisdom, power, healthfulness, and asks of him health, long life, power to conquer Drujas, Daevas, etc. He gives horses, might and strength, brilliant children to women, holiness and greatness to men, and husbands to maidens. Growing on the mountains, sweet and golden, the healing powers flow to him, through the wisdom of Vohu-Manô. He makes the soul of the poor in greatness like that of the richest, the mind of the poor so large in greatness that it soars on high with wisdom, and makes many men very holy and clothed with much wisdom. He is poured from the silver cup into the golden, nothing of him being spilled on the earth, since he has so high a value; and all the songs and hymns of praise are his. Ahura Mazda, says the *Mihr-Yasht*, first by means of a mortar uplifted it, by means of one adorned with stars, made in a heavenly way, on the high mountain. He is

> the promoter, the health-giver, fair, kingly, with golden eyes, who offered to Ashis-Vañuhi, on the highest height of the high mountain.

We find the bull adored also. Thus, in the Gâthâs:

> Praise to the two eyes of Ahura Mazda. Praise to the Fravashi of the bull, of Gayô (Marathan), of the holy Zarathustra . . . . Namely, the creatures of Ahura Mazda, of Vohu-Manô, of Asha-Vahista, of Khshathra-Vairya, of Çpĕnta-Ârmaiti, of Haurvaţ and Amĕrĕtâţ, which appertain to the body of the bull, to the soul of the bull, to the fire of Ahura Mazda.

So, in the *Yasht*, *Mâh Nyâyis:*

> Praise to Ahura Mazda, praise to the Amĕsha-Çpĕntas, praise to the moon, which contains the seed of the bull, to the only-born bull, to the bull of many kinds, the only-begotten bull, the bull of many kinds.

The same phrases are again and again repeated in the *Mah-Yasht* (*Kh.-Av. xxiii.*), which is addressed to the moon, mistress of purity, the bestower, shining, majestic, provided with water, with warmth, the beaming, supporting, peace-bringing, which brings greenness, which brings forth good things, the health-bringing Genie.

We have found the mystic numbers, three, five, seven and nine; and in Yaçna *i.* we find invited and announced to,

> all the lords who are lords of purity, the thirty-three nearest, who are round about Hâvani, of the best pure, whom Ahura Mazda has taught, Zarathustra announced. [In the prayer numbered *iii.*, it is said], may the three and thirty Amshaspands and Ormazd be victorious and pure.

The first of the Great Parsee prayers is called *Ashem Vohu:* the second, *Yathâ Ahû Vairyô*, but generally *Ahuna-Vairya.* The third prayer is the *Yênhê-hâtańm*, meaning, "to whom, to the Existing." Ahura Mazda is declared in Yaçnas *xix.* and *xx.* to have spoken the *Ahuna-Vairya* and *Ashem-Vohu.* The former commences thus, *Yathâ Ahû Vairyo athâ ratus;* and the latter, *Ashem vôhû vahistem açtî:* the third, *Yênhê hâtańm âaţ yêçnê paiti. Vohu-Vahistem* is, the text says, "the best good."

ZARATHUSTRIAN FAITH: THE GÂTHÂS.

It has been said that the pure faith taught by Zarathustra seems to have had engrafted on it, at a later day, the worship of fire, of the sun, the stars and the planets. That is true, but this was a return to the old Aryan faith older than the time of Zarathustra, and which he sought to suppress and extinguish. Undoubtedly it always continued dear to the popular heart, and was never wholly yielded up.

There are forty-two of the Gâthâs, of which the first thirty-two, with the exception of one and a portion of another, are unquestionably very ancient. The dialect in which they are written shows that, and their spirit and tenour show it still more clearly. We find in them no adoration of the heavenly bodies, nor the confused assemblage of the later Deities. They purport to be the direct utterances of Zarathustra, and evidently contain the teachings, by which he founded a new religion in Bactria.

They almost exclusively invoke Ahura Mazda, the holy spirit, and after him Vohu-Manô and Asha-Vahista, the first and chiefest of the Amĕsha-Çpĕntas. The other four are seldom named: and in the first (*Gâthâ Ahunâ-Vaiti*) Ahura is addressed as "You," in the plural, because in him are contained, and from him emanate the Amĕsha-Çpĕntas, which are his potencies in exercise, and with him they are seven. That he is the *substance*, of which they are the *subsistences* or *hypostases*, is evident from the name *Çpĕnta-Mainyus*, often applied to him.

> I praise ye, first, O Asha and Vohu-Manô, and Ahura Mazda, to whom belongs an imperishable kingdom,

is, as it were, the text which the Gâthâs develop, the key-note by which they are chaunted. They are eminently free of sensual ideas, pure and spiritual.

> Whom thou knowest, O Asha, as the creatures of Vohu-Manô (i. e., the children of good), the truthful, Mazda Ahura, to them fulfil completely their wishes . . . . I keep forever purity and goodmindedness. Teach thou me, Mazda Ahura, from out thyself, from heaven, through thy mouth, whereby the world arose [i. e., communicate to me, inspire me with, the wisdom emanating from thyself, by thy word and utterance which did create the world. We have here both the *Wisdom* of the Kabbalah, and the *WORD* of Plato, Philo and St. John; and at the same time the intelligent self-manifestation of the wise Agni of the Veda] . . . . Mazda remembers best the words that he has made of old, before Daevas or men were, and which he will make again. When Ahura is asked who can announce his holy doctrine to mortals, he says, 'This one is known to me here, who alone heard our precepts, Zarathustra, the holy.' He asks from us, Mazda and Asha [the Vedic Fire-Spirit, Agni], assis-

tance in proclaiming it. I will make him skilful of speech. But the bull, created for the industrious and active of mankind, said, 'I am not content with this man not invested with *power*, with the words to be spoken by one not clothed with the prerogative of action and accomplishing. I wish an absolute Ruler'; and he asked Ahura to give to Zarathustra, to assist him, Asha and Khshathra, with Vohu-Manô, that he might create good dwellings and comfort. And thus Zarathustra had the holy empire, as priest and king; the temporal as well as the spiritual power. The foundation of his divine right, the patent of his title is here, one that marks with singular distinctness the simplicity of manners and life of the primitive race of husbandmen and herdsmen whom he taught and ruled, as Samuel the prophet taught and ruled the Beni-Isral and Mahmoud the children of Islam.

He sang the praises of Ahura.

May we belong to thee [he cried], we who seek to improve this world. Whoso is obedient here, he will there unite himself with wisdom. [The words he speaks are 'the best for those who give their heart to Mazda.'] If the good man holds fast without doubt, to that which cannot be perceived with the eyes, then comes he to you all, since he desires Ahura Mazda . . . . Thee have I thought [he says], O Mazda, as the first to praise with the soul, as the father of Vohu-Manô, since I saw thee with my eyes, the active creator of purity, the lord of the world in deeds [i. e., manifested in act]. When thou, Mazda, first createdst the world for us, and the laws, and the understanding, through thy spirit; when thou didst clothe the vital powers with bodies, and didst create action and instruction to satisfy the wishes of the world that was to become.

All his prayer to Ahura Mazda is summed up in this:

All the enjoyments of life, which were and still are, and which will be, these distribute according to thy will . . . . Hear me and pardon me all, whatever it may be; purify me, O Lord, through Armaiti [Wisdom], give me strength. Holiest, heavenly Mazda, in thy goodness, give me at my supplication strong power through Asha, fullness of good through Vohu-Manô.

'If you really exist, Mazda,' cries the worshipper, 'together with Asha and Vohu-Manô, then give me this token . . . . that, offering, I may join myself to you in friendship, may, praising you, draw nigh to you. Where are thy worshippers, Mazda, who are known to Vohu-Manô? The intelligent carries out the excellent precepts, in joy and sorrow. O Asha, I know no other than you: do thou therefore save us.'

Even in the Gâthâs, Zarathustra inculcates purity, obedience, goodness.

'As is right,' he says, 'so he does, who created the first place [the home of the Aryans], the master; the most righteous dispensations for the evil as for the good. We approach ourselves, first, to thee, Mazda Ahura, through the service of the fire. O fire, son of Ahura Mazda, we draw near to thee with good mind, with good purity, with deeds and words of good wisdom. We praise thee, we acknowledge ourselves thy debtors, Mazda Ahura. With all good thoughts, with all good words, with all good works, we draw nigh to thee.'

And yet how natural for those only lately converted from the worship of the fire as a supreme God, to cry, as we have seen the worshipper do,

> dost thou really exist, Ahura Mazda, and thou, Vohu-Manô? I have seen thee, only, Asha, the fire: do thou, therefore, be our saviour. How very like to the plaintive cry, 'Lord, I believe: help thou my unbelief!' [And what a sublime confidence and trust in the words], Him will we serve with praiseworthy prayers, for now it is evident to the eyes that he who in works and words of the Good Spirit knows purity, he knows Ahura Mazda . . . . Him will we content with goodmindedness.

And what has in any age been said, more noble and more simply sublime than this:

> Through the Holiest Spirit, and through the bestmindedness, which springs from purity with words and works, Mazda Ahura has given to us fulness and immortality, good things and understanding. Of this Holiest Spirit he does the best, the best through the loud prayers, by the mouth of Vohu-Manô; with the hands of Armaiti he does pure deeds; through his own wisdom, Mazda is the father of Purity?

Ahura and Asha are "the wise Thinkers;" and through Vohu-Manô Ahura Mazda dispenses his favours and blessings to mankind. "He who resembles thee, Mazda," it is said in the *Gâthâ Çpěnta-Mainyû*,

> through the understanding of Vohu-Manô, whoso remakes the mind better and performs good works, he according to the law with word and deed, wealth unites itself with him, according to his desire and will, according to thy mind every one is at last.

Hear, finally, this prayer:

> May that man obtain the best, who teaches us to know the right path to profit, for this world, the bodily as well as for the spiritual. May there now come to this dwelling contentment, blessing, guilelessness, and wisdom of the pure. May there appear for this clan, purity, dominion, profit, majesty and brightness, long dominion of the Ahurian and Zarathustrian law.

The Bactrian Aryans had the same ideas in regard to Prayer and the Genius of Prayer as the Indian Aryans. They praised the *Ahuna-vairya* on earth and in heaven, and the *Yeňhe hâtaňm*, as potent to drive away Aňra-Mainyus, and Drukhs, all evil ones, all wizards and magicians. Ahura Mazda created the Gâthâs, the praiseworthy prayers, holy, the lords over the times, the pure, "which Gâthâs" it is said, "are ruling and protecting for us, heavenly food; which are for our souls both food and raiment."

The body of the holy Çraŏsha (obedience) is the Mañthra.

> He rejoices the Mañthra, who utters it for knowledge. To you come listening they who rule through your deeds, Ahura and Asha, with the prayers of Vohu-Manô, which thou, Mazda, has first taught.

"The victorious Çaŏshyañç" is mentioned barely twice, in one Gâthâ; Rashnu, the most righteous, once; and the Yazatas only twice, and in the same hymn. The stars, Tistrya, Vanaṇt, etc., are not mentioned at all, nor is the sun or the moon adored, and Mithra is barely mentioned, two or three times, and in later Gâthâs. There is a hymn to the fire, and there are three to the waters, all, probably, of a later period.

There is ample evidence in these hymns or prayers, of their great antiquity. Nothing in them alludes to cities, towns or even villages. Only the dwellings, the clan, the confederacy and the region are spoken of. Nothing is said of gold and silver as riches, nor of other riches than cattle. Not the wealthy or powerful speak in them, but the husbandman; and it is positively certain that when they were composed, the Bactrians, brave and warlike, and leading simple lives, had no other wealth than horses and cattle.

The first Gâthâ (*Ahunavaiti*), *Yaçna xxviii.*, begins with these words:

> I desire, by my prayer with uplifted hands, this joy; first, the entirely pure works of the holy spirit, Mazda, then the understanding of Vohu-Manô, and that which rejoices the soul of the bull.

In *Yaçna xxix.*, the soul of the bull complains to the Amĕsha-Çpĕntas,

> For whom have ye created me, who has created me? Aĕshma, Haza, Remô, Dere and Tavi defile me; I have not fodder save from you, teach me then the good things which know herbage. Then asked the fashioner of the cow (Ahura Mazda) of Asha; where hast thou a lord for the cow? That he may make mighty, provide with fodder those who apply themselves to breeding cattle . . . . Asha answered him, There is not a lord for the cow, who could be free from being tormented [by the plagues of Añra-Mainyus] . . . . Now call I with uplifted hands, zealously, to Ahura Mazda: for my soul, and that of the three-year-old bull.

Ahura Mazda then said to the bull,

> A lord cannot be found, nor a master who proceeds from purity. I, the creator, have created thee for the industrious and for the active. . . . . This Manthra of

increase Ahura Mazda created, in agreement with Asha, for the cow, and milk for those enjoying according to holy commands.

We have already cited the remonstrance of the bull, in regard to Zarathustra, as teacher merely, and his desire for a ruler.

Yaç. xxxix.—Here praise we now the soul and body of the bull, then our souls, and the souls of the cattle, which desire to maintain us in life.

xxxi.—To thee [Ahura] belonged Ârmaiti, with thee was the understanding which fashioned the cow, when thou, Mazda Ahura, the heavenly, createdst ways for her.

xxxii.—To these has Mazda announced evil, to them who slay the soul of the cow with friendly speech.

If he brings that which was spoken for slaying the cow, as protection to him who is far from death. (This, the note says, is unintelligible.) In the former verse, Mazda is represented as denouncing evil to those who, being fonder of meat than of purity (or honesty), kill the cattle of others, while professing friendship; and to those who by wrong and violence seek to rise to power. Then those are denounced as of the obedience of Aṅra-Mainyus, who by revolt and insurrection seek to rend asunder kingdoms—as public enemies: and everyone who, while Mazda grieves at it, labours to make wickedness so general, that the messengers of the Maṅthras of Mazda shall not be able to see purity anywhere. He, it is then said, is guilty of gross misconduct, and no longer governed by reason, who deceives the labouring men, and, induced by him, they accept the protection of the wicked, and if he uses the same language of friendship, which was resorted to for the purpose of gaining an opportunity to slay the cattle, to assure him of protection, who, being in no danger, does not need it.

The reader must judge whether this is too audacious an interpretation of the original translation; and especially of the phrase last cited above, and of these which precede it:

Whoso wishes the rending of the kingdom, he belongs to the abode of the most wicked spirit, as the destroyer of this world; and he who wishes, O Mazda weeping, he who wishes to keep the messengers of thy Manthras far from beholding purity. He makes himself guilty of great dismemberment, he gives his understanding to the Kavayas, he who deceives the Active, if they accept the wicked for protection.

They slay "the soul of the cow," because, though there are Fravashis of the living and the unborn cattle, the souls of animals perish with them, and are not, like the human soul, immortal.

Yaç. xxxiii.—Whoso is the best for the pure, be it through relationship or deeds, or through obedience, O Ahura, caring for the cattle with activity, he finds himself in the service of Asha and Vohu-Manô. [That is, as I understand it: 'He who best serves the righteous man (the upright worshipper of Ahura Mazda), whether by the kindly offices and sympathies of relationship, or by acts that he does to benefit him, or even as a hired labourer, a herdsman industriously caring for his cattle, he is in the service of Asha and Vohu-Manô.' It is the same doctrine that is embodied in the sentences, 'He best serves God, who serves his neighbour best'; 'Forasmuch as ye have done it unto one of these, ye have done it unto me,' and 'He prayest best who loveth best, all things both great and small.' Even the poor hired herdsman, in this simple and beautiful creed, could worthily serve the Deity, by faithfully and loyally doing his duty, in his humble place and sphere.

Throughout the Gâthâs there breathes the spirit and are uttered the words, of a sincere sympathy for the labouring man. Thus, in the next Yaçna, the worshipper, telling Ahura Mazda, what it is that he wishes and prays for, to be granted "to the soul endowed with body," asks first of all for the "works," the beneficial effects, of Vohu-Manô, not for kings or chiefs, or the priests or the rich, but "for those who labour with the walking cow," i.e., the husbandmen.

In the *Yaçna Haptañhaiti* (*xxxv.*) the worshipper asks that, by means of his prayers and good deeds, pleasantness and fodder may be distributed to the cattle, as well to those of the wise as to those of the unlearned, as well to those of the powerful as to those of the weak.

And, in the same:

we meditate your praise, Ahura Mazda, and his [Asha-Vahista's], and the best fodder for the cattle.

Yaç. xxxix.—Here we now praise the soul and body of the bull, then our souls, and the souls of the cattle, which desire to maintain us in life.

xliii.—For whom hast thou [Ahura] made the going cow, as a gracious gift? . . . . Who has created the desired wisdom, together with the rule? Who, through his purity created the love of father to son. [The importance of the gift of cattle, to the people among whom these hymns were sung, may be judged of by the other gifts that are named in connection with it.]

And, in the same,

who will war against these, through whom the Karapas and Uçikhschas give the cow to Aĕshma, the Kavas so greatly increased themselves. [Aĕshma is an evil spirit, one of the creatures of Añra-Mainyus. To give him cattle, and so enable the Kavas to grow rich, is deemed a great wrong; and the punishment denounced for it in the next line is, 'Fodder is not to be given to them through Asha, as a reward'.]

It is for their cattle and men, alone, that in Yaçna *xliv.*, increase is prayed, "through the purity of Vohu-Manô, unto the good birth." Evidently the wealth of the people consisted almost wholly in cattle: and hence the praises of Goshurim, the primitive ideal bull; and the title of Ahura, "maker of the cow."

> *Yaç. xlv.*—I desire thy instruction, O Ahura. The wicked man hinders those who act uprightly, prevents their cattle from going onward through the districts and regions—he, the tyrants, who by his deeds deserves death, whoso, resisting him, shall end his rule or his life, will obtain for the cattle the granaries of wisdom. [Evidently some predatory chief is meant, whose power prevented the herdsmen from driving their cattle from one region to another, for change of pastures, and to crush or slay whom would enable the cattle to go where there was abundant forage.]

In the *Gâthâ Çpĕntâ-Mainyû*, it is said to Ahura Mazda:

> Thou who art also the holy in heaven, thou who hast created the cow as a helpful gift, thou who givest her fodder and delight, according to thy wisdom.

And here we find the meaning, in the former passage, of the "granaries of wisdom." They were the food of the cattle, supplied by the wisdom or creative word, of Ahura Mazda.

In *Yaçna xlvii.*, it is said:

> Whoso makes the mind better, and does good works, he, according to the law with word and deed, wealth unites itself with him, according to desire and will [i. e., I think, wealth comes to him of *its* own accord, the *desire* and will being *its*, and not *his;* as the souls of the cattle are said to *desire* to serve men for food]; according to thy mind is at last every one [i. e., his fortunes such as Ahura Mazda thinks he deserves] . . . . Purity is to man the best thing after birth [next to life? or, from the time of his birth, during all his life?]: for the cattle is it laboured, the diligent us this for food. [Translated, '(let) the diligent (bestow) us this for food'.] This ['refers to the cattle', note] 'has to us brightness' this 'has to us strength, might, given, according to the desire [by the good will] of Vohu-Manô. So too has it made trees grow with purity for Mazda, at the birth of the first world'.

I do not see how "this" refers to the cattle. If, as food, they have brightness and strength, for men, they do not make the trees grow. The passage speaks of the priceless value of purity, i. e., of honesty and uprightness. The practice of it gives men cattle, and honest diligence secures food. It is this purity that gives reputation and influence and power; and these are legitimately gained by it, with the approval of the Divine wisdom.

However that may be, what we particularly seek to direct attention to, is that cattle and food are the only wealth spoken of; and that these are deemed to be worse than worthless, unless obtained by honest labour.

So, in the same Yaçna;

> when will Mazda, Asha, together with Ârmaiti, come; Khshathra, the good dwelling with fodder?

Yaç. xlix.—How and whose protection shall my soul desire, who is for the cattle, what man is acknowledged for my protector, besides Asha and thee, Mazda Ahura, the desired, the invoked, by the best spirit? [In the Yaçna immediately preceding, Zarathustra had asked for a particular ruler, one enjoying the friendship of Asha, and had prayed to be freed of wicked rulers, evil-doing and evil-speaking. The same subject is continued here, and it is very noticeable that the ruler is styled 'the protector'.] How shall he, Mazda, desire the helpful cow, who wishes her active for this world to live well during many years?'

I do not pretend to clearly understand this; but I *think* that "how shall he desire" means "in what manner shall he effectually pray for?" or, "how shall he have fruition of his desire?"

But it is again noticeable that cattle are regarded again, as the most valuable gifts to man from Ahura Mazda.

Gâthâ Vohu-Khshathra (*Yaç. l.*).—Do thou, holiest, heavenly Mazda, who hast created the cow and the water and the trees, give me immortality and plenitude, power and strength, instruction through the best spirit . . . . Grant thou also the cow fullness, through thy deeds and precepts.

Yaç. lvii.—O father over the cattle, and over those who belong to the Holy One: the pure, and those wishing purity in the world . . . . Thoughts, words and works, cattle and men, we commit to Çpĕnta-Mainyû. All cattle, the healthful goods, the healthful cattle, the healthful men, all healthful, pure.

Yaç. lix.—May there appear for this clan, purity, dominion, profit, majesty and brightness, long dominion of the Ahurian, Zarathustrian law; quickly may cattle arise out of this clan, quickly purity, quickly the strength of the pure men, quickly Ahurian custom.

lxi.—Then the fire of Ahura Mazda, content, without hate, satisfied, blesses [him who brings wood to it]. 'May there arise around thee herds of cattle, abundance of men. May it go according to the desire of thy spirit, according to the desire of thy soul. Be glad, live thy life, the whole time that thou wilt live'. This is the blessing of the fire.

Fargard *xxi.* of the Vendidad commences with an invocation to the holy bull and the cow, in these words:

Praise be to thee, O holy bull, praise to thee, well-created cow, praise to thee, thou who multipliest, praise to thee, thou who makest to increase, praise to thee, gift of the creator, for the best pure, for the pure yet unborn . . . . [And the Manthra-Çpĕnta says, in the same], I will purify thy body and thy strength; I will make thee rich in children and rich in milk; in activity, milk, fatness, bounds, and prosperity. For thy sake I will purify here a thousand-fold; riches in cattle, which runs about, and is nourishment for children . . . . Go up, O moon, thou who containest the seed of the cattle, over Harabĕrĕzaiti, and illumine the creatures.

In Fargard *xxii.*, Ahura Mazda, suffering from the venom of the serpent Añra-Mainyus, promises as a recompense for healing him, first to Mañthra-Çpĕnta and then to Airyama, not gold or gems, but horses, camels, horned cattle and small cattle.

ANCIENT BACTRIAN ARYANS.

There is a singular charm in these ancient utterances of the Aryan heart and intellect, that have caused me to linger among them longer than I intended. I must close the book for the present. It is eminently worthy of an extended and exhaustive commentary. For they strikingly prove the truth of this saying of Emerson:

> The religions we call false, were once true. They also were affirmations of the conscience, correcting the evil customs of the times.

They tell us of a pure, simple, honest, upright, industrious people, kind and affectionate, and not yet corrupted by prosperity or what we call civilization. We find in them no unchristian sentiments, except in regard to their enemies, as to whom they inculcate no pity or mercy, and use no words of charity. But this was a consequence of their belief in two principles or powers, each of whom was a creator, for they were twins. Añra-Mainyus was the enemy, the serpent; and not only were his Daevas hated as evil spirits, malicious and of malignant natures; but the Turanians, and all who would not adore Ormuzd (as Ahura Mazda) has long been called, were the offspring of Añra-Mainyus, whom it was a merit to annihilate. It was the same error that pervaded all the ancient religions, and was devised by them to Mohammedanism, and Christianity. Nor is it as yet by any means dead; but it is strongly rooted in the human heart, and every day bears fruit.

Some conclusions may, I think, be with very great confidence deduced from the Vendidad and Gâthâs.

1. It is absolutely certain that these were composed by the bards and prophets of a people of herdsmen and husbandmen, who journeyed from place to place, over wide regions of country, with their herds, seeking pastures—a simple, honest, frank and manly people, of free and independent spirit, brooking no tyranny, obeying their rulers from choice and not through fear, and having no other wealth than their herds; for not even sheep are spoken of in the oldest compositions.

2. It is plain that there were no large cities or even considerable towns, and no powerful monarchs or great nobles. They had simply chiefs, like the ancient Germans, their brethren, and like the American Indians, who in some way or other select those who govern them, and depose them when they prove unfit, or abuse their power. The aboriginal or indigenous

people of the country, the Turanians, still opposed the progress of the superior race, and predatory raids were of frequent occurrence, while revolts sometimes disturbed the land, led by disaffected chieftains.

3. They lived in a country, partially wooded, at least, well watered by rivers, that flowed into a great sea, having their sources in lofty chains of mountains, with many high summits, which overlooked the land they occupied.

4. Zarathustra was their ruler, as well as spiritual and moral teacher. Claiming to converse with Ahura Mazda the creator, to repeat his very words, and to communicate his commands, he succeeded in converting this people of industrious and honest herdsmen and husbandmen, to his singularly spiritual doctrine. He was evidently far in advance of his people, a profound thinker, a wise, pure, just, earnest and sincere man; and one is at first inclined to wonder how it was possible for him to persuade so primitive a people, until his time adorers of the fire and light, the luminaries of the sky, the winds, the dawn and the powers of Nature, to believe in a spiritual, invisible Deity, a Creator and Protector, and in the Spirits or Powers that were not only the Ministers of His will, but Himself manifested and in action in various modes.

If the Bactrian Aryans had been an idolatrous people, or had worshipped the sun, moon and stars, as themselves Gods, it might have been impossible for them to comprehend or have a genuine and real belief in the spirit, Ahura Mazda, or in the real existence of his personified potencies, or in the immortality of their own souls, their Very Selves, invested and supplied with temporary bodies, but themselves immortal, creatures of Ahura Mazda, having had pre-existence, and destined to continue to exist, when severed once more from their bodies.

But they had long before become familiar with the same spirituality and intelligence, in the Aryan conceptions of Agni and Indra, the Fire-Principle and Light-Principle, Deities of a nature wholly spiritual, of whom the visible fire and light were the manifestations. Zoroaster transferred to Ahura Mazda the more spiritual attributes of Agni, and Fire became the Son of Ahura Mazda, one of his Amĕsha-Çpĕntas, manifestations and emanations; the same Fire Essence and Principle, that he was before.

5. I conclude, also, that some even of the Priests and Bards were doubters, and distressed with uncertainty as to the reality of existence of these spiritual Deities. And I conclude that the concessions which Zarathustra had to make, in favour of the old popular worship of the powers of Nature and the luminaries, kept alive the old faith, and predisposed the people to return to it, as giving them something more real and tangible to worship, than the spiritual God of the prophet, to whom they were required

to ascribe the potencies which they saw and felt to belong to the heavenly orbs and to Nature herself. There are no such denunciations of the ancient worship, as are found in the Hebraic writings. There is no hint of any persecution of heresy, and faith is everywhere subordinated to works. The Bactrian worship seems to have been very simple. Nothing is said about temples, and there seems to have been no sacredotal pomp. Nothing is said of costly presents made by Princes to the Priests or even to the Bards. In fact, as an efficacy sufficient to propitiate the potencies of Ahura, and secure their favour, and thus to obtain all that the worshipper desired, was ascribed to three or four simple prayers, dictated by Ahura at the creation, and afterwards communicated by him to Zarathustra, and which do not seem to have had any additional virtue when pronounced by a Priest, there could have been but little need of the exercise of intercessory and mediatorial functions.

A divine efficacy was ascribed to the Mańthras, the individuals of the ideal universal, "Prayer," which was termed Mańthra-Çpĕnta, and addressed as a Deity, as the Vedic Brahmanaspati and Bṛihaspati were. The word *Çpĕnta* seems to have the same meaning as *Pati*, i. e., the ideal unit containing in itself in the creative mind all the manifold that are to become: as "humanity" existent *in intellectu Dei*, in the Divine Mind, before any individual man existed, *is*, in very truth, all that are afterwards to become and exist. But it does not appear that any peculiar or special class or family of men had particular and exclusive commission to repeat these prayers or sing the sacred hymns. The pure man, which every Zarathustrian and adorer of Ahura was, could with confidence and hope address himself directly to the creator or to his ministering potencies, the Amĕsha-Çpĕntas.

6. It is quite evident that as time passed, the old faith gained strength, and the old Gods asserted their right to worship and sacrifice. We find them complaining that they are not sacrificed unto, and offering to bestow great benefits on those who shall offer to them. By this time, it is evident, their ancient names had been forgotten, for the most part, and new ones were invented, or the indigenous ones adopted. Indra has been intentionally changed to an evil Deity, as Tuphon was in Egypt, as the easiest and most effectual mode of obliterating the memory of his worship. The name of Mitra had survived in Mithra; but his identity with the Morning Star seems to have been unknown, or only vaguely alluded to in a few passages. Ushas, as Ushahina, the dawn, still survives and is briefly praised, her original greatness long ago forgotten, as the very names of Varuṇa, Sûrya, Rudra, Vishṇu, Savitṛi and the Açvins are, and that of Aryaman, to identify whom with Airyama is a mere fancy from similarity of sound and letters, than which nothing is more deceptive.

The immense space of time that elapsed from the settlement in Bactria to the immigration of the Indian Aryans into the Indus country will hardly of itself account, either for the vast differences between the Zend and Sanskrit languages, or for the almost total dissimilarity of names of their Deities. We find each branch of the race, indeed, calling its Gods by names unknown to every other branch. There are none in the Sanskrit at all resembling those of the Keltic, Gothic or Sclavonic Gods, and the Greek and Roman names are almost as entirely different.

But each emigrating multitude found in the land in which it settled down, a much more numerous indigenous people, with which by degrees it intermingled, as the languages did. We can trace the Aryan type of face in families and individuals of every one of the existing races, even where the national type is widely dissimilar; the indigenous type prevailing more widely among some, the Irish and Russians, for example, and the Hindūs, than among others; and so we find the *debris* of the old Aryan language in every one of their tongues; but the great mass, the warp and woof of every one of their languages is from the indigenous sources. The Aryan emigrants must everywhere have adopted the indigenous names of the luminaries and the Gods.

7. It is certain that the people whom Zarathustra taught and ruled were acquainted with the steppes of the River Ranha (supposed to be the Jaxartes); and therefore they must have resided at no great distance from them. These steppes are on the north side of the Oxus, which forms the boundary of Bactria on the north, and the Jaxartes. Bactria is bounded on the south by the immense chains of the Paropamisus and the Asiatic Caucasus, and from these a great number of rivers run northward across Bactria, and fall into the Oxus, which carried their accumulated waters into the Caspian, though now it falls into the Sea of Aral. At what time this change took place, is not known; but it is certain that long after the time of Zarathustra the surface-level of the Caspian was at least three hundred feet higher than it is now, and that its waters then extended far to the eastward of their present limits, and the Sea of Aral formed a part of it.

The streams that flow northward across Bactria from the Caucasus and Paropamisus Mountains, may well have been the rivers

> that flow from Hukairya the lofty, by a thousand canals and channels, each forty days' journey long for a mounted man, watering all the seven Kareshvares, and falling into the boundary-sea Vouru-Kasha.

I am inclined to think that "the *Sea* Vouru-Kasha" was the river Oxus, and not the Caspian Sea. For the Fifty-fourth Yaçna says that the streams from the mountains

> all flow into the boundary-sea Vouru-Kasha, from whence Ardvî-çûra the pure has made them flow out, has poured them out.

In the *Aban-Yasht*, the same waters are spoken of,

> which flow mightily from Hukairya the lofty, away to the Sea Vouru-Kasha. They purify themselves all in the great Sea Vouru-Kasha, all the middle ones purify themselves; for she makes them flow out, she pours out . . . . The outflow of this my water alone comes down to all Kareshvares, the Seven.

The extreme southern point of Bactria is (about) Latitude 34° North, and the extreme northern point, about 39°. But nearly the whole of it lies between 35° and 37°; and it is divided into seven parts, by six rivers that flow into the Oxus. Neither in the countries that lie between Bactria and Media, nor in Media itself, do we find rivers answering the description of them in these hymns: and Media lying south and west of the Caspian, the steppes of Ranha were not north of it; but they were north of Bactria.

On the west of Bactria is the desert of Margiana, a vast sandy waste, interspersed with oases. Bactria is, on the whole, a mountainous country, but contains some very fertile steppes and valleys, the former of which anciently afforded pasture for a fine breed of horses, while the latter produced grain of all sorts and rice. It is now known as Balkh and Koondooz.

The Gâthâs and Vendidad display to us a more simple and primitive people than those among whom the Vedas were composed. It is not possible to doubt that their habits and manners of life were the same as those of the people of Turkestan are now; and they probably drove their herds, sometimes, across the Oxus, to pasture. They were at least familiar with the steppes.

Rawlinson thinks that Zarathustra was a Scythian, and that Magism was a Scythic faith. The Scythians, of whom the Tâtars and Turks are descendants (I do not include the Mongols among the Tâtars), unquestionably have what are called the Caucasian features; and the Aryans *may* originally have been but a Tâtar tribe. Their origin is hidden in a darkness impenetrable to us. We know that when the Bactrian Aryans occupied Media, they to a great extent blended with Scyths whom they found there, admitting whole tribes of them into their nation. It is no doubt true, that

> before the great immigration of the Aryan races from the east, Scythic or Tâtar tribes occupied the countries seized by them [and that] this population was, for the most part, absorbed in the conquering element; but in places maintained itself in some distinctness, and retained a quasi nationality.

It is probably true, as Rawlinson says, that the Aryans who overran Asia, from the Hindu-Kush to the shores of the Persian Gulf, were everywhere but a small element in the population of the countries subdued by them.

As the Aryans unquestionably had their origin in a country populated by Scythic tribes, by which they were surrounded, it is not easy to suppose that they were not themselves Scythic, i. e., Tâtaric or Turkic. It was in the very country between the Oxus and Jaxartes, that the Mongolian Dynasty long afterwards maintained itself; and thence it was that Baber, a descendant of Timur, conquered India, and founded there a Mongolian dynasty, that survived up to our own times, as the Great Moguls of Delhi. We need not wonder that the Aryan race, if it was originally Scythic, became what it did, when we remember the history and great deeds of the Osman Turks: and as to the perfection of the Sanskrit language, an eminent Orientalist has remarked that "we might imagine Turkish to be the result of the deliberations of some eminent society of learned men." The different Turanian languages have little in common with each other, and cannot be traced or referred to a common origin. As to the characteristics of the races, while most of the tribes in the Caucasus are Scythic, there is among them an Aryan race, calling themselves "Os," and "Iran." And they are in no respect superior to the other tribes.

The Finns are Scythic, and their literature and above all, their popular poetry bears witness to a high intellectual development in times which we may call mythical. Their songs still live among the poorest, recorded by oral tradition alone, and preserving all the features of a perfect metre and of a more ancient language. The Kalewala possesses merits not dissimilar from the Iliad, and is entitled to be considered the fifth national epic of the world, side by side with the Ionian hymns, the Mahabharata, the Shahnameh and the Nibelunge. While the language, as Professor Müller further remarks, might almost seem to have left the agglutinative stage, and entered into the current of inflection, with Greek or Sanskrit.

The Bulgarians are Finnic, the Finns having conquered Bulgaria in the Seventh Century; and the Hungarians are of the same race. The Georgians and the Basques are also of Tâtar or Scythic descent.

Originating in Turkistan, and having all the habits of the Tâtar race, what could the Aryans have been but Scyths, Turks or Tâtars? In this sense, Zarathustra was Scythic, and the worship of the Powers of Nature was a Scythic faith. Evidently a more intellectual race than those that surrounded them, and claiming that superiority by their name Arya, these Aryan, *noble* or *warlike*, Scyths advanced beyond the worship of the visible luminaries and material forces of Nature, to more spiritual conceptions and philosophical ideas, making it easy for Zarathustra to conceive of a Creative Deity, cognizable only by the intellect, and of the immortality and pre-existence of the human soul.

Thus the world owes to them all its profound religious and philosophical ideas, and Plato and Philo did but develop the great thoughts of the Vedic Poets and of Zarathustra.

Every one who has read the current works upon the ancient religions is familiar with the word *Honover*, by which Ormuzd created the universe. One does not at first recognize it in the prayer "Ahuna-Vairya," spoken by Ahura Mazda, before heaven, earth, the fire or the Daevas were. In Fargard *xi.* it is called the Prayer of Purification, and portions of it are given there. Its potencies are set forth in *Yaçna xix.*, and it is declared to have been spoken, "for every being, to learn and to meditate, on account of the best purity."

This Prayer, which is not said to be the Creative Word, is found at the commencement (*Number ii.*) of the Khordah-Avesta. The translation is as follows:

> As is the will of the Lord, so is he the Ruler out of purity.
> From Vohu-Manô gifts, for the works in the world for Mazda.
> And the Kingdom to Ahura, when we afford succour to the poor.

Neither do we find any creative word *Hom.* But it is curious that the three letters of the Hindū Ineffable Word, the initials of Agni, Varuṇa and Mitra, and so many other of the Vedic Deities, are also in the first syllable of the word Haŏma, in the name Ahu-Manô, and the name Ahura Mazda.

It is very likely that mystical meanings were attached to the words with which the two great prayers commenced—*Ashem Vohû* and *Yathâ ahû Vairyô:* but if so, there is no possibility of ascertaining what they were.

I dedicate what I have here written to that learned Scholar whose works have opened to me a new and wide field of thought, Professor Max Müller, in the hope that if these pages should be so fortunate as to be read by him, he may at least find in them some suggestions that may induce him to treat exhaustively the whole subject, and create between ourselves and our ancient Aryan ancestors a more intimate communion and conversation.

APOLOGETIC.

Since writing the pages to which these are supplemental, I have procured Volume *V* of Dr. Muir's *Sanskrit Texts*, the first volume of Professor Müller's *Translation of the Rig-Veda*, and Samuel Johnson's *Oriental Religions*. The following pages contain all that I have found in these works bearing upon the questions that I had discussed in the preceding volumes of this exercitation.

The new material thus supplied to me has not caused me to change my opinions in regard to the nature and character of the Vedic Deities; but has confirmed them, and enabled me to discover who and what Yama and Pushan were.

The translations of both Dr. Muir and Professor Müller are, of course, more correct representations of the original texts than those of Professor Wilson. But I have not found the difference, in the case of any text, between the translations, at all material, in their bearing upon any of my views; and, as even the later translations cannot be regarded as final, and are obviously often incorrect, because adapted to peculiar theories and obedient to certain preconceptions, I have concluded to retain those of Professor Wilson to the extent to which I had used them.

If I had had the egregious vanity to propose to place myself as a commentator by the side of these accomplished scholars, I should be very greatly discontented with what I have done, for it is very imperfect.

But I have no sort of pretension to that. At the beginning, I only proposed to myself, taking the texts in regard to Indra as I found them translated by Professor Wilson, to endeavour, by grouping them together and comparing them, to discover, if I could, what that Deity was. In doing that, I had to collect the texts in regard to Agni also, to understand the intimate connection and relations between the two Gods. This led to a like inquiry as to Mitra and Varuṇa, and from that the work has grown to its present proportions, and persuaded me also to engage upon and complete another, in regard to the next stage of intellectual development, as contained in the *Zend-Avesta*, of our Aryan race.

Of course I believe the views that are expressed in this inquiry to be in the main true. If I did not, I should incontinently burn the sheets, to propitiate and appease the insulted Aryan Gods. But so believing, I leave to others, more competent than I am, the task of proving them correct, and the book I surrender, with all its imperfections on its head, to the indulgent consideration of the craft of scholars, among whom I am but an apprentice.

Quod modò proposui, non est sententia; verùm
Credite me vobis folium recitare Sibyllæ.

THE VEDIC LANGUAGE.

Professor Müller, in Volume *I* of his *Translation of the Rig-Veda*, 121, has this passage:

> In *Vṛishan* we have one of those words which it is almost impossible to translate accurately. It occurs over and over again in the Vedic hymns; and if we once know the various ideas which it either expresses or implies, we have little difficulty in understanding its import in a vague and general way, though we look in vain for corresponding terms in any modern language. In the Veda, and in ancient languages generally, one and the same word is frequently made to do service for many. Words retain their general meaning, though at the same time they are evidently used with a definite purpose. This is not only a peculiar phase of language, but a peculiar phase of thought; and as to us this phase has become strange and unreal, it is very difficult to transport ourselves back into it, still more to translate the pregnant terms of the Vedic Poets into the definite languages which we have to use. Let us imagine a state of thought and speech in which *virtus* still meant manliness, though it might also be applied to the virtue of a woman; or let us try to think and speak a language which expressed the bright and the divine, the brilliant and the beautiful, the straight and the right, the bull and the hero, the shepherd and the king by the same terms, and we shall see how difficult it would be to translate such terms without losing either the key-note that was still sounding, or the harmonics which were set vibrating by it in the minds of the Poets and their listeners.

Now, we speak precisely such a language, every hour of our lives; and we need not go beyond the "key-note sounding" and "the harmonics vibrating" in our minds, for proof of it. "Virility" has just the same original and derivative meanings, in English, as *vṛishan* had in the Veda. The root *vṛish* meant emission. Hence *vṛishan* meant "virility" and "the virile energy"; and from that, of course, came many other meanings, suggested by concatenation of ideas. The word "emasculate" is another example of the same process of thought by which various meanings came to be attached to words. It is neither a peculiar phase of language nor a peculiar phase of thought, that words retain their general meaning and yet are evidently used for a definite purpose. Witness the phrase "circumcision of the heart." Nor has this "phase" become strange and unreal to us. It is the commonest of all the phases of language and thought. And what is it that Professor Müller means by the "definiteness" of the language that we use? No language has or ever had less right to claim to be "definite," than ours, except the German. All our writers are labouring, in prose and poetry, to make it daily less definite; for we and the Germans have the Aryan imagination, diseased.

It is not difficult to imagine a state of thought and speech, in which a word meaning "manliness" might also mean a virtue peculiar to a woman. Do we not use the expressions "the virtue of courage," and "manly virtue" yet? It is we ourselves who have applied to *women* the word *virtue*. And as to general and special meanings of the same word, our English tongue can defy competition. Take, for one example, the word "box." How many meanings has the word "fire"? We have "fires" of all sorts, of ambition, of love, and the popular heart is often enough "fired" by speakers who know how to use the huge quantity of words in our language that mean simply nothing at all. Let the reader look in any dictionary at the meanings of the words "reach," "draft or draught," "draw," "dream," "cónduct" and "condúct," and others to be seen on every page, and he will wonder at the idea or notion of Professor Müller that we have a "definite" language. Our uses of the words "pregnant," "seed," "green," "raw," and thousands of others are perfect parallels of those of the word *vṛishan* by our ancestors: and if, five thousand years from now, the writings in English of this age then surviving shall be no more in quantity than the Vedas, it will puzzle the scholar to ascertain the exact meaning of *our* words, infinitely more than it puzzles us to discover the exact meaning of the words of the Ṛich-Veda. The difficulty in this is, not that the words had, when used, so many various meanings, but that they had *not* many which they came to have afterwards, between which and those which they then had it is difficult and often impossible to distinguish: and that they then had meanings which afterwards became obsolete and were lost, being replaced by others. The same process is gone through with by every language. For example, in ours, the word "indorsed" no longer has the meaning which it had when Milton used it in the line,

An elephant indorsed with towers;

and while the French still speak of the "dispositions" of a statute, we talk about the good "disposition" of a man or woman.

Moreover, there was no system of grammar in the Vedic age, when the language was an unwritten one; and a peculiarly complicated and artificial one grew up ages afterwards. It was inevitable that when the old poems were reduced to writing there should be many errors committed, especially as to terminations, and the sounds of vowels determining cases, numbers and persons. It was also impossible that when poems had been retained in a multitude of memories, there should not be various readings and great uncertainty as to the true ones. During the long period of the retention of these poems in the memory, it was not in the Aryan nature to permit them to go unaltered and un-"improved." Every one is familiar with the incorrect quotations from accessible authors, that are constantly in use. Not one man in twenty who has used and written it, has repeated correctly the words of Juvenal:

Hoc volo, *sic* jubeo, *sit* pro ratione voluntas;

and the tomes written upon the meaning of words and phrases and the various readings in Shakespeare, are enough to prove to us that it is utterly impossible to know that the present reading of any line of the Ṛich-Veda is the original and perfectly correct one.

If we add to this the uncertainty as to the meaning of the particles, whether by themselves or in compounds, of course affecting, even when separate, the meaning of the nouns and verbs with which they are used, and the labourious industry and careful painstaking of the Brahmans to pervert the meaning of the Vedas and change the meanings of words, we shall not wonder at the discrepancies in the various translations.

It should be always remembered that the Vedic Poets lived ages before Hesiod and Homer, and that their poems expressed the faith, whatever it was, of the people at large, in whose hearing they were recited. And if then the translator will be deaf to Brahmanic babbling, and listen to the Vedic Poets as to men who repeated their songs to the contemporaries of the remote ancestors of the Greeks and Latins who worshipped the Olympian Deities, a race of herdsmen and husbandmen, knowing only so much of the universe as their naked eyes beheld, ignorant of all that we now call "knowledge," but thoughtful, reflective and of vigourous intellect and inclined to speculation upon the nature and causes of what they saw, he will not be likely to fall into the fatal error of ascribing to them ideas and notions that grew up ages afterwards, in regard to that region of the unknown that lies beyond the reach of human vision or to invisible existences wholly disconnected from everything cognizable by the senses: and he will then not find it so difficult to select the right meaning among the many of the same word; for he will find the simplest and most material meaning to be always the true one.

The writers of the Kabbalah did not know what they meant, for they, for the most part, meant nothing. The composers of the Veda always meant something, and knew what they meant. Their compositions are by far more purely poetic than devotional; and their poetry is not the poetry of sentiment or passion or description or of merely beauty and novelty of phrase, but of personification; and when we once understand them, they are as natural outflowings of the imagination and sequences of thought, as free from exaggeration and hyperbolism, as little strained and incoherent, as those of our own modern poets.

They knew nothing of a heaven beyond the sky, and had not conceived of a creative Deity outside of whom the universe made by him existed.

But they saw and felt that the fire which they saw generated and produced from the wood by friction, and then devouring that of which he was born, contained in itself light and heat; and they conceived that fire was one, and that light was one, variously manifested everywhere. I believe I understand as little as they did, how fire can extend itself and grow in spite of the most intense cold. I am sure that light is as profound a mystery to me as it was to them; and the brilliant and beautiful flame, joyous and mobile as if alive, is as great a wonder to me as it was to my Aryan ancestor. I know as little as they did how the heat and light from the sun comes to the earth, and how it is maintained there in the sky. And it was because it needed no teaching of science to enable them to speculate upon the nature and manifestations of fire and light, that they are the real authors of all religious philosophy, which has but conceived of a Supreme Creative Unity, and assigned to him the attributes and the mode of manifestation which they ascribed to the light and the substance from which it emanated.

Two things are very wisely said by Professor Müller, to appreciate which fully and bear them continually in mind are indispensable to him who cares to read understandingly the poems of the Veda and the even more ancient Gâthâs of Zarathustra.

1. Speaking, in *Chips ii.* 247, of the West Highland story of a frog that wished to marry the daughter of a queen, he remarks,

> We may ascribe to our ancestors any amount of childlike simplicity, but we must take care not to degrade them to the rank of mere idiots. There must have been something rational in the early stories and myths; and until we find a reason for each, we must just leave them alone, as we leave a curious petrifaction, which has not yet been traced back to any living type.

2. Speaking (*id.* 246) of different derivative languages, he says:

> No comparison should be made, before each word is traced back to its most primitive form and meaning. We cannot compare English and Hindustani, but we can trace an English word back to Anglo-Saxon and Gothic, and a Hindustani word back to Hindi and Sanskrit; and then from Gothic and Sanskrit we can measure and discover the central point from which the original Aryan word proceeded. We thus discover not only its original form, but at the same time its etymological meaning.

And thus it is only by assuming as certain, that in these ancient compositions of the two branches of the race whose separation by emigration was the latest of all, everything that is said had a natural, simple and intelligible meaning: and by giving to words their earliest meanings, that we can hope to attain unto any real knowledge of the thought and faith of these old singers of devotional and patriotic songs.

But etymology is only one of the handmaidens of investigation in this case. If we can once ascertain even the general nature of the ontological notions of the Indo- and Irano-Aryans, we shall then have to interpret their language by these known notions, and not impute to it meanings inconsistent with their ideas, and expressing only those of a later age.

ORIGIN OF THE VEDIC DEITIES.

Dr. Muir says, in Volume *V* of his *Sanskrit Texts:*

> The Rig-Veda consists of more than a thousand hymns, composed by successive generations of Poets, during a period of many centuries. In these songs, the authors gave expression, not only to the notions of the supernatural world which they had inherited from their ancestors, but also to their own new conceptions. In that early age, the imaginations of men were peculiarly open to impressions from without; and in a country like India, where the phenomena of Nature are often of the most striking description, such spectators could not fail to be overpowered by their influence. The creative faculties of the Poets were thus stimulated to the highest pitch. In the starry sky, in the dawn, in the morning scaling the heavens, in the bright clouds floating across the air, and assuming all manner of magnificent or fantastic shapes, in the waters, in the rain, in the storm, in the thunder and lightning, they beheld the presence and agency of different divine powers; propitious or angry, whose characters corresponded with those of the physical operations or appearances in which they were manifested. In the hymns composed under the influence of any great phenomena, the authors would naturally ascribe a peculiar or exclusive importance to the Deities by whose action these appeared to have been produced, and would celebrate their greatness with proportionate fervour. Other Poets might attribute the same natural appearances to the agency of other Deities, whose greatness they would in like manner extol; while others again would devote themselves in preference to the service of some other God, whose working they seemed to witness in some other department of creation. In this way, while the same traditional divinities were acknowledged by all, the power, dignity and functions of each particular God might be differently estimated by different Poets, or perhaps by the same Poet, according to the external influences by which he was awed or inspired on each occasion. And it might even happen that some Deity who had formerly remained obscure, would, by the genius of a new Poet devoted to his worship, be brought out into greater prominence. In such circumstances it need not surprise us if we find one particular power or Deity in one place put above, and in another place subordinated to, some other God; sometimes regarded as the creator, and sometimes as the created. This is very prominently illustrated in the case of the Vedic divinities, Dyaus and Pṛithivi, heaven and earth, and by other instances.

One cannot but place the very highest estimate upon the volumes of Dr. Muir, and should dissent from his conclusions with great caution. He unites to thorough and profound scholarship and an intimate acquaintance with the Vedic and Brahmanic literature, a perfect candour and fairness, a striking freedom from the itch for controversy and the desire to manifest his own learning in contrast with that of another. There are in his writings the seriousness, simplicity and gravity of a well-warranted confidence in his own acquirements and qualifications, a total absence of pretentiousness and freedom from the vice of an ambitious and gaudy style, inconsistent with that careful accuracy, always wanting in Dr. Cox and often in Müller, in their representations of the meaning of the Veda.

But I venture to suggest that Dr. Muir, in the passage quoted above, ascribes much too great a share in the production of the consequences of which he speaks, to the fancies of the Poets, and also that the inconsistencies of which he speaks are not so real as he supposes. Like apparent inconsistencies exist, in the writings of Christian Poets and divines, when they speak of the powers, operations and attributes of the Father and the Son. For when these are regarded as one, or even when the idea is always present that the Son is the Divine Logos of Philo and Saint John, the Very Deity manifested, and yet not the Deity's very hidden Self, it cannot but be that the Son will sometimes be spoken of as God, and sometimes as executing the will of God; and that His attributes will seem greater or less in the writings of different men, and even, at different times, in those of the same man. So, if Indra, Vishṇu, Pushan and Vayu are, as light, heat, flame, etc., all included in Agni, the fire, the powers that they exercise belong to Agni, he acts by them, and their powers and influences are his. So if the light of Varuṇa and Mitra, the planets Jupiter and Venus, or the Morning- and Evening-Stars, is the manifestation of Agni, and if the heat of Sûrya, the sun, and his light, are Agni's also, his powers will be ascribed to each, as if they were the powers of each.

For it is always, in the Aryan idea, even more fully developed in the *Zend-Avesta*, the Divine *Unity* that acts; and in the exercise of its own peculiar potency by one hypostasis, the concurrent or conjoint action of another often cannot be excluded. In other words, the wisdom of God does not act alone, but also His power intervenes and acts conjointly with it, concurring in producing the effect.

In the *Zend-Avesta*, the immanent Divine Intellect, Çpĕnta-Mainyu; the same Divine Intellect manifested and acting externally, Vohu-Manô; the Divine Strength or Power, the Divine Sovereignty, and even the Divine Productiveness (because the productions of the soil, and the cattle due to it feed the armies in the field), are by turns represented as winning victories for the Aryans.

Worship or Devotion is a warrior in the *Zend-Avesta*, because victory is owing to it also. Prayer and the Soma and even the fuel, and food, are Deities in the Veda, because they become of the fire, when consumed by it, and have the potencies of worship and sacrifice. The light of Ushas, the Dawn, is the light of Agni; and all the principal Deities are his subsistences.

It seems to me, therefore, that the varying representations of the powers, dignity and functions of the Vedic Deities, of which Dr. Muir speaks, are by far more philosophic than fanciful: and the legitimate fruits of the idea of substance and subsistences; of the Very Self and its hypostases.

THE VEDIC GODS.

THEIR NUMBER AND NATURE.

Yaska, as quoted by Dr. Muir, says,

> There are *three* Deities (*Devatâḥ*), according to the expounders of the Veda, viz.: *Agni*, whose place is on the *earth* (*pṛithivî-sthâno*); *Vayu* or *Indra*, whose place is in the *air* (*antariksha-sthânaḥ*); and *Sûrya*, whose place is in the *sky* (*dyu-sthânaḥ*).

And Rig-Veda *x*. 158. 1, says,

> *Sûryo no divas patu Vato antarikshât Agnir naḥ parthivebhyaḥ:* May the sun preserve us from the sky, Vayu from the air, and Agni from things on earth.

This notion has not only nothing in the ancient hymns to warrant it; but could not have suggested itself to any one, until the real meaning of those old hymns had been forgotten.

I take the following from Dr. Muir (*Volume* 9):

The Gods are spoken of in various texts of the Rig-Veda as being *thirty-three* in number. Thus it is said in Rig-Veda *i*. 34. 11:

> Come hither, Nâsatyas, Açvins, together with the thrice eleven Gods (*devebhir*), to drink our nectar.

Again, in *i*. 45. 2:

> Agni, the wise Gods (*devaḥ*) lend an ear . . . . bring hither those three and thirty.
>
> *i*. 139. 11. Ye Gods who are eleven in the sky (*ye devâso divi ekâdaça*), who are eleven on earth (*pṛithivyâm*), and who in your glory are eleven dwellers in the waters (*apsukshito*). [*Ap* is 'water': but *sukh* means 'to make happy, comfort, delight.']
>
> *iii*. 6. 9. Agni, bring hither, according to thy wont, and gladden the three and thirty Gods with their wives (*triñçataṁ triñç cha devân anushvadham*).
>
> *viii*. 28. 1. May the three over thirty Gods (*devâso*) who have visited our sacrificial grass, recognize us and give us double.
>
> *viii*. 30. 2. Ye who are the three and thirty Gods (*devaḥ*) worshipped by Manu (or man), when thus praised, may ye become the destroyers of our foes.
>
> *viii*. 35. 3. Açvins, associated with the thrice eleven gods (*devais*), with the waters, the Maruts, the Bhrigus, etc.
>
> *ix*. 92. 4. O pure Soma, all these Gods, thrice eleven in number, are in thy secret, etc. (*Viçve devâs trayaḥekâdaça*.)

It is only in the later writings that these thirty-three Devas are pretended to be identified or classified, and Dyaus and Pṛithivî, and Indra and Prajâpati included among them.

But in Rig-Veda *iii.* 9. 9, the Devas are spoken of as being much more numerous:

Three hundred, three thousand thirty and nine Gods (*devāḥ*) have worshipped Agni.

In Rig-Veda *i.* 27. 13, the "*devaḥ*" are spoken of as divided into great and small, young and old. They are, in many passages, spoken of as immortal; and yet there are many passages in which they are described as being the offspring of Dyaus and Pṛithivi. They are not, Dr. Muir says, regarded in general as unbeginning or self-existent beings. He says as follows:

The two (Heaven and Earth) [*Dyaus and Pṛithivi*], together are styled 'parents,' *pitarā*, or *matarā*, or *janitrī* (*dyāvā-pṛithivī-janitrī*, Rig-Veda *x.* 110. 9). In other passages, the Heaven is separately styled 'father,' and the Earth 'mother.' In the Atharva-Veda *xii.* 1. 12, the Poet says: 'The Earth is my mother, and I am the son of the Earth' (*Mātā bhūmiḥ putro aham pṛithivyāḥ*): *Parjanya* is 'the father.' And in *v.* 42 of the same hymn, 'Reverence be paid to the Earth, the wife of Parjanya, to her who draws her richness from showers': *bhumyai Parjanya patnyai.*

Heaven and Earth are regarded as the parents not only of men, but of the Gods also, as appears from the various texts where they are designated by the epithet *devaputre*, 'having Gods for their children.' In like manner it is said, in *vii.* 97. 8, that the divine worlds (i. e., Heaven and Earth) the parents of the God (*devī devadya rodasī janitrī*) have augmented Bṛihaspati by their power: and in *x.* 2. 7, they are described as having, in conjunction with the waters and with Tvashṭṛi, begotten Agni.

I have omitted most of the references given by Dr. Muir. Two of them are, Rig-Veda *x.* 35. 3, *mātarā yahvī ṛitasya*, "the great parents of sacrifice"; and *vi.* 51. 5, *Dyaush pitaḥ Pṛithivī Mātar*, etc.,

Father Heaven, unharming Mother Earth, Brother Agni, Vasus, be gracious to us.

On the other hand, Heaven and Earth are spoken of in other places as created. Thus it is said (*i.* 160. 4, *iv.* 56. 3), that he who produced Heaven and Earth (*dyāvā-pṛithivī jajana*), etc. Again, Indra is described as their Creator (*janitā divo janitā pṛithivyāḥ*); as having beautifully fashioned them by his power and skill, etc., [citing many passages, in regard to various Deities creating, or sustaining and upholding Heaven and Earth (*Pṛithivī*)].

In other passages we encounter various speculations about their origin. In *i.* 185. 1, the perplexed Poet enquires, 'which of these two was the first, and which the last? How have they been produced? Sages, who knows?' In *vii.* 34. 2, the waters are said to know the birthplace of Heaven and Earth (*viduḥ pṛithivyāḥ divo janitram*). In *x.* 31. 7, the Ṛishi asks, 'what was the forest, what was the tree, from which they fashioned the Heaven and the Earth' (*dyāvā-pṛithivī*); and in the same hymn, verses 2 and 3, the all-seeing Visvakarman is said to have produced the earth (*bhūmim*), and spread out the sky (*dyam*); . . . . producing the heaven and earth (*dyāvā-bhūmī janayam*).

There are, it will have been seen, two words that are supposed to mean "the earth,"—*bhûmi* and *prithivi*. *Bhûmi*, from *bhû*, "to become, to spring up, to be, to serve to, to cause," means, as *bhûman* also does, "the earth, land, estate, domain, place": and it is this which is fertilized by showers, and is the wife of Parjanya, and the great mother. *Bhûti* is "production, birth," as *bhavyâ* means "fruit and existence": and I imagine that the earth was called *bhûmi*, as the productive, the producer.

I have expressed the opinion that *Prithivî* did not originally and in the old hymns, mean the earth, but the expanse between earth and sky. Dr. Muir says (*v*. 33),

> The word *Prithivî*, on the other hand, which in most parts of the Rig-Veda is used for earth, has no connection with any Greek word of the same meaning [as *Dyaus*, 'sky,' has with *Zeus* and *Diespiter* and Θεος]. It seems, however, originally to have been merely an epithet, meaning 'broad,' and may have supplanted the older word Gau, etc.

In Rig-Veda *ii*. 15. 2, we read, *sa dhârayat prithivîm paprathatcha;* "He upheld the earth and spread it out": and the earth is imagined to have been called *prithivî* from its being extended, *aprathata*.

Benfey says:

> *Prithivî*, i. e., *prithvî*, fem. of *prithu;* the earth personified; earth as an element.

Prith or *prath* means "to throw, cast, extend, to be extended, to spread, to be unfolded." *Prithu*, i. e., *prathu*, means "large, great." And he also, incorrectly, says that the word *parjanya* (probably *sphurg*, for old *spharg*, whence Latin, *spargere*), means a rain-threatening cloud; and Parjanya was the Deity of rain. *Spurj* meant "thunder," and "the roar of the wind."

The Poet says, in the Atharva-Veda, as is above quoted, *mâtâ bhûmiḥ*, "the earth is mother": *putro aham prithivyaḥ;* "but I am the son of Pṛithivî; Parjanya is father: may he nourish us." Here the two words, *bhûmi* and *prithivî* may have been used as synonymous; or the Poet may have meant to say, "although the earth is mother, *I* was born of the expanse."

It is evident enough that the Vedic Poets had no settled belief in regard to the origin of things, or settled idea that things had an origin. As their principal Gods were powers and potencies of Nature, of the existence whereof apart from the material world they could not conceive, they as little could conceive of their creating or causing the material world, of which they were phenomena, for that involves pre-existence. It is expressly said, therefore, that the material world existed before Agni and the other Gods.

In Rig-Veda *i*. 113. 19, Ushas is characterized as the mother of the Gods (*Devânâm mâtâ*); in *ii*. 26. 3, Brahmaṇaspati (Prayer) is called their father (*devânâm pitaram*); in *ix.* 87. 2, Soma is said to be the father and skilful generator of the Gods (*pitâ devânâm janitâ Indaksha*). In *ix.* 96. 5, Soma is described as the generator of heaven, earth, Agni, Sûrya, Indra and Vishṇu (*janitâ divo, janitâ, pṛithivyâḥ janitâ Agner janitâ Sûryasya janitâ Indrasya janitotah Vishṇoḥ*). In *x.* 72. 5, the Gods are declared to have been born after Aditi; in *x.* 97. 1, certain plants appear to be described as produced three ages (*yugas*) before the Gods (*devebhyas*); while in *x.* 129. 6, the Gods are said to have been born subsequently to the creation of the universe, so that in consequence no one can declare its origin. Varuṇa and other Gods are sons of Aditi, and the birth of Indra is mentioned in several texts, and his father and mother alluded to. In *x.* 101. 12, we find him called the son of Nishṭigrî (*Nishṭigryâḥ putram Indram*). In *vi.* 59. 1, it is said,

> Your fathers, who had the Gods for foes, have been slain, O Indra and Agni; but you survive: *Hatâso vâm pitaro devaçatravaḥ Indrâgnî ||vatho yuvâm.*

In the next verse, both Gods are said to have had one generator, and to be twin brothers. The Atharva-Veda speaks of some of the Gods (*devâḥ*) as being fathers, and some sons.

In *iv.* 54. 2, Savitṛi is said to bestow immortality (*amṛitatvaṁ*) on the Gods (*devebhyo*): and *vi.* 7. 4, Agni is said by his power or skill, to confer immortality on the Gods (*devah*) who worship him when he is born like an infant, and shines forth from out of his parents (the sticks, by friction whereof, as it were by generation, the sacrificial fire was procured).

Dr. Muir says,

> Two of the passages above quoted imply that the existing Gods were successors of others who had previously existed . . . .

In *vii.* 21. 7, mention is made of earlier Gods:

> Even the former Gods (*devah*) admitted their powers to be inferior to thy divine prowess [or sovereignty—*Kshattrâya*].

Earlier Gods are also mentioned in *x.* 109. 4, though in conjunction with, unless we are to understand them as identified with, the Seven Ṛishis:

> In regard to her the former Gods said, the Seven Ṛishis who sat down to practise austerity: (*devâḥ etyasâm avadanta pûrve saptaṛishayas tapaseye nisheduḥ*).

An earlier age of the Gods is mentioned in *x.* 72. 2*f:*

> In the former age of the Gods (*devânâm pûrvye yuge*), the existent sprang from the non-existent. In the first age of the Gods (*devânâm yuge prathoma*) the existent sprang from the non-existent (*asataḥ sad ajâyata*).

And in Rig-Veda *i.* 164. 50, we have the following verse, which is repeated in *x.* 90. 16:

> with sacrifice the Gods worshipped the sacrifice (*yajnena yajnam ayajanta devas*): these were the earliest rites. These great powers sought after the sky, where are the early Sâdhyas, Gods (*yatra pûrve sâdhyâḥ Santi devâḥ*).

The *Devas* are, in their origin, simply the stars and other celestial luminaries. When the word is used collectively, it generally means, I think, the stars alone. The ancient Vedic belief was that the most eminent Ṛishis were transferred, at their deaths, to the sky, as stars. Mahîdhara, quoted by Dr. Muir (18) had a vague traditional recollection of this, when he said that

> there are two kinds of Gods, *karmadevâḥ*, work-Gods, and *âjânadevâḥ*, Gods by birth; the first being those who had attained to the condition of Deities by their eminent works, and the second those who were produced at the beginning of the creation. The second class [he says] is superior to the first.

The Seven Ṛishis (*saptaṛishayas*) were the stars of Ursa Major.

Of the thirty-three Devas, Dr. Muir says,

> It is also clear that the number of thirty-three Gods could not have embraced the whole of the Vedic Deities, as in some of the preceding texts Agni, the Açvins and the Maruts are separately specified, as if distinct from the thirty-three.

And as the stars were the Devas, we can understand why they are said to be 3,339 in number.

The number, 33, like this number, seems to have been specified on account of some mysterious significance ascribed to the number 3 and its combinations; and I do not at all doubt that by the 33 Devas, 33 particular stars were meant, that were in some manner related to each other or that together announced the advent of some season, or were especially noticeable, and found in one particular quarter of the heavens, or in groups of eleven.

C. O. Müller, in an article on Orion, from the *Rheinisches Museum für Philologie, zweiter jahrgang, Bonn*, 1634, to be found, translated, in the appendix to his *Introduction to a Scientific System of Mythology*, translated by John Leitch, says:

> Almost all the constellations which have furnished materials of any amount to the mythic poetry of Greece, are to be found in that division of the heavens, which lies to the south of the sun's path; not in the much larger space extending from the Ecliptic to the Pole. There Sirius, Orion, the Hyades and the Pleiades have their position nearly in a line. Of these, the Pleiades only are a few degrees distant from the Ecliptic to the north . . . . The circumstance that the constellations of most mythological importance lie south of the Ecliptic, is perhaps sufficiently explained

> by this, that they are not seen in the sky throughout the whole year, but are at times invisible, whereby their appearance became doubly remarkable, and gave occasion to all manner of combinations .... But the more northern constellations, which are every night for a longer or shorter time, or even constantly, to be seen in the sky, like everything which we see daily, appear less striking, and could not be so easily placed in relation to natural events, and thereby set in motion and brought into action.

He then remarks upon the very remarkable figure of Orion, with three stars of the second magnitude side by side in the belt, and six other bright stars, chiefly serving to mark the direction of the arms and legs, uniting with the others to complete the form of a man of gigantic size, with which the imagination also sought to connect Sirius, which is not far distant, and outshines all the other suns in the firmament of night; and when we consider all this, we must not wonder that such a constellation should, above all others, have given rise to legends and popular stories.

As the mighty constellation, Orion, proceeds along the sky,

> in the same path the two clusters of stars, the Hyades and Pleiades, move along in advance of Orion. The Pleiades or Seven Stars, a closely crowded group of small stars, are stationed over the right shoulder of Orion, a few degrees northward from the Ecliptic. In later times they were assigned to the neck of the Bull, as the Hyades represented the head of that Zodiacal animal. Homeric antiquity knew nothing of this distribution. The Hyades, somewhat south of the Ecliptic, are still nearer Orion. Aldebaran, the most brilliant star of the triangle which they form, stands on a line drawn from Bellatrix, the star in the shoulder of Orion, towards the Pleiades, and nearly at an equal distance from them.

No stars in the sky could so much and so constantly have attracted the attention of the Aryan herdsmen, as the stars thus spoken of. Those of the Great Bear, always pointing out the pole-star to the wayfarer, would of course be noticeable, and among the first of the constellations to be adored. It sanctified the number seven, as compounded of 3 and 4; and it was called in the Vedic age, by the Indo-Aryans, "the Seven Ṛishis," *Saptaṛishayah;* and by the Irano-Aryans *Hapto-iringa*.

I have slept in the open air a thousand nights, in Arkansas and the Indian country between the Arkansas and Red River, in about the latitude of the Punjab, and I never failed to greet with pleasure the appearance of the Three Kings of Orion. The stars of Ursa Major I seldom noticed—never, indeed, unless I desired to know where the North Star was. When I waked in the night, if the stars shone, I looked for the stars of Orion and for Jupiter, to tell me how the hours were passing.

There is no doubt, moreover, that at a very remote period, these stars, with the Pleiades and Hyades, became especially noticeable on account of their connection with the advent of spring and rainy weather. In the

Zend-Avesta, Tistrya and Çatavaêça bring rains; and there is no doubt that they are the Hyades and Pleiades.

We have seen that Rig-Veda *i.* 139. 11 says to the thirty-three Devas, as Dr. Muir translates it,

> who in your glory are eleven dwellers in the waters (*apsukshito mahinâ ekâdaça stha*).

Ap is "water." *Kshi* means "dwelling," but also the same verb, or another identical in letters, means "to possess," and "to rule." *Kshit*, as the latter part of a compound, means "ruling." *Su* is a Vedic adverb, meaning "very, much, easily, exceedingly," etc. It would hardly be said that stars "dwelt" or "abode" greatly or exceedingly, anywhere; but these adverbs could very well be added to "possessing," or "ruling."

The original meaning of *mah* (*magh*) was "to be great, powerful." *Maha* means "great," in the Rig-Veda; and *mahas*, "light, lustre," which is a meaning of *maha* also, in the later books. *Mahat*, "great, large, pre-eminent, excellent"; *mahi*, "great." The termination *na* forms possessive adjectives, and *mahina* means "gifted with, endowed with, or possessing, greatness, supremacy, excellence." So that I think the meaning of the words quoted above to be,

> Eleven of whom, pre-eminent, are the chief (or great) controllers (or possessors and disposers) of rain.

If this is so, we at once know that these eleven stars are the Pleiades and Hyades. The former constellation consists of only six noticeable stars, and never could have been deemed to consist of seven, until sayings that really referred to the Great Bear were supposed to relate to the Pleiades. Proclus states the number of stars of the latter to be six. O'Brien (*Mathem. Geography*, 37) says:

> The Pleiades are very small and close together; but they glisten with a remarkable degree of brightness. Only six of them can be seen by most persons, but a good eye detects a seventh; and sometimes one or two more; and hence the story of the Lost Pleiad.

And in Cicero's translation of Aratus, we find it said of the "*Vergiliæ*," as these were called by the Romans:

> *Hæc septem vulgo perhibentur more vetusto,*
> *Stellæ cernuntur vero sex undique parvæ.*

In the time of Hesiod (800 B.C.), these were seen rising near the sun in June, and indicated the season to begin harvesting. That Poet calls them "the Seven Stars." But in the very ancient times, size and brightness alone made stars noticeable; and then the six Pleiades and five Hyades were rulers of the rain.

The six great stars in Orion, with others near them, probably made another division of eleven; and the seven of the Great Bear and four others near them, the third division.

At all events, the Devas of the Veda were stars. The Daevas of the *Zend-Avesta* were not the same, but personifications of vices, wrongs and evils, the name being derived from, it is probable, a wholly different root.

EARTH, SKY AND HEAVEN.

Rig-Veda *i.* 6, 9 and 10 are as follows:

> *Ataḥ pari-jman â gahi divaḥ vâ rochanât adhi sam asmin riñjate giraḥ:* [which Professor Müller translates] From yonder, O traveller (Indra) come hither, or down from the light of heaven; the singers all yearn for it.
>
> *Itaḥ vâ sâtim îmahe divaḥ vâ pârthivât adhi, Indram mahaḥ vâ rajasaḥ:* or we ask Indra for help from here, or from heaven, above the earth, or from the great sky.

I take the following texts and remarks from his note on these verses (Rig-Veda *i.* 34 *et seq.*): in *v.* 9, *divaḥ vâ rokanât* (*rochanat*) is translated "the light of heaven." *Va* means "or." Professor Müller says:

> Although the names for earth, sky and heaven vary in different parts of the Veda, yet the expression *divaḥ rochanam* occurs so frequently that we can hardly take it in this place in a sense different from its ordinary meaning. Professor Benfey thinks that *rochana* may here mean 'ether,' and he translates, 'come from heaven above the ether'; and in the next verse, 'come from heaven above the earth.' At first, every reader would feel inclined to take the two phrases, *divaḥ vâ rokanât adhi*, and *divaḥ vâ parthivât adhi*, as parallel: yet I believe they are not quite so.

It is a very intractable fact that the expression is *divaḥ or rochanât;* when propriety requires it to be *of-divaḥ rochanât.* To show what it should be, several passages are quoted where it *is* so.

> *viii.* 98. 3. *Agachchah rochanam divaḥ:* Thou didst go to the light of heaven.
>
> *i.* 155. 3. *Adhi rochane divaḥ:* in the light of heaven.
>
> *iii.* 6. 8. *Urau vâ ye antarikshe . . . . divaḥ vâ ye rochane:* in the wide sky, or in the light of heaven.
>
> *viii.* 82. 4. *Upame rochane divaḥ:* in the highest light of heaven. [And in] *viii.* 1. 18. [is the phrase] *divaḥ bṛihataḥ rokanât adhi:* from the light of the great heaven.

The word also occurs in the plural; as *i.* 146. 1, *viçvâ divaḥ rochanâ;* where Müller translates it by "bright regions." It is joined with *Sûrya* and *naka*, in *Sûryasya rochanat*, "the light of the sun," or "the bright realm of the sun"; and *nâkasya rochane divi*, "the light of the firmament, in heaven"; where, Müller says, *divi*, "in heaven," seems to be the same as "the light of the firmament."

Rochana occurs also by itself, and then means "heaven." Three *rochanas* also are spoken of.

> The cosmography of the Veda [Müller says] is somewhat vague and varying. There is, of course, the natural division of the world into heaven and earth (*Dyu*

and *Bhûmi*), and the three-fold division into earth, sky and heaven, where 'sky' is meant for the region intermediate between heaven and earth. (*Prithivî, Antariksha, dyu*), to which the sea and rivers are added.

But very soon these three or more regions are each spoken of as three-fold; thus, *tisrah bhûmih, trinî rochanâ;* 'the three earths, the three skies,' in *i.* 102. 8, *trî rochanâ divyâ dhârayanta;* 'support the three heavenly skies'; *ii.* 27. 9, *trî rochanâ Varuṇa trin utadyûn trîni Mitra dhârayathaḥ rajâmsi;* 'Mitra and Varuṇa, you support the three lights and the three heavens and the three skies' (*rajâmsi*).

Here, Müller thinks, there seems some confusion; and asks what *rochana* can mean, as distinct from *dyu* and *rajas?* Benfey says that the original meaning of *rajas* was probably "dimness," and gives it the meaning of "sky." It is, he says, *rañj+as.* And *rañj* means "to dye, colour, glow"; part. *rakta*,"coloured, red, reddened"; *rakta*, noun, "red, blood, vermilion"; caus. *rañjaya*, "to colour, to illuminate."

But there is a still more complicated division alluded to, in *iv.* 53. 5,

triḥ antariksham, trî rajâmsi, trîni rochanâ, tisraḥ divaḥ prithivîḥ tisraḥ.

On the whole, he thinks that *divaḥ vâ rochanât adhi* must be read, "light *of* heaven"; and *divaḥ vâ pathiva adhi*, "heaven *or* earth."

The verb *ruch* means "to shine, to please"; and, noun, "light, splendour, beauty, lightning, desire"; *ruchî*, "light, a ray of light"; *rukma*, i. e., *ruch+ma*, "clear, bright," and (Vedic) "gold." *Rochana*, i. e., *ruch+ana*, adj. "irradiating, splendid"; noun (Rig-Veda) "the æther"; *rochis*, "light, flame."

I do not see why *rochana* should not sometimes be an adjective, "radiant," and sometimes a noun singular or plural, "radiance" or "splendours." "The heavenly splendours" and "the splendours of the sky" are common phrases now. *Dyu* is simply the sky; the blue and seemingly solid sky, in which the stars seem and were supposed to be. I do not believe that there is the least real evidence in the Veda of any conception of a "heaven" beyond the "sky." It seems to me absurd to represent the Vedic Poets as babbling about the visible radiance and splendours of a space unknown and invisible, beyond the blue sky.

Rajas evidently meant the ruddy and golden glories of the sky. The three skies may mean the sky of morning, that of noon, and that of evening, each with its different and peculiar radiance and glowing splendours: and the three earths must mean the earth, wearing its three different aspects at early morning, noon and evening-tide. Or, perhaps, the sky of the three seasons, the spring-season of greenness, the autumn of foliage brilliant with the painting of the frost, and the winter white with snow; and the earth at these three seasons, are meant. It is impossible that, not even knowing what the earth was, or that it had either shape or limits, the Vedic Poets should have talked about two other earths and two other skies.

In regard to *Pṛiṭhivi*, which presents the only real difficulty, Müller says:

> Pârthivâni also occurs by itself, when it means the earth, as opposed to the sky and heaven.

Thus, *x*. 32. 2, Indra is said to go between the *divyâni rochanâ* and the *pârthivâni rajasâ*, the resplendent radiance of the sky, and the crimson glowings of—what? Surely not the earth. The most brilliant of these flush the clouds with their magnificent and gorgeous glories, and these are *between* the earth and sky, in the wide expanse.

So, in *viii*. 94. 9, it is said that the Maruts spread out or expanded *viçvâ pârthivâna rochanâ divaḥ;* "all the splendours of the expanse and sky." In *vi*. 61. 11, Sarasvati filled *pârthivâni uru rajaḥ antariksham;* "the earthly places, the wide welkin, the sky." So Müller translates it, but says it is a doubtful passage.

Antariksha, i. e., *antar+iksh+a*. *Antar* is an adverb, "within"; a prep. "within"; and a part of compounds, where it means "interior, internal, what is between"; whence *antara*, a noun, "interior, internal, a hole, distance, etc." From it are the Latin *inter*, "between, among," and *antrum*, Greek, *αντρον*, "a cave." *Îksh* means "look, perceive, behold." As I have already said, it is that wherein birds fly, i. e., either the expanse or the air. We use the word "air" when we mean the space which it fills; and it is quite likely that while *Pṛiṭhivi* meant the whole expanse, *antariksha* meant that part of it immediately above the place or the earth, the cloud-region.

> Lastly [Müller says], *Pârthivâni*, by itself seems to signify earth, sky and heaven, if these are the three regions which Vishṇu measured with his three steps; or East, the Zenith and West, if these were intended as the three steps of that Deity.

For it is said in *i*. 155. 4, that he strode across *pârthivâni*, which Müller translates "regions of the earth."

In note at p. 42, Müller says,

> The sky or welkin (*rajas*), is the proper abode of the Maruts, ...

The passage referred to, *i*. 19. 3, is

> *Ye Mahaḥ rajasaḥ viduh viçve-devâsaḥ adruhaḥ, marutbhiḥ agne â gahi* [and he translates it], They who know of the great sky, the Viçve devas without guile; with *those* Maruts come hither, O Agni.

In the next verse he renders the latter phrase, "with *the* Maruts." I do not see why it should be "those" in the former. The *Viçve devas* are not the Maruts, but the whole host of the stars. *Adruhaḥ* is "uninjuring." The original meaning of *vid* was to "see," as the Latin *video* proves. To "know" is a derivative meaning. The verse seems to me to mean that the Maruts (winds) see the great splendour and the whole host of the uninjuring stars. Benfey so connects *viçve devâsaḥ* with the words preceding.

Professor Müller continues,

> The Vedic Poets distinguish commonly between the three worlds, the earth, *pṛithivî* (fem.) or *pârthiva* (neut.); the sky, *rajas;* and the heaven, *dyu.*

In another note (p. 43) he says that

> *nâka* must be translated by 'firmament,' as there is no other word in English besides heaven, and this is wanted to render *dyu.* Like the Jewish firmament, the Indian *nâka,* too, is adorned with stars; *i.* 68. 10, *pipeça nâkam stribhiḥ. Dyu,* heaven, is supposed to be above the *rajas,* sky or welkin.

The verse commented on is,

> *Ye nâkasya adhi rochane divi devâsah âsate.* [Wilson translates it] Who are Divinities abiding in the radiant heaven above the sun; [and Langlois] Under the resplendent celestial vault, these Gods rise and go to seat themselves. [*As* means 'to sit, abide, and stay.']

To *naka,* Benfey gives but the single meaning "heaven." *Nakasya* is the genitive singular. *Rochane* and *divi* are in the locative singular. *Adhi* is "on high, above." Müller translates the verse,

> They who in heaven are enthroned as Gods, in the light of the firmament.

May it not be, "Who, Deities of the sky (*devasah nakasya*) sit above, in the splendour of the firmament"; *naka* and *dyu* being synonyms?

In conclusion, I venture to suggest a doubt whether the Greek Zeus is really identical with the Sanskrit *div, dyu* or *dyo.* And as the reader must be at a loss to understand the formal changes of these words, I subjoin their declension:

1\. *Div* or *Dyu* (fem.), "sky."

Singular		Dual		Plural	
Nom.	*dyaúḥ*	N. A. V.	*dívau*	N.	*dívaḥ*
Abl.	*dívam*	I. D. Ab.	*dyúbhyâm*	A.	*diváḥ*
Instr.	*divâ*	G. L.	*divoḥ*	I.	*dyúbhiḥ*
Dat.	*divé*			D. Ab.	*dyúbhyaḥ*
Ab. G.	*diváḥ*			G.	*divâm*
Loc.	*diví*			L.	*dyúshu*
Voc.	*dyaûḥ*				

Dyo (fem.), "heaven."

Singular		Dual		Plural
N.	*dyaúḥ*	N.	*dyâvau*	*dyâvah*
A.	*dyam*		*dyâvau*	*dyâḥ*
I.	*dyava*			*dyóbhiḥ*
D.	*dyave*			
Ab.	*dyóḥ*		*dyóbhyâm*	*dyóbhyaḥ*
G.	*dyóḥ*		*dyávoḥ*	*dyávâm*
L.	*dyávi*			*dyóshu*
V.	*dyaũḥ*			

Forms of *dyu* which occur in the Rig-Veda: Sing. Nom. *dyaús;* Acc. *dívam*, *dyâm;* Instr. *dívâ;* Dat. *divé;* Gen. *diváḥ*, *dyóḥ;* Loc. *diví*, *dyáví;* Voc. *dyaũs;* Pl. Nom. *dyâvaḥ;* Acc. *dyûn;* Instr. *dyúbhiḥ;* Dual. Nom. *dyâvâ.*

Zeus, in the Greek, has for its Genitive, *Diŏs;* Dative, *Dii;* Acc. *Dia;* Voc. *Zeũ.* There is no doubt that *Diŏs*, and the other cases beginning with *d*, as well as *dios*, "divine," are identical with *Dyu* and *Dyaus.*

But I find no proof that *Zeus* is. I believe, on the contrary, it is from Ζαω, ζησομαι, "I live"; or from Ζεω, "I burn." For in the Doric, ζην, for ζαν, contracted, for ζαειν, is the present infinitive of ζαω; and Ζην, Ζηνος are forms of the name *Zeus*, as also Ζαν and Ζανος are.

The Hymns 159, 160 and 185 of Mandala *i.* are addressed to *Dyau* and *Pṛiṭhivi*, these names being, of course, rendered in the translations "heaven and earth." I extract the following passages, from Professor Wilson's *Translation*, omitting the Brahmanic conjectural additions in parentheses, as bearing on the question whether *Pṛiṭhivi* originally meant the *earth* or the *expanse.*

159. 1. I glorify with sacred rites the mighty Dyau and Pṛiṭhivi, the augmenters of sacrifice, who with devotion at holy ceremonies; those two who, having the Devas for children are reverenced by the Devas, and therefore with favour bestow desirable blessings.

2. Verily I propitiate, by my invocations the mind of the benevolent Father, and the great and spontaneous, and the mother. The parents, with kindness, have secured, by their excellent protections, the vast and manifold immortality of their progeny, the luminaries.

3. These, your children, the performers of good works [beneficent, working good] and of goodly appearance [shining brilliantly], recognize you as their great parents, through experience of former. Preserve uninterrupted stability in the functions of your progeny, whether fixed or moving [stars or planets], that have no other parents.

4. Those inspecting and intelligent sisters [stars and planets], conceived of the same womb, united, and dwelling in the same abode, measure it [i. e., move across

it regularly]; knowing and brilliantly radiant, they move without intermission, through the radiant expanse.

5. . . . . Benignant Dyau and Pṛiṭhivi, bestow upon us riches . . . .

160. *i.* Those two, the divine Dyau and Pṛiṭhivi, are the diffusers of happiness on all, encouragers of the truth [making things visible and real by their light], able to hold up the water [in the clouds that float there], auspicious of production [causers or favourers of it], and energetic [having direct influence on production, by their energy or inherent force]; in the interval between whom the pure and divine sun revolves for duties.

2. Wide-spreading, vast, unconnected [probably 'unlimited'], the generator and producer, they two preserve the worlds. Resolute as if of embodied, are Dyau and Pṛiṭhivi, and the Father [*Dyau*] has invested everything with forms.

Dr. Muir has "unwearied" for "unconnected"; and "creatures" for "worlds." The original of the former is *asaçchatâ*. *Ças* or *sas* is "to sleep." *Asaçchatâ* is "sleepless." The original of the latter is *bhuvanâni*, of which "worlds" is no translation. It means "the creatures," i. e., those created or produced, i. e., the children of Dyau-Pṛiṭhivi—the stars and planets.

The residue of the verse, Dr. Muir does not give; and I do not know the original of "resolute." In verse 3, Wilson applies it to the son of these parents. At all events, the "embodied," invested with "forms," are the luminaries, which are limited and defined portions of light.

3. The pure and resolute son of the parents, the Bearer, sanctifies the worlds by his intelligence [in the original we have *sa Vahni putrah pitroh*].

I think that phrase means "the sacrificial fire, one son of these parents." How the fire of the sacrifice "sanctifies" the stars and planets, by its "intelligence," I do not know. It strengthens and exhilarates them, by what it conveys to them. It is the "bearer," because it conveys the offering to the sky. It will be seen, by the next verse, that this "pure and resolute" son gave birth to his parents; and the words rendered by "pure" and "resolute" no doubt had some meaning in the original, as applied to Agni; as well as the milch-cow and the vigourous bull. Wilson makes these be earth and heaven,

and daily milks the pellucid milk [of the sky, according to Wilson; who thinks that this son is the Sun and Vahni an epithet].

4. He was the greatest worker of the working Devas, who produced the two all-originating regions [*rodasi*], who desiring to create an excellent work, stretched out these regions and upheld them by undecaying supports.

185, 1. Which of these two was prior, which posterior? How were they produced? Sages, who knows this? Verily, you uphold the universe of itself [the self-existent luminaries?], and the circling succession of days.

2. Stable and immovable, they sustain numerous moving and unstable bodies, even as a son is in the lap of his parents . . . .

4. May we always be to that heaven and Pṛiṭhivi, who are not subject to annoyance, who satisfy with food, who have the Devas for sons, and who are both endowed with the double of the divine days . . . .

5. Co-extensive, coeval and to end together, sisters, and kindred, and containing within them the source, generator-producer, of creatures . . . .

6. I invoke to the sacrifice, for the preservation of the Devas, the two vast, all-supporting and mighty parents [which, more probably, should read, 'to the sacrifice, for our preservation, the two vast, etc., parents of the Devas.' Wilson, following Sayana, inserts after 'parents,' 'of the rain and corn,' because Pṛiṭhivi was supposed to be the earth, and the ground is not parent of the stars]: who [the Devas], beautiful in form sustain ambrosial (showers).

What "ambrosial showers" are, I do not pretend to guess. In the remaining verses are the expressions:

I repeat to Dyu and Pṛiṭhivi this initial praise, to be heard around. May paternal and maternal preserve us . . . . May this, O heaven and Pṛiṭhivi [sky and expanse], be successful—which, O father and mother, I do, on this occasion, repeat to both of you.

In *v.* 84, Pṛiṭhivi is so plainly *not* the earth that even Sayana had to admit that it might have a *two-fold* meaning, and apply to *antariksha*, or the firmament. It should perhaps read as follows:

1. Verily, Pṛiṭhivi, thou dost replenish the exhausted mountains: Mighty and Most Excellent, thou art she who blessest the earth with abundant largess [*mahna jinoshi bhumim:* and as *bhumi* is, beyond possibility of question, the earth, it is equally sure that Pṛiṭhivi that blesses it with gifts or abundance, is not itself].

2. Wanderer in various ways, thy worshippers hymn thee [*Sic*, Wilson; but Pṛiṭhivi is 'footless,' and does not 'wander,' whether she is earth or expanse. It is most probable that we should read], Thy worshippers, journeying various ways, praise thee with songs; thee who bright-hued, tossest the swollen (cloud) like a neighing horse.

3. Thou who by thy sustenance maintainest the monarchs of the forest on the solid earth, when the showers of thy clouds fall from the shining sky.

In *vi.* 70, we find the following:

1. Radiant Dyau-Pṛiṭhivi, the abiding-place [home], of the celestial bodies, you are spacious, manifold, water-giving, lovely, ...

2. Uncollapsing, many-showering, water-retaining, yielding moisture, beneficent . . . . rulers over created beings . . . .

3. Firmly-established Dyau and Pṛiṭhivi, the mortal who has offered for your straight-forward course [has by offerings besought the continuance of your regular functions], accomplishes, and prospers with progeny; and invigorated by your action [by your impregnating influence, many beings, of various forms but similar functions are engendered].

4. You, Dyaus and Pṛiṭhivi have water everywhere; you are the home of water; are imbued with water, are the augmenters of water . . . .

5. May Dyau-Pṛiṭhivi, the outpourers of water, milkers of water, dischargers of the functions of water, divinities, promoters of sacrifice, bestowers of wealth, of renown, food, male children, combine together.

6. May Father Dyaus, may Mother Pṛiṭhivi, who are all-knowing and beneficent, grant us sustenance. May Dyau-Pṛiṭhivi, mutually co-operating and promoting the happiness of all, bestow upon us posterity, food and riches.

It surely needs no more to prove that Pṛiṭhivi was not the earth, but the expanse, the רקיע of the Book Barasith, which was

in the midst of the waters, to divide waters from waters, the waters under the expanse from the waters above it.

and which Alohim called שמים, *Shamayim*, the heavens. In the Septuagint it is called *στερεωμα*, and in our common translation, "firmament," meaning as the Greek word does, "a solid prop, stay" or "support." The Hebrew word does not mean that, but "expanse," from רקע, "to beat out, expand," whence רקעים, "plates," as "beaten out."

Antariksha seems to have been the lower region of this expanse, occupied by the atmosphere.

Connected with this, also, are "the three steps" of Vishṇu, of which I shall say a word further on a subsequent page.

AGNI.

A few of the texts in regard to Agni, cited by Dr. Muir in Section *xiii.*, and which were not at first within my reach, and some of those that were, but the originals of which I could not examine, may be referred to with profit.

That accomplished commentator says that Agni is the God of fire, the Ignis of the Latins, the Ogni of the Sclavonians. But, he says

> Agni is not, like the Greek Hephaistos (*Twashṭri*) or the Latin Vulcan the artificer of the Gods, ... but derives his principal importance from his connection with the ceremonial of sacrifice.

It is quite true that he is very often spoken of in connection with that, and as the sacrificial fire: but this is a special character, each one lighted being called Agni, as if each was all of that which bears the name. But, as I have already suggested, Agni is One, the Universal Fire, and each particular fire is that One, manifested and revealed, with a special individuality. In this, he is the Sage, a most eminent Ṛishi, the accomplisher of the sacrifice, the wise director, who worships the Devas, because by him men do sacrifice; a swift messenger, moving between sky and earth, commissioned both by the Devas and men to maintain their mutual communications, to announce the hymns to the Devas and convey to them the Soma and other oblations. He is the herald of men to summon the Devas to descend to the sacrifice, and comes with them, seated on the same car. He is the mouth and tongues through which the Devas and men participate in the sacrifice, and is himself asked to eat the offerings and drink the Soma juice.

In *x.* 51, there is a dialogue between Agni and the Devas, in which they desire him to come forth from his dark place of concealment in the waters and the plants, and endeavour to persuade him to appear and convey to them the customary oblations. In verse 6, he expresses his reluctance to do so, and gives the reason:

> Agni's former brothers have sought this goal [have endeavoured to reach this place?], as a charioteer passes along a road. But fearing this journey, O Varuṇa, I went to a distant place and trembled, etc.

Of course an absurd legend was invented, ages afterwards, to "explain" this passage.

The sacrificial fire is here intended by Agni; and he is finally induced, by the promise of long life and a share in the sacrifice, to accede to the request; and the particular fire is kindled. The *Agneḥ pûrve bhrâtaro* are, clearly enough, or were, former fires, that had been kindled there, and been short-lived.

So also each domestic fire is Agni, the lord of the house, *grihapati*, dwelling in every abode, a brilliant guest in every house, dwelling in every wood like a bird, and living in the midst of every family. He is father, mother, brother, son, kinsman and friend, and destroys the Râkshases.

He is said to have been brought from the sky or from afar, by *Mâtariçvan*, who is, Böhtlingk and Roth say, a divine being who, as the messenger of Vivasvat, brings down from heaven to the Bhṛigus, Agni, who had been before concealed; and also a secret name of Agni. And it is remarked that the word cannot be certainly shown by any text to be in the Vedic hymns a synonym of Vayu. Roth thinks that *Mâtariçvan* was not a man, but a demigod, half-divine.

Benfey has *Mâtariçvan*, i. e., *mâtṛi+i+çvan*, (vb. *çvi*), "air, wind." And this is what Roth controverts. It is the explanation given by Yaska. Also Benfey has, *îçvara*, i. e., *îç+van+a* (with *r* for *n* masc., fem., *ṛî*), "ruler, owner, lord, husband, king." *Iç* means "to possess, to be master, to be able"; and *van*, "to serve, to honour." *Vaiçvânara*, also, is a name or epithet of Agni. *Mâta*, *matṛi*, is "mother"; and *va* is "like, as." *Çvi* is "to swell, increase"; *çvas*, "to breathe," *çvasna*, *çvasa*, "air, wind, breath." In *i*. 164. 96, *Mâtariçvan* is said to be a name of Agni; as it is also said to be in *i*. 96. 3 and 4; *iii*. 29. 11; and *x*. 114. 1. I cannot find in the etymology of the name anything to support Roth's speculations. We neither know what the name means, nor who he was that is called by it; but as he brought the fire from the sky or from afar, and it is also called by his name, we are warranted in supposing that he was some legendary person, the original perhaps of the Greek Prometheus, after whom the fire is called because he once kindled it or is reported to have sacrificed by it; as Agni is called *Badhryasva* and *Daivodâsa*, after a priest or sacrificer and a king.

Agni is said to have been generated by Indra between two clouds, because there is a new birth of fire whenever the lightning flashes. So he is the son of Dyaus and Pṛithivi, and generated by the dawns, and by Indra and Vishṇu. It is unnecessary to discuss the multitude of texts which speak of the ordinary fire, of the sacrifice, of the hearth, or wherever the particular one is individualized. These are but the individualized manifestations of the one Universal, yet each considered as the whole partially seen.

This Universal is the source of all the Devas, *bhuvo devânâm pitâ portraḥ san* (*i*. 69. 1). In *viii*. 19. 33, what Dr. Muir calls the Fire-God, i. e., Fire's Very Self, is declared to be the tree of which all individual fires are the branches.

Fire is the radiant sovereign (*samrâjo asurasya*), as powerful as Indra is. He stretched out the heaven and the earth or expanse: he formed the mundane regions and the luminaries of the sky, begat Mitra, and caused the sun, the imperishable orb, to ascend the sky. He made all that flies, walks, stands or moves, and adorned the sky with stars. His extension is greater than that of the sky and all the worlds.

It is through him that Varuṇa, Mitra and Aryaman triumph. He knows and sees all creatures, is present in all recesses of the sky, knows all the secrets of men and all the laws that govern the movements of the luminaries (*daivyâni uratâ*).

The name or epithet *Vaiçvânara* is often applied in the Veda, to Agni, when he is the All of Fire: and this word, without the aid of any other explains and makes entirely clear the Vedic idea.

For *Vaiçvâ+nara* is the same as *Viçva-narâ* (as *Vaiçvâ-devas* is the same as *Viçva-devas*), the former part of the compound meaning "all, the whole, the wholeness, the universality." Benfey gives as the meaning of the compound "relating to, fit for, etc., all men." This is simply an unlucky guess. *Nara* means simply an individual, a person, and *Vaiçvâ-nara* means the totality, the whole or the oneness composed of the individuals.

Of all individual and particular fires, and also of all the luminaries of the sky; for these all shine by means of, and do manifest and reveal a portion of the great and eternal unity of fire. Wherefore it is said in *i.* 164. 46:

> They call him Indra, Mitra, Varuṇa, Agni; then there is that celestial well-winged bird. Sages name variously that which is but one; they call it Agni, Yama, Mâtariçvan.

"Him" and "it" are supplied in the translation. Perhaps *Indram, Mitram̃, Varuṇam, Agnim ahu* might be read, "They call Agni, Indra, Mitra, Varuṇa." The remainder of the verse is of uncertain signification. I do not know what is meant by *divyaḥ suparno garutmân*, "that celestial well-winged bird"; nor whether it is it, that is called Agni, Yama, Mâtariçvan: but *ekam̃ sad viprâḥ bahudha vadanti*, "the Poets address manifoldly what is only one," is plain enough. In *v.* 3. 1, it is said that all the Devas are comprehended in Agni; and in *v.* 13. 6, that he surrounds them as the circumference of a wheel does the spokes. The former of these sentences is *tve viçve sahasas putra devâḥ; putra* meaning "son"; and I take the meaning to be that they are contained in Agni and emanate from him.

In the Atharva-Veda it is said,

> Agni becomes Varuṇa (the Evening Star) in the evening; rising in the morning he is Mitra (the Morning Star); becoming Savitṛi (the moon), he moves through the air; becoming Indra, he glows in the middle of the sky.

And Agni and Indra are, as we have seen, constantly associated together, said to be twin brothers, and each exercising the functions of the other.

> It is Indra [Dr. Muir says], who is most frequently represented in the hymns as the patron and helper of the sacred race and the destroyer of their enemies;

for Indra is the Demiourgos, the manifestation as light of Agni, and the immediate agent by whom he acts. And in *viii.* 38. 1, where the two are called *Yajnasya ṛitvijâ*, two sacrificing priests, Indra shares in the character peculiar to Agni. There is no doubt as to the character of either; and nothing could be more expressly contradicted, than the idea that Indra was the firmament is by the Vedic texts.

Upon reperusal of the translation of Professor Wilson, I find some texts which are of more significance than they at first seemed, and some which I better understand. To these I will now briefly refer.

> *i.* 27, 6. Thou, *Chitra-bhânu*, art the distributor of riches, as the waves of a river are parted by interjacent (islets); thou ever pourest (rewards) upon the giver (of oblations).

Professor Wilson says, of *Chitrabhânu*,

> A common denominative of Agni, he who has wonderful or various lustre [Benfey has as its meaning, 'resplendent.' *Bhânu* means 'a ray of light, light, the sun, a sovereign']; the following simile is very elliptically and obscurely expressed; but such seems to be its purport, according to the explanation of the Scholiast.

The simile certainly seems not a very apt one.

Chitra means, among other things, "various" and "variegated"; and I think that *chitrabhânu*, here, means "variously manifested"; and that the whole verse means that Agni separates himself into various hypostases or persons, light, heat, etc., still remaining one, and these continuing to be of himself, as a river is divided by islands into various streams, all which are yet the one river. And the phrase "Thou ever pourest upon the giver" means, I think, that in these hypostases, beneficently manifested, Agni continually flows forth, or pours into them his own substance.

In another form of expression this contains the same idea as is expressed in *i.* 68. 1,

> radiant among the Devas, and in himself alone comprehending the virtues of all these. [So in *i.* 69. 1], Thou, as soon as manifested, hast pervaded all the world with devout acts, being the father and son [source of light and heat to them and shining forth from them. In *v.* 3], Thou, Agni, assumest all celestial natures (*tad devatarupo bhavati*), thou becomest the state, figure, condition, form or appearance of the Devas [i. e., manifested as them, and they being his revealings, in form and vigour].
>
> [In *i.* 96. 7, Agni] now is and heretofore has been, the abode of riches, the receptacle of all that has been, and all that will be born; and the preserver of all that exists,

and that are coming into existence. [In *i.* 127. 8, it is said], We invoke thee, who art the guest of men, to whom all these immortals apply for sustenance, as to a father; thee, to whom the priests offer oblations among the Devas.

For, as the luminaries are Agni manifested, the sacrificial flame, ascending towards the sky and becoming invisible, was deemed to feed them with that which was their life or spirit. It was the same fire that shone there. He is, as is said in *i.* 149. 3, "identical, with many forms, and, as the sun, radiant"; i. e., always one and the same, he has many manifestations by limited forms, and, in the form of the sun, is resplendent. So in Verse 2 of the same, "being, as it were, the generator of men, as well as of the sky and expanse," because if darkness were perpetual, nothing could be said to exist. He abides with his glories, i. e., he is himself wheresoever his emanations are and shine.

The connection of Agni with the waters is difficult to understand, and the commentators hardly attempt to explain it. In *i.* 149. 4, he is said to be present at the place where the waters are gathered together (*apam sadasthe*). In *i.* 151. 1, it is said that the pious worshippers have generated him by their acts, amidst the waters, at the sacrifice.

In *ii.* 35, *apam napat*, "the grandson of the waters" is invoked; and the last verse shows that the name is an epithet of Agni. Some waters, it is said in Verse 3, collect together; others unite with them, as rivers they flow together, to propitiate (according to Wilson) the ocean fire; the pure waters are gathered round the pure and brilliant grandsons of the waters. The young and modest wait upon the youth, assiduous in bathing him, and he, though unfed with fuel, yet cleansed with clarified butter, shines with bright rays amidst the waters, that abundance may be to the worshipper. Three divine females present food to him; as if formed in the waters they spread abroad, and he drinks the ambrosia of the first-created. He, the grandson of the waters, who abides in his own dwelling, he, gathering strength in the midst of the waters, shines for the sake of conferring wealth upon his worshipper. And those who give no offerings do not attain to this inconceivable Deity, whether abiding in the immature or the perfect waters.

The three maidens are no doubt three rivers. The Scholiast says, *Ilâ*, *Sarasvati* and *Bhârati*, personifications of sacred prayer or praise. They were unquestionably rivers. "They flow together to propitiate the ocean-fire" pretends to be a translation of *ûrvam nadyah prinanti*, and Sayana gives *ûrva* "its usual acceptation" of "submarine fire." "Shines with bright rays amidst the waters" alludes, according to Professor Wilson, either to the submarine fire, or to the lightning amidst the rain-clouds.

The only meaning of *ûrva* given by Benfey is,

the name of a saint from whose thighs (*ûru*), the submarine fire proceeded.

The same hymn continues, as translated by Professor Wilson, as follows:

> 8. All other beings are, as it were, branches of him, who, truthful, eternal and vast, shines amidst the waters with pure and divine; and the shrubs, with their products are born.
>
> 9. The grandson of the waters has ascended the firmament above, of the tortuously-moving, arrayed in lightning: the broad and golden coloured spread around, bearing his exceeding glory.

Professor Wilson, in note to *ii.* 35. 1, says that *apâm napât* means "the son of the trees or fuel, which are the progeny of the rains." But in note to *i.* 22. 6, where he makes the text say, "Glorify Savitṛi, who is no friend to water" (a clear mistranslation, since Savitṛi is eminently the mother of waters), he says that *napât* is here taken in its literal import, "who does not cherish," *na-pâlayatî*, but dries them up by his heat, *santâpena çoshakah.* But Savitṛi was not the sun, but the moon. And the derivation is merely fanciful, and unsound. Benfey has *na-pâ+t, naptṛi*, i. e., *na-pâ+tṛi*, "a grandson," with no other meaning; but I do not see how, if compounded as he thinks, it has that meaning. *Pâ* means "to drink" and "to protect." *Nor* generally expresses negation; but in the Veda, he says, "like, as."

As to the propitiation of the ocean-fire, I do not find that *priṇânti* means "they flow together." Benfey gives three verbs *pṛi*, neither of which has any such meaning. One means "to bring over, protect, fill"; one, "to be busy or active"; and one, "to be pleased with." The phrase is *Ûrva nadyah priṇanti. Nadyâḥ* is, according to Müller (*Grammar*, 104), the nominative or vocative plural of *nadî* or *nady*, of which *nadyâh* is ablative and genitive singular. *Nada*, fem. *nadî*, means "a river." I think that the phrase means, simply, "the rivers fill the lake."

> 10. The grandson of the waters is of golden form, of golden aspect, of golden hue, and seated on a throne of gold: the givers of gold present to him food.

Gold was not offered, given or presented at the sacrifices, nor is it anywhere included among the presents received by the priests or bards: and the food presented to Agni was whatsoever was burned in the fire, and supposed so to become part of the fire and light. "The broad and golden coloured," in Verse 9 are, no doubt, the great clouds, flushed with light, and the allusions in Verse 10 are also to the clouds.

> 11. Beautiful is his form, is the name of the grandson of the waters; flourish though hidden; the youthful waters collectively kindle the golden-coloured divinity in the firmament, for water is his food.

13. Vigourous, he has generated himself as an embryo in those; he is their infant; he sucks them; they bedew him; the grandson of the waters of untarnished splendour has descended to this, in the form of a different.

14. The abundant waters, bearing sustenance to their grandson, flow round him with spontaneous movements; when abiding in his supreme sphere, and shining daily with imperishable.

And then the worshipper declares that this is a hymn to Agni.

Compelled to accept the interpretations of Sayana, Yaska and others, Dr. Wilson has had to make the Vedic Poets utter a great deal of that sort of utter nonsense which is never found in the very early Poets of any people; the Veda thus interpreted bearing much the relation to the original that the Kabbalah bears to the ancient Hebrew writings.

But also one would think, in reading this translation, and seeing how inappropriately words are conjoined, and what strange relations are established between adjectives and substantives always before entire strangers to each other, that the scanty resources of the English language did not afford equivalents for very many Sanskrit adjectives.

In *iii*. I. 3, we have,

The Devas discovered the graceful Agni amidst the waters of the flowing, for the purpose of acts.

What possible meaning does the last phrase convey? And it continually happens that the interpretation itself needs an interpreter.

In subsequent verses we read that the seven great rivers augmented Agni in might, as soon as he was born; the Devas cherished the body at his birth. Then he sanctified the rite, and spread through the firmament with intelligent and purifying. He everywhere repairs to the undevouring, undevoured, the vast of the firmament, not clothed, yet not naked, seven eternal ever youthful rivers, sprung from the same source, received Agni as their common embryo. These seven rivers, Professor Wilson supposes, are the seven great rivers of India.

Aggregated in the womb of the waters, spread abroad; and, omniform, are here effective for the diffusion of the sweet, like milch-kine full-uddered; the Mighty are the fitting parents of the graceful Agni . . . . When the vigourous Agni is greatened by praise, then the showers of sweet rain descend. At his birth, he knew the udder of his parent, and let forth its torrents and its speech; there was no one to detect him, lying hidden in the deep, with his auspicious associates, and the many of the firmament.

He cherishes the embryo of the parent, and of the generator; he alone consumes many flourishing; the associated brides, who are kind to man, are both of kin to that pure showerer; do thou, Agni, ever preserve them!

The great Agni increases on the broad unbounded, for the waters supply abundant nutriment; and placid he sleeps in the birth-place of the waters, for the service

> of the sister streams. He, the generator, the embryo of the waters, has begotten the waters for the offerer of the libation. The auspicious wood has generated the graceful and multiform embryo of the waters and plants; the Devas approached him with reverence . . . . Mighty suns, like brilliant lightnings, associate with the self-shining Agni, great in his own abode, as if in a cavern, as they milk forth ambrosia into the boundless and vast ocean.

In *iii.* 3. 5, it is said,

> The Devas have placed in this world the delightful Agni in a delightful chariot, the tawny-hued Vaiçvanara, the sitter in the waters, the omniscient, the all-pervading, the endowed with energies, the cherisher, the illustrious.

In *iii.* 5. 3. 5. 6. 7. 8, we find:

> Agni the embryo of the waters, has taken his station on high (*saṇvasthâi*). He protects the seven-headed in the center; he protects the exhilarating of the Gods. He made the commendable and beautiful water, the glossy skin, the station of the diffused slumbering, and, ever vigilant, preserves it. Radiant, pure, vast and purifying, he repeatedly renovates his parents. As soon as generated, he is borne aloft by the plants, which grow flourishing by moisture, as the beautifying waters descend. May he in the bosom of his parents protect us.
>
> Stationed on the navel of the expanse, in the form of the firmament, he shines: he respires in mid-heaven (*mâtariçvan*).

It is the Scholiast that makes this word mean "he respires in mid-heaven," or "acts in the form of the sun": or, Yaska says, it may mean, "he who abides in the forest." The more usual sense of it, Wilson says, is "the wind," as in the next stanza, where it kindles the fire of the sacrifice. In this next verse (10), we find what is meant by the continually recurring phrase "sustains, supports, upholds the sky, the heavens, etc." For here we read,

> The mighty Agni, best of the luminaries of the sky, *sustained* the sky with radiance when the wind kindled the bearer of oblations [the fire of the sacrifice].

In *iii.* 27. 12, Agni is the grandson of food (*ûrjjo napat*), which, in a note, Professor Wilson renders "son of the oblation" shining above in the firmament.

No poetic fancy could have conceived of Agni, the fire, as born of the streams of water, or as latent in their depths: and accordingly we find, by comparison of the texts, that the place of his imagined birth is among the rain-clouds, in which concealed, he is suddenly manifested as lightning, making visible with a sudden glare the whole expanse. And when he was thus conceived of as the child of the waters, a wide field was opened for fanciful conceits. Among the enigmatic passages relating to Agni, are the following:

iii. 2. 9. The Immortals, desirous, sanctified the three radiances (*tisrah samidhah*) of the great circumambient Agni: one of them they have placed in the world of mortals as the nourisher; the other two have gone to the neighbouring sphere.

These other two, Professor Wilson thinks, are that of the firmament, or the lightning, and that of the sky, the sun. To get at this he has to hold that *samidhah*, which means "fuel, wood, and grass," here intends the three forms or conditions of fire. *Samidh* is *sam+indh;* and *indh* means "to kindle" and "to shine."

iii. 17. 3. Three are thy existences, Jâtavedas; three, Agni, are thy parent-dawns (*tisra âjânirushasah*).

The three existences (*triṇyâyûnshi*) are said by Professor Wilson to be

three lives, as supported by butter, by fuel, and by the Soma plant.

Âjâni, he says, may mean "sisters" or "mothers." Why there should be three dawns personified as Agni's parents or sisters, he does not clearly see, unless the three diurnal fires are alluded to.

I cannot find for *yâyûnshi* the meaning of "lives," nor for *âjâni,* that of "mothers or sisters." The former it seems to me, from *yâ*, "to go," means "issue, outflowing, emanations, subsistences": and *âjâni* means, I think, "children, products." Both are, I think, the flame, light and heat, of the fire.

In *iii.* 20. 2, it is said to Agni,

born of sacrifice, ... thy viands are three, three thine abiding-places, three the tongues satisfying; three verily are thy forms, ... [In *iii.* 26. 7], I, Agni, am the living breath of three-fold nature, the measure of the firmament, eternal warmth, I am also the oblation.

In *iii.* 6. 2, it is said to Agni,

may thy seven-tongued fires be glorified,

which hardly permits us to doubt that the seven colours of the ray of light were well known. In *i.* 141. 2, Agni dwells among the seven auspicious mothers (*saptasivâshu mâṭrishu*). If in *sapta-siva*, *siva* is from *siv*, the compound words mean the seven united ones, and they are either seven stars that form a constellation, or the seven colours. *Maṭri* is "mother," both words being here in the locative plural.

The essence of the Indo-Aryan faith is expressed in *viii*. 19. 16:

> ***Protected by Indra, well knowing the path that through thy power, Agni, we should follow, we adore of thyself that by which Varuṇa, Mitra, the Nasatyas and Bhaga shine.***

INDRA.

In Section *v.* of Volume *V.*, Dr. Muir has furnished a complete collection of the texts of the Veda and other works in reference to Indra. A careful examination of them confirms my conclusion, arrived at upon consideration chiefly of the translation by Dr. Wilson, that Indra was the Universal, or Substance of, Light.

In *iii.* 48. 2, it is said that on the day when Indra was born, he drank, through fondness for it, the juice of the Soma plant; that of old, the mother who bore him satiated him with it, in the house of his mighty father; that approaching his mother, he desired sustenance, and saw the Soma on her breast.

iv. 17. 4, as Müller translates it, makes Dyu to be the father of Indra; but Dr. Muir does not so translate it. The first verse is,

> *Suvîras te janitâ manyata Dyaur Indrasya kartta svapastamo 'bhût, yaḥ îm̃ jajâna svaryam̃ suvajram, anapachyutam̃ sadaso na bhûma.*

Muir reads it,

> Thy father was, as the sky thought, a most stalwart being; the maker of Indra, he who produced the celestial thunderer, immovable as the earth, he was a most skilful workman. [Müller]: Dyu, thy parent, was reputed strong; the maker of Indra was mighty in his works; he (who) begat the heavenly Indra, armed with the thunderbolt, who is immovable as the earth, from his seat.

He was full of vigour, when born, and his mother concealed him. But he uplifted himself, clothed with a robe, and filled both worlds as soon as he was born. She bore him in order that he might range abroad, and desiring full scope for himself. He was born fierce to exercise impetuous strength; exulting, fiery, full of confidence; and the Maruts augmented him, when his mother brought him forth. He filled the two worlds like the dawn.

For the light is continually reborn, and when it appears, it floods all the sky, fills the expanse, and makes visible all the earth, as it were in an instant. And as Agni and Indra have one generator, and are twin brethren, Indra is born again whenever a fire is kindled. Agni is said to confer immortality on the Devas, who worship when he is born like an infant, and shines forth from out his parents. For every sacrificial fire, kindled by its parents, the two pieces of wood, is a manifestation of Agni, the Universal; and each of these and the fire of the domestic hearth is Agni, and the light of each, Indra.

Every exertion of strength, too, even the slightest, is an exertion of the universal strength, of the one power, called *Daksha*, and this strength is the father of both Agni and Indra, Strength, or the virile erotic vigour.

It is *the same* mighty Divine Power, in *our* conception also, which wafts a feather and crushes a world. And Agni and Indra give the luminaries of the sky immortality, because they *continue* to manifest themselves in radiance by them. The Devas drink Soma to obtain *this* immortality, because the Soma juice, feeding the fire, becomes *of* the fire, a component portion of it.

In *x.* 167. 1, it is said of Indra, *tvaṁ tapaḥ parîtâpya ajayaḥ svaḥ;* which Dr. Muir reads, "conquered heaven by austere fervour": but the primitive meaning of *tapas* is "fire," from *tap*, "to warm, heat, shine"; and *pârîtapa* means "heat, warmth": and the meaning clearly is that emanating from fire and heat he attains, i. e., extends to, the sky. So in *x.* 159. 4, Indra is said to have become resplendent and supreme, by means of the offering of an oblation. Dr. Muir renders *dyumnî uttamaḥ*, "glorious and exalted": but the primitive meaning of the former, is "illuminating"; and the latter is a superlative. The oblation feeds the fire, and thereby increases the light. Every *particular* light, as well as *all* light, is Indra.

The Devas that are said in Atharva-Veda *xi.* 5. 19, to have overcome death by *brahma-charya* (studentship, religious study, pious austerity, chastity), and *tapas* (fire, penance, mortification, religious austerity, devotion), are the pious men, saints, Ṛishis, who, departing from this earth were transferred to the skies and became stars. And we see that here, in this much later hymn, *tapas* has the derivative meaning, while in the older ones, and applied to Indra, it had the original and primitive one. *Tap* meant "to warm, heat, be warm, shine, illuminate, burn up, consume"; and thence, "to give pain, to suffer pain, to mortify one's flesh." *Tapta*, part. of perf. pass. meant "hot" and "molten"; and *tapa*, "illuminating, heat, and tormenting."

Indra is spoken of as undecaying; and it is said that neither autumns, months or days cause him to grow old, or make him feeble (literally, "thin, emaciated").

Ushâḥ iva, is rendered "*like* the dawn," making in *x.* 134. 1, Indra fill the two worlds (*rodasî*), like the dawn. *Iva* means "like"; but Benfey gives, as other meanings, "in some way, almost, scarcely." Müller, in his *Grammar* renders it by "as," and I have before said, of this or a like expression, that I believed the meaning to be *as* the dawn, the dawn being a hypostasis of himself, filled the worlds; i. e., the dawn filled them with light.

[Benfey]: *Rodas*, i. e., *rud*+*as* (the seat of the roaring storm), n. Heaven, dual *sî*, and as former part of a compound, Heaven and Earth.

To *rud* he ascribes the meanings of "to weep, cry, bewail"; and to *rudra*, "one who roars." It does not seem probable that from a verb meaning "to weep" only, would come a derivative meaning "roaring" or "roarer."

It is natural enough to speak of the clouds, the upper air, the heavens, as "weeping" rain; for the raindrops are the tears of the clouds. And I cannot but believe that *rodas* meant that upper region, sky, or heaven, as that which weeps, or rains. In that case, *rodasî* could not mean heaven and earth; nor could it in any case, for the earth neither weeps, cries nor roars. I think, therefore, that *rodasî* does not mean the "two worlds," but the two *regions*, the air or cloud-region, and that above the clouds. It often happens, daily, almost, that we see bodies of cloud far above a lower stratum of cloud; and the two of these may have been *rodasî*. At any rate, even the savage sees that the clouds are far below the sun and moon, below each other, too, and move different ways.

Indra is once addressed as an Aditya, along with Varuṇa; is identified with Sûrya, and receives once the epithet of *Savitṛi*. There must be some sensible reason for this. There was no confusion or muddle of ideas, with the composers of the Veda; and there is but the one single sensible reason possible to be imagined, that Indra was *light*, and manifested himself by and through every luminary, and therefore *was* every one. So "*the Word*" was not only, in the beginning *with* God; but it *was* God; as Yehuah *was* the Elohim, and the messengers who talked and ate with Abraham and Lot.

In *viii.* 58. 4, Indra is called *sûnuṁ satyasya*, "Son of Truth." *Satya* means truth; but it is the same as *sant* present participle of *as*, "to be."

In *iii.* 49. 1, he is said to have been produced by the Devas (*janayanta devâḥ*) as a destroyer of enemies (*vṛitrâṇâṁ*), which may mean "enemies" or "shadows," or "clouds." And that he was produced by the Devas means merely that he manifested himself through them, was emitted from them.

We must always bear it in mind that Agni is sometimes fire, in that sense which includes all particular fires that ever have been or will be kindled; and sometimes a particular fire, sacrificial or domestic, kindled on a particular occasion, and that the kindling of each such particular fire is the birth of Agni: and that, whenever Agni is born, Indra is born also, being included in Agni, as thought is in the mind.

In *vi.* 59. 2, Agni and Indra are said to be twin brothers, having the same father, and whose mothers are, one here, the other there. It is strange that, in view of even one text like this, Indra should ever have been supposed to be the firmament. Dr. Muir remarks that the sense of this verse is not very evident, unless it simply means that the mothers are different. I think it means more than that. These adverbs of locality are never mere expletives in the *Zend-Avesta;* and I think they are never so in the Veda. Here the *locus in quo* is probably considered as the mother; and that of Agni is imagined to be the earth, and that of Indra, the sky.

In *vi.* 55. 5, Pushan also is called *bhrâtâ Indrasya*, the brother of Indra.

In *i.* 82. 5, 6, the wife (*jâya*, "the bringer forth or producer," and *patni*, "the one subject to or governed by") of Indra, is spoken of: in *iii.* 53. 4, *et seq.*, the wife (*jâya*) and pleasant home of Indra are spoken of; and this wife is probably the Goddess Indrânî, several times mentioned elsewhere.

In *x.* 112. 3, Dr. Muir reads,

> He assumes the most beautiful forms, and is invested with the ruddy lustre of the sun.

Sparçayasva ("is invested") is the [Illegible—W] of *sparç*, "to take, embrace." And the meaning is, that Indra is embodied in, makes himself visible as, the crimson radiance of the sun. So, in the *Zend-Avesta*, the sun is said to be the body of Ahura Mazda.

One of the epithets most frequently applied to Indra is *suçipra* or *çiprin*. Sayana doubts whether this means "with handsome cheeks," or "with handsome nose." I do not find either of these words in Benfey.

In *vi.* 46. 3, he is styled *Sahasra-muskha*. Sayana interprets this, "having a thousand genital organs": but where it occurs in *viii.* 19. 32, he explains it as meaning, "having great brilliancy." Dr. Muir does not offer any explanation of his own, of either this or the former phrase. Benfey gives, as meanings of *mushka*, "a thief, a testicle, the scrotum, a heap, a multitude, the name of a plant"; and of *mushkara*, "a man with large testicles." I find no root from which to derive the word, in either sense. No doubt it means "having a thousand testicles," thus figuratively expressing the power of generation of light.

He is called *hari-sipra* ("ruddy-jawed,"—*Muir*); *hari-keça* "ruddy- or golden-haired," *hari-çmaçâru*, "the ruddy- or golden-bearded or moustached," and his whole appearance is ruddy or golden, *hari-varpas*. So he is golden, *hiraṇyaya*, and golden-armed, *hiraṇya-bâhu*, carries a golden whip, and rides in a shining golden car, drawn by two ruddy or golden (*harî*) steeds, with flowing golden manes, with hair like peacocks' feathers and peacocks' tails.

Harit and *hari* mean "green, tawny, yellow"; but also "a ray of light, a fire." The colour expressed by it is, no doubt, that of fire.

The origin of the idea of Indra rending the clouds with his thunderbolts, slaying Vṛittra and other enemies, and causing the rain to pour down, was not that his beneficence caused him to do so, in order to give the earth rain; but that thereby, as is said in *i.* 32. 4, and *i.* 51. 4,

> the gloom which had overspread the sky is dispersed, and the sun is restored, thereby, to his place in the sky. The heavy rain-clouds hide the sun, and enshroud the earth with a heavy gloom, which when a great storm is at hand alarms the animals and oppresses men with a sense of danger. The darkness is then at war with light which can prevail against it, and reoccupy its sovereignty, when the clouds shall

> have poured out their waters upon earth. To effect this, and not for the beneficent purpose of refreshing and fertilizing the earth and filling the rivers, Indra launches his thunderbolts against the storm-clouds. The Maruts aid him, striving to drive the clouds before them and unveil the sun; and Vishṇu, the heat, because the lightning is one species of fire and includes both light and heat. The enemies who confront Indra and Vishṇu are the seven Dânus or Dânavas, issue of Dânu, the mother of Vṛittra also. They are named Namuchi, Kuyava, Çushna, Çambara, Varchin, Ahi, Pipru, Uraṇa, Ranhiṇa, Arbuda, etc., if the Dânus are more than seven in number, and if some of these were not chiefs of the native tribes, against whom Indra was imagined to assist the Indo-Aryans in battle.

Dr. Muir thinks that all of these represent the malignant influences at work in the atmosphere, to prevent the fall of showers, of which the parched fields were often so much in need. He thinks that all the imagery in regard to Indra and these combats grew up from the need of rain, and the supposed beneficent influence of Indra in producing it; and as the rains did bless the thirsty earth after long droughts, and make it fruitful, there is no doubt that this came to be imagined to be the sole purpose of Indra's combats.

But Parjanya and not Indra was the Rain-God. Indra is compared to, and therefore distinguished from him, in *viii.* 6. 1. In *viii.* 82. 1, 4, he is identified with Sûrya, the sun, because he is the light of the sun. In *i.* 32. 4 and *ii.* 19. 3, he is said to have generated the sun: for the sun, as a body of pure light, proceeds from the otherwise unseen Universal Light. So the Logos, manifesting the Father, is said to be Protogenes and Monogenes, the first-*begotten* and only-*begotten* Son, of God. In *x.* 89. 2, Dr. Muir says,

> Indra seems to be identified with the sun (*sa Sûryah*), and to have destroyed the black darkness by his light (*kṛishṇâ tomâm si twishyâ jaghâna*). *Kṛishnâ* is, literally, 'black' or 'dark blue'; *tamas*, 'darkness, gloom'; *twish*, 'light, splendour,' from *twish*, 'to shine'; and *han*, 'to kill, destroy, remove, etc.'

If I am right, the names of the enemies of Indra ought to have meanings significant, not of demons of the drought, but of antagonism to the light, of gloom and darkness.

Vṛitra means among other things, "darkness," and "a cloud." *Vṛi* means, "to cover, conceal, surround, envelop." *Namuchi* is, Benfey says, *na+much+i*. *Much* (among other things), "to shed, effuse, pour out." *Na* is the particle of negation; and *Namuchi*, therefore, means "not pouring out," or "the not-pourer-out," the refuser to shed rain. *Çushna* is from *çush*, "to dry up, wither," and means "the sun and fire," and, as drying up, "drought." One meaning ascribed to *Çambara* is "water." *Varch*, "to shine"; *varchas*, "lustre." *Uraṇa* is probably from *ûrṇu*, "to cover": *ranhiṇa* is probably the same as *rohiṇa;* and that means "redness," and *rohiṇî*, "lightning."

Some of these abstract conceptions, therefore, represent antagonisms of light, and others, preventers of production. But there is no doubt as to the original notion, i. e., that Indra, the light, when darkness caused by storm-clouds encroached upon his sovereignty and domain, rent the clouds with the lightnings, that, losing their burden of rain, they might disappear, or become so thin and fleecy as to cause no gloom in the atmosphere.

> *vi.* 30. 5. Indra is said to have become the king of things moving, and of men, generating at once the sun, the heaven, the dawn. The original here of 'generating,' is *janayan*, from *jan*, 'to bring forth, produce'; caus. *janaya*, 'to beget, bring forth, produce, cause.'

"Things moving" or "moveable" is a very indefinite phrase; and the original, *jagataç*, is not much more definite. *Jagat*, an old participle of the present of the verb *gam*, as an adjective means "moveable," as a noun, "race of men, the world"; dual, *jagati*, "heaven and earth"; fem. *jagati*, "the earth, the world." *Tṛi-jagat*, "the three worlds," means heaven, earth and the lower regions. So much we are told by Benfey. *Gam* meant, originally, "to go, to move"; and *gama* "going, moving, moving in the sky, like a bird." *Charshaninam*, rendered "of men," is from *char*, "to move, go, graze, behave, live, act, make, perform, spy"; whence *charishnu*, "moveable, belonging to the animal world"; *charshani*, "men," which may have meant, originally, "wanderers, graziers, spies, travelers." These "things moveable" are evidently living creatures. The meaning of "earth" or "world," derivatively attached to *jagat*, after the Sanskrit had become a dead language, must have been owing to its including *all* living creatures, and was not warranted. The Poets of the Vedas never thought of the earth itself as moveable, any more than the children do. And the *tṛi-jagat* were probably the air, earth and water, inhabited, one by the birds and other winged creatures, one by animals, reptiles and men, and one by the fishes. And the dual *jagati* no doubt meant the earth and air; i. e., the creatures inhabiting each.

And of what but the light could it be said that it produced the sun, sky and dawn? The three words personified the light of these three.

In *viii.* 12. 30, it is said that Indra placed the sun a brilliant light (*çukram jyotir*), in the sky, and then all the worlds (*viçvâ bhuvanâni*) submitted to him. *Bhuvana*, i. e., *bhu+ana*. *Bhû* is "to become, to spring up, to be, to live, to exist." Therefore the primary meaning of *bhuvana* is, as it is given by Benfey, "a being, a creature." These are the Vedic meanings. In the later books it means "the world, heaven and water," as well as "man, mankind." And when first used to mean "the world," it must have signified the world of living creatures. Afterwards the phrase, "the three worlds," was used; and meant, no doubt, "air or space, the earth and the waters."

> *viii.* 14. 9. The lights of the sky (*rochanâ divo*) have been fixed and established [i. e., the light selected the places where it would shine as heavenly bodies; and, 'those once established, he has never removed'].
>
> *viii.* 85. 9. The Asuras are without weapons, and are no Gods: *anayudhâso asuraḥ adevâç*.

As *yudh* means "to fight," and, noun, "war, battle, or warrior"; and *yuddha* "the *use* of arms, war, battle," I should render *ayudhâso* "unwarlike," or "unused to," or "unskilled in arms." Therefore Indra is asked to sweep them away with his wheel: *chakrena tam apa vapa ṛijîshin*. *Vapa*, "cause to go." *Chakra*, "a potter's wheel, a discus, or sharp circular weapon, (a missile) especially of Vishṇu." It seems more likely that this was intended here, than that the word means a wheel. That Indra should be armed with a weapon of circular shape, was natural, since the sun, the great antagonist of darkness, is of that shape. The discus was a quoit, and was used in the gymnastic games of Greece; and we perpetuate the remembrance of the discus of Indra, when we speak of the disk of the sun.

> *x.* 54. 3. Thou didst produce at once the father and the mother, from thine own body (*tanvâḥ svâyâḥ*).

But *sva* means "one's own self"; and not "body." Whatever the father and mother were, they flowed out or were produced from the Very Self or being, of the light. Very probably the sun and moon are meant.

> *v.* 6. He placed light in light (*jyotishi jyotir*), and imparted to sweet things their sweetness (*madhunâ sam madhûni*).

The meaning is that he supplied light to the luminaries, and gave its sweetness to the honey. The bees work only by day and love the light.

In *i.* 174. 1 and *viii.* 79. 6, Indra is designated as "*Asura*"; while we have seen him in another passage driving away the *Asuras*. *Asura* came to mean a demon, at last, we know. Benfey gives it that meaning, and also that of "eternal," from *as*, "to be." I think it is from *as*, "to burn" or "shine" (*ash*, *ush*), and that *Asura* is "shining one," that is, "luminary." But the *Asuras* whom Indra routed were not luminaries. They were *without* light. *Sur* means "to shine," whence *sura*, "the sun"; and *sura-dvish* meant "an Asura or demon"; "light-hater."

Originally, we are warranted in supposing that one of the two words, which meant, "the shining ones," followed the old form of its proper root, and was *Ashura* or *Ushura*. When this was changed to *as-ura*, it was still not the same as *a-sura*, "lightless." The *A-suras* were the shades or dusky glooms of night, which Indra drove, routed, from the sky. The *As-uras*, "the shiners," were the Devas or "denizens of the sky," generally the stars only; but the other luminaries being sometimes called by each name.

Dr. Muir says, of these passages, that the attributes which they ascribe to Indra

> are chiefly those of physical superiority, and of dominion over the external world. In fact, he is not generally represented as possessing the spiritual elevation and moral grandeur with which Varuṇa is so often invested.

For a much higher degree of definite and pronounced personality could be ascribed to a planet, visible nightly, than to a Universal without form or limits, and, moreover, Varuṇa was one of the manifestations by limitation of Indra, and through him exercising his potencies. Precisely in the same way, we ascribe to Christ, as the revealed and manifested Word in human form, a much more definite personality than we can possibly ascribe to the God of whom we can have no conception, and who has been truly said to have no name and no sex.

Dr. Muir quotes texts, in which faith in Indra "is confessed or enjoined." They amount to this: that men have "faith" (*çrad*) in him, when he hurls his lightnings. Is this a *religious* faith? In *i.* 102. 2, it is said that the sun and moon move alternately, that we may behold and have faith (*çraddhe*). In *i.* 103. 5, it is said,

> Behold this his great abundance, and have faith in the prowess of Indra: *çrad Indrasya dhattana vîryâya*. [The last word means 'virility' as well as 'heroism.' In *i.* 104. 6] We have put faith in thy great power: *nah çraddhitam̃ te mahate indriyaya* . . . . faith has been reposed in thee: *çrad te asmai adhâyi*.

It is but a belief in his power, a confidence in the regular return of day, after night. This is the *satya çraddha* spoken of in *i.* 108. 6, a real belief and confidence. In *ii.* 12. 5, the hearers are advised to put faith in Indra: *çrad asmai dhatta*. In *vi.* 18. 4, in answer to a question, assurance is given that Indra's strength is really existing: and in *viii.* 89. 3, he is himself represented as asseverating that he is here, can be seen, and surpasses all creatures in greatness.

Dr. Muir has collected a multitude of texts in which the powers, beneficence and liberalities of Indra are enlarged upon. He gives wealth, cattle, protection and content, and takes the field with the Aryans against the Dasyus, striding forward, wielding the thunderbolt, and shattering their cities.

> Chastising the lawless (*abratan*), he subjected the dark skin to Manu, or the Aryan people.

Vrata means "rule, action, work, devout act." *Avratan* probably meant "impious."

He is not alone, as protector and friend of the Aryans. It is said to the Açvins, in *i*. 117. 21,

> sweeping away the Dasyu with the thunderbolt, ye have created a great light (*uru jyotir*) for the Arya (*âryâya*).

In *vi*. 21. 11, it is said of all the fire-tongued and frequenting-religious-rites Devas (*agnijihvâḥ ṛitasâpaḥ*) that they have made the race of Manu superior to the Dasa.

> *ii*. 11. 18. Thou, Indra, hast revealed the light to the Aryans. The Dasyus are gone, defeated, backward: *ni savyataḥ sâdi Dasyur Indra*.

Dr. Muir translates this "the Dasyu was placed on the left side." *Sad* means "to *sink down*, to sit down (Vedic), to become helpless, be in distress, be dejected, to perish, decay"; and in the passive, "to be diminished, gone, lost, oppressed, spoiled," etc. *Sadita*, "exterminated, exhausted, decayed, broken, distressed." *Savya* means "left, left hand"; but also "southern, south," and "backward, reverse, contrary." "Placed on the left side" has no definite meaning, while that the Dasyus were forced back, by the aid of Indra, perhaps to the southward, seems a far more natural interpretation.

In *iii*. 34. 9, it is said here, that Indra, "destroying the Dasyus, has protected the Aryan colour." *Varṇa*, "colour," from which the denominative *varṇ*, "to colour," came at last to mean "caste, class, tribe," etc.; but it originally meant the colour of the skin.

> *vi*. 18. 3. Then thou didst subdue the Dasyus, and didst give the people (*kṛishtîr*) to the Aryans.

The verb *kṛish* means "to draw, bear, plough." *Kṛishṭa*, "ploughed"; *phala-kṛishṭa*, "tilled ground, produced by cultivation"; *kṛishi*, "ploughing, agriculture." As *jyotir* means "brightness," why may not the meaning here be, that Indra gave to the Aryans the cultivation of the land won from the Dasyus?

In *vi*. 25. 3, it is said that Indra had subjected all the Dasyan tribes to the Aryans; and in *viii*. 24. 27, that in the land of the Seven Rivers (*Sapta Sindhushu*), he turned away from the Aryans the weapon of the Dasyu. In *viii*. 87. 6, Indra is the destroyer of many cities and the slayer of the Dasyus, the prosperer of the race of Manu, and Lord of the sky (*patir divaḥ*). In *x*. 49. 2, he says that he has stayed the weapon of *Çushna* (drought), and does not abandon the Aryan race to the Dasyus.

In *vi.* 60, we find that there were hostile Aryans also; for Indra and Agni are besought to slay all enemies, Aryas and Dasyus; and in *x.* 38. 3, he is asked for help to enable the worshippers to slay all ungodly men (*adevah purushṭuta*), whether Dasas or Aryas, who fight with them; and in several other passages there is like prayer as to both.

The Reverend William Arthur, in his *Mission to the Mysore*, is greatly disgusted with the bacchanalian character and absurdities of the Sama-Veda, which he considers a heap of hymns without coherency or sense, and woefully devoid of pure theology or morals. He had not read the Rig-Veda; but would, no doubt, have had the same opinion of that. A Brahman would express very much such an opinion in regard to much of the contents of the Hebrew books. Dr. Muir endeavours, not very satisfactorily, to explain the sensual character, generally attributed to Indra, and which

> appears in opposition to the moral perfection which is elsewhere described as an essential feature of his nature.

He thinks that the Poets regarded him

> as anthropopathically partaking, in a higher degree, of the elements, sensuous, as well as intellectual and moral, which, on the evidence of their own consciousness, they knew to be equally constituent parts of their own nature. [And, then] these ancient authors did not connect the same low associations as we now connect with the sensuous, or even sensual, principle in the character of the God, which is exemplified in his love for the exhilarating draughts of his favourite beverage.

They certainly had no idea that Indra actually drank, as a man drinks, the juice of the Soma. It is, I think, very doubtful whether it had any intoxicating quality at all. All the ancient peoples had their sacred plants and herbs, for the sanctity attributed to which no satisfactory reason can be given. Instances of this are the *verbenæ* or sacred branches of the myrtle, olive and laurel, of the Latins; the *bareçma* or bundle of twigs of date and pomegranate, of the Irano-Aryans; and the *misseltoe*, the *pren awyr* or tree of the air of the ancient Britons. Also the *briw* or *vervain*, which, Pliny tells us, the Druids used in casting lots and foretelling events; and the *selago* a *hedge hyssop*, in modern Welsh, *grâs dnw*, or the Grace of God, which, we learn from Pliny, the Druids gathered with great care and superstition, permitting nothing of iron to touch or cut it, nor the bare hand to touch it; and which could only be gathered by some sacred person privately, with the left hand, and that enveloped in a peculiar vesture, he being clothed with white, his feet naked, and washed with pure water, and after the offering by him of a sacrifice of bread and wine.

If the intoxicating qualities of the Soma plant had been the reason of the sanctity and potency attributed to it, this quality of the Haöma would equally have been celebrated in the *Zend-Avesta*. Among the extraordinary virtues imputed to the misseltoe, was that of promoting the increase of the species, or preventing sterility; and there are expressions in the Veda which indicate that the Soma plant was supposed to possess aphrodisiac virtues. Its sacred character came, most probably, from this.

We find the fuel which fed the fire of the sacrifice, invested with the divinity of Agni, because it was, when consumed, transformed into the fire. So the Soma juice fed the fire, and became a part of it, and it was, of course, regarded as feeding and increasing the light that flowed from the fire. It was in this sense that Indra drank the Soma and was enlarged and exhilarated. All the rest was the mere wantonness and license of the Aryan imagination.

Professor Roth thinks that Varuṇa belongs to an older dynasty of Gods than Indra, and that during the Vedic age, the high consideration originally attaching to the former was in course of being transferred to the latter. I have no doubt that the visible luminaries were first worshipped, long before the conception of fire and light as universals was formed in the Aryan intellect: of the latter part of Roth's proposition I find no convincing proof. Mitra was certainly an ancient Deity, because both the branches of the race, the Indians and the Iranians revered him. I doubt if Varuṇa was known at the time of the separation of these races. If he had been, the Irano-Aryans would have continued to revere him jointly with Mitra. Professor Roth says:

> The course of the movement was therefore this, that an old God, common to the Aryans (i. e., the Persians and Indians), and perhaps also to the entire Indo-Germanic race, Varuṇa-Ormuzd-Uranos is thrown back into the darkness, and in his room Indra, a peculiarly Indian, and a national God, is intruded. With Varuṇa disappears at the same time the ancient character of the people, while with Indra there was introduced in the same degree a new character, foreign to the primitive Indo-Germanic nature.

The first remark that suggests itself, in reading this passage, is that Ormuzd is most unfitly coupled in it with Varuṇa and Ouranos. One of these was the planet Jupiter, and the other the sky; while Ahura Mazda was, in every lineament of the Zarathustrian conception of him, the same Essential Light and Supreme Intelligence, single and infinite which the intellect of the present day reveres as God.

The Aryan conception of Varuṇa did not change during the Vedic period, nor did that of Indra enlarge. Indra was, from the beginning to the close of that period, light, and Varuṇa, the same Light, limitedly manifested, as the planet Jupiter. He thinks,

> Viewed in its internal aspect, this modification of the religious conceptions of the Aryas consists in an ever-increasing tendency to attenuate the supersensuous, mysterious side of the creed, until the Gods who were originally the highest and most spiritual, have become unmeaning representatives of Nature, Varuṇa being nothing more than the ruler of the sea, and the Adityas merely regents of the sun's course.

The highest Deity of the Vedic period was Agni, the fire. Conceived of as a Universal, having personality and unity, it was inevitable that the imagination should invest him with the attribute of intelligence, and ascribe to him feelings and sympathies. After a time, this led to the conception, among the Irano-Aryans, of a being superior to and source of the fire, to whom these attributes were transferred, and by degrees ceased to be considered to belong at all to the fire. So, among the Indo-Aryans, Brahm was conceived of, as the Infinite and Absolute Source, and, as emanating from him and being the hypostases of his substance, Brahma the creator, Vishṇu the preserver, and Çiva the destroyer. Indra continued to be adored as a subordinate Deity; but that he was light was forgotten. Mitra, Varuṇa and Aryaman, only recognized as luminaries, were naturally repudiated by the new spiritual faith, and disappeared, as Indra would have done, if he had not originally been the light, of which Brahm never ceased to be regarded as the Essence and Very Substance. I do not see, in either the Indian or Iranian branch of the Aryans, "the ever-increasing tendency to attenuate the supersensuous"; but precisely the reverse, a continual struggle towards the idea of an intellect, supreme, infinite, absolute source and origin of all things, beings and intellectual powers.

Professor Benfey and Mr. Bréal are quoted by Dr. Muir as expressing the opinion that Indra was the successor of Dyaus, the sky. The radiance of the sky, Benfey says, appeared to the Ayra, before they left the common country, as, in consequence of the climate there prevailing, the holiest thing; and that to those who settled in India, where the glow of heaven is destructive, and its rain alone acts beneficently,

> this aspect of the celestial Deity must have appeared the most adorable, so that the epithet *Pluvius* in a certain measure absorbed all the other characteristics of *Dyaus Pitar*. [This found its expression, he thinks, in the name *Indra*], in which we unhesitatingly recognize a word (which arose in some local dialect, and was then diffused with the spread of the worship), standing for *sind+ra*, which again was derived from *syand*, 'to drop.'

The conceptions that had been attached to Dyaus were then, he thinks, transferred to Indra. Professor Müller assigns the same sense to *Indra*. It is, he says, "a name peculiar to India, and admits of but one etymology"; i. e., it must be derived from the same root, whatever that may be, which in Sanskrit yielded *indu*, "drop, sap." It meant originally the "giver of rain," the *Jupiter Pluvius*, a Deity in India more often present to the mind of the worshipper than any other.

Roth thinks that *Indra* is from the root *in* or *inv*, with the suffix *r*, preceded by *d*, and means "the overcomer, the powerful." Mr. Bréal says that Indra is an exclusively Indian God, created after the ancestors of the European races had emigrated from Asia; and that he occupies the place of some more ancient divinity. He says,

> The name of this God, which we may give with perfect certainty, is *Dyaus*, or *Dyauspitar*, the heaven, father of beings.

Of course, if Indra was rain, or the sky as raining, he was not light, and most of the passages in which he is spoken of become nonsense. No one has more emphatically warned us of the danger of etymological speculations, based on similarity of words, than Professor Müller. I have not found a Sanskrit word *indu*, meaning "drop" or "sap." *Indu*, in the Ramayana, is "the moon." *Syand* does mean "to drop, to flow," and Benfey thinks that *Sindhu*, "a river" (the Zend *hendu*), "the Indus," comes from it. If so, the fact that *Sindhu* retains the *s*, proves that *Indra* is not from the same root.

But for the preconceptions in respect of the character of Indra, there would never have been a doubt as to the root of the word. It is the verb *indh*, "to kindle, to shine." "Power" is a derivative meaning of *indriya*, as "virility" is; both owing to the attribution of generative potency to light. *Indu* was a name of the moon, as "shining," from the same root; and *Indh-ra* or *Aindh-ra* literally signifies "that which is kindled or shines, radiance, splendour, light."

Dr. Muir says (*v*. 121):

> Beyond the fact noticed by Roth, that Varuṇa is much less frequently mentioned in the last, than in the earlier books of the Rig-Veda, I have not observed in the hymns themselves anything that can be construed as a decisive proof that the worship of Indra was superseding that of Varuṇa during the period of their composition. It is true that even in the earlier parts of the Veda, the number of hymns addressed to the former God is much greater than that in which the latter is celebrated. But I have not discovered any expressions which would distinctly indicate that the popularity of the one was waning, and that of the other increasing.

There are, he says (referring to them), several hymns, however, in which Indra is associated with Varuṇa as an object of celebration, and where the two are described as acting in concert; he says,

> and this association of the two *might* have arisen from the worshippers of Indra desiring to enhance the dignity of that God, by attaching him to the older and more venerable Deity.

There seems to be no reason for making that admission. There is no proof of any struggle for precedence between the worships of Indra and Varuṇa. The worship of the latter was the worship of Indra and Agni, who were manifested by him, whom he *was*, as the Word *was* God. That known, it is easily understood why Agni and Indra, Indra and Vayu (fire and its flame), Indra and Pushan (the planet and its light), Indra and Soma (the light of the fire, and that which increases it), and Indra and Vishṇu (light and heat) were adored together. Therefore Vishṇu is called *yujyah sakhâ*, "the intimate friend," of Indra; and Varuṇa, *Indra-sakhâ*, "the associated or coherent with" Indra. They are *samrâjâ*, "the two kings," and together launch the thunderbolts.

In *vii.* 82. 5, it is said that they together, by their power, produced or made all the creatures of the sky or heavens; and that Mitra contentedly honours Varuṇa, while Indra shines accompanying the Maruts.

Jâtâni bhuvanasya I take to mean the luminaries of heaven. It is to be remembered that to these Poets the lights of heaven were not imagined to be bodies like the earth, but orbs of light; and therefore Indra had produced them all. And, as to the other phrase, Venus could properly be said to honour or wait upon Jupiter, when they appeared together in the same quarter of the sky, he being the more regal.

Indra and Varuṇa are called *dharttârâ charshaṇînâm*, which Dr. Muir reads "supporters of all creatures"; and the same epithet is applied to Mitra and Varuṇa. So Varuṇa is called *charshaṇî-dhrit*, which Dr. Muir reads "supporter of creatures." Benfey gives us *charshaṇi*, meaning "men," from the verb *char*, which means "to move, go, live, act, spy," etc.; whence *chara*, "moveable, moving, a spy"; and as *ku-chara* means "a fixed star," *charshaṇi* may mean the planets, called by the Greeks, πλανηται, "wanderers."

In *viii.* 83. 9, it is said that Varuṇa always maintains (keeps or observes) his ordinances. In *i.* 25. 1, the laws (*vratam*) of Varuṇa are spoken of, which the worshipper admits breaking daily. The laws of Indra (*Indrasya vratâni*) are said not to be broken by any of the Devas, in *iii.* 32. 8; the three-fold law (*tri-dhâtu vratam*) of Agni, in *vii.* 5. 4; and in *ii.* 28. 8, it is said that in Varuṇa all laws (*vratâni*) are grounded, immovable as a rock.

Indra and Varuṇa are said to have dug the channels of the rivers (the water, raised by the rains which they cause, washing them out); and to have caused the sun to journey in the sky; because when Jupiter is the Morning Star, he and the light precede the sun in the eastern sky, and seem to lead him up.

In *vii.* 82. 2, all the Devas in the highest sky (*vyoman*, from *vye*, "to cover") are said to have given or added vigour and power to Indra and Varuṇa.

x. 48. 11, as translated by Dr. Muir, represents Indra as saying,

> I, a Deva, do not assail the rank (or glory) [it might also be rendered 'do not diminish the dignity, light or splendour'] of the Devas the Adityas, the Vasus or the Rudriyas, who have fashioned (*tatakshur*) me for glorious power, and made me unconquerable, irreversible and unassailable.

"Irreversible" must be a misprint. It represents *astṛitam* from *stṛi* (with negation), which means "to hurt, kill." But if Indra is the Universal Light, how can it be said that he has been "fashioned" by the Adityas, Vasus and Sons of Rudra?

Taksh originally meant "to hew," and derivatively "to prepare, to fashion, to give form to." *Tatakshur* is the third person singular of the reduplicated perfect: and the meaning must of necessity be that these Deities gave limitation by form to Indra; i. e., that they were manifestations of the light, in form and limitation, each a limited revealing, in permanent form, of the immeasurable Universal Light.

In *viii*. 51. 7, it is said:

> All the Gods yield to thee, Indra, in vigour and strength.

In *iv*. 30. 1 *et seq*., he is described as having no superior or equal, and as having alone conquered (surpassed?) all the Devas in battle. In *vii*. 21. 7, it is said that the ancient (or many) Devas subordinated their powers to his splendour and royalty.

In other passages it is said that all the Devas are not able to frustrate the mighty deeds and counsels of Indra; that Varuṇa and Sûrya are subject to his law; and in *x*. 89. 8, 9, he is besought to destroy the enemies of Mitra, Varuṇa and Aryaman.

> All these texts, however, which are so laudatory of Indra, may be paralleled in the Rig-Veda, not only by similar ones [Dr. Muir remarks, referring to Mitra and Varuṇa], but also by a farther set of texts, in which other Gods are magnified in the same style of panegyric. This is in accordance with the practice of the Indian Poets to exaggerate (in a manner which renders them often mutually inconsistent), the attributes of the particular Deity who happens at the moment to be the object of celebration. Thus it is [he says] that in *ii*. 38. 9, it is said that neither Indra, Varuṇa, Mitra, Aryaman nor Rudra can resist the ordinance of Savitṛi, *vratam na minanti*. *Mi*, whence *minant*, partic. pres., means 'to hurt'; and *vrata* means not only 'a law or ordinance,' but also a 'voluntary act, rule, work.'

It cannot mean that the law or rule of Savitṛi is for the government of Indra and Varuṇa; but that the law of his own being and movement cannot be abrogated or changed by them. So in *vii*. 38. 4, it is said that the Devî Aditi and the Kings Varuṇa, Mitra and Aryaman unite to magnify the moon

(Savitṛi). For, when the full moon shines in the sky, these planets grow pale and seem to be her attendants.

In *i.* 156. 4, it is said that King Varuṇa and the Açvins submit to the power of Vishṇu. For they receive their light from Agni, of whom Vishṇu is a hypostasis, or a part included in the whole, Agni manifested as heat.

In *i.* 141. 9, Varuṇa, Mitra and Aryaman are said, for the same reason, to triumph through Agni, when he blazes forth.

Dr. Muir concludes by saying, that

> if we were to infer from some of the passages, that the worship of Indra was beginning to gain ground on that of Varuṇa, we should have, in like manner, to conclude from others, that the worship of Savitṛi, Vishṇu or Agni was beginning to supersede that of all the other Deities who are there subordinated to them, not excepting Indra himself.

I have thus referred to all the materials additional to those within my reach before, to enable me to decide what Indra was, which are furnished by Dr. Muir: and I am more than ever satisfied with the conclusion that he was the Universal Light. There is no text really inconsistent with this, and very many that directly sustain it, and that have, on any other hypothesis, no sensible meaning. Indeed, it seems to me that not even the lingering shadow of a doubt remains. I can anticipate, nevertheless, that it will be thought that the conceptions which I ascribe to the Aryan Poets are entirely too modern, too metaphysical, too much in advance of their age.

It might be enough to reply, that it is too plain to be denied, that such conceptions and ideas were entertained by them, unless the Veda is nonsense, pure and simple; or to answer that these ideas and conceptions are found to have been possessed by the Brahmans, the Bactrians, the authors of the Hebrew Kabbalah, and the oldest among the Grecian philosophers; and that they are the fruits, not of learning but of reflection, needing for their birth in the human mind only eyes with which to see the world, and intellect and imagination to speculate upon what the eyes saw.

The relation between Indra and the luminaries, as conceived of by these old Poets, is simple enough. If there were beyond the sky a limitless ocean of light, and each luminary were an aperture through which there flowed portions of this light, each would be the light, although it might be individualized and called a ray; for when the light expanding fills the space between earth and sky, the Light, the Universal, is itself there, so far as that which is of limitless or even very great extent, can be in one limited space. The moment anything is conceived of as a unit, the whole of it is conceived of as being where any part of it is. It is *the sea*, that chafes against a particular shore, or lifts the pebbles gently on the shore of a particular bay.

It is *the air*, that breathes upon us, in at our window. And so every ray of the light is *the whole light*, except in quantity.

Now, if the light of the sun is conceived of as not generated in the sun, by any power inherent in the sun, but as being itself the sun, the Very Light, revealed and manifested within a limited space or investing a body of limited form, then all the energies and potencies of this body, *being* those of the light so manifested, and the existence there of any thing except this light not being apparent, and probably not thought or conceived of, light would be considered by the mind as its being, and it would be to the intellect the Very Light itself, limitedly revealed. And in attributing to this limited portion of the light the attributes, energies and potencies of the whole, we should do only that which every man does, who speaks of "the sea" as breaking over a particular rock, or in its wrath dashing against the rocks of a particular shore a single vessel.

The idea of emanation is equally as simple. Flame, light and heat are all conceived of, naturally, even by the child, as separate and distinct things. Yet they are all included in the fire, and are of it, and flow forth from it. It is the fire, we say, that burns us. It is the fire that blazes; it is the fire that shines. The flame, the light and the heat are distinct revealings of the fire, yet each the fire itself, in that particular mode and aspect; and when we, in our ordinary language, ascribe to the fire the burning of our flesh that is the effect of the heat, we do precisely what the Aryan Poets did, in ascribing the same potencies to Agni and Vishṇu alike. And the inconsistency which commentators find in the Veda is precisely the same as that found in our expressions of thought, when we speak at one time of fire and at another time of heat, as producing a particular effect.

In Rig-Veda *iii*. 50. 4, Indra is called

> *kshapâm vastâ janitâ sûryasya*, the lighter up of nights, the parent of the Sun.

One such passage seems to me sufficient to prove that he is light. And I am firmly convinced that whatever expressions seem to be inconsistent with this, are mistranslations, owing to misconceptions of his nature, when they cannot be shown to be in harmony—attributes ascribed to him as personified wisdom, power, bravery, etc. What particular meaning of a word is the right one, when it is used with reference to a particular Deity, will necessarily depend on the real character of that Deity.

Take, for example,

> *iii*. 32. 8: *Indrasya karma su-kritâ purûṇi vratâni devâḥ na minante viçve:* the *deeds* of Indra are well done and many: all the Devas do not break his *laws* [or, do not injure his *ordinances:* as Professor Müller translates it].

Karma certainly means "deeds" and "actions," being from the verb *kṛi*, "to make, do, perform, utter," etc. The *deeds* of Vohu-Manô are very often spoken of in the *Zend-Avesta*, and are the Manthras and prayers that are his utterances, the expressions of the Divine Intellect. *Indrasya karma* means the manifestations of the light, and its effects—all that the light does, in the performance of its varied functions. But what are Indra's laws or ordinances?

Professor Müller has, in Volume *I* of his *Translation of the Rig-Veda*, an interesting discussion as to the meaning of the word *vrata*, which is, he says,

> one of those words, which, though we may perceive their one central idea, and their original purport, we have to translate by various terms, in order to make them intelligible in every passage where they occur.

Originally, he thinks, *vrata* meant "what is enclosed, protected, set apart": secondly, "what is fenced off, determined, settled," and hence, like *dharman*, "law, ordinance."

Any regular action gives us the idea of a law that causes and regulates it. We do not mean by the phrases "the laws of Nature," "the laws of growth," etc., laws imposed on Nature, growth, etc., by the supreme outside Power; but merely the regularity of the mode of action. Electricity and magnetism have their laws, i. e., their regular modes and processes of action. I think that a great truth was expressed by the philosopher who said,

> The laws of Nature are the varied action of God.

And, accordingly, *vrata* is found to mean "voluntary act, action self-willed, rule, action, doing, work," and even "eating,"—i. e., whatever is regularly *done*. *Mî*, whence *minanti*, *miyâte*, etc., has but the single meaning "to hurt," given to it by Benfey, but it no doubt meant "to break, to violate," also. *Yasya vratam na miyâte* may mean, as Müller renders it,

> whose law is not broken [or, it may as legitimately mean], whose regular action is not [cannot be] interfered with, prevented, affected.

In *ii.* 24. 12, it is said,

> *viçvam satyam maghavânâ yuvoh it âpah chana pra minanti vratam vam:* all that is yours, O potent Ones, is real: even the waters do not break your law.

What "law" do the heavenly bodies enact for the waters? But if we reflect a moment, we may discover the meaning. The water does not obstruct or hinder the light of the sun, moon or other luminaries, on the contrary it illuminates and fills the water, making objects visible on the bottom of lakes and streams; and, to one who knows nothing of the cause of the visible image of a luminary in the water, of the laws of reflection, the orbed lights of the sky seem to have their doubles or second selves radiant in the bosom of the still waters, as real, apparently, as brilliant certainly, as the orb itself in the sky. The water does not prevent or hinder the action of the light or of a luminary, in that sense.

But, it is plain how the Devas, the stars, planets, sun and moon, do not break the laws of Indra, in that sense, there are laws of Aditi for men to perform, and laws of Varuṇa which men break: and Professor Müller renders

> *aminatî daivyâni vratâni*, not injuring the divine ordinances.

There is a three-fold law (*tridhâtu vrata*) of Agni Vaiçvanâra, which Dyu and Pṛithivi follow: but this is his three-fold action, as fire, light and heat.

I do not believe that it was ever imagined by the Vedic Poets that Varuṇa had enacted any moral laws for the government of their conduct. If it had been, some of those laws would have been specifically stated and the duty of obeying them inculcated; but not even one is particularized.

Now, the Deities are represented in the Veda and *Zend-Avesta* as pleased with sacrifice and offering, as enjoying the Soma juice, as expecting, desiring and demanding to be sacrificed to. One of the two original meanings of *vṛi* was "to choose." And as the sacrifice was *desired* by the Devas, the sacrifice was called *vrata*. And the phrases *vratam chakrima, vratam minîmasi*, etc., do not, I think, mean overstepping and breaking *laws*, but neglecting the duty of sacrifice, as disappointing the desires and disregarding the wishes of the Deva mentioned. I should read,

> *kat asya ati vratam chakrima*, which of his desires have we disregarded? [and] *yat chit hi te viçaḥ yathâ pra deva Varuṇa vratam minîmasi dyavi-dyavi*, whatever desire of thine we disappoint, Varuṇa, day by day, men as we are.

Yehuah, the Deity of the Hebrews, their Alohai, chief or substance of the Alohayim, was the God of Hosts, or of the celestial armies of the stars. And so in the Veda we have (*vii.* 44. 5),

> *çrinotu naḥ daivyam çardhaḥ Agniḥ sṛinvantu viçve mahishâḥ amûrâḥ:* may the army of the sky, may Agni hear us! May all the potent wise ones!

So Agni is invited to bring the Devas to the sacrifice, that the *çardhaḥ divyam* may be sacrificed unto.

There is no doubt that intellectual and moral characteristics and qualities were ascribed to Indra. The rudest savage Kamschatkan ascribes these to his ugliest idol. The Poet ascribes them to everything that he personifies, and his fancies become mythology. And even the philosophers have deemed that the stars were wise and rational beings, with power over men's fates and fortunes.

It seems that even the early Vedic Poets had the notion of the identity of light and intellect: and what is the source or essence of intellectual light, if not God? In *iv.* 26. 1 and 2, Indra says:

> I was Manu, and I was the Sun. I am the wise Ṛishi Kakshîvât . . . . I am the Sage Uçanas. Behold me! I gave the earth to the Ârya, and rain to the sacrificer . . . . The Devas have followed my will: *Aham Manur abhavam̃ Sûryaç cha aham̃ Kakshîvân ṛishir asmi vipraḥ*, etc.

It was but a little way from this to Zarathustra's conception of *Vohu-Manô*, the Manifested Wisdom or Intellect of the Primal and Eternal Light; Ahura Mazda, becoming, in every true Aryan believer, the human intellect, and every prayer, and every hymn its utterance.

So, in *i.* 4. 3, it is said to Indra,

> we recognize thee in the midst of the right-minded, who are nearest to thee. Come to us! Pass not by us, to reveal. [And, in *v.* 4] Go, worshipper, to the wise and uninjured Indra, who bestows the best on thy friends, and ask him of the learned.

That he is the light is clearly shown by *i.* 6. 1, in which it is said that with him "associate" those that stand around (the sentinels of the sky, the unimpassioned, those that revolve, the lights or brilliant ones that shine in the sky). The same phrase, "associate with" is used in the same sense in the *Zend-Avesta*, meaning that they shine by his light. The word in the text here is *yunjanti*, from *yuj*, "to join, to unite with, to become one with."

In *i.* 9. 3, Indra is said to be *viçva-charshane*. Sayana of course perverts this into "worshipped by all institutors of sacrifices," after explaining it as "who art joined to all men." *Charshaṇi* is said by Benfey to mean "men," from *char*, "to move, go, graze, live, act, perform, spy." So "spy" is one of the meanings of *chara*, "moveable." I think that *charshaṇe* here means the celestial bodies, often styled "moveable" and "spies." Indra is not all men, but he is all the luminaries.

I do not believe that the epithet *su-sipra*, applied to Indra, means either "handsome-nosed," "handsome-jawed" or "handsome-chinned." Benfey has *sipra* with the meanings, "perspiration" and "the moon," but not with that of "nose," "jaw" or "chin." As *sṛibh* and *sibh* are the same, and *sṛimbh* and *simbh*, and as *sṛipra* also means "the moon," I take it and *sipra* to be the same word, from *srip*, "to creep, go, glide, move"; and that *su-sipra* means "well-going" or "swiftly moving one."

His "good deeds," it is said in *i*. 51. 1,

> spread abroad for the benefit of mankind, as rays of light.

His good deeds are not things that he does, but, as in the *Zend-Avesta*, his utterances or revealings. The good deeds of Vohu-Manô are the Manthras and prayers which he inspires. Here the good deeds or utterances of Indra are diffused or flow abroad, as rays of light, emanating from him.

In the same verse he is called *Mesha*, which is supposed to mean "a ram." I hardly think that he was called that animal. *Mesha*, it is said, meaning "a ram," is from *mih*, "to sprinkle, effuse, give." The last is a Vedic meaning; and I think that *Mesha* originally meant "giver," or "source of emanation." In *i*. 52. 1, he is again called "that *Mesha* who makes the sky known," i. e., by whom it becomes visible.

Not only do the libations sprinkled on the sacred grass replenish him (by being consumed in the fire and becoming a part of it and of its light), "as the *kindred* rivers hastening to it fill the ocean," as is said in *i*. 52. 4; but also the hymns that glorify him attain unto him, as rivulets a lake. The *thoughts*, as well as the light, become part of himself.

In *i*. 102. 2, it is said,

> The seven rivers display his glory; heaven, earth and sky display his visible form; the sun and moon, Indra, perform their revolutions, that we may see, and have faith in what we see.

Here the distinction is plainly expressed between the Very Self of Indra, and his revealings and manifestations, in visible form, and through the sun and moon, compelling us to believe in the invisible, which we can know only by its revealings or manifestations to our senses.

The seven rivers that display the glory of Indra, are, no doubt, the seven actual streams of the Indus country, owing to him the increased volume of their waters. So there were seven Kareshvares (districts or divisions), of the Irano-Aryan land, formed by different streams flowing to the Oxus. We find mention made of "the seven rays," also, as in *i*. 105. 9,

> Those which are the seven rays, in them is my Source (*nâbhi*, 'navel') expanded. Trita Aptya knows that, and praises them for his extrication.

Rosen renders this,

> Those which are the seven rays of the sun, among them is my domicil placed.

The Scholiast identifies the solar rays with the seven vital airs abiding in the ruling spirit. In the *Zend-Avesta* there are seven Amĕsha-Çpĕntas, or emanations from the supreme Deity, Ahura Mazda; and to these answer seven of the ten Sephiroth of the Hebrew Kabbalah. It is hardly to be believed that the Indo-Aryans of the Vedic period had learned that the white light of the sun was compounded of seven distinct rays, three primary and four secondary, curiously corresponding with the scale of musical notes and with the seven stars (3+4) of Ursa Major.

In the fifth verse of this hymn, the Devas are invoked,

> who are present in three regions, who abide in the light of the sun [and in the tenth, it is said], May the fire shedders [effusers or pourers-out], who abide in the center of the expanded heavens, having together conveyed my prayers quickly to the Devas, return.

These are the Hyades; and the seven "rays" mentioned in Verse 9, may be the stars of the Great Bear. The "navel" is perhaps the pole-star.

It is doubtful whether we shall ever understand some of the expressions used in connection with Indra; as, for example, in *i.* 121. 2,

> The mighty Indra manifests himself after his own daughter: he made the female of the horse unnaturally the mother of the cow. [So the expression in *i.* 130. 9], Endowed with augmented vigour, he hurled the wheel of the sun (*Sûraschakram, pravrihid*); and, ruddy of hue, deprived them (the black enemies of the Ârya) of existence; he, the sovereign lord, deprived them of existence (*vacham mushayati*, literally, 'steals, or takes away speech').

"Hurling the wheel of the chariot of the sun" at the Dasyus, and taking away their speech, whether that means killing them, or silencing their clamour, or suppressing his own exclamations (which are the guesses of the evidently puzzled Scholiast), was, no doubt, something that Indra was imagined to have done; but what, one may well despair of understanding.

Vṛih, according to Benfey, means "to raise"; and *pravṛih* would mean "to raise up," or "lift on high." *Chakra* is the disk or orb, of the sun. *Mush* means "to steal, rob, plunder, take away, deprive of." The Dasyus, like the American Indians, probably made their attacks, and certainly their forays, under cover of the darkness, and with hideous yells; and Indra, instead of hurling the orb of the sun at them, probably caused it to rise, and silenced their clamour.

In *i.* 133. 6, it is said,

> most powerful with mighty energies, thou assailest, Indra, with terrible blows; and doing no injury to man [to the Ârya], invincible, hero, by enemies; attended, hero, by three or seven followers (*trisaptaih, çûrasatwabhih*).

In a note, Professor Wilson seems to consider that *trisaptaih* means "thrice-seven." Who then are the three, seven or twenty-one "followers" of Indra? He says that the Maruts are *forty-nine* in number, and that *satwabhih* must mean something else, perhaps the seven platters offered to the Maruts, repeated at the three daily rites; or, attended by the beings, i. e., the Maruts, to whom the thrice-seven offerings are presented.

Satwan means, according to Benfey, "a warrior." *Çûrasatwabhih* means, I think, "by heroic warriors"; and these were probably twenty-one stars, in groups of seven each, that appeared with the dawn, and were deemed to assist Indra.

> *i.* 139. 9. The ancient Dadhyanch, Angiras, Priyamedha, Kaṇva, Atri, Manu, have known my birth: they who were of old and Manu have known. For long life among the Devas is theirs, and in them our origins are (*asmâkam teshu nâbhayah*, 'in them are our navels').

The phrase, "navel of the waters" often occurring in the *Zend-Avesta*, means there "the source or place of origin of the streams or rains." *Nâbhi* is not only "the *navel*," but also "the nave" of a wheel, "the center."

In *ii.* 12. 3, 7 and 12, it is said of Indra,

> He who, having destroyed Ahi, set free the seven rivers . . . . he who gave birth to the sun and to the dawn, and who is the bringer-forth of the waters. . . . . He, the seven-rayed, the showerer, the powerful, who set free the seven rivers to flow.

And, in *ii.* 13. 7 and 10,

> Thou who hast generated the various luminaries of the sky, and who, of vast bulk, comprehendest the vast ones . . . . thou art he who has regulated the six expansive, and art the protector of the five that look up to thee.

Wilson adds "races" after "five." *Shad vishṭirah* is the original of "the six expansive," said to be heaven, earth, day, night, water and plants. *Vish* means "to pervade, to embrace"; and *vishṭi*, "working, a workman, occupation, act, action, sending, dispatching." "The six workers" are, probably, the six Pleiades, whose rising at the Vernal Equinox announced the arrival of the season of labour for the husbandman; and "the five" were, undoubtedly, the Hyades.

I think I have left nothing unnoticed, that is worthy of note, in the Veda, in regard to Indra; and nothing, it seems to me, can be clearer than that he is the Universal Light.

The name *Vishṇu* is from *vish*, also *viç*, "to pervade, to embrace." Nothing could more aptly be styled "Pervader," than Heat.

Upon considering and reconsidering the passages of the Veda, in regard to the "three steps" of Vishṇu, a possibly correct explanation has suggested itself to me.

The Hymn *i*. 22 first invokes the Açvins to come to the sacrifice at dawn of day, and drink the Soma juice; then Savitṛi, "the golden-handed" (*suvarṇa-hasta*), child of the waters, enlightener of men; then Agni, to bring the wives of the Gods, and Tvashṭṛi, and the Goddesses themselves to come. Then the sky and expanse are invoked to blend the sacrifice, i. e., to unite it with the general light that pervades them. Then, in *v*. 14, it is said that the Sages, by means of pious acts, i. e., of sacrificial acts of devotion, taste the ghee-resembling waters of these two in the permanent region of the Gandharbas. "The ghee-resembling waters" is very probably a mistranslation. The meaning of the verse certainly is that the Sages who have become stars, taste, either by means of the present sacrifice, or in consequence of their own piety as sacrificers, while on earth, the melted butter and Soma juice intermingled, of the sacrifice, which ascends into the expanse, transmuted by the fire into light.

Verse 15 is translated by Wilson,

> Earth, be thou wide-spreading, free from thorns and our abiding-place. Give us great happiness.

It was hardly necessary to request it to be "wide-spreading," as it could not well become any more so, to gratify Priest or Poet. Besides it is not the earth that is addressed, but the expanse. The worshipper did not need to beg the earth to be his abiding-place, as he had, just then, no other. Besides, Wilson says, *syona* "has sometimes the sense of expanded, sometimes of pleasant, agreeable." Benfey is not of that opinion. He gives us *syona*, "handsome, pleasing, a ray of light, the sun, a sack, happiness"; and *syûna*, "a ray of light, the sun, a sack." I do not know what the original word is, that is rendered "thorns." But I have no doubt that the verse should be read,

> O Expanse, beautiful (or brilliant), be thou . . . . and our final abode.

Then follows Verse 16:

> May the Devas preserve us from that of the earth whence Vishṇu by the seven metres stepped; [or, according to Dr. Muir] May the Gods preserve us from that

> whence Vishṇu strode across the seven regions of the earth (*pṛithivyâḥ sapta dhâmabhiḥ*). [And, 17], Vishṇu traversed this: three times he planted his foot, and the whole was collected in the dust of his. [Or, according to Dr. Muir], Vishṇu traversed this: in three places he planted his foot, and was enveloped in his dust.

The original of the two verses is:

> *Ato devâḥ avantu no yato Vishṇur vichakrame pṛithivyaḥ sapta dhâmabhiḥ. Idam Vishṇur vichakrame tredhâ nidadhe padam samûlham asya pâṁsure:* May the Devas receive pleasure from this [sacrifice], whence Vishṇu strode across the seven regions of Pṛithivi.

Vikrama means "step, proceeding, overpowering, strength, heroism." *Krama*, "a step, a foot, a bound, regular order, course, method, way, etc." *Krameṇa*, "by degrees"; from *kram*, "to step, walk, etc." *Vi-kram*, "to walk along, enter, proceed." *Dhâman*, "an abode, state, host, dignity, light, splendour." Also, *dhmâ*, part. *dhama*, "to blow (as breath, wind), to melt, to throw." *Dhâ* has many meanings—among them, "to generate, carry, bear, nourish, preserve, get, show, put, grant." Unless the meaning of the phrase, *pṛithivyâḥ sapta dhâmabhiḥ* may be, "with (i. e., accompanying) the seven splendours of the expanse," alluding to the seven rays of Indra, it is an enigma to me.

This (i. e., the expanse) Vishṇu traversed (*vichakrame*, in Verse 16 rendered "strode across"): then follows, in Verse 17, *tredhâ nidadhe padam. Tredhâ*, i. e., *tri*+ *dhâ*, "three-fold, in three places, in three parts." *Pada* means "a step, a footstep, trace, mark, sign, place, a foot." The latter part of the verse is rendered by Muir,

> and [the world] was enveloped in his dust; [and by Wilson] and the whole (world) was collected in the dust of his (footstep).

There are in the original only the three words, *samûlham asya pâṁsure.* There is no meaning whatever, in either translation, and of course each is worse than no translation.

Ûh is the same as *vah*, but used only after prepositions. *Vah* is "to draw, carry, bear, have, bring, etc." *Samûh*, i. e., *sam*+ *ûh* or *sam*+ *vah* is "to bring near, to bring together." *Samûlḥam* may mean "was collected, was gathered together, cohered." *Pâṁçu* or *pâṁsu* is "dust, a particle of dust." Here, I think, it means "particles," of the vapour rising from the fire; and the phrase means that Vishṇu was conjoined with or cohered with these particles as they ascended.

In Verse 18, we have *trîṇi padâ vichakrame Vishṇur*, "three steps stepped Vishṇu"; the epithets *gopâh*, "cowherd, protector, warder, concealer," and *adâbhyah*, "not to be checked or impeded," being applied to him. And then follows *ato dharmâṇi dharayan;* which Wilson renders by "upholding thereby righteous acts"; and Dr. Muir, "upholding thereby fixed ordinances." *Dharma* means "virtue, merit, right, law, duty, justice, a sacrifice"; and *dhri*, "to bear, carry, maintain, support, retain, keep." I think the phrase means "carrying hence the sacrifice," or "giving effect to the acts of worship."

> *v.* 19. *Muir:* Behold the deeds of Vishṇu, through which this intimate friend of Indra has perceived the established laws.
>
> *Wilson:* Behold the deeds of Vishṇu, through which (the worshipper) has accomplished (pious) vows: he is the worthy friend of Indra.

I think it should be read,

> *Vishṇoḥ karmâni paçyata,* know the operations (the efficient action) of Vishṇu; *yato vratâni paçpase,* whereby he has given effect to, has accomplished, has been a party to, acts of worship.

And Vishṇu is here styled *Indrasya yujyaḥ sakhâ,* "the intimately united with, or the closely united twin-brother, of Indra," on account of the intimate union between light and heat.

The twentieth and twenty-first verses speak of the *parama pada* of Vishṇu, which both Wilson and Muir render by "supreme station." If *pada* meant "foot" or "footstep" before, it means the same here. It is the third and highest stage, step, degree or term, of that action or operation, whatever it was, of Vishṇu, by which the sacrifice was made effectual, i. e., was made to reach the stars.

This "supreme station," Wilson has it,

> the wise ever contemplate, *sadâ paçyanti sûrayaḥ,* as the eye ranges over the sky.

Dr. Muir's reading of the first clause is the same. *Sûrayaḥ* is "the Sages," from *Suri, Sûrya,* the sun—the root being *svar,* "the sun, splendour, heaven." And these Sages are *Sûrayaḥ,* because they are stars that shine in the sky. And they do not contemplate, but know and have perception or intuition of this last stage or step in the process by which Vishṇu makes the sacrifice and worship effectual.

They do or have this, Dr. Wilson says, "as the eye ranges over the sky." It is, Dr. Muir says (this "station"), "placed like an eye in the sky." The original is, *divîva chakshur âtatam.* Müller does not give *divîva* as a form of *div, dyu* or *dyo,* "sky." *Chakshas* is "an eye," and *chaksh* means "to see": but also *chak* and *chakas* mean "to shine," and *âtatam* means "effused"; so that I read this clause, "effused as radiance in the sky."

Finally, in Verse 21,

> The wise, ever vigilant and offering praise (or diligent in praise), kindle that, or amply glorify that, which is the supreme station of Vishṇu.

So Professor Wilson and Dr. Muir read it. I do not think that the original means that the station was kindled. The expression is nonsense. *Indh* means "to shine," and "to kindle"; and *samindh*, Benfey says, "to kindle." But, undoubtedly, when the priests (*vipraso*) kindled the sacrificial fire, they kindled that which was to cause the last stage, step or term in the action or operation of Vishṇu.

For I believe the three steps of Vishṇu to have been, the change of the Soma juice, cast into the fire, into vapour, the change of the vapour into invisible spirit or air, and its reappearance as light, on reaching the stars; during all which steps of the process the heat was deemed to cohere with or be conjoined with its particles. Or, the three steps may have been the change of the Soma juice into flame, the ascent of the flame, invisible, and its reappearance as light, uniting with that of the stars.

In *i*. 154 and 155, the exploits of Vishṇu are glorified, "who made the three worlds," according to Professor Wilson—*pârthivâni vimame rajânsi*, literally, he says, "he made the earthy regions." It is Sayana who says that *pṛithivi* is used here in the sense of the three worlds. Mahidhara suggests that *pârthivânî rajânsi* may mean "atoms of earth." I take the phrase to mean,

> who poured out the colours of the expanse. [Also, he] sustained the lofty aggregate site, thrice-traversing, and is praised by the exalted; *uttaram sadhastham askabhâyat, vichakramânas tredhâ*.

Professor Wilson makes it "the lofty aggregate site of the spheres." *Sadhastha*, i. e., *sadha*+*stha* means "permanent place of abode": and *skambh*, "to make firm, create, support." That Vishṇu supported the loftiest or upper abiding-place, stepping three times, means that he supplied it with light. And it may mean that this highest region is one of his own abiding places, since heat comes to us from the sun, or that it is the future (which *uttara* means, as well as "higher") abiding place of pious men.

The "exalted" who praise him, are the Sages who have become stars.

In subsequent verses of this hymn, Vishṇu is called *giri-sthah* and *girikshit*, which, Professor Wilson says, may mean either "dwelling on high," or "abiding in prayer or speech." And it is said of him:

> in his three paces all the worlds abide; who alone made, by three steps, this spacious and durable aggregate; whose three imperishable paces, filled with ambrosia, delight with sacred food; who verily alone upholds the three elements (*tridhatu*) and the expanse and sky; in whose favourite path Deva-seeking men delight; that wide-stepping Vishṇu, in whose exalted station there is a flow of felicity. [And in Verse 6], We pray that you may both go to those regions where the many-pointed and wide-spreading rays are; for here the highest station of the many-hymned, the showerer, shines, great.

Dr. Muir, for the "exalted station" and "flow of felicity," has "a spring of honey in the highest sphere of Vishṇu"; and, instead of "path" he has "abode," as the meaning of *pâtho*. The original of the whole verse is,

> *Tad asya priyam abhi pâtho açyâm naro yatra devayavo madanti urukramasya sa hi bandhur itthâ Vishṇoḥ pade parame madhvaḥ utsaḥ:*

and Dr. Muir reads it,

> May I attain to that his beloved abode where men devoted to the Gods rejoice; for that is the bond of the wide-striding God, a spring of honey in the highest sphere of Vishṇu.

There is no particular reason for holding that the spring up there in the star-country is one from which *honey* flows. *Madhu* is anything sweet, liquorice, honey, the nectar of flowers, sugar, spirituous liquor, milk and water. And also it means the season of spring. And it is much more probable that this upper region, the chief home of the genial heat that causes production was called by the Poets the fountain of spring and its sweets, than that it was styled the flow of felicity or spring of honey.

Then, how is the abode of Vishṇu his bond? It is true that *bandha* means "binding" and "laying snares," but also it means "the body, building, forming, agreement, union"; and heat may be considered, perhaps, as the soul of this upper region, and it as the body or home of the generative potency of heat.

There is, however, another possible explanation. *Nara* means "a man," but also simply an individual, applied to the Deities; and the *naro devayavo* mentioned in the first clause of the verse are the stars that once were Sages. They "rejoice" (*madanti*) in that abode of Vishṇu, but *mad* means also "to get drunk"; and *madanti* may here mean "become intoxicated, or, exhilarated, with the light derived from the sacrifice"; and this may be the *madhva*, whereof that region is a fountain.

That the "three steps" of Vishṇu are upward from the earth is evident. And in *iii*. 55. 10, we find,

> *Vishṇur gopâḥ paramam pâti pâthah priyâ dhâmâni amṛitâ dadhânah;* Vishṇu, the preserver, guards the highest abode, occupying the delightful imperishable regions.

The "ambrosia," in *v*. 4, according to Wilson, is the sacrifice, transmuted by the fire, and ascending to the sky, to invigorate the Devas. *Tridhâtu*, i. e., *tri+dhâtu*, in the same verse rendered "the three elements", which Vishṇu is represented as "upholding," does not mean earth, water and light. *Dhâtu* means, it is true, "a primary or elementary substance"; but also any constituent part of the body; and *tridhâtu*, Benfey says, means "three-fold." Here it means the one expanse, composed of three parts.

In *i.* 155, Indra and Vishṇu are "the two invincible Deities who ride upon the radiant summits of the clouds." And in verses 3, 4 and 5, we find it said that Indra's mighty virility makes parents capable of generation and enjoyment,

> whereby, in the upper region of the sky, the sun has an inferior and superior appellation, and a third of father.

The original of this last clause (which Professor Wilson says is very obscure) is,

> *Dadhâti putro avaram param pitur nâma tritîyam.*

Dhâ means, among other things, "to bear, carry, get"; and the phrase seems to me, literally, to mean,

> the son bears (or, receives) a lower and higher name, and the father a third one (i. e., one higher than the higher of the others).

Probably the words "in the upper region of the sky" should follow the rest of the sentence. There is no difficulty as to the literal meaning of the words or of the phrase. The only difficulty is to ascertain what the son and father are. Indra and Vishṇu are addressed together in the second verse, and in this, the third. The name of Indra is in parentheses, *his* virility being supposed to be spoken of. But in the next verse the virility of Vishṇu is distinctly mentioned, and it would therefore seem clear that it is Vishṇu who is spoken of in the third; and whatever may be meant by this last clause, the effects spoken of seem to be ascribed to that virility. Perhaps the lower name may be "rain or water," the next above, "vapour or cloud," and the highest that which produces or causes the vapour, i. e., "heat."

In Verse 4, the virility of that Lord, the preserver, the innocuous and vigourous, is praised, and he is said to have traversed the three regions with three wide steps, in different directions, for the many-praised existence. And in Verse 5, we have,

> man, glorifying, tracks two steps of that sky-beholding [that which *reaches* the sky]; but he apprehends not the third; nor can the soaring-winged birds.

The worshipper sees the flame and the vapour ascending, the clouds, and the light of the fire in the air; but the vapour, still ascending, becomes invisible, and the flame and light also disappear, or are lost in the light that shines from the sky. The three steps are, clearly, the transformations, in ascending, of either the flame or the vapour of the sacrifice, or of both.

In *i.* 156. 3, Vishṇu is said to be known by the singers of hymns, "as the germ of sacrifice" (*ritasya garbham*), meaning, Wilson says, "born as one with sacrifice." *Garbha* means "fœtus, embryo or sprout." *Ṛita* is "true, truth." Benfey does not give to *ṛita* the meaning of "sacrifice." If it meant that, the heat could well be said to be in embryo in the sacrificial fire.

In *v.* 3. 3, we have, in Wilson's translation,

> For thy glory the Maruts sweep, when thy birth, Rudra, is beautiful and wonderful: the middle step of Vishṇu has been placed, so thou cherishest the mysterious name of the waters (*paçi guhyam nâma gonâm*).

Paç means "to bind," and *go*, "cattle, rays, waters," etc. It is impossible to say what the phrase really means.

It is quite likely that after it had been forgotten that Vishṇu was heat, and when it was no longer known what was meant by his three steps, the texts in relation to them and to his "stations" were corrupted by emendations made for the purpose of suiting them to the supposed various meanings. The only real ground for wonder is, not that the texts are so obscure, but that they retain enough of the originals to enable us to say with certainty that Vishṇu was heat.

In *i.* 127. 1, it is said that Agni desires for the Devas the blaze of the clarified butter which is offered in oblation with his flames. And in *i.* 135, Vayu, the flame, is invited to come and partake of the food, and the Devas are said to hold back for him, as the one first entitled to drink: the sweet effused juices, it is said, are ready for his exhilaration, and for their function, the Soma is offered as his portion among men and Devas. In *i.* 134. 5, the Soma juices, for him, are said to be eager for the oblation, eager for the cloud (showering waters).

As the flame of the sacrificial fire conveyed both the butter and the Soma juice to the stars, it is most probable that the three steps of Vishṇu were the transformations of these into flame by the heat, and then into somewhat invisible, that continued to ascend, and to which the heat was supposed still to cohere.

PARJANYA.

Dr. Bühler, quoted by Dr. Muir (*v.* 142), holds Parjanya to have been decidedly distinct from Indra. He says,

> Taking a review of the whole, we find that Parjanya is a God who presides over the lightning, the thunder, the rain, and the procreation of plants and living creatures. But it is by no means clear whether he is originally a God of the rain, or a God of the thunder.

He inclines, however, to think, that from the etymology of his name, and the analogy between him and Perkunas, the Lithuanian God of thunder, he was originally the thunder-God. In another essay, his conclusion is, that he was

> the God of thunder-storms and rains, the generator and nourisher of plants and living creatures.

That is to tell us, not what he *is*, but what effects he *produces*.

In *vii.* 102. 1, Parjanya is called "the son of the sky," *divas putrâya.* In *vi.* 52. 16, he is conjoined with Agni (*Agniparjanyau*), and in several places with Vâta, the wind (*Parjanya-vâtâ, Vâtâ-parjanyâ*).

Benfey has

> *Parjanya* (and incorrectly *paryanya*) probably *sphurj*, for old *sparj+ana+ya*, a rain-threatening cloud, rain, the Deity of rain.

But *sphurj* means "to thunder." *Sphur*, from which it comes, is "to tremble, palpitate, struggle, break forth, flash, shine, sparkle," and (Vedic) "destroy." Benfey derives from it the Anglo-Saxon *spurnan*, and the Greek *σφυρυν*, the Latin *sperno*, which have no relation to rain or thunder, and *σπειρω*, "sow," *σπερμα*, "seed," and *σπορασ*, "scattered, dispersed." And he thinks that the Latin *spargo* is from the old form *sparj*. As *spargo* means "sprinkle, scatter," *sphurj* and *sparj* must have meant "to rain," to be identical with it.

On the whole, etymology proves of little use here. The texts may serve us more profitably.

In *v.* 83. 1 to 10, Parjanya is addressed and lauded as follows:

> Laud Parjanya; the procreative and stimulating fructifier, resounding, sheds his seed and impregnates the plants. He splits the trees, he destroys the Rakshas; the whole creation (*viçvam bhuvanam*) is afraid of the mighty stroke; even the innocent man flees before the vigourous God (*vṛishṇiyâvato: vṛish*, 'to rain, shed, moisten,' perhaps 'to engender'; *vṛishṭi*, 'rain'; *vṛishan*, 'raining, a bull, a horse'; *vṛishṇi*,

'passionate, angry'; *yava*, 'velocity,' from *jû*, 'to push on, impel.' If the word means 'vigourous,' it is the vigour of virility. It seems more probable that it means 'rain-impelling'), when Parjanya, thundering, smites the evil-doers (*dushkṛitaḥ*). Like a charioteer urging forward his horses with a whip, the God brings into view his showery scouts. ['God' has no equivalent in the original] . . . . Parjanya charges the clouds with rain. The winds blow; the lightnings fall; the plants shoot up; the sky makes fruitful; food is provided for all creatures, when Parjanya, thundering, replenishes the earth with moisture; Parjanya, before whose agency the earth bows down (*yasya vrate Pṛithivî namnamîti*, 'before whose law Pṛithivi submits'); by whose action plants are, of every form, grant us thy powerful protection (*mahi çarma*, great blessing). Grant to us, Maruts, the rain of the sky. . . . . Come hither with this thy thunder, our divine father (*asuraḥ pitâ*), shedding waters. Resound, thunder, impregnate, rush hither and thither with thy watery chariot. Draw on forward with thee thy opened and inverted water-skin; let the hills and dales be levelled. Raise aloft thy great water-vessel, and pour down showers: let the discharged rivulets roll on forward: moisten the sky and expanse (*dyâvâ-pṛithivi*) with fatness; let there be well-filled drinking-places for the cattle. When thou, Parjanya, resounding and thundering, dost slay the evil-doers, everything here rejoices, and whatever lives in the expanse. Thou hast shed down rain: now desist: thou hast made the waterless deserts fit to be traversed; thou hast generated (produced) plants for food, and thou hast fulfilled the desires of living creatures.

In *vii.* 101, Parjanya is represented as the ruler or proprietor of all living creatures (*Yo viçvasya jagato devaḥ îçe.* It represents all creatures, and the three spheres as abiding in him, *tasthus tisro dyâvaḥ*); that in him is the life of all things, moveable and stationary; and he is called, in *ix.* 82. 3, the father of the great leafy plant, Soma.

What Parjanya *does*, is plain enough. He causes thunder and rain. But what he *is*, is another thing altogether. He is a Deva, an Asurah, and the son of Dyaus. Müller agrees with Bühler, that Parjanya is cloud. I do not believe that the names *Asura* and *Deva* were ever applied to clouds.

I return again to etymology, and find that Benfey, who has given several Greek and Latin words as cognates of *sparj*, which clearly are not so, has furnished one that is identical with it, Σπαίρω, "palpitate, vibrate, tremble"; and under *sphur* we find *spharaya*, "to cause to flash"; *visphurita*, "tremulous, shaken"; *visphur*, "to tremble, to glitter," and for the root itself, "to flash, shine, sparkle"; and partic. *sphurita*, "trembling, glittering, shining, quivering, throbbing."

One would hardly, at first sight, identify the Latin *fulgeo*, *fulgur*, as identical with *sparj*, *sphurj* in Sanskrit. The latter form, with *u*, is probably the older, as it is found also in the Latin, which greatly affects the *u*. Thus the Greek words αμελγω and αρκος become *mulgeo* and *ursus:* and the Sanskrit *a* changes in Latin into *u* and sometimes *o* in a multitude of words; e.g., *makshika*, *musca; nabhas*, *nubes; vanas*, *venus; marmara*, *murmur; manda*, *mundus; nava*, *novus; agnata*, *ignotus; anj*, *ungo; vam*, *vomo; vach*, *voco; akshi, oculus.* The change of the Sanskrit *r* into *l* in Latin is not common; but it sometimes occurs, as in *pṛich, parch, plecto; pṛikta, plexus; ruch, luceo, lux.* The Sanskrit *p* rarely changes into *f* in Latin; but it does so in *fluo*, from *plu;* and in the root under consideration *p* and *ph* (=*f*) are both found in Sanskrit.

Moreover, Benfey has *sphal* and *spul*, as originally=*sphur*, and as meaning "to tremble, throb," from which *sphalaya* means "to strike, crush."

Fulgeo, Latin, means "to flash, lighten, glitter, gleam, glare, glisten, shine"; and *fulgor, fulgur*, "flashing, lightning," or, rather, "vibrating, zigzagging lightning."

I think it very clear, therefore, that Parjanya is Indra, the light, manifested and personified as the lightning.

ADITI, DITI, DAKSHA.

Aditi is an object of frequent celebration in the Veda, and yet the commentators utterly disagree as to what she was or represented.

She is supplicated for blessings on children and cattle; for protection and forgiveness.

In Rig-Veda *i.* 113. 19, Ushas is styled "the mother of the Devas, and the manifestation of Aditi" (*mâṭâ devânâm Aditer anîkam*): Müller translates *Aditer anîkam* by "the face of Aditi." In numerous texts, she is styled "*devi*": in *ii.* 40. 6, the irresistible *devi* (*devî Aditir anarvâ*); the luminous, the supporter of creatures, the celestial" (*jyotishmatîn Aditim̃ dhârayat-kshitim̃ svarvatîm*); the widely-expanded; the friend of all men. In *v.* 69. 3, the Ṛishi says:

> In the morning I continually invoke the Deva Aditi (*devim Aditim̃*), at midday, at the setting of the sun.

Her gifts, pure, unassailable, celestial, imperishable and inspiring veneration, are supplicated; and the large blessings conferred by the Maruts are compared to the beneficent deeds of Aditi. In *iv.* 55. 3, she is styled *Pastya*, which Roth understands to mean a household Goddess. I cannot find that meaning for it, nor any root from which to derive it, except *spaç*, "to embrace."

She is invoked as the great mother of the devout, the mistress of the ceremonial, the strong in might, the undecaying, the widely-extended, the protecting, the skilfully-guiding Aditi.

Böhtlingk and Roth take the word *Aditi* to mean, among other things,

> infinity, especially the boundlessness of heaven [the sky], in opposition to the finiteness of the earth, and its spaces.

This signification they consider to be personified in the Goddess Aditi. In his illustrations of the Nirukta, Professor Roth had understood the word to mean "inviolability," "imperishableness"; and when personified as a Goddess, to denote eternity, her sons the Adityas being the sons of eternity, and the solar and luminous Gods, Varuṇa, Mitra, Aryaman, Bhaga, etc., being pre-eminently the eternal Deities; as light was regarded as the immaterial and eternal principle.

In his essay on *the Highest Gods of the Aryan Nations*, he says:

> Aditi, eternity, or the eternal, is the element which sustains and is sustained by the Adityas. This conception, owing to the character of what it embraces, had not in

the Vedas been carried out into a definite personification, though the beginnings of such are not wanting . . . . This eternal and inviolable principle, in which the Adityas live, and which constitutes their essence, is the celestial light.

And Professor Müller says (*Trans. of Rig-Veda i.* 230):

Aditi, an ancient God or Goddess, is in reality the earliest name invented to express the infinite; not the infinite as the result of a long process of abstract reasoning, but the visible infinite, visible by the naked eye, the endless expanse, beyond the earth, beyond the clouds, beyond the sky.

I do not understand how the endless expanse, beyond the sky, can be visible to the naked eye. We must remember that to the Vedic Poets, the sky was what it is to children, a solid vault, overarching the earth. If they conceived of anything beyond it, they could only have conceived of it as empty space, certainly not of it as having any potencies or influences to affect themselves, not as a being, a thing or a power, or as an actuality.

Neither do I believe that the Vedic Poets adored a deified infinity or eternity, or the infinite or the eternal, any more than they did the fixed and firm, fixedness and stability (by words equivalent whereunto they designated the earth), or largeness or extension, because they designated the expanse between sky and earth (or the earth) by the epithet *Pṛithivi.* To adore was to ascribe powers and influences unto that which was supposed to possess them.

viii. 25. 3. *Tâ Mâtâ viçvavedasâ asuryâya pramahasâ mahî jajâna Aditir ṛitâvarî* [which Dr. Muir translates]: The Mother, the great, the holy Aditi, brought forth these twain (Mitra and Varuṇa), the mighty lords of all wealth, that they might exercise divine power.

I do not think that *ṛitavarî* means "holy." Its ordinary interpretation is "true," or "possessing truth"; but it means "real," "actual," "possessing reality." Nor do I think there is anything about "exercising divine power" in the text. The "*viçvadevas*" are all the heavenly bodies together. *Asura* is said to mean "eternal" in the Veda; but it meant "burning" or "shining," or merely "existing," according to the root from which it came. *Pramahasa* is "very resplendent."

viii. 47. 9. May Aditi defend us, may Aditi grant us protection, she who is the mother (*mâtâ*), of the opulent Mitra, of Aryaman, and of the sinless Varuṇa (*mâtâ Mitrasya revato Aryamṇo Varuṇasya cha anehasaḥ*).

Anehas, according to Benfey, means "without a rival." I can find no derivation for the word that will make it mean "sinless." Benfey gives, also *revant*, i. e., *rayivant*, "wealthy." *Rayi* is "wealth"; and *raya*, "swift, impetuous."

Jajana, rendered "brought forth," in the former passage, is the reduplicated perfect of the root *jan*, from which "*Genesis, generation, gigno, genus, γιγνομαι*," etc., come, and means "to produce," as well as "to give birth to." *Mata*, "mother," is that which "produces," as well as "that which gives birth to"; and also means that *in* which anything begins to exist—one of its meanings being "space or æther."

In *ii*. 27. 7, Aditi is styled *râja-putrâ*, "the mother of kings"; in *iii*. 4. 11, *su-putrâ*, "the mother of excellent sons"; in *viii*. 56. 11, *uqra-putrâ*, "the mother of powerful sons"; in *ii*. 27. 1. the epithet *râjabhyaḥ*, "kings," is applied to all the six Adityas there named.

The original meaning of the verb *raj* is "to shine." In the Rig-Veda it is used in the sense of "to govern." Indra and the moon were called *râja*, which means "a king, master, one of the Kshatriya caste." *Rajâ-putrâ*, in the oldest sense, meant "shining issue, children, or sons." *Su* is "good, beautiful"; *uqra*, "very strong."

All these epithets, Dr. Muir says, obviously have reference to Varuṇa and the other Adityas as her offspring.

In *viii*. 90. 15, Aditi appears to be described as the daughter of the Vasus (*duhitâ vasûnâṁ*) the sister of the Adityas (*svasâ adityânâm*), and mother of Rudras (*mâtâ rudrâṇâṁ*).

> *x*. 63. 2. All your names, ye Gods (*devaḥ*), are to be revered, adored and worshipped; ye who were born from Aditi (*ye stha jâtâḥ Aditer*), from the waters, ye who are born from the earth (*pṛithivyâs*).
>
> *x*. 63. 3. Those Adityas . . . . to whom their mother the sky, Aditi (or, the infinite sky), towering to the empyrean, supplies, etc.

The original of "the sky, Aditi," or "the infinite sky," is, here, *dyaur aditir*. The words *Dyaus* and *Aditi* are similarly united in *v*. 59. 8: *mimâtu dyaur aditiḥ*, etc. Dr. Muir says,

> Professor Müller takes *aditi* in *x*. 63. 3, as well as in *v*. 59. 8, for an adjective, meaning 'unbounded': but we should have thus to take *Aditi* in different senses in two adjoining verses. In Verse 2 of this hymn, Prof. Müller himself takes *Aditi* as signifying the Goddess.

In *x*. 49. 2, we have *devatâḥ divas cha, gmas cha, apâṁ cha*, "the Devas, offspring, *jantavah*, of the sky, of the earth, and of the waters." And in *vii*. 35. 11, the Devas are classed as *divya, pârthiva* and *apya:* in Verse 14 of the same hymn, as *divya, pârthiva* and *gojâta;* and in *vi*. 50. 11, as *divya, pârthiva, gojâta* and *apya*. In *x*. 65. 9, Parjanya, Vata, vigourous, shedders of rain, Indra, Vayu, Varuṇa, Mitra and Aryaman are all styled *devân Âdityân*, and said to be, *ye pârthivâso divyâso, apsu ye*, "terrestrial (?), celestial, from the waters." Dr. Muir renders *devân Âdity-ân*, "the divine Âdityas." Originally its meaning certainly was "celestial Âdityas," or "Âdityas of the sky."

Dr. Muir is puzzled by these classifications of the Devas. He tells us that Sayaṇa explains *gojâta* as *Pṛiçner jâtâh*, "born of Pṛiçni," and that Roth explains it as meaning the Gods of the starry heavens. But *go* means the earth, and then how is it that there are a class *pârthiva* and a class *gojâta* together, if *pṛithivi* also means the earth?

> Even if we suppose [Dr. Muir says], that in the preceding passages it is intended to identify Aditi with the sky, this identification is very far from being consistently maintained in the hymns. And it is equally difficult to take the word as a constant synonym of the earth.

In *iii*. 54. 19, Aditi is invoked, with *pṛithivi dyaur*, the water (*utapaḥ*) and the sun with the stars (*Sûryo nakshaṭṭrair*) and the wide atmosphere (*antariksham*): in *v*. 46. 3, *Indrâgnî Mitrâvaruṇa Aditim̃ svaḥ pṛithivîm dyâm Marutaḥ* are invoked: in *vi*. 51. 5, father-sky (*dyaush pitaḥ*), mother Pṛithivi beneficent, brother Agni, the Vasus, with all the Adityas and Aditi: in *ix*. 97. 58, Mitra, Varuṇa, Aditi, Ocean, Pṛithivi and sky: in *x*. 36. 2, sky and Pṛithivi, and Aditi, mother of Mitra and Varuṇa (*Aditiḥ mâtâ Mitrasya Varuṇasya*): in *x*. 63. 10, *Pṛithivim Dyâm*, and the sheltering and guiding Aditi.

In *v*. 62. 8, Mitra and Varuṇa are invited to ascend their car, of golden form at the break of dawn, with iron supports at the setting of the sun,

> and thence ye behold Aditi and Diti (*atas chakshâthe Aditim̃ Ditim̃ cha*).

Roth translates these two words by "the eternal" and "the perishable." But in his *Lexicon*, he describes *Diti* as

> a Goddess associated with Aditi, without any distinct conception, and merely, as it appears, as a contrast to her.

Dr. Muir says, that *Aditi* may here represent the sky and *Diti* the earth;

> or, if we are right in understanding the verse before us to describe two distinct appearances of Mitra and Varuṇa, one at the rising and the other at the setting of the sun, Aditi might possibly stand for the whole of nature as seen by day, and Diti for the creation as seen by night. At all events, the two together appear to be put by the Poet for the entire aggregate of visible nature.

Diti is also mentioned alone, in *vii*. 15. 12, as conferring what is desirable: and in *iv*. 2. 11, Aditi and Diti occur together, and Roth renders them by "wealth" and "penury." Elsewhere he considers *Diti* to be a personification of liberality or opulence; i. e., he derives the word from the verb *dâ*, "to give."

But I think it indisputable that Diti and Aditi are opposites, the *a* prefixed in the latter name meaning negation or privation, like our prefix *un*. And I think it equally clear that Diti is from another verb *dâ*, meaning "to cut," whence *dita*, fem. *diti*, "cut-off," and that *Diti* means, literally, "the limited," and *Aditi*, "the unlimited or unbounded." The latter, I think, is the concave which bounds and limits the earth; and the former, the earth so limited.

As to what is said about Mitra and Varuṇa, connected with sunrise and sunset, it is easily explained by the fact that one of these was the Morning Star, and the other the Evening Star.

Dr. Muir says:

> Perhaps Aditi may best be regarded as a personification of universal, all-embracing Nature, or being, with which she is in fact identified in the following remarkable verse. She is the source and substance of all things, celestial and intermediate, divine and human, present and future. [What then is Diti? Nothing?] Aditi is the sky (*dyaur*); Aditi is the air (or intermediate firmament—*antariksham*); Aditi is the mother and father and son (*Aditir mâtâ sa pitâ sa putraḥ*); Aditi is all the Gods and the five tribes (*viçve devâḥ Aditiḥ panchajınâḥ*); Aditi is whatever has been born; Aditi is whatever shall be born (*Aditir jâtam Aditir janitvam*).

In *vi*. 51. 11, Aditi is invoked, along with Indra, the earth, the ground (*kshama*), Pushan, Bhaga and the five tribes (*panchajanâḥ*) to bestow blessings. So in *x*. 53. 4, 5, "ye five tribes, welcome my offering"; in *x*. 55. 3, *pancha devaḥ*, the five Devas, are mentioned; and in *x*. 60. 4, "the five tribes in the sky" (*divîva pancha kṛishṭayaḥ*). Some of the old commentators understand by the five tribes the Gandharvas, Pitris, Devas, Asuras, and Râkshasas. Manu thinks the phrase means the whole pantheon, or a particular portion of it.

Jana, originally "creature," i. e., what is born or produced, means "man collectively, men, crowd, man individually, class, set," etc. But of what the five classes are, there is nothing that can inform us. The commentators know nothing about it.

Benfey gives *antariksha*, i. e., *antar*+ *iksh*+ *a*, "the sky"; but *antarikshaga*, moving in the air, "a bird." *Antar* means "within"; *antara*, "the interior, interval." *Antariksha*, therefore, is not the air or atmosphere, but the space in which it is.

Benfey says that the conception of Aditi "is still dark." Regnier that she is "a personification of the all, the mother of the Gods."

> [In *i*. 24. 1], who shall give us back to the great Aditi, that I may behold my father and my mother? . . . . the divine Agni, the first of the immortals, he shall give us back to the great Aditi, that I may behold my father and my mother.

"That I may behold" (*driçeyam*). *Driç* means "to see, behold, declare, acknowledge, know." "That I may behold my father and my mother" is, *pitaram̃ cha driçeyam mâtaram̃ cha.* I do not see that the word "my" is necessarily in the translation. "That I may see *the* father and mother," or, "that which both generates and produces." Dr. Muir suggests that these are heaven and earth. Why may they not be applicable to Aditi? She is elsewhere said to be father, mother and son.

Agni is invoked, that he may "give back" the worshipper to Aditi (*ko no mahyai Aditaye punar dat*). *Dâ* means "to give, grant, bestow, return," etc. Agni is fire, and the light included in the fire. I think the meaning is,

> who will, by removing the darkness, enable us to see the sky, the generator and producer?

Benfey thinks that *Aditi* here is a proper name, and explains it as denoting "sinlessness." It would not be more absurd to undertake to spiritualize Ushas into an abstraction. One wonders, indeed, that no one has thought to do that.

Undoubtedly, Dr. Muir says,

> Aditi is in many other texts connected with the idea of deliverance from sin.

He instances the following:

> *i.* 162. 22. May Aditi make us sinless (*anagastvam̃ no Aditiḥ krinotu*). [*Âgas* means 'crime, fault, sin.' The *an* prefixed means 'without.']
>
> *i.* 24. 15. Varuṇa, loose from us the uppermost, the middle and the lowest bond. Then may we, O Aditya, by thy ordination, be without fault (*anâgasaḥ*) against Aditi.

Other passages cited by Dr. Muir ask to be made free of sin, and pardoned for sins or faults, against Aditi, by Agni, by the help of Savitṛi; that Aditi, Mitra and Varuṇa will be gracious, if any sin has been committed against them; that, through the ordinances (*vratâni*) of Aditi, the worshipper may be without sin towards Varuṇa; that Aryaman and Agni will sever from him any sin he has committed; and that Mitra, Aditi and Savitṛi will declare him sinless (*anâgân*) towards Varuṇa. Similar petitions are elsewhere addressed to the sun, dawn, heaven and earth, and to Agni.

It is difficult to conceive of any other possible fault against most of these, than that of omitting to sacrifice to them.

In other parts of the Veda, Aditi is represented as playing a subordinate part.

In *vii.* 38. 4, she is mentioned as celebrating the praises of Savitṛi, along with her sons, Mitra, Varuṇa and Aryaman, and welcoming his aid; and in *viii.* 12. 14, she is declared to have produced a hymn to Indra.

I have before referred to Rig-Veda *x.* 72, a hymn of comparatively late date, in which Daksha is said to have sprung from Aditi, and Aditi from Daksha, produced by him, and being his daughter.

> Of the eight sons of Aditi [it is said here], who were born from her body, she approached the Devas with seven, and cast out Mârttâṇda, the eighth. With seven sons Aditi approached (*upa prait, upa pra ait*) the former generation (*pûrvyam̃ yugam*). She again produced Mârttâṇda, for birth as well as for death.

It is uncertain what was meant by Mârttâṇda. Benfey gives *Martanda*, i. e., *Mṛitanda*+ *a*, "the sun," "a hog"; and *Mṛitaṇḍa*, "the father of the sun." *Mṛi* means "to die"; *mṛita*, "dead, death"; *mṛitaka*, "a dead body"; *mṛiti*, "death." On the other hand, from *mṛid*, "earth," we have *mṛida* and *mṛittika*, "earth." Professor Müller explains *Mârttânda*, briefly, as "addled egg"; and the Hindū commentators say that it means

> one in consequence of whose birth the egg had become dead; [one called so] because born when the egg was dead; [one] undeveloped into any distinctions of shape.

Dr. Muir quotes these, but offers no suggestion of his own.

All this leaves us wholly uninformed as to what was really meant by this eighth son of Aditi. Müller says that it cannot be supposed that the seven planets were known to the Vedic Poets, even 1,000 years before Christ. I do not think that Mercury and Saturn were known as planets to the most ancient Poets; but I think they were known to those who composed the hymns of the eighth, ninth and tenth Mandalas.

Whatever Aditi was, the Adityas were luminaries; and they were finally considered to be seven in number. In Rig-Veda *ii.* 27. 1, we have a list of six names only: Mitra, Aryaman, Bhaga, Varuṇa, Daksha and Am̃saḥ. In *vi.* 50. 1, we have Aditi, Varuṇa, Mitra, Agni, Aryaman, Savitar, and Bhaga: but Aditi could not have been one of the Adityas, supposed to be her own progeny.

May not Mârttâṇda have been the earth, which, having no limits to the ancients, could not have had a definite shape; and which may have been called dead, as not shining or emitting light and radiance?

In *x.* 5. 7, is an interesting text, which, if it could be properly understood, might help to possess us of the Vedic idea embodied in the names Aditi and Daksha. It is, as translated by Dr. Muir:

> (a principle) not existing (actually), but existing (potentially) (*asach cha sach cha*) in the highest heaven, in the creative potency of Daksha, and in the womb of Aditi

—Agni (became) in a former age the first-born of our ritual, and is both a vigourous bull and a cow.

Professor Müller's translation of the first of these verses is:

Not-Being and Being are in the highest heaven, in the birthplace of Daksha, in the lap of Aditi.

Janman is translated by Muir, "creative potency"; by Müller, "birth-place"; *upasthe*, "womb" by Muir, and "lap" by Müller. The former means, according to Benfey, "birth, production, sowing, planting, father, a creature." The words that in other languages come from *jan*, show that its primitive meaning was "to beget." The latter word, according to Benfey, means "lap," and "the male and female organs of generation."

I think that the former word means here "the generative potency," and the latter, "the productive capacity." So, in the Hebrew writings, unbegotten descendants are in "the loins" of their ancestors. The reference here seems to be wholly to Agni. *Achach cha sach cha*, "existing and not-existing," i. e., latent and not manifested, as when he is in the wood from which he is to be generated by friction, he is in the loins of Daksha and in the conceptive organ of Aditi, to be begotten by one and produced by the other. In a former age or period (*âyuni*), he was the first-born (*prathamajâḥ*) of "our ritual" (*ṛitasya*). So Dr. Muir renders the last word; but I hardly think it means that. *Ṛitu* means "order, right time, a season of the year, the season approved for sexual intercourse." The primary meaning of *prathama* is "first, primal, primary." Is not the meaning here, that Agni was born at the beginning of things, the first-born, at the beginning of generation and production?

Agni is, it is said in this hymn, *vṛishabhas cha dhenuḥ*. *Vṛish* means "to rain, shed, moisten, to engender and to have power." *Vṛisha* is "a bull" (as a type of the generative energy, originally); and *vṛishan* is "a bull or horse." *Vṛishaṇa* means "the testicles"; and *vṛishabha* is "a bull," and as the latter part of compound words, "pre-eminent, excellent." *Dhenu*, i. e., *dhe+nu*, is "a milch-cow," and "the earth," from *dhe*, "to suck, to drink, to suck in, to absorb." The true *original* meaning of the two words is, that Agni both emits and absorbs the seed of generation; but this grosser meaning had changed into that of generator and producer, or, simply, male and female.

There may have been a reference, in this, to that generation and production, as it was regarded, with two pieces of wood, by means of which the sacred fire manifested itself; but the principal meaning, couched in the figurative language, no doubt was, that Agni produced from himself, generating within himself, and producing outwardly, his hypostases or subsistences, his issue and progeny, Indra, Vishṇu, Vayu, Ushas, and the rest—light, heat, flame and the golden glories of the dawn.

We find here identically the idea, which, developed, became that of Brahm, separating himself into Brahm and Maya, and begetting and producing his progeny, the three persons of the Trimurti: and in the male-female nature of Agni, the *Hu-Hi*, He-She of the Hebrews. And here, also, in this figurative and symbolic expression, "the bull and the cow," is the origin of the sanctity and creative potencies, in the Brahmanic and later age ascribed to the bull, as well as that of the Grecian fables in which the bull bears a part.

In *x*. 72. 2, we have, according to Professor Müller:

> In a former age of the Gods (*devânâm pûrvye yuge*) Being was born from Not-Being (*asataḥ sat ajayata*); [according to Dr. Muir:] In the earliest ages of the Gods, the existent sprang from the non-existent.

In Verse 3, the same is repeated, changing *purvye* to *prathame*.

Sat, *sant* is the present participle of *as*, "to exist, to be." *Sat* means "being, existing," and, as a noun, "entity." *Asat* is "non-entity."

In the same hymn, Verse 5, it is said that after Aditi was born from Daksha, the propitious (or excellent) Devas were born, who possess immortality.

> *x*. 64. 5. Thou, O Aditi, dost tend the two kings, Mitra and Varuṇa (*râjânâ Mitra-Varuṇa*), after the production and by the will (*janmani vrate*) of Daksha.
>
> *vi*. 50. 2. . . . . the resplendent Devas, the sons of Daksha (*Daksha-pitṛin*) [or, possessors of powers], who have two births (*dvijanmâno*), are holy, true, celestial, adorable, and have Agni in their tongues (*Agni-jihvâḥ*, organs of his utterances).

These Sûrya is asked to visit in sinlessness (*anâgastve*). As neither sin nor sinlessness can be imputed to Sûrya, the sun, the use of the word *anâgastve* here satisfies me that I guessed rightly, in the work to which this is a supplement, that the word or words in the Veda, rendered by "sin" originally meant "losing one's way." And it seems plain that here the invocation to the sun is, that without wandering from his path he will punctually return to the sky, and visit the stars there, the sons or progeny of Daksha.

> *vii*. 66. 2. Which two wise Devas (i. e., Mitra and Varuṇa), the mighty sons of Daksha (*Daksha-pitarâ*), the Deities (*asuryaya*), have established to exercise divine rule.

In these texts the general opinion seems to be that *Daksha* is not the name of a Deity. Roth assigns to *dakshapitaraḥ* the sense of "preserving, possessing, bestowing powers." Dr. Kuhn approves this. Müller translates the word by "fathers of strength." And Dr. Muir reads in the alternative, "possessors of strength."

In Rig-Veda *ii*. 27. 1, Daksha is named with Mitra, Varuṇa, Aryaman, Bhaga and Aṁsa, as an Adityah.

Professor Müller (Rig-Veda *i*. 230), after saying that *Aditi* meant the visible infinite, adds:

> That was called A-diti, the un-bound, the un-bounded; one might almost say, but for fear of misunderstandings, the Absolute, for it is derived from *diti*, 'bond,' and the negative particle, and meant therefore originally what is free from bonds of any kind, whether of space or time, free from physical weakness, free from moral guilt. Such a conception became of necessity a Being, a Person, a God. To us such a name and such a conception seem decidedly modern, and to find in the Veda, Aditi, the infinite, as the mother of the principal Gods, is certainly at first sight, startling. But the fact is that the thoughts of primitive humanity were not only different from our thoughts, but different also from what we think their thoughts ought to have been.

"Unbound" and "unbounded" have nothing of meaning in common with each other. If *diti*, in *Aditi*, means "bound," it did not originally mean bound by bonds of any kind, of space, time, weakness or guilt. The ideas which such words originally express, are always simple ones. The more complex ideas are annexed to them long after they begin to be in use. After a time, they obtain figurative meanings, very different from the simple, actual fact which they at first announced. When the word that means "circumcision" was first used, and for a long time afterwards, nobody thought of the "circumcision of the heart." It was a long time after any people had the word that meant "blind," before they used the phrase "blindness of heart." These meanings are the creations of the imagination; and *diti* originally meant, simply, "tied" by a rope, cord, etc.

Neither do I see how the word "untied" (for that is the synonym of "unbound") could ever come to mean "infinite." One verb *dâ* undoubtedly means "to bind, to tie"; and, with the preposition *sam*, its participle of the perfect passive is *saṁdita*, "tied." But another verb *dâ* and *do*, means "to cut"; and its participle of the perfect passive is also *dita*, "cut off." A part is limited and bounded by separating it, cutting it off, from the whole; and *aditi*, derived from that verb, really means "unbounded, unlimited, limitless, boundless." A "section" of country is so much cut off, from *secare*, "to cut."

The original conception of Aditi was, therefore, I think, not at all that of the Absolute, or of any freedom from bonds, but only of bounds. The "infinity" expressed by it was infinity of extent. Nor, indeed, *was* it infinity, but only indefiniteness, the Indefinite. If Aditi meant the *visible* Infinite, i. e., the Infinite that one *sees*, it was no infinity at all. No one can see the

Infinite. He *may* see the Indefinite. But if infinity *was* meant, it could have been no other Infinite than that of space; and it is not in the least "startling" to find it said in the Veda that this infinite or indefinite space was the mother of the stars, for it simply means that their being commenced in it, as we say that events are in the womb of time, which is only the reproduction in a different form of the saying in the *Zend-Avesta* that certain things were born or produced in the Infinite Time.

The thoughts of the Vedic Poets were not as different from ours as we think. It is only that we do not understand theirs nor analyze our own. They were not "startled" at the idea that Indra had a mother, because they did not mean that he was born as a human child is born, any more than we, when we say that a nation is *born*, and that thoughts are *born* in the mind, and that the Word was the only *begotten* Son of God, mean that one is born or the other generated, as a babe is.

The mode, fashion and processes of imaginative thought, of these old Poets, both of the Veda and *Zend-Avesta*, were simple enough, and only seem to us to be different from our own. If we call a spring or fountain an "eye," and then invest it with all the attributes of our own eye, we shall do precisely what the Vedic Poets did. Indra was the light. They represented this light as a warrior, armed with the flashing thunderbolt, the lightning, and then invested him with the weapons and armour, and all the characteristics of a warrior. When they compared a lake or a river to a maiden, they described the person and the dress of a beautiful girl, bearing the name of the lake or river. In short, when they personified anything, they let their fancy run without rein, in investing the person so imagined with all the attributes and characteristics it could have had, if really such person. It was doing in words what the Greeks did in marble, when they represented the Divine Wisdom by the statue of Minerva, and Love by that of Venus; as we put wings of feathers on our angels. Spenser has so personified in the true old Aryan spirit, all the human passions.

Proclus argued that place was a body: and Simplicius, discussing this, and saying that Plato, in his *Commonwealth*, said that light was place, adds,

> For this is the light which is above the empyrean world, and is a monad prior to the triad of the empyrean, ethereal and material worlds. This light, too, is the first recipient of the eternal allotment of the Gods, and unfolds self-visible spectacles in itself to those that are worthy to behold them. For in this light, according to the Chaldæan Oracle, things without figure become figured. And perhaps it is on this account called place, τοπος as being a certain type, τυπος of the whole mundane body, and as making this which are without interval to possess interval.

The Vedic Poets had no such notions as these. They had vivid and fertile imaginations, and with them philosophic ideas; but they clothed these ideas in the language of the imagination. They said that Agni was *born* of the friction of two sticks, and compared this to the act of generation. Philosophic language would express the phenomenon differently; but the meaning would be no more plain. Their idea was that the fire *existed* in the wood, and was not *created* by the friction but *brought forth* and *manifested* by it. Manifestation was birth to them, the production outwardly of the thing or being; and to a birth, a father and mother are necessary. When we say that miasma generates fever, and that evils are born of war, we merely mean that one is caused by the other: but when we say that Time gives birth to great events, that islands were born of the ocean, or the world born of chaos, we do not express causation. And if we said that the ocean was mother of islands, we should express precisely the same simple and natural idea that the Vedic Poets did, when they said that Aditi, the sky, was mother of the stars.

Nor was it unnatural, that when Indra, light, was born, i. e., was manifested and revealed, the sky should pay it homage, "and Aditi produce a hymn for Indra the king." Varuṇa and Mitra were "nursed in the lap of Aditi," and this idea did not "startle" the Vedic Poet, any more than it startles us to hear said,

La nuit, mère des songes
A la naissance de l'aurore.
Il repose dans le sein du sommeil.
Dans le sein de la mort.
Rocked on the bosom of the deep,

or

Le vent, ce fougueux enfant du Nord.

"The *children* of the *desert*," and the "*sea-born Venus*" are expressions that have never startled anybody.

The truth is that all the eloquent pictures in words of the sensations produced in the men of the early ages by the marvels of the heavens and of the phenomena of Nature, are merely fanciful. They were no more impressed by the wonders of the sky than we are, unless they were of a nature to alarm them. I never knew an American Indian exhibit any curiosity in regard to the real nature of the sun, moon and stars. To the child, they are no more wondrous than the household lamps are; and to the grown man noticeable only by their real or supposed connection with the material interests of his daily life. The dawn and sunrise no more impressed the ancient Aryan than they do us; and "that silent aspect" did not "awaken in the human mind the conception of the Infinite, the Immortal, the Divine." These conceptions were the fruits of calm and thoughtful speculation.

I am sure that "*Aditi*" was not originally conceived of as the Infinite, the visible Infinite, or Infinitude. It must originally have been a mere adjective, applied indifferently to anything the bounds of which were not visible, or, as our words "infinite" and "boundless" were, to anything very large; as *amṛita*, which is rendered by "immortality," meant "long life." After a time *Aditi* became an epithet peculiarly applied to space, and then its name, when it was personified. The figurative language in which the sky and its stars were spoken of, gave rise to new ideas and notions concerning it and them, until the one became a potent Goddess, and the mother of the others, and these others, Gods; and she, with the Adityas, the planets, heard the invocations of the worshippers, and gave them aid and relief. But the original character of the Devas and Adityas was never forgotten in the Vedic times. In *iv*. 25. 3, we read :

> who now chooses the protection of the Devas? Who ask the Adityas, Aditi, for their light (*jyoti*)?

Jyut=dyut means "to shine"; causal, *jyotaya*, "to illuminate"; *jyutimant*, "shining."

Professor Müller says:

> We are not justified in saying that there ever was a period in the history of the religious thought of India, a period preceding the worship of the Adityas, when Aditi, the Infinite, was worshipped; though to the Sage who first coined this name, it expressed, no doubt, for a time, the principal, if not the only object of his faith and worship.

If not in degree, this is at least in kind, a perversion of the meaning of the Veda like those of the Brahmans. For no Sage coined the name "*Aditi*." Whether it meant "untied" or "unlimited," it was originally a word of the common people, no more coined by a Sage than the words that meant "black," "white," "long" and "short." And there is no reason whatever to believe that when the space was first called Aditi, the word meant what we mean by "Infinite"; or that at that time space was the object of worship, or that the infinite was, at any time.

Of the name or word *Daksha*, Professor Müller says:

> *Daksha*, in the sense of 'power' or '*potentia*,' may have been a metaphysical conception.

But it may also have been suggested by a mere accident of language, a never-failing source of ancient thoughts. The name *Daksha-pitaraḥ*, an epithet of the Gods, has generally been translated by "those who have Daksha for their father." But it may have been used originally in a very different sense. Roth proves, he thinks, that it originally had the simpler meaning of "fathers of strength," or, as he translates it, "preserving, possessing, granting faculties."

In *iii.* 27. 9, Agni is called *Dakshasya pitaram*, the father of strength. In *vi.* 50. 2, the shining Devas (*su-jyotishaḥ devân*) are called *Daksha-pitṛîn*. In *vii.* 66. 2, we read,

> Mitra and Varuṇa, who are of good strength (*su-dakshâ*, exceeding powerful), *daksha-pitara*.

And in *viii.* 63. 10, the suppliants call themselves *daksha-pitaraḥ;* unless the accent is wrong, in which case the word applies to the Deities invoked.

In these passages, Müller prefers the original and simple meaning of *Daksha;* but says,

> the fact remains, that in certain hymns of the Rig-Veda (*viii.* 25. 5), *Daksha*, like *Aditi*, has become a divine person, and has retained his place as one of the Adityas, to the very latest time of Puranic tradition.

He thinks that if Aditi is looked upon as the Infinite personified,

> most passages, even those where she is presented as a subordinate Deity, will become intelligible.

And he says:

> Aditi, in her cosmic character, is the Beyond, the unbounded realm beyond earth, sky and heaven, and originally she was distinct from the sky, the earth and the ocean. Aditi is mentioned by the side of heaven and earth, which shows that, though in more general language she may be identified with heaven and earth in their unlimited character, her original conception was different. This we see in passages where different Deities or powers are invoked together, particularly if they are invoked together in the same verse, and where Aditi holds a separate place by the side of heaven and earth.

And he quotes the following:

> *i.* 94. 16. May Mitra and Varuṇa grant us this, may Aditi, Sindhu, Pṛithivi and the sky (*dyauḥ*).
>
> *i.* 191. 6. The sky (*dyauḥ*) is your father, Pṛithivi your mother, Soma your brother, Aditi your sister.

vi. 51. 5. In this verse, Aditi and the Adityas are invoked, with sky, the father (*dyauḥ pitar*), Pṛithivi mother, Agni brother; all invoked together, with all the shining ones (*viçve sagoshâḥ*), unless *sagoshâḥ* is connected with *âdityâḥ*.

In *x.* 63. 10, the well-protecting Pṛithivi, the unrivalled sky, and the well-shielding Aditi, the good guide, are invoked: in *x.* 66. 4, *Aditiḥ dyâvâ-pṛithivi*, Aditi, sky and Pṛithivi.

In *x.* 36. 1, we have, in one and the same verse, *dyâvâ kshâmâ*, and *dyâvâpṛithivî*. *Kshâmâ* means "enduring, durable, the earth" (of course, as "stable, fixed, permanent"). In Verse 3 of the same, Aditi is called the mother of Mitra and Varuṇa.

Of Aditi as mother, Professor Müller says:

> In this character of a Deity of the Far East, of an Orient in the true sense of the word, Aditi was naturally thought of as the mother of certain Gods, particularly of those that were connected with the daily rising and setting of the sun. If it was asked, whence comes the dawn, or the sun, or whence come day and night, or Mitra and Varuṇa, or any of the bright, solar, eastern Deities, the natural answer was that they came from the Orient, that they are the sons of Aditi.

Where the passage was effected from "the visible Infinite, the Unbounded," "to the Orient," as the meaning of *Aditi*, I have not discovered. Certainly, one of these things is very different from the other. I do not find that Aditi is mentioned before, as a Deity of the Far East. How is the Infinite a Deity of the Far East, in particular, or any more than of the Far West, or Far North, or Far South?

And it is quite evident that this question of source, origin or starting place could only be asked of something that the questioner saw. The "Gods," and Mitra and Varuṇa, and the bright, solar, eastern Deities, must therefore have been simply heavenly bodies.

> *ix.* 74. 3. Wide is the space for him who goes on the right path of Aditi: *urvî gâvûtiḥ aditeh ṛitam yâte.*

It is uncertain, I think, whether the translation is right *urvi*, fem. of *uru*, means "large," and *gavûti*, "a pasture-ground": and also *urvî* means "the earth." *Ṛita* is "true, truth, just"; and *yâ*, "to go." What *is* "the right path of Aditi"? Who is it goes on it, and how? And what is the meaning of a wide space or pasture-ground being for him?

We have already seen that in *i.* 89. 10 (final), Aditi is *Dyau* and *antariksha*, generator, producer and progeny or issue; all the Devas are Aditi, the five families, the produced and the to-be produced. Müller thinks that no passage occurs in the Rig-Veda, where the special meaning of heaven or earth is expressed by Aditi. He thinks it does not mean sky, in *x.* 63. 3, but is either a masculine, meaning Aditya, or an epithet, "unbounded" or "immortal." And in *i.* 72. 9, we should read, he thinks,

> the wide Aditi, the mother with her sons.

And in the passage, *i.* 24. 1, where he reads,

> who will give us back (*kah punaḥ dât*) to the great Aditi, that I may see father and mother?

He says it is more difficult to determine whether Aditi is not used in the sense of life after life, or as the name of the place whither people went after death, or of the Deity presiding over that place. And he thinks that we may choose between the two meanings, of "earth" or "liberty," and translate, either,

> Who will give us back to the great earth? [or], Who will restore us to the great Aditi, the Goddess of freedom?

If *Aditi* had really, at first, only the meaning of "sky," it probably came afterwards to mean the whole space not occupied by the earth. Even when it meant only the former, it must have been regarded as the place of production of the Devas, and, it would seem from this verse, if correctly translated, of men, or of the intellectual portion of man, also. But *punar*, an adverb, not only means "back," but also "again, in an opposite way, but, on the contrary, nevertheless." And Müller says (Rig-Veda *i.* 251):

> Nothing is more difficult in the interpretation of the Veda, than to gain an accurate knowledge of the power of particles and conjunctions. The particle *chana*, we are told, is used both affirmatively and negatively, a statement which shows better than anything else the uncertainty to which every translation is as yet exposed.

Punaḥ, in the text may not mean, and probably does not mean, "back" or "again," in the sense that the worshipper had been once before at the place; but back to the beginning of things.

However that is, and accepting *punaḥ* as meaning "back," may not the meaning of the sentence be this?—

> Who will return us to, take us back, to the great Aditi, the source of production of all things where I may see the generation and production of things?

That is, is it not saying, in the form of an interrogation, that it is not possible for one to penetrate into the great womb and source where all things are generated and produced, and to see the process of the generation and production, that is, the origination, of things?

Of "the very prominent moral character of Aditi," Professor Müller says that we can understand how she came to be considered as delivering from sin,

> if we watch the transition which led from a purely cosmical conception to a moral one, of Aditi.

And that transition, he thinks, was, that sin is conceived of in the Veda as a bond, rope or chain confining the sinner; and this naturally suggested the idea that A-diti, the un-bound or un-bounded, was one of those Deities who could best remove the bonds of sin or misery. If we once realize this concatenation of thought and language, he thinks, many passages of the Veda that seemed obscure will become intelligible.

And, reading *anagaḥ-tve aditi-tve*, in *vii.* 51. 1, "guiltless*ness* and Aditi-*hood*," translating these words literally, in order to make their meaning quite clear, he says that *âgas* has the same meaning as the Greek ʽαγος, "guilt, abomination"; *an-âgâstva*, therefore, as applied to a sacrifice or to the man who makes it, means "guiltlessness, purity." *Aditi-tva, Aditi-hood*, has a similar meaning, it means freedom from bonds, from anything that hinders the proper performance of a religious act. It may come to mean "perfection" or "holiness."

There is hardly any limit to the transmutations of meaning of words. When sin was once called a bond (and "the bonds of iniquity" is an expression familiar to our ears), one free of bonds was free of guilt, crime and wrong, if the expression was meant in that sense, and as the condition of being unbound is that of freedom, it might mean holiness or perfection, since these are freedom from sin.

But how could all this be derived from the idea of unlimited extension, of the Infinite in extent? The Untied is not the Infinite. There is no connection of sense between the two phrases; nor is there between the words "unbound" and "unbounded."

The idea of power in Aditi to assist in trouble, to give wealth, to forgive errors, could not have come from the idea that it was free from guilt and sin, because unbound. The atmosphere and sky and wind are free of sin and guilt, also; but the idea of their potencies did not come from that mere negation.

The Greek word ʽαγος is from the verb ʽαζω, ʽαζομαι; and it means "veneration, propitiation, etc."; and this word (in English letters "*hagos*" is also said in the dictionaries to mean crime. The Greek word given by Müller, as meaning "guilt, abomination," is not *hagos*, but ʽαγος, *agos*, which is from αγω, "lead, rule, etc." and means "leader."

The whole sentence is thus translated by Professor Müller:

> May the quick Maruts listen and place this sacrifice in guiltlessness and Aditi-hood.

What this means is not clear to me. The original, with the corresponding English words, as given by Müller, are,

anagah-tve	*aditi-tve*	*turasah*	*imam*
in guiltlessness	in Aditi-hood	the quick Maruts	this
yajnam	*dadhatu*	*çrosha manah*	
sacrifice	may place	may listen	

Âgas, in Benfey, is "crime, fault, sin." Its derivation is not given, and he does not refer to any passage in the Veda, wherein it occurs. *Âgatva*, i. e., *â*+ *ga*+ *tva* (verb *gam*), "concern," i. e., "concern with, having something to do with"; *âgati*, i. e., *â*+ *gam*+ *ti*, "arrival, concern"; *agama*, "arrival, occurrence, stream, knowledge, sacred science, a precept, etc." *Gam* means "to go, to move, to turn to, to pass." Also the verb *gâ* means "to go ," and "to come," "to undergo." With *â* prefixed, it means "to approach," and "to befall."

Âgas, no doubt, originally meant "to go astray, to lose one's way," i. e., "not to go to the place intended."

The suffix *tva* forms abstracts from adjectives and substantives; such as *amṛitatva*, "immortality"; *nagnatva*, "nakedness"; *bahutva*, "multitude." —*Bopp*, *Section* 834.

Turâsâh (in Benfey), i. e., *turâ*+ *sâh*, a name of Indra and of Vishṇu. *Turaga*, *turañga* and *turañgama*, each mean "a horse." *Tur* means "to hasten"; and, as an adjective, "hastening," and "a warrior"; *tûr*, "to go quick, to hurt," and "swiftness." Is it not possible that *turâsaḥ* meant "riders, as swift ones, horsemen"; and that this was the origin of the name of the *Turanians*, in the *Zend-Avesta?*

Dadhatu is from *dhâ*, "to put, grant, confer, generate, undertake, carry, bear, nourish, preserve, get, undergo, and show."

I venture to suggest this reading of the sentence: the worshipper, in the first part of the verse, had asked the favour and protection of the Adityas; and now adds:

> May the swift ones (the horsemen, or the Açvins?) hear, and maintain this sacrifice in orderliness and completeness:

i. e., that it be duly ordered and regularly performed, without deviation (going astray from the regular formulas of procedure), and not diminished or cut short.

In *i*. 24. 5, the prayer is,

> O Aditya, let us be in thy service (*vratê*, work, devout act), *anâgasaḥ Aditaye:* [and in *v*. 82. 6] May we, *anâgasaḥ Aditaye devasya Savituḥ save*, obtain all good things.

Müller renders *anâgasaḥ Aditaye*, "free of guilt, guiltless, before Aditi." Roth translates *Aditaye*, in the latter verse, by "freedom" or "security." *Devaya Savituḥ save*, "in the keeping of the God Savitar."—*Müller*. I think that *save* means "a sacrifice," or "sacrificial ceremony"; and that the prayer is not that the worshipper may be free of guilt or guiltless, but may without irregularity or omission perform all the ceremonies of sacrifice.

So, in *i*. 162. 22,

May Aditi give us sinlessness, *anâgâḥ tvam nah Aditiḥ kṛinotu*, the last word meaning 'do, make, perform,' etc.

I think the real meaning of *anâgâḥ* is "regularity or order," perhaps in the course of Nature. So the sin (*agah*), committed through thoughtlessness (forgetfulness) against Agni, in *iv.* 12. 4, I believe to be omissions of duty in the details of the sacrifice to him.

Aditi, like all the other Vedic Deities, was the giver of wealth and health, and was implored for these and for protection. She was asked to protect the cattle, to give happiness, to drive away enemies. She is asked to bring Rudra's favour, and is called the milch cow that gives food to the true man, who offers to the Gods. She is invoked to grant light, and is called "luminous or shining" (*jyotishmatî*), and *svarvati*, "resplendent." She is said to support the earth and is styled "all production."

In two passages we find the words *dyauḥ aditiḥ* together. Here Müller thinks it an adjective meaning "unbounded." In *iv.* 1. 20, it is said of Agni, *viçveshâm aditiḥ yajñiyânâm*, which Müller renders "the freest among all the Gods."

The original meaning of *dâksha*, from a Vedic verb *daksh*, meaning, according to Benfey, "to act in a satisfying manner," "to be strong," "to act quickly," "to go or move," was either "strength" or "motion." The adjective *daksha* has not the meaning of "strength," according to Benfey, but those of "clever, able"; and *dâkshya* is said by him to mean "ability, skill."

The fire for the sacrifice, when the Vedic sacred songs were composed, was procured by means of friction produced by motion, the motion produced by strength. A flat piece of wood was laid upon the ground, and a sharp pointed stick, set upright upon that, was made by the hands of the priest to revolve rapidly, until heat enough was generated to set on fire the piece of wood underneath. To the imagination of the Aryan Poets, this operation was a veritable generation and production, resembling the animal act, the upright stick representing the male organ, and the flat piece of wood the female one.

Thence Agni was said to be the son of Daksha, of motion, produced by strength. And when the active and acute Aryan intellect began to speculate in regard to the origin of the material world, and of the lights of the sky, the idea of Being, produced by motion, strength or energy, was transferred to that field of thought, and Daksha was said to have produced in space the heavenly bodies, through which Agni manifested himself as Indra, the light. And this was the first real idea of a Veritable God, i. e., of a Creative Energy; which they did not attempt to define. Nor, indeed were their ideas certain and definite as to this: for Aditi was said to have sprung from Daksha, and Daksha from Aditi. They were not certain whether energy or motion was the First Cause, or itself caused by a First Cause. But it is at least certain that the general idea was, that Aditi was the mother; not the mother of Daksha, but of the Adityas, the sun, moon and three known planets.

There is great uncertainty and dubitation, it will have been seen, as to the real personality of Aditi. Its etymological lineage is doubtful, and whatever meaning is given it that ascribes to it locality, some other and well-known word contests its claim. There are other names for the sky or heavens and the expanse or firmament.

The chief attribute of Aditi seems to be production. It is the great Mother, and it continually reminds us of our own quasi-Deity, "Mother-Nature," the Isis of the Egyptians. It will be seen hereafter, that in Book *x*. of the Rig-Veda, where the beginning of things is described, a vast mass without form and in darkness is imagined, upon which, at length, the creative energy brooded, and from this commerce the first germ of thought and of being began.

We cannot wink so hard as not to see that the ancient thought, always and everywhere, explained the origin of things by generation. We have already seen the creative potency of Daksha spoken of, his generative energy; and the productive capacity of Aditi, *janman* and *upadthe*, the originals of the *linga* and *yoni* of the Brahmanic age.

Benfey gives, as a meaning of *daksha*, in the Parasmaipada, "to act in a satisfying manner"; and in the Âtmanepada, "to be strong." These are Vedic meanings. Other certain meanings are, "to act quickly, to go or move." *Dâkshya* is "ability, strength." *Daksha* is "clever, able, suitable." The derivative meanings, as found in words formed from *daksh*, lead us to suspect that it had other meanings that became obsolete. *Dakshiṇa* means "clever, right (side or hand), south, southern, upright, honest." *Dakshinâ* is "a good milch cow." That the right hand was called *dakshiṇa* is explainable by the fact that it is the stronger and more the instrument of skill, than the left. But how it came to mean "southern" and "south" is not so easily understood. Was it once an epithet of the sun; and if so, of him as generator? I think so; and that *daksha* originally meant the generative energy, as well as other strength. *Aditi* was either space, imagined to be the womb wherein *daksha* causes impregation and the birth of things, or the uncreated, which the ancients with like indefiniteness, called "Nature." I think that *Aditi* was, as an abstract, that capacity to produce; and that it came to mean, specially the womb of Nature, space, in which an unknown masculine energy generates all things. As the unbounded, it specially meant the space below the sky, and as that, was the mother of the planets. Sometimes it was conceived of as containing in itself both the generative and conceptive and productive potencies.

If one were to ask us what we mean when we speak of "Nature" or "Mother-Nature," "Nature, the Great Mother," "the forces of Nature," we should find it as difficult to reply, as we do to explain what our ancestors meant by *Aditi*. The definition of one of the words will define the other.

Diti is undoubtedly from *dâ;* and the meanings of other roots nearly identical may serve to indicate its original meaning. *Dhâ* means "to generate, to carry, bear and nourish." *Dhita* and *hita* are participial forms of this verb. *Dî* means "to shine"; whence *didhita*, "light, splendour," and *dîdhî*, Vedic, "to shine"; *dîp*, "to blaze, shine"; *dîpti*, "splendour"; and *dah*, originally *dagh*, "to consume by fire."

But fire, light and heat are not the original creative or generative power. Agni himself is born, generated in the great bosom of Nature: and of this original generation, that of the sacrificial fire by friction was always a symbol, and the virile member and female womb symbolized the great potencies by which that original generation was effected.

Mitra, Varuṇa, Aryaman and the other Devas are called sons of Daksha. So the Hindū commentators explain *Daksha-pitarâ*, and in this they are clearly right. For we find that Mitra and Varuṇa are not only called the "strong sons of Daksha" (*sûnû Dakshasya sukratû*), but also the "grandsons of mighty strength" (*napâtâ çavaso mahaḥ*). *Çavas* (Vedic) means "power, strength"; and here, I think, *Daksha* is clearly the generative energy, father of Agni whose sons the planets are.

Various epithets are applied to the Adityas, by which name Mitra, Varuṇa and Aryaman only are in general intended. They are *çuchayah*, "shining, resplendent, white"; *hiraṇyayâḥ*, "golden"; *dhârapûtâḥ*, "observing purity, pure or causing purification, or absolving"; *avṛijinâḥ*, "without wickedness" (from *vṛij*, "to bend," whence *vṛijana* "crooked"; and probably the real meaning of the epithet being "unswerving"); *anavadyâḥ*, "blameless"; *ṛitâvânaḥ*, "possessing truth" (but probably the original meaning of *ṛita* is better preserved in the Latin *ratus*, "fixed, firm, stable, sure, certain, unalterable"); *kshattriyâḥ*, "rulers"; *arishṭâḥ*, "unharmed, victorious"; *uravaḥ*, "great, or protectors"; *gabhiraḥ*, "dwelling in the depth"; *asvapnajaḥ*, "sleepless"; *animishâḥ*, "unwinking" (which plainly indicates that they are planets, as not twinkling like the fixed stars, by which peculiarity they were, no doubt, first distinguished from them); *bhûryakshâḥ*, "many-eyed"; *dîrghadhiyaḥ*, "far-knowing"; *dhṛitavratâḥ*, "steadily working," or "with uniform motion."

They support or maintain and preserve things, both moving and stationary. They see the good and evil in men's hearts, and know the sincere from the deceitful; for that they are worshipped implies that they know when they are sincerely worshipped. They are true and worshipful, and hate falsehood, and punish nonobservance of ceremonial rites; and they give protection, length of life, offspring, guidance and light.

For it is Agni that is adored in adoring them. Their light is the manifestation and outshining of himself and Indra; and light is the very life and being of all things: it gives health, makes things real by making them visible, enables men to find their way and not wander and stray from the right paths, and enables them to labour and earn wealth: and light is the good of the universe, as darkness is its evil.

The Morning Star, large and brilliant in the clear, pure atmosphere, announced to the worshippers that this darkness was about to flee routed away, and casting long lines of light upon the tremulous waters and the grass sparkling with dew, seemed to their imagination to come down and be present, by that light, at the sacrifice that awaited the first blushes of the golden dawn: and from the still bosom of the lake or the deep waters of the stream, the orb itself smiled upon those who seemed to be its favourites. The Evening Star remained after the sun had set, to delay the coming of the darkness, and seemed to promise the worshipper protection. Unfailingly returning at the appointed time to him who watched and waited for them to appear, they seemed incapable of deceiving, and human truth was but the likeness of their faithfulness. Their calm, grave stateliness, and the ever-benignant regard with which they looked on men and their affairs, gave the idea of power, of self-reliance, of judicial impartiality, of kindliness and of protection, and for the unfortunate, of grave sympathy and compassion.

And we, their descendants, still love these beautiful wayfarers of the unfathomable depths of heaven, and look anxiously for and welcome their coming. To him who, waking before the dawn, waits upon the great plains for its coming, or on the ocean, marks the hours that pass wearily, by the slow progress of the three glittering Kings of Orion, nothing gives such comfort and content as the rising of the Morning Star above the far horizon of land or water with promise of the glorious coming of the dawn and of the renewed life of the world. For, darkness is death, and silence and oblivion, and "Light is the life of men," in the most literal and sober sense of the words; and it is still to us, as it was to Plato and Philo and to St. John and Paul, the Very Effluence of the God.

MITRA AND VARUṆA.

One is grateful to Dr. Muir for quoting what is said by Sayana and other Hindū commentators, in regard to the specific personality of Mitra and Varuṇa, since nothing more is needed to disillusionize one who imagines that these perverters of the meaning of the Veda can be of the slightest aid towards its true interpretation. They make Mitra to be the God over the day, the sun, the producer of the days, the ruler of the terrestrial world; and Varuṇa the representative of the night, the ruler over it, one who envelopes like darkness, the producer of the night, the setting sun, who by his departure creates the nights.

All this is mere nonsense. The setting sun was not conceived of as a distinct individuality, that could be the object of adoration. To say that Mitra was the God that presided over the day, leaves the question wholly unsettled, *which* God or *what* orb he was. *What* is that Varuṇa that envelopes like darkness? What was Varuṇa, who produced the night; that by his departure creates the nights?

The explanation of the whole blunder is very simple. Mitra was the Morning Star, and Varuṇa, the Evening Star. Read the commentaries with that key.

The Mithra of the *Zend-Avesta* also was the Morning Star; and therefore it was that Mitra was said to have been a Persian *female* Deity; for the Morning Star was Venus, and Varuṇa was the royal star of the evening, Jupiter.

I cite the following passages, from those collected by Dr. Muir:

> Rig-V. *i*. 25. 18. I beheld him who is visible to all; I beheld his chariot (*ratham*) upon the ground (*kshami*).

Ratha is (in Benfey) "a car, a war-chariot, any vehicle, a foot, and the body." *Rathā* is "the name of a river"; *patra-ratha* ("wing or feather chariot") is "a bird." The word is derived from *ṛi*, "to go, to go to, to undergo, to rise, move, raise, open." Dr. Muir precedes this citation with the remark that

> Varuṇa is, sometimes at least, visible to the mental eye of his worshippers.

The word rendered "I beheld," is *darçam*, as that rendered "visible" is *darçatam*, both from the verb *dṛiç*, which means "to see, behold, look at, inspect, look upon, search, discover, learn and know," and means *actual* seeing with the eyes. The noun *kshami* means the actual solid earth or ground. And the "chariot" of Varuṇa is the long trail of the light of the

Morning Star, lying upon the ground. It is perfectly clear that the Poet speaks of an actually visible luminary, and of some particular one. Originally the Evening Star, when his individuality was not known, Varuṇa had become, long before the Vedic times, the planet Jupiter. We find that in Greece also, the Morning Star was at first supposed to be all the time the same star, Venus.

> *vii.* 88. 2. When I have obtained a vision of Varuna, I have regarded his lustre as resembling that of Agni (*Agner anîkam̃*).

Here also actual sight is spoken of; and the worshipper regards the radiance of the planet as being the very presence and manifestation (*anîka,* face) of Agni. *Îkh* means "to go," as *Îj* does also, and *Ay, I* and *Î*. *Ikh* has the same meaning: and *an* means "to breathe, to blow, to live." Does not *an*+ *îka* mean, then, the breathing forth or flowing forth; i. e., the effluence or emanation from Agni?

He is arrayed in golden mail, surrounded by his spies (or outlookers, the stars), and, potent and punctual, sits in his station, exercising sovereignty. Dr. Muir translates *dhrita-vrato,* "fixed of purpose." *Vrato* means "a voluntary act, rule, action and work": and I think the allusion is to his undeviating and punctual regularity. The house with a thousand doors, the palace which he and Mitra occupy, with a thousand columns, is the sky. *Dvâra* means "a door, gate, entrance, pass," i. e., the aperture, opening, or way of either; and the allusion is to the stars as openings through which the light issues. The columns are supplied by the Poet's imagination; and Ovid says, "*Regia Solis erat sublimibus alta columnis.*"

Mitra and Varuṇa are styled "kings," and monarchs of all things. They, and especially Varuṇa are often termed *Asuras*, which Dr. Muir renders by "divine"; but which means either "being" or "shining"; I think, the latter. They are designated as *rudra,* which Dr. Muir renders by "terrible." The meaning of *rudra* given by Benfey is "one who roars."

The grandest cosmical functions are, as Dr. Muir says, assigned to Varuṇa. He measures and upholds heaven and Pṛithivi, and embraces all the three worlds, for the light that flows from him is the manifestation of Indra, and it pervades and envelopes everything. He is said to *cause* the sun to shine, because when he is the Morning Star he *precedes* him, and sunrise follows his rising, as the effect follows the cause. The wind is his breath, because his potency is that of Agni manifested. He opens boundless paths for the sun, because he goes before him, on the way that he is to travel. He sees, beholds and knows various things, because he shines on everything, and to shine is to see, as we say that the sun and moon look down upon the earth; and that the stars are the eyes of the sky.

In short, the expressions which seem to attribute to him divine potencies and moral qualities, and which came to be so understood, if traced back to their original and material meaning, and if we can catch and follow the thread of the poetic Aryan thought, will be found to have had, at the beginning, a sensible and natural application to him as a planet. The potencies ascribed to the Soma plant and its expressed juice are equally as great, and, to our way of thinking, much more extraordinary; and even these are all capable of explanation, and are perfectly simple developments of a luxuriant imagination, fettered by no rules and by no consideration of well-ordered thought, or fear of exaggeration.

In Rig-Veda *vii.* 86. 3, where the worshipper "seeks to perceive," i. e., is anxious to know, what "sin" he has committed, and the Sages can only tell him that Varuṇa is angry with him, he asks Varuṇa himself to inform him, and promises that, freed from sin, he will come to him with adoration. He prays to be released from the sins (*drugdhani*, "wrongs, injuries, hurts") of his ancestors, and from his own; and protests that it was not his will, but some seduction that led him astray; wine, anger, dice or thoughtlessness, or even sleep. Evidently it is a wrong done to Varuṇa himself—the omission of due attention to his worship, neglect or dilatoriness, and even, as it seems, some error or omission of ceremonial, of which the offender was not conscious.

In *iii.* 59. 1 to 8, the character of Mitra is plainly enough defined. Calling to men, he causes them to come forth to their labours. He holds (*dadhâra*) the earth and sky (*pṛithivîm uta dyâm*), i. e., he fills the sky and expanse with his light. With unwinking eye he looks upon all creatures. He is son of Aditi, the great Aditya, who rouses men to their labours, confers benefits on his worshipper, and is to be approached with reverence. By (or with) his radiance (*mahina*, from *mahas*, "light, lustre"), he transcends the sky: with his glory (*çravobhiḥ*) the earth (*pṛithivi*). *Çravas* is "renown" from *çru*, "to hear"; but there is another verb *çru* or *sru*, which means "to flow, to let flow, to shed"; and *çravas*, from this, would mean "outflow, effluence," and when used in speaking of a planet, "radiance or splendour." As to *pṛithivi*, I am quite as certain as ever that it originally meant the expanse, and not the earth.

However it may seem to others, I, looking for the explanations of the texts of the Veda that are most consistent with Aryan naïveté of thought, and the simplicity and material character of the primitive meanings of words, find in this hymn conclusive evidence that Mitra was the Morning Star. And undoubtedly the reason for the close connection between Mitra and Varuṇa, the former being mentioned alone in only one hymn, was that when one was the Star of the Morning, the other was the Star of the Evening, and that each was alternately one and the other.

Professor Roth says that this dual invocation is preserved in the *Zend-Avesta*, in regard to Ahura and Mithra, but that, I think, is a mistake. He says also that the essential character of the two Gods, Mitra and Varuṇa, as distinguished from one another, is nowhere distinctly expressed in the hymns, and was in fact originally one which could not be defined with intellectual precision. That too, I think is all an error. But in the following remarks he is near putting his hand upon the very truth; and that he did not, is because he looks *over* the truth, with a preconceived opinion that it lies beyond. He says:

> The stage of religious culture which lies before us in the Rig-Veda, enables us to distinguish this difference as one already existing, viz.: that Mitra is the celestial light in its manifestation by day, while Varuṇa, though the Lord of Light and of all time, yet rules especially over the nightly heaven. A hymn of Vasishṭha (*vii.* 36. 2) says: 'One of you (Varuṇa) is the lord and unassailable guide, and he who is called Mitra (i. e., the friend) calls men to activity.' Here so much at least is declared (and the same thing is expressed in nearly the same words in other places), that the light of day, which awakens life, and brings joy and activity into the world, is the narrower sphere of Mitra's power; though, however, Varuṇa is not thereby relegated to the night alone, for he continues to be the Lord and the First.

And this curiously hazy and indistinct view of Varuṇa is then presented:

> If Varuṇa is, as his name shows, that one among the lucid Adityas [What is a 'lucid' Aditya, if not a luminary visible to the eye?], whose seat and sphere of authority is the bright heaven, in whose bosom is embraced all that lives, and therefore also the remotest boundary, beyond which human thought seeks nothing further, then is he also one who can scarcely be attained either by the eye or by the imagination. By day the power of vision cannot discover this remotest limit, the bright heaven presents to it no resting place. But at night this veil of the world, in which Varuṇa is enthroned, appears to approach nearer and become perceptible, for the eye finds a limit. Varuṇa is closer to men. Besides, the other divine forms which, in the clouds, the atmosphere, the rays of light, filled the space between the earth and yonder immeasurable outermost sphere have disappeared [Where are the stars?]: and no other God now stands between Varuṇa and the mortal who gazes at him.

Dr. Muir thinks that these are "ingenious and interesting observations." Perhaps they are. If so, the ingenuity is displayed in carefully putting words together so that they shall sound well and mean nothing. Let the reader read it once more, and then answer, if he can, the question, "*What*, in Professor Roth's opinion, *was* this God Varuṇa?" One might as well say that he was the Gyascutas. *What* was that "lucid" Aditya, whose *seat* and sphere of authority was the *bright* heaven; whose bosom either was or embraced the remotest boundary; who could scarcely be attained by the eye or the imagination; who was *enthroned* in the *veil* of the world (darkness?); who comes closer when this *veil* becomes more perceptible, and every other divine *form* and ray of light has disappeared; and on whom, so shrouded in the perceptible and palpable darkness, the mortal eye *gazes?*

The Vedic Poets had no such vague and hazy imaginings of airy nothings, less real than impossible monsters seem in feverish dreams. They well enough knew what their Deities were and what they meant; for they were neither silly nor insane.

Dr. Muir also has the truth in his hand, and does not know it, but lets it escape from him, where he considers the identity of the Vedic Mitra and the Mithra of the *Zend-Avesta*. There is no doubt, he says, from the correspondence of the two names, that they were originally the same Deity. Dr. Windischmann, he says, regards it as established, that this God was known, and common, to the old Aryan race, before the separation of its Iranian from its Indian branch, though the conception of his character was subsequently modified by Zarathustrian ideas. Herodotus speaks of Mitra, not as a God, but as a Goddess. His words are (*i.* 131),

> *Ouranē thuein, para tĕ Assuriōn mathŏntēs kai Arabiōn: Kalĕŏusi dĕ Assuriŏi tēn Aphrŏditēn Mulitta, Arabiŏi dĕ Alitta, Pĕrsai dĕ Mitran.*

He says that she was identical with Urania.

Max Müller says, in the Preface (*xii.*) to his *Translation of the Rig-Veda*, Volume I:

> I feel convinced that on many points my translation is liable to correction, and will sooner or later be replaced by a more satisfactory one. It is difficult to explain to those who have not themselves worked at the Veda, how it is that, though we may understand almost every word, yet we find it so difficult to lay hold of a whole chain of connected thought, and to discover expressions that will not throw a wrong shade on the original features of the ancient words of the Veda. We have, on the one hand, to avoid giving to our translations too modern a character, or paraphrasing instead of translating; while, on the other, we cannot retain expressions which, if literally rendered in English or any modern tongue, would have an air of quaintness or absurdity totally foreign to the intention of the ancient Poets. There are, as all Vedic scholars know, whole verses which, as yet, yield no sense whatever. There are words, the meaning of which we can only guess. Here, no doubt, a continued study will remove some of our difficulties, and many a passage that is now dark, will receive light hereafter, from a happy combination.

Undoubtedly it is true that one chief cause of the uncertainty as to the meaning of words and phrases in the Veda, is, that the meanings which a multitude of words had, when the hymns were composed, had been lost when they were reduced to writing and compiled, no one knows how long afterwards.

If we add to this the resolute persistency of most translators in making the old Poets talk as men now do, and accept the translator's language as their own; and the constant use of English words, that, in their present acceptation misrepresent the Sanskrit words that are rendered by them, and even have no equivalents at all in Sanskrit, because they express ideas that then had no existence, or imply knowledge which the old Poets did not possess, we shall find ample explanation for a large part of the uncertainty as to the meaning of a great number of Sanskrit texts.

What is most wanted is a *Vedic* dictionary, the ripe fruits of the long labours of years and of the most careful study and investigation by an acute intellect, that shall give the *Vedic* meanings of all the words, as far as it is possible to ascertain what they were—the later meanings being separately subjoined.

There is no doubt that very many words have had ascribed to them meanings entirely wrong, by the mistaking one root for another. The roots of many words are only recoverable by conjecture, but the Zend, Greek and Latin derivatives will enable a profound scholar to recover many lost roots, and correct many established errors in regard to the meanings of words.

Take as an example the word and name Mitra. Benfey gives, as meanings of the word, "*Mittra*, commonly written, *Mitra*, i. e., *Mid*+ *tra*," 1. a Vedic Deity, referring to the Rig-Veda; 2. the sun (the *Panchatantra*); 3. a friend (the *Râmâyana*); 4. an ally. Then he gives us *mith*, *midh*, *mid* and *med*, as meaning, 1. to understand; 2. to hurt; 3. (Vedic) to rival; and *mid*, to be unctuous; to liquify and to love, for which two meanings he admits there is no authoritive reference; and to rejoice (Vedic).

Then we find *Mithas*, "mutually, reciprocally, with each other, from each other, privately"; *mithuna*, "a couple, copulation, union, the sign of the Zodiac, Gemini." And *Mithyâ* means "falsely, untruly, feigned, wrong, what does not concern one." *Mittratâ* is friendship; *mittra-yu*, "acquiring friends"; *mittravant*, "one who has friends." So *Maitra* and *Maittra* is "a friend," and also the name of a particular kind of alliance, proceeding from friendship.

In the Vendidad and elsewhere, in the *Zend-Avesta*, *Mithra* means "a promise, contract, an engagement."

There is also a verb *mâ*, whose participle of the perf. pass. is *mita*, and which means "to measure," whence *miti*, "measuring, determining, knowledge."

It is evident that there is a confusion of roots here, and that it is uncertain to what roots some of the derivatives are to be assigned. No one root could have meant, originally, "to hurt, to understand, and to rival." We find no root from which to obtain the adverbial meanings, "mutually, reciprocally," etc.; and yet the meanings "friend" and "ally" must go back to the same root as the adverbs; and *Mithra*, a promise or contract must have come from the same.

The Latin equivalents will often shed light upon the developments of meaning of Sanskrit and Zend words. I am satisfied that the meanings of words originally common to both languages, or rather, belonging to the one language from which both descended, found in the Gâthâs or hymns composed by Zarathustra, are older than the Sanskrit meanings; and here I think that the oldest meaning of Mitra is cognate with that of "promise" or "contract." Now *promissio*, "promise," in Latin, is from *pro+ mitto*, "send forward, send forth, send in advance, foretell, etc., cause to expect, give hope or promise of"; and *contractus*, "a contract," from *con+ traho*, "to draw or bring together." One contracts by a promise; and from the meaning "promiser" would naturally come those of "ally," "friend," etc., meanings of *Mitra* in Sanskrit.

I think, therefore, that *Mitra* is from a root that meant "to promise," and that the name meant "promiser" because the Morning Star, rising, gives assurance of, foretokens, heralds and promises the speedy rising of the sun; whose friend and ally, also, he was no doubt considered.

Varuṇa, i. e., *vṛi+ una*, Benfey says; and *vara*, i. e., *vṛi+ a*, "better, excellent, precious, beautiful, eldest, a blessing, a husband." He thinks that the Greek 'αρειων, "αριστος, came from this. Also, *vîra*, i. e., *vṛi+ a*, (probably for original *vâra*, "heroic, strong, powerful, eminent, a hero, heroism, fire"). As Jupiter is the largest star in the sky, the name Varuṇa probably meant "pre-eminent," and caused his common title of "King Varuṇa." That this planet bore the name of the King of the Olympian Gods, also, shows the estimation in which it was held by the Aryan race.

As to the powers ascribed to Varuṇa, they are the powers of Agni. In Rig-Veda *i*. 164. 46, it is said,

> They call him Indra, Mitra, Varuṇa, Agni (or, they call Agni, Indra, Mitra, Varuṇa), ... Sages name variously that which is but one. They call it Agni, Yama, Mâtariçvan (or, they call Agni, Yama, Mâteriçvan).

For the first phrase is, *Indram Mitram̃ Varuṇam Agnim âhur:* and the second, *Agnim Yaman Mâtariçvânam âhuḥ*. The readings in parentheses agree better with the known character and meaning of Agni, and with other passages. All Devas are declared to be contained in Agni, as the spokes of a wheel are in its circumference or circularity.

And this, and what Varuṇa and Mitra *are*, are very clearly expressed in the Atharva-Veda, *xiii*. 3. 13:

> Agni becomes Varuṇa in the evening; rising in the morning he is Mitra; becoming Savitṛi he moves through the air; becoming Indra he glows in the middle of the sky.

It seems clear, also, that the planet Varuṇa was regarded as having control over the rain, and therefore as protector of the rivers which the rains made to swell and flow. In *vii.* 49. 2, it is said,

> May the waters of the sky, and those that flow (rain and the rivulets), those for which channels are dug (for irrigation), and those which are self-produced (the springs), those which are proceeding to the ocean (*samudrârthâḥ;* for which I do not find that meaning), and are bright and purifying, preserve me. May those in the midst of which Raja Varuṇa goes, beholding the truth and falsehood of men, etc. . . . . May those waters in which Varuṇa, Soma and all the Devas (*viçve devaḥ*) are exhilarated by food, into which Agni Vaiçvânara has entered, etc.

So, in *vii.* 64. 2, Mitra and Varuṇa are called *Sindhupati*, which Dr. Muir renders "Lords of the sea" (or, "of rivers"). But there is no doubt that *sindhu* meant originally "river," and nothing else: and Varuṇa and Mitra are masters or lords of the rivers, because they are supposed to control the rains.

> *v.* 24. 4, 5. *Varuṇo 'pâm adhipatiḥ*, 'Varuṇa, Lord of the waters': *Mitrâvarunau vṛishtyah adhipati*, 'Mitra and Varuṇa, Lords of rain.'

The idea of Professor Roth, that

> when, on the one hand, the conception of Varuṇa as the all-embracing heaven had been established, and, on the other hand, the observation of the rivers flowing towards the ends of the earth, had led to the conjecture that there existed an ocean enclosing the earth in its bosom, then the way was thoroughly prepared for connecting Varuṇa with the ocean,

—this notion, for it is no more, is hardly plausible as a conjecture. While the Indo-Aryans remained in the Punjab, where most of the hymns of the six or seven first Mandalas were composed, they knew nothing about any ocean, to which the rivers there ran. *Sindhu* meant a river, and gave name to the Indus. *Samudra*, which in later days came to mean the "sea or ocean," is given by Benfey as *sam*+ *und*+ *ra*. *Sam* means "with, together, much, wholly, beautifully." *Und* is "to wet or moisten"; and *udan*, i. e., *und*+ *an* is "water." Unless the Indo-Aryans knew something of the Caspian and Sea of Aral, or unless their ancestors had known them, and applied the word to these bodies of water, the people of the Punjab could have had no noun that meant "sea."

But the Indus ran along the western boundary of their country, and all their rivers fell into it; and the Evening Star set behind and beyond it. Reflected in the water, it seemed to dwell there; and there is no doubt that he was supposed to control the rains. Why, it is not easy to say with certainty. Perhaps because he and Mitra shone by Indra, and he was manifested in their light, and he was the great causer of rains. Whatever its origin, it is certain that the planet Jupiter was supposed to have power over the rain, and this notion long survived in the name *Jupiter Pluvius* of the Latins. Appian (*de Mundo*) says,

> *Juppiter dicitur etiam Imbricitor* (is called shower-sender), *et item serenator.*

And Tibullus says (*Eleg. i.* 7. 26),

> *Arida nec pluvio supplicat herba Jovi.*

There are abundant illustrations of Vedic thought in the Latin writers, two of which I may pause to notice: the chariots, with their wheels, and the swift horses, of the sun and other Aryan Deities, figure in Tibullus, who says (*Eleg. i.* 9. 61. 2):

> *Illam sæpe ferunt convivia ducere Baccho,*
> *dum rota Luciferi provocet orta diem;*

and (*Eleg. i.* 3. 93. 4):

> *hunc illum nobis Aurora nitentem*
> *Luciferum roseis candida portet equis.*

Professor Westergaard says of Varuṇa, that

> he has, in the later Indian mythology, become God of the Sea, whilst in the Vedas he appears first as the Mystic Lord of the Evening and the Night.

But the identity which he imagines to exist between *Varuṇa* and the Zend word, *Varena*, a name of a country, is merely imaginary.

Professor Müller, and indeed all the commentators, identify *Varuṇa* with the Greek Ουρανος, used in Hesiod as a name of the sky, "a firm place for the blessed Gods." *Ouranos* is said by Hesiod to cover everything, and to be stretched out everywhere, embracing the earth. And Müller says (*Chips, ii.* 65),

> This sounds almost as if the Greek myths had still preserved a recollection of the etymological power of *Ouranos*. For *Ouranos* is, in the Sanskrit, *Varuṇa*, and is derived from a root *var*, 'to cover'; *Varuṇa* being in the Veda also a name of the firmament, but especially connected with the night, and opposed to Mitra, the day.

But, as Dr. Muir remarks, the parallel between *Ouranos* and *Varuṇa* does not hold in all points. There is no relation of husband and wife between Varuṇa and the earth, as there is between Ouranos and Gaia; nor is Varuṇa represented as the progenitor of Dyaus, as Ouranos is of Zeus.

Moreover, Varuṇa is neither the expanse, sky, firmament or heaven (whatever the two latter words may mean, if anything); and Dyaus is the sky, and husband of Pṛithivi, if she is the earth.

Certainly Varuṇa was nothing more than the Evening Star, or Jupiter, when the Greek Exodus took place, whatever he may have become ages afterward: and as Ouranos was certainly the sky, one cannot help suspecting that similarity here is not identity; especially as the Doric form of Οὐρανὸς is Ὠρανὸς. It is true that one of the meanings of *vṛi* and *var* is "to cover"; but some other root is wanted for *vara, vîra, vîrya*, and others, in all of which the original idea of "strong" is included. The Zend *vairya* is from the same root, *vaira*, in Sanskrit, i. e., *vîra*+ *a*, meaning "heroism," and *vairaya*, "to fight."

Ûrṇu means "to cover," *uru*, "large," and *uras*, "the breast." The Greek *Ouranos* may be cognate with these, but I doubt its connection with *Varuṇa*.

It is noticeable that *Varuṇa* means belonging to *Varuṇa;* and *Vâruṇî*, fem., "the West, the region of Varuṇa." The attribution to Varuṇa of the function of producing rain may have been the consequence of the supposed derivation of the name from *vâr*, *vâri*, "water," whence *vârida*, "a cloud," and *vâruṇî*, "spirituous liquor."

Dr. Muir says (*v*. 77):

> According to the Greek geographer, Strabo, the Indians, as known to him by the report of other writers, worshipped Jupiter Pluvius, the River Ganges, and the Gods of the country. This Jupiter Pluvius was no doubt Indra.

May it not, more probably, have been Varuṇa?

Varuṇa seems to have been considered peculiarly the planet of rain. Thus, in *ii*. 28, we find,

> 4. . . . . The rivers flow by the power of Varuṇa: they never weary, they never stop. . . . .
>
> 5. Cast off from me sin [harm, misfortune, ill-luck], Varuṇa, as if it were a rope: let us obtain from thee a channel with water. Cut not the thread of me weaving pious works [i. e., thwart not my undertakings in husbandry]; blight not the elements of holy rites [the productions that are to be offerings], before the season.

In *i*. 139. 2, we have,

> Mitra and Varuṇa, bestow abundantly that unenduring water, which you obtain from the sun, through your own energy; through the inherent energy of the vigourous.

In *v*. 68, we have:

> 2. The Mitra and Varuṇa who both are sovereign rulers, originators of the rain, eminent Devas among the Devas.

> 3. They two are able, of great terrestrial and celestial riches: great is your might among the Devas.
>
> 4. Rewarding with rain the holy rite, they favour the zealous worshipper. . . .
>
> 5. Senders of rain from the sky, granters of desires, Lords of Sustenance. . . .

And, in *v.* 69. 2:

> Mitra and Varuṇa, the cows are full of milk through you, and the rivers yield sweet water through you; through you, the three radiant receptacles and showerers of rain stand severally in their three spheres.

This function, of benefactor of the earth by means of rain, was undoubtedly attributed to Varuṇa and Mitra, on account of their association with the stars whose appearance before the dawn announced the coming of the Vernal Equinox. It is somewhat to be wondered at that their planetary character should ever have been doubted. A single verse completely identifies them, *iii.* 55. 6:

> The child of two mothers [night and day] sleeps in the West: the other infant journeys unobstructed: these are the functions of Mitra and Varuṇa.

The reference to the Evening and Morning Stars is unmistakable: as it is in *iii.* 61. 7, in the words,

> The mighty Ushas, the golden light, as it were, of Mitra and Varuṇa, diffuses her radiance in different directions.

SÛRYA AND SAVITṚI.

Dr. Muir considers Sûrya and Savitṛi as exact personifications of the sun, and says,

> It is under these two different appellations that the Sun is chiefly celebrated in the Rig-Veda; and although it may be difficult to perceive why the one word should be used in any particular case, rather than the other, the application of the names may perhaps depend upon some difference in the aspect under which the Sun is conceived, or on some diversity in the functions which he is regarded as fulfilling. Different sets of hymns are, at all events, devoted to his worship under each of these names, and the epithets which are applied to him in each of these characters are for the most part separate. In some few places, both these two names, and occasionally some others, appear to be applied to the Solar Deity indiscriminately; but in most cases the distinction between them is, nominally at least, preserved.

As we *know* that Sûrya was the sun, we have by that knowledge a sure key of interpretation of many expressions which are used in regard to him and other Deities alike.

He is the vitality (*âtmâ*, rendered "soul" by Muir), of all those that move and that are stationary; and their preserver (*gopaḥ*, "cowherd, guide?"). He is the arouser (*pravasitâ*, "vivifier," *Muir*) of men, impartial, or the same ("common," *Muir*) to all. *Sâdhâraṇa*, "belonging to many, common, equal, like, similar"; *Prasû*, "a mother, a mare"; *prasûti*, "offspring, bringing forth, birth:" *prasava*, i. e., *prasû+a*, "bringing forth, being in labour, offspring, blossom, fruit;" *prasavitṛi*, "father, forefather;" *prasavitṛî*, "a mother."

Sû and *su* mean "to beget, bear, bring forth"; another verb *su*, "to possess power or supremacy"; and another, "to go"; but for these two there are no authoritative references. There is also another verb *sû*, "to cast, send, incite, impel."

Where Dr. Muir translates *prasavitâ jajânâm*, "vivifier of men," I think it means "arouser, awakener" of them, at rising in the morning. And in *vii.* 63. 4, instead of "enlivened," I read

> awakened by him men pursue their purposes and do their work.

The path of Sûrya is prepared, i. e., he is preceded by the Adityas Mitra, Varuṇa and Aryaman. His chariot is drawn by sometimes two and sometimes several or seven horses. For his rays are of one colour, white, and yet when they form the rainbow, they are of seven, no doubt the origin of the veneration paid to that number.

He *sees* and *beholds*, is far-seeing and all-beholding, seeing all creatures and the good and evil deeds of mortals. He is the eye of Mitra and Varuṇa, and sometimes that of Agni (*chakshur Mitrasya Varuṇasya Agneh*). For Agni is manifested in his light; and when he rises, the planets that preceded him shed no light distinguishable from his, and see the world by his light.

Like most other expressions of the Vedas, this of the sun's "seeing" survives today. The Aryan intellect, thought, imagination and speculation were the same then that they are now. The race is unchanged, in all its essential characteristics. We say, as the Greek and Latin Poets did, that the sun, stars and moon *look down* upon the earth. Ushas is said to precede the brilliant eye of the Devas and lead upward the white horse *with beautiful eyes*.

In *x*. 85. 1, it is said that the earth is upheld by "truth" (*Muir*) i. e., actuality, reality, existence, being, is self-existent; the sky is upheld by the sun. He is the radiant chief of the luminaries (*devânâm asuryaḥ purohitaḥ*), by his magnitude, or the largest of all. He is identified with Indra, for it is Indra who is manifested by him: and each of them is *Viçvakarman* (who acts in all) and *Viçvadeva*, who *is* all the luminaries: and in *vii*. 60. 1, and *vii*. 62. 2, Sûrya is prayed at his rising to declare men sinless to Mitra, Varuṇa, etc., i. e., not in fault for adoring him and not them, after they have disappeared or faded.

"In many passages, however," Dr. Muir says, "the dependent position of Sûrya is asserted." Plainly because he is sometimes regarded as Indra manifesting himself, and sometimes as merely the sun, caused and produced by Indra. Thus he is said to have been produced or caused to shine, or to have his path prepared, by Indra, and by Indra and Soma. But when similar expressions are used in regard to Sûrya and Ushas, Dhatṛi, Varuṇa, Mitra, and others, the meaning simply is that they *precede* him, and therefore are imagined to *cause* him to rise. It is even said that the Angirasas, by their rites or sacrifices *cause* him to ascend. It is but a figure of speech.

"In passages of this description," Dr. Muir says, "the divine personality of the sun is thrown into the background; the grand luminary becomes little more than a part of Nature, created and controlled by those spiritual powers which exist above and beyond all material phenomena."

The Poets of the Veda had no idea or conception of any "divine personality," in our sense of that phrase. The highest idea that they had in regard to the sun, was that he was a shining-forth of Indra, the universal light. If they attributed to Indra and Agni, either as universals, or as manifested by the sun, moon and planets, potencies and faculties that we now call "divine," intellect, benignity and others, they attributed these to the fire and the light, and not to any divine being above them, their creator or cause, or to a spiritual being, but to fire and light *as* fire and light, as these were visible to them and known by them. They knew of no spiritual powers, existing above and beyond all material phenomena. They attributed to Indra and Agni powers purely human, and a purely human intellect and temper.

I know it may be said that I might show that the original meaning of all our Theosophic language was material, "celestial" meaning "skyey," and "spirit, breath," etc., and that as this would by no means prove that such words have not now entirely other meanings, so the material meanings of the Vedic words do not prove that they had not higher meanings, as the words have into which we translate them. And if I were reading the Bhagavadgîtâ or Hitopadeça, I should give them those meanings, because that they had them when used there is manifest. But in the Vedic hymns it is equally manifest that they were not so used; and that the ideas that they now convey were then unknown. One cannot mistake Agni for God or a Spirit; nor Ahura Mazda, in the Gâthâs for anything else than God, in our meaning of that name.

The celestial splendour of Mitra and Varuṇa is unreal (i. e., invisible), in the sky, when Sûrya moves there, radiant, and a brilliant opponent; whom nevertheless they by and by hide by clouds and rain. Dr. Muir translates *Mâyâ vâm Mitrâvaruṇâ divi çrita*, "The divine power of Mitra and Varuṇa is *shown* in the sky;" but *çrita* means "fortune, bliss, light, splendour," and Mitra and Varuṇa do not shine when the sun is high in heaven. And *mâyâ* means "illusion, unreality."

"Sûrya is declared to be god-born:" but the word rendered by "god-born" is *devajataya*, which, like *dus-jâta*, "miserable" and *yathâ-jâta*, "foolish, a fool," means merely a Deva, i. e., literally, "born a Deva." Also he is called *divas putrâya*, "son or child of the sky;" and is said to have been drawn by the Devas from the ocean where he was hidden; i. e., induced by them to rise out of the sea; to have been placed by the Devas in the sky, i. e., to have been induced by them to rise into and have place in the sky, and to have sprung from the eye of Purusha. *Puras* means "first, before," and also "the east," or "eastward." *Chakshas* means "the eye;" and here, I think, "the opening or window," of the east.

And he is said to have been overcome and despoiled by Indra; who, in some verses in Mand. *i*. 4. 5, is alluded to as having carried off one of the wheels of his chariot; by which was no doubt meant an eclipse, annular, perhaps, or total, in which Indra withheld his light, and ceased for the time to manifest himself. One such phenomenon was a demonstration of the truth of the doctrine that the luminaries are dark bodies, when Indra ceases to reveal himself through them. Even large spots on the sun might cause the use of like expressions.

In *i*. 50, the avant couriers of Sûrya precede him in the sky, seeing all things and to be seen of all men. Before his rays, the stars steal away like thieves; before him, the all-beholding luminary. His rays, that are his revealing, are seen by all mankind, flaming like fire.

> With that glance of thine, wherewith, O Illuminator, O Varuṇa, thou surveyest the busy race of men, thou, O Sûrya, penetratest the sky, the broad firmament, measuring out the days with thy rays, spying out all creatures.

The words rendered here by "With that glance of thine, wherewith, O Illuminator," are *yena pavaka chakshasâ anu*. *Pavaka*, i. e., *pû+aka*, is rendered by Benfey "fire." *Pû* means "to purify." *Chakshasâ* is the instrumental of *chakshas*, "eye." I do not see why *pacyasi* should mean "surveyest," and *pacyan*, "spying out." *Eshi*, rendered by "penetratest," means "goest, strivest to attain, searchest." And *mimâno*, in the phrase *ahâ mimâno aktubhiḥ*, "measuring out the days with thy rays," means determining their length, in the sense of causation. I do not see how it could ever have been said that Sûrya searches the sky with that glance of Varuṇa's, with which he, Varuṇa, surveys men.

Pâvaka came to mean, according to Benfey, "belonging to Agni." The meaning of the verse must originally have been that by that light of Agni whereby Varuṇa as its eye viewed living creatures, Sûrya also searches the sky, measures the days and views all living beings.

Seven mares, of the colour of gold, bear onward in his chariot the much-seeing Sûrya with flaming hair. He has yoked the seven brilliant mares, the daughters of the car: *ayukta sapta çundhyuvaḥ Suro rathasya naptyaḥ*. *Ayukta*, "yoked." *Yuj* means "to join, connect, put to." *Çundhyu*, "brilliant," is from *çundh*, *çudh*, "to purify;" and Benfey gives *çundhyu* as meaning "purifying."

What is noticeable here is, that these mares or rays are said to be "grand-daughters of the chariot;" and in the next verse *svayuktibhih*, which Dr. Muir renders "self-yoked;" it meaning that in their very self they are one, united by their inherent essence,—meaning perhaps that, united, they constitute a single white light; or else that they are but effluences from one and the same substance of light.

Finally, Sûrya is styled in this hymn *deva-devatrâ* a God among the Gods. *Trâ* is an adverbial suffix, and Bopp (Sec. 991) thinks that it is the origin of the comparative suffix *tara*. Perhaps it is the oldest form of that. And I think that here it means superiority; and as in Hebrew the *Kadosh Kadoshim* "Holy of Holies," means "the holiest," so here, I think, the meaning is "the superior among the Devas;" i. e., the largest of the heavenly bodies.

The root *su* or *sû*, from which the word *Savitṛi* is derived, has, it is said by Dr. Muir, three principal significations: 1. to generate or bring forth; 2. to pour out a libation; 3. to send or impel. To the third, add "to incite." We have seen what is meant by *pra+su;* and that *pra+savitṛi* means "father," and *pra+savitrî*, "mother;" i. e., "begetter" and "bringer-forth." Dr. Muir adds;

> The word *prasavitṛi*, as well as various other derivatives of the root *su* are introduced in numerous passages of the Rig-Veda, relating to the God *Savitṛi*, with evident reference to the derivation of that name from the same root, and with a constant play upon the words, such as is unexampled in the case of any other Deity.
>
> *i.* 124, 1. The Deva Savitṛi has incited (*prâsâvîd*) both men and animals to pursue their several ends.
>
> *i.* 157, 1. The Devah Savitṛi has aroused (*prâsâvîd*) every moving thing.

In *v.* 81. 2, Savitṛi the Wise (*Kavi*) is said to put on (or manifest) all forms. He sends (*prâsâvîd*) good fortune (or happiness) to men and animals. He illuminates the sky, and shines after the going of the dawn. He alone is the lord of generative power (*prasavasya*), and by his movements becomes Pushan. It would seem from this that Savitṛi, shining after the going, or after the path, of the dawn, must be the sun: but *anu* means "along," "like," "according to," as well as "after."

> *iii.* 33, 6. The God (*Deva*) Savitṛi has led us (the waters). By his incitation (*prasave*), we flow on broadly.
>
> *ii.* 38, 1. The God Savitṛi has risen to incite us; he who continually so works, the supporter.

In *iii.* 56. 6, it is said that three times a day, Savitṛi sends desirable things from the sky, and that so also do Mitra and Varuṇa.

He stretches out his arms in his vivifying energy, establishing and animating all moving things by his rays. He stretches out his golden arms to vivify, or impart energy (*savanaya*).

He is pre-eminently the golden Deity, being *hiraṇ-yâksha*, golden-eyed; *hiraṇya-pâṇi*, *hiraṇya-hasta*, golden-handed. *Hasta* is "hand;" *pâṇi*, Benfey says, is "hand," perhaps akin to *parṇa*, "wing." He is *hiraṇya-jihva* and *sujihva* and *mandra-jihva*, golden-, sweet- and pleasant-tongued. He invests himself with golden mail, or brown or ruddy armour; assumes all forms, and is yellow-haired or has hair of rays. Luminous of aspect, he ascends a chariot with radiant, brown, white-footed horses, and beholding all creatures, pursues an ascending and descending way.

Surrounded by a golden lustre, he illuminates the atmosphere, and all the regions of the expanse. His robust and golden arms, which he stretches out to bless and to infuse energy into all creatures, reach to the utmost ends of the sky. Indra, also, is called "golden-armed." Agni is said to raise aloft his arms, like (or, as) Savitṛi: The dawns are said to send forth light as Savitṛi stretches out his arms: and Mitra and Varuṇa are supplicated to stretch out their arms.

He impels the car of the Açvins, before the dawn; is called *viçve-deva*, and bestows immortality on the Devas, as he did on the Ribhus, who by the greatness of their merits attained to his abode. Of course he dispenses benefits and blessings, sends food, removes sickness and forgives sins.

It is nowhere expressly said that he is the sun. That can, at the utmost, only be implied from a very small number of expressions, none of them by any means conclusive. One is *v*. 81. 2,

> he shines after the path of the dawn (*anu prayâṇam Ushaso*).

Prayâna, in Benfey, is "going forth, march, going:" and the full moon may be distinctly seen after the day has dawned, and after sunrise. And he impels (or directs) the car of the Açvins before dawn; which the sun cannot be said to do; but the moon, rising before day, and following the twin horsemen up the sky could naturally be deemed to do.

It more sustains the theory that he is the sun, that he is said to arouse men and animals, to follow their pursuits as Ushas is said to do. But when the summer days are excessively hot, and the moon shines clear at night, men travel by her light, to avoid the heat. The American Indians make their night-attacks when the moon rises: and I have often, on the plains and in Mexico, journeyed and marched troops by night.

The sun does not assume many different forms. The moon continually changes form. The crescent moon may well be said to haṿe golden arms. The horses of Savitṛi are white-footed, which those of Sûrya are not.

In *x*. 139. 1, we have,

> *Sûryaraçmir harikeçaḥ purastât Savitâ jyotir ud ayân ajasram.*

Raçmi means "a ray of light." So that Savitṛi is here said to be "Sûrya-rayed," i. e., shining by the light with which the sun, Sûrya, invests him, and with radiant hair; and thus continually to uplift his splendour in the east.

In *i*. 35. 9, he is said to approach or bring Sûrya (*veti Sûryam*): in *i*. 123. 3, to declare men without fault before Sûrya; and in *v*. 81. 4, to combine (or be conjoined with) the rays of Sûrya (*vita Sûryasya raçmibhiḥ samuchyasi*. In *vii*. 66. 4, he is prayed to arouse the worshipper after the rising of the sun (*Sura*), along with Mitra, Aryaman and Bhaga, all of which are planets. This is Dr. Muir's translation. The original is,

> *Yad adhya Sûre udite anâgâḥ Mitro Aryamâ suvâti Savitâ Bhagaḥ.*

Adya, in Benfey, is not "after," but "now, today." And I venture to think that the proper rendering is, that Mitra, Aryaman, Savitṛi and Bhaga may now arouse (or awaken) the innocent man, at the rising of the sun.

In *vii.* 35. 8 and 10, Savitṛi the Deva and the large-eyed Sûrya are separately mentioned; as both are mentioned in juxtaposition with Dhâtṛi and Vishṇu, in *x.* 181. 3.

In *i.* 157. 1, we read,

Agni has awoke from the earth: Sûrya rises: the great and bright Ushas has dawned with her radiance: the Açvins have put the steeds to their car, to retire; and the Deva Savitṛi has aroused all moving creatures.

The texts in *iv.* 14. 2, and *x.* 158. 1, cited by Dr. Muir, as employing the two names indiscriminately, to denote the sun, are not by any means conclusive. And that in *i.* 124. 1, and *vii.* 63. 1 to 4, where the functions generally assigned to Savitṛi, are ascribed to Sûrya, is of no weight, as the functions of both are those of Agni and Indra acting through them. In *v.* 81. 4 and 5, Savitṛi is represented as fulfilling the proper functions of Mitra and Pushan; and in *v.* 82. 1 and 3 and *vii.* 38. 1 and 6, seems to be identified with Bhaga.

I have not found anything in the additional texts furnished by Dr. Muir, to unsettle my opinion that Savitṛi was originally the moon. *Savana* is the moon: *Sava* is the sun, and also the moon; and *Savitṛi* means "mother." The root of all is *sû* or *su.* That Savitṛi came to be understood to be the sun, perhaps soon after the Vedic period, perhaps long afterwards, is certain enough: and it was inevitable that the text should be changed, to be in some degree accommodated to that hypothesis. The single fact that if Savitṛi was not the moon, that great and adorable luminary was not worshipped at all, and is hardly mentioned, goes a great way to prove that she was Savitṛi, which, also, was then probably Savitṛî (feminine) meaning "mother."

PUSHAN.

This Deity, the nourisher, cherisher, augmenter (from *push* and *pûsh*, "to nourish, cherish and augment"), has hitherto proven an enigma to me.

As the reader will have seen, I was not able to come to any definite conclusion, when the chapters were written to which this is a Supplement, as to what Pushan was to the Vedic Poets. And Dr. Muir, after comparing all the texts, confesses a like inability. He says:

> It will appear that the character of this God is not very distinctly defined, and that it is difficult to declare positively what province of Nature or of physical action he is designed to represent.

It will assist us in the inquiry, first to determine, if it is possible to do so, what he cannot be.

The God who conducts men over roads, and protects men while journeying, driving away the wolf, the waylayer, the thief and robber; who makes paths easy to traverse, and leads people over them to a country of rich pastures; who carries a spear of gold and a goad with leather-thongs, for driving cattle; who follows the kine and protects horses, and compels hospitality to the wayfarer; who brings the cattle home safe, and drives them back to the owner when they are lost; who has braided hair and is drawn by goats; who is a skilful charioteer, and drives the golden wheel of the sun through the clouds, who moves onward, beholding all creatures, and with his golden ships that sail across the ocean of the air acts as the messenger of the sun, desiring food and subdued by love; and whom, vigourous and rapid, the Devas gave to Sûrya; who and Soma hide the hated darkness, and impel the chariot with seven wheels, that is not all-pervading, that revolves in all directions, is yoked by the intellect, and shines with seven rays; who abides in the sky and moves onward beholding the universe; this being is not "a province of Nature or of physical action."

He is either a potency or particular energy of Indra, or he is a luminary. He is a radiant Deity. Indra and he are invoked together; Indra drinks the Soma, and Pushan desires meal and butter. Indra seeks to slay his enemies in company with him, his friend. When Indra brought great rains, Pushan was with him: and they together bring prosperity.

It might seem from this association that Pushan, like Indra, was a subsistence of Agni, some quality or potency of fire, personified. But no potency or energy so personified, moves onward, i. e., revolves, looking down upon the earth and its creatures, or is a messenger of the sun, or lord of roads, guide and protector of travelers, and restorer of strayed cattle.

That he is the fulfiller of prayers, and the inciter of Sages, promoter of sacrifices, impeller of chariot-horses, a Ṛishi friendly to men, and a protecting friend of the wise man, the unshaken friend, born of old, of every suppliant, may consist with either character.

I think that he must be a luminary. He is called the lover of his sister, and the Poet addresses the husband of his mother; and he is the brother of Indra. Whether these relationships can be explained is very doubtful.

The functions ascribed to Pushan at once remind us of the Deity whom the Greeks called *Hermes* and the Latins *Mercurius*. Cicero says that there were five of this name, the first of whom was the son of *Cælus* and *Lux*, of the sky and the light. The planet Mercury is so close an attendant upon the sun as to be almost always within the sphere of his radiance, and therefore seldom visible. The Mercury of the Poets was the son of Zeus or Jupiter, by Maia, one and the most luminous of the Pleiades, daughter of Atlas and Pleione, one of the Oceanides, who had twelve children, which became the Pleiades and Hyades. Atlas, one of the Titans, was said to have been King of Mauritania, master of a thousand herds, and to have been changed into a mountain, running east and west across the deserts of Africa, and so high that the heavens were said to rest on its summit. According to Appolodorus, his mother's name was Asia. Others say that Hesperis was the wife of Atlas and mother of the Atlantides.

Mercury was the messenger of the Gods, and especially of Jupiter, as Pushan was of the sun. He was the patron of travelers, as Pushan was, and of shepherds. He conducted the souls of the dead, another function ascribed to Pushan. He was the patron of orators and merchants, and also the protector of thieves, pickpockets and other dishonest persons, and when just born, stole and drove away the oxen of Admetus, which Apollo tended: and was made not only the messenger, but the interpreter and cup-bearer of Zeus, who presented him with a winged cap called *petasus*, and wings for the feet, called *talaria*. He bore also a short sword called *herpe*. He invented the lyre with seven strings, and gave it to Apollo, receiving in exchange the celebrated *caduceus*, with which the latter had driven the herds of Admetus.

He was called Cyllenius, Trikephalos, Agoneus, and by other names. In Bœotia he was worshipped under the name of Kriophoros, and is represented carrying a ram on his shoulders. Offerings of milk and honey were made to him, because he was the God of eloquence.

The *caduceus*, originally something by which cattle were driven, became at last a rod, entwined at one end by two serpents, in the form of two equal semicircles. It is said to have been originally a herald's staff, an olive stick, with garlands upon it, which were changed into serpents.

Hermes was supposed to effect the universal fecundation, in the spring, when the celestial ram opened the year, by communicating the solar influences to the moon, which, vivifying the germs deposited in her bosom, produced all living creatures.

By Penelope he was the father of Pan; and this paternity sufficiently designates him as the God of flocks and herds and pasture-grounds, whence he received the characteristic epithet of *Nomios*, pasturer, feeder, distributor, administrator. At Tanagra, in Bœotia he had two temples, one dedicated to him as *Kriophóros*, ram-bearer (from κριός, "a ram;" as "horned," from κέρας, "a horn"); the other as *Promachos*, defender, champion. It is said that to win Penelope, he assumed the form of a *goat* (*Lucian, Dial. Deorum*). So his son, Pan, is said to have seduced the moon, taking the shape of a white *ram*.

From the *caduceus*, a rod of gold (*rabdos*) he was called *chrusorrapis* (χρυσόῤῥαπις) "having the rod of gold;" *rabdos* meaning a stick, twig, rod, staff, etc. This epithet is found in the Homeric hymn to Vesta and Hermes, in lines 8 and 13. Lines 7, 8 and 9 are:

> Καὶ σύ μοι, 'Αργειφόντα, Διὸς καὶ Μαιάδος υἱέ,
> Ἄγγελε τῶν μακάρων, Χρυσόῤῥαπι, δῶτορ ἐάων.
> Ναίετε Σώματα καλά, φιλα φρεσὶν 'αλλήλοισιν.

Which Chapman translates

> And thou that of the adorned-with-all-delights
> Art the most useful Angel, born a God
> Of Jove and Maia, of Heaven's golden rod
> The sole Sustainer, and hast power to bless
> With all good all men, great Argicides,
> Inhabit all good houses, seeing no wants
> Of mutual minds' love in the inhabitants.

So in Rig-Veda *vi.* 58. 1, Pushan is implored that his gifts may be beneficent, as Mercury in Homer is *dōtŏr eaōn*, giver of good things. He is borne by goats, guardian of cattle, lord of a house overflowing with plenty, and messenger of the sun: he follows the kine and protects the horses. He compels hospitality to the wayfarer, piercing the hearts of niggards, penetrating them with the prayer-stimulating goad.

In the Hymn to Hermes, Apollo says to Mercury:

> I'll make thee
> Amongst the Gods of glorious degree,
> Guide of men's ways and theirs;

and when Hermes had given Apollo the lyre, he placed in the hand of Hermes to be his own, *a shining goad*, and put the oxen in his charge;

> And gave again a *goad*, whose bright head cast
> Beams like the light forth;

the rod, which became the *caduceus* not being given until afterwards. Not it, but the *mastix phæinos*, the shining goad, is the goad of Pushan.

He is also *nuktos opōpētēra*, the watchman of the night, and *pulēdŏkŏn*, the guardian of doors. He assists at the birth of all beings, even of the Gods, and is entrusted with the conduct of souls to the infernal regions. He is the bringer of dreams, also (ἡγήτωρ ὀνείρων). He presides over the principal relations of men with one another, in matters of commerce and business; and he shows the road to travelers, and guides and escorts them.

Before the invention of the telescope, Mercury was visible only when near the sun, and for a short time after his setting or before his rising. But Mercury was very early discovered by the observers of the ancient nations, to be a planet; and to them perhaps the most striking phenomena of the planetary motions were the limited deviations of this planet and Venus from the sun. There is no doubt that the movements of all the planets, as soon as they were discovered, were attentively observed and studied. The Morning Star first attracted attention, and it was adored, by the name of Mitra or Mithra, before the separation of the Irano-Aryan and Indo-Aryan branches of the race. And there was no reason why Mercury should not have been discovered by the Aryan observers, as he was discovered by the Chaldæans; for the atmosphere is peculiarly clear at Bokhara and Samarcand and few vapours dim the sky near the horizon, the consequence being that even small stars can be seen when only two or three degrees above it.

Mercury is alternately visible and invisible. After being invisible for several days, he will be seen to emerge from the light about the setting sun, and will then daily recede from it, toward the southeastern side of the horizon till the deviation is equal to that which has been observed on the eastern side of the horizon. Then it returns to the West, is again concealed for some days in the solar light, then re-appears before sunrise in the east, and the phenomena are repeated in the same order as before. Venus follows the same law, except that her deviations are twice as great as those of Mercury. Macrobius seems to say that the ancient Egyptians supposed that Mercury and Venus moved round the sun (*in Sorun. Scip. Lib. i. Cap. xix.*). He gives their reasoning thus:

> *Circulus, perquem Sol discurvit à Mercurió circulo ut inferior ambitur, illum quoque Superior Cuculus Veneris includit: atque ita fit ut hæ duæ stellæ cùm per superiores circulorum Vertices curvunt, intelligantur supra solem locatæ: cùm verò per inferiora commeant circulorum; sol eis superior æstimetur*, etc.

And Copernicus said that Martianus Capella and some others of the Latins, *existimant enim quod Venus et Mercurius circumervant Solem in medio existentem;* and gave the reason assigned by them why these planets could not go to a greater distance from the sun.

Cicero calls Mercury and Venus *comites Solis*, because they never go beyond a given distance from him.

Mercury never appears at a greater distance from the sun than 28° 48′, and seldom so far: and where the twilight is long, he can rarely be seen with the naked eye. Copernicus is said to have lamented, on his deathbed, that he had never seen it; and Delambre, a great French astronomer, saw it but twice.

I think there can be no doubt of the identity of Pushan and Mercury; and if there is none, the interesting consequence follows, that the planet Mercury had been observed and known to be a planet in close and intimate connection with the sun, before the emigration from the cradle of the Aryan race, of the Grecian branch of it, and of course long before the separation of the Indo- and Irano-Aryan branches.

How his peculiar functions, of guarding houses, enforcing hospitality, caring for cattle, and guiding and protecting travelers came to be ascribed to him, will probably never be discovered. It may be that the cause was his association with particular stars, when visible in the morning or evening. Nor can we account for his connection, or that of Hermes, with goats or a ram.

His close association with Indra is explained by his being most of the time within the bright radiance of the sun. So, rising at times a little before the sun, he was called his skilful charioteer.

In *vi*. 58. 1, which Dr. Muir reads,

> one of thine (appearances) is bright, the other is venerable; thy two periods are diverse: thou art like the sky,

alludes, I have no doubt, to this planet being alternately visible and concealed. The original is,

> *Çukram̃ te anyad yajatam̃ te anyad vishûrûpe ahanî dyaur ivâsi.*

If this has any meaning at all, the translation cannot be correct. *Dhyam̃ jinvo*, in the next line, is rendered by Dr. Muir, "inspirer of the soul." *Dhyai* means "to contemplate, think of, meditate on;" and *jinv* is "to further, to help." *Bhuvane viçve arpitaḥ* he translates "abiding within the whole creation." I do not find *arpitaḥ* in Benfey. *Rap* means "to speak" and "to praise" (Vedic). Is not *arpitaḥ* the past participle passive of it, and the meaning "praised in or throughout all the creation"? And does not *dhyam jinvo* mean "furthering contemplation, or meditation"?

The Greek Hermes was the God of persuasion by eloquence, and the suggester of shrewd devices and cunning plans. Moreover, he was considered as the institutor of divine worship, and the first sacrificer.

Pushan is the nourisher and dispenser of food, blessings, prosperity; and one of the epithets of Hermes (*Iliad, xx.* 34. 72) is εριούνης, εριούνιος, "beneficent, greatly useful or profitable." So he is called (*Iliad, xvi.* 185: *Oduss. xxiv.* 10), 'ακακητα, "doer of no harm;" and elsewhere, κερδωος, "astute," and σῶκος, "preserver, averter of danger, benefactor, protector, prosperer, giver of health;" ποικιλομητης, "of varied counsels;" σοφος, "wise;" and he was the minister, the messenger, and the herald of the Gods.

Pushan is said to have grasped *ashtrâm çithirâm*, which Dr. Muir translates "his relaxed goad." I do not see how a goad could be "relaxed;" nor do I find *çithira* in Benfey. *Çithila* is "loose, flaccid, feeble, languid, ineffective, relaxed," etc. *Ço* and *çi* mean "to sharpen." May not *çithera* be an adjective, formed from *çi* with the suffix *ira* and the mute *th* interposed?

Pushan is a protector or multiplier of cattle; and Hermes took charge of those of Admetus: each carries the ox-goad; each is a solar Deity, and accompanying the sun, aids in the revolutions of day and night. Pushan is called *kapardin*, *kaparda* being supposed to mean "braided hair." If that is its meaning, it is simply absurd. The derivation of *kapardin* is unknown. *Kaparda* means a small shell, a cowrie. *Kapata* is the half of a folding-door. *Kaparda* was probably the name of a cap or bonnet, as the *petasus* worn by Mercury was a closely fitting cap, with a broad flap, and so called from πεταω, "expand, spread out," which may have been the meaning of the root from which *kapata* and *kaparda* came.

As Mercury was called "wise," so Pushan is called *purandhi*, "wise," and *mantumat*, "wise in counsel," and *viçvavedas*, "knowing all things."

In *x.* 17. 5 and 6, it is said:

> Pushan knows all these regions: may he conduct us in perfect security; blessing, glowing, all-heroic, may he go before us, watchful and understanding. Pushan was born to move on distant paths, on the far road of the sky and the far road of the expanse. He goes to and returns from both the beloved abodes.

In Rig-Veda *i.* 23. 13 and 14,

> the glowing Pushan is prayed to bring hither, like a lost beast, the supporter of the sky, who is surrounded by brilliant grass; and said to have found the king so designated, who had been concealed.

"Surrounded by brilliant grass" represents *chitrabarhisham* of the original text. *Chitra* means "visible, clear, shining, variegated, various, fluctuating, wonderful." *Barha* and *varha* is "a peacock's tail;" and the compound *chitra-barha*, Benfey says, means "having a variegated peacock's tail." It is a prayer to Mercury to rise, and bring with him Indra, the light, glowing and radiant with all the colours of the rainbow. Roth understands *chitra-barhis* to mean "having glittering straw," or, "having around him straw in the form of jewels;" and Benfey, Dr. Muir says, thinks that Soma is intended, and renders the word by "reposing on a rich covering." Dr. Muir thinks that the reference is obscure. If Benfey is right, in his Dictionary, the word means "radiant with many colours, like a peacock's tail."

In *i.* 23. 8, the other Devas are styled *Pûsharâti*, which Dr. Muir translates into "bestowers of Pushan's gifts" or "having Pushan as their chief giver." *Râti* is "gift, present," but I do not see how either of those meanings could belong to the compound. It is more probable that the latter part of it should be *rati*, without the accent, and that the whole means "fond of Pushan."

The origin of the Greek legend, that Hermes on the very day of his birth stole the oxen that Apollo tended, is to be found in his habitancy among the rays of the sun, and in the fact that one and the same word in Sanskrit means "cattle" and "rays of light." One is at a loss to understand how rays of light could have been compared to a herd of bulls, and the same word *go* have meant both; and I do not believe that this double meaning of the plural of *go* came from any supposed resemblance between them. The bull was the symbol of virile potency or the generative power; and of the words that mean the semen virile, *çukra* meant light, also; and *hiraṇa* and *hiraṇya*, gold, the synonym of light: and in the Kabbala the light that flows from the Deity is the life-producing seed. It is probable that the rays of the sun were called *go*, as being the impregnating effluences of the sun.

That Apollo became reconciled to Hermes, and consented that he should remain in charge of the cattle, and transferred to him his golden and shining goad, meant that he permitted him to remain amid his rays. And from this legend of his theft of the cattle came, no doubt, the idea that he was the patron and protector of thieves; while in the Veda he protects the traveler against the waylayer, the thief, the robber and the wolf, whom the light scares away from the roads.

The wisdom and beneficence ascribed to Pushan naturally seemed to belong to one who dwelt almost continually in the very bosom of that light which was the effluence of the highest Deity conceived of by the Aryans. And thus it naturally came that the Greek Hermes was regarded as the Divine Word, in which resided the creative potency of the Deity, and the Divine Intellect.

We are not left in doubt of the ascription of functions, energies and potencies to the Greek Hermes and Latin Mercurius, of the same kind and degree as those ascribed to Pushan; and Cæsar tells us that similar potencies were imputed to Mercury by the Gauls. The name Mercury was given to the metal quicksilver, "living silver," because it represented the divine spirit in men.

We know the *fact*, and we know that there were sufficient reasons for ascribing these energies to that planet, although these reasons may not now be discoverable. The Vedic Poets were as rational and sharp-witted as we are, thought as coherently, and their imagination, though vivid, quick, and somewhat extravagant, was not the imagination of delirium. There were fitness, consistency, appositeness and *logical* appositeness in their ideas; which will continually become more manifest to us, in proportion as we succeed in identifying ourselves with them, and in thinking as they thought, divesting ourselves for the time of all ideas which they had not, and, as it were, of all knowledge which they did not possess. To understand them, we must look at so much of the universe only as we can see, look at it with their eyes, think it to be what they thought it, know only what they knew of it, and conceive of no other Divinity than that of light and fire.

Considering this planet as nearest of all to the source of light, and as the agent, herald and messenger of the sun, with whose rays his mingled and united; and light being the very life of men, the cause of all production, the cause of all reality, that whereby men are enabled to travel and to labour, to avoid dangers and find their cattle that have strayed, there is nothing in the hymns to Pushan which it was not natural for a Poet to say.

A very modern writer thus personifies Spring:

> Spring, with dainty foot and ankle, steps lightly over the golden line that parts the seasons. She shivers a little, glancing backward at the snow and ice and the big black rains, then smiles ahead at the soft air full of a filtered gold, the singing of birds, the fragrance of flowers, and the aroma of the new-mown hay.

If we found this in Sanskrit, in the Veda, it would be thought that the ancient Aryans worshipped Spring as a Goddess; and nothing in the descriptions of Indra as a warrior or Sarasvati as a girl would be considered more fancifully extravagant. And in the same spirit and no other, many of the Vedic hymns were composed. Neither were they all hymns of worship and adoration, but many of them simply imaginative poems, in which only the Poet's thick-coming fancies were expressed, without any intermingling of devotion. I doubt if these Poets really worshipped the winds and rivers, any more than the Poet Wordsworth did. Yet the line between the mere poem and the devotional hymn may often be difficult and often impossible, to trace. The following hymn (*i.* 42. 1.) is in form the expression of adoration and prayer, but certainly for the most part merely a poem:

> Conduct us, Pushan, over the road! remove trouble, offspring of the emancipator! Beneficent Deva, lead us on! Smite away from our path the destructive and injurious wolf, which lies in wait for us. Drive away from our path the way-

layer, the thief, the robber. Tread with thy foot upon the burning weapon of that treacherous wretch, whoever he may be. O wonder-working and wise Pushan, we desire that thy assistance, wherewith thou didst favour our fathers. Bringer of all blessings, distinguished by thy golden spear, make wealth easy of acquisition by us. Lead us past our antagonists; make our roads easy to travel on; acquire strength for us here. Lead us over a country of rich pastures; let there be no new hindrance in our way. Bestow, satisfy, grant, fill our stomach. We do not wrong Pushan. We praise him with hymns; we ask the helper for wealth.

In *i*. 23, there are several verses, in two of which Pushan is named, which seem to me to have been totally misunderstood:

13. Resplendent and moving Pushan, bring from heaven the (Soma) juice, in combination with the variegated sacred grass, as an animal that was lost.

So Professor Wilson reads it. Dr. Muir says that in it

the glowing Pushan is prayed to bring hither, like a lost beast, the supporter of the sky, who is surrounded by brilliant grass.

The original of the verse is:

â Pushan chitrabarhisham âghṛiṇe dharuṇam̃ divah âja nashṭam̃ yathâ paçum.

I return to this text, to consider it with those that follow it. Dr. Muir translates *dharuṇam̃ divah* by "supporter of the sky;" Professor Wilson by "from heaven the (Soma) juice." I do not see whence the meaning of "juice" is obtained for it. Benfey has not *dharuṇa;* but *dharaṇa*, i. e., *dhṛi*+*ana*, "preserving, supporting, support;" *dhṛi*, "to bear, carry, maintain, support, retain, have and keep."

Verse 14 is,

Pushâ râjânam âghṛiṇir apagûlham guhâ hitam avindach chitrabarhisham.

This Wilson translates into

The resplendent Pushan has found the royal (*Soma* juice), although concealed, hidden in a secret place, strewed amongst the sacred grass.

The meaning ascribed to it by Dr. Muir is that Pushan had "found the King so designated, who had been concealed."

The former of these verses seems to me to invoke the radiant Pushan to bring up the maintainer of the sky, many-coloured as a peacock's tail, who has strayed away and is lost, like an animal. And in the latter, Pushan is said to have found this King (either Indra or the sun), the many-coloured, hidden away and shut up in a secret place, the "royal juice" and the "variegated sacred grass," amongst which the *juice* was found "*strewed*," are fair specimens of Brahmanic nonsense.

15. Verily he has brought to me successively the six, connected with the drops, as repeatedly ploughs for barley.

16. Mothers (*ambayah*), to us, who are desirous of sacrificing, the kindred flow by the paths, qualifying the milk with sweetness.

17. May those waters which are contiguous to the sun, and those with which the sun is associated, be propitious to our rite.

18. I invoke the divine waters [waters from the sky], in which our cattle drink: offer oblations to the streams.

And the remaining verses praise the waters as medicinal and purifying.

I have no doubt that the meaning of Verse 15 is, that Pushan brings in due succession, at the same time annually, the six Pleiades, to whom the spring-rains are owing, or whom these accompany, at the season of ploughing for the sowing of grain. In 16, *ambayah* may mean, Wilson says, either "mothers," or "waters." *Amba* means "a mother," and *ambu*, "water." *Ambara* means "sky," *ambudhi*, "ocean." *Ambu* is, Benfey says, akin to *ambhas*, which means "water." I incline to believe that the Pleiades were not called "mothers," and that the word means "waters." If so, the verse should be read,

For us who desire to sacrifice, the kindred waters flow by the paths [along the routes on which we drive our cattle, pasturing them], making rich and sweet their milk; and the waters contiguous to the sun, and with which he is associated, are the rains.

THE AÇVINAU.

Dr. Muir (V. Sec. *xv.*) says that the Açvins seem to have been a puzzle even to the oldest Indian commentators. But so were nearly all the Vedic Deities. He quotes as follows, from Yaska in the Nirukta:

> Next in order are the Deities whose sphere is the sky: of these the Açvinau are the first to arrive. They are called *Açvinau* because they pervade (*vyaçnuvâte*) everything, the one with moisture, the other with light. Aurṇabhâva says they are called *Açvinau* from the horses (*açvaiḥ*), on which they ride. Who, then, are these *Açvinau?* Heaven and Earth, some say; Day and Night, others say; and others the Sun and Moon. The legendary writers say, two Kings, performers of holy acts. Their time is subsequent to midnight, whilst the manifestation of light is delayed, and ends with the rising of the sun. The dark portion denotes the intermediate (God), the light portion, Aditya (the sun).

Professor Goldstücker reads the latter portion of this differently, and does not think, with Roth, that Yaska identifies the Açvins with Indra and the sun. This is his version:

> Their time is after the (latter) half of the night, when the (space's) becoming light is resisted (by darkness); for the middlemost Açvin (between darkness and light) shares in darkness, whilst (the other) who is of a solar nature (Aditya) shares in light.

And he quotes Durga, the commentator on Yaska, who so interprets the passage.

On which one cannot help remarking that if scholars so disagree as to the reading of a simple passage in Sanskrit, found in an author comparatively modern, there cannot be any great certainty as to the interpretation of very much of the Veda.

Professor Roth, also, as quoted by Dr. Muir, says:

> The two Açvins, though, like the ancient interpreters of the Veda, we are by no means agreed as to the conception of their character, hold, nevertheless, a perfectly distinct position in the entire body of the Vedic Deities of light. They are the earliest bringers of light in the morning-sky, who in their chariot hasten onward before the dawn, and prepare the way for her.

Rig-Veda *i.* 181. 4, is,

> Born here and there, these two have striven forward with spotless bodies, according to their respective characters. One of you, a conqueror and a sage [is the son] of the strong one; and the other is borne onward, the son of the sky.

The Açvins are in several places called *divo napâtâ*, "sons of the sky;" and in *i.* 46. 2, *Sindhumâtâra*, "whose mother is the river, or sea." Their sister is mentioned, also, by whom the commentator understands Ushas: and they are in many parts of the Rig-Veda connected with Sûryâ, the youthful daughter of the sun, called also, in one place, *Urjânî*, as Sayana understands it, *Sûryasya duhita*, who is represented as having, for the sake of acquiring friends, chosen them for her two husbands.

What this wife of the Açvins was or represented, or what the wives of Indra, Agni, Varuṇa and other of the Deities were or represented, no one even endeavours to guess.

In *i.* 116. 17, it is said,

> The daughter of the Sun (*Duhitâ Sûryasya*) stood upon your chariot, attaining first the goal as if with a race-horse. All the Devas regarded this with approbation in their hearts (saying), Ye O Nasatyas, are in alliance with good fortune.

But in *x.* 85. 9, it is said,

> Soma was the wooer, the Açvins were the two friends of the bridegroom, when Savitṛi gave to her husband Sûryâ (fem.), consenting in her mind. When ye came, Açvins, to the marriage procession of Sûryâ, to make inquiries, all the Devas approved, and Pushan, as a son, chose you for his parents.

In *vi.* 58. 4, the Gods are said to have given Pushan to Sûryâ.

It may be that these spouses of the various Deities were stars that occupied particular positions, at particular times, probably about sunrise, with reference to the sun and planets, so as to seem to be in conjunction with one or the other. I do not believe that they were merely imaginary beings; and I have a very strong impression that Sûryâ was Sirius. Hevelius states that on the morning of the 2nd of October, 1661, he saw Sirius with the naked eye, when the sun had already ascended above the horizon. The meridian of Sirius passes through the middle degrees of Gemini, and therefore, when the equinoctial colure intersected the sign of the Two Horsemen, and the year opened at their heliacal rising, Sirius rose with them, and was the daughter of the sun. This is the explanation of that star, then deemed a female, having selected the Two Horsemen for her husbands; and in the later passage, of their being the friends of Pushan (Mercury), the bridegroom, when the moon gave the star Sûryâ to her husband Sûryâ, the sun, to rise with him and Mercury at the Vernal Equinox.

The Açvins are described as coming from afar, from the sky or lower part of the expanse, as being in or arriving from, different unknown quarters, above or below, far or near, and among different races of men, because during part of the year they are not seen. Therefore the worshipper sometimes inquires as to their locality, and in one place they are said to have three stations. They are said to yoke their horses to their car at early dawn, and descend to the earth, because the ceremonies were held at the Vernal Equinox, when their rising announced the coming of the dawn, twenty-five hundred years before the stars of the Celestial Bull opened the year.

Thus, in *vii.* 67. 2, it is said,

> Agni [the sacrificial fire] being kindled has shone upon us; even the furthest ends of the darkness have been seen; the light that precedes Ushas, the daughter of the sky, has been perceived, springing up for illuminating. Now, Açvins, the Poet invokes you with his hymns.

In *viii.* 5. 1:

> When the rosy-hued dawn, though far away, gleams as if she were near at hand, she spreads the light in all directions. Ye, wonder-working Açvins, like men, follow after Ushas in your car, which is yoked by your will, and shines afar.
>
> *x.* 39, 12. Come, Açvins, with that car swifter than thought, which the Ṛibhus fashioned for you, at the yoking of which the daughter of the sky is born, and day and night become propitious to the worshipper.
>
> *x.* 61, 4. When the dark stands among the dark-red rays, I invoke you, Açvins, sons of the sky (*divo napâtâv Açvinâ*).

In *i.* 34. 10, Savitṛi is said to set their shining car in motion before the dawn.

Dr. Muir accounts for the enthusiastic worship of which these Deities were the object, by saying that "the reason may have been that they were hailed as the precursors of returning day, after the darkness and dangers of the night." The truer reason was that, when their worship commenced, their rising with the sun announced the coming of spring; to which coincidence twenty-five centuries afterwards the worship of the Bull was owing, and still twenty-five centuries after the heliacal rising of the Bull at the Vernal Equinox, the Ram or Lamb took the place of the Bull, about the beginning of our era.

Among the many epithets applied to the Açvins are, "honey-hued," "of a golden brilliance," "fleet as thought," "swift as young falcons," "many-formed," "mighty," "of wondrous powers," "profound in wisdom," etc. Their car is in all its parts golden, is three-wheeled, and triple in other respects, of which I have spoken before. It is drawn by birds, or by horses like birds, swift-winged, golden-winged, falcon-like, swan-like.

Their close connection is shown by their being compared to many twin objects, among which are two eyes, two hands, two feet, two ears, two lips, breasts, nostrils, and two wings of the same bird. Why they are asked to move three times by night and three times by day, to bestow nourishment thrice, at evening and at dawn, to bestow riches thrice, and the devotions of the worshippers thrice, etc., is not so easy to explain. All this is connected, no doubt, with the three wheels, fellies, supports, etc., of their chariot.

They place the productive germs in all creatures, and generate fire, water and trees; because they announced the opening of spring; and for the same reason they were connected with marriage, procreation and love. They are said to have restored the Sage Chyanâna to youth, and to have renewed the youth of Kali. They brought to the youthful Vimada (a Ṛishi) a bride named Kamadyû; restored Vishṇâpû, like a lost animal, to the sight of Viçvaka, son of Kṛishṇa, their worshipper; and intervened in favour of Bhujyu, son of Tugra, as is described enigmatically in *i.* 116. 117 and 182. Abandoned by his father in the water-cloud, in the sea, and clinging to a log amid the waves, Bhujyu invoked the Açvins, and they rescued him, conveying him to a place of safety in animated water-tight ships, that traversed the air, three days and three nights in three flying cars, with a hundred feet and six horses, on a ship propelled by a hundred oars, with their headlong flying horses, with their well-yoked chariot, swift as thought; in an animated, winged boat, in four ships, when he was sunk in bottomless darkness.

When Viçpatâ's leg had been cut off in battle, the Açvins supplied her with an iron one. They restored sight to Rijrâçva, who had been blinded by his father, for slaughtering one hundred and one sheep, and giving them to a she-wolf to eat, she having supplicated them in behalf of her blind benefactor. They restored to sight and the power of walking Parâvṛij, who was blind and lame; drew up the Ṛishi Rebha out of the waters, delivered Vandana from some calamity, and restored him to the light of the sun, bestowed wisdom on their worshipper Kakshîvat, and caused a hundred jars of wine and honied liquor to flow forth from the hoof of their horse, as from a sieve. They assisted the Sage Atri Saptavadhri, when plunged into a gloomy and burning abyss; which act of beneficence is, in *x.* 80. 3, attributed to Agni. They gave the wise Vadhrimati a son called Hiraṇyahasta (hand of gold); Vadhrimati meaning "modest-spoken." They gave a husband to Ghoshâ when she was growing old in her father's house; caused Sayu's cow, that had ceased bearing, to give milk; gave Pedu a horse animated by Indra, which conquered all his enemies; and rescued from the jaws of a wolf a quail by which they were invoked.

Benfey, Dr. Kuhn and Müller think that these deliverances refer to certain physical phenomena with which the Açvins were connected. They sound very much more like tales composed for children: and Dr. Muir thinks this allegorical method of interpretation unlikely to be correct, and that the Ṛishis merely referred to certain legends then popularly current. Most of these legends are in *i.* 112 to 119; and in these are recitals of succours rendered to numerous other persons.

As to the names, *rebha* is from *rebh*, "to sound, to praise," whence *rebhaṇa*, "the lowing of kine;" *vandana*, "praise, prayer, worship;" *paravrij* "humbled, miserable, an outcast;" several are names of Ṛishis; and the rest have no meanings that help to explain the legends.

The Açvins are connected with Indra, in *x*. 73. 4, and in one place are said to ride in his car. At other times they accompany Vayu, the Adityas or the Ṛibhus, or participate in the strides of Vishṇu. They accompany Vayu and Vishṇu, because they are manifestations of Indra and Agni. They accompany the Adityas, because these are the planets, which are often near the Twins. The Ṛibhus are Sages transferred to the sky, and become stars,—the three, probably in the belt of Orion.

In *i*. 181. 2, the Açvins are styled *Indratamâ* and *Maruttamâ*. Dr. Muir gives to *tamâ* the sense of "possessing strongly the qualities of." In *x*. 131. 4 and 5, they assist Indra in his conflict with the Asura Namuchi, and are styled *vṛitrahantamâ*, in *viii*. 8. 22, "vigourous, slayers of Vṛitra or of enemies,"—Dr. Muir here giving *tamâ* the sense of "vigourous."

They are worshipped with uplifted hands, and supplicated for a variety of blessings, for long life, deliverance from calamities, offspring, wealth, victory, destruction of enemies, preservation of the worshippers, their houses and cattle; and are exhorted to overwhelm and destroy the niggard who offers no oblations, and to create light (bring on the daylight) for the priest or Poet who chants their praises.

Professor Goldstücker, in a note with which he favoured Dr. Muir, says:

> It would appear, then, that these Açvins, like the Ṛibhus, were originally renowned mortals, who, in the course of time, were translated into the companionship of the Gods; and it may be a matter of importance to investigate whether, besides this *à priori* view, there are further grounds of a linguistic or grammatical character for assuming that the hymns containing the legends relating to these human Açvins are posterior or otherwise to those descriptive of the cosmical Gods of the same name. The luminous character of the latter can scarcely be matter of doubt . . . . Their very name, it would seem, settles this point, since *açva*, the horse, literally 'the pervader,' is always the symbol of the luminous Deities. The difficulty, however, is to determine their position amongst these Deities, and to harmonize with it the other myths connected with them.

Always the same vague babble!

Yaska's opinion, he says, is that the Açvins represent "*the transition* from darkness to light, which the intermingling of both produces that inseparable duality expressed by the twin nature of those Deities." And this interpretation, he thinks, is the best that can be given of the character of the *cosmical* Açvins. Vivasvat, he thinks, "implies the firmament expanding to the sight through the approaching light;" and Saraṇyu "the moving air, or the dark and cool air, heated, and therefore set in motion, by the approach of the rising sun." Sûryâ, he thinks, is "the representative of the weakest manifestation of the sun;" and the sister of the Açvins, Ushas, the dawn. And he concludes by saying that

> the mysterious phenomena of the intermingling of darkness, which is no longer complete night, and of light which is not yet dawn, seems to agree with all these conceptions.

It certainly does not agree with the *texts*, at least a score of which are utterly inconsistent with this thin and unsubstantial notion that the two horsemen of the sky represent the "*transition*" from darkness to light.

Professor Müller, commenting on the passage in the Tenth Book of the Rig-Veda, in which the Açvins are said to be children (twins) of Vivasvaṭ and Saraṇyu, says:

> The idea of twin powers is one of the most fertile ideas in ancient mythology. Many of the most striking phenomena of Nature were comprehended by the ancients under that form, and were spoken of in their mystic phraseology as brother and sister, husband and wife, father and mother. The Vedic pantheon particularly is full of Deities which are always introduced in the dual, and they all find their explanation in the palpable dualism of Nature, day and night, dawn and gloaming, morning and evening, summer and winter, sun and moon, light and darkness, heaven and earth. All these are dualistic or correlative conceptions. The two are conceived as one, or belonging to each other; nay, they sometimes share the same name.

Life and death, good and evil, health and sickness, motion and fixedness, and any other two opposites, would be "correlative conceptions": but it could hardly be said that they are "conceived of as one, as belonging to each other." We find, Professor Müller says, *Ushâsânaktâ*, dawn and night; *naktoshâsâ*, night and dawn, and also *Ushâsau*, the two dawns, i. e., dawn and night. He instances also *Dyâvâpṛithivi*, heaven and earth (sky and expanse); *Pṛithivîdyâvâ*, earth and heaven, and also *Dyâvâ*, etc.; and says that *Dyu* and *Pṛithivî* are spoken of, in *i.* 159. 4, as sisters, as twins, as living in the same house, etc.

The Açvins, he says, are always spoken of in the dual. A sufficient reason for that is, that they were but two in number.

> The same conception [he thinks], underlies their name, and the names of the sun and dawn, when addressed as horses. The sun was looked upon as a racer, so was the dawn, though in a less degree; and so were, again, the two powers which seemed incorporated in the coming and going of each day and each night, and which were represented as the chief actors in all the events of the diurnal play.

He admits that this character of the two Açvins is "somewhat vague," but *for this very reason*, all the more correct. And yet, only two or three pages before, he had asked whether it was possible to form a clear conception of Saraṇyû, "of such a being," as described by Roth and Kuhn.

The Açvins are called *ihehajâtau*, "born here and there," i. e., as Professor Müller thinks, "on opposite sides," or "in the air and in the sky." One is *jishṇu*, "victorious," he who bides in the air; the other is *subhaga*, "happy," "the son of Dyu or the sky, and here identified with Aditya or the Sun." *Jishṇu* means "overpowering, excelling, victorious," and *subhaga*, "splendid, beautiful, or happy." *Jatau* in the compound, does not necessarily mean "born." It may mean merely "being." And the explanation of the whole of this, and of one of the Açvins being in the sky and one in the air, is, that when Castor rises, Pollux, being due east of it, remains for some time below the horizon, so that one is "here," in the visible world, and one "there," i. e., somewhere else. Castor is the more exalted or higher, and Pollux, beautiful, though not yet seen. When they approach the meridian, one is due south of the other, Castor being above.

Professor Müller quotes,

> Wake the two who harness their car in the morning. Açvins, come hither!

and

> Sacrifice early, hail the Açvins; not in the dreary evening is the sacrifice of the Gods;

and yet says that Yaska rightly placed the activity of one of the Açvins at the very beginning of day, and hence that of the other at the very beginning of night. If we remove the mask, he says, we find behind it

> Nature in her two-fold aspect of daily change—morning and evening, light and darkness—aspects which may expand into those of spring and winter, life and death, nay, even of good and evil.

Indra and Agni are addressed together in the dual, *Indrâgnî*, but likewise as *Indrâ*, the two Indras, and *Agnî*, the two Agnis. Of this, Müller says,

> Indra is the God of the bright sky, Agni the God of fire, and they have each their own distinct personality; but when invoked together, they become correlative powers, and are conceived as one joint Deity.

In one passage they are actually called *Açvinâ*, and share several other attributes in common with the Açvins. They are called brothers and twins, and, when invoked together *ihehamâtarâ*, "they whose mothers are here and there." But still it must not be supposed, he says,

> that Indra and Agni together are a mere repetition of the Açvins. There are certain epithets constantly applied to each of them that are not applied to the other, and certain legends told of the Açvins, that are not transferred to Indra and Agni. But Indra coincides in some of his exploits with one of the Açvins or Nasatyas, as is shown by the compound *Indra-Nasatyau*.

It seems strange that Professor Müller could have come so near the truth, without opening his eyes to see it. But nothing blinds a man like a theory. Just so he persists in considering Mitra and Varuṇa to be day and night. It is even more singular that he should have so utterly mistaken the character of the Açvins, when he quotes a hymn in which he says that the dual character of "these Indian Dioscuroi" clearly appears. It is a wonder that he never asked himself if the Dioscuroi (Castor and Pollux) and the Açvins were not the same. Nor is this so singular as his adherence to his theory that one was morning or dawn, and the other evening or the gloaming, while reciting the words of Hymn *ii*. 39. For by it the Açvins are declared to be like the two stones used for the single purpose of grinding the Soma; like two hawks rushing towards the same nest; like two priests reciting one prayer together; like twin goats, like husband and wife; two heroes on their chariots, two horns on one head, two hoofs, two birds, two ships, yokes, naves of one wheel, spokes, felloes; like two eyes, hands and feet, hips, breasts, nostrils and ears, of one body.

Śayaṇa explains the name or epithet *dasra*, often applied to them or to one of them, as signifying "destroyers of enemies," or "of diseases," or "beautiful." Roth understands it to mean "wonder-workers." In one place, *Indrâ-Vishṇû* are called *dasrâ*. *Nâsatyâ*, another epithet commonly applied to the Açvins, is regarded by Sayaṇa as equivalent to *satya*, "truthful." It is only in the later literature that these are regarded as the separate names of these Deities. One of the Vedic Poets uses the compound *Indra-Nâsatyau*, which, Müller says,

> on account of the dual that follows, cannot be explained as Indra and the two Açvins, but simply as Indra and Nasatya;

which is to say that it is the name of one of them. But I imagine that its meaning is, Indra as, or manifested as and by, the two Açvins.

Nothing, it seems, is really known as to the meaning of *dasra*. Benfey gives as its meaning, "helping?" but without even a conjecture as to its derivation. *Das* means "to become exhausted;" *dasyu*, "a ruffian;" *dâç*, "to worship, make oblations, bestow;" and *dâ*, "to give." In Greek δὰς means "a torch or light," from δαιω, "burn;" and an old root *daṁc* or *daṁs* in Sanskrit meant "to speak or shine." The Latin verb *do* "give," had an old infinitive, *dasi*.

Benfey gives us *nâsatya*, i. e., *na*+*a*+*satya*, without meaning, merely as a name. *Nâça* is "disappearance," from *naç*, "to disappear, be lost, go away, perish." And I think there is good reason for believing that, as Castor rises before Pollux, and when rising not long before the sunrise, must have been visible when Pollux did not rise soon enough to be seen at all, and at least was often visible before Pollux had risen; and as, on the other hand, at certain seasons and for some days in succession, Castor was visible after Pollux had set, or when the latter had not been seen at all, *dasra* meant "the one that is seen or shines," and *nâsatya*, "the one that has disappeared, or perished." Hence the Greek legend of their alternation of life and death. *Nâsatya*, it may be added is from the verb *as*, with the *a* of negation and privation prefixed; but this verb was, probably, not *as*, "to be," but *as*=*ash* and *ush*, "to burn, to shine."

The two names will thus mean "shining" and "not shining," or "visible" and "invisible."

I cannot see any reason to doubt the identity of the Açvins and the Grecian *Dioscouroi*, the Θεοὶ Σωτῆρες, or "mighty helpers of men," the Ἄνακες or Ἀνα κοὶ, kings, the Ἱπποδαμοι, "tamers or controllers, of horses." Yaska says that the legendary writers called them "The two *kings*, performers of holy rites."

A few passages in regard to the Açvins, in addition to those already noticed, deserve a moment's consideration, as some do that have alrêady been quoted, for various reasons.

Verses 1, 2 and 3, of *i.* 3, deserve notice, if only for their ingenious perversions of meaning in the translation. In that of Professor Wilson, they read as follows:

> 1. Açvins, cherishers of pious acts, long-armed (*purubhujâ*), accept with outstretched hands the sacrificial viands.

"Pious acts" are not acts of piety as part of individual conduct and conversation; but acts, ceremonial performance, of worship or devotion. These the Açvins encourage, by appearing in the east, at the time of the sacrifice, i. e., at daybreak. *Purubhujâ* may also be rendered, Professor Wilson says, "great eaters."

Puru means "much, many, exceeding, very exceedingly." *Bhujâ* means "the arm, hand;" *bhuj*, "to bend, to make crooked," and "to eat and drink, enjoy, endure, govern, possess;" *bhuji*, "fire." Evidently it is very doubtful whether *purubhujâ* means "long-armed;" and yet, if these stars were to receive the sacrificial food with outstretched hands, they may have been imagined to have long arms.

> 2. Açvins, abounding in mighty acts, guides, endowed with fortitude, listen with unaverted minds to our praises.

Many great deeds are elsewhere ascribed to the Açvins; they were guides, perhaps, because they rose in advance of the dawn; and as they were horsemen and warriors, it was natural to ascribe to them courage.

3. Açvins, destroyers of foes (*dasra*), exempt from untruth. . . . .

I have already inquired as to the meaning of *dasra*. "Exempt from untruth" means that they never fail to appear, and thus, as it were, break their promise and prove false and faithless.

In *i.* 34 is a succession of enigmas. It rings, to use Professor Wilson's expression, a variety of changes on the number 3. Some of these changes are:

> Açvins, be present with us thrice today. Three are the solid wheels of your abundance-bearing chariot, three are the columns set for support, and in it you journey thrice by night and thrice by day. Thrice in one day you repair the faults; thrice today sprinkle the oblation; and thrice, evening and morning, grant us food.

They are asked to visit the worshippers, grant favours, give food, and riches, come to the rite, preserve intellects, etc., thrice. They are to be thrice worshipped, day by day, and are asked to repose on the triple of sacred grass, to repair from afar to the three-fold, to come thrice with the seven mother-streams, for the three rivers, the triple oblation prepared.

The key to the enigma is the reference to the three daily sacrifices, at morning, noon and evening, to each of which ye Açvins are invited to come, and each time to grant favours and dispense blessings. Here the Deities seem, like the Grecian Twins, to assume human attributes and to become deified men, capable of leaving the stars, and of journeying where and when these do not. But I am not satisfied about the *trivṛito rathasya*, the three-wheeled carriage with its three supports. As to the powerful ass, *râsabha*, although it no doubt means an ass, I do not believe it originally meant that, as used in connection with the Açvins. *Bha* means "a star, a lunar asterism, a planet," and is a modern name of the planet Venus. *Bhâ* is "light, splendour" and "the sun"; and, as a verb, "to shine, to appear." *Rasa* means "to roar, sing," and probably "to bray"; but also a verb of the same letters means "to taste, to love," being probably a denominative from *rasa*, "taste, pleasure, charm, love, affection, passion, juice, essence, the essential juice of the body, the semen virile."

So in the Greek, *lúkē* meant "light," and *lúkos*, "a wolf and the sun," and one of the names of Apollo was *lúkeios*.

The hymns to the Açvins were certainly recited or chanted, before daybreak, and at a time of the year when their rising a little way preceded the dawn. It is probable that there was a regular festival, each year, at that time, and that new hymns were produced at each, while the old ones were occasionally repeated. Those to Pushan were no doubt composed on the various occasions when Mercury was visible before sunrise at the same time. And it seems also that with the exception of the Great Bear, the stars adored as Devas were those of Taurus, Gemini, Orion and others in their vicinity; for which only one reason can be rationally imagined—that they all rose towards morning, at the Vernal Equinox.

In *i*. 46. 14, it is said to the Açvins,

> May Ushas follow the radiance of your approach, revolving Açvins. [And, in *i*. 47, 7 and 9]: Nâsatyas, whether you are abiding far off or near at hand, come to us, in your well-constructed car, with the rays of the sun . . . . Come Nâsatyas, in your sun-clad chariot.

From which it is evident that the hymn was composed when the stars of Gemini rose heliacally, i. e., when the sun was in that Sign at the Vernal Equinox.

In *i*. 119. 2, *Ûrjâni* is said to have ascended the car of the Açvins. *Ûrj* means "strength, food"; *ûrja*, "strength"; and the verb *urj*, "to nourish, strengthen." In the preceding verse, the worshipper, desiring food, to support life, invokes the wonderful car of the Açvins, swift as thought, drawn by fleet horses, many-bannered, and bringing rain. Upon its moving, the voices of the worshippers are raised in praise; their hymns ascend, and the sacrifice begins. Evidently this was early in the morning at the time of the rising of the twins, at the season when rains were expected, and when they would fertilize the ground and cause production. That is what we learn from the ascent of *Ûrjâni*, that power of Nature, which feeds, nourishes, strengthens and sustains life, *production* or *growth*, the *Parendi* of the *Zend-Avesta*, into the car of the Açvins, in which, generally Sûryâ, daughter of the sun, *splendour* or *radiance*, rides, whose two husbands the Açvins are styled, in *ii*. 31. 4.

SMITHSONIAN INSTITUTION:
Washington: August 25, 1873.

Times of rising of certain stars, reckoned in apparent solar time, at the epoch of the Vernal Equinoxes of the years B.C. 2500 and B.C. 5000.

	B.C. 2500			B.C. 5000		
	Lat. +30°	Lat. +35°	Lat. +40°	Lat. +30°	Lat. +35°	Lat. +40°
The Sun	6.00	6.00	6.00	6.00	6.00	6.00
Pleiades	5.40	5.39	5.37	4.05	4.10	4.16
Hyades	6.44	6.45	6.46	5.09	5.17	5.27
Belt of Orion	8.33	8.40	8.48	7.03	7.19	7.38
Capella	5.21	5.04	4.46	3.54	3.44	3.38
Sirius	10.20	10.31	10.45	9.12	9.32	9.56
Castor	7.38	7.22	7.05	6.00	5.52	5.44
Pollux	8.04	7.51	7.36	6.24	6.18	6.11

The Sun was within the limits of the constellation Gemini, at the Vernal Equinox, from the year B.C. 6800, till the year B.C. 4700.

(Prepared by Professor William Harkness, at the request of the Smithsonian Institution, for Albert Pike.)

TVASHṬṚI.

The original meaning of *Tvashṭṛi*, as that potency of fire which softens and melts metals, was of a character to be speedily lost sight of; and this potency being personified at the very beginning as a worker in metals (the prototype of Hephaistos or Vulcan), whatever befitted the character of a most skilful smith and artificer was ascribed to him. This is especially the case in the later hymns. In *x*. 53. 9, he sharpens the axe of iron of Brahmaṇaspati (prayer); and in the earliest hymns forges the thunderbolts of Indra. We need not be surprised at this particular quality or potency of fire becoming anything or doing anything, when prayer, because believed to be the efficient instrument that won victories for the Aryans, and therefore poetically represented as a warrior, got itself at last armed with a battle-axe. Even in the earlier poems, the original character and meaning of Tvashṭṛi were much lost sight of; but enough remains whereby to detect them and be sure of them.

He is styled, in Mandalas *i*. and *iii*., *supâṇi*, *sugabhasti* (the bountiful- or skilful-handed; *gabhasti* meaning "an arm, a ray of light"); *svapas*, *sukṛit*, "the skilful worker"; *viçvarupa*, "omniform, taking all forms," also an epithet of Vishṇu (Heat); and Savitṛi, the generator; and he imparts generative power and bestows offspring; either because he is confounded with the heat that melts and softens, and thence with the vital heat, or because he gives form to that which is generated and conceived. I think it is the latter, because in *i*. 188. 9, he develops the seminal germ in the womb, and is the shaper of all forms, human and animal, in that and other passages.

This was the earlier idea. At first fabricator, as worker in metals, he became the maker of all forms, the fashioner, and thence the generator. In *iii*. 55. 19, *iv*. 42. 3, and *x*. 110. 9, he is said to have produced and nourished a great variety of creatures, that all beings are his, and known to him, and that he has given their forms to the sky and expanse and all things else. In *ii*. 23. 17, he is said to be skilled in all Sama-texts, and to have made Brahmaṇaspati above all creatures. In *x*. 2. 7, and *x*. 46. 9, he is said, along with heaven and Pṛithivi, the waters and the Bhṛigus, to have generated the fire. He is master of creation (*bhuvanasya sakshaṇi*), in *ii*. 31. 4; and in *ix*. 5. 9, a first-born protector and leader. He knows, i. e., frequents, the region of the Devas, is a companion of the Angirasas (as the heat which effects the sacrifice), and is supplicated to nourish the worshipper and protect his sacrifice. He is *draviṇodos*, "giver of wealth or strength," and *suratna*, "having abundant wealth."

He is thus the heat, of which he was originally but a single one of the potencies, and all these expressions, attributing to him the same powers and qualities as are ascribed to Vishṇu, are but the figurative representations of the powers and benefits and effects of heat.

In several passages he is connected with the Ṛibhus, who also are represented as skilful workmen, that fashioned Indra's chariot and horses, and made their own parents young.

I find still no explanation of the making by the Ṛibhus of a single new sacrificial cup that Tvashṭṛi had fabricated: nor do I find with any certainty what the Ṛibhus were, or what their name means. It is said that this exhibition of skill by the Ṛibhus was performed by the command of the Devas, and in consequence of a promise that they should be transferred to the sky; and Tvashṭṛi is represented as having hidden himself among the Goddesses, ashamed, when he saw the work of the Ṛibhus, and as having sought to slay them. But in another place he is said to have praised them and admired their work. In *x*. 66. 10, the Ṛibhus are called the happy supporters of the sky.

That Tvashṭṛi was originally a potency of Agni appears from the identification of Agni with him, in *ii*. 1. 5. And in *i*. 95. 5, Agni appears to be designated by the word Tvashṭṛi. As to the name itself it is from *twaksh*, "to produce, to work." This is Benfey's derivation of the name. Also, *twish* and *twesh* meant "to shine, light, and splendour."

In *x*. 17 we have an account of the giving in marriage by Tvashṭṛi of his daughter Saraṇyû to Vivasvaṭ (the Vivaṅhao of the *Zend-Avesta*, first teacher of the Ahurian faith, and father of Yima). According to Dr. Muir, this is the legend:

> Tvashṭṛi makes a wedding for his daughter. (Hearing) this, the whole world (*viçvam bhuvanam*) assembles. The mother of Yama, the wedded (*paryuhyamânâ*) wife of the great Vivasvaṭ, disappeared. They concealed the immortal from mortals. Making one of like form, they gave her to Vivasvaṭ. Saraṇyû bore the two Açvini, and when she had done so, she deserted the two twins.

Upon the face of these verses, it is uncertain whether Saraṇyû was the first or second wife; whether she was the daughter of Tvashṭṛi or the mother of Yama, or the one who disappeared. It is profitless to repeat the legends of the Nirukta and Bṛihaddevatâ, invented ages afterwards, to explain this legend, by those totally ignorant of its real meaning.

Benfey gives us *sarayu* (from vb. *sri*, "to flow, blow") as meaning "air, wind"; and *saraṇyu* (vb. *sṛi+ana+ya+u*) as "air, wind, water, a cloud." Heat produces wind, which may be said to be its daughter; but how did wind or air produce the Açvinî, and desert them?

Vivasvat, i. e., *vi+vas-vant*, is given by Benfey as meaning "the sun." *Vi* means "a bird, the eye, heaven, the sky, the region of the wind." *Vas* means "to dwell, live, shine, wear." *Yama* means "a twin," and in the dual, "twins." It also means "restraining, taming," etc., and is the name of a Deity, and of the planet Saturn. *Yam* means "to tame, restrain, govern" (horses), etc. But the original here is *Yamasya Mâtâ*, "Mother of Yama," *Yamasya* being the genitive singular.

I cannot make "wedded" out of *paryuhyamânâ*. Benfey gives *paryukshaṇa*, "sprinkling"; *paryupâsaka*, "one who honours"; *paryupâsana*, "honouring somebody," and *paryupâsitṛi*, "one who honours"; and makes the former part of each compound to be *pari*, "round, about, against, to, over, from, out, except, after, full, quite, excessively." *Yamânâ* I do not find. *Yamânâ* is *Yama*, and "restraining, binding, cessation." Why Benfey so often picks out two or three compounds, gives them a place, and omits others quite as much entitled to respect one fails to see, and is the more provoked at it as capricious.

It is to be said, also, and apropos of *paryuhyamânâ*, that one is continually compelled to wonder how the compound obtains from its components the sense imputed to it, and need only read a few of Sayana's preposterous interpretations of single words, to be convinced that there must be a vast deal of guessing in all the translations. As to the particles, they are generally ignored.

It is reasonably clear, I think, from the text itself that Saraṇyû was the daughter of Tvashṭṛi; and that it was she who disappeared, and who bore the Açvini and deserted them. *Yama* means "a pair" as well as "a twin," and it and *yamânâ* in *paryuhyamânâ* may refer to the Açvini.

At all events, we may be able to discover the original idea out of which the legend grew. A people living in a land overlooked by immense mountains, could not but know that the clouds were composed of the same kind of vapour as that which rose from boiling water; for when they ascended the mountains they would often pass through the clouds. Tvashṭṛi, the heat, producing the steam by boiling, was the father of Saraṇyû, the cloud. Married to the sun, imbued with his light, and glowing as with the ardour of passion, under the influence of his rays, the soft clouds of the morning sky melt away and disappear as he rises; and this hymn may have been composed when the twin horsemen of the constellation Gemini, rising before the sun, seemed to be born of the soft cloud through whose rifts they shone, when these glowed with the light of the yet unrisen sun.

In *viii.* 26. 21 and 22, Vayu, the flame, is said to be the son-in-law of Tvashṭṛi. The flame of the sun upon the cloud may be meant by Vayu, or the flame of the sacrificial fire, causing the steam from the Soma juice thrown into the fire, to become invisible.

Tvashṭṛi is represented as having for his most frequent attendants the wives of the Devas, which, according to Professor Roth results from the fact that his creative energy is chiefly manifested in the wombs of females.

In *x*. 49. 10, Indra is said to place in the rivers a lucid element, which Tvashṭṛi, though a Deva, could not do: for heat, without light, cannot illuminate; in *iii*. 48. 4, it is said, Indra overcame Tvashṭṛi, carried off his Soma juice, which he drank from the cups; and in *iv*. 18. 3, that Indra drank off the Soma in the house of Tvashṭṛi. The fire is the house or abode of the heat, and when the Soma juice is poured upon the fire, it does not remain there to be consumed, but rises in clouds of vapour, which, seized on by the flames becomes invisible and seems to be consumed by the light.

> This Trita Aptya, being skilled in the use of the weapons of his father, incited by Indra, fought against the three-headed and seven-rayed (*triçîrshaṇaṁ saptaraçmim*), and, slaying him, carried off the cows even of the multiform son of Tvashṭṛi. Indra, the lord of the good, pierced this arrogant being, who boasted of his strength; seizing the cows, he struck off the three heads even of the omniform son of Tvashṭṛi (*x*. 8. 8).

(See also *ii*. 11. 19.) And in *x*. 99. 6, a loud-shouting monster with three heads and six eyes is mentioned as overcome by Trita.

Trita is not explained by Benfey, but merely given as a name. Evidently it means a triad, perhaps fire, flame and light, as one. *Âptya* is not in Benfey. The only word resembling it is *âpti*, "acquisition." *Âp* means "to attain, incur, obtain;" whence *âpta*, "fit, trusted, near, a friend, large"; *vyâpta*, "that which has inherent properties." The gerund of *âp* would be *âptya*. This word, also, may perhaps be *ap*+*tya*, *ap* meaning "water," and *tya* being the base, "he, this or that." *Apatya* means "offspring, child."

In the verses quoted above, Trita first, and then Indra, slays Viçvarupa, or the omniform. They must therefore either be the same, or Indra must be one of the Triad. Fire, light and flame are three in one, and as Indra is light, Trita must be this triad. I do not see how he could be called "son of the waters." The son of Tvashṭṛi or heat is something produced by heat, without flame or light. What can this be but smoke, which ascending in volumes from a fire of wood just kindled, assumes a thousand shapes as it eddies upward, and is blown to and fro by the wind? The struggle of the incipient blaze, fanned by the wind, with the heavy masses of smoke from the green wood would naturally suggest the idea of a contest for the mastery; and the final overcoming by the clear flame and brilliant light, leaping up and causing the smoke to cease and disappear, hailed with joy by the worshipper or wet and chilled traveler, would be considered a victory of Indra and the slaying of an enemy of most unwelcome presence, from whom no one, on any side of a fire in the open air can escape. The three heads, six eyes and seven rays were the additions of a later age.

SARAṆYÛ

In the legend of Saraṇyû we find, probably, the origin of that of Ixion, who became enamoured of Juno, and instead of her, met a cloud formed by Jupiter in the shape of Juno, and embracing it begat the Centaurs, part man and part horse.

Professor Müller says (*Science of Language, 2nd Series*), that where *Saraṇyû* is used as a masculine, its meaning is by no means clear. He says,

> In the sixty-first hymn of the tenth book, it is almost impossible to find a continuous thread of thought. The verse in which Saraṇyû occurs is addressed to the Kings Mitra and Varuṇa, and it is said there that Saraṇyû went to them in search of the cows.

If Saraṇyû was the vapour that, rising as a cloud becomes invisible, the meaning here may be that this vapour ascends towards Mitra and Varuṇa, to unite itself with the clouds in the sky. In the next verse, Müller says, Saraṇyû is called a horse, just as Saraṇyû (fem.) is spoken of as a mare; but he is called the son of him, i. e., according to Sayaṇa, of Varuṇa. In *iii.* 32. 5, Indra is said to cause the waters to come forth, together with the Saraṇyus (mists or fogs?), who are here mentioned, Müller says, very much like the Angiras in other places, as helpers of Indra in the great battle against Vṛitra or Vala. In *i.* 62. 4, the common epithets of the Angiras (*navagva* and *daçagva*) are applied to the Saraṇyus; and there, too, Indra is said to have torn Vala asunder with the Saraṇyus. I believe, therefore, we must distinguish between the *Saraṇyus* in the plural, a name of like import as that of the *Angiras*, possibly as that of the *Maruts*, and *Saraṇyû*, in the singular, a name of the son of Varuṇa or of Yama.

The Angiras were a family of Ṛishis, whose ancestor or ancestors had been translated, as some expressions indicate, to the sky as stars. It does not seem to me that the word *Saraṇyû* is of like import. It means a somewhat that *goes* or *moves*, as *Vala*, whom Indra shatters, is a whirlwind or cyclone, a somewhat that *whirls*.

The "explanations" of Yaska and Çaunaka, quoted by Professor Müller, I pass by. He says that it is difficult to say how much of the legends that they repeat is old and genuine, and how much was invented afterwards, to explain certain mythological phrases occurring in the Rig-Veda. I think they are wholly of the latter class, so far as they are additions to what is found in the Rig-Veda. And even what is found in the Tenth Book, is not to be depended upon as of like antiquity with the contents of the books that precede it.

Professor Müller remarks that Professor Kuhn has identified *Saraṇyû* with the Greek *Erinys;* in which identification he agrees, but only as to the name, adhering to his own view as to *Saraṇyû*, entertained from the first. Professor Kuhn, he says, adopting in the main the views of Roth, explains the myth as follows:

> Tvashtar, the Creator, prepares the wedding for his daughter Saraṇyû, i. e., the fleet, impetuous, dark storm-cloud, which in the beginning of all things soared in space. He gives to her as husband Vivasvaṭ, the brilliant, the light of the celestial heights,—according to later views, which, for the sake of other analogies, I cannot share, the Sun-God himself. Light and cloudy darkness beget two couples of twins: first, Yama, i. e., the twin, and Yamî, the twin sister (a word which suggests itself); secondly, the two Açvins, the horsemen. But after this the mother disappears, i. e., the chaotic, storm-shaken dimness; the Gods hide her, and she leaves behind two couples. To Vivasvaṭ there remains, as his wife, but one like her, an anonymous woman, not further to be defined.

Upon which Müller says:

> Was this the original conception of the myth? Was Saraṇyû the storm-cloud which in the beginning of all things was soaring in infinite space? Is it possible to form a clear conception of such a being, as described by Professor Roth and Professor Kuhn? And if not, how is the original idea of Saraṇyû to be discovered?

If no interpretation of the character and meaning of a Vedic Deity is to be accepted, that does not give us a clear conception of him or her, so far as the guesses of commentators go, the number of those Deities of whom we are entitled to say that we know anything, becomes very small.

Professor Müller thinks that there is but one way for discovering the original meaning of Saraṇyû; namely,

> to find out whether the attributes and acts peculiar to Saraṇyû are ever ascribed to other Deities whose nature is less obscure.

But, unfortunately, this community of attributes and functions, between two or half a score of Deities, is an impediment, too often, to the discovery of the peculiar and especial functions of each. Tvashṭṛi has many, common to himself and other Deities, but none of these assist us to ascertain that in the latter part of the Vedic period, he had usurped upon Vishṇu, and become heat, of which at first he was but one function, that of changing the forms of things, by the power of melting, softening and sublimating to vapour. But wherever a Deity is spoken of in many texts, some epithet will be found applied to him, some action or mode of action imputed to him, which suits his peculiar and especial character alone: and thus Tvashṭṛi was not originally called "the begetter," or invested with any of the functions or attributes of light; but he was the artificer, the forger of the thunderbolt, and *viçvarûpa*, "the omniform or maker of all forms." And if he was ever called, in the earlier Vedic period, *Savitâ*, as he is in *x.* 10. 5, that epithet meant "maker and artificer," and not "begetter or creator."

Ushas also, Professor Müller says, is said in *iii.* 39. 3, to have borne twins, who assume form, the conquerors of darkness, who have come at the foot of the sun. When the two stars Castor and Pollux rose at the opening of the dawn, they were naturally said to be born of that flushed and glowing eastern sky, in which they appeared.

So he says that Ushas, the dawn, is also spoken of as a horse, and as a mare and the friend of the Açvins; and

> here then [he says], we have a couple, the sun and the dawn, that might well be represented in legendary language as having assumed the form of a horse and a mare.

But, in the first place nearly every Vedic Deity has horses; and to speak of one as a horse was as warrantable in the case of many others as in that of the sun or of the dawn: and, in the second place Saraṇyû is not called a mare in the Veda, but only in the commentaries or embodied nonsense of a later age.

The conclusion of Professor Müller is, that Saraṇyû, "the running light," was a name of the dawn; and her twin children, Yamau, "the twins," were day and night, in giving whom birth the dawn dies. And he tells us that his own researches lead him again and again to the dawn and the sun as the chief burden of the myths of the Aryan race. He says,

> The whole theogony and philosophy of the ancient world centered in the dawn, the mother of the bright Gods, of the sun in his various aspects, of the morn, the day, the spring; herself the brilliant image and visage of immortality.

Again he says:

> I look upon the sunrise and sunset, on the daily return of day and night, on the battle between light and darkness, on the whole solar drama in all its details, that is acted every day, every month, every year, in heaven and in earth, as the principal subject of early mythology. I consider that the very idea of divine powers sprang from the wonderment with which the forefathers of the Aryan family stared at the bright (*Deva*) powers that came and went, no one knew whence or whither, that never failed, never faded, never died, and were called immortal, i. e., unfading, as compared with the feeble and decaying race of man. I consider the regular recurrence of phenomena an almost indispensable condition of their being raised through the charms of mythological phraseology, to the rank of immortals, and I give a proportionately small space to meteorological phenomena, such as clouds, thunder and lightning, which, although creating for a time a violent commotion in Nature, and in the heart of man, would not be ranked together with the immortal bright beings, but would rather be classed either as their subjects or their enemies. It is the sky that gathers the clouds, it is the sky that thunders, it is the sky that

> rains; and the battle that takes place between the dark clouds and the bright sun, which for a time is covered by them, is but an irregular repetition of that more momentous struggle which takes place every day between the darkness of the night and the refreshing light of the morning.

Professor Kuhn and other eminent men in Germany maintain the opposite theory, holding that clouds, storms, rains, lightning and thunder were the spectacles that above all others impressed the imaginations of the early Aryans; that they viewed the coming and going of the celestial luminaries without wonder or emotion; but could not so view the meteoric changes, so lawless and mysterious, so exceptional and apparently out of the regular course of things, that wrought such immediate and palpable effects, for good or ill, on the lives and fortunes of the beholder. And Professor Schwartz thinks that

> originally, the sun was conceived of implicitly as a mere accident in the heavenly scenery, and assumed importance only in a more advanced state in the contemplation of Nature and the formation of myths.

And Professor Kuhn, taking Saraṇyū as the storm-cloud, and Vivasvaṭ as one of the many names of the sun, considers Yama to be their first-born son, and to mean Agni, the fire, or rather the lightning, followed by his twin-sister, the thunder: and the second couple, the Açvins, he considers to be Agni and Indra, the God of the fire and the God of the bright sky; and solves the myth thus:

> After the storm is over, and the darkness which hid the single cloud has vanished, Savitar (the sun) embraces once more the Goddess, the cloud, who had assumed the shape of a horse running away. He shines, still hidden, fiery and with golden arm, and thus begets Agni, fire; he lastly tears the wedding-veil, and Indra, the blue sky, is born.

Professor Müller, though placing himself in their point of view, cannot grasp any clear or connected train of thoughts in the mythological process which they describe, nor conceive of men standing on a level with English shepherds, talking in that fashion.

> However [with great modesty he adds], it is not for me to pronounce an opinion, and I must leave it to others, less wedded to particular theories, to find out which interpretation is more natural, more in accordance with the scattered indications of the ancient hymns of the Veda, and more consonant with what we know of the spirit of the most primitive ages of man.

It is clearly impossible to defend the theory of Professor Kuhn. Agni and Indra were never imagined to be the Açvins, or children of Saraṇyū, whatever she was. The most superficial reading of the Veda proves *that*.

The latter part of the text in question (*x.* 17. 2) seems to me to repeat the former part, and Yama, the twin, mentioned in the former, to be one of the Açvins or the pair of Açvins mentioned in the latter.

But it seems also to me that Professor Müller makes the dawn and the alternations of day and night play by far too great a part, in the Vedic mythology. It is always to be remembered that very much of what we consider mythological and religious in these Vedic writings or compositions, was simply poetry, in which the composer laboured to invent and express poetical fancies and imaginings in appropriate language. Personification was, of course, his chief resource. There is little of the poetry of mere description in the early compositions of any people. No poetry could be composed about light and fire, metaphysically expressing the philosophical ideas in regard to them. The field of the Poet was among visible objects. The sun and other luminaries of the sky, the dawn, the Morning Star heralding it, the winds, offered the most inviting, the most available and natural subjects of song. He could personify Indra, the light, as a warrior hurling the thunderbolt into the bosoms of the clouds, in order to restore the reign of light, and praise the Soma and prayer: but the phenomena of Nature would most commonly occupy his thoughts. But none of the theogony or philosophy of the Vedic world centered in the dawn, the sun or the seasons.

I do not think that the sky has ever been accepted by any people as a Deity. It and the earth, alike, I think, have been personified by the Poets alone. I do not believe that Ouranos and Gaia ever were Gods to the Greeks, or Cœlum and Terra to the Latins. The sky was as fixed, solid and immovable, to them, and as little of a sentient being, as the ground under their feet was.

As to the "wonderment" with which they regarded the phenomena of dawn, and the battle, daily, between darkness and light, I am quite sure that the latter idea never presented itself to them. Nothing is less like a battle or an angry struggle, than the peaceful, gentle, soft and silent coming of a lovely dawn, after a spring or summer or autumn night.

And as to the former, I imagine that they no more wondered at the sky and its phenomena, than ordinary children do. All that is regular in Nature excites no wonder. The unlettered herdsmen and even the Bards and Priests of those days, looked upon everything within the range of their vision as a red Indian does. The rising of the sun gladdened them, of course, for all men love the day and its light; but it never excited even curiosity. I have been much among both civilized and wild tribes of Indians, and learned from the Comanches their names for the Great Bear and some other constellations; and I never yet heard a single expression of curiosity in regard to the regular phenomena of Nature.

Every ancient people, and every uncivilized race of men have adored the sun. That, I believe, had been the earliest worship everywhere: and the Peruvians and Natchis are, in that respect, but the types of every people in its infancy. In the Vedic period, our forefathers had advanced beyond that, and though the sun and other luminaries were still adored, they were revered as manifestations of the light and fire, of Indra and Agni. The Poets sang of many beings that never were worshipped: and their laboured conceits and personifications became at a later day mythology.

And even these, I think, were by no means as vague and misty and incoherent as they are represented to be by the commentators. Delirium alone could account for some of their verses as the translations represent them to us. But, as I have said before, I believe that their conceptions and ideas were always clear, distinct and coherent; and that if they seem to us not to be so, it is only because we do not understand them.

Saraṇyû, I think, was certainly not the storm-cloud, but the soft, fleecy vapour often seen in the eastern sky at sunrise, or on the summits of the hills, and which, ever-shifting, and flushed with the changing hues, roseate, crimson and purple, which the sun's light creates, constitute the peculiar and magnificent splendour and glory of the morning; for the storm-clouds do not disappear from the sky, but retire angry and sullen, lingering long upon the horizon: and when they rise in the east in the morning, or settle down upon that horizon after sunrise, remain there, ordinarily, the sure beginnings of storm and tempest.

I only add that I do not find any sufficient evidence of the identity of Saraṇyû and the Greek Erinnus. The most that can be said is that one name possibly became the other. There is no reason, that I can see, for believing it, nor do I believe it.

When the Soma juice was thrown into a blazing fire, it made, of course, a cloud of steam, which rising a little way and then disappearing, seemed to appear again in the soft white clouds of the morning sky. The vapour and the cloud were Saraṇyû. It was the child of heat, because it equally rose from water boiled in a vessel, and not touched by the flame. And long after the older Vedic hymns had been composed, some new Poet, diligently and laboriously seeking for new conceits, hit upon that expressed in the passage on which we are commenting.

USHAS.

As Ushas is, beyond any question, the dawn, i. e., the light and glow that in the east precede the sunrise, the hymns addressed to her and the texts in which she is mentioned are chiefly valuable by the aid they afford towards understanding what is said of other Deities and avoiding misconceptions. She is *duhitâ divaḥ*, the daughter of the sky: she brings horses and cattle, and is all-bestowing; for the light that enables men to see what, if darkness were perpetual, would be as if it were not, to them, may easily be conceived of as bringing and giving that which it enables men to have and use. Like an active woman, she advances, giving strength, and arousing men and animals. She has yoked, i. e., she brings, her rays, from the remote rising-place of the sun, and advances with a hundred chariots. Everything that moves bows down before her glance (every luminary that traverses the sky fades before it). The beautiful female creates radiance. The potent daughter of the sky appearing drives away the haters of the worshippers. She brings abundant prosperity.

> In thee [says the hymn], when thou dawnest, O Beautiful, is the life and the breath of all creatures

(because they wake when her light falls upon their eyes). She is asked to hear the invocation, and to come to the Soma-offerer's house, and to protect the prosperous man with her chariot. She moves in a chariot drawn by bright and ruddy steeds; and is asked to bring all the Devas to drink the Soma.

I regard this as simply a poem; and do not believe that it was one whit more devotional than Coleridge's "Hymn to Mont Blanc." The dawn never could have been seriously conceived of as a being having knowledge, power and sympathies; and that alone which was venerated in her was the light, in which the dawn consists.

The hymn *i.* 92. 1, is even more poetical; and as one of the most interesting of the Veda, I borrow here the translation of it by Dr. Muir:

> These dawns (*Ushasaḥ*) have become conspicuous: they display their lustre in the eastern hemisphere. Like bold warriors drawing forth their weapons, the ruddy mother-cows (*gâvo arushîr mâtaraḥ*) advance. The rosy beams have flashed up spontaneously; they have yoked the self-yoked ruddy cows (*svâyujo arushîr gâḥ ayukshata*). The dawns, as heretofore, have brought us consciousness; the red cows (*arushîr*) have assumed a brilliant lustre. Like women active in their occupations, they shine from afar along a common track, bringing sustenance to the pious and liberal worshipper, and all things to the man who offers libations of Soma. Ushas, like a dancer, puts on her gay attire; she displays her bosom as a cow her udder: creating light for all the world, she has dissipated the darkness . . . . [*i.*

123. 10. Like a maiden glorying in her form, thou, Deva, advancest to meet the Deva who seeks after thee. Smiling, youthful and resplendent, thou unveilest thy bosom in front. Like a fair girl adorned by her mother, thou displayest thy body to the beholder. *i.* 124. 4. She has been beheld like the bosom of a bright maiden. Like Nodhas, she has revealed things that we love. Awaking the sleepers like an inmate of the house, she has come, the most constant of all the females who have returned. 7. As a woman who has no brother, appears in presence of a man, as a man mounted on a chariot goes forth in pursuit of wealth, as a loving wife shows herself to her husband, so does Ushas, as it were, smiling, reveal her form. *v.* 80. 5. She displays her person like a fair woman, like one rising out of the water in which she has been bathing. *vi.* 64. 2. Thou, full of brightness, displayest thy bosom, Deva, shining in thy glory.] *i.* 92. 5. Her bright ray has been perceived; it extends and pierces the black abyss. [*iv.* 51. 9. The bright lucid dawns concealing the black abyss with their radiant bodies.] The daughter of the sky has assumed a brilliant glow, like the decorations of the sacrificial post on festivals. We have crossed over this darkness [i. e., have passed through the darkness of the night]; Ushas, dawning, restores consciousness; radiant, she smiles like a flatterer seeking his own advantage: fair in her aspect, she has awakened all creatures to cheerfulness. The shining daughter of the skies, bringer of excellent songs, has been praised by the Gotamas. Ushas, thou distributest resources in offspring, men, horses and kine. Blessed Ushas, thou who, animated by strength, shinest forth with wonderful riches, may I obtain that renowned and solid wealth, which consists in stout sons, numerous slaves, and horses. Directing her eyes towards all creatures, the Deva shines before them far and wide. Rousing to activity every living thing, she notices the voice of every adorer. Born again and again, though ancient [*i.* 123. 2. The youthful, born anew has shone forth on high. *iii.* 61. 1. Thou, Devi, old, young, wise, movest at thy will], shining with an ever-uniform hue, wasting away the life of mortals, carrying it away as a clever gambler the stakes. She is perceived revealing the ends of the sky; she chases far away her sister (night). Wearing out the lives of men, the lady shines with the light of her lover [*i.* 115. 2. The sun follows the shining Devi Ushas, as a man, following, overtakes a woman. *vii.* 75. 4. Daughter of the sky, mistress of the world (*bhuvanasya patnî*), food-providing wife of the sun]. *i.* 92. 12. The bright and blessed one has widely diffused her rays, as if she were driving forth cattle in various directions, or as a river rolling down its floods; maintaining the ordinances of the Devas (*daivyâni vratâni*) she is perceived, made visible by the rays of the sun. Ushas, provider of food, bring us that brilliant fortune whereby we may possess offspring. Ushas, resplendent, awaking excellent songs, dawn richly upon us today bringing cows and horses. Yoke today, Ushas, thy ruddy steeds, and then bring us all blessings.

In *i.* 113, the sun is her child, and the night her younger sister: and inasmuch as she has been produced for the production of Savitṛi, it is said, the night has made way for Ushas. She disobeys not the settled ordinance, but comes daily to the appointed place. She yearns longingly after the former dawns, and gladly goes on shining with the others. And she is called "Mother of the Devas (*Mâtâ Devânam*), manifestation (*anikam*, face) of Aditi, and forerunner of the sacrifice."

In other hymns she is called the sister of Bhaga and kinswoman of Varuṇa. She brings the eye of the Devas (the sun) and leads up the beautiful white horse. She is called the wife of the sun; and the dawns are even said to *generate* the sun, sacrifice and Agni, because they *precede* them. So Agni is called her *lover*, and is said to appear with or before the dawn; for it is his light which is revealed by her. In one place he is represented as going to meet her as she comes, and to beg for riches; which simply means that the sacrificial fire will be kindled at the early dawn, and is to be well fed with offerings of the best.

In *vii.* 6. 5, Agni is said to have made the dawns the wives of the heroic shining one. Ushas is also often connected with the Açvini, the twin horsemen, the time of whose manifestation Yaska regards as being between midnight and sunrise; and which rose with the dawn, 5,000 years B.C. at the Vernal Equinox. They are said to "associate" with her; and she is said to be their friend (*divo duhitrâ Ushasâ sachethe*); *sach* meaning "to follow, obey, favour, honour"; according to Benfey; but also "to associate with, minister to, give counsel to, advise." *Sachi* means "friendship," and *sachiva*, "friend, companion, minister, counsellor;" and *sakhâ bhûd Açvinor Ushâḥ*, and *Uta sakhâ si Açvinoḥ—sakhâ* meaning "friend, associate, companion."

In *viii.* 9. 17, Ushas is called upon to awaken the Açvini; and in *iii.* 58. 1, her hymn is said to have awakened them. But also, in *x.* 39. 12, we are told that when the car of the Açvini is yoked, the daughter of the sky is *born*. That Ushas is the *daughter* of the sky, and *born* daily, explains how Aditi is *Mother* of the Adityas, and how Agni is *born* whenever a fire is kindled. In *x.* 85. 19, the moon is said to be born again and again, ever new, and to go before Ushas as the herald of the day.

Indra is said, in several places, to have created or lighted up Ushas. But in *ii.* 15. 6, he is said to have crushed her chariot with his thunderbolt. And in *iv.* 30 he is commended for a deed of might and manliness, in smiting Ushas, the daughter of the sky, a woman who was bent on evil, who was exalting herself. He crushed her, and she fled away in terror, from her shattered car, when he had crushed it, and it lay broken and dissolved. In *x.* 138. 5, it is said that the bright Ushas was afraid of the destructive thunderbolt of Indra, and departed, and abandoned her chariot. And in *x.* 73. 6, it is said that Indra destroyed certain foes, like the chariot of Ushas.

All of which must mean that when the sun had risen, and before his more brilliant light the rosy colours of the dawn disappear, which are the chariot of Ushas, she flees away; and this was imagined by the Poets to be an act of hostility on the part of Indra, by which, if she had not fled, she would have been annihilated.

So much we can understand: but if the radiant colours of the dawn are her chariot, how could Indra crush it with his thunderbolt? The lightning does not flash in a clear sky. How could it be said of Ushas that she was *dushaṇḍyuvaṁ*, united with evil or wickedness? That she was exalting herself might mean that, becoming more and more bright, she endeavoured to become the rival of the sunlight, and so provoked Indra to crush her chariot: but the same question presents itself, how this could be done by the thunderbolt; and how she, afraid of his destructive thunderbolt, departed and *left* her chariot, and he destroyed it as he destroys his foes?

In all this there seems to be what some writers would style a "startling" inconsistency, certainly an incoherency and incongruity and contradiction calculated to make one doubt the sanity of the poetic imagination of the Vedic Bards.

But I believe, as I have said, that when this is the case, the fault is in our interpretation, in our failing to follow faithfully the train of thought of the Poet and to comprehend his conception. Müller has a very beautiful passage, in which he describes the dawn as a beautiful maiden consumed in the too ardent embrace of her lover, his love proving more fatal to her than hate. But this is not the Vedic idea. It represents Indra as hostile to her, as launching the thunderbolt against her, because she had united herself with evil; and Dr. Muir says that the Poet,

> with the want of gallantry which was so characteristic of the ancients, does not hesitate to admire the manliness and heroism of Indra in overcoming a female.

I think there is no want of gallantry shown, either in the Veda or the *Zend-Avesta*.

If we suppose that at the first faint glancings of the dawn in summer, a heavy thundercloud rises, and by degrees thrusts up its black masses into the sky; thus forbidding the sun to pour his light upon the earth, when he shall have risen; that in this war of darkness against light, Ushas unites herself with the clouds, as the stars fade out of the sky, and flushing all their summits with her golden glories makes these glories of the clouds her chariot, we can understand how the Poet could imagine her uniting herself with the evil, the dark clouds, the enemies of Indra; and how he could be said to crush her chariot with the thunderbolt and compel her to flee in terror.

In *i.* 113. 4 and 5, it is said,

> Ushas enables those who were almost sightless to see distinctly,

and that she gives back all the regions. Illuminating the world she makes our property manifest (i. e., enables us to see it). Therefore in *v.* 7, she is called "the mistress of all earthly treasure." For what we cannot see, of material things, is to us as if it were not. The dawn restores them to us; and to be able to do that, must have them in her gift, and be mistress of them, "possessor of affluence," "source of wealth."

VAYU AND VATA.

Dr. Muir, like the other commentators, considers Vayu to be the wind, and Vata as only another name of the God of the wind.

It is said in *i.* 135, that it belongs of right to Indra and Vayu to take the first draught of the Soma; for when the liquid is poured upon or into the sacrificial fire, it is first received by the flame and the light. He is said to have sprung from the breath of *purusha* (man), because by the breath, the coals are blown into flame. He is said to be the son-in-law of Tvashṭṛi, who is said to have had a daughter Saraṇyû (air, wind); and the air or wind causes the flame of a fire to increase and become more light, and emit a more brilliant light, and this in larger quantity.

Vayu is called *darçata*, "visible," *supsara stama*, "most beautiful"; *krandad-ishti*, "rushing on with a roar." He is spoken of together with Indra, as touching the sky, swift as thought, priest or sacrificer, thousand-eyed, etc. He goes in a shining car, drawn by a pair of red or purple horses, or by many, ninety-nine, a hundred, a thousand horses. He and Indra often occupy the same chariot, i. e., there is close and intimate union between the light and the flame of fire. Their chariot has a frame-work of gold, that touches the sky, and it is drawn by a thousand horses.

It is singular, Dr. Muir says, that he is rarely connected with the Maruts or Deities of the storm. But it is not singular, if he is the *flame*, of the sacrificial or domestic or other fire. If he *were* the wind, he would be constantly spoken of in connection with the Maruts, and could not be dissevered from them or from the storms. But, Dr. Muir says,

> in one place [*i.* 134. 4] he is said to have begotten them from the rivers of heaven (*ajanayo Marutŏ vakshaṇâbhyo divaḥ â vakshaṇâbhyaḥ*); and in another place [*i.* 142. 12], to be attended by Pushan, the Maruts and the Viçve Devas (*Pûshaṇvâte Marutvâte Viçvadevâya Vâyave*).

I do not appreciate the phrase, "the *rivers* of heaven." Benfey has *vaksh* (Vedic) "to grow, to become tall," and *vakshas*, "the breast, the bosom." And what these "rivers of heaven" *are*, if the translation is correct, from which the winds are begotten, any one, I think, would be puzzled to say. *Vakshaṇâbhyo* seems to be an epithet of the Maruts. That flame produces movement of the air is a physical fact which no one can help knowing.

In *x.* 168. 1, the glory of Vata's chariot is celebrated; and its noise is said to come, rending and resounding. Touching the sky he moves onward, making all things ruddy, and he comes, sweeping the dust from the expanse. The gusts of the air rush after him, and congregate in him, as women in an assembly. Sitting along with them, on the same car, the Deva who is ruler of all the world (Indra) is borne along. Hasting forward, by paths in the atmosphere, he never rests on any day. Friend of the waters, first-born, true, in what place was he born? Whence has he sprung? Life of the Devas (*âtmâ devânâm*), source of production (*garbho*, "womb") of created beings (*bhuvanasya*), this Devaḥ moves as he pleases. His sounds have been heard, but his form is not (seen): this Vata let us worship with an oblation.

x. 186. 1. May Vata waft to us healing (medicine), salutary and giving satisfaction to the heart. May he prolong our lives. And, Vata, thou art our father, our brother and our friend: cause us to live. From the abundance of undyingness which is deposited yonder in thy house, O Vata, give us to live.

I do not see how it could be said that the wind or air was the life or vitality of the Devas, when their vitality is light; nor how, if Vata is the air, the gusts of air rush after him. How does the *air* make all the heavens red? And how is the air the source of *bhuvana*, whether that word means "the world," "heaven," or the aggregate of living creatures?

The same Deity, Vayu, is found in the *Zend-Avesta*. There also he is called by the translator "the *air* that moves on high," and yet is evidently flame. It is impossible to doubt that he is the same in the Veda. Indra and Vayu are offered unto together, in *i.* 2. 4. 5 and 6; are said there to abide in the sacrificial rite, for they are hypostases of the fire, *in* it and *of* it. In *v.* 1, Vayu is "pleasant to behold." That was never said of the *air*. In *i.* 23. 3, Indra and Vayu are said to have a thousand eyes, i. e., reveal and manifest themselves and are visible by, a thousand luminaries.

In *i.* 134. 1, Vayu is invoked to come to the sacrifice with his swift coursers, with *niyutwatâ rathena*, which Wilson translates "steed-yoked car," saying that the horses of Vayu are called *Niyuts*. It is incomprehensible that the air should have been said to yoke to his car red and purple horses; to arouse men from sleep, and summon heaven and earth, to light up the dawn, to beget the Maruts, to protect from the fear of evil spirits.

In *i.* 134. 4, 5, it is said, as Wilson translates, "*for* thee," etc. I think the "*for*" manifestly wrong, and I read,

by thee [i. e., *by means of thee*], the brilliant dawns, from afar, spread abroad their auspicious raiment (*bhadrâ Vasira*) in inviting rays (*dansu raçmishu*), in variegated and glorious rays: by thee the cow that yields ambrosia (*savardugha*) milks all kinds of treasure: . . . . for thee the bright, pure, quick-flowing, potent for exhilaration, are eager for the oblation.

And, if this were not enough, we find, in *i.* 135. 4, and elsewhere, the expressions *Vâyavâgatam; Indrascha-âgatam*, the name in the nominative *singular* being in conjunction with the verb in the *dual*, and, so implying that to name one is to name both, or that Vayu and Indra are inseparably united.

In *iv.* 46 and 47, Indra and Vayu, with a thousand steeds, ride in the same chariot, and Indra is the charioteer: and in *iv.* 48, it is repeated, that Vayu is drawn by the Niyuts and has Indra for his charioteer. He is called (as Wilson translates it)

> the represser of calumnies (*niryur vâno asastih*); and the dark nurses of wealth (*krishne vasudhitî*), the universal forms (heaven and earth), attend upon him.

"Represser of calumnies" is, Professor Wilson acknowledges, only a substitute for a blank. And "the dark nurses of wealth," and the "universal forms" are very mysterious personages.

Indra and Vayu are so commonly addressed together as to show that there is an intimate connection between them. In *vi.* 49. 4, Vayu is praised alone, as possessor of vast riches, most adorable, filler of his chariot, riding in a radiant car, and driving the Niyuts. And in verse 6 of the same hymn, Parjanya and Vata are addressed together, as showerers of rain, and asked to send from the firmament waters to be of benefit. In *vi.* 50. 12, Vishṇu and Vayu are asked to make the invoker happy, sending rain; and Ṛibhukshin and Vaja; and Parjanya and Vata are prayed unto for abundant food.

In *vii.* 5. 7, it is said to Agni:

> Born in the highest sky, thou like (as) Vayu, ever drinkest the beverage; generating the waters, thou thunderest.

By which I understand that the fire is addressed in its manifestation as flame.

In *vii.* 90. 3 and 5, Vayu is styled

> the white-complexioned dispenser of wealth, whom heaven and earth bore for the sake of riches:

and Indra and Vayu are styled "two sovereigns," to whom a hero-bearing chariot is presented: and in this hymn and 91, Indra and Vayu are several times invoked together, and said to have a common chariot; and the latter is "the white-complexioned Vayu, intelligent glorious with the Niyut steeds." In 92, he is mentioned alone and with Indra; and in *viii.* 9. 12, the Açvins ride in the same chariot with Indra, and are domiciled with Vayu.

Indra and Vayu are thus shown to be of one nature, as Agni and Indra are; and there cannot be the least doubt that Vayu is Flame.

Vâtâ is the perfect participle of *vâ*, which in Benfey means "to blow," as the wind does, "to become dry, to dry." The meaning of *Vâta* is given as "blown": and also *vâta*, as a noun, "air, wind, breeze, rheumatism, gout." *Vâti* is "air, wind, the sun, the moon." *Vâtika* is "fever, inflammation."

I think that the original meaning of *vâ* was "to dry," and that Vata was fire or heat, as producing dryness. And as the wind dries the wet ground, I think Vata came to mean "wind," as that which "dries up;" and *vâ*, "to blow," because the wind that blows does dry up moisture. In *vii*. 40. 6, "the circumambient Vata" is invoked to send rain. There it must be the air or wind.

In *vii*. 36. 8, Vaja is invoked as "the sustainer of old, the liberal of gifts," with Pushan and Bhaga: and *Ṛibhu*, *Vibhva* and *Vâja* are named as the Ṛibhus, in *i*. 161. 6; while in *vii*. 48, addressed to the Ṛibhus, we have *Ṛibukshâno Vajah* addressed, without *Vibhu* or *Vibhva*, in the first verse; and in the second, the *Ṛibhus* and *Vibhus;* and Vaja is invoked to defend in battle: while in verse 3, the invocation is to *Vibhvan*, *Ṛibukshin* and *Vaja;* the Ṛibhus thus being three in number, named respectively *Ṛibhu*, *Vibhu* or *Vibhva* and *Vaja;* and the three being called *Ṛibhus*, *Vibhus* and *Vajas*, indifferently. I shall speak of the Ṛibhus hereafter.

YAMA.

The passages in regard to Yama and the Fathers, quoted by Dr. Muir (*V. Sec. xviii.*) from the ninth and tenth books of the Rig-Veda (unknown to me until recently), prove to be of the greatest interest and value, connecting as they do with the historical account in the *Zend-Avesta*, of settlement and colonization by Yima, son of Vivanhao, identical with Yama, son of Vivasvaṭ.

When I considered the texts until lately within my reach, in regard to Yama, I was at a loss to determine what was intended and understood by him, and I offered to the reader the only conjecture that seemed to me even plausible. I leave it to stand, as an example of the difficulties of interpretation.

Dr. Muir first discusses, in the section devoted to Yama, "the references to immortality in the earlier books of the Rig-Veda." One cannot but feel greatly interested in an inquiry as to the real notions of the most ancient of the Aryan Sages, Priests and Poets, in regard to the condition of man after death, and whether they possessed clear and settled ideas of the survival of existence of the intellect, soul or spirit, and of an inherent immortality of the soul.

Dr. Muir says:

> It is in the ninth and tenth books of the Rig-Veda, that we find the most distinct and prominent references to a future life. It is true that the Ṛibhus, on account of their artistic skill, are said, in some texts in the earlier books, to have been promised, and to have attained, immortality and divine honours.

For this he refers to *i.* 161. 2, where it is said that they shall be made worshipful as Devas; and in *iv.* 35. 8,

> Ye who on account of your skill have become Devas, and sit like falcons in the sky: do ye, children of strength, give us riches: ye, O sons of *Sandhanvan* (or *Sudhanvan*) have become deathless (*abhavata amṛitâsaḥ*). [And, *v.* 3 of same], Then, skilful Vâjas, Ṛibhus (*Vâjâḥ Ṛibhavaḥ*), ye went, on the path of deathlessness (*amṛitasya panthâm̃*) to the multitude (or troop) of the stars (*gaṇam̃ devânâm*).

Sandhanvan, I think, means "the twilight," as *Sam̃dhiya* and *Sâm̃dha* do. *Ṛibhu*, i. e., *rabh+u* and *vâjâ* are epithets that do not give us any clue by which to identify the Ṛibhus with any particular stars.

> This, however [Dr. Muir continues], is a special case of deification, and would not prove that ordinary mortals were considered to survive after the termination of their earthly existence.

I think that it, and the case of the Seven Ṛishis or Sages, who became the stars of Ursa Major, distinctly prove the reverse. It is very evident that these and other favoured individuals were supposed to have become stars; and the same notion obtained among the Greeks.

> There are, however [Dr. Muir continues], a few passages which must be understood as intimating a belief in a future state of happiness. Thus Agni is said, in *i.* 31. 7, to exalt a mortal to immortality (*tvaṁ tam Agne amṛitatve uttame martaṁ dadhâsi*), and to be the guardian of immortality (*adabdho gopâḥ amṛitasya rakshitâ*).

But it is not at all certain or even likely that the Vedic Poets had any conception of existence absolutely without end. *Marta*, from *mṛi*, "to die," means "a man, a mortal": but *amṛita*, i. e., *a*+*mṛita*, did not mean "immortality." We know what its ante-Vedic signification was, from the meaning of the Zend words *amĕrĕ* and *amĕrĕtat*, in the older portions of the *Zend-Avesta*. *Amĕrĕtat* was merely "life" as the opposite or negation of "death," i. e., lengthened or protracted life. This length of days, Agni and the other Gods were implored and believed to give; and in the Gâthâs of Zarathustra, it is often spoken of as one of the results of victory, peace and security.

The same power of lengthening life, by giving good health and averting danger, was ascribed to the Soma, because it was a part of the sacrifices and when thrown into the fire became an undistinguishable portion of Agni. In *i.* 191. 1, it is said,

> By thy guidance, Soma, our wise ancestors obtained riches among the Devas.

Ratna, which Dr. Muir renders by "riches," is said by Benfey to be *ram*+*tna*, and to mean "a gem, jewel, treasure, anything the best of its kind." But *ram* means "to rest, to like to stay, to be delighted, to rejoice, to sport, etc."; so that *ratna* may have meant originally "pleasure, rest, felicity." So, in verse 18 of the same,

> *apyâyamâno amṛitâya Soma:* becoming abundant for long life, grant the most excellent wealth in the sky.

So in *i.* 125. 5 and 6, the liberal man is said to go to the Devas, and to remain permanently in the high place of the sky. This brilliancy is the portion of those who bestow largesses, they are honoured as suns in the sky; they attain *amṛita*, they prolong their lives. Here *amṛita* means good health. In *i.* 154. 5, the worshipper prays that he may attain to the dwelling of Vishṇu, where men devoted to the Devas rejoice. In *i.* 179. 6, a Ṛishi is said to have attained the object of his aspirations, among the Devas. In *v.* 4. 10, the worshipper prays to Agni, that he may attain *amṛita* ("long life"). Mitra is prayed for rain, wealth and *amṛita*. In *x*. 107. 2, the givers of largesses have abiding-places on high, in the sky; the givers of horses live with the sun; the givers of gold enjoy *amṛita*, the givers of raiment prolong their lives. In *vii*. 57,

6. *Dadâta no amṛitasya prajâyai*, Add us to the men of long life [i. e., make us such].

In *i*. 159. 2, the sky and expanse are said to bestow on their offspring long life; *uru prajâyâḥ amṛitam*. *Prajâyâḥ* means "offspring, progeny, subjects, people."

In *vii*. 86. 4, it is said,

> *Te id devanam sadhamâdaḥ âsaun ritâvânaḥ kavyaḥ pûrvyâsaḥ:* They were dwellers with the Devas, those ancient righteous Sages. [*viii*. 58. 7], When we two, Indra and I, go to the region of the sun, to our home, may we, drinking nectar, seek thrice seven in the realm of our friend. [In *viii*. 48. 3], We have drunk the Soma: we are become long-lived; we have entered into light; we have known the Devas.

In *x*. 186, Vata is declared to have a store of long life, or health, in his house. And in *x*. 95. 18, the Devas promise Purûravas, the son of Iḷâ, that though he is a mortal, yet when his offspring shall worship them, with oblations, he shall enjoy happiness in *Svarga;* said to mean Paradise. It is from *svar*, "the sun, splendour, the sky." *Svaru* is "sunshine."

I have already given the enigmatical myth of the marriage of the daughter of Tvashṭṛi, at which all the world assembled (as Dr. Muir translates *viçvam bhuvanam*, *bhuvana* meaning "being, creature," and if "world" also, the aggregate of living beings); when the mother of Yama, becoming wedded, the wife of the great Vivasvaṭ, disappeared, immortal and concealed from mortals, and another of like form was given to Vivasvaṭ, who bore the Açvins—Saraṇyû, who abandoned the twins.

Professor Müller proposes the inquiry whether *Yama*, meaning originally "twin," could ever be used by itself as the name of a Deity. We can speak, he says, of two twins, but could a single Deity or month be properly called "a twin." In the passage above quoted, the wife of Vivasvaṭ is said to have been *Yamasya mâtâ*, *Yamasya* being the genitive singular: but Benfey gives, as one meaning of *Yama*, "a pair."

The word *Yama* occurs in Rig-Veda *i*. 66. 4, which Professor Müller thus translates literally—it is addressed to Agni:

> Yama is born, Yama will be born, the lover of the girls, the husband of the wives.

But, remembering the twinship of Agni and Indra, as representatives of day and night, he translates:

> One twin is born, another twin will be born [i. e., Agni, to whom the hymn is addressed, is born, the morning has appeared; his twin, or, if you like, his other self, the evening, will be born].

Rosen translates this:

> *Sociatæ utique Agni sunt omnes res natæ, sociatæ illi sunt nasciture;* all things born are associated with Agni; all that are to be born, are associated with him.
>
> *Langlois: Jumeau du passé, jumeau de l'avenir*—twin of the past; twin of the future.
>
> *Wilson:* Agni, as Yama, is all that is born; as Yama, all that will be born.
>
> *Kuhn:* The twin (Agni) is he who is born; the twin is what is to be born.
>
> And *Benfey:* A born Lord, he rules over births.

The verse first says of Agni, that like an army let loose, he wields his force, like the flame-pointed arrow of the archer. The residue of the verse follows:

> I think that this was said at the Vernal Equinox, when the stars of Gemini rose heliacally, and their rising was waited for by the sacrificer, as announcing the coming of dawn and the opening of spring; and that when Castor rose he said, 'a twin, or, one of the twins, is born, i. e., has risen; a twin, or, the other twin, will be born, i. e., will shortly rise.'

The words "the lover of the girls, the husband of the wives," contain, Müller thinks, a mere repetition of the first hemistich. The light of the morning, or the rising sun, he thinks, is called "the lover of the girls," these "girls" being the dawns, from among whom he rises.

Thus, he says, in *i.* 152. 4, it is said,

> we see him coming forth, the lover of the girls (*kanînâm*), the unconquerable.

Sâyaṇa explains *kanînâm* by *ushasam*, dawns. *Kanyâ* means "a girl, a virgin, a daughter." *Kanîyaṁs* means "very small"; *kanishṭha*, "smallest"; *kanîyasa*, "smaller"; and there must have been an adjective *kani*, "small." *Kan* meant "to love, to be satisfied," and perhaps, "to shine." In Zend, *kainin* is "girl," and *khanha*, "sister."

In *i.* 163. 8,

> after thee the cows, after thee the host of the girls;

which are, he thinks, merely two representations of the same thing, the bright days, the smiling dawns. So in *ii.* 15. 7, "the hiding-place of the girls" is spoken of, and is, he thinks, the hiding-place of the cows, the east, the home of the ever-youthful dawns. *Jâraḥ*, "lover," is applied to the sun, in *vii*. 9. 1, and *i*. 92. 11;

> The lover woke from the lap of the dawn.
> The wife, dawn, shines with the light of the lover.

"The husband of the wives," he thinks, meant the evening sun, as surrounded by the splendours of the gloaming, as it were by a more serene repetition of the dawn. The dawn is likewise called "the wife"; but in *ix*. 86. 32, it is said of the sun,

> The husband of the wives approaches the end.

And so he makes "the lover of the girls" to be the young sun, and the husband of the wives the old sun, the girls and wives being the dawns and gloamings.

The original of *i*. 66. 4, in part, i. e., of so much as speaks of Agni as Yama, is *Yamo ha jâto yamo janitvam*. The phrase ought to have some connection with what precedes or what follows it, in the same verse. Now, the whole verse, as Wilson renders it, is:

> He (Agni) terrifies like an army sent, or like the bright-pointed shaft of an archer. Agni, as Yama, is all that is born; as Yama, all that will be born. He is the lover of maidens, the husband of wives.

As Agni is the vital heat and generative power and so *causes* and *is* concupiscence, I suppose the meaning of the last clause to be that it is he that causes love for virgins and coition with wives. And the second clause may allude to his same potency as generator of twins. At all events, it seems clear enough that *yamo* here is not a proper name.

In *i*. 152. 3 and 4 are, in Wilson,

> who knows, Mitra and Varuṇa, that it is your doing that the footless (*apad*) dawn is the precursor of footed beings, and that your infant sustains the burthen of this? He diffuses truth and disperses the falsehood. We behold the lover of the maidens, ever in movement, never resting for an instant, wearing inseparable and diffusive, the beloved abode of Mitra and Varuṇa.

Here Wilson has "the maiden (dawns)." In *i*. 163. 8, it is said,

> The car follows thee, O Horse: men attend thee, cattle follow thee; the loveliness of maidens upon thee; troops of demigods following thee have sought thy friendship; the Devas themselves have been admirers of thy vigour.

The "horse" is the sun, it is said. That seems doubtful. The whole hymn needs an interpreter, for notwithstanding all attempts at explanation it still remains an enigma. It is as follows, as translated by Wilson:

1. Thy great birth, O Horse, is to be glorified [in 162, 1, the horse sacrificed is called 'the swift horse sprung from the Devas,' *devajatasya*, whether first springing from the firmament or from the water (*samudrâd-uta va purîshât*), as to the meaning whereof I will inquire hereafter] inasmuch as thou hast neighed, for thou hast the wings of the falcon and the limbs of the deer.

2. Ṭrita harnessed the horse which was given by Yama. Indra first mounted him and Gandharba seized his reins. Vasus, you fabricated the horse from the sun.

It follows that the horse was not the sun.

3. Thou, Horse, art Yama; thou art Aditya; thou art Ṭrita by a mysterious act; thou art associated with Soma. The Sages have said there are three bindings of thee in the sky. [The original of 'three bindings' is *bandhanâni trîni.*]

4. They have said that three are thy bindings in the sky, three in the waters (*trîṇyapsu*), and three in the firmament. Thou declarest to me, Horse, who art Varuṇa, that which they have called thy most excellent birth.

5. I have beheld, Horse, these thy purifying; these impressions of the feet of thee who sharest in the sacrifice; and here thy auspicious reins, which are the protectors of the rite, that preserve it.

6. I recognize in my mind thy form afar off, going from below, by way of the sky, to the sun. I behold thy head soaring aloft, and mounting swiftly by unobstructed paths, unsullied by dust.

7. I behold thy most excellent form coming eagerly to thy food in thy place of earth; when thy attendant brings thee nigh to the enjoyment, therefore, greedy, thou devourest the fodder.

8. The car follows thee [etc., as above].

9. His name is of gold; his feet are of iron; and fleet as thought. Indra is his inferior. The Devas have come to partake of his oblation. The first who mounted the horse was Indra.

11. Thy body, Horse, is made for motion: thy mind is rapid as the wind: the hairs are tossed in manifold directions; and spread beautiful in the forests. [Here, Wilson says, 'the horse is identified with Agni, whose flames consume the forests'].

12. The swift horse approaches the place of immolation, meditating with mind intent upon the Devas: the goat bound to him is led before him; after him follow the Priests and the Singers.

13. The horse proceeds to that assembly which is most excellent; to the presence of his father and his mother. Go, today, rejoicing to the Devas, and may they grant blessings to the offerer.

Of this hymn, Professor Wilson says that, although more mystical than 162, especially in regard to the intimations of the identity of the horse with the sun, there is nothing in it incompatible with the more explicit description in the former of the actual sacrifice of a horse. And certainly the last two verses announce thc coming of an actual horse to the place of sacrifice, there to be immolated, and in the flames to ascend to the stars in the sky.

The preceding hymn describes the sacrifice of the horse "sprung from the Devas," preceded by a goat offered to Indra and Pushan. The slaughtering, cutting up and roasting of the animal are described in detail. The flesh is in part given in alms to be eaten. But *v.* 19 is,

> There is one immolator of the radiant horse, which is time [*ṛituḥ*, properly 'season'; by metonomy, 'time']: there are two that hold him fast. Such of thy limbs as I cut up, I offer them, made into balls, upon the fire.

Ṛitu means "order, right time, season of the year, menstrual discharge, the season approved for sexual intercourse." But probably *Ṛituḥ* in the text was the title of the priest who slew the horse, aided by two others holding the animal fast to receive the blow.

Then it is said to the horse;

> Verily at this moment thou dost not die, nor art thou harmed, for thou goest by auspicious paths to the Devas.

The horses of Indra, the steeds of the Maruts and a courser with the ass of the Açvins are to bear him to the sky. And, finally, among the gifts which it is hoped that the oblation will bring them, the last named is "bodily vigour."

In *iv.* 38, 39 and 40, the war-horse *Dadhikrâ* is extolled, and language of adoration used, as to a Deity. Until we reach verse 5, of 40, he is simply and plainly the war-horse, giver or winner of victories; but that verse is:

> He is Hansa, dwelling in light; Vasu, dwelling in the firmament; the invoker of the Gods, dwelling on the altar; the guest, dwelling in the house; the dweller amongst men [as consciousness, Wilson adds]; the dweller in the most excellent; the dweller in truth (reality); the dweller in the sky; born in the waters, in the rays of light, in the verity, in the mountain, The (Very) Truth.

The commentators all agree that this verse (known as the *Hansavatî Ṛich*) means the identification of Aditya, or the sun in the type *Dadhikrâ*, with *Parabrahma* or the Universal Deity, and consequently his identity with all the other types of the Supreme Being.

The "explanations" of the terms or types, as given by the commentators, are worthless. They are, in the original and as rendered by Wilson, as follows:

> 1. *Hansa*, said to be from *han*, 'to go.' That verb means 'to strike, wound, hurt, injure, kill, destroy, blot out, remove, impede'; and, without authoritative reference, 'to go.' All its derivatives have meanings that flow from its first and primary meanings, as e. g., *hana*, 'killer'; *hantṛi*, 'murderer'; *hanana*, 'striking, wounding, killing.' But *haṁsa* means 'a goose, gander, swan, a sort of horse, the sun,' and other later meanings.

2. *Vasu*, from *vas*, 'to shine,' and meaning 'a ray of light, the sun,' and, later, or from *vas*, 'to wear, put on,' etc. 'Wealth, gold,' etc.

3. *Hotâ*, 'a worshipper or sacrificer.'

4. *Atithi*, 'a guest,' from *at*, 'to go, move continually,' and thus meaning originally 'a traveler receiving hospitality.'

Both of the words are often applied to Agni, one to designate the sacrificial fire, "invoker of the Devas," and the other, "the domestic fire."

5. *Nṛishad*, i. e. (according to Benfey, *nṛi-sad*), 'understanding.' *Nṛi* is 'man'. *Sad*, as the latter part of compound words, 'sitting, dwelling.' *Nṛishad*, therefore, is *something* inherent in man, variously supposed by the commentators to be 'consciousness, vitality, eye-sight.'

6. *Varasad*, 'dweller in the most excellent,' i. e., according to the commentators 'the solar orb.' *Vara*, i. e., *vṛi*+*a*, and the same as *vîra*, gives *virya*, 'virility'; *vir*, 'a hero,' etc., and means among other things, 'best, excellent'; and also 'one who solicits a girl for his wife, a bridegroom, a son-in-law, a husband, a catamite, a sparrow,' as salacious.

7. *Ṛitasad; ṛita* meaning 'truth.'

8. *Vyomasad; vyoman*, 'the sky.'

9. *Abjah*, 'born in the water'; *ap*, 'water.'

10. *Gojah*, 'born among the rays,' or 'ox-born.'

11. *Ṛitajah*, 'born of truth' or 'of the sacrifice.'

12. *Adrijah*, 'born of *Adri*,' 'a stone, mountain or cloud.'

Finally, he is said to be *Ṛitam*, "truth or reality."

In *vii*. 44, Dadhikrâ is invoked first, then the Açvins, the dawn, Agni, Bhaga, and others. Dadhikrâ is aroused and animated, and Dadhikrâvan propitiated, and termed the swift steed, the first, knowing, in the front of the chariots, consentient with Ushas, Sûrya, the Adityas, Vasus and Angirasas: and Dadhikrâ is invoked to sprinkle the worshipper's path, that he may follow the road of sacrifices. Here some constellation would seem to be meant, then known as the Horse, perhaps Pegasus, in which is Markab, a star of the first magnitude. As we have seen, the horse, about to be sacrificed, was assured that he would not die, but would be translated to the sky.

It is quite likely that in these hymns, composed by different persons, at different periods, the horse had more than one symbolic meaning. We are now concerned with that which he has in *i*. 163. There he is fleeter than thought, and was first mounted by Indra, when Tṛita had harnessed him, and Gandharba held the reins. The Vasus fabricated him from the sun. He is Yama, Aditya, Tṛita by a mysterious act, and associated with Soma.

The mysterious act is "explained" by the commentators, as being "a secret of the nature of a cloudy day, or an act of a universally penetrating character." These explanations, Professor Wilson thinks, "are not very obvious."

Tṛita is evidently from *tṛi*, "three," and like *tṛitaya* must mean "a triad." With this, here, it agrees that there are three "bindings" of the horse, in the sky, three in the waters and three in the expanse. The commentators make *tṛinyapsu* mean "three upon earth,"—food, site and seed, or tillage, rain and seed; in the firmament, cloud, lightning, thunder.

Bandh means "to bind, fasten, gain, get, bear (as fruit)," whence *bandha*, "binding, holding in fetters, the body, building, forming, agreement, union"; and *bandhana*, "binding, fastening, confining, a rope or chain." *Bandhu* is "a kinsman, friend." The "three bindings," *bandhanâni trini*, are three *somewhats* connected and united, forming, as it were, a trinity. But what of this kind can be imagined, that has anything to do with a horse? And did the horse spring from *samudra*, "the sea," or *purîshâ*, whatever the latter may be?

The horse, bull and goat are all symbols of virility. The idea of generation after the human manner, i.e., by connection of male and female, union of the male and female organs, and impregnation by semenation, itself a profound mystery, and *in* itself no more indecent than sexual reproduction in the vegetable world, suggested itself to the Aryan imagination as naturally as it did to the Semitic, as the mode of emanation of the universe from the womb of the Infinite. That creation was a genesis and a birth, though not prominent in the Veda, is to be found in it: and as the continuation of men and things is due to generation or impregnation and production, it was natural that these should be personified. Light was the great impregnator, and heat was vitality and also a potency of generation: but the sexual desire, which afterwards, in Brahm, was said to have caused self-separation into male and female, connection between the two, Brahm and Maya, and thence the universe—sexual desire, called *Kama*, "Love," had, naturally, entered the circle of potencies that the imagination personified; for it is a force, and the cause of the perpetuation of all the animal creation. It is especially potent in the stallion, and he became the symbol of it, as the bull and goat did, for the same reason. It seems to have its seat in the genital organs, and to its existence and activity there, hope, cheerfulness, courage are in a great measure due. Those organs therefore, and especially those of the male, became symbols of it; and in the Kabbalah, borrowed by the Hebrews from the *Zend-Avesta*, the Sephirah *Yesōd*, *Fundamentum*, is the *membrum virile*, and the Sephiroth *Hōd* and *Netsach*, Glory and Victory, are the *testiculi;* Light the Divine Seed; and the process of divine generation is described again and again, in the plainest language possible.

Moreover, this symbol was triune, three uniting in a single act, to produce a single result and effect. And, of the Sanskrit words that mean the *semen virile*, *çukra* also means "light"; *hiraṇya* and *hiraṇa*, "gold";

indriya, "power"; *Vija*, "divine Truth," as cause of being; and *retas* is a name of Agni; while *ruch*, "light and splendour" also means "desire."

The conviction has been forced upon me that the horse, in *i.* 162, is at once the actual animal, sacrificed, and sexual desire symbolized by the horse. If this is so, perhaps the expression in *v.* 19, that there is one immolator of the radiant horse, time, means that age extinguishes this desire. In *i.* 162, this symbolization becomes more distinct. The horse is here to be glorified, whether springing from *samudra* or *purîshâ*. *Samudra*, i. e., *sam+und+ra* means "the sea, ocean": *sa-mudra*, "sealed." *Samud*, i. e., *sam+ud*, whence *samudâya*, "rising, a day, effort"; *samutsedha*, "height, elevation"; *samût-thâna*, "rising, getting up, increase," etc., is compounded of *sam*, "with, together, much, very," etc., and when followed by a prefix, as in *sam-ud-kship*, generally without a special signification; and *ud*, "up." *Ud-ayudha*, "with raised weapon." And *sam-ud-ra* would mean "elevation, erection." *Purîsha*, in Benfey, is "fæces, excrement, remains of food." It is, he says, akin to *pṛi*. Of course this meaning does not belong to the word in the text under consideration. *Puṛa* (probably *pṛî+a*) means, among other things, "the body," and "skin"; and *puri* and *purî* the same. *Pṛi* and *pûṛ* mean "to fill" and "satisfy," "cover."

Tṛita harnessed the horse. Is this the triad or trinity, wherein the desire resides? Indra first mounted him, for it is light that impregnates and fructifies. The Vasus or rays, fabricated the horse from the sun: for their heat is the vital principle and generative potency. The horse is Tṛita by a mysterious act (operation), in allusion to the triune symbol and its effect. He is Aditya, a potency of Nature. He is associated with Soma, because the Soma juice was believed to possess aphrodisiac virtue. The *banhanâni trini* refer to the same symbol, and to the trinity of generator, producer and issue, on the earth, in the waters and in the air.

Also the horse is Yama, and Yama gave him to Indra. What is Yama here? He is, we have seen, "all that has been and all that will be," or, "all that is born, all that will be born," being Agni, Agni as Yama; and he is the lover of maidens and husband of wives. He is simply, then, the generative potency of heat, Agni manifested and acting as that animal heat which causes desire, and generation and production.

Gandharba or *Gandharva*, it is said, held the reins. The meaning of the name is unknown. *Gandha* means "smell, odour and perfume." When Somaçâ, in *i.* 126. 7, solicits the approach of her husband, she says,

> deem me not immature. I am covered with down like a ewe of the *Gandhârius;*

and Professor Wilson says,

> another meaning is also assigned to *Gandhâri.*

How the meaning "twin" is obtained for Yama, does not appear. *Yam* means "to tame, restrain, govern, give"; and the meanings of all the other derivatives come from these. No doubt there was some connection between Yama as the generative potency of Agni, Yama, twin, and Yama, son of Vivasvaṭ. It may have been the duality between Hūd and Netsach in the Kabbalah.

In the Grecian legend, Castor and Pollux, or, more correctly, Poludeukēs, becoming enamoured of Phoebe and Talaria, resolved to carry them away, from the feast in celebration of their marriage to Lynceus and Idas; and to marry them; in consequence of which a conflict ensued, in which Castor killed Lynceus and was killed by Idas, whom afterwards Poludeukēs killed. Castor was afterwards restored to life, and one of them had a son by Phoebe, and the other by Talaria.

Referring to the passages in Mandala *x.*, in which Yama is spoken of, Professor Müller inquires whether it is possible to discover, in Yama, the God of the Departed, who is there spoken of, one of the twins?

> I confess [he says] it seems a most forced and artificial designation; and I should much prefer to derive this *Yama* from *Yam*, 'to control.' Yet his father is Vivasvaṭ, and the father of the twins was likewise Vivasvaṭ. Shall we ascribe to Vivasvaṭ three sons, two called the Twins, Yaman, and another called Yama, the Ruler? It is possible, yet it is hardly credible; and I believe it is better to learn to walk in the strange footsteps of ancient speech, however awkward they may seem at first. Let us imagine, then, as well as we can, that Yama, Twin, was used as the name of the evening, or the setting sun; and we shall be able, perhaps, to understand how, in the end, Yama came to be the King of the Departed, and the God of Death.

In *viii.* 67. 20, "the shaft of Vivasvaṭ, the poisoned arrow," is spoken of. Müller thinks that Vivasvaṭ, like Yama, was sometimes considered as sending death. The shaft or arrow was, I believe, sun-stroke, a frequent cause of death in that latitude.

Yama, I am quite sure, never was the name of the setting sun or of the evening. He did not, from that, become King of the Dead or God of Death. He is spoken of in only three or four passages of the first Mandala, in one of the second and in two of the sixth, and the passages in relation to him in the subsequent books are of much later date, and were composed when a long time had elapsed after he led to the southward a body of emigrants, to the southward and towards the setting sun.

In *vi.* 33. 9, it is said,

> The Apsarasas sit down, wearing the vesture spread out by Yama: [and in *v.* 12 it is said], He, the Sage, cognizant of both worlds, was the donor of thousands: he was verily donation: wearing the vesture spread by Yama, Vasishṭha was born of the Apsaras.

As Mitra and Varuṇa are said, in verse 11, jointly to have begotten Vasishṭha, it must be they who are styled Apsaras. In verse 9, the original is, *Yamena tatam paridhim vayanto apsarasa upasedui Vasishṭhâh*, and Wilson says it is somewhat dark. He says:

> The garb *paridhim, vastram*, spread, *tatam*, by him, is the revolution of life and death.

The residue of the explanations that he quotes may be omitted without serious loss.

Paridhi, in Benfey, "that by which something is bordered, a halo, the horizon, a circumference." *Pari* is an adverb and a preposition, meaning "round, all round, about," etc., *dhâ* means "to put," passive, "to be contained." *Paridhi*, therefore, means an "envelope, that which invests, encloses, enwraps, environs," etc., and "the body, as containing within it the vital Soul and intellectual Spirit." *Vastra* is, "that which *invests*" (Latin *vestis*), and hence, derivatively, "garments, clothes," from *vas*, "to wear, put on."

In verse 10 of the same hymn, it is said,

> when Mitra and Varuṇa beheld thee, Vasishṭha, quitting the lustre of the lightning, then was one of thy births.

They begat him, it is said, by pouring a common effusion into a sacrificial water-jar, whence Mâna arose and Vasishṭha. The body which then enveloped each, and those that enveloped the Apsarasas, children of Vasishṭha, and which each dwelt in, came from Yama, Generation. In it, coming from the sky, where they are stars, they sit near.

In *i*. 35. 6, it is said:

> Three are the spheres [heavens: Müller]: two are in the proximity of Savitṛi, one leads men to the dwelling of Yama.

Müller has it,

> two are said to belong to Savitṛi, one to Yama.

The word rendered "spheres" or "heavens," is *lokas:* and these, the commentators say, are heaven, earth and Antariksha, "the firmament." It is very doubtful what is meant here by *loka*. It is, Benfey says, *loch*-or *ruch*+*a*, with *l*. for *r*. *Ruch* means "to shine, light, splendour," and *ruchi* is "light, splendour, a ray of light." *Loka* means, according to him, "seeing, sight, the world, the universe, a world, man, mankind." *Loch* is "to see, behold, perceive, regard, consider." The "three regions" are said in verse 7, to be illuminated by *suparṇa* (radiance). Sûrya is said in verse 8 to have lighted up the three regions of living beings. In verse 9 Savitṛi is said to travel between the two regions of heaven and earth. And here, I imagine, it is the earth that is the sphere or region of Yama, the generative potency of material Nature.

If Yama, in the hymn *x*. 17 means "Twins," they and the Açvins, sons of Vivasvaṭ, are the same, the great stars of the constellation Gemini. And in the much later hymn, *x*. 10. 1, where these have become male and female, and Yamî, the sister, solicits Yama to have intercourse with her, I think that the same two stars are referred to. But it is difficult to determine what the real meaning of the hymn was. She wishes the sage, after traversing a vast ocean, to beget a son, and look far forward over the earth. The undying ones, she insists, desire this of him, a descendant left behind by the one sole mortal. The Devas Tvashṭṛi, she insists made them husband and wife, in the womb. Though she should wait upon him (submit her body to his embraces?), by night and day, still the eye of the sun would open again. Such, with repeated solicitations, is her part of the poem. He refuses, declaring it would be unrighteous. The heroes (*vîrâḥ*), Sons of Splendour, he says, look far and wide around. Their parents he says, were *Gandharva apsu* and his water-wife (*apya yosha*). Of course, no one endeavours to explain why Saraṇyû is styled the "watery" wife of Gandharva. Explanation of it is simply impossible, on any of the theories that we have quoted. But if Saraṇyû is vapour and the vapourous clouds, then the epithet at once appears to be perfectly appropriate and proves the conjecture correct. As *Gandha-vaha* meant "that which conveys fragrance," and therefore "the wind," Gandharva may have meant the air of spring, agitating the clouds.

Yama asks her, who knows that first day, when they were in the womb together, who has seen it, and who can declare it. Vast, he says, is the realm of Mitra and Varuṇa. (For that realm, of the Morning and Evening Stars, is the whole sky and expanse, everywhere in which have always been the clouds.) And when she proposes to bare her body to him, he answers, that these spies of the Gods (*devânâṁ spaçah*, outlookers of the Devas), who here revolve, neither stand still nor wink. Both in the sky and expanse, she tells him, twins are closely united; but he declares it to be sinful, and commends her to some other male.

Notwithstanding the grossness of expression here, apparently only fit and appropriate in a conversation between material creatures capable of copulation, I think it quite clear that the whole is merely figurative, and merely a poetic expression of the fact that, although always moving together, the two stars Castor and Pollux never are in conjunction, but always at the same distance from each other. At the same time there is no doubt that at this comparatively modern period, these stars were beginning to be, or had become, to the mind of the Poets and still more to the people, actual persons and beings like the Grecian Dioscuri.

I come now to that which is of much more living interest to us, to a great fact in the history of our race.

In Fargard *ii.* of the Vendidad we have a historical recital of the emigration of Yima, son of Vivanhao, from the original mountain-home of the Aryans, to the southward, to a more genial climate, in consequence of the severity of the winters, by which the pasturage was destroyed and the cattle starved. With a large body of followers, driving with them their herds of horses and cattle, and accompanied by their wives and children, they went from the high valleys of the western slope of the Bolor Tagh or Comedarum Montes, in which the Oxus and Jaxartes (Sihoun or Sirr and Jihoon) have the sources of their many heads, and either crossing part of these, and descending into the open country to the southwest of the sources of the Jaxartes, or crossing those of the Oxus, and finding their way into Bactria, they settled, and built a walled city, and established a great system of irrigation, in some alluvial plain through which a large, swift, clear river ran. This region, thus settled by Yima and his colonists, was the Airyana Vaeja of the First Fargard of the Vendidad.

And it was either that fertile valley in which the city of Samarcand now stands, where three rivers from the mountains come together, and the Sogd, Zohik, Sirafshan or Polymetus flows to the west, then bends to the northwest, and then to the southward, towards the Oxus; or it was the equally fertile and level plain around the present city of Bokhara, on the same river, far below Samarcand; or it was the great plain of the city of Balkh or Bactria, on the south side of the Oxus.

The Zohik now falls into Lake Denghis, near the Oxus, a body of salt water, of great depth, and about twenty-five miles in length. Parallel to it runs the river, Kurshee, which now sinks in the sand: and both, there is no doubt, at one time fell into the Oxus, which itself, there is little doubt, then flowed into the Caspian. On each side of each of these streams, formerly much larger, it is evident, than they are now, stretched a zone of most fertile land, but cultivable only by irrigation. Running out of and parallel to the Zohik were many long deep channels, which were extended by art, or new ones made, by which the whole valley was abundantly irrigated, and with these the whole country on the rivers, from Samarcand to Bokhara, and all the country around Balkh, and in the valley or alluvial bottom of the great river Oxus, on both sides, are intersected still.

One of the principal sources of the Oxus is in Lake Siricol, at an elevation of 15,600 feet above the sea, in Latitude 37° 27′ North. Samarcand is in 39° 32′; Bokhara in 39° 25′ and Balkh in 36° 35′. To know that Madrid is in 40° 30′, Genoa in 44° 22′, Rome in 41° 52′, Seville in 37° 10′, and Constantinople in 41° 05′, will give one a better idea of the climate and temperature of these early homes of the Aryan race. In all the valley of the Zohik are grown rice, tobacco, cotton, oranges, pears, apricots, grapes in great variety, figs and peaches, the best of these being raised at Samarcand, and the apricots as large as apples.

Excepting the valleys of the rivers, the country is a desert, for the most part of sand of no great depth, and in which water can everywhere be had by digging a few feet.

How long before the time of Zarathustra, this emigration of Yima took place, we have no certain means of determining. Twice before his death he was deprived of the royal power, for infidelity to the Ahurian religion, and twice restored to it. How many kings succeeded him, before Zarathustra, we do not know. It is said more than once in the *Zend-Avesta*, that Zarathustra sacrificed to Ahura in Airyana Vaeja; and unless this name was merely descriptive and laudatory (it meaning "the good creation"), and given to Bactria as it had been given to Sogdiana, he must have lived at first, in the valley of Samarcand. If so, he must have emigrated to Bactria, or else all tradition on the subject is unreliable: and moreover, the descriptions of the country in which he fought against and conquered the Tâtars or Toorkhs and native tribes, Turanians, Çaimirians and others, and where he reigned as a king, too evidently agree with Bactria to permit of any doubt.

Zarathustra, it is to be added, in the Gâthâs or patriotic exhortations addressed to his people and their chiefs, urging them to rise against and expel the infidels who had invaded and held a large part of the country and marauded upon the rest, does not claim to have been the author of what we call the "Zoroastrian" religion: and it is elsewhere stated that it was first preached by Vivanhao, the father of Yima, a priest. Yima was not a teacher, but a soldier and a king.

Now, there is no doubt at all in regard to the meaning of that part of the *Zend-Avesta* in which these historical facts are stated. And there is no doubt that Yima emigrated from the high valleys in the mountains. As he settled Airyana Vaeja, which the First Fargard designates as the first of the countries created by Ahura, it would seem that the country on the Zohik at Samarcand could not have been settled when he emigrated. Yet that is possible, and that he passed by it, leading his mountaineers, and settled in the plain of Bokhara, or even crossed the Oxus and established himself in the plain of Balkh. And as the bands which he led and which afterwards followed him became the Irano-Aryan, and the Medo and Perso-Aryan branch of the race, and the old original tongue became with them by slow degrees and after a long period, the Zend, while those who became the Indo-Aryan branch remained behind, and at a later day, perhaps when pressed upon by the Tâtar and Toorkhish hordes, crossed the Oxus into Eastern Bactria, and thence through the passes of the Hindu Kush or Paropamisus into Kabul, ultimately occupying the country of the Seven Rivers, on the upper waters of the Indus, by which time the old language had with them become the Vedic Sanskrit, I think that Yima emigrated long after Samarcand and Bokhara had been settled, and into Bactria, settling in the plain of Balkh. Whether the Samarcand country was settled before the Greek, Latin, German or Gothic, Sclavonic and Keltic emigrations, or before even the latest of these, we shall never know.

I may here add, that, in my opinion, the Zend is nearer the original language that the Sanskrit, having the oldest forms; and that the Latin is nearer to it than the Greek.

We are on firm ground in regard to the emigration of Yima; and he never became a Deity to the Irano-Aryans; but continued a historical personage.

And we are on equally firm ground in asserting the perfect identity of names and persons, between *Yima* the son of *Vivanhao* and *Yama* the son of *Vivasvaṭ*. The change of *a* into *i* in Yima is paralleled by that in many words where *a* changes into *ai*, as in *pari*, *pairi; madhya*, *maidhya; prati*, *paiti;* while, on the other hand, *çiras*, "head" becomes *çara; hiraṇya*, *zaranya; pitar*, *patar;* while *jani* becomes *jêni*, and in Greek *gunē;* the Sanskrit *panchan* becomes in Latin *quinque;* and the Sanskrit *a* always changed into *e* in Zend, before a final *m*. As to Vivasvaṭ, the change of *s* into *ṅh* in Zend is common. *Manas* becomes *manaṅh; aṁhas*, *azaṅh; ojas*, *aonjanh*, etc. I do not enlarge on this, since the identity of Yama and Yima and that of Vivasvaṭ and Vivaṅhao are admitted by every commentator.

I return now to the Veda. Rig-Veda *x*. 14. 1, of which Dr. Muir (*v*. 291) gives the original and a translation, is also to be found, with slight variations, in Atharva-Veda *xviii*. 1. 49. It is as follows:

> 1. Worship with an oblation Yama the King (or Chief), son of Vivasvaṭ, the assembler of men, who departed to the mighty streams, and explored the road for many.

The words rendered "to the mighty streams" are *pravato mahîr anu*. This rendering is adopted by Roth. He had before translated the words, "from the deep to the heights," and Dr. Haug had rendered them "from the depths to the heights." But, says Dr. Muir, in the Atharva-Veda, *xviii*. 4. 7, where the same words occur, in the sentence,

> they cross by fords the great rivers, which the virtuous offerers of sacrifice pass,

they seem more likely to mean "the mighty streams." But Roth thinks they are mighty *celestial* waters. One fails to see why they should. So in Atharva-Veda *vi*. 28. 3, Yama is said to have first reached the river (*pravatam̃*) looking out a road or route for many. *Pravata* is not in Benfey. It is added in the hymn last cited, that Yama is master of the two-footed and four-footed creatures.

We shall never have any wholly true interpretation of the Veda, until translators permit the Vedic bards to speak for themselves, without putting words in their mouths to make the expression of their thoughts correspond with a preconceived theory. It is evil enough that it is so often unavoidable that the first meanings which words had when they were uttered must be replaced by the meanings that they had come to have two thousand years afterwards, or be guessed at by the aid of these. It is worse when words are added because a given theory requires it. Taking the words of the first verse of this hymn in their natural import and meaning, it records this historical fact, agreeing with the other ancient record of the Vendidad; that Yama, an Aryan chieftain, organizer of a body of emigrants, went from the home of his people to the great rivers, opening a way which many after him were to follow. The Atharva-Veda adds to this, by interpolation, that he was the first of men that died, which is mere nonsense.

2. Yama was the first who found for us the route. This home is not to be taken from us. Those who are now born (go) by their own routes to the place whereunto our ancient fathers emigrated.

The country which Yama discovered and occupied has become permanently a home of the Aryans, now too powerful to be in danger of expulsion from it: and the men of the present day can go, by routes selected by themselves (not following that taken by Yama), to the country whither our ancestors emigrated.

The next verse names, as I understand it, some of these earliest emigrants: *Matâlî* magnified (*vavṛidhânah*, "invested with power") by the Kavyas, Yama by the Angirasas, and Bṛihaspati by the Rikvans, both those whom the Devas magnified (or exalted), and those who (magnified) the Devas (but as each word is *devâḥ*, and the latter may as well be taken to be in the nominative as in the accusative, I think we should read, "both those whom the Devas invested with authority, or, made great, and those who are Devas, i. e., who have become so by translation to the sky) of these some are gladdened (gratified) by *Svâha* (expressions of veneration at the sacrifice), and others by *Svadhâ* (the food sacrificed).

4. Place thyself, Yama, on this sacrificial seat, in company with the Angirasas and the fathers. Let the texts recited by the Sages persuade thee hither. Be gratified, O King, with this oblation.

5. Come with the worshipful Angirasas: be satisfied here, with the children of Virûpa. Seated on the grass at this sacrifice, I invoke Vivasvaṭ, who is thy father.

6. May we enjoy the good will and gracious benevolence of those worshipful beings, the Angirasas our fathers, the Navagvas, the Atharvans, the Bhṛigus, offerers of Soma.

7. Depart thou, depart, by the ancient paths, whither our early fathers departed. Thou shalt see the two Kings, Yama and the Deva Varuṇa, exhilarated by the oblation.

8. Meet with the Fathers, meet with Yama, meet in the height of the sky with the sacrifices thou hast offered. Throwing off all imperfections, return to thy home. Become united to a body, and clothed in a shining form. Go ye, depart ye, hasten ye from hence.

These verses are now addressed at funerals, to the souls of the departed, while their bodies are being consumed in the funeral pile. It would seem from the text itself that they are addressed, and were addressed when first composed and whenever repeated, to a deceased person, whose body was present, and upon a funeral occasion. That is the traditional and accepted interpretation, and of course every translation conforms to it.

If this is what the passage is, the "hymn" is not a hymn, but a collection of incoherent fragments that got together by accident. The occasion of the first six verses was a sacrifice to Yama, supposed to have been translated to the sky, at which he was earnestly invited to be present, with the fathers and Angirasas, persuaded by the texts to be recited by the ministering Priests; and to accept with graciousness and satisfaction the oblation, the sacrifice of food, about to be burned in the fire, kindled in the open air. His father also is invoked to be present. Seated on the grass, and inviting them also to be seated there, the worshippers pray for the good will and gracious favour of the various deified men whom they invoke, and then, suddenly, some dead man is exhorted to depart and go to the sky, to meet the fathers, Yama and Varuṇa, and the sacrifices he has offered; to go, depart, hasten. The fathers, it is said then,

have made for *him* this place.

For *whom*, and *what* place? Yama gives him an abode. He is exhorted to hasten past two dogs, and dwell in festivity with Yama, entrusted by him to the same dogs. And then it is said that these two brown messengers of Yama wander about among men; and *they*, the brown, insatiable, broad-nosed dogs are invited to give the worshippers again today the auspicious breath of life (as if *they* were dead), that they may behold the sun. And then again, with verse 13 comes the direction to pour out the Soma and sacrifice the butter to Yama; with prayer to him for long life among the Devas, and salutation to the ancient Ṛishis.

It is evident that this was a sacrifice, not to Yama alone, but to him and many other deified persons, made at early dawn, and while the stars still shone. I do not believe that any corpse was present at such a sacrifice, and certainly it was no funeral. The oblation is just about to be made, the *svadhâ*, when this apostrophe (the *svâhâ*, I take it to be) is pronounced. Taking Dr. Muir's translation to be correct, and without comparing it with the original, I found it impossible to understand the meaning of a part of what is supposed to be an address to the soul of the deceased. Finally I came to believe that it was misunderstood, even when it was incorporated in the Atharva-Veda. And I am now convinced that it was addressed to the *oblation* or *sacrificial food*, and *Soma juice*, about to be cast into the fire, there to become of the fire, as an undivided portion of a unit, and to ascend in flame and vapour to the sky and Devas.

I undertake, with very great diffidence, to give my own reading of these verses, for my knowledge of Sanskrit is very limited, and but for a tolerable acquaintance with several of the languages derived from it, I should hardly endeavour to read the simplest sentences.

> 7a. *Prehi prehi pathibhiḥ pûrvyebhir yatra naḥ pûrve pitaraḥ pareyuḥ:* Depart thou, depart, by the ancient paths (to the place) whither our early fathers have departed.

So Dr. Muir reads it. *Prehi* and *pareyuḥ* are from *pra-ya*, which means according to Benfey, and by the natural signification of the prefix *pra*, the Latin *pro*, "to go forth, proceed, proceed to, rise to." And *yatra* means, according to him, "where, in what place," and not "whither." I think it nearer the original to read, "go forth," or, "ascend, ascend, by the ancient ways whereby our remote ancestors ascended."

> 7b. *Ubhâ râjânâ svadhayâ madantâ Yamam paçyâsi Varuṇam cha Devam:* (There) shalt thou see the two Kings, Yama and the God Varuṇa, exhilarated by the oblation (or, exulting in independent power).

Svadhâ means "spontaneity, self-will, strength," according to Benfey, as well as the food offered to deceased ancestors. But as it has been twice used, before, in this hymn, in the sense of "oblation" (of food), I think it is hardly used in another sense here. *Paçyasi*, future of *dviç*, means "wilt see, discover, search, learn, know." So I read the line:

> Thou wilt see (or, know) both the Kings exhilarated (or, intoxicated) by the oblation (or, oblation-intoxicated), Yama and the Deva Varuṇa.

For the oblation, becoming fire and light, ascends to the sky, to feed with light the stars that once were holy men or leaders, and thus know, i. e., unite with, Yama and Varuṇa.

8a. *Sangachhasva piṭṛibhiḥ saṁ Yamena ishṭâpûrttena parame vyoman:* Meet with the fathers, meet with Yama, meet with the [recompense of] the sacrifices thou hast offered in the highest heaven.

Sangachhasva, rendered "meet with" in this line, is in the next rendered "become united to," because there a wrong theory required it. It is the imperative of *sangam*, which means "to meet with, unite with, connect with." Dr. Haug explains *ishṭâpûrta* thus: *ishṭa* means "what is sacrificed," and *âpûrtta*, "filled up to."

For all sacrifices go up to heaven and are stored up there, to be taken possession of by the sacrificer on his arrival in heaven.

The texts quoted to sustain this, do not sustain it. They only express the worshippers' desire that they may follow their sacrifice, i. e., go, by and by, where it has gone. The sacrifices were not supposed to be stored up for the sacrificer, but to be consumed by and exhilarate the Devas.

Ishṭi,=yajti, means "sacrifice"; and *pûr, pṛi*, "to fill, collect, satisfy," whence *pûrtta*, "completed." And I think that the line should be read:

Unite with the fathers, with this Yama, with this completed sacrifice [i. e., with the whole, of which the particular oblation addressed was a part, when the residue should reach the sky, to unite with the light whereby Yama and the fathers shine], in the heights of the sky.

8b. *Hitvaya avadyam punar astam ehi. Sangachhasva tauvâ suvarchâḥ.* Throwing off all imperfection, again go to thy home. Become united to a body and clothed in a shining form.

Tauvâ means "body," but also "one's self, person." *Suvarchaḥ* is, it seems to me, an adjective, meaning "shining brilliantly." Perhaps the line means,

Freed of all impediment, return to thy home, and, shining brilliantly, unite with that which is thy self [i. e., from which thou didst emanate or flow forth].

9. Go ye, depart ye, hasten ye from hence. The fathers have made for him (*asmai*) this place. Yama gives him (*asmai*) an abode, distinguished by days and waters and lights [*aktubhir: aktu*, 'night,' Benfey].

10. By an auspicious [good or proper] path, do thou hasten [run] past the two four-eyed brindled dogs, the offspring of Saramâ. Then approach the benevolent fathers who dwell rejoicing with Yama.

11. Intrust him, O Yama, to thy two four-eyed protecting, road-guarding, man-watching dogs; and bestow on him (*asmai*) prosperity and wealth. [A strange prayer in behalf of a soul ascending to heaven.]

12. The two brown messengers of Yama, broad of nostril and insatiable, wander about among men (*janan*, 'creatures, beings,' probably the stars). May they give us again today the auspicious breath of life, that we may behold the sun.

13. Pour out the Soma to Yama: offer Yama an oblation. To Yama the sacrifice proceeds, when heralded by Agni and prepared. 14. Offer to Yama an

oblation with butter, and be active. May he grant to us to live a long life among the Devas. 15. Offer a most honeyed oblation to King Yama. This salutation to the earliest-born the ancient Ṛishis, who made for us a way.

It is probable that this hymn underwent modifications after its original composition, when part of it came to be supposed an address to the soul of a person deceased. But the changes could not have been very great, for they did not obscure its original meaning. I think it cannot be doubted that whatever it became afterwards, the apostrophe was the *svâhâ* addressed to the oblation, when about to place it in the fire. The exhortation to run or hasten by the dogs of Yama was naturally regarded as proving that it was a soul of a man that was addressed. But these dogs were no doubt stars, Sirius and Procyon, probably, or Canes Venatici, in the North; and Yama either Arcturus in Boötes, or a star in Orion. Four minor stars near each dog, it is probable, caused them to be styled "four-eyed."

It is said that the fathers made for "him" "this place"; and that Yama gave "him" an abode. Yama is asked to place "him" under the protection of his dogs; and these dogs are then asked to give the worshippers the breath of life (i. e., to bring on the daylight). The word rendered "him," in each case, is *asmai*, dative of the base *idam* and nominative *ayam*, meaning "this" (indefinitely). So *etasmai* is the masc. and neuter dative of the base *etad*, "this" (very near). Now, the base of the first person, "I" is *asmad*, and we have in the declension of *aham*, "I"; acc. *asman*, "us"; instr. *asmabhih*, "by us"; dt. *asmabhyam*, "to us"; abl. *asmat*, "from us", etc.; while *tasmai* is dat. masc. of the base *tad*, "he"; and *tyasmai* is dat. masc. of the base *tyad*. *Asmi*, "I am," is the first person sing. pres. indic. of *as*, "to be"; and in the Vedas we find *asme* for *vayam*, "we." In *asmê*, the simple vowel *a* is the characteristic element of the first person, for the rest of the word (*smai*) is found also in the second person, *yushmê*, "you." And so in *aham*, "I," *am* is but termination.

Bopp thinks there was originally a pronominal base, I, expressing the idea "he," and in Sanskrit and Zend meaning "this," which has left in those languages no proper declension, but only adverbs, as *i-tas*, "from here," "from there," etc. Of this base he gives *iṣhmâi* as the dative.

As the *a* of *aham*, "I," is found in *asmâi*, *huic*, *asmât*, *hoc* and *asmin*, *in hoc*, while the Latin *isti* and *isto*, "to him" and "by him," are represented by *tasmâi* and *tasmât*, I believe that *asmai* was used to designate sometimes the party speaking, sometimes the party spoken of; and that originally, perhaps, it may have belonged especially to the first person altogether.

For a party to designate himself as "this one" was as natural as it is now to say "this deponent further sayeth not." And I think that *asmai*, in the text, meant the Poet himself, who, in speaking of or for himself, spoke of all who worshipped with him, abundant examples of which may be seen in the *Zend-Avesta,* the number of the pronoun and verb changing in the same verse from singular to plural and from plural to singular again.

When the address to the oblation and the prayers for protection, wealth and prosperity are ended, the direction is given to pour out the Soma and offer the oblation. The sacrifice to Yama proceeds, it is said:

> offer the oblation and be active.

Long life is prayed for. Then a honeyed oblation is offered: and it is declared that the hymn is chanted to Yama who opened the way for emigrants.

I have only to add that the translation of Dr. Muir makes the dogs "wander about among men." But *Charato*, from *char*, means "move, go, and spy"; and *janan*, meaning "creatures or beings," also properly designates luminaries. The dogs revolve, along with the stars and planets.

I think it conduces to show that the address in question was to the oblation, that in *i.* 163. 13, the horse that had been immolated is said to have gone to the highest abode, to the Devas.

> *iii.* 55, 2. May the Devas not harm us here, nor our ancient fathers who know the realms (*padajnaḥ*).

But the original of the latter clause is, *mâ pûrve Agne pitaraḥ padajṇaḥ*, and Agne is omitted in the translation. *Pada* means "step, footstep, trace, mark, sign, place, abode," and also "a ray of light." *Jnâ* means "to know, to consider, perceive, think of." I think the meaning is that they shine as stars, by the rays received from Agni.

In *viii.* 48. 13, Soma, in concert with the fathers, is said to have extended the sky and expanse. In *ix.* 82. 3, they are called beholders of men: and in *x.* 68. 11, the fathers are said to have adorned the sky with stars. In *x.* 88. 15,

> I have heard of two paths for mortals, that of the fathers and that of the Devas: [and in *x.* 107. 1], the great light [daybreak] given by the fathers, has arrived.

In *x.* 15. 1, the lower, upper and middle fathers are invoked to rise.

> May these fathers [it is said], who have attained to higher life (*asu*) protect us in the invocations.

But *asu*, here, is not from *as*, "to be," I think, but from *as*, "to shine."

> 2. Let this reverence be today paid to the fathers who went forth first, and who last, who are sitting in the expanse, or among the chiefs of splendour in the sky. . . . . May Yama feast as amply as he desires, on the oblations, eager, and

sharing his gratification with the eager Vasishṭhas, our ancient ancestors, who, officiating at sacrifices, offered the Soma. 16. Come, Agni, with a thousand of those exalted [translated to the sky] ancient fathers [who were], adorers of the Gods and sitters of the fire [of sacrifice], who are real, who are eaters and drinkers of oblations, and are received into the same chariot with Indra and the Devas. . . . . 13. Thou knowest, O Jâtavedas (probably shortened form of *jâta*+ *vedasya*, 'Son of wisdom') how many those fathers are who are here and who are not here, those whom we know and whom we know not. Accept the sacrifice duly offered with the oblation. Do thou, O self-resplendent (*svarâṭ*) Deva, along with those who, whether they have undergone cremation or not, are gladdened by our oblation, grant us this (higher) vitality (*asunîti*), and a body according to our desire.

Sva undoubtedly meant "self," and that which Spinoza called "substance." Fire, as Unity, was the *sva*, self, of every particular fire; as the Divine Wisdom, of Zarathustra was the Wholeness in Unity, the *Self*, of all individual intellects; each of which was Itself, in limited quantity of extent.

Svar was "the sun," and also splendour or radiance. *Sura*, also, from a supposed verb *sur*, was "the sun," and there was probably a verb *svar*, meaning "to shine," of which *svarâṭ*, for *svarant*, was the present participle, meaning "splendent, resplendent, radiant, shining." So in Zend *hvô* is "self," and *hvare*, "the sun." The epithet *svarâṭ* is here applied to Agni, source of all light, and perhaps involves more than the mere idea contained in the word "resplendent, radiant or shining," which could be applied to a star or lamp. It probably meant "emitting *all* splendour," i. e., from whom all light, splendour and radiance flow.

Asunîti occurs again in verse 2 of the next hymn. In *x*. 59. 5 and 6, it seems to be employed as the personification of a God or Goddess: but Müller considers that there is nothing to show that *Asunîti* is a female Deity. He renders it "guide of life." Roth thinks it a name for Yama. In the Atharva-Veda it is joined with *svarâṭ*. *Asu*, from *as*, "to be," is "life, vitality"; and also, I think, "light, splendour, radiance," from *as* = *ash*, *ush*, "to burn." *Asunîti* means "life-giver" or "light-giver," or causer or producer of life or light.

If *Jâtavedas* means "born of wisdom," which it seems it must, *jâta* being the past partic. pass. of *jan*, then, as it is an appellation of Agni, we have in it the very first hint that I have found, in the Veda, of an Entity superior to and the origin of Fire and Light; a divine creative or productive Wisdom, the *Çpĕnta-Mainyu* of the doctrine of Zarathustra, of the Holy Spirit, which became the Holy Ghost, the *Pneuma Hagion* of the later Christianity.

In *x*. 16, Agni is prayed to, not to burn up or consume a party, not to dissolve his skin or his body; but when he has matured him to send him to the Fathers, to consign him to them (*pra hinutat* and *pari,dattât pitṛibhyaḥ*, "deliver to and leave with, the Fathers"). That is, Agni is besought not to annihilate the body of the deceased, not even his skin or body, but transmuting all and absorbing it into himself, and making it part of himself, to convey it to the Fathers, in the sky.

> When he shall reach that state of vitality, he shall then fulfil the pleasure of the Gods.

So Dr. Muir translates the latter part of verse 2. I think he utterly misunderstands it. The original is

> *yadâ gachhâti asunîtim etam atha devanam vaçanîr bhavati.*

I do not believe that *asunîti* means "state of vitality"; but I think it means "source of splendour" or "resplendent place." Benfey gives to *vaçi-bhûta* the meaning of "subject to the will"; but a literal rendering of the phrase here does not express the real meaning, which is, that the burned body converted into fire and manifested as flame and light, ascends to where the light's Self abides, unites with it, and afterwards assists in enabling the celestial bodies to shine.

> Let his eyes [it is then said], go as light to the sun, and his breath to the wind. Go [it is said], to the sky, to the expanse, to the rains, as Nature directs, and let the limbs, changed into light and heat, nourish the plants.

This is, of itself a magnificent idea, and explains the preference of the Indo-Aryans for the custom of burning the dead. It is the body's destiny to be reconverted into fire, flame, light and heat, and ascending as a sacrifice, to gratify the Devas. To bury it in the earth is to deny it this destiny and leave it to rot in foul corruption; when, if burned, it would become immortal, as light, and bless the earth with warmth and nourishment. What higher destiny could the body have? The chemist has long since taught us that when a body is burned, every particle of it mingles again with the elements. I do not know that we are any the better or the wiser for knowing it.

> 4. As for his uncreated part, do thou, Jâtavedas, refine it with thy heat, and let thy flame and splendour illuminate it; in those forms of thine that are auspicious carry it to the place of the pious. Restore to the Fathers, Agni, him who comes offered to thee with oblations, etc.

So far as the Rig-Veda goes, I do not find in it the least real ground for the representation that the deceased goes in person to meet his forefathers, and enters upon a more perfect life in a more delectable abode; where a life crowned with the fulfilment of all desires is passed in the presence of the Gods, and employed in the fulfilment of their pleasure.

The men of thought of this day have found out that what the Brahmans thought or wrote, in the post-Vedic age, is of little or no interest or value. Is it indispensable that in the later ages of every religion, its ancient books shall be misunderstood and perverted? It was so in India, at least. In that nightmare age of the intellect and imagination, when everything grotesque and hideous, repulsive and disgusting, beastly and monstrous, that the imagination could conceive in its long period of delirium was embodied and personified as divine (the growth, chiefly, of misunderstood expressions of the Vedas), everything in the Rig-Veda was distorted, perverted and misinterpreted; and so it continues to be in India to this day.

Now, what we want to have put before us in English is the Veda of the Vedic age, and not the Brahmanic Veda. The notions of the Brahmins are now well enough known, and are found not worth the knowing. Neither is the Veda worth knowing, as it has been to this time translated, nor the *Zend-Avesta* as the Parsees misread it. I may be widely, immensely, utterly mistaken, in my understanding of the two works: but, at all events, *as* I understand them, the Rig-Veda and the five Gâthâs of Zarathustra are by far the oldest books in the world, and from them all our religious and philosophical opinions, doctrines and notions have flowed.

I believe that the Veda and *Zend-Avesta* are very different books from what they are currently supposed to be, and of infinitely more value: and some day a scholar will appear who, first comparing all the derivative languages and ascertaining the ancient roots and the first meanings of the Vedic words, will then, setting out with a sound knowledge of the notions, conceptions and Deities of the Veda, give us the thoughts of its authors, as they were understood by themselves and by those who first heard them repeated; as genuine poems, the creatures of an opulent fancy and vivid imagination, but without incoherency or inconsequentiality, and with no notions vague, absurd, inconsistent or contradictory as to the personality and attributes of their real Deities, or of those potencies of God and Nature which their poetic fancy invested with a personal being and moral and intellectual attributes, as well as material forms and physical powers.

In Rig-Veda *ix.* 113. 7, *et seq.*, the enjoyments "of the future state," Dr. Muir says, are to be conferred by the God Soma, and are described as follows:

> 7. Place me, O Purified One (*pavamâna*), in that imperishable and unchanging place, where perpetual light and glory are found (*Indrayendo parisrana*).

Dr. Muir omits the first half of the verse: and does not translate the last two words literally. *Pavamâna*, Benfey says, is the present participle *âtmanepada* (intransitive) of *pû*, "to purify," and means "wind, and Agni." When applied to Agni, it of course has the transitive meaning, "purifying, purifier." Applied to Soma, it may mean "purified"; but I doubt it. Verbs often have a transitive meaning when in the form *âtmanepada;* and the distinctions are difficult to make, and not to be accounted for.

> 8. Where King Vaivasvata is, and the solid obstacle of the sky, where the great waters flow, there make me undying.
>
> 9. Where actions are unrestrained (*Yatrânukâmam charaṇam*), in the third heaven, third sky (*trinâke tridive divaḥ*), where the places are luminous, there make me undying.

Yatra is "where." *Anukama* means, as ordinarily translated, "according to will, or, desire." *Charaṇa* is a noun, from *char*, "to move, go, act," and is said by Benfey to mean "fixed observances." It means simply the movements or revolutions of the stars: and *anukama*, literally, "according to will, or, pleasure," means, no doubt, "regulated by a sovereign will," or "in accordance with fixed laws."

The phrase *trinâke tridive divaḥ*, literally, it is supposed, "third heaven, third sky, of the sky," needs much more consideration than it has ever received. Whenever the old Poets can be rescued of the imputation of writing nonsense, something is done towards understanding them.

Nakta is "night." Compare Latin *nox, noctu;* Gothic, *nahts;* Anglo-Saxon, *naht, niht;* English, *night;* Greek *νυξ*. *Naktaṁdiva* is "day and night"; and *div* means "day," and *diva*, "by day." Compare Latin *diu* and *diuturna*, and *dies*. The ancient Aryans knew no other "heaven" than the sky; and if *naka* means anything more than "night," it is the night-sky. But how could the expression possibly have been used, "three *nake* and three *dive*," or "third *naka* and third *div*, of the sky," if *naka* meant "heaven" and *div* meant "sky"?

The question what the phrase really meant, is by far more interesting than very many that the commentators have discussed, certainly more so than the meanings of *Arusha;* for it relates directly to the intellectual and spiritual development of the race at that time. I do not pretend to explain the phrase. I only say that I do not believe that the Vedic Poets knew or said anything about any other heaven or sky than that which they saw; and that it is absolutely certain that they believed the old Ṛishis to have become well-known stars, every night seen in the visible sky; and that they did not expect or ask to be themselves translated to invisible stars in an invisible sky. The triple sky or heaven may have been that of the sun, planets and fixed stars. The old observers could easily learn by observation, that the moon came at times between the earth and sun, and was therefore the lower of the two, and that the planets were below the fixed stars. And this is what was meant, is made probable by the fact that the Ṛishis, which were certainly stars, are sometimes said to be in the highest heaven, and the worshipper here asks to become a Deva in the third.

And as the same differences of height are discoverable by day, the sky of the day and the sky of the night are both named. And whether this be or be not the real meaning, it is at least absolutely certain that the sky or heaven in which the fixed stars shone was the highest heaven.

> 10. Make me immortal in the world where there are pleasures and enjoyments, in the sphere of the sun, where ambrosia and satisfaction are found.

It is hard to say what is the meaning of *kâmâḥ nikâmâs*, rendered "pleasures and enjoyments." *Kâmâ* means, in Benfey, "wish, desire, love." *Ni*, prefixed, seems generally to add little to the meaning: and Benfey gives "desire" as the meaning of *nikâma*. *Svadhâ* rendered "ambrosia" is the food sacrificed; and *ṭriptis*, rendered "satisfaction," means that, and also "satiety and exhilaration."

> 11. Make me immortal in the world (place) where are joys and delights and pleasures and gratifications; where the objects of desire are attained.

Dr. Muir says that the pleasures here referred to, by the words *ânandâç*, *modâç*, *mudaḥ* and *pramudaḥ*, are most probably to be understood as of a sensual kind. Roth thinks otherwise. He insists upon ascribing to the author of the hymn (a very late one) his own Christian idea of heaven. But there is no doubt that the words or most of them meant sexual pleasures. The Vedic ideas in regard to the celestial or starry existence of men translated to the skies, had already disappeared when this hymn was composed.

Dr. Muir remarks that

> it is clear that in the Vedic age, the Gods themselves were not regarded as possessing a purely spiritual nature, but as subject to the influence of various sensual appetites.

He instances their exhilaration by the Soma juice, and Indra, in Rig-Veda *iii.* 53. 6, being said to have a handsome wife, and pleasure, in his house. Other passages, imputing revelry and sensual and even sexual enjoyment to some of them, he quotes from Rig-Veda *x.* and the Atharva-Veda. But these are not of the ancient Vedic age. As to the Soma, it went to the Devas and Gods as light and heat, and thus only exhilarated them; and the passage in regard to the wife of Indra, or the light, is purely imaginative. Vishṇu is represented as possessing generative ardour and capacity; but this, also, is as purely imaginative as the gay clothing of the Goddess of Rivers, as a maiden.

What a "purely spiritual nature" is, I do not know. Light is not material, nor did flame seem so to the ancients, and certainly heat is not. We can conceive of nothing more immaterial and spiritual, than light.

The Irano-Aryans made worship or devotion a Deity, called Çraŏsha, and ascribed to him valour, as a warrior, armed with the ordinary weapons of the soldier. Did they, by this poetic personification, cease to regard him as purely spiritual?

Ushas, the dawn, is the manifestation of light and colour. The sun is her lover, and impregnated by his rays she blushes rosy red. Saraṇyû, the vapourous cloud, bears children, begotten by Vivasvaṭ. Our gospels say that Mary was found to be with child by the Holy Ghost. If Vivasvaṭ, Indra or the Holy Ghost were poetically represented as men, producing conception in the human manner, with any amplitude imaginable of description and detail, would any sensible man say that the Poet believed them to have virility and its organs, and to receive sensual enjoyment as men do?

It is time, it seems to me, that we should at least *begin* to understand the Vedic Poets; and I think it is worth endeavouring to do. If, a thousand years hereafter, as many amours should be ascribed to the Holy Ghost, effected in as many various shapes, as those of Zeus, they would be owing, no doubt, to what is said by Matthew; but they certainly would not prove that any such notion was entertained by Matthew.

The truth is that there are no sexual or even sensual ideas in the ancient Vedic hymns, ascribed to the Deities, otherwise than poetically and figuratively; and but one or two brief passages that could, being misunderstood, justify subsequent intellectual abuses in the phallic and linga worship. The gross ideas of the later Kabbalists cannot justly be attributed to the original idea of divine generation. The symbols of the wise always become the idols of the vulgar; and the inevitable progress of every religion is, from the adoration of the potency or principle symbolized, to the idolatrous worship of the symbol itself.

In another late hymn, *x*. 154, it is prayed that some one may go to those for whom the honeyed beverage flows, to those who by *tapas* have become unconquerable, unassailable, or beyond the reach of harm (*anâdhṛishyâs*), who, through or by *tapas* (*tapasâ*) have gone to the sky, to those who have performed *tapas* (*tapo ye chakrire mahas tâṁç chid*).

Dr. Muir renders *tapas*, "rigourous abstraction," which is the very latest and Brahmanic meaning of it; and we shall find in a subsequent verse *tapasvato*, rendered by him "austere," and *tapojan* rendered "born of rigourous abstraction."

3. Let him go to the combatants in battle, to the heroes who there sacrificed their lives, or to those who have bestowed thousands of largesses (*sahasradakshiṇâs*).

4. Let him depart, Yama, to those austere (*tapasvato*) ancient fathers, who have practised and promoted sacred rites (*ṛitasâpaḥ, ṛitâvânaḥ, ṛitâvṛidhaḥ*).

5. Let him depart, Yama, to those austere (*tapasvato*) Ṛishis, skilled in a thousand sciences (*sahasranîthâḥ kavayo*) who guard the sun (*gopâyanti Sûryam*).

That these Ṛishis "guard" the sun, i. e., are his guards or attendants, proves that the Ṛishis were deemed to have become stars. *Nîtha*, "guiding," from *nî* "to conduct, guide, lead away, lead to." *Nî-ti*, "guidance, moral behaviour, prudent counsel, etc." *Kavi* is "wise." I cannot find any warrant for the use of the word "sciences." There were no sciences in the Vedic days, but there were prudent counsels and wise advice.

The "largesses" bestowed were gifts for the sacrifices—later, for the Brahmins.

Tapas has several meanings. *Tap* meant, at first, "to warm, heat, shine, illuminate, to burn up," and thence, "to give pain, to suffer pain," and finally, when the practice of mortifying the body by penance and austerities grew up, it came to mean them. Its original meaning certainly appears in the participle *tapta*, "hot, melted, refined."

So *tapas* at first meant "fire," and afterwards "penance, mortification, religious austerity, devotion." And I greatly doubt whether it is used in this hymn in its later sense. I think it means sacrifice by fire. I think, even, that the Poet said of those who had become stars, that by sacrifice they were invincible and had gone to Heaven. There, I think, the *tapas* was their own cremation, by which becoming fire, they had ascended to the sky. How could a Sage, a Ṛishi, a star, be said to be "*born* of rigourous abstraction," or even of the sacrifice? I think the meaning is, that as stars they were born of the fire. There is no evidence elsewhere of the practice of austerities by the ancient Ṛishis, nor do I believe they did practice them. They sacrificed; and they chanted their songs, and received large presents for doing it, and became rich, being simply travelling Bards or officiating Priests, fed upon the sacrificial food, and exacting largesses.

In Rig-Veda *x*. 14. 4 to 6, and *x*. 15. 8, the different races of the fathers are mentioned by name, viz., Angirasas, Vairûpas, Navagvas, Atharvans, Bhrigus, Vasishthas, etc. In *x*. 15. 13, though not all known to their worshippers, they are known to Agni. For it is Agni that shines in each, even of those that are not visible, or, perhaps, of those not distinguished and known as particular stars.

Dr. Muir's references, to passages ascribing potencies to the fathers, and adoring them or praying for favours, are all to the tenth Mandala and to Atharva-Veda *xviii*. In these they are worshipped, and oblations offered to them; their good will is supplicated, and their anger deprecated; they are entreated to hear, intercede for and protect the worshippers, and to bestow on them opulence, length of life and children. They are represented as thirsting for the oblations prepared for them on earth, and are invited to come with Yama, Vivasvaṭ and Agni, and feast on the sacrificial food. They accordingly arrive by thousands, borne on the same car with Indra and the other Devas (i. e., as indivisible portions of the one light from all the orbs in the sky), and range themselves in order on the sacrificial grass. What is more natural than the idea that the Heavenly were pure light, concentrated, or divided into fragments; and that the light which reached the earth was a part of the Very Self of each, itself coming down, to return again when the star ceased to shine? As Agni was every particular fire, so he was the Very Self of every luminary, and Indra, his subsistence, emanating from him, came to the earth in every ray of light.

It is very evident that all this was but a rank growth from an original idea resembling that of the translation to the sky of Enoch in the Hebrew Book Barasith or of Generation, which appeared again in the ascent of the Prophet Elijah, and finally in that of Yesūs in the sight of his disciples. At first attributed to a few, perhaps only to the seven Ṛishis, it came at length to be considered the general destiny of all, until even bad men were smuggled in among the good, and became baleful stars. There was no other heaven, until the Brahmins invented one.

How the idea first came into being, that certain stars were ancient heroes or Sages, can, even with the aid of etymology, only be conjectured. At first, perhaps, it may have been a poetic fancy, embodied in a name, or it may have been the outgrowth of popular names applied to certain stars and groups of stars. The popular fancy gives such names before it is done by the Poets, and then the Poets weave legends to correspond with the popular names.

The three stars in the belt of Orion are popularly called the Three Kings. We have no legend, to which to assign the origin of the name. In such cases, the name precedes the legend; and we should have, no doubt, a legend of the Three Kings, but for our having outgrown that state of the intellect in which legends are invented.

I say that *we* have no legend of the Three Kings. But the name has begotten legends, and somewhat, more; for these stars are the three wise men of the East that came at dawn, bringing perfumes, to salute the newly born Saviour; and there remain still more modern legends in the folk-lore of various countries, naming the same origin.

So the stars in Gemini were called "twins" and "the twin horsemen," *Açvinau*, before they became children of Leda, by Tyndarus and Zeus; and the Pleiades were called the "girls, virgins or daughters," before a legend made them Atlantides. The popular fancy never is at rest, and is never content until it personifies and gives name to everything that the eyes behold.

The origin and derivation of the word *Ṛishi* are easily discovered. *Ṛî*, *ṛish*, *ṛij*, *ṛit* are all from the original biliteral root *ṛi*, "to go, to move," the primitive form of which was *ar*. There are a hundred derivative words in

Sanskrit from this root. In Zend, the old root *ar*, "to go," remains unchanged. In Latin it became *ire*, "to go," whence *iter*, "journey"; in Greek *eō* (εω) and *iēmi* (ιημι). *Ṛij* and *ṛish* meant originally "to go," and *ṛishi* simply "itinerant" or "journeyer": and the *Ṛishi* was an itinerant bard or minstrel.

The Seven Stars of the Great Bear, which never disappear or pause in their movement, were also naturally called the *Seven Ṛishis*, as in the Zend, *Hapto-iringa*. *Îr*, also, in Sanskrit, meant "to go," as *ish* did: and the name of this constellation therefore meant, in both languages, "The Seven Goers."

Kshi meant "to possess, rule," and also "to dwell"; and *ṛikshi* probably meant "moving without deviation, on a fixed and unchanging circuit."

Ṛiksha was probably from *ṛich*, "to shine"; for it meant "a star" as well as "a bear." *Arch* is the same word, and is found in the Greek *Arktos*, "a bear." Any one who has ever seen a bear chained to a stake will understand why *ṛiksha* may have been formed from *ṛi*, "to go"; for it is the most restless of animals, continually travelling round its stake in a circle: and the comparison of the Seven Stars to a bear would inevitably suggest itself to any one who knew a bear's habits.

By and by, of course, the derivation of *ṛiksha* as well as that of *ṛishi* was forgotten, and the *Ṛishis* became saints, the Great Bear the *Seven Ṛishis*, and so many saints translated to the skies.

SARASVATÎ.

Sarasvatî, Dr. Muir remarks, "appears to have been to the early Indians—what the Ganges became to their descendants." The texts which he cites from the Mandalas of the Rig-Veda not translated by Professor Wilson, do not enable us to identify the river, and otherwise do not give us much additional information in regard to the Vedic conceptions of this Deity. Even in the Atharva-Veda she continues to be both river and Goddess. It is as a river, that she is called "purifier"; and in the passage (Rig-Veda *x.* 17. 10; Atharva-Veda *vi.* 51. 2), where the waters, the mothers, are asked to purify the worshippers, Sarasvatî having been mentioned immediately before, it is said,

> for these Goddesses bear away defilement: I come up out of them pure and cleansed.

The purification ascribed to Sarasvatî has nothing to do with sacrifice. It is simple baptism, washing.

In *x.* 64. 9, and 75. 5, etc., she is specified along with the other well-known streams that are there named, the Sarayu, the Sindhu, the Gangâ, the Yamunaâ and the Sutudri. In *iii.* 23. 4, she is named with the Dṛishadvatî and Apâyâ. In *vii.* 96. 2, and *viii.* 21. 18, reference is made to the chiefs and people living along her banks.

A striking example of the fallibility of interpretation of difficult passages of the Veda, as well as of the resoluteness with which the simplest passages are spiritualized, is afforded by the translations of Rig-Veda *i.* 3. 12, the original of which is

> *Maho arṇaḥ Sarasvatî pra chetayati ketunâ dhiyo viçvâḥ virâjati.*

Sâyaṇa understands it of the river, and explains it thus:

> The Sarasvatî, by her act (of flowing), displays a copious flood.

Roth makes it

> A mighty stream is Sarasvatî; with her light she lightens, illuminates all pious minds.

He considers the commencing words as figurative, and not as referring to the river. Benfey renders:

> Sarasvatî, by her light, causes the great sea to be known; she shines through all thoughts.

He understands "the great sea" as the universe, or as life, which he says is often designated in common Sanskrit also by the word *sâgara*. And Dr. Muir thinks that

> the conceptions of Sarasvatî as a river, and as the directress of ceremonies, may be blended in the passage.

Dhiyo viçvâḥ virâjati certainly means, literally, "illuminates all minds, or, intellects." *Chetayati*, which Roth renders "lightens," and Benfey, "causes to be known," is third pers. sing. of *chetaya*, causative of *chit*. *Chit* means "to perceive"; and *chetaya*, "to perceive, get consciousness, think, cause to think, know." Both translates *ketunâ* by "light." *Kit* is "to perceive, to know"; and *ketu* is "a sign by which objects may be recognized." *Ketunâ* I do not find in Benfey. *Arṇa* is the ocean. If by it was meant the Indian Ocean, this hymn was composed after the Indo-Aryan emigration had reached its shores. If it was, as I believe, the Caspian, then the Sarasvatî was originally the Oxus, the Ardviçura, probably, of the *Zend-Avesta*.

May not the former portion of the verse mean that Sarasvatî makes known or enables men to find, the great sea, by being the means of reaching it, or by showing the way to it? And the latter part, that she removes all doubt as to the existence of the sea from all men's minds? I am sure that the correct interpretation must mean something, and not be nonsense pure and simple. Even Sâyaṇa felt that, as to this verse.

I am chiefly led to believe that Sarasvatî was originally the Oxus, because another stream is called Sindhu; and if she was not the Indus, I do not know where else except in Bactria, called in the *Zend-Avesta* the land of the Seven Kareshvares, she could have been called *saptasvasâ*, *saptathî sindhumâtâ*, "having seven sisters," "one of seven rivers," and "mother of streams." Nor should I think that if the Indus had once been so celebrated as Sarasvatî, it would even have lost the name, and been called simply "the river." Yet Sarasvatî *may* have been the Indus, and that river have ceased to be called so, after the Indo-Aryans had occupied the Ganges country.

In *v.* 43. 11, Sarasvatî is called on to descend from the sky, from the great mountain, to the sacrifice; and in *vi.* 49. 7, she is called the daughter of the lightning, and *Vîra-patni*. Dr. Muir renders this "wife of a hero." I find that *vîra* means "fire" as well as "hero"; and *vîra-patni* may mean "wife of fire," because water, heated by the fire, gives birth to the vapour and clouds.

She is said to descend from the sky (*divo*) and mountains, because her sources were on the heights of the immense mountains, on whose summits the sky appears to rest. Atlas, we remember, was said to bear up the sky on his shoulders.

Sarasvatî is described as bestowing wealth, fatness and fertility; and prosperity and riches of all descriptions flow from her fruitful breasts. She is the receptacle of the powers of life, and bestows offspring, and in *x*. 184. 2, is associated with the Deities who assist procreation. These attributes would indicate a river that enriched and made fertile the country by irrigation.

In *x*. 75. 1, the Indus is especially lauded as the Sindhu and as the mother-river, into which the others flow. Among eighteen other streams, the Sarasvatî is named, with the Gangâ, Yamunâ, Sutudrî, Parushṇi. Described as flashing, sparkling, gleaming, the most abundant of streams, the Sindhu is said to roll her waters over the levels; and yet is mistress of a chariot with noble horses, richly dressed, etc.

In Rig-Veda *vii*. 33, the Ṛishi Vasishṭha is said to have sprung from an *Apsaras, Urvaçi*. Böhtlingk and Roth describe the *Apsarases* as female beings of a ghost-like description, whose abode is in the atmosphere. They are the wives of the *Gandharvas*, have the power of changing their forms, love playing at dice, and impart good luck. Professor Goldstücker says that originally they seem to have been personifications of the vapours which are attracted by the sun, and form into mist or clouds. We have already seen, in *x*. 10. 4, Gandharva in the waters and his aqueous wife designated as the parents of Yama and Yamî.

Ap is "water." *Saras* is "a lake," *sṛi*+*as*, *sṛi* meaning "to flow, extend, spread, spread out." So *Sarasa* is "a pond," and *sarasija* "a lotus," which grows in ponds. *Sarasvant* is "the ocean"; *sari*, "a water-fall," and *sarit*, "a river." *Apsaras* is simply a lake of water, as *nabhas-saras* is a lake or expanse of clouds: and the *Apsarases* were, no doubt, the lakes in which the various rivers, or part of them, had their rise. *Urva*, fem. of *uru*, is "large"; and *Urvaçi*, the *Apsaras*, was, no doubt merely a large lake, like Siricol, out of which the main branch of the Oxus flows. Vasishṭha was born, probably, near some lake, so called.

ÇRADDHÂ.

Rig-Veda *x*. 151, is addressed to Çraddhâ, or "religious faith." By her, it is said, the fire is kindled, and the oblation offered. She is asked to prosper the liberal worshippers of the Gods, and to impart faith, and is said to be an object of adoration in the morning, at noon and at sunset.

Çraddhâ is unmistakably the Çraŏsha of the *Zend-Avesta*, "worship" or "devotion," supposed by the commentators to have become one of the Amĕsha-Çpĕntas at a comparatively late period. But, Çraŏsha was not an Amĕsha-Çpĕnta. As worship was the efficient cause of prosperity and victory, Çraŏsha was represented as a warrior, fighting on the Aryan side.

THE ṚIBHUS.

In note to *i.* 51. 2, the protecting and fostering Ṛibhus are said to mean the Maruts. They hastened to the presence of Indra, and uttered encouraging words. Hymn 110 of Mandala *i.* is addressed to them, and they are invited to drink to their utmost content of the Soma juice, when it is offered in the fire. They are, therefore, Light-Gods, i. e., stars; what stars, it may not be possible to ascertain.

And they were mortals deified, translated to the sky as stars, for in verse 2, the Ṛishi Kutsa, author of the hymn, calls them sons of Sudhanvan, and says that when they were amongst his own ancestors, they went to the forest to perform (penance), being desirous of enjoying (the Soma libations), and while immature (*apâkâ*, literally, Wilson says, "unripe," and meaning here "immature in wisdom").

When they so retired, it is said, then, through the plenitude of their completed, they came "to the hall of the worshipper Savitṛi."

> (3). 'Then Savitṛi bestowed upon you immortality, when you came to him who is not to be concealed, and represented to partake of the libations; and that ladle for the sacrificial viands which the Asura had formed single, you made four-fold.' [*i.* 20. 6. 'The Ṛibhus have divided into four the new ladle, the work of the divine Tvashṭṛi:' (2). 'They created (*tatakshuh*) mentally (*manasâ*) for Indra the horses that are harnessed at his words:' (3). 'They constructed (*takshan*) for the Nasatyas, a universally-moving and easy car, and a cow-yielding milk'.]

Lauded by the bystanders (*i.* 110. 6), the Ṛibhus, with a sharp tool meted out the single sacrificial ladle, like a field, soliciting the best, and desiring sacrificial food amongst the Devas.

> 6. To the leaders, dwelling in the firmament, we present . . . . the bûtter, and praise with knowledge those Ṛibhus, who, having equalled the velocity of the protector, ascended to the region of the sky, through of food.

And then Ṛibhu is declared in strength the defender of the worshipper, and his asylum through gifts of food and wealth. This must mean that *each* of the Ṛibhus is so; for the functions of all are the same.

They are styled *nṛibhyah*, "leaders" (*yajnasya*, "of the sacrifice," being according to the commentators, understood); as in the text *Ṛibhava hi yajnasya netârah*, "the Ṛibhus are the leaders of the sacrifice." Rosen thinks that in the text first quoted they are leaders or chiefs of the air. But *nṛi* means, simply, "a man," and *nṛibhyah* is its dative plural. The meaning of the text is, "To the mortals who abide in the firmament" (*antarikshasya*), i. e., to those who once were mortals.

In note to *v.* 6, Professor Wilson says that a text of the Veda identifies the Ṛibhus with the solar rays (*Âdityarasmayo api Ṛibhava uchyante*). But *uch* means only "to like, to be accustomed to," and the text does not *identify* them with the *Âditya-rasmayo*, even if *Âditya* there means "the sun." But Wilson adds, "the Ṛibhus are, indeed, said to be rays of the sun." Where?

Benfey considers *Ṛibhu* to be *rabh+u*. And *rabh*, originally *grabh*, *labh*, according to him, means "to seize, to take:" but it must have had other meanings; or its derivative *rabhas* would not mean, in the Veda, "zeal, strength, strengthening food, sacrifice": nor *rabhasa*, "joyful, joy, passion, speed, velocity, precipitation, regret, sorrow" (though all these are later meanings). Accordingly, *labh* means "to obtain, get, acquire, enjoy, undergo, perform"; and *grabh* or *grah*, not only "to take," but "to captivate, gain, undergo, perceive, learn," and many other things. But I am skeptical as to this derivation. The change of *rabh* into *ṛibh* is, to use a pet word, "startling." It is quite as likely that *ṛibhu* is from *rebh*, "to praise."

In *i.* 161, the legend of the ladle is more fully given, but none the less remains an enigma. In verse 1, the Ṛibhus, sons of Sudhanvan are represented as saying,

> Is this our senior or our junior who has come? Has he come upon a message? What is it we should say? Agni, brother, we revile not the ladle (*chamasa*) which is of exalted race. Verily, we assert the dignity of the wooden.

In verse 2, the messenger replies:

> Make four-fold the single ladle: so the Devas command you, and for that purpose I am come, sons of Sudhanvan. If you accomplish this, you will be entitled to sacrifices along with the Devas.

They replied, that having made a horse, a car and a cow, and two persons young, they were ready to execute this new order. They did so, and then asked for the messenger, Tvashṭṛi; but when he saw the one ladle become four, he disappeared among the women (*gnâsu antar nyânaje;* but what *gnâsu* means is uncertain).

> 5. When Tvashṭṛi said, 'Let us slay those who have profaned the ladle for the drinking of the Devas,' then they made use of other names for one another, as the libation was poured out; and the maiden propitiated them by different appellations, *anyair enân kanyâ namabhih sparat.*

Benfey gives, as meanings of *spṛi*, "to gratify, protect, live." Who the girl or virgin was that protected the Ṛibhus, is unknown: probably the dawn, Ushas.

> 6. Indra has caparisoned his horses: the Açvins have harnessed their car: Bṛihaspati has accepted the omniform: therefore, Ṛibhu, Vibhwa and Vâja, go to the Gods, doers of good deeds, enjoy your sacrificial portion.

7. Sons of Sudhanvan, from a hideless (cow) you have formed a living one; by your marvellous acts you have made your aged parents young; from one horse you have fabricated another: harness now your chariot, and repair unto the Devas.

8. They have said, 'Sons of Sudhanvan, drink of this water, or drink that which has been filtered through the Munja grass; or if you be pleased with neither of these, be exhilarated at the third sacrifice.'

9. Waters are the most excellent, said one: Agni is the most excellent, said another: the third declared to many, *vardhayantim* [said by the Scholiast to mean either a line of clouds, or the earth. *Vardhaya*, causative of *vṛidh*, means 'to augment, to make powerful, to exalt.' But what 'that which augments, enlarges or makes powerful' is, is to be ascertained from the preceding verse. It is, of course, the third thing named there,—that which, when drunk, exhilarates, i. e., the Soma juice, or, more probably, that aliment of the stars which ascends to them from the fire of the sacrifice]: and thus speaking true things, the Ṛibhus divided the ladle.

10. One pours the red water upon the ground: one cuts the flesh, divided into fragments by the chopper: and a third separates the excrement from the other parts. In what manner may the parents render assistance to their sons?

Nothing more is said in this hymn, in regard to making the ladles. In *iv.* 33, addressed to the Ṛibhus, we find as follows:

5. The eldest said, 'let us make two ladles': the youngest said, 'let us make three': Tvashṭṛi, O Ṛibhus, applauded your proposition.

6. The men kept their word, for such they made, and thereupon the Ṛibhus partook of that libation. Tvashṭṛi, beholding the four ladles, brilliant as day, was content.

iv. 35. 2. May the munificence of the Ṛibhus come to me on this occasion; there has been the drinking of the effused Soma, in consequence of one ladle having been made four-fold by their dextrous and excellent work.

3. You have made the ladle four-fold, and have said, 'assent!' therefore have you gone, Vâjas, the path of the undying: dextrous-handed Ṛibhus, the company of the Devas.

4. What sort of ladle was that which by skill you have made four? . . . .

5. . . . . By your deeds you have made the ladle for the drinking of the Devas.

iv. 36. 4. You have made the single ladle four-fold . . . . therefore you have obtained immortality amongst the Devas. . . . .

Other things said to and of the Ṛibhus are:

i. 161. 11. Ṛibhus, leaders, you have caused the grass to grow upon the high places: you have caused the waters to flow over the low places; for good works [for abundant production? Thus the spring rains are attributed to them, causing the grass to grow on the high grounds, and enabling the husbandman to irrigate the alluvial lands]: as you have reposed for awhile in the dwelling of the unapprehensible (*agohyasya gṛihe*), so desist not today from this.

Gṛiha is "a house." *Guhya*, partic. of the fut. pass. of *guh* "to conceal," means "to be concealed, hidden, mysterious." *Agohyasya* must mean "the unconcealable." In verse 13, the translation has,

> Ṛibhus, reposing in the solar orb, you inquire, 'who awakens us, *Agohyasya*, to this office?' The sun replies, *çvânam bodhayitâram*, 'the awakener or arouser is the dog'. [The commentator 'explains' *çvânam* as 'the wind'. It is Sirius, the Dog-Star, which we have elsewhere seen called the dog]: and the year (being ended), you again today light up this.
>
> 12. As you glide along enveloping the regions, where, then, are the parents? Curse him who arrests your arm: reply sternly to him who speaks disrespectfully.

In *iv.* 33 are noticeable these passages:

> 1. I send my prayer as a messenger to the Ṛibhus. I solicit the milch cow, the yielder of the white milk . . . . for they, as swift as the wind, the doers of good works, were borne quickly across the firmament by rapid steeds.
>
> 2. When the Ṛibhus, by honouring their parents with renovated, and by other works, had achieved enough, they thereupon proceeded to the society of the Devas; and, considerate, they bring nourishment to the devout.

It is then recited that they made their aged parents young, and investing a cow with flesh, continued its beauty for a year, and so obtained immortality.

> 7. When the Ṛibhus, reposing for twelve days, remained in the hospitality of the unconcealable (sun), they made the fields fertile, they led forth the rivers, plants sprung up on the waste, and waters were on the low lands.

Unmistakably, this means that these three stars rose, for twelve mornings so short a time before the sun, as to be enveloped by the light that preceded his coming in the east.

> 8. . . . . those Ṛibhus who constructed the firm-abiding, wheel-conducting car; who formed the all-impelling multiform milch-cow. . . . .
>
> 9. The Gods were pleased by their works . . . . Vâja was the artificer of the Devas, Ṛibhukshin of Indra, Vibhvan of Varuṇa.

In verse 10 they are said to have constructed for Indra his two docile steeds. In *iv.* 34. 6, it is said of them,

> associated with Indra, with whom you are intelligent,

i. e., their light is his manifestation; and in verse 7 they sympathize in satisfaction with Varuṇa, as, in verse 8, they are said to sympathize with the Adityas, Savitṛi and others. In verse 9, they are the all-pervading leaders. In *iv.* 35. 8, they are

> Sons of strength, who have become Devas by soaring aloft in the sky like falcons.

And in *iv.* 37. 4, where they are called Vâjins, they are said to be borne by stout horses, mounted on a brilliant car; and they are called *ayahsiprâ* and *sunishkâh*. The latter means "beautifully ornamented": the meaning of the former seems undiscoverable. And, in the same verse, they are

> Sons of Indra and grandsons of strength:

or rather, *they* are *son* and *grandson;* for the two nouns are in the singular, though followed by *vah*, "you" in the plural.

These Deities are munificent, givers of food, and showerers, and also intelligent and wise, and are prayed unto for many blessings.

Vâja means "a wing, food, feather of an arrow, battle, speed, sound." It is from *vâj*, "to go." Another *vaj* means "to strengthen," and Benfey thinks there was probably a verb *vaj*, "to increase, to be strong." From it are the Latin *vigor* and *vigere*.

Vibhâ is "light, lustre, a ray of light"; *vibhâvan*, "shining"; *vibhava*, "power"; *vibhu*, "omnipresent, all-pervading, eternal, solid, master, lord."

It is very clear that these Ṛibhus were three stars, large and brilliant, and near enough to each other to be deemed a trinity or single constellation. They were in the same quarter of the heavens, also, as the Açvins, and Sirius rose before them, leading them up. Originally, also, they were real or legendary personages, to whom, if real, many legendary tales had attached. What was meant by their having made the car and horses of Indra, I cannot even conjecture; and the multiplication of the sacrificial ladle or cup is as great an enigma to me as ever. No doubt, those who heard the hymn, when it was composed and long after, knew what it meant; but the allegory has lost its meaning for us.

As to the stars so named, I think they were the three in the belt of Orion.

RUDRA.

In *i.* 114. 1, in the translation of Professor Wilson, Rudra is called "the Destroyer of Heroes." The original of this is *Kshayad Vîrâya*, of which he says,

> in whom heroes (*virâ*) perish (*vinaçyanti*); or it may mean, of whom the imperial (*kshayantah prâptaisvarayâh*, heroes, i. e., the Maruts) are the sons.

In the *Zend-Avesta*, the fourth Amĕsha-Çpĕnta, or emanation from Ahura Mazda, is *Khshathra-Vairya*. The two names or epithets are evidently identical. *Khshathra* means "sovereignty, royalty, dominion." *Vairya* means "heroic," from the Sanskrit *vaira*, "heroism, prowess." In those ages, sovereignty was won only by heroism and prowess in war. *Vîra* is the same word as *vaira*, meaning "heroic, strong, powerful, eminent, a hero, a soldier"; and *vîrâya*, a denominative from it, means "to show one's heroism." *Vîrâya* or *virya* is "strength, power, fortitude, heroism, dignity, splendour, virility"; and it is also an adjective, and means "strong, potent, heroic," etc.

Kshaya, in Benfey, is *kshi+a*, "loss, destruction," etc., from *kshi*, "to destroy." But also he gives *kshi*, part. *kshaya*, "to possess, to rule"; and from this come *kshatra*, "dominion, sovereignty," and the *kshayad* of the text; and also the *Khshathra* of the *Zend-Avesta*, the Russian *Tzar*, and the word *Tarshatha* in Nehemiah.

So that the epithet, applied to Rudra is, "heroic sovereign." And it is an interesting fact that this epithet of one of the potencies of fire should have become, with the Irano-Aryans, the name of an Amĕsha-Çpĕnta, the original of *Malakoth*, the Tenth Sephirah or Emanation, of the Hebrew Kabbalah.

UNITY OF INTELLECT AND POWER.

I have endeavoured all the time to keep in mind that those men whose uttered thoughts in the Veda and *Zend-Avesta* I have endeavoured partially to understand and interpret were my ancestors, with intellects of like nature as my own, and who thought and sung as Wordsworth and Shelley would have done, if they had been of that age. It is necessary to identify ourselves as perfectly as possible with them, to imagine ourselves, with as little knowledge of Nature as they, living when and where they did, subject to the same influences, encompassed by the same surroundings, unacquainted with the causes, even proximate, of the phenomena of Nature, having their intellectual wants and aspirations, with no restraints such as modern good taste and chaste refinement imposes, to hinder the most audacious flights of the imagination, and with that ungovernable fancy for personification which filled the temples of Athens with male and female statues of the Gods and peopled the poetry of every branch of the race with a thousand graceful and beautiful beings, creatures of the imagination, making the seasons, the years, the potencies of Nature, the virtues and the vices, Fortune with her blinded eyes, Hope leaning on her anchor, and Charity, beings like ourselves.

And we must not only make ourselves to be, for the time, what they were intellectually; but we must live their life, be with them herding their cattle on the steppes, sacrificing at dawn in the open air, cultivating their fields and subjugating the native tribes.

We must be with them in their own land also; for no one is ignorant of the influence on the intellectual character of a people, exerted by the scenery with which it is familiar. It is to their mountains the Swiss owe their continued freedom.

Samuel Johnson, in his *Oriental Religions*, very lately published, speaking of "the Bactrian Highlands, at the northeastern extremity of Iran, nestling under the multitudinous heights of the Bolur-Tagh and Hindū-Kush," says:

> They who have penetrated farthest into these mountain ranges report that the silent abysses of the midnight sky, with its intensely burning stars, and the colossal peaks lifting their white masses beyond storms, impress the imagination with such a sense of fathomless mystery and eternal repose, as no other region on earth can suggest. The mean altitude of these summits of Himâlaya, the Home of Snow, is loftier than that of any other mountain system in the world; and their mighty faces, unapproachable by man, overlook vast belts of forest which he has not ventured to explore. From one point, Hooker saw twenty snow peaks, each over twenty thousand feet in height, whose white ridge of frosted silver stretched over the whole horizon for one hundred and sixty degrees. Here are splendours and glooms, unutterable powers, impenetrable reserves, correspondent to that spiritual nature in whose earlier education they bore an essential part.

This writer has the key of interpretation of the Veda, and has, I think, in a few sentences expressed more of the real meaning of its hymns, than any other commentator. For example:

> The word *Div*, designating at once the clear light of the sky [which is an error, since *dyu* meant the sky itself, and only that]; and whatsoever spiritual meanings these simple instincts intimately associated therewith, has endured as the root word of worship for the whole Aryan race: in all its branches the appellatives of Deity are waves of this primal sound, flowing through all its manifold and changing religions with the serene transcendence of an eternal law. . . .
>
> We may infer, from the testimony of the two related Bibles, *that the oldest Aryas found God in all the forms and functions of fire* . . . . The Sacred Fire, kept kindled on the domestic altar, as the centre of religious sentiment and rite, and as consecrating all social, civil and political relations, is found to be a common heritage of all Aryan races. Its flame ascended from every household-hearth, watched by the Pitris, or fathers, alive and dead, of this primitive civilization.

Here Dr. Johnson loses sight of the idea which, reflected upon and developed, would have been fruitful of truth; and wanders into a by-path that "gives out" in the woods. He adds,

> Modern scholars have traced its profound influence, as type and sacrament of the family, in shaping the whole religious and municipal life of ancient Greece and Italy.

But every people has had the household fire and the family. These are not peculiar to the Aryan race. The "sacred" light was in every house, also, whether of the sun by day or the fire or lamp at night: but it was not its connection with family that was most excellent in either. Nor does it appear that the household fire was kept always burning, or was regarded as entitled to veneration, except as a part of the Universal Fire.

But in a subsequent page he is in presence of the truth again, when after an interesting discussion of the character of the Hindū mind, he says,

> To appreciate the results of these contemplative tendencies, we must recall *the old Aryan worship of the clear Light of Day.*

And further on, treating of the Rig-Veda, he says:

> These hymns are outcomes of a yet remoter past; they point us beyond themselves to marvellous creative faculty in the imagination and faith of what is otherwise wholly inaccessible, the childhood of man. They present a language already perfected without the aid of a written alphabet [one of two, itself and the Zend, dialects of one older language spoken before the separation, ages before, of these two branches of the Aryan family, itself the development of one still older, spoken by the ancestors of Kelt, Goth, Sclave, Latin and Greek, before any of them emigrated]; a literature already preserved for ages in the religious memory alone. They sing of older hymns, which the fathers sang—of 'ancient Sages and elder Gods.' They were themselves old, at the earliest epoch to which we can trace them. Their

> religion, like their language, was already mature, when they were born. Do not seek in them the beginning of the religious sentiment, the dawning of the idea of the Divine. Their Deities are all familiar and ancestral. It is already an intimate household faith, which ages have endeared. 'This is our prayer, the old, the prayer of our fathers.' 'Our fathers resorted to Indra of old; they discovered the hidden light and caused the dawn to rise; they who showed us the road, the earliest guides.' 'Now, as of old, make forward paths for the new hymn, springing from our heart.' 'Hear a hymn from me, a modern bard.' As far back as we can trace the life of man, we find the river of prayer and praise flowing as naturally as it is flowing now. We cannot find its beginning, because we cannot find the beginning of the soul.

That is true of the Aryan race. But we know nothing of the lacustrine dwellers or the Troglodytes of the Quaternary period, or the indigenes of various countries, of the age or period of stone. And we find prayer and praise flowing among the Egyptians, Hebrews and Chinese also, as far back as we can trace them.

What is much more important, of incalculable importance to us, is this, that if the ontological conceptions which I think are really contained in the Veda and *Zend-Avesta*, *are* really there, it has needed neither special inspiration nor special incarnation of God to teach men any truth of which the human intellect is now possessed. The Aryan human intellect was able to discover them all.

For as to the perfection of the language, the Turkish is said to be so much so that it might seem to have been invented by a Congress of most accomplished men of learning. And there are languages of very barbarous tribes that astonish us by their wealth of forms. The thoughts of the Vedic poets are of far greater import to us than their language.

Again Dr. Johnson says:

> This infantile nature *nevertheless adored the light.* The dawn and the decline of day, and the starlit night that hinted in its splendours an unseen sun returning on a path behind the veil, were dear to its imagination and its faith; and fire, in all its mysterious forms, from the spark that lighted the simple oblation, and the flame that rose from the domestic hearth, to that central orb, in which the prescience of their active instinct saw, so long ago, an all-productive cosmic energy, was everywhere one and the same, alike mysterious, alike divine. And this vital Fire of the Universe was everywhere within call, stooping to human conditions, respondent to their need and will; at once a father and a child; born when the seeker would, out of dark wombs in herb and tree; waiting there to kindle at the touch of his hand, when he rubbed the two bits of wood, or turned the wheel of his fire-churn, as if his busy fingers reach through the bright deeps on high, and brought life at their tips, *kindled life*, fresh from the central flame.
>
> Light, as element of Nature, as vision of the Soul! The symbol is forever dear. And it was *as* symbol, not as mere material element, that it had religious homage in the early ages. Unconscious symbolism [he thinks it is], a sense of help, beauty, power, in the elements, already obscurely suggesting the intimate unity of Nature with man; the condition and germ of all later development in man. And this is what we find in the Veda.

The old Vedic Deities all center in this purest of the elements [Light].

But neither is this Vedic worship the mere personification of the elements, the mere calling the thing fire, or cloud or moonplant, a God. What we do in fact note here, in the not yet differentiated instinct, is a predominance of the spiritual element, and this not only in its constant recognition of intelligence as everywhere, the substance of Nature, and in its admiration of conscious energies and volitions, etc. . . . . It is indeed what Quinet finely declares to be the meaning of the whole Vedic religion—'*Revelation by Light.*'

That a profound theistic instinct, the intuition of a divine and living whole, is involved in the primitive mental processes we are here studying, I hold to be beyond all question. For these hymns are in reality not so much the worship of many Deities, as the recognition of Deity everywhere . . . . there is manifold revelation, but there is also unity of impression. The response to these divine invitations takes outwardly different directions, is addressed to different objects; but intrinsically it is seeking the same spirit in all.

It is not mere element-worship [he says]: the religious sentiment recognizing the æsthetic faculty, rather; an assertion of inherent rights and capacities of the soul. It is, 'no mere element-worship,' and the Grecian cosmogonies, like it, clearly indicate the recognition of life and mind as the essence of these outward forms.

In no other way can we explain the fact that these Vedic Deities are in no essential respect distinguishable from each other. It is not merely that *they are mostly forms of light or fire:* this recognition of unity in the symbol points back to the intuition of a deeper spiritual and moral oneness. They are all described in the same way, all are truthful, beneficent, generous, omniscient, omnipotent. All are bestowers of life, inspirers of knowledge. They are alike the refuge of men, alike immortal; creators and measurers of the world, for the benefit of men; radiant with all-searching light, transcending and pervading all worlds. . . . They have all equal praise. . . . All are invoked for the same blessings. They are even mutually interchangeable, ... and all alike are supreme.

These mysterious forms and processes of light, to which diverse names were attached, really flowed into one another; sometimes by imperceptible gradations, sometimes by instantaneous shift, as of feeling or mood.

Even so is this whole religion contained in the adoration of light; in the sense of *a vital fire* in the universe, one with the life that stirred within the soul; in the search for this through all disguises, and the recognition of it in all visible powers.

The Vedic hymns belong to different epochs, and must represent many changes in the special ideal associated with each of the Gods; and that every fresh form would naturally be held the offspring of the last. Doubtless, too, these images of birth and youth in part refer to natural transitions or phases of the heavenly bodies, the visible symbols of Deity; and report the ever-fresh productive vigour of their outgoings and renewals.

The good man ascends to heaven and stands among the Gods. The stars of the generous shine in the firmament. They partake of immortality.

I quote these passages for that of truth in them which others than their author have failed to discover. What there is of error I do not care to point out. And I conclude with this sentence:

For the germs of this our larger opportunity, which guarantees wisdom and gladness to man's present and future thought; of his genial outlook upon life as a

> home, and his fearless hospitality to its forces and laws; of the home-born courage to use all faculties and open all paths; of the assurance that we are not slaves of prescription, whether to person, creed or distinctive religion, but natural heirs to universal truth; of the self-respect whose religion is rational, and the liberty whose ideal is endless progress, we must go back to the frank Aryan herdsman, inviting his Gods to sit as guests beside him on his heap of kusá-grass.

And for all our conceptions of God as an Universal Substance, a Supreme Unity infinitely extended and containing in Its Self all manifoldness, as the One Essential Light that is the Life of the Universe; the One Intellect that is revealed and manifested in all Intellects, as it is manifested as Light wherever Light is; of a Deity beneficent, indulgent, protecting and not merciless, cruel and vindictive like the Semitic Gods that have so long been the Christian God; for our conceptions of the creative Wisdom and the Word that is the Deity's very Self manifested; of Spirit, of the immaterial soul, of immortality, we must go back to the Poets who chanted their devotional songs in the hearing of the same herdsmen, at the morning-sacrifice, to the dawn, to Mitra the Morning Star, and Varuṇa, the regal Jupiter, as manifestations of the Light.

For all these are either their conceptions, or have grown out of theirs.

And there is an immense wealth of content and satisfaction, to me, in surely knowing that nothing which is known to us in regard to God, ourselves or Nature, nothing of true religion, nothing of sound ontology, has come to us from the race that had its origin in the low flat alluvion of the Euphrates and the Tigris; and we no more think the Semitic thought than we have in our veins Semitic blood, or speak a Semitic tongue.

ADVANCE OF THE ARYAN INTELLECT TOWARDS REASON.

In Section *xxi.* of Volume *V.* of the *Sanskrit Texts*, Dr. Muir considers "The Progress of the Vedic religion towards abstract conceptions of the Deity."

After quoting the notions of Yaska, he proceeds to say:

> These, however, are the views of men who lived after the compilation of the Brâhmaṇas, at a period when reflection had long been exercised upon the contents of the hymns, and when speculation had already made considerable advances. In the oldest portions of the hymns themselves, we discover few traces of any such abstract conceptions of the Deity. They disclose a much more primitive stage of religious belief. They are, as I have already remarked, the productions of simple men, who, under the influence of the most impressive phenomena of Nature, saw everywhere the presence and agency of divine powers, who imagined that each of the great provinces of the universe was directed and animated by its own separate Deity, and who had not yet risen to a clear idea of one Supreme Creator and Governor of all things. This is shown, not only by the special functions assigned to particular Gods, but in many cases by the very names which they bear, corresponding to those of some of the elements, or of the celestial luminaries.
>
> Thus, according to the belief of the ancient Ṛishis, Agni was the divine Being, who resides and operates in fire; Sûrya the God who dwells and shines in the sun; and Indra the regent of the atmosphere, who cleaves the clouds with his thunderbolts, and dispenses rain.

Agni is not a divine being, who resides and operates in the fire. He is the Fire or Fire, Itself; that which is limitedly manifested in every particular fire. To this Universal or Unity, only visible in diversity, the Poets ascribed intellect, wisdom, power, will, foresight and beneficence; and these being human attributes, the ascription of them to Agni made him a Deity, precisely as we make ourselves a God, by imagining non-matter having being and extension, and investing this creature of the intellect with our own intellectual and moral attributes; and it being very doubtful whether we do not, in spite of our resolution not to do it, ascribe to him our physical attributes, as well, being only semiconscious of it.

Neither is Sûrya the God who dwells and shines in the sun. He is the sun, by whom Agni and Indra shine, the Very Orb itself. And Indra is not the regent of the atmosphere. He is Light, and has nothing to do with the atmosphere. He cleaves the clouds with his lightnings, to dispel the darkness which they create, that darkness being, *protanto*, the annihilation of himself. The rains that follow are but the incidental result.

> While, however, in most parts of the Rig-Veda, we not only find that such Gods as Agni, Indra and Sûrya are considered as distinct from one another, but that various other Divinities, more or less akin to these, but thought of as fulfilling

> functions in some respects distinguishable from theirs (such as Parjanya, Vishṇu, Savitṛi, Pushan, etc.) are represented as existing along-side of them, there are other hymns in which a tendency to identification is perceptible, and traces are found of one uniform power being conceived to underlie the various manifestations of divine energy. Thus Agni is represented as having a threefold existence, by which may be intended, first, in his familiar form on earth; secondly, as lightning in the atmosphere; and thirdly, as the sun in the heavens. In other passages, where the same God is identified with Vishṇu, Varuṇa, Mitra, etc., it is not clear whether this identification may not arise from a desire to magnify Agni, rather than from any idea of his essential oneness with other Deities with whom he is connected.
>
> In *iv*. 42. 3, too, where Indra appears to be represented as the same with Varuṇa (*aham Indro Varuṇah*, etc.), the design of the writer may have been to place the former God on a footing of equality with the latter.

There is a singular want of logical coherency in these notions of Dr. Muir. How could Indra be made *equal* to Varuṇa, by declaring him to be one and the same? Does a desire to magnify Agni (as if each Deity had his partizans) explain the Vedic idea of the oneness of Agni and any other Deity? This idea of oneness is a distinct, peculiar and striking one, like that of the oneness of the Logos and Father of Philo and St. John. It is a peculiar metaphysical conception, not in the least explained by a desire, however great, to *magnify*, and especially not by a desire to magnify the greater, Agni or the Father. When it is said in the *Zend-Avesta* that Çpĕnta-Mainyu, the Divine Intellect abiding in the Very Deity, *is* the Amĕsha-Çpĕntas, which are emanations from the Deity, no desire to magnify can explain this. The emanation-theory explains it. But Dr. Muir, missing that idea of emanation and manifestation by limitation, which explains everything that seems obscure, is continually engaged in endeavouring to explain inexplicable contradictions, incoherencies and absurdities, which the texts, as he interprets them, present. He continues to say:

> There are, however, other passages, in the earlier works of the Rig-Veda, which suffice to show that the writers had begun to regard the principal Divinities as something more than mere representations or regents of the different provinces of Nature.

That is true. There is nothing in the earlier books to show that they *ever* regarded them as "mere *representations* or *regents*" of any provinces of Nature. But on the other hand, there is nothing to show that they had any conception of "one uniform power underlying the various manifestations of divine energy," as distinct from or as superior to the fire. Fire itself, invested with the attributes of intellect, with an intellectual and moral nature, was itself the one uniform power; but there were supposed Deities whose power was not the power of Agni, nor they any manifestation of Him. Such were the Maruts and Sarasvatī.

> Varuṇa, Indra, Sûrya, Savitṛi and Agni are severally described (in strains more suitable to the Supreme Deity than to Subaltern Divinities exercising a limited dominion), as having formed and as sustaining heaven and earth, and as rulers of the universe [and the Soma-juice may be added to the list]; and Varuṇa in particular, according to the striking representation of the hymn preserved in the Atharva-Veda *iv.* 16 (though this composition may be of a somewhat later date), is invested with the divine prerogatives of omnipresence and omniscience.

This is a very great and grave error. All luminaries are said to *see* all things, meaning that their light shines throughout the expanse, and over all the sky, and on all the earth below them; and light, whether called Indra, or, as manifested by one orb, Sûray or Varuṇa, is said to be everywhere, for the same reason. That is not what divine omnipresence and omniscience are, for us.

> Although the recognized co-existence of all these Deities is inconsistent with the supposition that their worshippers had attained to any clear comprehension of the unity of the Godhead, and although the epithets denoting universal dominion, which are lavished upon them all, in turn, may be sometimes hyperbolical or complimentary, the expression of momentary fervour, or designed to magnify a particular Deity at the expense of all other rival objects of adoration, yet these descriptions no doubt indicate enlarged and sublime conceptions of divine power, and an advance towards the idea of a Sovereign Deity.

Agni was God, as we understand that word, but not God as Creator. There is no speculation in the Veda as to his existence without beginning, and he is not represented as having created the material universe. Neither does his unity include all the Deities; but the Aryan Poets had a perfectly clear idea and comprehension of his unity, so far as other Deities were manifestations of him. If the Divine Unity, to be such, must include in itself all Deities, must it not also include in itself all intellects, and our creed be Pantheism?

Agni had the essential attributes of God and was veritably God, as being without form or shape or limitation, or local habitation, indefinable and not cognizable even by the intellect; as a power, intellectual and moral, with no idea of materiality connected with a pure and perfect Spirit, an intellect, one, simple and without body or limitation. It needed only the one step further that Zarathustra took, to give the universe a God as pure and perfect, as inaccessible and immaterial, as any religion or any philosophy has ever imagined. There is nothing whatever of the Bâl, Al or Yehuah of the miscalled Semitic race, in the character of Agni. No human form or sensual appetites or detestable passions were ascribed to him; but chiefly truth, wisdom and beneficence. To obtain the Veritable God of our own conception, The One Pure and Perfect of the highest Hindū, Bactrian and Grecian Philosophy and of Christianity (which began as a reform of Hebraic morals and ended in a revolt against the Hebraic creed), it was only necessary to separate the intellectual and moral attributes of Agni from his nature as simple fire, give the former personality and indefiniteness, and call them Ahura and Mazda. Neither philosophy not religion ever has procured or ever will procure for itself a more perfect and spiritual conception of Deity, than that of Zarathustra the Great Bactrian, or the Unknown Thinker, earlier than he, who first taught the being of such a Deity, Supreme Power and Wisdom, Substance of all Light, Source of all Intellect, Author of all Good, supremely just and right and perfectly beneficent.

> When once the notion of particular Gods had become expanded in the manner just specified, and had risen to an ascription of all divine attributes to the particular object of worship who was present for the time to the mind of the Poet, the further step would speedily be taken, of speaking of the Deity under such new names as *Viçvakarman* and *Projâpati*, appellations which do not designate any limited function connected with any single department of Nature, but the more general and abstract notion of divine power operating in the production and government of the Universe.
>
> It is perhaps in names such as these that we may discover the point of transition from polytheistic to monotheistic ideas. Both these two terms, which ultimately came to designate the Deity regarded as the Creator, had been originally used as epithets of Indra and Savitṛi, in the following passages: Rig-Veda *iv.* 53. 2, 'Savitṛi the supporter of the sky and the Lord of creatures' (*divo dharttâ bhuvanasya prajâpatiḥ*). *viii.* 87. 2, 'Thou, Indra art most powerful; thou hast caused the sun to shine; thou art great, the universal architect, and possessest all Godlike attributes' (*tvam Indra abhibhir asi tvam Sûryam arochayah viçva karmâ viçvadevo mahânasi*).

As I am convinced that the Aryan intellect was the same and its laws of thought and modes of thinking were the same, seven thousand, and ten thousand, years ago, that it and they are to-day, and that the intellectual characteristics as well as the physical and moral ones, of race are unchangeable otherwise than in the line of development and progress, I do not believe that these ancient Aryan Poets ever uttered so perfect an absurdity, such a specimen of nonsense, as that the sun or moon "supported" the sky. Even the Negro intellect is too high above the ape's to have uttered that.

Dharttâ is the past participle passive of *dhṛi;* and the meanings of this verb are, as given by Benfey, "to bear, carry, maintain, support," and, passive, "to exist, live, stop, retain, resist, have, keep;" and the casual, *dhâraya*, means "to bear, hold, weigh, continue to live, support, keep, possess, practice, endure, contain, recover." There is nothing more ridiculous in the translations of the Veda than the phrase "supporting the sky," applied to a star or planet.

Besides, *dharttâ* is a *passive* participle, and *divo* is not in the genitive or accusative; and I think that *divo dharttâ* means "being, or dwelling, in the sky; a denizen of the sky." There is not a figure of speech in the Veda that might not occur or suggest itself to an English, French or German Poet, and if we meet with one in the translations of the Veda, that never would occur to *us*, we may be quite sure it never *did* occur to *them*. It is very certain that no Poet not insane would at this day think of saying that a star or planet or the moon or sun *held up* the sky.

Prajâ means "progeny, offspring, creature, subjects, people." *Pati* is "master, governor, lord, husband"; and *bhuvanasya* is gen. sing. of *bhuvana*, "being, creature, world, man, mankind, heaven, water." I think that *bhuvanasya prajâpatiḥ* means "chief of, or among, the beings of the sky."

Indra, being the light that flows forth through the sun, of course makes him to shine. Neither the firmament nor the atmosphere could be said to do *that;* and all the commentators make one or the other of these Indra.

Viçva-karmâ is *viçva*, all+*karma*, from *kṛi*, "to make, produce, cause, utter forth." I think that *viçva-karmâ viçvadevo* means "producer, or, causer, of all, *and* all, the Devas"; i. e., that they are all manifestations of the light, and all *are* the light or Indra.

Soma, also, is called *prajâpati*, "chief or master of beings, progeny or people," in *ix*. 5. 9: and in *x*. 170. 4, Sûrya is called *viçvakarman* and *viçvadevyavat*. The attributes and potencies of the light, of which the sun is the manifester, the utterer-forth, in later language the Logos or Word, are ascribed to him, as the powers of the Father are to the Logos; and so Sûrya *is* Indra and *viçvadevo* and *viçvakarman*, as the Logos, *is* the Father, and as the Kabbalistic emanations *are* the Deity whom they express and whose utterances they are, and as the Amĕsha-Çpĕntas are Ahura.

Therefore it is said in *x*. 114. 5,

> The Bards in their songs represent in many modes the well-winged (*suparṇam*) who is one.

Su, so prefixed means "good, well, beautiful, beautifully, much, very, easily." *Parṇa* is "a wing, feather, leaf, tree." *Tâmra-parṇi* is the name of a river. *Parṇin* is "a tree"; and *parṇ*, "to be green"; but for this there is no authoritative reference. *Parṇin* is the name of an *Apsaras*, i. e., of a lake or pond; and it was so styled, no doubt, from being covered with the broad leaves of the lotus or water-lily. Benfey suggests that *parṇa* may be *prî+na;* but the past part. pass. of *pṛi* is *purṇa*, and it forms also *pṛina*, *pṛinî*, and moreover has no meaning from which "wing" or "leaf" can be obtained. The true root may be *pṛi*, to "protect" or "shelter."

In *i*. 164. 46, we have,

> They call him Indra, Mitra, Varuṇa, Agni, and (he is) the celestial, well-winged *garutmat*. Sages [Poets] name variously that which is but one. They call it Agni, Yama, Mâteriçvan.

As *garut* means "a wing," *garutmat* must mean something winged, a bird. *Çveta-garut* is "a goose."

What was meant by these "wings," unless the *flame* of the fire, I am at a loss to imagine.

In Rig-Veda *ii.* 35. 8, all other creatures (*bhuvanani*) are said to be branches of *Apâṅmnapat*, "grandson of the waters." Müller understands the words *mahad devanam asuratwaṁ ekam*, with which all the verses of Rig-Veda *iii.* 55 conclude, to mean

> The Great Divinity of the Gods is *one* [which, says Dr. Muir], might be understood as if they asserted all the Gods to be manifestations of one Supreme Deity.

They *do* assert that all the Devas of the sky are manifestations of Agni.

> But [he says], the cause need not mean anything more than that the divine power of the Gods is unique.

Asuratwa is *asura*+*twa*, the suffix making an abstract noun, like *amṛitatwa*, "undyingness," from *amṛita*, "undying." And *asuratwa* does mean divine power, but "being, existence," from *as*, "to be," or "radiance, shiningness," from *as*, "to burn, to shine." I think the meaning clearly is,

> the great radiance or light of the Devas is one.

Or *mahad* may mean "light," which *is* one of its meanings; and we should read,

> the radiance of the Devas is one light.

Hymn 129, Rig-Veda *x.*, acquaints us with the later speculations of the Poets as to the origin of things, out of which grew the Brahmanic ideas as to Brahm and Maya. It is thus translated by Dr. Muir:

> 1. There was then neither non-entity nor entity (*na asad âsîd no sad âsît tadânîm*).

In a note at page 359, Dr. Muir says that in *x.* 5. 7 it is said that Agni, being "a thing both *asat*, non-existent (i. e., unmanifested) and *sat*, existent (i. e., in a latent state or in essence) in the highest heaven, etc., became, etc."

There was no atmosphere nor sky above. What enveloped, where, in the receptacle of what? Was it water, the profound abyss? (*Kim âsîd gahanaṁ gabhîram.*) *Gahana* is "impervious obscurity"; *gabhîra* is "deep, unfathomable."

> 2. Death was not then, nor undyingness; there was no distinction of day or night. That one breathed calmly, self-supported: there was nothing different from or above it. 3. In the beginning darkness existed, enveloped in darkness.

All this was undistinguishable water. That one which lay void, and wrapped in nothingness, was developed by the power of fervour (*tapasas*). 4. Desire (*kâmas*) first arose in it, which was the primal germ of mind (*manaso*). Sages, searching with their intellect have discovered in their heart to be the bond which connects entity with non-entity (*sato bandhun asati*). The ray which stretched across these, was it below or was it above? There were there impregnating powers (*retodhâḥ*) and mighty forces (*mahimânaḥ*), a self-supporting principle (*svadhâ*, 'spontaneity, self-will, strength,' according to Benfey:), beneath, and energy (*prayatiḥ*, erotic energy in action), on top. Who knows, who here can declare whence has sprung, whence, this creation? The Devas are subsequent to the development of this: who then knows whence it arose? From what this creation arose, and whether (any) made it or not, he who in the highest heaven is its ruler, he indeed knows or he does not know.

Evidently there is nothing about One Supreme Divine Creator here. There is nothing but a mystical copulation, impregnation and production. *Kama* arose in the Primal Unity, as it lay dark and undistinguishable; and *kamas* is simply the sexual impulse and desire. The ancients called it love. We call it concupiscence. *Retas* (nom. of *retodhaḥ*) is that which impregnates, literally the *semen virile*. From this hymn and other like passages, all or almost all post-Vedic, grew after a long time, the Linga and Yoni worship.

It is said in *x*. 97. 1, that certain plants are older than the Devas, by three *yugas*.

The first movement in the process of generation of things (or of creation by generation) is the development of the Primal Unity by the potency or energy of *tapas* by its own inherent heat, Müller says; by rigourous and intense abstraction, Professor Roth says, and Dr. Muir recites the passages in which *tapas* is mentioned, to show that there is reason for taking this to be the meaning. In every one of the texts cited by him *tapas* has either its original meaning of "fire," from *tap*, "to heat, warm, shine, burn up," or that of sacrifice. Here it is simply the heat of the organs of generation, which excites *kama*, "desire." There is no doubt that nothing imaginable is so absurd that some one may not be expected to say it. But one *is* a little "startled" to learn that the great, dark, indistinguishable mass of inert chaos, in a condition half-way between being and non-being, the crude raw mass of material, without form or life, entered upon and persisted in a course of "rigourous abstraction," long before the sexual impulse stirred, that was the first germ of intellect, mind and thought; and that by means of this "rigourous abstraction," erotic desire or the sexual impulse to libidivate was developed, and caused the first small and undeveloped germ of intellect to spring up. It is beyond all comparison more absurd than any notion of Dr. Haug.

PURUSHA.

Dr. Muir says:

> Another important but in many places obscure hymn of the Rig-Veda, in which the Unity of the Godhead is recognized, though in a Pantheistic sense, is the ninetieth of the tenth Book, the celebrated *Purusha Sûkta.*

From the sixth verse onward, the hymn recites the offering and cutting up of Purusha by the Devas, they and the Sâdhyas and Ṛishis sacrificing. From this sacrifice came the hymns Rich and Saman, the Metres and Yajush. The four castes came from different parts of the body, as did the moon and sun, Agni, Indra and Vayu, the atmosphere, sky and earth. It is no wonder Dr. Muir thinks some parts of it obscure.

I think that the first five verses may be of the later Vedic period. The residue is later than the establishment of castes and the compilation of the Rig-Veda and Sama-Veda. The first five verses are thus read by Dr. Muir:

> 1. Purusha has a thousand heads (a thousand arms, *A.-V.*), a thousand eyes and a thousand feet. On every side enveloping the earth (*sabhûmim viçvato vṛitva*), he transcended [it] by a space of ten fingers (*aty atishṭhad daçângulam*).
>
> 2. Purusha himself is this whole Universe (*Purushaḥ evedam sarvam*), whatever has been, and whatever shall be (*yad bhûtam yach cha bhavyam*). He is also the Lord of Immortality (*ûtam ṛitatvasyeçâno*), since through food he expands (*yad annenâti-rohati*). [Does the Supreme Being *expand* by *food?*]
>
> 3. Such is his greatness, and Purusha is superior to this (*ato jyayamç*, more powerful than this). All existing things (*viçvâ bhûtâni*) are a quarter of him (*pâdo 'sya*), and that which is immortal in the sky is three quarters of him (*tripâdt asyâmṛitam divi*).
>
> 4. With three quarters Purusha mounted upwards (*tripâd ûrddhvah ud ai Purushaḥ* [went up above or on, high]). A quarter of him again was produced here below (*pâdo 'syehabhavat punaḥ*). He then became diffused everywhere (*tato vishvan vyakrâmat*) among things animate and inanimate (*sâçanânaçane abhi*).
>
> 5. From him Viraj was born, and from Viraj Purusha (*tasmâd Virâḷ ajâyata Virâjo adhi Pûrushaḥ*). As soon as born, he extended beyond the earth, both behind and before (*sa jâto aty arichyata paçchâd bhûmim atho puraḥ*).

In these verses I find nothing like the Unity of the Godhead, in a Pantheistic sense or in any other. *Puru*, the Zend *pouru*, in the Veda also *pûru*, means "much, many," and *purusha* or *pûrusha*, "a man generally or individually a male, mankind." Its true primal meaning is "man, mankind, humanity," the unit of the race: thence, the first man, as containing all the race; and the Universal Soul of mankind, the Supreme Being.

It is perfectly clear that in this hymn, Purusha is humanity, mankind, in the first five verses. Therefore he is said figuratively to have had a thousand heads, arms, eyes and feet. He does not "envelope" or "pervade" the earth. He "spreads over it, occupies it, covers it, fills it." Those are equally meanings of *vṛitvâ*. Nor did he "transcend it by a space of ten fingers." *Sthâ* is "to stand, stop, wait, stay, abide." *Adhi* and *ati*, prefixed, mean "above, beyond, over on." And *sthâ*, with *adhi* prefixed, means "to stand on, to be supported by, to rest on, to stay, to remain, to inhabit, to command, govern, lead, pass over, surpass, overcome, subdue." *Adhishṭhita* means "guided, occupied, fixed, established, overpowered, subdued." *Aty*, by itself, means "over, exceedingly, in a high degree, much," as an adverb; and, as a preposition, "over, beyond, more than." I take the phrase clearly to mean that Purusha subdued and subjected to his will, occupied and cultivated, the earth, extensively, by his ten fingers, that is, by or with the labour of his two hands.

He is not said to be "the whole universe." *Evedam sarvam* does not necessarily mean that. It may quite as well mean all the race; all the individuals, that is, of the race: and *yad bhûtaṁ yach cha bhavyam*, "whatever has been born and whatever is to be born."

Man is *utâmṛitatwasyecâno*, also i. e., *ut+amṛitat+vaça+yeçano*, "able to secure for himself long life"; for, *annenatirohati*, i. e., *annena+ati+rohati*, *annena* meaning "food," *ati*, "abundantly," and *rohati*, third person sing. pres. of *ruh*, meaning "grows": and the whole, "for food grows abundantly."

Such is his present greatness; but he is even more powerful than this. There is in him an indefinite capacity for increase and extension, and he is to spread more and subdue new lands.

It is not said that all existing things are a quarter of him. *Viçva bhûtâni* does not necessarily mean "all beings or creatures." *Bhûta* means "a living being, a creature"; but also "an element," and five *bhûtas* are enumerated, earth, fire, water, air and æther. One fourth of man is composed of the several elements; three immortal or undying parts of him are of the sky, and with these three he ascended to the stars, when burned upon the pyre. The one fourth composed of the elements remained, resolved into its component parts. One of the parts that ascended was so much of the body as was by burning changed into light. The others were probably the soul and spirit, as distinguished from each other. The light was vitality, and this and the other parts were undoubtedly those which, borrowed by the Hebrews from the Magi were called *Nephesch*, *Ruach* and *Neschamah*, or, in the Latin of the Kabbalah, *Psyche*, *Spiritus*, *mens*.

The quarter that was of the elements, was produced again, below and diffused among the various portions, animate and inanimate, of the physical creation.

When thus burned, *Virâj*, splendour or radiance, was born of or produced from Purusha, and this, feeding the stars and invigorating Indra, became again the vitality of men.

Finally, it is said that, as soon as born (*sa jato*), as soon as man began to exist, he began to spread over the earth, *paçchâd atho puraḥ*, behind and before, or westward and eastward.

All this is mere poetry, with certainly no purpose of establishing a new Deity. It is all easily enough understood, and must be an old fragment, to which ages afterwards, the succeeding verses were added. It is impossible to believe that any sane human being ever imagined Universal Humanity sacrificed, cut to pieces, burned, by the stars, Sâdhyas and Ṛishis. Nor is that a possible allegory.

The old verses of the hymn are valuable for the conclusive corroborating evidence which they give upon several points. They prove that the Devas were the heavenly bodies, and that many of the stars and Devas were ancient Sages, supposed to have been translated to the sky. They prove that this translation and the existence of the stars were the only other life and immortality known to the Indo-Aryans; and they leave no doubt in regard to the fact that the moving cause of sacrifice and offering was that the oblations were deemed to become light, to replenish the stars and invigorate Indra himself; and that this was also the reason for the adoption of the custom of burning the dead.

The nonsense of the Bhâgavata Purana, and even of the Atharva-Veda, about Virâj and Purusha is only worth referring to, as it is quoted by Dr. Muir, to show how the Brahmanic stupidities had their origin. Virâj was the earth, all the universe; she entered into the sacrificial horse. Purusha is all that has been, is or will be, enveloping the universe, and occupying but a span. He kindles Virâj, and is Lord of Immortality and Security, because he has transcended mortal nutriment. Everything exists in his feet, which are the worlds; immortality, blessedness and security abide in the heads of the three-headed.

But there is by far more warrant for the modern nonsense, in what remains of the hymn, if it is correctly translated, and if it really represents Purusha as immolated, sacrificed, cut in pieces, by the Devas, Sâdhyas and Ṛishis, or by the Sâdhyas and Ṛishis who became Devas.

That it is correctly translated, I doubt exceedingly, and should feel quite sure, but for the fifteenth verse.

Sâdh means "to finish, accomplish, effect, perform, overcome, conquer, and learn." *Sâdh*, "perfect, good, a Muni or Sage"; *sâdhya*, "accomplishment, perfection." The *Ṛishis* were the itinerant bards; the *Sâdhyas*, Sages, perhaps skilled in medicine, as *sâdhya* also means "to be cured, curable"; *sâdhaka*, "an adept," and *sâdhana*, "medicament, drugs." These being men, could not have sacrificed humanity or mankind, of which they were a part:

and the idea of such an immolation and burning, and of the production of Vedas and Castes, atmosphere, sun and moon, by cutting the body of humanity into pieces, is so supereminently preposterous that one can find no allegorical meaning in it. Let us scrutinize the translation, and see if the Vedic Thinker cannot be relieved of the imputation of babbling nonsense without a redeeming feature.

> 6. When the Devas offered up Purusha as a sacrifice (*yat Purushena havishâ devâḥ yajman atanvata*), the Spring (was) its clarified butter, Summer its fuel, and Autumn the (accompanying) oblation (*vasanto asyâsîd âjyam grîshmaḥ idmaḥ çarad haviḥ*).

Havis means, according to Benfey, "clarified butter, oblation, sacrifice," from *hu*, "to sacrifice, to worship by oblations." *Hava*, also, is "oblation, sacrifice." *Yajna* is "a sacrifice," from *yaj*, "to sacrifice, to worship." *Tan* means "to spread, direct, arrange, cause."

As Bopp shows, Section 933, the suffix *as* forms equivalents of English present participles, e. g., in *manas*, "thinking"; *srôtas*, "flowing"; *çrâvas*, "hearing"; *chakshas*, "seeing"; whence, for these, the substantive meanings, "mind, stream, ear, eye," all of which include the idea of *action*. The suffix *is*, he regards (Section 937) as a weakening of *as*. For examples, he gives *çôchîs*, "lustre" (shining); *archîs*, "lustre" (shining); *havis*, "butter clarified" (from *hu*, "to sacrifice"); *chadis*, "roof" (covering); *jyotis*, "splendour" (shining).

In all these, except *havis*, the noun includes and expresses the active present participle meaning: and I cannot but think that this word, instead of meaning the oblation, or that which *is* offered or sacrificed, means the offerer of the oblation, the one who furnishes it.

If that is so, the first clause of the verse would be read,

> when the Devas arranged, directed, or prepared the sacrifice, Purusha furnishing the oblation, or being the offerer.

In the second clause I do not think the word "was" belongs. I think the verb used in the first clause, or the participle, is understood, and that it should be read,

> Spring furnished the clarified butter for it; Summer, the fuel, and Autumn, the oblation.

It seems to me that the whole of these verses refers to the supposed first sacrifice offered by men, mankind or humanity, the Sâdhyas and Ṛishis who thereby became Devas, officiating.

> 7. This victim, Purusha born in the beginning, they immolated on the sacrificial grass (*tam̃ yajnam barhishi praukshan Purusham̃ jâtam agrataḥ*): with him as their offering, the Gods, Sâdhyas and Ṛishis sacrificed (*tena devâḥ ayajanta sâdhyâḥ ṛishayas cha ye*).

Agrataḥ means "in the presence of"; and I venture to submit that the verse means,

> This oblation they sacrificed on the sacred grass, in the presence of mankind, then already old; with it the Devas worshipped, the Sâdhyas and the Ṛishis.
>
> 8. From that universal oblation (*sarvahutaḥ*) were produced curds and clarified butter. He (it) formed those aërial creatures, and the animals, both wild and tame.

The first three words, *tasmâd yajnât sarvahutaḥ*, mean, "from that oblation all consumed"; and the evident meaning is that such oblations, by the changes effected by the fire, enter into new combinations, replenish the orbs (*chakre*) of the sky, with light, and become parts of the animals.

> 9. From that sacrifice all consumed sprang (*jajnire*, were born or produced) the Rich- and Sama-Veda, the metres and the Yajush.

Because these were the consequences and outgrowth of worship.

In Verses 11 to 14, it is asked,

> when they divided Purusha, into how many parts did they distribute him.

The answers are

> The Brahman was his mouth; the Râjanya his arms; the Vaiçya his thighs, and the Sûdra sprang from his feet.

These are merely subdivisions of humanity. Then it is said that the moon was produced from his soul (or vitality); the sun from his eye, Indra and Agni from his mouth, and Vayu from his breath; the atmosphere from his navel; the sky arose from his head; the earth came from his feet; the four quarters from his ear: and "so they made the worlds." Any explanation of this must be merely conjectural.

> 15. When the Gods, in performing their sacrifice, bound Purusha as a victim (*devah yad yajnam̃ tanvanah abadhnan Purushan paçum*), there were seven pieces of wood laid for him round the fire, and thrice seven pieces of fuel employed.

Abadhnan Purusham paçum certainly means "they bound the victim, Purusha." Benfey informs us that *purusha-paçu* means "a beast-like man"; and *nṛi-paçu*, "a man destined to be immolated." And it is very probable that the reference is to the immolation, in ancient times (then long disused) of human victims, prisoners of war, perhaps; as there is reference elsewhere to ancient sacrifices of horses.

16. With sacrifice the Gods worshipped the sacrifice (*yajnena yajnam ayajanta Devas*, which means, I think, 'with worship, the Devas performed the sacrifice'). These were the first institutions (*tâni dharmâṇi prathamani asan;* these were the most ancient, or first, ceremonials of worship). These great beings (*mahimânaḥ*, great men) attained to the heaven [sky] where the Devas, the ancient Sâdhyas, reside (*santi*, are).

It is clear enough that Purusha was not the Supreme Being, and that no sacrifice of the Supreme Being is thought of here. It was a sacrifice performed by men, the first of all ceremonial acts of worship, a sacrifice of clarified butter and the productions of autumn; and by such pious acts the Sâdhyas and Ṛishis earned the right to be translated to the sky and become stars.

Purusha, originally humanity, may have come to be virility of the universe, by the action whereof upon the dark undistinguishable chaos, the generation of things began. But in *this* hymn, there is no such idea.

PRAJÂPATI.

HIRAṆYAGARBHA AND SKAMBHA.

The word *Prajâpati* was originally employed as an epithet of Savitṛi and Soma, and it then meant "Lord of Creatures, Beings or Luminaries." Afterwards it came to mean, probably, that Unity or Universal, in which all creatures are included, as Brahmaṇaspati meant prayer and Vanaspati, fuel. He certainly became that in the Brahmanic period, and is in the Çatapatha Brâhmaṇa identified with the universe of creatures, and described as having alone existed in the beginning, as the Source out of which creatures were evolved. In the Atharva-Veda he is identified with breath, *Prâṇa* or vitality and said to have been generated by *Kala*, Time.

Mahîdhara speaks of *Prajâpati Hiraṇyagarbha*,

> existing as an embryo in the egg of Brahma, which was golden, consisting of the golden male Purusha.

Hiraṇa, i. e., *haran+a* means "gold, a cowry, the *semen virile*." *Hari* and *harit* mean "green, tawny, yellow, a ray of light," and birds and animals that are yellow or green, as a lion and a peacock. *Hiraṇya* is "gold, silver, substance, imperishable matter, the *semen virile*." We have already seen that *çukra*, "resplendent," means also the *semen virile*. Gold has always been the metal of the sun, and synonymous with light: but why should the words that mean "gold" and "light" also mean the human semen? The Kabbalists give us the answer to this question.

Rabbi Chajim Vital says (*Discursus Initialis i., Libri Sohar*),

> *Exinde et post modum describitur lux [quia dicitur, Fiat Lux. Ubi indigitatur semen, quod provenit per gradum Fundamenti], quæ creata est, et occultata et comprehenditur in fædere illo [id est, illa Lux occultata, quæ est Benignitas, occultata est in membro fæderis], [circumcisionis, quod est quasi membrum virile, numeratio (Sephirah) scil, nona] quod ingreditur in Rosam [Basiliam quasi membrum fæmininum, dum conjunguntur gradus (Sephiroth) Yesod and Malakoth] et producit in illa semen, et hoc vocatur lignum faciens, fructus, cujus semen in eo, et hoc semen revera manet in Signo fæderis [id est: non est sicut semen humanum quod non manet in membro, sed prodit: nam lux ista quæ influit in Basiliam etiam in fundamento manet].*

And in the Commentary of Rabbi Jizchak Lorja in these *Discursus*, enough more will be found, on the same subject, of which I quote only a part of one sentence:

> *Fundamentum [the Sephirah Yesod], quod dicitur omnis vivens, et est effluxus guttæ seminalis è cerebro, quod vocatur Sapientia.*

The Divine Creative and vivifying Light and Wisdom were thus designated.

Garbha, from *grah*, original *grabh*, "to take, seize, marry, hold, bear, catch, receive, etc.," means "the womb, the interior, fœtus, embryo, a sprout, conception." As the latter part of a compound, "holding in one's interior, containing."

The Hymn *x*. 121, which celebrates Hiraṇyagarbha, may enable us to understand the meaning of the name. As given by Dr. Muir, it is as follows:

> 1. Hiraṇyagarbha arose in the beginning (*samavarttatâgre*, which rather means 'included' or 'contained,' 'aggregated' or 'assembled,' at the beginning): born (*jâtaḥ*), he was the one Lord of things existing (*bhûtasya patir ekah âsît*): he established (*sa dadhara*) the earth and this sky (*pṛithivîm̃ dyâm utemâm̃*): to what Deva shall we offer our oblation (*kasmai Devâya harishâ vidhema*)?
>
> 2. He who gives breath, who gives strength, whose command all the Devas reverence (*yasya viçve upâdate praçisham̃ yasya Devaḥ*); whose shadow (*chhâyâ*, 'shade, reflected image, reflected light, splendour, colour') is immortality, whose shadow is death; to what Deva, etc.?
>
> 3. Who by his might (*mahitvâ*) became the sole King (*râjâ*) of the breathing and winking world (*prâṇato nimishato jagato*); who is the Lord of this two-footed and four-footed [creation] (*ya içe asya dvipadaç chatushpadaḥ*); to what Deva, etc.?
>
> 4. Whose greatness (*mahitvâ*) these snowy mountains (*himavanto, himavant*, 'cold,' the Himalaya), and the sea with the Rasâ (river) declare (*samudram̃ rasayâ Sahâhuḥ*)—of whom these regions (*yasyemâḥ pradiço*), of whom they are the arms (*yasya bahu*): to what Deva, etc.?
>
> 5. By whom the sky is fiery (*yena dyaur ugrâ*), and the earth fixed (*pṛithivî cha dṛilhâ*), by whom the firmament (*svaḥ*), and the heaven (*nakaḥ*) were established (*stabhitam̃*); who in the atmosphere (*antarikshe*) is the measurer (*vimânaḥ*) of the aërial space (*rajaso*): to what Deva, etc.?
>
> 6. To whom two contending armies (*krandasî*) sustained by his succour (*avasâ tastabhâne*), looked up (*abhy aikshetâm*) trembling in mind (*manasâ rejamâne*); over whom the risen sun shines (*yatrâdhi Suraḥ udito vibhâti*): to what Deva, etc.?
>
> 7. When the great waters pervaded the universe, containing an embryo, and generating fire (*âpo ha yad bṛihatîr viçvam âyan garbham̃ dadhânâḥ janayantîr Agnim*), thence arose the one spirit (*tato samavarttatâsur ekaḥ*) of the Devas: to what Deva, etc.?
>
> 8. He who through his greatness beheld the waters which contained power (*daksham̃*) and generated sacrifice (*yajnam*), who was the one (or, only, or chief, pre-eminent) Deva above the Devas: to what Deva, etc.?
>
> 9. May he not injure us (*mâ no himsîj*), he who is the generator of the earth (*janitâ yaḥ pṛithivyâḥ*), who ruling by fixed ordinances (*satyadharmâ*, acting with unvarying regularity?) produced the heaven (*divam̃ jayânâ*), who produced the great and brilliant waters (*châpaç*, in Benfey, 'bow;' *Indra-châpaç*, 'rainbow'): to what Deva, etc.?
>
> 10. Prajâpati, no other than Thou is Lord over all these created things (*viçvâ jâtâni pari*): may we obtain that, through desire of which we have invoked thee: may we become masters of riches!

The breathing and winking world *prâṇato nimishato jagato*, in Verse 3, is the living and twinkling creation, i. e., the stars. *Samudram̃ rasayâ*, in

Verse 4, means, I think, "the sea with its water." *Ugra*, rendered by "fiery" in Verse 5 means "very strong."

Krandasî, Dr. Muir says, is explained in Böhtlingk and Roth's Lexicon, as meaning two armies engaged in battle. Mahîdhara thinks it means heaven and earth. In *ii.* 12. 8, speaking of Indra, it is said,

> *Yam Krandasî sanyatî vihvayete* [which Wilson renders by], Whom crying aloud, encountering (two) invoke.

There is, he says, no substantive, and Sayaṇa proposes *rodasî*, "heaven and earth," or *dve sene*, "two armies."

Krand and *krad* mean "to cry miserably, to roar, and to implore." There is certainly no reason for interpolating anything about armies. *Krandasî* probably means the two implorers or suppliants, and the reference may be to the Priests or Atharvas, and the Bards or Ṛishis. This would explain the phrase, "when the risen sun shines"; since that was the time for completing and ending the sacrifice.

The phrase in Verse 7, "when the great waters *pervaded* the universe" conveys no meaning to me. *Î* or *Ay* not only means "to pervade," but also "to conceive" and "to desire." And there is no doubt that *apo ha yad bṛihatîr viçvam ayan* means, "And when the vast water conceived the all" (the water meaning the abyss of infamous and weltering matter), and then there is sense and connection in this that follows,

> containing the embryo, and producing (or giving birth to) Agni, or the fire, then the one light or radiant splendour (*asû*) of the Devas went forth thence, or emanated from it, or, was contained in it.
>
> He who through his greatness beheld the waters which contained power,

does not, I think, express the meaning of the original. *Paryapaçyad*, i. e., *pari+apaçyad* is a compound of the adverb and preposition *pari*, "round, all round," and *paçya*, which forms some tenses of *driç* (the same as *paç* and *spaç*, meaning "to see, behold, look at, discover, search, learn, know," and with *pari*, "to frequent, see, consider, search, know"). But the true meaning *here* is that of *sparç*, *spaç*, "to embrace," whence, *sparça*, "touching, contact, *sexual intercourse*." *Paç*, *pas* and *pash* mean "to bind" and "to touch."

So in the Hebrew, the verb ירע, *yedang*, in the phrase translated "and Adam *knew* Eve his wife," means "saw, knew, and to have carnal connection with."

And the meaning of the eighth verse is, that Hiraṇyagarbha through his greatness *knew* the waters that contained *daksha*, power, and produced worship, or the sacrificial fire. He, therefore, was the one Deva, pre-eminent above all the others, or the source of all, or Unity including them all.

He is called in Verse 9, generator (*janitâ*) of the expanse, and is said to have generated also (*jajânâ*) the sky. That he "rules by fixed ordinances," does not express the meaning of *satyadharmâ*. *Satya* means "truth, reality," and *dharma*, "law, justice, right, virtue, duty, custom, necessity, etc." It is from *dhṛi*, which means "to bear, carry, maintain, support, exist, live." The meaning of the compound word probably may be, "acting in accordance with the laws of Nature, or the laws of things." It is certainly not meant that Hiraṇyagarbha rules according to ordinances fixed by himself, or "rules" at all; but that in obedience to a law already existing, a law of the True and Real, he generated the sky and expanse: and that "*law*" is the law of sexual desire, which was considered as inherent and self-existent in Nature. He was the generative energy personified, supposed to have existed as an energy, before the existence of either beings or things.

In the Atharva-Veda, *x*. 7. 28, is this verse:

> Men knew Hiraṇyagarbha, the Supreme, the Ineffable (*Hiraṇyagarbham paramam anatyudyam janâḥ viduḥ*): before him Skambha shed forth gold in the midst of the world (*Skambhas tadagre prâsinchad hiraṇyaṁ loke antarâ*).

Janâḥ may mean either "creatures," "beings," or "men": *Parama*, "most excellent, highest, first." "Ineffable" means "unspeakable," and may apply to the *Name* of a Deity, but not to the Deity or energy itself. *Anatyudyam* means "unsurpassable"; *an* prefixed meaning negation or deprivation, and *ati*, "over, on," and *udyama*, "raising, effort, energy."

Skambh means "to make firm, to support, to stop, obstruct, inpede." *Stambh*, another form of the same verb, "to make firm, to stop, make immovable": *stabdha*, "stopped, blocked up, immovable, firm": *stambha*, "a post, a pillar, a stem, obstruction," as "supporting, upholding, stopping."

Skambha is "the fixed, the immovable, that on which a superstructure rests." Before *Hiraṇyagarbha*, i. e., before the mysterious union of the male energy and the female capacity to produce, in the womb of Chaos and Darkness, Skambha poured forth the seed of impregnation, the virile or generative energy in the midst of the universe.

Skambha, as a name, at least, does not occur in the Rig-Veda. Hymns *x*. 7 and 8 of the Atharva-Veda are devoted to him. The whole of the former and a portion of the latter are quoted by Dr. Muir, in Volume *V*. of his Texts, and a small portion of each in Volume *IV*. pp. 18ff. It would be profitless to copy all these portions. It is inquired in them who that Skambha is, on whom Prajâpati supported and established all the worlds: how far Skambha penetrated into that highest, lowest and middle universe, comprehending all forms, which Prajâpati created; how far into the past; and how much of the future is contained in his receptacle? How far he penetrated into that one *membrum virile* (*aṅga*), which he separated into a thousand parts? Skambha established both these, the earth and sky, the wide atmosphere, the six wide regions and pervaded the entire universe. He who knows the golden reed (*vetasaṁ hiraṇyayaṁ*) standing in the water (*tishthantam salile Veda*), is the mysterious Prajâpati.

Vetasa is a cane or rattan. But *hiraṇyaya* has the same meaning as in the name *Hiraṇyagarbha* and *vetasa hiraṇyaya* here means the virile member, the Linga, capable of impregnation, standing in the chaotic abyss or waters.

These two, the earth and sky, stand, supported by Skambha. Skambha is all this which has vitality which breathes, which twinkles. Whatever moves, flies or stands, whatever exists breathing or not breathing, or twinkling, that omniform sustains the expanse; that, combined, is one only.

These notions are dreamy enough, and incoherent as the vagaries of nightmare. The later books rioted in wilder extravagances, of which one can have but a faint idea from these vague utterances in regard to Skambha.

Skambha was but a word, a name for an unknown somewhat, of which the mind endeavoured in vain to form or grasp an idea; of an unknown, stable, permanent and fixed; self-being, and not matter, but from which matter was born. It would be idle to endeavour to explain or understand that of which the mind can have no comprehension.

EVIL SPIRITS.

In speaking of Agni, I have cited the passages in the first five Mandalas, in which the *Râkshasas* are mentioned.

In *vi.* 62. 8, the anger of the Devas is invoked against "him who is associated with the Râkshasas (*Râkshoyuje*)." And in the next verse it is said,

> He hurls his weapon against the strong Râkshasa, against the malignant menaces of man (*droghâya chid vachase ânarâya eva*).

In *vi.* 63. 10, the Açvins are prayed to give horses to the worshipper.

> Achievers of great deeds [it is said to them], may the Râkshasas be slain!

In *vii.* 1. 13, Agni is prayed to protect from the odious Râkshasas, and that protection is also asked "from the illiberal, the malignant, the iniquitous;" and it is added,

> may I, with you for my ally, triumph over the hostile.

In *vii.* 16. 10, Agni is prayed to keep off the Râkshasas. In *vii.* 21. 5,

> Let not the Râkshasas, Indra, do us harm, not the evil spirits do harm to our progeny.

In *vii.* 38. 7, it is prayed that the Vâjins may destroy the murderer, the robber, the Râkshasas. In *vii.* 73. 4, the Açvins are called "destroyers of Râkshasas." In *vii.* 85. 1, it is said to Mitra and Varuṇa,

> I offer adoration to you both, uninterrupted by Râkshasas.

In *vii.* 104. 1, 2, 3, 4, 7, etc., the Râkshasas are specially denounced. Indra and Soma are asked to afflict and destroy them, to cast down those who delight in darkness, the destructive, malignant; to put to flight the stupid, and consume, slay, drive away and utterly exterminate the cannibals. They are the haters of Brahmans, hideous, vile; and it is prayed that they may perish like the offering cast into the fire, and be chastised, being plunged into surrounding and inextinguishable darkness, so that not one of them may again issue from it. And verses 4 and 5 are

> Indra and Soma, display from heaven your fatal, the extirpator from earth of the malignant ones: put forth from the clouds the consuming, wherewith you slay the increasing Râkshas race. Indra and Soma, scatter around from the sky, pierce their sides with fiery searching undecaying, so that they may depart without a sound.

7. Come with rapid steeds, slay the oppressive mischievous Râkshasas: let there be no happiness, Indra and Soma, to the malignant who harasses us with his oppression.

16. May Indra slay with his mighty weapon him who calls me the Yâtudhâna, which I am not; the Râkshasa who says, 'I am pure.' May he, the vilest of all beings, perish.

17. May the stones that grind the Soma destroy the Râkshasas by their noise.

18. Maruts . . . . seize the Râkshasas, grind them to pieces; whether they fly about like birds by night [on marauding raids?], or whether they have offered obstruction to the sacred sacrifice [by attacking the worshippers at dawn].

19. Hurl, Indra, thy thunderbolt from heaven . . . . slay with the thunderbolt the Râkshasas, on the east, on the west, on the south, on the north.

20. They advance, accompanied by dogs: desirous to destroy him, they assail the indomitable Indra. Çakra whets his thunderbolt for the miscreants; quickly let him hurl his bolt upon the fiends.

21. Indra has always been the discomfiter of the evil spirits coming to obstruct the offerers of oblations: Çakra advances, crushing the present Râkshasas, as an axe cuts down a forest, as the earthen vessels.

22. Destroy the evil spirit, whether in the form of an owl, or of an owlet, of a dog or of a brown goose, of a hawk or of a vulture: slay the Râkshasas, Indra, with the thunderbolt as with a stone.

23. Let not the Râkshasas do us harm: let the dawn drive away the pairs of evil spirits, exclaiming, 'What now is this?' May the earth protect us from terrestrial, the firmament protect us from celestial mischief!

24. Slay, Indra, the Yâtudhâna, whether in the form of a man or of a woman, doing mischief by her deceptions; may those who sport in murder perish decapitated: let them not behold the rising sun. [Which certainly alludes to marauding bands that plunder at night, and advises their summary execution, when captured, before return of the daylight.]

25. Soma, do thou and Indra severally watch, be wary, be vigilant: hurl the thunderbolt at the malignant Râkshasas.

In *iv.* 4. 15, it is said to Agni,

consume the unadoring (*açaso*, 'who offer no praise') Râkshasas: deliver us from the reproach of the oppressor and reviler.

It is evident that the Râkshasas were native tribes, encountered by the Aryans in the Punjab. They are mentioned in the Ramayana, also, where, in all the country south of the Jumna, it is said that wild beasts and Râkshasas everywhere abound. Though the Ramayana describes them as huge, beastly, disgusting demons, cruel, terrible, ugly, huge-bellied, loud-shouting, etc., they were plainly the aborigines of the country, who slew the Brahmanic hermits, in the country south of the Vinhya range. Kabandha, a Râkshasa whom Rama encountered was burned on a funeral pile in a trench by Laksmaṇa. Khara, one of their chiefs, describes them in the Ramayana, as being "of fearful swiftness, unyielding in battle, in colour like a dark blue cloud." Khara was "the perpetual enemy of the Brahmans, cruel, hated of the Brahmans, devoid of righteousness and wicked." Ravana, another chief, is stigmatized as wicked and cruel, a killer of Brahmans, polluter of sacrifices and ravisher of wives. *Sanskrit Texts, Muir, ii.* 409 to 416.

In the Mahabharata, the Râkshasas are described as following Brahmanical observances, and a thousand learned Brahmans are entertained by Virûpaksha, a Râkshasa king.

VṚITRA, AHI.

Vṛitra, sometimes termed Ahi, Professor Wilson says (*note a. to i.* 32. 1),

> is nothing more than the accumulation of vapour condensed, or figuratively, shut up in, or obstructed by a cloud. Indra, with his thunderbolt, or atmospheric or electrical influence, divides the aggregated mass, and vent is given to the rain, which then descends upon the earth, or passes off in rivers. Later writers [he says (those of the Puranas)] converted this into a literal contest between Indra and an Asura, or chief of the Asuras; but it is merely an allegorical narrative of the production of rain.

This is dwelt on in *i.* 32 and subsequent Sûktas. Indra clove the cloud, broke a way for the torrents, sent the waters down to the earth. With his thunderbolt, sharpened by Tvashṭṛi, he struck the first-born of the clouds (the first-formed cloud: *Wilson*). He struck the darkling mutilated Vṛitra: Ahi lies prostrate on the earth like a tree felled in the woods. Vṛitra, arrogant, having neither hand or foot, defied Indra, who struck him with the thunderbolt on his mountain-like shoulder, like one emasculated who pretends to virility. Then Vṛitra, mutilated of many members, slept. As he lay recumbent on the earth, the waters flowed over him: Ahi was prostrated under the feet of the waters that Vṛitra had obstructed.

The mother of Vṛitra was bending over her son, when Indra struck her buttock with his shaft; so she lay above and Vṛitra below, Danu sleeping like a cow with her calf. The waters carry off the nameless body of Vṛitra, tossed into the midst of the never-stopping, never-resting currents. The foe of Indra has slept a long darkness.

> When the single resplendent Vṛitra returned the blow, Indra, by thy thunderbolt, thou becamest like a horse's tail [whisking off flies: *Wilson*]. Neither the lightning, nor the thunder, nor the rain which he showered, nor the thunderbolt harmed Indra, when he and Ahi contended, and Maghavat triumphed also over other. But had entered his heart, when about to slay Ahi, and he traversed ninety-nine streams, like a hawk, and then became sovereign of all things, movable and immovable, of the cattle hornless and horned, the monarch of men, comprehending all things, as the circumference of a wheel comprehends the spokes.

Ahi and *Vṛitra*, Wilson says (*note c. i.* 32), are both given as synonyms of *Megha*, a cloud, in the Nighantu; the former is derived from *han*, "to strike," with *â* prefixed, arbitrarily shortened to *a:* the latter, literally the "encompasser" or "concealer," is from *vṛi*, "to enclose," or *vṛit*, " to be or to exist," or from *vṛiddh*, "to increase," a choice of etymologies intimating a vague use of the term. He is said to be *vyança*, having a part, or metaphorically a limb, detached, thus confounding things with persons, as is still more violently done in a following verse, where he is said to have neither hands nor feet.

Vṛitra is clearly "darkness," and nothing more or less, from *vṛi* and *vṝ*, "to cover, conceal, overspread, enwrap, enclose, surround, envelope." To "conceal" is its Vedic meaning: and literally, *Vṛitra* is "the concealer, the coverer, the enveloper." *Ni-vṛita* is "a wrapper, cloak, veil." And it means "a cloud," only because a cloud covers and darkens; and "an enemy," only because darkness is the opposite, antagonist and enemy of light. And Vṛitra is said to be *vyança*, i. e., *vi+aṁça*, "without parts or limbs," as if *vi+aṁçu*, "without rays, rayless," because darkness is without form, shapeless.

But what, then, is Danu, the mother of Vṛitra? Benfey gives *danu* as a proper name in the Ramayana; and *danuja* as a *danana* or demon; without indicating its derivation. Nor do I find any other meaning for *Ahi*, except "snake." *Vṛitra* and the *Dasyus* are often named together, as will be seen; and Benfey gives us merely, *dasyu*, "a ruffian, a thief, the name of one of the mixed classes": and *dânu, danu, dânana, danuja*, "a demon." *Daṁç, daṁs* and *das* mean "to bite"; and *danta* is "tooth."

In the next hymn, it is not so plain what Vṛitra is. In verse 4, Indra has slain "the wealthy barbarian, with his adamantine" (bolt), and Professor Wilson adds in a note to this,

> Vṛitra, the *Dasyu*, literally a robber, but apparently used in contrast to *Ârya*, as if intending the uncivilized tribes of India. 'Thou, singly assailing him, although with auxiliaries at hand. Perceiving the impending manifold destructiveness of thy bow, they, the *Sanakas*, the neglecters of sacrifice, perished.'

The *Sanakas*, Wilson says, are the followers of Vṛitra, called *ayajvânas*, non-sacrificers, in contrast with the *yajvânas*, sacrificers;

> here, apparently, also identifying the followers of Vṛitra with races who had not adopted or were hostile to, the ritual of the Vedas.

Vṛitra, then, must have become, in this hymn, something more or other than "the accumulation of vapour condensed."

These non-sacrificers (opposed to the worship of the fire and light), contending with the sacrificers, fled with averted faces, when Indra blew the disregarders of worship from off sky, expanse and earth. Scattered before him and the holy men who encouraged him, conscious, like the emasculated contending with men, they fled by precipitous paths (retreated through the mountain-passes?). He destroyed them "on the farthest verge of the sky"; consumed the robber, from heaven. Decorated with gold and jewels, they were spreading over the circuit of the earth (over the whole country, to the mountains, or from the mountains, "the farthest verge of the sky"): but mighty as they were, Indra dispersed them with the sun.

Here it seems doubtful whether it is the shades and glooms of night that are meant, or the native tribes. Were the shades non-sacrificers, merely because the sacrifices were made at dawn, and therefore considered to be *opposed* by the darkness?

In verse 9, Indra has blown away the robbers, with or by means of prayers. But in 10 and the following verses the hymn returns to the original idea of Vṛitra. The waters flowed to provide the food of Indra, but increased in the midst of the navigable: then Indra with his fatal and powerful shaft slew Vṛitra, whose thoughts were ever turned towards him.

In 12, Indra set free the obstructed by Vṛitra, when sleeping in the caverns of the earth, and slew the horned dryer up (*çringinam çushṇam*).

> Thou, Maghavan, with equal swiftness and strength, didst kill with thy thunderbolt the enemy defying thee to battle.

In the following verses, Indra destroyed "their cities," and then reached Vṛitra with his thunderbolt and slaying him, exhilarated his mind. He protected Kutsa, grateful for his praises; defended the excellent Daçadyu engaged in battle. The dust of his courser's hoofs ascended to heaven. The son of Switrâ rose up, to be again upborne by men. He protected the excellent son of Switrâ, when combating for his lands and encouraged when immersed in water (i. e., when struggling to protect his lands against inundation): and he is prayed to, to inflict sharp pains on those of hostile minds, who have long stood against the Aryans.

In *i.* 51. 4, it is said to Indra:

> Thou hast opened the receptacle of the waters: thou hast detained in the mountain the treasure of the malignant (*parvate dânumad vasu*): when thou hadst slain Vṛitra who is Ahi, thou madest the sun visible in the sky.

Here *Ahi* is explained "*hantṛi*, the slayer." *Dânumad* may mean "one doing an injury," or one descended from *Danu*, as Asura, or it may be an epithet from *danu*, "giving."

Here Vṛitra is the dispeller of the darkness caused by the clouds, and enables the sun to shine out. In the next two verses, he is lauded for having humbled the deceivers who ate the oblations; for having, propitious to the Aryans, destroyed the cities of Pipru and assisted Rijiswin in destroying robbers. He defended Kutsa in deadly fight with Çushṇa, destroyed Çambara in defense of Atithigva, trampled under foot the great Arbuda, and from remote times was born for the destruction of oppressors. "In destroying robbers" is in the original, *dasyu hatyeshu*, "killing the Dasyus."

And in *v.* 8, Indra is besought to discriminate between the Âryas and those who are Dasyus; and subjugating those who perform no religious rites, to compel them to submit to those who do sacrifice, to humble the neglecters of holy acts, in favour of those who observe them.

In *i.* 52, the slaying of the stream-obstructing Vṛitra is spoken of; and he is termed the "wide-extended," who, having obstructed the waters, reposed in the region above the firmament. In *v.* 10, the strong heaven was rent asunder at the clamour of Ahi, when the thunderbolt of Indra struck off the head of Vṛitra, the obstructor of heaven and earth.

In *i.* 53 and 54, Indra is lauded for slaying Namuchi, Karanja and Paranaya, demolishing the hundred cities of Vangrida, besieged by Rijisvan overthrowing twenty Kings who came against Suçravas, preserving him and Tûrvayâṇa, and making Kutsa, Atithigva and Ayu subject to the mighty though youthful Suçravas, slaying Çambara, defeating the Asuras, protecting Narya, Turvasa, Yadu and Turvîti, of the race of Vayya, guarding their chariots and horses in battle and demolishing ninety-nine cities of Çambara. Then, in *v.* 10, it is said that the darkness obstructed the current of the waters, the cloud was within the belly of Vṛitra, but Indra caused them to flow down. In *i.* 55. 6,

> destroying the well-built dwellings of the Asuras, expanding like the earth, and setting the luminaries free from concealment, he enables the waters to flow.

This would seem to mean by the dwellings of the Asuras, either the clouds or darkness, covering the whole extent bounded by the horizon; but it is not possible that the cities and kings spoken of were merely the clouds and their potencies personified. We have, in what is said of them, references to wars of a time then very remote at the first settlement of the country, against the native tribes, and the names are those of Aryan heroes and leaders of the aborigines.

In *i.* 74. 3, Agni is the slayer of Vṛitra, and winner of booty in many a battle. In *i.* 80, Indra is lauded for slaying Vṛitra, striking him off from earth and heaven, striking his jaw and letting the waters flow, striking him from the sky, and on the temple. In *i.* 63. 4, he slew Vṛitra and put to flight the Dasyus in battle. In *i.* 101. 2, he slew the mutilated Vṛitra and Çambara and the unrighteous Pipru, and extirpated the unabsolvable Çushna (*açusham çushṇam*). *Çush* means "to become dry, to be withered, afflicted, emaciated, destroyed": *çusha*, "drying": *çushna*, "the sun, fire, as drying": *çushma*, "strong, the sun, fire, wind, light": *çushman*, "light, lustre, strength." The phrase is a peculiar one, to be applied to a man: and rather seems to mean that Indra extinguished a fire that could not be diminished, or confined within due bounds.

But the exploits of Indra are singularly intermixed. In *i.* 100. 18, attended by the moving (Wilson adds, *Maruts:* more probably Aryan troops, the "active" of the Gâthâs), he attacked the Dasyus and Çimyus, slew them with his thunderbolt, and divided their lands among his white-complexioned friends (*sakhibhih çvitnyebhih*), and rescued the sun and set free the water. In *i.* 103. 2, 3, 4, 5, 7, and 8, he has slain Ahi, pierced Rauhiṇa and destroyed the mutilated Vṛitra; has destroyed the cities of the Dasyus, and is prayed to direct his shaft against them and augment the strength and glory of the Ârya. He has destroyed the Dasyus and recovered cattle, horses, plants, waters and woods; takes from him who performs no sacrifice, and gives to him who sacrifices; awoke the sleeping Ahi with his thunderbolt, and slew Çushṇa, Pipru, Kuyava, Vṛitra and destroyed the cities of Çambara.

In *i.* 174. 2, he humbled the people who sued for pardon, when he had destroyed their seven new cities; and dispersed the flowing waters, destroying Vṛitra for the sake of the youthful Purukutsa. In verses 7 and 9, he destroyed Kuyavâcha for Duryoṇi, made the land productive, made the waters overspread the earth like flowing rivers, but protected the property of Turvaça and Yadu against inundation.

In *i.* 177. 1, Tṛita slew the mutilated Vṛitra, Tṛita being the trinity, Agni, Indra and Vishṇu. In *ii.* 14, Indra slew Vṛitra, Dṛibhika, Bala, Uraṇa, Arbuda, Svaçna, Çushṇa, Pipru, Namuchi and Rudhikrâ, and the assailants of Kutsa, Ayu and Atithigva, demolished the hundred ancient cities of Çambara, and cast down (defeated) the hundred thousand (followers, troops) of Varchin. In *ii.* 15, he slew Ahi, carried off Dabhîti, burned all their weapons in a fire, and enriched the Aryans with their cattle, horses and chariots; turned the Sindhu to the north, ground to pieces with his thunderbolt the wagon of the dawn, scattering the tardy enemy with his swift horses, destroyed Bala, forcing the mountain passes, and slew the Dasyus, Chumuri and Dhuni, having cast them into sleep; protected Dabhîti, while his Chamberlain (*rambhî*) gained in that the gold. In *ii.* 11. 18, he crushed the spider-like son of Danu (*danum aurṇavâbham*), Vṛitra, and let open the light to the Ârya, the Dasyu being set aside on his left hand: and men are spoken of who, through his protection surpass all their rivals, as the Aryans surpass the Dasyus.

In *iv.* 19. 3, Ahi, whom Indra slays, is styled

> the insatiable, unnerved, ignorant, unapprehending, slumbering Ahi, obstructing the downward flowing of the streams:

and in verses 1 and 2, the Devas send Indra to destroy Vṛitra, and slay the slumbering Ahi for the water, and mark out (the channels of) the rivers. He shatters the clouds and sets free the obstructed rivers, releases the imprisoned rivers: and in *v.* 8, having slain Vṛitra, he has liberated many mornings and years, swallowed up by darkness, and has set the rivers free.

In *vi.* 17. 9 and 10, we have the assailing Ahi, the ambitious, audacious, loud-shouting Ahi, crushed by Indra.

In *vi.* 20. 2, strength has been given to Indra, that, associated with Vishṇu, he may slay *Ahim Vṛitram*, obstructing the waters. Wilson renders those words, "the hostile Ahi." In this hymn all the exploits of Indra are recited. The Paṇis, by hundreds, fled from the Sage, his worshipper, in battle: he conquered Çushna and deprived him of sustenance, and when Çushna fell, the infidel power was broken, and the Aryan faith extended far and wide. He bruised the head of Namuchi, protecting Nami, son of Saya: he demolished the strong cities of the Pipru, and gave spoil to Rijisvat, his worshipper: he compelled the submission to Dyotana of Etasa, Dasoṇi, Tûtuji, Tugra and Ibha; shattered the seven cities of Çarat, killing the enemies and giving them to Purukutsa: benefited Uçanas, son of Kavi, slew Navavâstva, and saved Turvasa and Yadu when the rivers overflowed; and, finally, he killed Dhuni and Chumuri, and thereupon Dabhiti sacrificed to him.

In *vi.* 22. his aid against the Asuras, Râkshasas and Dasyus is magnified and extolled. In *vi.* 35. 2, he is besought to overthrow, in favour of the Aryas, all the servile races everywhere abiding (*Viçva abhiyujo vishûchîr âryâya viço ava târû-dâsih*).

In *vi.* 27, new names appear. Indra has slain the race of Varaçikha, favouring Abhyavartin, son of Chayamâna, killing the descendants of Vṛichîvat, on the Hariyûpîyâ, on the eastern part, whilst the western was scattered through fear. *Hariyûpîyâ*, Professor Wilson says, is the name either of a river or a city. *Hara*, in Zend, is "a mountain"; *Harabĕrĕzaiti* being the Bolor Tagh range. Three thousand mailed warriors (Aryans) assembled on the Yavâyatî to acquire glory. The Vṛichivâts advanced against them and were annihilated. *Yavya* is "fit for producing barley," and *yavyavati* would mean a place or ground where it was produced, barley-fields. Turvaça submitted to Sṛinjaya, and the Vṛichivâts to the descendants of Devavâta: and Abhyâvartin, son of Chayamâna, an opulent Raja, presents to the Ṛishi who composed the hymn two girls riding in cars, and twenty cows.

In *vi.* 31. 4, Çambara is called a Dasyu. Elsewhere he is called an Asura. A hundred of his cities were destroyed. In *vi.* 33. 3, it is said that Indra destroyed both enemies, Dasa and Arya. It would seem from this and some other passages that there were feuds among the Aryans. It would be strange if there were not. There have been ever since.

In *iv.* 28. 1, 2 and 3, Indra has slain Ahi, sent forth the seven rivers, and opened the shut-up sources; taken off the wheel of the chariot of the sun, and slain the Dasyus in battle, and Agni consumed them before noon. And in verses 5 and 6 it is said that Indra has made the Dasyus devoid of all, the servile races abject; and that Indra and Soma have distributed great numbers of horses and cattle that had been concealed, and land won by their power.

In *iv.* 38. 1 and 2, two *Deities* not named give the Aryans, it seems, the open land and forests of the Dasyus, and horses for their subjugation. Wilson follows Sayaṇa, under protest, in reading

> you two have given a horse, a son (*kshetrâsâm urvarâsâm*), a weapon, of the Dasyus.

Kshetra means "landed property, a field" (from *kshi*, "to possess, rule"). *Urvara* is not in Benfey, who has only *uru*, fem. *urvî*, "large"; but in the Zend *urvara* is "a tree." The suffix *sâm*, Sayaṇa says, is from *san*, "to give."

In *vii.* 19. 4 and 5, Indra is said to have slain with the thunderbolt the Dasyus Chumuri and Dhuni, on behalf of Dabhîti, and also Vṛitra and Namuchi. In *viii.* 3. 19, Indra has extirpated Vṛitra and destroyed Arbuda and Mṛigaya. In *viii.* 6. 6, he has cloven with his thunderbolt the head of the turbulent Vṛitra: and in verses 13 and 14 has divided Vṛitra joint by joint, and sent down the waters to the ocean, and hurled his thunderbolt upon the impious Çushna.

> Yaska says, in the Nirukta, who was Vṛitra? A cloud, say the etymologists; an Asura, son of Tvashṭṛi, the tale-tellers say. The fall of rain arises from the mingling of the waters and of light. This is figuratively depicted as a conflict. The hymns and Brâhmaṇas describe Vṛitra as a serpent. By the expansion of his body, he blocked up the streams. When he was destroyed, the waters flowed forth. *Muir: Sansk. Texts, ii. 174.*

Dr. Muir conclusively shows (*Texts, ii.* 359 *et seq.*) by many of the texts above quoted, and many others, that the Indo-Aryan bards called their own race Ârya, and expressly distinguished them from another people or other tribes called by them Dasyus,

> a race of distinct origin from the Aryans, and perhaps different from them in colour, as they certainly were in language, in religion and in customs, who had been in occupation of India before it was entered by the Indo-Aryans from the northwest:

and that these, as they advanced eastward and southward, drove these indigenous tribes before them into the mountains and forests, and took possession of their territory.

These indigenous "tribes" seem to have been, nay, certainly were, a settled, civilized and powerful people. They wore ornaments of gold, and jewels, and had builded great, strong cities. They had, no doubt, a history reaching back many centuries: and their languages, which still exist among their descendants, yet numerous in Northern India, are no doubt much more ancient than Sanskrit or Zend. The whole world swarmed with a busy population, hundreds of thousands of years before what we call "history" began. The true history of man is found in language, in the bogs of Northern Europe, the caves of Central Europe, the lacustrine habitations recently discovered, and the weapons and domestic utensils, of stone and bronze, that attest the antiquity of the race and the absurdity of the legends that have so long amused the world.

Dr. Muir also shows that fundamental differences exist between the Sanskrit and the languages of the South of India, proving that the tribes among which the latter dialects were originally vernacular, were of a different race from the Indo-Aryans, as the ancestors of those tribes were, which in the mountain regions of the sources of the Indus and Ganges still preserve their ancient tongues.

Many passages, quoted by him, of which I have cited only a part, prove that the Dasyus were a native people, or that the word was a general name, given by the Aryans to the natives generally, though they may have spoken many different tongues and were divided into a multitude of small tribes. They are described, by a general characterization, as non-observant of the sacred rites. They are termed *Dâsa* as well as *Dasyu*, as contradistinguished from the *Âryâ;* as having cities; as being of black skin or dark complexion, *tvachaṁ kṛishṇâm*, and thus distinguished from the Aryan colour, *ârya varṇa*.

We find also prayers to Indra for victory over kinsmen as well as strangers hostile to the worshippers, against both *Dâsa* and *Ârya* enemies: and Indra is said to have slain the two Âryas, Arṇa and Chitraratha, on the opposite bank of the Sarayu, and to have averted the bolt of the Dâsa from the Ârya in the land of the seven streams, *saptasindhushu*.

Dr. Muir, after deciding that the Dasyus were the indigenous people, hostile and observing different rites, and regarded with contempt and hatred by the superior race, says:

> It is, of course, not to be expected that we should find the Indian commentators confirming this view of the matter more than partially; as they had never dreamt of the modern critical view of the origin of the Aryas, and their relation to the barbarous aboriginal tribes.

They generally understood the Dasyus to have been superhuman beings, demons or Titans, rather than human enemies. But the author of the Aitareya-Brahmana represents Vaiçvamitra naming, as progeny of his disobedient sons, the Andhras, Puṇḍras, Çabaras, Pulindas, Mûtibas and other numerous frontier tribes, and adds,

> most of the Dasyus are descended from Vaiçvamitra.

And Manu tells us that without the pale of the castes are those who speak the language of the Mlechhas, or of the Aryas, all of whom are called Dasyus. The Mahâbhârata says,

> Having vanquished the Paurava in battle, the Pandava conquered the Utsavasanketas, seven tribes of Dasyus inhabiting the mountains.

It says that Pâkaçâsăni conquered the Daradas, with the Kâmbojas, and the Dasyus who dwell in the northeast region, as well as all the inhabitants of the forest, with the Sohas, the furthest Kâmbojas, and the Northern Ṛishikas. And in another place, that Çaineya conquered thousands of Kambojas, Çăkas, Çăvăras, Kirâtas, Varvaras; and that the ground was covered with the helmets and shaven and bearded heads of the Dasyus; this word being evidently a generic term denoting the whole of the tribes previously mentioned.

But there are many other passages of the Rich-Veda, Dr. Muir says, in which the words *Dasyu* and *Dâsa* are applied to demons of different orders, or goblins (Asuras, Râkshasas, etc.).

Professor Benfey, quoted by Dr. Muir, says, that in several passages, the *dasyu* and *dâsa* are the races that were subjugated by the Aryans, while in not a few those names

> are applied to the demons with whom the Gods are in conflict, and whose defeat is a condition of the earth receiving the heavenly blessing which is bestowed by the Gods.

The essential similarity of the words *dâsa* and *dasyu* he considers to be beyond doubt, *dâsa* meaning "slave."

He says,

> Both *dâsa* and *dasyu*, in contrast with the *Ârya*, at first designated the original population subjected by the latter at the time of their diffusion; and this relation which subsisted on earth, which no doubt was not rarely interrupted by revolts of the subject people, was transferred by the Aryans to the domain of the Gods, whose harmful demons were represented as the rebellious slaves of the Deities.

There are two errors in this, I think. I do not find that the demons were considered to be rebellious slaves: and it is not possible that *dâsa* and *dasyu* originally meant "slave." Each *came* to mean it, because the Dâsa and Dasyu were enslaved. In the same way we have the word "slave" itself. It was originally the name or an epithetical designation of the Bulgarians, and came to mean "subjects or those who serve," when they became subjects of the Greek Empire. The Slaves or Sclaves, themselves, derive it from *slava*, "glory." Others derive it from *slovo*, "to speak." But both are from the same root, for glory or renown consisted then as it does now, in being spoken of. The original root of it is the Sanskrit *çru*, "to hear," whence *çrava* and *çravs*, "the ear," "renown"; *su-çravas*, "famous"; *prithu-çravas*, "widely renowned."

Professor Roth, always on the spiritual side, when there is question between a spiritual and material meaning, naturally defines *dasyu* as 1st, superhuman beings, and 2d, as hostile, wicked or barbarous men. And he thinks that

> many of the demons subdued by Indra, designated by particular names, as Çambara, Çushna, Chumuri, etc., bearing the general appellation of *dasyu*, are not only spirits of darkness like the Râkshasas, but are extended over the widest spheres.

He deems it advisable seldom to consider the word as meaning "men." I think that it is impossible to hold that the word originally meant both barbarians and demons. It was originally an appellation of the native tribes, and came at a much later day to mean "demons," and it is an infallible test, where it occurs, by which to determine the greater or less antiquity of a hymn.

The Dasyus are particularly designated in several places as *anindra*, without or despisers of Indra. In *ii.* 20. 7, they are called the *dâsîḥ* of black descent, *kṛishṇayariḥ*, which, as well as *kṛishṇagarbhaḥ*, in Rig-Veda *i.* 101. 1, Roth explains as descriptive of the black clouds. Benfey also explains as clouds, "the black skin" (*kṛishṇa twacha*), in *ix.* 41. 1. In *vii.* 5. 3, the "black tribes" (*viçah asiknir*), who fled, scattered, relinquishing their possessions, when their cities were demolished and burned, are held by Roth to have been "spirits of darkness." The value of such perversions of plain language and perversions of meaning is little greater than those of the delirious glosses of Philo Judæus and the Kabbalah, on what they consider the allegories of the Hebrew Scriptures.

The epithet *mṛidhravach* is applied in the Riçh-Veda to the native tribes, and the meaning of the word has been much discussed. Dr. Muir renders it

> injuriously speaking [but thinks it], too uncertain to admit of our referring it with confidence to any peculiarity in the language of the aborigines.

I do not think that it had the meaning of "speechless," or "bereft of speech," or "softly-speaking," or "stuttering." *Ravach* is "speech." *Mṛidh* means "to kill," and *mṛidha*, "war, battle." *Mṛidhravach*, I imagine, means, simply, "hostile," or "openly hostile," or, literally "maledictory." Kuhn thinks it refers to the gradual dying away of the distant thunder, which is regarded as the voice of the vanquished demon. It is astonishing into what absurdities a theory can lead a man; and with what exemplary patience a sensible and sedate scholar like Dr. Muir listens to and repeats such worthless vagaries.

So the aborigines are called *anâsas*, which Müller thinks means "noseless," and Sayaṇa says means "devoid or deprived of word;" *âsya*, "face" or "mouth;" being put by metonomy for *çabda*, "the speech" that comes from the mouth. *A* is a negative prefix, and so is *an;* and the word may either be *a-nasas* or *an-asas*. *Nâsâ*, compounds, *nasa*, means "a nose;" but it is not permissible to suppose that the indigenes had no noses. *Asant* means "wicked, a heretic." *Âs* means "to sit, abide, stay"; whence *âsana*, "sitting encamped, dwelling," and *âsyâ*, "sitting"; and *anasa* may mean "unsettled, wandering, nomadic."

Çambara, whose towns Indra destroyed, is styled the Dâsa, son of Kulitara, in *iv.* 30. 14, and to have been hurled down from the great mountain; which proves that he was a mountain chief, and that the hymn was composed at, or refers to, a time when the Indo-Aryans still resided near the mountains and were at war with the North Indian tribes.

Dr. Muir says:

> I have gone over the names of the Dasyus or Asuras mentioned in the Rig-Veda, with the view of discovering whether any of them could be regarded as of non-Aryan or indigenous origin; but I have not observed any that appear to be of this character. But we should recollect that the Aryans would not unnaturally designate the aboriginal leaders (if they specified any of them in their sacred hymns), by names of Ayarn origin, or at least softened into an Aryan form. The Greeks introduced Greek modifications into Persian and other proper names, and the Chaldæans are stated in the book of Daniel to have given Chaldæan appellations to the Jews.

We know how the Romans Latinized Keltic, German and British names, and how *we* have Anglicized, with the most ludicrous results, French, Spanish and Indian ones. We have, among our Indian tribes, the Snakes, Creeks, Blackfeet and Sacs and Foxes, and have given English names to hundreds of chiefs, whose real names we have never known.

The texts in which the Dasyus seem to be spoken of as demons or superhuman, are but few. In *x.* 99. 6, the loud-shouting *Dâsa*, with six eyes and three heads, is spoken of, which reminds us of the snake Dahaka of the *Zend-Avesta*, with several heads, which was evidently a tribe of several villages or bands. In *viii.* 14. 14, Indra hurled down the Dasyus, when they were mounting upwards and seeking to scale heaven; and in *ii.* 12. 2, to Dâsa are said to have regarded themselves as immortal (*amartyaṁ*), which is no more than if it had been said that they regarded themselves as invulnerable.

In the recitals of the contests of Indra and Vṛitra, Dr. Muir says, we are, no doubt, to understand both the God and his adversary as personifications of atmospherical phenomena. In the same way, he thinks, Çambara,

Çushna and Namuchi are to be regarded as mythical personages, of a kindred character with Vṛitra. And yet there are many passages in which the word *vṛitra* has the signification of enemy in general; and Spiegel thinks that *Vṛitrahan* had originally nothing more than a general signification, and that it was only at a later period that it came to be a special designation of Indra. The mythical narratives generally identify Çambara with Vṛitra; and Roth says:

> It is true that Çambara is employed, at a later period, to designate an enemy in general, and in particular the enemy of Indra, Vṛitra; but it is not improbable that this may be the transference of the more ancient recollection of a dreaded enemy to the greatest of all enemies, the demon of the clouds.

Çambara is not spoken of in the Riçh-Veda as identical with Vṛitra. He is clearly a powerful chief or King of the aborigines. Vṛitra is nowhere mentioned as having cities that Indra demolishes. If the cities of Çambara and others were cloud-cities, would they not have been called cities of Vṛitra? Nor is Vṛitra called a Dâsa or Dasyu in any hymn composed before the Dâsa or Dasyu had become in the popular opinion demons or superhuman beings. The special and highest appellation of Indra, often repeated and with emphasis, is "slayer of Vṛitra"; and as no other foe of the Aryans is thus eminently distinguished, it is clear that Vṛitra was his principal antagonist. But it seems hardly probable that the "greatest of all enemies" was the demon of the clouds, who prevented the falling of the rain.

Müller says that *dasyu* simply means "enemy," and that even Aryan tribes may be so called, as Vasishṭha himself, the very type of the Aryan Brahman, when in feud with Viçvamitra, is called not only an enemy, but a Yâtudhâna, and other names which, in common parlance are only bestowed on barbarian savages and evil spirits. In Rig-Veda *x*. 87. 16, it is said that the Yâtudhânas gloat on the bloody flesh of men or horses, and drink the milk of the cow, meaning, probably that they marauded upon the Aryan settlers and drove away their cattle. Yâtu means a traveller, but what *dhâna* means is uncertain. Benfey says it is "the latter part of compound words, implying especially the place of the preceding notion," "residence." *Dhana* means "property, abundance, gold, cattle, booty." *Dhanu* is "a bow," and *dhanus*, "armed with a bow, an archer"; and *Yâtudhâna* may have meant, originally, "swift bow-men." *Râkshas*, Müller says, originally meant "strong, powerful," but it soon took the sense of "giant and barbarian." *Râksh* meant "to preserve, spare, guard, keep, tend, govern, protect"; and *râksha*, "one who guards; preserving, guarding, protection, protecting." I do not see how a word with this meaning could have produced the meaning of "demon," or "evil, harmful spirit," in *râkshasa:* but I do not find for it the meaning of "strong, powerful."

The aborigines are also called *kravyâd* and *âmâdas*, "flesheater" and "raw eaters," because they ate uncooked meat. Another epithet applied to them is *çiçna-devâ*, rendered "lascivious wretches," but meaning, more probably, "phallus-worshippers."

The process of Aryan settlement and conquest has been repeated in North America, as it is described by Dr. Muir (*ii.* 392). The warfare waged by the Dasyus was like that of the American Indians, and, in the words of Dr. Muir, their black complexion (only dark, probably), ferocious aspect, barbarous habits, rude speech and savage yells, and their stealthy and sudden attacks, under cover of the night and of the impenetrable forest, naturally led the Aryans to speak of them as demons. The return of day would cause them to retire and restore the bewildered and harassed Aryan settlers to security, and sunrise be said to drive the demons away. To the settlers of New England, Ohio and Kentucky, the Indians were the "red devils," "fiends in human shape," and similar figurative expressions in the ancient Vedic hymns came after a time to be accepted literally.

And Dr. Muir well remarks that the Vedic poems were composed at different dates during a long period of time; new compositions being continually added, in which many thoughts and phrases were incorporated, borrowed from the older hymns. The old hymns did not remain unchanged, either, for that was simply impossible.

> And, as circumstances changed, the allusions and references in the older hymns might be forgotten; and it might happen that some of the expressions occurring in them would no longer be distinctly understood, and might in this way be applied to conditions and events to which they had originally no reference. The same thing might happen by way of accommodation; phrases or epithets referring to one class of enemies might be transferred to another . . . . Hints and allusions in the Vedas have been often developed in the Purâṇas into legends of an entirely different character and tendency; the functions and attributes of the Vedic Gods were quite changed in later ages, and even in the Brâhmanas the true meaning of many of the Vedic texts have been misunderstood.

And hence, he concludes, and it is not possible to deny, that even in the age when the later hymns were composed, the process of misapplication may have commenced, and that their authors may, in various instances, have employed the words of the earlier hymns in a different manner from that in which they were at first applied.

> In this way [he says], it is conceivable that what was originally said of the dark-complexioned, degraded and savage aborigines, of their castles or rude fortifications, and of their conflicts with the Aryas, may have been at a later period transferred to the foul spirits of darkness, to the hostile demons of the clouds, and to the conflicts of the Gods with the Asuras and the Daityas. Or, it is, perhaps, a more probable supposition, that in the artless style of early poetry, the earthly enemies of the worshipper were mentioned in the hymns alongside of the malicious spirits of darkness . . . . or the aërial foes of Indra.

There are two or three things in this passage that deserve a moment's notice.

The Vedic poems cannot properly be styled *early* poetry, nor was their style *artless*. Logical evidence (the testimony of words or language, for "philology" means love of words, as "philosophy" means love of wisdom) infallibly establishes it as a proven and demonstrated *fact*, that great intervals of time elapsed between the successive out-flowings of the several streams of Aryan emigration; and that, when the Vedic hymns were composed, the race had an immense antiquity, and Aryan thought and imagination had been busy during great cycles of centuries. The ancestors of the Kelts, Goths, Germans and Sclaves, as well as those of the Greeks and Latins, were men of full intellectual stature, and in no sense barbarians; and these had gone with their herds to conquer Europe, ages before the separation of the Irano- and Indo-Aryan branches of their race: and centuries more had passed, after that separation, before the ancient tongue spoken in the valleys of the Bolor Tagh and in the valleys of Samarcand and Bokhara, had become the Sanskrit of the Veda and the Iranic of the *Zend-Avesta.*

It is not so certain that the aborigines of either India or Bactria were so degraded or savage as they are supposed to have been. There were Turanian chiefs who were honoured by the Irano-Aryans; and there were, undoubtedly, powerful indigenous races in India. The *puro* spoken of in the Veda, of which Çambara had a hundred, were, it is far more probable, not castles, but towns. These people were by no means savages. They had gold and jewels and wore helmets, and were unquestionably brave and formidable antagonists. All the intellect of the world was not confined to the Aryan race. Not to speak of the Egyptian and Semitic intellect, we know that the Etruscans, Lycians and Circassians (except the one tribe, the Os) were not of Aryan blood.

Dâsa has in Benfey the single meaning "slave," as, probably, *dam+sa*, *dam* meaning "to be tamed, to tame, to subdue." But those not subdued, and who were open and dangerous enemies, numerous and powerful, were called by this name, and also *dasyu*. The latter was probably their real name, and the other probably was applied to them on account of its resemblance to the latter, and by way of contumely. I do not believe that the two were synonymous, or from the same root. *Dasyu* may have come from *dâ*, "to cut off, destroy."

When the Dasyus had become evil spirits, the original character of Vṛitra had changed also, and what was at first the gloom or darkness, the direct opposite and negation of light and therefore the mortal enemy of Indra, came to be considered one of the Dasyus or demons. What *Ahi* meant and what *Danu*, the mother of Vṛitra, was, it remains to discover. It would seem from some of the texts that Ahi was the cause of the obstruction of the flow of water in the rivers by ice, by melting which, Indra set the waters free and filled the river channels. In the 1st Fargard of the Vendidad, the "opposition" which Añra-Mainyus created in Airyana-Vaêjâ was "a great serpent and winter," or "a mighty serpent and snow." I have not been able to see how a serpent could have been appropriately spoken of in connection with intense cold and a winter of ten months, and either as a symbol of it, or a figurative expression for it, or an agent in producing it. The Sanskrit *ahi*, "snake" became *azi*, in Zend. I am now more than ever convinced from the stoppage of the waters (of the flowing of the rivers) being attributed to Ahi, that neither it, in this connection, nor *Azi* in the Vendidad, meant "serpent." It must have meant "cold." The adjective and noun *hima* (Latin *heims*, "winter"; Greek χιων, "snow") i. e., Benfey says, lost *hyam*+*a*, means "cold, frost, snow"; and *himâ* (fem.) "winter." Hence the name *Himâlaya*, of the great Asian range of mountains. *Haima* is a variant of *hima*.

We recognize, Bopp says (Section 80), the simple pronominal base *ma* in the Sanskrit suffix *ma*, which in adjectives or substantives denotes the person or thing that completes the action expressed by the root, or on whom that action is accomplished. Abstracts also are formed by this suffix, which, however, is seldom adopted in that state of the language which has descended to us. Examples are, *rukma*, "gold," as "glittering," from *ruch*, "to shine"; *yudhma*, "combatant," from *rudh*, "to fight"; *bhama*, "the sun," as "giving light"; *çushma*, "fever," as "drying."

Hâ means "to abandon, leave, forsake, lose, resign, let fall"; and the participle passive perf., *hina*, "deprived, wasted, decayed, vile, bad, low, deficient"; and *hâni*, noun, "loss, privation, absence, want." From this verb, perhaps, cáme *hima* or *haima*, as a name of winter, the season of desolation, decay and abandonment or forsaking by light and warmth. And from this, also, with the augment *a*, *Ahi*, the wintry cold. *Vṛitra*, *Ahi* and *Danu* are evidently very ancient words, belonging to the old Aryan tongue. The root from which *Danu* came, if it still exists, has lost its original meaning. There are three verbs *dâ*, two of which mean "to bind," and "to cut" or "to cut off." It would seem that *Night* must be the Mother of Darkness: but there is now no evidence that *danu* meant "night" and *danam*, "children of night." But who of us knows the derivation and real meaning of our own words "night, winter and summer?"

In the first passage in which we find the name of *Vṛitra* (*i.* 4. 8), we have it in the plural, and seeming to be the name of human enemies of the Aryans. Indra, by the appellation of *Çatakratu* ("honoured by a hundred sacrifices," 'εκατομπαιος: *Benfey*. *Çata*, like 'εκατον and *centum*, an indefinite number) is said to have become the slayer of *the Vṛitras* (*Vṛitrâ-nâm*), and to defend the warrior in battle. And in *i.* 23. 9, the Maruts,

> liberal donors, along with the mighty and associated Indra,

are invoked to destroy Vṛitra, and let not the evil one prevail against the Invoker.

Çatakratu means just what *centum virilis* would mean in Latin, i. e., a hundred-fold strong or mighty.

In *i.* 84. 13 we have,

> Indra, with the bones of Dadhyanch, slew ninety times nine Vṛitras.
>
> [In *ii.* 11. 5 and 9]: Indra, Hero, thou hadst slain by thy prowess the glorified Ahi, hidden privily in a cave, working in concealment, *covered* by the waters in which he was abiding, and arresting the rains in the sky . . . . The mighty Indra has shattered the guileful Vṛitra, *reposing* in the cloud.
>
> [And in *ii.* 12. 3]: He who, having destroyed Ahi, set free the seven rivers.
>
> [And in *iii.* 32. 6 and 11]: Thou hast slain with active strife the slumbering, darkling, water-investing Vṛitra, thou hast let forth the bright waters like horses into battle . . . . Thou hast slain Ahi, enveloping the slumbering water and confiding in his prowess.

These passages clearly show that Vṛitra was Darkness and Ahi Cold. The latter not only obstructed the flowing of the rivers, but arrested the rains in the sky, turning them, there, into snow and hail. And if Ahi is ever used as a name of Vṛitra, the reason is that as light and heat are manifestations of the one substance, and the rays of sunlight are hot, so darkness may be regarded as the cause of cold, and the cold only the darkness itself.

INDEX

Açvinau....530–541
Açvins, names of.... 534
Aditi....480, 490–500
Aditi, Diti, Daksha....480–501
Agni....43, 111–125, 309, 437–446, 605, 607, 629
Agni and Indra....138–147
Agni, epithets applied to.... 62
Agni, texts relating to....53–67
Agni, the domestic fire.... 438
Ahi.... 628
Ahi-Vṛitra.... 626
Ahuna-Vairya.... 412
Ahura Mazda....371–380
Ahura Mazda, the Creator.... 372
Akô-Manô.... 373
Aldebarân.... 323
Alexander the Great, period of.... 24
Ameretâṭ.... 373
Amĕsha-Çpĕntas....373–378
Andar.... 373
Aṅra-Mainyus....371, 372
Ansa.... 301
Antar—within.... 431
Apologetic.... 413
Apsaras.... 593
Arcturus.... 322
Ardibehest....373, 375
Arian a primitive language.... 27
Arian languages, radical affinity of.... 27
∀rṇa.... 592
∀rushâ....178–185
∀rya.... 412
∀rya, the word.... 26
∀ryaman.... 44
∀ryaman—Mitra—Varuṇa....252–279
Aryan and Semitic.... 1
Aryan emigrants.... 409
Aryan intellect, advance of....605–611
Aryan language, branches of....35–41
Aryan numerals, coincidences of.... 40
Aryan race, cradle of....17–18
Aryan race never barbarians.... 13
Aryan separation, period of.... 365
Aryans, early.... 639
Aryans, feuds among.... 631
Aryans preceded in Europe by savages.... 35
Asha.... 390
Asha-Vahista.... 373

Ashis-Vanuhi.... 394
Asterisms.... 322–324
Aṣwins, texts relating to.... 87–93
Aṣwins, the.... 283–298
A. U. M.... Preface vii, 46
Author, modesty of.... Preface vi-vii

Bactrian Aryan religion.... 407
Bactrian Aryans, ancient.... 406–412
Bactrians and Scyths.... 410–411
Bhaga.... 326–327
Bhuvanani.... 190
Bleeck, Mr.... 365
Bokhara.... 21–22
Brahm.... 329
Brahma.... 346
Brahmanas.... 212
Brahmaṇaspati.... 204–216
Bṛihaspati.... 204–209
Bulgarians are Finnic.... 411
Bunsen, Baron.... 2, 363–365

Canopus.... 322
Castor and Pollux.... 293, 323
Çatavaêça.... 391
Çaurva.... 373
Common terms, origin of.... 37–39
Çpĕnta.... 408
Çpĕnta-Ârmaiti.... 373
Çraddhâ.... 593
Çraŏsha.... 373, 378, 379
Çraŏsha—Çraddhâ.... 593
Create, definition of.... 15

Dadhikra.... 301
Daksha.... 498, 500
Danu.... 627
Dasyu.... 637
Dasyus.... 633
Date of this volume, 56 years since.... Preface ix
Decimal numeration known early.... 39
Deioces.... 365
Deities of Veda.... 300
Deities of Veda all beneficent.... 131
Deities offered by Nature to the Aryans.... 94–109
Denghis, Lake.... 573
Devas and Gods—3,339.... 422
Devas, Vedic, were stars.... 428
Dioscuri.... 293
Diti.... 483–484
Drvâçpa.... 392

Earth, Sky and Heaven....429–436
Emanation, idea of.... 463
Emerson, saying of.... 406
Emigration, sequence of Aryan.... 39
Etymology....16–17
Evil spirits....623–625

Family names, comparative philology of.... 36
Family names, origin of.... 37
Family relationship names had early meanings.... 36
Finns are Scythic.... 411
Fire, adoration of.... 125
Fire in the Zend-Avesta....367–370
Fire, domestic.... 369
Fire, sacrificial.... 369
Fire, why produced by attrition.... 6
Fravashis.... 393

Gangu.... 302
Garbha.... 619
Gâthâs, the....398–406
Gnostics, the....127, 128
God, Aryan name for.... 3

Hâ.... 640
Haŏma.... 396
Haŏma—Soma.... 369
Haurvat.... 373
Heat....200–201
Hermes.... 526
Hesiod and Homer compared.... 32
Higgins, Godfrey.... 358
Hom.... 412
Horse, the....567, 568, 569
Horsemen, the two.... 294
Hotra.... 303
Hungarians are Finnic.... 411
Hyades.... 360

Ila.... 303
Indian text, example of.... 42
Indians, American.... 638
Indo-Aryans, cosmic ideas of....97–98
Indo-Aryans, immigration of....23–24
Indo-Aryans, the....Preface v-vi
Indra....44, 138–168, 413, 447–469
Indra and Varuṇa, texts relating to....77–78
Indra, Asuras slain by.... 72
Indra, epithets applied to....71–72

Indra is all of the luminaries 466
Indra, texts relating to 68–71
Indra, the Universal Light 447, 462, 469
Irano Deities and religion 407
Irano-Aryan religion older than Veda 125
Irano-Aryans and Scyths 411–412

Jajana 482
Janman 487
Jâtavedâs 67, 582
Jaxartes river 573
Johnson, Samuel 600–604
Julian, the Emperor 129

Kabbalah, the 127, 416
Khordad 373
Khshathra-Vairya 373
Kṛttikâ 321
Kshi—dwelling 427

Language and translation 11–24
Languages, derivative 417
Languages, origin of present Aryan 28
Light 183–184
Logos, the 127

Maghavan 165
Maha—great 427
Mâh Nyâyis 397
Mantras 212
Maruts 332, 361
Mary 587
Mata—mother 482
Medes and Arioi 26
Mercury 521
Metals, some known early 39
Method of inquiry 52
Mithra and the Sun 383–390
Mitra 44, 413
Mitra and Mithra 506
Mitra and Varuṇa 502–512
Mitra, the Morning Star 439
Mitra-Varuṇa-Aryaman 252–279
Mitra, Varuṇa and Aryaman, texts relating to 78–86
Mṛigaçîrsha 323, 324
Muir, Dr 331, 419–420
Mulciber 329
Müller, Max 412
Müller *versus* Aryan polytheism 133
Mythology, dualism 535

Nasatyas.......... 327
Night.......... 585
Numbers.......... 359–360

Oneness.......... 606
Origen.......... 129
Oriōn.......... 323, 324, 425–426
Oriōn, three stars in.......... 589
Ouranos.......... 510
Oxus river.......... 573, 575

Pan.......... 522
Parjanya.......... 165–166, 477–479
Parṇin.......... 609
Parsee prayers, the great.......... 397
Pegasus.......... 322, 567
Periods shown by constellation.......... 541
Philo.......... 124
Philo—Agni.......... 124
Philosophical definitions.......... 126–131
Pitu.......... 313
Plato.......... 124
Pleiades.......... 426, 529
Pleiades and Hyades.......... 427
Plotinus.......... 130
Prajâpati.......... 618–622
Prayers, Aryan.......... 400
Pṛiṣni.......... 305–306
Pṛiṭhivi.......... 306–307, 435–436
Proclus.......... 130
Punjab, the.......... 19–20
Purusha.......... 612–617
Pushan.......... 44, 314–325, 520–529
Pushan and Mercury.......... 524

Râkshasas.......... 624–625
Regulus.......... 322
Religion, Irano-Aryan.......... 407
Religion of the author.......... 5
Ṛibhu.......... 559
Ṛibhus.......... 347–349, 594–598
Ribukshin.......... 301
Rig-Veda.......... Introduction xi
Ṛiksha.......... 590
Ṛishis.......... 215, 589
Ṛishis, the seven.......... 425
Ṛitu.......... 566
Rodasi.......... 303
Rohini.......... 321

Rudra....330–339, 503, 599
Rudrasya....332
Rudrâya....332

Sabellius....129
Sanakas....627
Sanskrit and Greek and Latin....3
Sanskrit and Latin, common origin of....41
Sanskrit letters....Preface x
Sanskrit, perfection of....13
Sapandomat....373
Saramâ....350–358
Sarameya....356
Saraṇyû....546–551
Saraṇyû, wife of Vivasvaṭ....543
Sarasvatî....342–346, 591–593
Savitṛi....231–242
Savitṛi, the Moon....240–242, 519
Siricol, Lake....573
Sirius....358
Sîta....305
Skambha....310
Sky never deified....550
Soma....246–251, 609
Soma—Haŏma....369
Soma and Haŏma....247
Spiegel, Professor....365
Stars, the....391–397
Substance, definition of....126
Sun adored by the ancients....551
Sun, the child of Ushas....553
Supreme beings and emanations....127
Sûrya....44, 229–230, 605
Sûrya and Savitṛi....513–519
Sûrya, the Sun....513

Tamerlane, period of....24
Tanûnâpat....67
Tertullian....128
Theosophy, Vedic....132–137
Tishya....301
Tistrya....391
Triple triangle....362
Tṛita....301, 545, 630
Turanians....407
Turkish language, the....602
Tvashṭṛi....542–545
Tvashṭṛi, a potency of Agni....543
Tvashṭṛi, father of Yima's wife....543
Tvashṭṛi—Vulcan....542
Twashṭṛi....328–329

Ushas....280–282, 340–341, 587
Ushas bore twins.... 548
Ushas, daughter of Agni.... 123
Ushas, the Dawn....552–555

Vahni.... 228
Vaiṣwânara....223–227
Vanaṇt.... 391
Vanaṇt-Yasht.... 395
Vanaspati....217–222
Varuṇa....44, 413, 481
Varuṇa-Mitra-Aryaman....252–279
Varuṇa, texts relating to....74–76
Varuṇa, the Evening Star.... 439
Vasus....311–312
Vayu....169–177
Vayu and Vata....556–559
Veda and Zend-Avesta.... 584
Veda, difficulty of translation of.... 32
Veda later than Zend-Avesta.... 125
Veda, meaning of.... 1
Veda, misunderstanding of in Brahmanas.... 31
Veda not Brahmanic Veda.... 584
Veda, other Deities of....300–312
Veda, the....1–10
Veda, the age of.... 10
Vedas.... 639
Vedas, age of compilation.... 1
Vedas and their age....25–34
Vedas, collections of.... 2
Vedas, Deities of.... 47
Vedas do not teach an anthropomorphic God.... 133
Vedas, Hindu idea of the origin of.... 34
Vedas not *Indian* writings.... 25
Vedas not monotheistic.... 3
Vedas, origin of.... 34
Vedas, when compiled.... 26
Vedic Deities....Preface vii
Vedic Deities, origin of....419–420
Vedic Gods their number and nature....421–428
Vedic Gods, thirty-three in number.... 421
Vedic hymns, their characters.... 4
Vedic language....414–418
Vedic Poets, period of.... 416
Vedic theoṣophy....132–137
Vedic worship and interpretation....48–52
Vega.... 322
Vendidad, the....365, 406
Vernal equinox, the.... 254
Vibhwan.... 302

Viçpatâ.... 533
Vishṇu.... 44, 186–203, 470–476
Vishṇu, three steps of.... 473–476
Vîstâspa.... 363
Vivaṅhao, father of Yima.... 543
Vohu-Manô.... 373–400
Vouru-Kasha, the sea.... 409–410
Vṛishan.... 414
Vṛitra.... 451
Vṛitra, Ahi.... 626–641
Vulcan.... 329

Yama.... 243–245, 560–590
Yazatas.... 381–382
Yima and Zarathustra.... 574

Zarathustra.... 363–366, 407
Zarathustra and Scythians.... 410–411
Zarathustra, home and period of.... 23
Zarathustrian Gâthâs, the.... 398–405
Zend-Avesta.... 365, 574
Zend-Avesta and Vedas.... 574
Zend-Avesta, fire in the.... 367–370
Zend-Avesta older than Veda.... 125
Zeus–Dyu.... 432–433
Zohik.... 573